The Man Who Ran
WASHINGTON

The Man Who Ran
WASHINGTON

The Life and Times of
JAMES A. BAKER III

Peter Baker and Susan Glasser

DOUBLEDAY / NEW YORK

AUTHORS' NOTE:

James Baker and Peter Baker are not related.

Copyright © 2020 by Peter Baker and Susan Glasser

All rights reserved. Published in the United States by Doubleday,
a division of Penguin Random House LLC, New York, and distributed
in Canada by Penguin Random House Canada Limited, Toronto.

www.doubleday.com

DOUBLEDAY and the portrayal of an anchor with a dolphin
are registered trademarks of Penguin Random House LLC.

All photographs are courtesy of the Baker Institute
for Public Policy except as otherwise noted.

Jacket photograph: James Addison Baker III by
Michael Arthur Worden Evans, ca. 1984. Gelatin silver print.
National Portrait Gallery, Smithsonian Institution;
gift of the Portrait Project, Inc.

Jacket design by Michael Windsor

Library of Congress Cataloging-in-Publication Data
Names: Baker, Peter, [date], author. | Glasser, Susan, author.
Title: The man who ran Washington : the life and times of
James A. Baker III / Peter Baker and Susan Glasser.
Description: First edition. | New York : Doubleday, [2020] |
Includes bibliographical references and index.
Identifiers: LCCN 2019038715 (print) | LCCN 2019038716 (ebook) |
ISBN 9780385540551 (hardcover) | ISBN 9780385540568 (ebook)
Subjects: LCSH: Baker, James Addison, 1930– | Statesmen—United States—
Biography. | Cabinet officers—United States—Biography. |
United States—Politics and government—1981–1989. | United States—
Politics and government—1989–
Classification: LCC E840.8.B315 B35 2020 (print) |
LCC E840.8.B315 (ebook) | DDC 973.92092 [B]—dc23
LC record available at https://lccn.loc.gov/2019038715
LC ebook record available at https://lccn.loc.gov/2019038716

Manufactured in the United States of America
1 3 5 7 9 10 8 6 4 2
First Edition

For Theo

Contents

The Man Who Ran
WASHINGTON

The Velvet Hammer

A little more than a week before the 2016 presidential election, Jim Baker was obsessing over what to do about Donald Trump. Baker's wife, daughters, and closest advisers were urging Baker to vote against him. Baker's best friend, former president George H. W. Bush, his partner for nearly a half century on the tennis courts, on the campaign trail, and on the world stage, had made it clear that he would vote against Trump. So had Bush's son, former president George W. Bush, and other members of the Bush family.

Throughout the long, nasty campaign, Trump had been attacking the Bushes and pretty much everything they—and Baker—stood for. Trump had asked for an endorsement and Baker had refused, but he still was not sure what to do in the privacy of the voting booth. He saw the modern Republican Party as a global bulwark of open markets, free enterprise, and the American way of life. He had helped to build it and he was used to winning. Now Trump, vain and bombastic, a flashy New York real estate mogul who boasted of grabbing women's private parts and seemed like a sure loser, threatened to upend all that. But Trump was the party's nominee, and Baker, late in life, remained a party man.

We sat down with Baker in his favorite suite at the Willard Hotel, the ornate Victorian landmark barely a block away from the White House. Baker was eighty-six years old at the time, although you would not have known it. He wore his customary dark suit with money-green tie, a habit he picked up when he became secretary of the treasury in Ronald Reagan's second term and had continued ever since. A courtly lawyer with a Texas twang, a perpetual twinkle in his eye, and an ear for gossip, Baker dominated both American politics and policymaking through much of the 1970s, 1980s, and early 1990s with a mastery rarely seen before or since. But for the last several years, over the course of dozens of hours of interviews, it had become clear that Baker thought the country had gone seriously off course. "The point of holding power is to get things done and accomplish things," he told us once in the summer of 2014, his voice rising almost an octave in exasperation. He pressed that point whenever the current generation called for advice, which they still did fairly often, but he seemed mystified that the message was not getting through. "The argument I've been making," he said, "is that we're not *leading*."

Now, on that Halloween morning in 2016, Trump seemed like a catastrophic herald of the system's breakdown. "The guy is nuts," Baker sighed as we talked in the sunny oval sitting room of his suite. "He's crazy. I will not endorse him. I've said that publicly. I've told him that." Trump was promising a destructive end to the Washington-led world order that Baker and others had spent a generation designing. He disparaged longstanding alliances, vowed to rip up free trade pacts, decried American leadership outside its borders, casually embraced a new nuclear arms race, and sought to reverse the globalization that had defined international politics and economics since the end of World War II. He opposed just about everything that Baker and the modern Republican Party supported and Baker ticked them off for us again that morning: "He's against free trade. He's talking about NATO being a failed alliance. He's dumping all over NAFTA," the trade pact with Mexico and Canada that Baker had helped set in motion. Baker still backed it, as did the vast bulk of his party. "That was a hell of a deal," he said, shaking his head. Yet in Trump's view, the leaders of the past—Baker and his contemporaries—had bungled their chance and squandered American greatness. Trump's campaign, as quixotic as it originally seemed, had tapped into a powerful strain of resentment with his pledge to blow up Washington and remake it in his own image. He promised to drain the very swamp on which the Willard stood.

Voting against Trump should have been an easy call for Baker. Trump, after all, was "a guy who's his own worst enemy," as Baker reminded us. "He can't keep his mouth shut." But Baker also was not quite ready to walk away from the party to which he had devoted so many years. He knew what it felt like when political power shifted and he knew that it was much better to be on the winning side. He had fought against the Reagan Revolution inside the Republican Party on behalf of Gerald Ford and George Bush, then became the revolution's most capable executor as Reagan's White House chief of staff. As Bush's secretary of state, he had watched the unraveling of the Soviet Union and its empire in Eastern Europe, another revolution that Baker did not start but figured out how to channel. The lesson he had taken from these events was simple and it was clear: When the tectonic plates of history move, move with them.

When it came to Trump and the nationalist-populist backlash that he represented, however, Baker just could not decide. It was only days before the election, and he went back and forth. At the end of our long conversation, after touching on Middle East peacemaking and the inner machinations of the Bush White House and the bipartisan prayer group he used to attend on Capitol Hill, we circled back to the subject at hand.

Could Jim Baker, the very definition of the establishment, really vote for Donald Trump?

Baker looked stricken. "Well," he said, "I haven't voted for him *yet*."

DELEGATE HUNTER, campaign manager, White House chief of staff, treasury secretary, and secretary of state, James Addison Baker III played a leading role in some of the most critical junctures in modern American history. For a quarter century, every Republican president relied on Baker to manage his campaign, his White House, his world. Baker brought them to power or helped them stay there, then steered them through the momentous events that followed. He was Washington's indispensable man.

Any chronicle of the modern presidency would find Baker at the heart of virtually every chapter, for his was an unmatched case study in the acquisition, exercise, and preservation of power in late-twentieth-century America and into the first decade of the twenty-first. He was the campaign operative who secured the Republican nomination for Gerald Ford against a relentless challenge from the right by Ronald Reagan in 1976, then four years later managed George Bush's first presidential campaign, which proved successful enough to earn Bush the vice presidency and Baker a spot by the new president's side. He set up and ran Reagan's White House as chief of staff for four years, securing many of the achievements that shaped the legacy of the fortieth president. In Reagan's second term, with nothing more than an undergraduate course in economics, he took over as secretary of the treasury and rewrote the American tax code from top to bottom in collaboration with leading Democrats. He returned to the campaign trail in 1988 to win the presidency for Bush in a harshly negative election that foreshadowed some of the political nastiness of races to come, then switched back into statesman mode as America's top diplomat, from which perch he effectively managed the most tumultuous period in international politics since World War II.

Over the following few years, as Washington presided over the end of the Cold War, Baker shaped a new American approach to a reordered world. Through it all, he was the archetype of a style of American politics and governance that today seems lost, an approach focused on compromise over confrontation, deal-making over disagreement and pragmatism over purity. He negotiated with Democrats at home and Soviets abroad, assembled the coalition that won the Gulf War and brokered the reunification of Germany in the heart of Europe. He was the "gold standard" among White House chiefs of staff, as virtually everyone put it, and went on to become the most consequential secretary of state since Henry Kissinger. In short, he was the un-Trump.

We had set out to write a biography about Baker during Barack Obama's presidency, when the nation was already starkly divided but Trump's ascendance was still unthinkable. As we interviewed Baker and his contemporaries for the book, the increasingly real prospect of a President Trump suggested an even more urgent reason for the project than we had originally envisioned: the unraveling of the political system that Baker had learned to operate so skillfully, at just the moment when the post–Cold War international order that he and his generation had established was fraying. At least to start, a book about Baker had seemed like escapism, offering an opportunity to time-travel back to Washington at the tail end of the Cold War, as the fractious 1980s evolved into a 1990s when America, suddenly, reigned supreme. That was Baker's moment. Freedom, and McDonald's, had come to Red Square; apartheid had ended peacefully in South Africa. History was not over, but it was definitely happening, right there for everyone to see on twenty-four-hour cable news. Although that did not erase the partisan conflicts and bitter discord roiling American politics through the Reagan years, and the city had its usual supply of hypocrites and charlatans, demagogues and dilettantes, it was a far more optimistic Washington than today's angry, anxious capital, a Washington where getting things done was not just possible but required.

Baker seemed to us the representative of that time; certainly, he was the uniquely successful exemplar of it, a hard-edged partisan who nonetheless believed in bipartisanship and thought elections required a record to run on, not merely a provocative position to tweet. But if Baker's Washington was a more functional, fundamentally more civil place, it was still a capital whose currency was power, populated by political animals for whom access, influence, and image were paramount. Baker was one of them. He was calculating and canny and opportunistic in all the ways that reflected the city whose top jobs he had conquered, one by one. He did not question its injustices, or the insularity of a world populated by white men who looked and sounded like him. Then again, neither did he come to Washington to fight the culture war that animated so many of his fellow Republicans. As our conversation on the eve of Trump's election suggested, Baker had not become the ultimate Washington player because of his ideological fervor, but because, better than anyone of his generation, he figured out how to wield the levers of power. His doctrine was dealmaking. Real deals, ones that stuck, deals that changed the world. And you cannot make deals and get things done while criticizing from the outside. Baker knew that. You have to be on the inside. You have to be allowed to play the game before you can win it.

"WASHINGTON LOVES the ones who grease its gears. But history only remembers the ones who shift them," the late *Washington Post* writer Marjorie Williams wrote of Baker. The man she profiled in the *Post*'s Style section upon his ascension to secretary of state in January 1989 was confident in his stature in the imperial capital at its twilight-of-the-Cold-War apogee, yet insecure enough to wake up each morning ready for battle to prove it. He represented the city's ideal of itself, a relentless but nonetheless patrician competitor willing to drink a Scotch with his rivals after hours, an Ivy League country-clubber equally at home in tennis whites or toting a shotgun to a duck blind in predawn Texas. This Baker was a master of Washington at the end of almost a decade at its heights; he was smooth and smart and disciplined, "a man in whom drive is more important than destination," as Williams wrote, but also a gentleman for whom recklessness was as inconceivable as incivility. Baker was a "player," the capital's ultimate accolade, and no matter what the game, he figured out a way to come out on top. As Haley Barbour, who worked in the Reagan White House with Baker and went on to become chairman of the Republican National Committee and governor of Mississippi, observed to us, "In the two-party system, purity is the enemy of victory, and Jim Baker was a winner."

Williams, though, had not been entirely right about Baker. Her impeccable eye caught the man who yearned to be more than just the staffer in the gray pinstriped suit behind Ronald Reagan in all those Oval Office pictures. But she missed how much the moment mattered too. Baker was no mere fixer. He was a doer as well, at a time when that was still possible in American politics. The end of the Cold War was a period of unparalleled American power. It was also, and we tend to forget this because of how it turned out, a moment of great risk. The gears were shifting. Politicians did not have the present-day luxury of permanent feuding as a substitute for action. Baker's skill set turned out to be suited for the era. He excelled not just in the Washington arts of self-promotion, palace intrigue, and blame-shifting (although he was world-class at all of them), but also in putting them into service for the real art of the deal, whether it was saving Social Security with congressional Democrats or persuading Soviet leaders to allow two Germanys to become one again or jaw-boning Arab sheikhs into contributing so much money for the liberation of Kuwait that the Gulf War against Iraq became the first American conflict to nearly turn a profit.

He divided problems into three categories, according to David Gergen, a former adviser from his White House days: easy; hard but doable; and impossible. The first category he left to others, the last he wrote off, and the middle is where he focused his energies. As inconceivable as it seems amid our state of endless partisan warfare, getting things done was in fact the currency of the realm in the Washington of Baker's era and this is what drove him with a ruthless focus and confidence that infuriated others who were ideologically purer and far less effective. Washington has and always will be a town that struggles between outcomes and principles; it is a place where compromise is both necessary and invariably suspect. Did Baker actually stand for anything other than his own advancement? Was it just power for power's sake? What would he be willing to give up to cut a deal? His critics were not the only ones to wonder. But what was remarkable about Baker was the extent to which his deals stuck.

At the end of his run, when the Berlin Wall had fallen and the Soviet Union was no more, when colleagues from the Reagan White House were out of the power game entirely or writing bitter memoirs about the Iran-contra scandal, Baker had somehow escaped the humbling comedown that is usually a part of the Washington narrative. Instead, Baker's reputation only grew in the years of gridlock and dysfunction that followed, and he has more recently become a figure of surprisingly bipartisan nostalgia for a different time and a different sort of leadership. "He was the most important unelected official since World War II," the former national security adviser Tom Donilon, a Democrat, told us.

Many have compared Baker at his height to the Wise Men of earlier Washington eras, pillars of the postwar establishment such as Dean Acheson. But Baker flourished in a succession of jobs that not even an Acheson could have imagined. Clark Clifford, the legendary Democratic fixer for decades in the capital, built his reputation off a four-year tour as counsel in Harry S. Truman's White House before returning to office for a short stint as Lyndon B. Johnson's defense secretary. In more recent times, political strategists such as James Carville, Karl Rove, and David Axelrod became household names after running one or two White House campaigns. Baker ran *five*. He also ran three cabinet departments, the achievement he preferred to highlight.

Baker always longed to be a statesman, not a hack. When *Time* magazine put him on the cover along with a Democratic operative under the word "Handlers," Baker hated it. But by the time he was called out of political retirement in Texas to help his best friend's son in the Florida recount that followed the too-close-to-call 2000 presidential election, Baker's reputation was so formidable that Democrats knew they would lose the moment they heard of his selection. And lose they did. "Baker somehow understood the billiards of politics, understood the ricochets," said Hedrick Smith, who followed him in the 1980s for *The New York Times*. "He understood how balls careened off each other." Baker knew when not to exercise power, too, whether it was letting his outmaneuvered White House rival Ed Meese save face with a symbolic but meaningless title or avoiding the temptation to gloat to the Soviets about their geopolitical humiliation.

For an operative who lived in fear that Marjorie Williams had been right, that he was just a glorified gear greaser after all, it was a record that few would match. In a city where powerful staffers are celebrated but also understood to be basking merely in the reflected glory of their presidential patrons, Baker transcended his many titles. He was not defined by his era; he helped to define it.

IN THE COURSE of writing this book over the last seven years, we conducted more than two hundred interviews with Baker, his family and friends, his admirers and detractors, and many of today's Washington players in both parties who expressed awe at Baker's accomplishments— and wanted to know how he had done it. What was Baker's secret, the clue to how an obscure corporate lawyer could come to the capital, *their* capital, and succeed at a series of the hardest, most consequential jobs in the world?

The answer that Baker himself would give to this inevitable question was both practiced and unsatisfying. He would grin and summon a Texas accent and talk about his father's maxim, the one that was beaten into him when he was a privileged mama's boy in Depression-era Houston. "Prior preparation prevents poor performance" became such a familiar mantra to those who worked with, and for, Baker over the years that they were not surprised when the Five Ps became the centerpiece of his post-Washington political memoir, *"Work Hard, Study . . . and Keep Out of Politics!"*—itself titled after one of his grandfather's most memorable sayings.

Washington is filled with careful lawyers who do their homework and stay up late cramming for meetings. No doubt Baker excelled at this. He was legendary for not going home from the office when he was Reagan's chief of staff until he had returned every last phone call from irate members of Congress and importuning journalists alike (and also for the neat pre-email trick of making many of the calls so late at night that he knew the recipients would no longer be at their desks to pick up the phone). But he was far from the only workaholic in a city where identity and status derive from one's position and not the other way around.

Still, Baker's work ethic and preparation were formidable. He was fanatically competitive and fanatically well organized. In his eighties, preparing to take us on a tour of the Houston neighborhoods where he grew up, lived, and worked for the entirety of his life outside Washington, Baker greeted us in the back of his black sport-utility vehicle with a yellow legal pad scratched full of notes. It turned out to be a carefully constructed itinerary of every place he wanted to show us. Baker was not satisfied, however. He had already driven the route in advance of our visit and decided to make a few last modifications. The man was and is a perfectionist.

But that too hardly explained his ability to navigate the upper reaches of Washington as it recovered from the anger and malaise of Vietnam, Watergate, and the Iran hostage crisis to regroup for the last gasps of the Cold War. And besides, you could study his early history forever and come away concluding that Baker was not actually very well prepared for the challenges of leading the greatest superpower the world has yet known through the volatile late twentieth century, when both its domestic politics and its international position would be fundamentally transformed. Baker came to Washington and won its highest prizes not because of what he studied or what he knew. He was not a war hero or a sage expert on balance-of-power politics. Nor did he get there on the basis of his family name or wealth, although his early years were marked by the benefits of both.

In many ways, in fact, it is hard to distinguish Baker's life from those of many other late-twentieth-century American worthies. As the unilateral rule of the predominantly white male American gentry was coming to an end, Baker could have been the emblem of a Cold War fraternity on its way out. A Texan by birth and breeding later pedigreed in the halls of

Princeton, Baker crossed easily between the worlds of Western frontier and East Coast clubs. He favored tailored shirts with "JAB III" monograms and would rarely be seen at work with so much as his tie loosened. He also wore cowboy boots and chewed Red Man tobacco and thought nothing of spitting into a Styrofoam cup in the middle of meetings on tax policy. He was rich, but not as rich as people thought. When on vacation, he could usually be found shooting quail in South Texas or fishing the Silver Creek near his ranch in Wyoming. He kept a bottle of Chivas Regal in a desk drawer for an afternoon drink when needed. He swore profusely and told dirty jokes. "Did you get laid last night?" he would ask his young advance man, Ed Rogers, each morning when they were on the road together during the Reagan years. It was not a throwaway line. "He'd look me in the eye and want an answer," Rogers recalled.

A lawyer from a storied clan of lawyers who spent the first few decades of his professional life tending to the business disputes of the oilmen and bankers who ruled Houston, Baker did not come to American politics animated by a desire to save the world or even much of a worldview at all, and most of what the law had taught him before he entered public life was about the perils of risk-taking. He was profoundly careful—"Mr. Caution," his close adviser, Margaret Tutwiler, dubbed him. "A shrink would have a field day with Jim Baker," Tutwiler observed. "The man is so realistic, without emotion, that even though he's an emotional, sensitive guy, sometimes it's so clinical. But he lives in the real, real world. He does not delude himself over fairy tales." Dispassionate and ever to the point, Baker brought discipline and endless handwritten lists to the challenge of running the world. He was "somebody who likes making order out of chaos," as his son Will Winston put it. He defined himself as the opposite of an ideologue. "I didn't have any overarching paradigm for politics," Baker told us as he reflected on his career years later. "My view was you try to get things done."

It was in the doing, then, that Baker excelled, in his genius ability to read what others required in a situation and find a way to give some version of that to them while still walking away from the table with whatever prize he sought. Baker was a compulsive winner, but he also had a way of making rivals feel like they had not entirely been defeated. "The Velvet Hammer," his cousin Preston Moore called him, and Baker was much more pleased when *Time* used that phrase to headline another cover story about him, this time referring to him not as The Handler but as "a gentleman who hates to lose." Anyone who had ever tangled with him knew that was true. Baker was that way because of who he was and where he came from, and it was his strange luck, and the country's, that he happened to be ready to leave his hometown and legal career behind at just the moment when the entire Republican elite had been decimated by Richard Nixon's Watergate disaster.

And here the story was rich, complex, and surprising in ways we did not expect. The man who would dominate Washington turned out to be an accidental political savant. He did not spend his childhood obsessing over electoral votes or memorizing congressional district boundaries. His Texas clan had viewed politics as a dirty business ever since the Civil War, when the family patriarch, a slave-holding Alabama émigré, had been booted out of a Texas judgeship after the Confederacy's defeat. "This is not a man who sat back and read Machiavelli or read the great books about influence and power," noted David Gergen. "It just came naturally to him."

A nominal Democrat until the 1970s, Baker never would have come to Washington if not for tennis, the preppy old boys' network, and a family tragedy. And even then it might not have happened if his domineering micromanager of a father had still been alive, for his dad, a stickler who billed his son if he had more than one soda at the country club as a child, who dictated which law school he should attend, and who even decreed what kind of car he should drive long after his son was already a married man with children of his own, had strictly enforced the ban on all things political.

That Baker's success was the kind that books would be written about was hardly foreseeable. He never even began working in Washington until he was already in his forties, starting his climb to the top from the obscurity of a political appointment in the Commerce Department. Yet his just might be the most consequential middle-age career switch in modern American politics. His timing, if accidental, was also impeccable: The gears were changing in history, and Baker would get his chance to move them. He was truly the Man Who Ran Washington back when Washington still ran the world.

But that is getting ahead of the story, which, as any good tale of America's capital should, begins far away, in this case a Houston mansion in the early days of a decade marked by crisis.

Part One

CHAPTER I

In the Magnolia City

Just six months after the stock market crash that would bring America into the Great Depression, James Addison Baker III arrived at Baptist Hospital in Houston at 7:31 a.m. on April 28, 1930, the long-awaited son of James Addison Baker Jr. and his wife, the elegant society hostess Bonner Means Baker. In the spidery handwriting on his birth certificate, his father's occupation was listed simply as "Lawher," although in actuality he was not only a prominent attorney but a banker, a builder, a war hero, and a demanding taskmaster who would expect much from the son for whom he had waited through thirteen childless years of marriage.

Already the Depression raged, in Houston and across America. But when baby Jimmy—a big child, weighing in at more than eight pounds, three ounces—came home to the imposing Spanish-style house at 1216 Bissonnet Road that his father had commissioned for the family a few years earlier, he would encounter none of it. The street had recently been renamed for one of his father's fellow World War I heroes, but was still known as Old Poor Farm Road and, in fact, the poorhouse was still there, a few miles away, besieged now with families seeking shelter. But the Bakers were insulated by wealth and color from the economic ravages of the time and the baby was welcomed home to a newly decorated nursery with a cook, a nanny, and a chauffeur to tend to him.

The world that Jimmy was born into had been shaped, to a remarkable degree, by his father, grandfather, and great-grandfather before him. He lived in a neighborhood of their design, in the shadow of a great new institution of higher learning that they had built and whose affairs they oversaw. He would grow up to play tennis and swim and hunt at clubs they had helped to found. The city of Houston that boomed around him was named for his great-grandfather's friend, its buildings financed by the bank his family helped to run. The art museum and the city's leading social-service charity were both started by his grandparents. When he got old enough to go to school, Jimmy would attend Houston's most prestigious private academy; his father, naturally, was chairman of the board.

Jimmy would soon grow into a tall boy with a lean, athletic build, a shock of dark, curly hair, an easy disposition, and eyes that gleamed over a good joke. He was smart, crazy about sports, and an indifferent student at best. He saw no injustice he yearned to correct or wrongs to right. As a boy, he wanted nothing more than a rifle and a chance to hunt something; as a young man, he thought mainly of creating a home for his own growing brood. The diplomat who would come to see himself as a guardian of the free world grew up in a very small universe.

He had inherited a lot more than a name from his distinguished, demanding forebears. Eventually, it would be his turn to take a place in the law firm that they had built and that had built the family fortune and reputation along with it. He had known this was his course in life since he had known pretty much anything at all. Privilege was his birthright, but it came with formidable demands of duty and discipline. His mother made clear to her son the expectations that awaited him, the fourth James Addison Baker. "Jimmy," she would say, "you have quite a legacy to live up to." He would be raised to follow the family tradition more than any of the hordes of cousins he grew up with or the younger sister, named Bonner after their mother, who came along just eighteen months after he was born. "He was the hero son," said his cousin Stewart Addison Baker. "He was the person who was expected to succeed in a grand way and I think even when he was a young man, it was assumed that he would fulfill those expectations."

THERE IS NO UNDERSTANDING Baker without understanding his family. The Bakers of Texas had always been lawyers and they passed the profession down to their sons along with the name—and the burden of living up to it. The first James Addison Baker, Jimmy's great-grandfather, born in 1821, had read law after serving as a schoolteacher near Huntsville, Alabama, hitting the books at night until he was admitted to practice at the age of twenty-two. By his early thirties, James Baker was young and ambitious and alone—his first wife, Caroline Hightower, died three years after they married. Just a few months after her death, he and his four brothers abandoned Alabama for Huntsville, Texas, the frontier namesake of their hometown. His late wife's parents had already moved there, part of a wave of slave-holding settlers who embarked on "patriarchal migrations" from north Alabama, "with hundreds of Negroes and their flocks and chattel in heavy wagon trains," as an early historian of the town wrote, coming to Texas "in search of cheap land now that the slave economy was exhausting the old states."

By 1853, Baker had met and fallen in love with another Alabama transplant, Rowena Beverly Crawford. Crawford was seven years younger, the headmistress of the new town's school, known as the Brick Academy, and in June of that year, Baker wrote to her father "to attain approbation of my suit" to marry her, acknowledging that while he was a "gentleman," he brought neither wealth nor high connection to the match. "I am not one of fortune's favorites, otherwise than in receiving the rewards of my own exertions," he wrote. The Crawfords came from more distinguished stock, a plantation family that traced its arrival in the colonies to an ancestor who landed in Virginia in 1654 from Presbyterian Scotland. Nonetheless, Baker was granted permission and the two married in 1854. Their first son died a year after birth, as did two later daughters, but their second son, James Addison Baker Jr., came along in 1857, one of five children who would live to maturity.

By the time Baker settled there, Huntsville, Texas, was barely removed from its origins a few years earlier as a Native American trading post, fortuitously sited near a spring in the midst of a grove of oak trees surrounded by red-clay hills. It had been founded by two brothers from his hometown, Pleasant and Ephraim Gray, in 1835, when Baker was already a teenager. The Brick Academy where Rowena had taught was the town's first chartered school and, soon after arriving, Baker sat on the committee that set up the first law school in the state of Texas. Huntsville was a "town of growing importance," wrote one of its notable early residents, the New England missionary Melinda Rankin, in a memoir of Texas in the 1850s. Rankin, Rowena's successor as headmistress of the Brick Academy, would have known the Bakers well and she saw the small settlement of émigrés from the Deep South among whom she had chosen to live as "rivalling in growth and prosperity other towns in the State of older standing," a boom she attributed to its becoming "the seat of justice" for newly incorporated Walker County. Lawyers like Baker were much in demand down at the brand-new brick courthouse on the town square.

Still, when his son James Jr. was born, the town was barely more than a crossroads, and its official population stood at just 939 in 1860 on the eve of the Civil War. The town's most famous citizen was General Sam Houston, the legendary hero of the Texas Revolution, who became president of the briefly independent Republic of Texas and later the state's governor and senator. He was also, according to family lore, Baker's friend and fellow Mason.

In 1860, Baker was elected to the Texas state legislature meeting in Austin, but he resigned a year later. The Civil War had erupted by then and Baker, although already forty years old, signed up for a six-month enlistment with Huntsville volunteers fighting for the Confederacy. His family owned a number of slaves, according to county records, and he brought one of them to the war, a man named Bill, who cooked for Baker and his tent mates. They saw little action and Baker, while serving in the unit, ran for and was elected a judge for the district that included Houston, the booming new town seventy miles due south from Huntsville that bore his friend's name.

Baker resigned from the army and went to Houston to take up his judgeship; he would keep the title and the connection to the city for the rest of his life. But with the Northern victory in 1865, Union troops occupied the courthouse and the Reconstruction governor of Texas removed Baker and other Confederate officials from their posts. Baker never forgot it. His short, bruising experience in elective office as a judge and in the legislature during the year when Texas voted to secede from the Union left him bitter about politics, an aversion that would grow through the years of postwar Republican rule in Texas and eventually be passed down to generations to come.

Judge Baker, as he was now known, soon began practicing law again in Huntsville, where he took on a sensational case, representing four white defendants arrested for murdering a freed black man in a dispute over a crop-sharing agreement. After three of the four were convicted, two of the defendants brandished hidden guns, opened fire at police officers, and escaped. When sympathetic white men in the area refused to form a posse to hunt them down, the Reconstruction governor declared martial law and sent in the state militia. Eventually the defendants were caught but they were later pardoned.

Beyond his representation of such men, little is known about Baker's personal views on the subject of the bitter racial politics of the day, although he named his son born after the war Robert Lee Baker in honor of the South's most famous general. Yet in one of Baker's most notable cases as a lawyer, just three years after the Civil War, he represented Eliza Stoneum, a freed African American woman who was being deprived of her white common-law husband's estate by his family and sued to be recognized as his lawful spouse and heir. In a moving decision, a white district judge reversed the original verdict against Stoneum, writing that a court is "a place where *justice* is administered" and concluding that "this old and faithful woman, the mother of the children of the deceased, after her forty-six years of toil" should not be deprived because she was believed to have "African blood in her veins."

Just a few years later, in 1887, Judge Baker's nephew Andy Baker, born in Huntsville at the tail end of the Civil War, had a son, Jesse, with an African American woman. Jesse, a farmer who took the Baker name, ended up having eleven sons and daughters of his own, making him patriarch of a vast African American branch of the Baker family whose existence may or may not have been known to Judge Baker.

Huntsville after the Civil War was no longer the center of business and opportunity it had seemed when Judge Baker first moved there as a young man. Bypassed by the railroad after the town leaders failed to offer a generous enough financial inducement, Huntsville was becoming a sleepy cul-de-sac after the war and, in 1867, was decimated by a yellow fever epidemic that killed more than 150 of its residents. By 1872, Judge Baker had decided to leave, and he moved to Houston to join a law firm formed just after the Civil War by Peter Gray and Walter Browne Botts, both Confederate veterans like himself; their two-man shop specialized in work for banks and railroads. With his move, Gray & Botts became Gray, Botts & Baker, then a couple years later, after Gray left, Baker & Botts.

FOUNDED IN 1836, Houston had grown far more rapidly into a commercial center than Judge Baker's adopted hometown to the north. But it was still a small place with an uncertain future, home to just nine thousand residents when Judge Baker moved there. An island of wooden buildings surrounded by cotton farms, the city was known for its "oceans of mud, and submerged suburbs, the home of the frog and the cradle of the mosquito, the birthplace of fever," as a newspaper put it at the time. Called the Magnolia City for its fragrant groves, it was smaller than the port town of Galveston, but the arrival of railroads was already transforming Houston into a vital transit point for timber, cotton, and other agricultural products. By the turn of the twentieth century, its population had nearly quintupled, overtaking Galveston to make Houston the largest city in Texas. The opening of a ship channel to the Gulf of Mexico in 1914, presided over by Judge Baker's son, sealed the city's rise as a major center of commerce and its emergence as a swaggering metropolis.

The out-of-state railroad companies that dominated Houston in its early days needed help navigating the populist laws of Texas, which is where Judge Baker and his firm came in. In the first decades of the firm's existence, as much as half of its income came from railroads. "The law firm and the city literally grew up together," according to a history of the firm. Jay Gould, the capitalist titan of the era, seized control of many smaller railroads and Baker & Botts became the Texas representation for his Missouri Pacific. After Gould was beaten out and several Texas lines were consolidated under Southern Pacific, the firm became the new combined company's general counsel in 1893. The firm also represented many of the city's other industries. "There is scarcely a great enterprise in Houston or the surrounding country in which we have not figured in some way," wrote Clarence Wharton, the firm's unofficial historian.

Judge Baker was determined to have his oldest son and namesake follow him into this thriving legal business. Jimmie, "a dashing handsome person with a twinkle in his eye," attended Texas Military Institute, then joined Baker & Botts alongside his father. Genial and confident, sporting a thin mustache, often wearing a white summer suit and smoking a cigar, Jimmie read law at the firm, but found time outside of studying to join the Houston Light Guards, a uniformed company of the state's National Guard formed by Confederate veterans after Reconstruction that became a favorite sideline of the city's emerging business elite. Jimmie rose to captain in the militia, and for the rest of his life he would go by Captain Baker, never mind that it was purely an honorific and he never served in a genuine military outfit.

Captain Baker, grandfather of the future secretary of state, was a lively presence in Houston and a savvy manager of people. He charmed ladies and was said to be a riveting storyteller and a nimble dancer. He loved hunting, fishing, hiking, and playing cards. In 1882, he met Alice Graham of Waco, Texas, one of four daughters in a family with its own Scottish roots. They married the following January, on his twenty-sixth birthday, and nine months later came their first son, Frank Graham Baker, born on Alice's nineteenth birthday. They were later joined by a daughter, Alice Graham Baker, and a second son, James Addison Baker Jr. By this point, Captain Baker had dropped his own Junior and gave the title to his son, even though the boy was the third James A. Baker. Later in life that James Baker would name his son James III, even though he really was the fourth to hold that name. In years to come, the family would explain the confusing numerology by joking that they never could count.

By 1887, Captain Baker made partner at the family law firm, which marked the occasion by renaming itself Baker, Botts & Baker. But successful as he was, Captain Baker was still in his father's shadow at work and at home, where he and his growing family lived with his parents in a Greek Revival–style house. Eventually they would move into their own home, a grand Victorian pile with a turret at 1416 Main Street, and have three more children, for a total of six. A decade after Captain Baker made partner and the firm became a family business in the true sense of the word, Judge Baker died, on February 23, 1897, at the age of seventy-five. The old frontier lawyer was buried back in Huntsville in the Oakwood Cemetery not far from where Sam Houston was laid to rest.

Turn-of-the-century Houston was Captain Baker's time, and he would come to dominate the city and its fledgling institutions more than any Baker before or since. As he built what became known again as Baker & Botts and later just Baker Botts into a powerhouse, Captain Baker operated as far more than simply a lawyer. Over the years, he served as a partner, vice president, or president of everything from an electric utility to an oil company. The merger of two financial institutions in 1912 produced the South Texas Commercial National Bank, the second largest in Houston. Captain Baker served as its president or chairman from 1914 until his death twenty-seven years later.

Burly and formidable as he grew older, Captain Baker was a founder by nature and inclination. He helped create many of the institutions that still shape Houston today. When the Houston Country Club opened, Baker was on the board—same for its rival, the River Oaks Country Club. He was president of the Houston Bar Association, a founder of the Houston Gas Company, and an organizer of the Galveston, Houston and Henderson Railway. Together with his wife, he helped establish the Houston Museum of Fine Arts.

Alice Baker was a force of her own, a pillar of liberal causes inspired by the good works of Progressive-era activists such as Jane Addams in Chicago and her Settlement House movement. She raised money to build a new wing for the Houston Tubercular Hospital, personally pouring the first shovel of concrete in the foundation. Appalled by what she had heard about the poor living conditions for immigrants in the city's booming, squalid Second Ward, she invited a dozen women to her house in February 1907. The Houston Settlement Association was born in the Bakers' elegant living room that day and it soon opened a community center, organized English classes, established a clinic for babies, offered playground activities, and provided day care for working mothers. "Residents of every section of the city should have a fair chance at proper living conditions and moral surroundings," she said.

AT THE FIRM, one of Captain Baker's most important clients was William Marsh Rice, the richest man in Houston and a major patron of the city. Rice's untimely death in September 1900 resulted in what newspapers at the time described as "America's most remarkable murder case" and "one of the most remarkable trials in all history." It would, in the end, redraw the map of Houston and reshape the history of the Baker family.

Rice was a transplant from Massachusetts who arrived in Texas "a penniless youth without resources, friends or even acquaintances," as a historian put it. But Rice made a fortune in almost every trade conceivable, from ranching and railroads to timber and cotton. Although he relocated to New York, he made plans to use his wealth to create a school in Houston in his name, the William M. Rice Institute for the Advancement of Literature, Science and Art. But when Rice's wife died in 1896, she left a will that sought to give part of her husband's property to her own family along with various churches and charities. Furious, Rice instructed Captain Baker to contest the will, arguing that as a New York resident, he was not subject to Texas law.

The dispute remained unresolved four years later when Rice himself suddenly died in his Madison Avenue apartment in New York at age eighty-four. Captain Baker received a telegram notifying him of the death—and then a second telegram from Rice's bankers warning that his client had died "under very suspicious circumstances." Baker leaped into action, arranging for New York authorities to prevent the body from being cremated and rushing north. Arriving in New York, he was met, oddly enough, by Albert Patrick, a lawyer who had been working on the other side of the legal battle over the will of Rice's wife but who now claimed to be acting on the dead man's behalf. Tall and balding with a red beard, the thirty-four-year-old Patrick contended that Rice had died after eating nine bananas, five baked and four raw. He asserted that before his death, Rice had soured on Captain Baker and had a new will drawn up leaving Patrick in charge of the bulk of the $8 million estate, or roughly $245 million in today's dollars. If that were not dubious enough, the morning after Rice's death, Patrick sought to cash four checks made out to him, signed "W.M. Rice" and dated the day before the mogul perished, totaling $250,000.

Captain Baker and New York authorities investigated and determined that the checks and the new will were forgeries. Baker along with a prosecutor interrogated Charlie Jones, Rice's valet, who confessed that he had helped Albert poison the magnate—in other words, the butler did it.

Authorities later concluded that a towel bathed in chloroform had been held over Rice's face, leading to his death. Patrick's trial in 1902 was a sensation, the longest on record in New York City to that date, covered breathlessly by local newspapers and followed across the country. Captain Baker sat in the courtroom, serving as the foil for Patrick's defense attorney, who described the Texan as a "wily, astute and crafty lawyer" who manipulated "the weak individual Jones" against his client. The jury was unmoved and convicted Patrick of first-degree murder, leading to a death sentence.

But the verdict was not universally accepted. Nearly 3,500 doctors signed a petition questioning the medical evidence that Rice was poisoned. Other notables of the day, including former president Grover Cleveland and Mark Twain, signed a statement on Patrick's behalf. Sir Arthur Conan Doyle called the case a "gross miscarriage of justice." With two former senators taking on his appeal, Patrick won a commutation from one New York governor, reducing his death sentence to life in prison, and a full pardon from a subsequent governor, who freed him outright. A law professor who examined the case nearly a century later concluded that Patrick was guilty of forging the checks and the will, but probably not the murder; the idea of chloroform may have been the power of Captain Baker's suggestion to the butler.

However Rice had actually died, Baker had secured the estate from being stolen and he soon put it to work developing the Rice Institute. He doubled the endowment to nearly $10 million by the time the school formally opened in 1912 on the anniversary of Rice's death, serving seventy-seven male and female students in a single building in western Houston. Baker served as chairman of the board of trustees, a post he would hold for more than fifty years. The institute was later renamed Rice University and it eventually grew into one of the premier institutions in Texas. Baker tended to it so assiduously that he sent his own gardener to campus to plant oak trees and then, when walking by the saplings, would urge them on: "Damn it, grow." Rice may have given the school his name, but *The Houston Post* called Captain Baker "the foster father of Rice Institute."

The Rice trust that Baker controlled was also perhaps the largest source of capital available to developers putting up office buildings in downtown Houston, financing the construction of a modern metropolis as well as whole neighborhoods of comfortable Arts and Crafts bungalows around the institute Baker was nurturing from the "barren wasteland," as Rice's first president, lured south from Princeton, put it. He was now a banker, a lawyer, and an urban visionary. "Baker and his friends literally helped build the city," according to a book chronicling the history of Baker Botts.

By 1922, Captain Baker was ready for a grand home of his own too, one that would announce his place in the emerging city. He paid about $125,000, or just under $2 million in today's dollars, to buy The Oaks, a seven-acre property blocks from downtown Houston where skyscrapers would eventually rise. The imposing estate on the corner of Baldwin and Hadley Streets was filled with tall oak trees and a rose garden that Alice Graham Baker tended with the help of a half dozen gardeners. The three-story, dark-red-brick home, designed by the Houston architectural firm of Sanguinet and Staats, had an impressive foyer, marble fireplaces, a billiards room, an extensive household staff, and a set of stables for the horses. It would be the family seat for years to come.

Baker loved surrounding himself with his large clan and everyone was expected for Sunday dinner at The Oaks in the dark wood-paneled dining room. In later years, the grandchildren were convinced ghosts lived there, a fear the old Captain would do little to allay when he promised them a nickel if they ran around the room in the dark. At home as well as work, he was a forbidding figure; when riled, Captain Baker "could turn quickly from the affable uncle to the stern patriarch," as the firm's history put it. Preston Moore, one of his grandchildren, recalled him as a strict, intimidating man. "He was a tough taskmaster," he remembered. Another grandson, Addison Baker Duncan, said the Captain would "scare you to death."

Captain Baker certainly had very definitive ideas about what was expected of a Baker and he was not hesitant to make his expectations for the family clear. One of his rules was to avoid politics, an antipathy he inherited from his father, Judge Baker. When *The Houston Post* profiled Captain Baker a few years before his death, he was asked his secret for success. "Work hard, study and apply yourself closely, stay on the job and keep out of politics," he had said.

CAPTAIN BAKER KNEW exactly what he wanted for his sons—all the benefits of the first-rate Eastern education he had never received, then a return to Texas to take up the law in Houston as he and his father had done. In the fall of 1899, he sent his oldest son, Graham Baker, to the Hill School, a strict Presbyterian boarding academy outside Philadelphia that was beginning to attract the sons of the South's newly wealthy postwar magnates. Baker chose it, according to family lore, because it was the best he could find without looking at New England, where Texans were wary of sending their children for fear that they would "lose their Southern connection," as Duncan put it.

But in February 1902, in the midst of his senior year, Graham was struck by pneumonia. A telegram summoning the Captain and his wife found him in New York City, in the midst of the sensational trial over William Marsh Rice's death, and the Bakers rushed to the train to make it to their son in time. They were at his bedside when he died three days later, a tragedy of the pre-antibiotics era that made front-page news back in Houston, where he was mourned as "the idolized treasure of a happy household." When he died, Graham Baker was eighteen years old and set to go to Princeton University that fall.

Instead, his younger brother James Jr. would go east a few years later in his place, taking up all the burden of his father's expectations. The fact that Captain Baker and his wife would send James Jr. to the Hill School despite the memories of loss spoke to how much they still venerated it. Years later, Captain Baker would extol the place as a model for "the efficiency of its teaching," the strict "discipline," and "particularly, the wonderful moral influence thrown about the student body."

After graduating, James Jr. headed to Princeton University, another favorite of the Southern elite where many of the Hill School graduates went. Known to friends as "Bake," the transplant from Houston assembled the sort of résumé that the family back home expected of him—vice president of his freshman class, president of his sophomore class, manager of the musical clubs, a member of the Cap and Gown Club, circulation manager of *The Daily Princetonian*. In sports, he was a star at both pole-vaulting and wrestling. His was to be the last real class of the prewar era, a group that would soon find its future in the trenches of the Western Front but spent its four years in Princeton in genteel partying of the sort that F. Scott Fitzgerald, just a couple of years behind Baker, would portray in *This Side of Paradise*, his novel about a social-climbing Princeton man from the hinterlands who wooed and lost a beautiful debutante.

During a visit home to Houston, Baker attended a high school dance where he met a debutante of his own named Bonner Means. The daughter of John Coalter Means, a "not particularly successful" businessman trading in timber, oil, and cotton, and his wife, Stella Bonner Means, Bonner was just fifteen when she came upon Baker, but she would always describe their chance encounter as love at first sight.

History, and the demands of Baker's position as the family scion, would make it a long courtship. First, Baker put off the wedding to graduate from Princeton in 1915, after which he went, per the Captain's orders, to the University of Texas at Austin law school. A long career at the family firm beckoned, but Baker graduated in 1917, soon after the United States entered World War I. The law would wait. In August 1917, James Jr. finally married his sweetheart at Houston's Christ Church, then honeymooned not very romantically at The Oaks, the family estate, ten months before he shipped off to Europe as an Army lieutenant to fight the Germans. His father, domineering but proud, advised him in a letter sending him off to the bloodiest war yet known to mankind to pay attention to the "bearing and deportment of a young officer," urging him to "wear a neat white collar and cuffs and see that your trousers and coat are well pressed, your shoes neat and tidy."

A member of the Ninetieth Infantry Division, known as the "Pride of Every Texan," James Jr. would see for himself the full horrors of the war, serving in the trenches of Verdun, where more than 700,000 were killed or wounded in an epochal battle earlier in the war. At one point, he later told his son, when troops under his command were reluctant to clear out an enemy bunker, he went in himself and captured three German soldiers with only a .45 caliber revolver. His cousin Alice Gray's husband Albert wrote after returning home to describe running into Baker, "bedraggled with mud" and wearing a trench helmet, a dirty private's uniform, and a pistol. A captain in the battalion told him that Baker had "covered himself in glory."

His unit fought under the command of General John "Black Jack" Pershing in the Battle of Saint-Mihiel, an open hellscape of bombed fields and deafening artillery rounds, then, after a short break, returned for forty-five days straight in the trenches, from which Baker was the only officer in his unit to survive uninjured. By the time the war was over, he had been promoted to captain and earned a post as an aide to a general, an assignment he considered "a snap," as he put it in a letter to his sister, after the ordeal at the front. "There's nothing to do except stick around with him, drink Moselle wine, and ride in his six-cylinder car," he wrote. It was lost on no one in the family that his father was called Captain Baker even though he never served in the actual military, while James Jr. was a real captain cited for his valor in combat.

Returning to Houston after the war, James Jr. bowed to the inevitable and joined his father's law firm in 1919, becoming a partner in 1927. Although he wanted nothing more than to be a trial attorney, his father did not want him to focus on the courtroom. He pressed his son to devote time to business as he did; James Jr. was soon on bank boards and making the city grow, supervising the building of subdivisions and managing

Baker Botts as it expanded from a collection of solo practitioners into more of a collective enterprise.

As Houston grew, so did the firm. The late-nineteenth-century arrival of the railroads had made the city, and the lawyers at Baker Botts who served them ("Houston: Where Seventeen Railroads Meet the Sea," as the city's boosterish slogan of the era had it). But in the early twentieth century, it was the discovery of oil transforming Texas, starting with the 1901 eruption of a great gusher in a well at Spindletop in the southeast corner of the state that sent oil a hundred feet into the air and would not be capped for nine days. Wildcatters flocked to the region and with them came a wave of new service, supply, and manufacturing businesses, not to mention the accompanying speculators, gamblers, and prostitutes. In effect, it was the Texas equivalent of California's gold rush a half century earlier, "with rotary drill bits and derricks instead of pick axes and gold pans," as the Texas State Historical Association put it. Within a few years, the first offshore drilling began and by the 1920s Texas was the largest oil-producing state in the nation. The discovery of a giant field in East Texas in 1930 followed by additional finds in West Texas later in the decade accelerated the state's emergence as an energy powerhouse.

By that point, Houston had surged to a population of nearly 300,000 and become a national destination, the "Chicago of the South," as the city's promoters dubbed it. Now largely under James Jr.'s leadership, the firm expanded along with its hometown, serving newfound energy giants such as Texaco, Sinclair Oil, Atlantic Refining, Continental Oil, and Standard Oil. Captain Baker had a worthy heir in his son. "He was a central figure in the coming of age of both his law firm and his city," as the firm's history put it.

THE NEXT JAMES ADDISON BAKER, namesake of these formidable lawyers and the future secretary of state, was born a princeling of the newfound Houston aristocracy. For thirteen years, his parents had tried to have a baby without success, leading eventually to a train trip to Baltimore for his mother to have an unspecified "procedure." Having almost given up, the Bakers took a trip to Hawaii, a long journey in those days. When they returned, Bonner Baker discovered she was pregnant.

As a boy, Jimmy spent Sunday dinners and Tuesday afternoons with his grandfather at The Oaks, surrounded by his flock of first cousins, five of whom were born within a few years of each other. When his mother needed food for dinner, she sent Jimmy with Beatrice Green, his nanny, to Jetts Grocery on nearby Montrose Boulevard, where they would order a chicken and the owner would go out back where he kept live birds, pick one out, wring its neck, and then pluck its feathers off.

Jimmy's early years were a round of basketball and football and, especially, tennis. Each morning, Green woke him up and got him ready for school. Then after the last class, she took him over to the Houston Country Club. He started tennis lessons early and became addicted. "He is a very, very competitive person," said Preston Moore, his cousin and best friend throughout childhood. Once while playing tennis, another young boy hit Jimmy in the hip with an errant ball. "He said, 'Watch this,'" and sent one back across the net, giving the other boy a black eye, Moore recalled.

In Depression-era Houston, the initial impact of the nation's economic collapse was tempered by the burgeoning oil business, but soon enough the advent of cotton compresses resulted in lower worker pay as crop prices fell. A wave of anti-immigrant sentiment washed over the city as white workers complained that Mexican migrants were taking their jobs. Texas was further ravaged by the Dust Bowl of the 1930s, the swirling windstorms and relentless droughts that eroded millions of acres of land and drove farmers out of business and toward the cities. When Houston's two biggest banks teetered on the edge of collapse, the city's leading businessman, Jesse Jones, stepped in to broker a deal to save them, bolstered by a 2 a.m. phone call he placed to Captain Baker. The captain's support for the rescue plan "gave us real courage," Jones said later, and brought the holdouts into the deal.

In his memoir, the future secretary of state never even mentioned the Depression, but he did remember how much his father and their friends hated Franklin D. Roosevelt and New Deal programs like the Works Progress Administration. Like many wealthy white Texans in that era, his parents were conservative Democrats who believed in limited government and low taxes, saw FDR as a class traitor and voted Republican at the national level. They hosted dinner parties serving pheasant under glass and assigned young Jimmy to memorize anti-Roosevelt poems, then had him come downstairs and recite for the guests. "They were all about WPA and the big government," he recalled. His father's philosophy was summed up in an interview he gave to a reporter in 1951 at the height of the Korean War. "Even if we win a military victory," he said, "under our national policy we may lose the war and our individual freedom by undue regulation and by a bad fiscal and monetary policy of not balancing the national budget. The days of soak the rich are over. They have been soaked."

In the home he had commissioned for his family in the new development he built near Rice Institute called Broadacres, James Baker Jr. had emerged as a figure every bit as formidable as the father who had dominated his own life. Jimmy remembered him as tough and inflexible, with "an austere demeanor." His father, Jimmy said years later, "was a strict disciplinarian." He set high expectations and insisted on his children living up to them—drilling into them the Five Ps mantra of prior preparation that would stick with his son for the rest of his life. "He was brought up in a demanding household," said Preston Moore, his cousin. "They were stern disciplinarians." Moore, as close as a brother to Jimmy, moved in with the family for a time after his own father died at the end of World War II; he and Jimmy went to bed at night together on the second-floor outdoor sleeping porch, a relic of those pre-air-conditioning days, falling asleep to the roar of the lions in the nearby zoo.

The senior Baker worked weekends, often bringing Jimmy into the Baker Botts office with him, and when his son finished a tennis match, he would make him stay on the court to keep practicing. The father did not shy away from corporal punishment, viewing it as a way to teach children to keep in line. If Jimmy did not wake up by 7 a.m. on a Saturday, his father would splash cold water on him. He would chastise Jimmy because his sister was doing better than he was in school. Jimmy's friends "were a little bit afraid" of his dad, recalled one, Wallace Stedman Wilson. Together, they came up with a nickname for the old man: the Warden.

When a teenage Jimmy came home late one night with his friend Jimmy Bertron, he apologized for their tardiness, telling his father that they had had a flat tire. Suspicious, the father separated the boys, sending his son to the dining room and Bertron to the living room, then interrogated them separately to see if their stories matched, much like a prison boss might do with two inmates accused of stealing extra food.

When Jimmy was about fourteen or fifteen, he spent the night with a friend and they along with some other boys decided to have a little fun. They went out with a Benjamin pump air rifle and shot out some streetlights, only to be rounded up by police officers and taken to the local station. The officers called the boys' parents and one by one they arrived to take their sons home. Not Jimmy's dad. "He said, 'Let him stay there for the night,'" Baker recalled decades later. "It didn't surprise me. That's the way he was." Jimmy was the only one of the group to spend the night in jail. The Warden hoped to teach him a lesson.

HIS MOTHER WAS the protective one. As David Paton, a lifelong friend of Jimmy's, put it, "The father was the person who was very much in command and Jimmy respected that. His mother was the melody to which he responded beautifully."

Bonner Means Baker loved to read to Jimmy and was considered a witty storyteller; her son would inherit her facility for a good joke. Complimented years later on her skill at spinning a tale, she responded, "Darling, I had to be a good storyteller because we didn't have movies or radio. We didn't have anything and if you wanted a beau, you had to be able to—if you wanted to entertain friends, you had to really be able to tell a story."

She was also the one Jimmy sought out for emotional support. He called her "Mamish" and thought of her as "doting" and "cuddly," "warm" and "spirited." Mamish would do almost anything to protect her children from what she saw as a hostile outside world, even if it meant unintentionally humiliating them in front of their schoolmates. Eight decades later, Baker would remember the indignity of the hot lunches she insisted on sending him at the Kinkaid School. Every day at midday he would have to go over to the side entrance of the school building to meet the family chauffeur to collect the black metal lunchbox of hot fried chicken, rice, and gravy that his mother had dispatched. There would be no bagged lunch like the other children. For a young boy trying to fit in, the whole exercise was mortifying. He dreaded it, but no matter how much he pleaded with his mother, she refused to stop. "It was demeaning," he recalled, the memory still searing late in life. "It was so embarrassing." Mamish, a perfectionist, had a strict sense of what she considered right and wrong and, especially, what was proper for the Bakers. She was, her son concluded, "sort of a Victorian."

There were few other slights that stuck. Asked years later about the most traumatic experience of his childhood, Baker could only remember the time when he was playing with his black-and-white cocker spaniel, Gyp, and spotted an orange in the gutter. Jimmy tossed it for the dog to fetch, only to watch in horror as Gyp raced into the road and was run over right in front of him. "That just killed me," he said later.

In the summer of 1941, when the grandson who would bear his name into the twenty-first century was just eleven years old, Captain Baker died at the age of eighty-four, having amassed a large estate and an even larger reputation. The funeral procession stretched two miles long as much of Houston turned out to pay respects. "Few men have had so much influence on Houston, its growth and development as had Captain Baker," the *Houston Chronicle* wrote. "It would never have been the city it is without him." Indeed, the *Chronicle*'s own headquarters was built with the help of financing from the Rice trust managed by Captain Baker. His "was no commonplace life," noted a long tribute to him by the Philosophical Society of Texas, one of the many groups of which he had been an esteemed member. Captain Baker, it concluded, "was rarely endowed to make the most of the great transitions in which the old South became the new."

A few months later, on December 7, 1941, Jimmy had just finished playing tennis at the River Oaks Country Club and was walking over to the main clubhouse when he overheard the radio in the caddy shack announce the news that Japanese forces had attacked Pearl Harbor. He watched an uncle and cousin head off to the military, while his family planted a Victory Garden and limited their driving to ration gas.

Like much of the South before the war, the Texas that Baker grew up in was riven by bigotry, hatred, and organized violence against blacks. The state's last recorded lynching took place in Texarkana in 1942, when Jimmy was twelve, the culmination of generations of Jim Crow repression. The only African Americans he knew, however, were on his family's household staff—his nanny Beatrice Green and the nanny who came before her, Maybelle Cosby, plus the family chauffeur, Rufus Lockett, and the cook, Belle Jones, who fed them a steady diet of Southern home cooking, including delicacies such as pig's feet that Baker's father refused to eat. "It was segregated and that's what he knew," recalled Green, who remained close to the family well past her one-hundredth birthday.

Green said she never discussed race with Jimmy when he was growing up. "No one was talking politics," she said. Preston Moore remembered riding a bus through the Southampton neighborhood not far from home one day when Jimmy was about twelve and discovering the rules of segregated seating when they unknowingly sat in the back. "The bus driver told us we couldn't sit back there," Moore said. But they stayed in their seats anyway. "That was the only political stand that I remember."

Every summer during the war, Jimmy's parents sent him off to camp and, in all the letters back and forth over the next four years that survived, not a single mention was made of the war or the latest from the front lines. The only reference was a passing mention of their Victory Garden and war shortages. "Of course, World War II was going on," remembered Mike Kelley, another boy from the neighborhood who went to camp with Jimmy, "but we were in our early teens and weren't terribly aware of that."

During his summers away at Camp Rio Vista, Jimmy received regular reminders from his father about the man he was expected to be. "I hope you will try to get along with every boy in the Camp, no matter whether you like him at first or not," his father wrote in the summer of 1941 when Jimmy was eleven. "I know you have been homesick a little of the time," he added a few weeks later, "but that you are and will be too much of a man to show it or let this worry you to any extent."

Jimmy got similar advice about the masculine requirements from his grandfather before he died. "I am very glad indeed to note the genuine interest each of you is taking in many of those games known as 'Manly Sports,'" Captain Baker wrote Jimmy and his other grandsons. He urged them to get to know the names of the top baseball stars and leading players from other sports like tennis, football, and basketball. He sent each of them a $3 check to spend as they wished. "Please acknowledge receipt," he added in lawyerly fashion, signing off, "With assurances of my abiding admiration and love for you, I am, now as always, Yours affectionately." He signed "Grand-father" over a typewritten "James A. Baker."

In 1944, even as American troops were landing at Normandy and liberating Europe, Jimmy spent part of the summer at the St. John's Military Academy in Delafield, Wisconsin. He saw the Mississippi River for the first time on the train ride up north. He learned combat training, unarmed defense, and jiujitsu as well as how to use .30 caliber machine guns, 60 mm mortars, and .50 caliber machine guns. He proudly sent home three targets he shot with a rifle at fifty yards, all in or near the bull's-eye. By the end of camp, he weighed 124 pounds, a full fifteen pounds more than when he arrived.

He then headed west, riding a train by himself from Wisconsin all the way out to Wyoming, where his father had planned a grand adventure for them. They were headed into the backcountry near Yellowstone Park for nearly a month to hunt elk; Jimmy would even get to miss the first two weeks of school, an unheard-of dispensation from his father. Both Bakers already loved hunting and it was one thing they cherished doing together. His father had first taken Jimmy out shooting when he was only six years old. "His mother thought that was too early," remembered Beatrice Green, "but he loved it." Later, his father regularly drove him sixty miles west of Houston to the Eagle Lake Rod & Gun Club, where they spent early morning hours shooting ducks and dodging alligators that sometimes tried to take their birds. The club, founded in 1920 with his father and grandfather among the original members, was a bastion of Houston's elite, its membership of bankers and oilmen and lawyers capped at sixty, with individual slots handed down from generation to generation. Jimmy's mother hated it. After one too many predawn mornings and a particularly icy dunk in the lake when his father tipped over their boat, she refused to go any longer, telling James Jr., "You have a son now, take him." The two went so often that one time when Jimmy was around twelve, his nearsighted father had him drive all the way down. Eventually, he got to know the lake so well he no longer needed the guides.

But even by Texas standards, this Wyoming trip would be a major undertaking. Neither James Jr. nor his teenage son had ever hunted big game. Before they left, Baker bought two .30 caliber hunting rifles, one for himself and one for Jimmy. The two Baker women, mother and daughter, were left behind at the Valley Ranch in Cody, Wyoming, while Jimmy and his father met up with the hunting party, a distinguished group that had been put together by the elder Baker's Princeton roommate, William Spencer, and that included a general and the governor of Wyoming, Lester Hunt, who later became the inspiration for one of the main characters in Allen Drury's classic political novel *Advise and Consent*. Jimmy was the only boy.

They rode twenty-six hours on horseback into the wilderness, stopping along the way in unspoiled mountain meadows filled with elk. They made camp on Open Creek near the headwaters of the Yellowstone and Jimmy and his father shared a tent. Every morning, after Jimmy's father had taken his customary ice-cold dip in the stream as a substitute for the freezing showers he took at home, they rode out to hunt. Once, his father watched two big bulls fight—then shot the winner. "Boy, that wasn't fair," he told his dad. In the end, though, it was Jimmy who bagged an impressively large elk—the biggest of the whole hunt. The trip to the West, free from the constraints of their Houston life, solidified Jimmy's relationship with his father, who was raising him in the Baker family tradition of rugged play matched by professional excellence.

Back at the Kinkaid School, the private coed academy where his father was chairman of the board, Jimmy played on the varsity basketball team and on a six-member football squad as backup quarterback. When he turned fourteen that year of the Wyoming adventure, his parents gave him a Cushman motor scooter so he could ride to school in the morning and then to the River Oaks Country Club in the afternoon to play tennis with a Russian pro, Andrew Jitkoff, with whom he grew so close that he was "like a second father to me."

But Kinkaid could only take him so far. The Warden had bigger plans for him.

CHAPTER 2

The Warden's Son

Jimmy Baker got off the train in Pennsylvania after a long ride from Texas in the fall of 1946. Following his father's footsteps, Jimmy was arriving in Pottstown to spend his final two years before college at the Hill School, the elite boarding school that James Baker Jr. had attended after his brother Graham's tragic death there at the turn of the century. A generation and two world wars later, not all that much had changed. The Hill, as it was known, was still strict, Presbyterian, all boys, and decidedly old-fashioned.

Jimmy was hardly a natural fit. "It was the first time I ever saw anybody in cowboy boots," marveled his new roommate, William Barnabas McHenry, whose illustrious forebears went back to the Revolutionary War and, before that, to a castle in Ireland. Barney, as he was known, had never experienced anyone like Baker, who bragged of the elk he had shot in the wilds of Wyoming and was unsure of what to make of the spartan prep school. Yet Baker accommodated himself to his new surroundings, demonstrating an ability to shed his skin that would prove useful later in life. "He became un-Texan very quickly," McHenry said. But when he went back home, "he became very Texan again. The accent returned."

Founded in 1851, the Hill School boasted that it was the first school in the nation where the students lived on campus with faculty members. In the spirit of reconciliation, it had adopted both blue and gray as its colors after the Civil War. By the time Jimmy arrived, the legendary headmaster James I. Wendell, a silver-medal Olympic hurdler, had been in charge for years, fashioning the institution in his own image as a school that valued athleticism as well as scholarship. Baker found himself in a small campus in a small town. It was all white and all boys. The students wore coats and ties to class, and the main excitement of the year was the annual football contest against archrival Lawrenceville. "There was no friction," McHenry said. "There were no girls. There was no protest—nothing to protest against." Nothing much to do, either. The Hill had a heavily chaperoned dance in junior and senior years, but otherwise lights went out at 10 p.m. "Pottstown, Pennsylvania's not exactly the center of the universe," McHenry noted. "Where could you go? What could you do?"

Jimmy found himself lost at first. Life at the Hill was constricting. He was unhappy. Salvation came on the tennis court. By his second year, he was named captain of the team. He made friends, who predictably called him "Tex." The student newspaper, the *Hill School News*, dubbed him "'Smiling' Jim" and even undertook to report on his love life. "Jim mused over the female situation for quite a while," it said, "but came to the conclusion that his attentions were divided among many."

He was not an academic star. The Hill required much more work than Kinkaid did. Jimmy struggled with French and was in danger of failing geometry. On a paper about Shakespeare, a teacher noted, "Your subject and at times your generalizations were so big that it is hard to find much of value here. Besides you had a tendency here to wander and to be wordy."

Back home in Houston, from his desk at the firm, his father did not think much of Jimmy's work ethic. "He is a fine boy with plenty of ability and, I am afraid, a strong lack of inclination to do any hard work except under pressure," he wrote to one of Jimmy's teachers. At times, his father had a hard time restraining himself. "I am sorry you thought my last letter was rough," he wrote to his son. "It wasn't nearly as rough as the letter I wrote you yesterday but did not send when your mother phoned me that she had finally received a reply from you. This will not be nearly as rough as I am afraid I am going to have to be if you don't remove that French condition by maintaining a passing grade."

Not content to leave the matter to his son's haphazard academic record, the elder Baker began lobbying Princeton, his alma mater, more than a year in advance to admit the young man, while frankly acknowledging his shortcomings. "Jimmy has always passed without difficulty," Baker wrote a Princeton official, "but so far has never made any particularly high grades."

The son, grandson, and great-grandson of lawyers, Jimmy now set his sights on breaking out of the family pattern. He thought about becoming a doctor and spent a summer at St. Joseph's Infirmary, Houston's first hospital. His job was to hold the vomit tray and, if that were not enough to knock the romance out of medicine for him, he found himself horrified at the sight of blood. "For someone who likes to hunt," he discovered, "I'm a little squeamish."

So he applied to Princeton, once again heading down the path set for him by the Warden.

WHEN JIMMY BAKER ARRIVED at Princeton in the fall of 1948, one of the first things he did was to join a student organization with a provocative name—the Right Wing Club. This was no sign of his future politics. The club was so named because its members used their right arms to lift their beers, of which there was no shortage. "When I got to Princeton, I just went nuts having so much fun, I damn near flunked out," he recalled years later. "The freedom was more than I could handle."

For the first time in his life, Baker felt liberated. When Jimmy became a teenager, his father had offered him $1,000 if he would refrain from smoking or drinking until he was twenty-one years old, huge money in that era. But Jimmy turned it down. The Warden was not going to college with him.

Those early days at Princeton were wild ones. Baker was willing to do almost anything. When a fellow freshman who also loved to party feared that he was about to be drummed out of school, he roamed the dormitory halls begging anyone to break his fingers on the theory that the injury would give him an excuse to get out of final exams. Everyone said no—everyone, that is, except Jimmy Baker. As long as the other student really wanted him to do it, Baker was game. The other freshman put his hand on a wooden chair. "Obviously we were having a few pops," Baker said. "I took a fire poker and went *whack* and I broke his fingers."

Living on a $75-a-month allowance from his father, Baker spent the first half of his first year in Campbell Hall, rooming with three friends from the Hill School, David Paton, Barney McHenry, and James Detmer. Baker and his roommates were assigned a suite with two small bedrooms with a sitting room where Detmer kept an upright piano. Baker and Paton shared one of the bedrooms, Baker taking the bottom of a rickety bunk bed and Paton the top. "If he was out to party or whatever, he didn't stand climbing to the second deck as well as I did," Paton explained. Halfway through the year, a suite opened in 1879 Hall. The only dormitory on the east side of campus and once home to the office Woodrow Wilson used while university president, it was normally barred to freshmen. Baker and his friends were assigned a corner suite on the second floor. All four would remain there together for the next three years until Detmer left during senior year to join the military.

Arriving just three years after World War II, Baker's cohort at Princeton saw itself as the "first normal post-war class." With the draft now suspended, they were "anticipating an education and a future unmarred by the prospect of any immediate national or world crisis," as the *Nassau Herald* yearbook put it. Theirs was the largest class in Princeton history and, while homogenous by later standards, it was more diverse than many of its predecessors, with the largest share of public high school students (37 percent) and the widest national distribution that the university had yet seen. The members of the Class of 1952 were abandoning some of the traditions that had shackled their prewar predecessors. Freshmen were supposed to wear black caps known as "dinks," but a poll that fall found that only 20 percent of the class were obeying, despite the risk of retaliation from sophomores.

Still, it was a genetically conservative campus. The yearbook described President Harry Truman's win in 1948 as "a somewhat upsetting presidential election." The world had changed since the war, but Princeton had not done as much as other schools to change with it. There were no women among its students and it had been the last of the Ivy League schools to admit African Americans. Indeed, Princeton had only graduated its first black students the year before Baker arrived, more than three quarters of a century after Harvard and Yale did, and it still had no African Americans on its faculty. The school had also tried to limit Jewish admissions. Nearly one out of every five members of the incoming class was, like Baker, the son of a Princeton alumnus and more than half were either Presbyterian, as Baker was then, or Episcopalian, as he would become later in life.

Princeton did not seem as foreign to Baker as might have been expected. Of all the Ivy League schools, Princeton was considered the most Southern. There were twenty Houstonians in the Class of 1952 along with Baker. His father and other relatives had gone there. He may have been called Tex by the Easterners from time to time but, with his ready stock of jokes, sharp tongue, and prep school background, they did not pick on him, and the nickname that stuck was "Bake," the same name his friend George H. W. Bush would prefer to call him years later. Bake quickly became co-captain of the freshman tennis team and a popular fixture on campus. "Princeton was known as the elite school," recalled Frank Carlucci, a classmate who went on to serve as secretary of defense in the

Bush cabinet with Baker. "He moved easily in those circles. A good cultural background and first-rate mind."

Yet Baker did not use his first-rate mind to much advantage with his professors. In his first semester, he took the basics—English, French, history, geology, and politics—and his grades proved uninspired. His average for the first term was a middling 3.88 on a seven-point scale in which a one was the best. Baker did not worry about it too much. "There wasn't an awful lot of talk about academics, at least not in our group anyway," said Barney McHenry.

The future secretary of the treasury scored a meager 5-plus in economics. "I am greatly disappointed that you have flunked an important economics exam," his father wrote him. "There is no reason why, with proper application, you should flunk any of them. If I were you, I would not make any trips away from Princeton, except for tennis, until you are through with your examinations this June."

IN THE SUMMER OF 1949, Baker's parents got him a job with an oil driller in East Texas run by his mother's brother, Coalter Means, a wildcatter in every sense of the term. His uncle was known as Uncle To in the family ever since a younger brother had been unable to pronounce his real name. On the rig, he was known as Drill Stem. He was brash and lived a fast life and "didn't pay much attention to the law," as Baker remembered later. He drove a Cadillac, racing it around Texas. When he got pulled over for speeding and taken to a local courthouse, he would peel off large bills to pay his fine on the spot. The opposite of the Warden in so many ways, he considered Jimmy the son he never had.

For a young Princeton student, summer on the oil rig in the tiny town of Woodville, about a hundred miles northeast of Houston, was a radical break. From early in the morning until sunset, he worked as a roustabout, helping the roughnecks man the pipes and drills. Newcomers like him, called boll weevils, underwent an initiation, and he was no different just because he was the boss's nephew. The first job the roughnecks gave him was bailing out the rat hole, where the next piece of drill pipe was stored. With all the drilling mud, the rat hole collected liquid. The roughnecks gave Jimmy a little can tied to a string and had him drop it down into the hole and pull it out repeatedly as the water filled in whatever he took out. "It took me about a couple hours to catch on," Baker recalled years later.

Fortunately for him, a welder nicknamed Smooth took him under his wing. When Jimmy did get into a minor altercation with another worker,

Smooth backed him up. "Jimmy, you tell old John that Smooth said to take a flying leap at his ass," he instructed.

The days were hot and sweaty. Every morning Jimmy brought a black lunch kit lined with wax paper and ate the same thing the others did—cold rice and gravy with a big white onion washed down with plenty of coffee. At the end of the day, exhausted and drained by the heat, he retired with the other workers to a boardinghouse, where they drank a cold beer, ate a little supper, and collapsed into bed. He netted about $10 a day.

His parents were a little shocked by his appearance when they visited but satisfied that he was learning the value of real work. "I have thought of you constantly since we left you at the oil well," his mother wrote after returning home. "It is with a great deal of love and pride that I recall your face—so covered with black grease and red clay that only the whites of your eyes were visible." His father wrote separately: "We both feel that you have been very courageous to take your present job and that, while the experience is hard, it will be of great benefit and you will never regret it."

Baker would later say that summer matured him more than any other experience to that point. Not all of the lessons he learned would earn his parents' approval. Once, he brought home a friend from the rig and set him up on a date, only finding out later that the friend was married. Bonner Baker was not happy when she heard about it, to say the least.

RETURNING TO PRINCETON for sophomore year, Baker and his three roommates reunited. Beer was their staple on Saturday nights followed by a milk punch concoction on Sunday mornings. It was hardly the Jazz Age, but the boys reveled in what they took to be Gatsbyesque levels of dissipation. "Scott Fitzgerald was our hero," Barney McHenry said. The roommates took the train to New York on weekends for still more partying, or sometimes McHenry drove them in the black Chevrolet he kept against school rules and named FitzRandolph after the wrought-iron Fitz-Randolph Gate that served as the university's official entrance on Nassau Street. Once, the police stopped Baker and some friends hitchhiking to Trenton. "They picked us up and took us to the Princeton jail, which was almost a colonial-times-type jail," Baker said. "It was a real dump and I had to spend the night." This time, his father could not come to bail him out even if he had wanted to.

The social whirl in New York—balls, coming-out parties, and the like—exposed Baker to a different world, one where, as he put it scornfully, some families dressed in tuxedoes for dinner at home. For a tobacco-chewing Texan, even a wealthy one, it was more than a little alien. The tycoons of Long Island were not at all impressed with his family name and did not care a bit about his position back home. They had never heard of Captain Baker or even been to Houston for that matter. "I've really been cruising with some of the 'upper crust,' and some of the homes (estates) would put The Oaks to shame," he wrote home to his parents. "The only really good thing I can say for it all is that at least I'm learning how to act at terrifically formal dinners and dances. The people, though, at these affairs are all so stuffy, social-minded and supercilious that they make me think about home and how friendly people are, and I wouldn't switch ways of life with any of them. Some of the people, of course, are very nice, but I can't help thinking how lucky I am to live the life I lead. Nothing like us good ole upper middles!"

On campus, Baker spent time not devoted to partying on sports. As much as he liked tennis, Baker dropped off the team in sophomore year, in part because of the stiff competition and in part to take up rugby, which held particular appeal because the team went to Bermuda for spring break. While on the island in the spring of 1950, Baker went to a party on the beach, where he met Mary Stuart McHenry, the daughter of an insurance salesman from Dayton, Ohio, who was studying at Finch College, a small finishing school on the Upper East Side in New York City. No relation to his McHenry roommate, she was eighteen, attractive, and full of life. They kissed on the beach. Baker fell hard.

"I've got the screaming A-Bomb hots for you," Baker wrote to her from Princeton as soon as he returned. A few weeks later, he switched his nuclear-era vernacular to make the same point. "Mary Stuart, I've known I had a bad case of the H-bombs for you for quite a while, but tonight I found out just how bad a case—and it's much worse than I suspected before," he wrote. "I just kept wishing that you were here; all night I wished." After adding, "I'm mad for you," he stopped and looked at what he wrote. "I just reread this and it doesn't quite live up to our motto of 'Don't Get Serious,' but I don't guess you can change the way things are—at least I can't. All love to you, Jimmy."

By chance, Mary Stuart's roommate at Finch was Patricia Honea Schutts, a cousin of Baker's. "She was absolutely crazy and devoted to Jimmy from day one," Schutts recalled. Mary Stuart soon was taking the train down to campus from New York for long weekends. "It was just a wonderful love affair," David Paton, Baker's roommate, remembered. "She was this very simple, pretty, unaffected, cheerful girl who just adored him, and I think that simplicity and that uncomplicated love was something that was just unusual for him. He'd been dating people in the Houston area for years—and often pretty girls with fast snaps and probably more educated than Mary Stuart, at least reflected that education more. She had just a certain simplicity, charming and real. She was very real."

Princeton, then and later, was a tribal environment and the end of sophomore year was the time to apply to the selective eating clubs on Prospect Avenue, known as "The Street," in an admission process called "Bicker." The seventeen eating clubs delineated campus pecking order and dominated social life. They later served as a lifelong professional network. Applicants were subjected to a grueling series of ten interviews, judged not just on their own merits but on family stature and the friends they hung out with; for some, the process was validation, for others, a humiliation.

The class that rebelled against the dinks decided to do the same against Bicker. The vast majority of sophomores Baker's year signed a petition declaring that every member of the class should receive at least one offer from an eating club. No one was to be left behind. "We argued that if a classmate was good enough to be admitted to Princeton, he should be good enough for its eating clubs," said Don Oberdorfer, a classmate who would later cover Baker as a diplomatic correspondent for *The Washington Post*. The clubs resisted and, seeking compromise, the school administration proposed creating an eighteenth nonselective club that would take the rejects. The sophomores dismissed the idea and, when the clubs defied them by passing over twenty-six applicants, the rest of the class stood firm until places were eventually found for all of them—the first time that would happen in school history, effectively ending the practice of excluding some students. *The Daily Princetonian* student newspaper trumpeted the victory with a banner headline larger than any in its seventy-five-year history to that point: "ALL SOPHS GET BIDS!"

There is little record of Baker being a leader in this effort, but he and his friends made a similar stand of their own. Along with David Paton and about a half dozen friends, Baker formed what was called an "ironbound," meaning that if a club wanted to sign up any single member of the group, it would have to take them all. It worked. Baker and his friends received an offer early in the process from the Ivy Club, the oldest and most patrician of the eating clubs, once described by Scott Fitzgerald as "detached and breathlessly aristocratic." Not bad for a Texas kid from the good ole upper middles. "Ivy was the snobbish club," said Richard Riordan, a transfer student who later in life became mayor of Los Angeles, "although I would have gladly accepted it had they offered it to me." Still, Riordan knew

Baker and thought he was no snob. "He treated everyone equally, the big shots and the little shots."

THAT SUMMER OF 1950, as Baker spent another couple months as a rough-edged Texas roustabout, the "unmarred future" that his Princeton class had looked forward to was shattered when the United States found itself back at war. The Stalinist government of North Korea, a Communist enclave that had emerged after the Japanese occupiers were pushed out at the end of World War II, had invaded South Korea and President Truman sent American troops to defend its ally as part of a United Nations force. They would not be "normal postwar" graduates after all.

The nuclear era was no longer the abstraction it had seemed when Baker was writing his first love letters to Mary Stuart McHenry and listening to Princeton's most famous resident, Albert Einstein, lecture on world peace with his "long uncombed gray hair" and clothes "like a tramp," as Baker wrote home. The draft was soon reinstated and while college students were supposed to be exempt for the next year, many Princeton students feared what was to come as they returned to campus that fall of Baker's junior year. "Everybody had to scurry around because you wanted to get a safe harbor," said Barney McHenry. "At least you wanted to graduate, anyway."

By Christmas, Baker was anxious. It seemed that all of his friends had already received their draft classifications, while he was still waiting. A couple of them had been called up by the Marines. Back home in Houston for the holiday, he went to the local draft board to find his classification. "They told me it had been sent to Princeton the day I left and that I'm 1-A!" he wrote Mary Stuart, referring to the most eligible category. "That was quite a shock 'cause I was hoping for a 2-A," he continued, "but they said that they're having to change 2-A's to 1-A now 'cause they've got to take so many men. Now if I want to get in something beside the infantry I'll have to enlist before I get my physical notice which I'll get in either Feb or March. My one out it seems might be the Army Air Force. They might let me finish school this year but I don't know."

As nervous as everyone was, there were no protests against the war. "Nobody questioned it," Riordan said. It was a time of rising tension, from the Communist takeover of China to the Soviet Union's acquisition of the atom bomb to the advent of McCarthyism, but the Princeton students remained in their bubble, where the intense focus was on a campaign to end mandatory Sunday chapel attendance. "In Princeton, the number one characteristic of the year was a remarkable normalcy," *The Daily Princetonian* editorialized in June 1951.

Baker remained socially prolific. He became president of the 21 Club, another drinking organization. "The efforts of Jim Baker and an all Junior '21' Club kept party spirit alive throughout the Fall," the yearbook reported. Baker, a history major by now, also finally buckled down in academics, and even earned a top grade of 1 in a history class, the only one he would receive in all four years at Princeton. He took an interest in Russia, which until then he knew about mainly from his tennis pro back in Houston whose family had been run out of the country by the Bolshevik Revolution. Inspired by Professor Cyril Black, who had spent part of World War II as a State Department officer and eventually was part of a delegation to the Soviet Union, Baker decided to write his junior paper on the brief transitional government of Alexander Kerensky. After the war, Black introduced Russian history to the Princeton curriculum for the first time and Baker found it riveting. Black was certain that the two Cold War adversaries would eventually get over their animosity.

For his senior thesis, Baker made a point of seeking out Professor Walter Hall, who had been his father's thesis adviser four decades earlier. Once described as "probably the most popular teacher of Princeton undergraduates in the first half of this century," Hall was known for his fancy vests and knickerbockers, an ever-present pipe, and an unorthodox teaching style. He sometimes stood on his desk during a lecture and once taught a class in his underwear. By the point when Baker studied with him, Hall was in his last year of teaching and dependent on hearing aids that made a constant buzzing sound, so everyone called him Buzzer.

Baker picked a topic that would prove meaningful in shaping his views of politics and diplomacy, the conflict between two towering figures of Britain's Labour Party: Aneurin Bevan, who had just stepped down as health minister after helping to launch the National Health Service, and Ernest Bevin, who had just resigned as foreign secretary after working with the Americans to form institutions of the Cold War such as NATO.

The paper was a challenge he dreaded. "Things look darker around here with every passing day," he told Mary Stuart in January 1952. "Right now I plan to get pitifully drunk on the Saturday night of my last exam, spend Sunday recuperating, and put in 8 days—starting Monday—on my thesis." He planted himself in a green carrel in Firestone Library and got to work. The resulting 150-page paper, titled "Two Sides of the Conflict: Bevin vs. Bevan," was largely a straightforward history of the clash between Bevin, a Bristol truck driver who had risen through the trade unions to become labor minister in Winston Churchill's wartime unity government and foreign secretary under Clement Attlee, and Bevan, an ardent socialist who represented the left wing in Parliament.

Reading between the lines, the paper could be seen as a road map of the fundamental tension that would define Baker's own time on the public stage. He described Bevin as a pragmatist and "expert negotiator" who was accused of sacrificing the values of the party and as a result developed "a genuine dislike of these dreamers," as Baker put it. "In spite of all the socialist activity and trade union agitation that was going on around him," he wrote, "Bevin never became lost in the idealistic. He was always very practical." In words that could have described himself later in life, Baker added: "Bevin was not interested in theories, but in practicalities. He knew that when men were unemployed they wanted bread and work, not an oration on the coming revolution. Bevin believed in solving the problems of the present before tackling the problems of the future. The solution of the immediate difficulty outweighed consideration of the long-term goal." By contrast, the Bevan wing with its emphasis on purity and push for a broader welfare state struck Baker as impractical in the extreme as the West faced the larger existential crisis of the Cold War. "One is left with the impression that these left-wingers resolve a planetary crisis by a discussion on the advantages of free false teeth," he wrote dismissively.

Baker graduated on June 17, 1952, after spending much of his final months at Princeton trying to figure out how to avoid getting drafted to serve in the Korean War. Eventually, rather than wait for the draft, Baker decided to sign up, which would give him more choice in where he would be deployed. An inner ear problem kept him out of the Navy and Air Force and an interview with a Central Intelligence Agency recruiter during a campus visit did not go well.

"One of the questions they asked me was would you have any problems jumping out of an airplane with a parachute behind enemy lines?" he remembered.

The answer was a definite yes. "I said, 'This interview is over.'" So he opted for the Marine Corps.

BAKER ARRIVED at the Marine base in Quantico, Virginia, that August. Afraid that being known as James A. Baker III would seem "sissified" among the tough young men surrounding him, he put down his name as James A. Baker Jr., as if that would solve the problem.

He had spent the two previous summers while still an undergraduate in Marine camps, the first in San Diego, where he made good enough marks that he was chosen as the bearer of the guidon, the unit pennant, until he mouthed off to a drill instructor and was sent back into the ranks. "I get a little big for my britches and they take it away from me and taught me a lesson," Baker said.

Commissioned as a junior officer at Quantico, he spent the next five months in basic training. His hunting experience made him a good rifle shot. "Did an excellent job in carrying the good orders he gave for a nite attack," his captain wrote on an evaluation. "The weather was unfavorable for a nite attack, but Lt. Baker led his squad to within 10 yards of the enemy and was not discovered until he gave the order to assault the position."

At the end of the course, Baker was told he would be sent into the infantry as a platoon leader, but being in charge of forty-four men seemed distinctly unappealing. Instead, he asked to become a naval gunfire spotter. It could be a dangerous job—spotters were often in the first wave of an amphibious landing—but intended or not, the assignment got him out of the Korean War. Of the sixty members of his basic training class who signed up for artillery, fifty-nine were sent to Fort Sill in Oklahoma and from there to Korea. Some of them never made it home. Baker, the sixtieth member of the class, was dispatched to the naval gunfire school at Little Creek, Virginia, and then assigned to the Second Marine Division at Camp Lejeune before being deployed to the USS *Monrovia*, a troop transport patrolling the Mediterranean Sea. "I fought the Korean War on the French Riviera," Baker became fond of saying later in life.

Before shipping out, Baker and Mary Stuart had a few days together in Washington. Walking down the street in his uniform in January 1953, Baker was stopped by a stranger who thanked him for his service and offered tickets to Dwight D. Eisenhower's inauguration the next day. The young couple watched as the famed general was sworn in and warned in his inaugural address about a worldwide "time of tempest." They found themselves in seats for the inaugural parade within sight of the White House as the new president and first lady waved to massive crowds from a white Cadillac with the top down on an unexpectedly sunny day. It was the closest Baker had ever been to the executive mansion.

His ship set sail three months later at 10 a.m. on April 22 and while it was nowhere near a war zone, life on the *Monrovia* had physical hazards all its own for a young man who grew queasy on boats and airplanes. "I was sick the entire time," he remembered. Baker shared a single compartment with a dozen other officers, each of them taking turns with two washbasins and one shower—which was better, at least, than the enlisted men had it, stacked like cordwood in the lower holds. "But I can see where this looking out and seeing nothing but sea and other ships for 2 or 3 weeks at a time will get very boring," he wrote to his parents.

Baker's assignment was to work with NATO forces. During a training exercise, he was assigned to adjust fire from a Turkish destroyer and a Greek destroyer, only to find himself unable to communicate with either since no one spoke English. "It was a disaster," he said, an inauspicious debut in international diplomacy.

He spent nearly a week on the Greek island of Zante as part of a relief operation after a deadly earthquake. The island was "shattered, split wide open and sowed with death" by waves "like those which Homer described overtaking the Ionian king, Ulysses, on his way home to ancient Ithaca," reported *Life* magazine, which had a photographer accompanying the Marines. Baker and the others delivered food, water, and tents, set up aid stations, inoculated survivors against typhus and typhoid, repaired roads and a power plant, and, most haunting of all, burned or buried hundreds of bodies. For a young man from a sheltered background, the experience was searing. "I don't think the devastation could have been much worse if it had been caused by an atomic bomb," Baker told his parents.

Still, Baker's ship managed to stop in some of the most picturesque places in the Mediterranean and the Marines were allowed to explore as long as they were back on board by 2 a.m. After Zante, he found himself in Naples, where he took three days of liberty to see his parents, who traveled to meet him there. "It bolstered my sagging spirits considerably," he told them later. He did not get to see Mary Stuart, but the two had gotten engaged at a posh New York hotel before the Marine deployment. In Florence, he bought silver ashtrays at $10 each as gifts for his ushers at the upcoming wedding, proud of negotiating a 10 percent discount.

By the time his Mediterranean tour was over, so was the Korean War. Like many young men of his generation, Baker had not questioned the wisdom of the American intervention in Korea. He had spent little time thinking about the geopolitical logic behind investing American lives in a grinding conflict in Asia that risked escalation with the Soviet Union or China. To the extent he thought about it at all in those terms, he considered Korea a necessary front in the Cold War, part of a broader mission to contain the spread of Communism, and he shared the sentiment that, as he put it, "these sorry bastard Chinese were screwing us around."

After returning from the Mediterranean, Baker headed to Ohio, to marry Mary Stuart. The ceremony was held on November 7, 1953, at

Dayton's Christ Episcopal Church. It was not a modest affair. Mary Stuart wore a gown of ivory satin and a full-length veil of Point de Rose lace arranged in mantilla fashion, while carrying a bouquet of lilies. Baker wore a morning suit. She had nine bridesmaids. He had ten groomsmen, including David Paton as his best man. She was twenty-two; he was twenty-three. Afterward, the newlyweds honeymooned in Bermuda, where he had first caught the screaming A-bomb hots for the young woman from Finch College.

ONCE AGAIN, Baker's father would be the driving force in determining what came next. Uninterested in staying in the military, Baker began considering law school. His father had always told him that he did not have to become a lawyer just because everyone else in his family with the same name had, but it was clear the elder Baker thought it was the course that the fourth James Addison Baker should pursue.

The Warden got his way. Baker, while maintaining he was not sure he would practice law once he got out, prepared his applications. With a Princeton degree, he might have set his sights on Harvard Law School or one of the other top national schools. But that was not the path his father had chosen for him. Baker was told to apply instead to his father's alma mater, the University of Texas School of Law. The elder Baker argued that it would be better to learn in the state where he would practice and make contacts that would serve him well in the working world. A compliant Baker arrived at the Austin campus in the fall of 1954.

But it was not enough to go to the same law school his father had—the Warden insisted that his son pledge the same fraternity too. Never mind that Baker was now twenty-four years old and married with a baby on the way and two years of the Marine Corps under his belt. He signed up for Phi Delta Theta as ordered and gamely endured hazing rituals administered by undergraduates. "I did it for my dad and I went through hell," he said years later. "I had these young kids that were five and six years younger than I was telling me, 'Sit on that ice block in burlap,' and they would drop raw eggs down my throat. I did all that for my dad. He wanted me to do it."

In the midst of this, Mary Stuart gave birth to their first son, James Addison Baker IV, on October 9. They called him Jamie. Two years later, another boy came along, Stuart McHenry Baker, whom they called Mike. Baker's father gave him an allowance of $90 a month, which together with $160 from the G.I. Bill was hardly enough to care for a family of three, much less four. "But he was smart enough to know that that kept me focused on the job at hand and it did," Baker recalled. "I saw so many of my contemporaries who grew up with me under the same circumstances, good opportunities and never lacking anything—they were ruined by having too much money too soon."

This time, Jimmy bore down on his classes, diligently writing out long, detailed briefs about the cases they studied each night. He was put to the test right from the start. During the first week or so of his property class, the professor picked Baker out of a large class.

"Mr. Baker, Mr. James Addison Baker the Third," the professor called out. "Would you give us the case of *Ghen vs. Rich?*"

Baker was as nervous as he had ever been, but he stood up and managed to recount the details of an 1881 case about who owned a harpooned finback whale that washed up on a Massachusetts beach, the whaler who killed it or the owner of the land where it ended up. (The court sided with the whaler.)

As he headed toward graduation in 1957, near the top 10 percent of his class, Baker had assumed he would go to work at the family firm. The problem was that Baker Botts now had an anti-nepotism policy, meaning that relatives of its current partners and employees were not supposed to be hired. Baker's father thought he could finesse that. "You got good grades and your name is James A. Baker," he told his son.

But his father came home that night with bad news. The firm had rejected his request for an exception to the nepotism policy. Baker was crushed. "Everything I had ever known in my life was Baker Botts and it had always been held up to me as *the firm,*" the younger Baker later reflected. It would be years before he realized that the rejection was a blessing in disguise. Had he succeeded, everyone would have assumed it was because of his name, and if he had failed, everyone would have tut-tutted that he had nothing going for him but his lineage.

For the moment, however, all he knew was that he had disappointed his father. "I was devastated," he said, "absolutely devastated."

CHAPTER 3

God Came Today

O n the wall of the Houston Country Club, the winners of the annual tennis tournament were listed in long rows on large wooden plaques. On the one titled "Men's Singles Championships," the name James A. Baker III was engraved next to the year 1958. Also next to 1959. And 1960. And 1961. By the time a young oilman named George Herbert Walker Bush moved to Houston and joined the country club looking for someone to team up with in doubles, all he had to do was check the plaque to find a promising partner.

Bush was a Yankee émigré who had spent the last decade searching for oil in Texas. Tall and proper, with a New England accent and an Ivy League pedigree, he was not a natural fit in Texas. But he was a "friend maker," as his brother Jonathan Bush put it, the kind of person who would meet someone during the day and bring him home for dinner that night unannounced, much to the chagrin of his wife, Barbara, who was left scrambling to add another plate at the table.

The son of an investment banker who later served as a senator from Connecticut, Bush headed to Texas a few years after returning from a heroic stint as one of the youngest Navy pilots in World War II. He took a job as an oil field equipment salesman for Dresser Industries, on whose board his father sat. His first home in Texas was a rented two-room duplex in Odessa, where the family had to share a bathroom with a mother-and-daughter prostitute team next door. They later moved to nearby Midland. By the time Bush made the 492-mile move to Houston in 1959 and enrolled his oldest son, George W., in the same Kinkaid School that Baker had attended, he was president of his own small oil firm, Zapata Offshore Company.

Bush and Baker first met through a small-world connection involving Mary Stuart. Growing up in Dayton, Mary Stuart had been friends with a girl named Teensie Bush, who was a cousin of George Bush. When the Bush family moved to Houston, Teensie got in touch with Mary Stuart to suggest they meet. George was also using Baker Botts for some legal work for Zapata. And they would discover that Barbara's aunt had taught Mary Stuart in school in Dayton. So one Sunday afternoon after they moved to Houston, the Bushes invited the Bakers over to their house at 5525 Briar Drive for hamburgers and a swim in their pool.

Bush was six years older than Baker and, when they relocated to Houston, Barbara was pregnant with their sixth child, Dorothy, who would be called Doro. Their first daughter, Robin, had died of leukemia several years earlier, so Doro's arrival was greeted joyfully in a household that otherwise included four rambunctious boys. The families had much in common. Jim and Mary Stuart's two sons, Jamie and Mike, were roughly around the same age as Jeb, Neil, and Marvin Bush. Two more Baker boys would come along soon, John Coalter Baker in 1960 and Douglas Bland Baker just thirteen months later. All of them loved the Baker family dog, a black Labrador named Cinderella by the boys and eventually known just as Cinders. The families lived not far apart and would regularly get together for Sunday barbecues and games of touch football. At Christmas, the Bushes would invite the Bakers over for cocktails.

But the friendship between Baker and Bush would truly be forged on the tennis courts of the Houston Country Club, which Baker's grandfather had helped to found in 1908 when it opened the first eighteen-hole golf course in Texas. In 1957, the club moved to the exclusive Tanglewood neighborhood, where Bush would build a relatively modest two-story house on an oversized plot of land. Baker had practically lived on the courts as a boy growing up in Houston, and his father had won the doubles tennis championship three years in a row in the 1940s. Thanks to the obsessive practice sessions ordered by his father, Baker more than lived up to the paternal legacy—all told, he won the singles tournaments six years and won his first doubles championship in 1961.

By the mid-1960s, the tennis pro at the club put Baker and Bush together for doubles. Neither had a particularly strong serve. Baker used to joke that Bush's was so weak that the future president could hit the ball and run over to the other side of the court in enough time to return it himself. Bush kidded that Baker needed him to back up his "powder puff serve." Still, he admitted in retirement, "Baker's the better tennis player than I am." But Bush played the net well and with Baker's killer ground strokes, they made a formidable team. Together, they won the doubles championship at the club two years in a row, in 1966 and 1967. They found that they complemented each other and soon learned to anticipate what the other was thinking on the court without being told, a connection that would prove crucial later in life. "They're both enormous competitors," George W. Bush reflected years later. "They want to win."

At the time, their relationship had little to do with politics. With his father still representing Connecticut in the Senate, Bush was years away from his own first run for office and unsure about his prospects as a Republican in an overwhelmingly Democratic state, while Baker was a relatively apathetic Democrat who took seriously his grandfather's warning about staying away from politics.

Mary Stuart was the politically active member of the Baker family in the Eisenhower era, an Ohio Republican among the Southern Democrats. She once hosted a Republican precinct meeting in their living room and only one other person showed up. "I served him drinks," Baker liked to tell people years later. Otherwise, Baker could hardly be bothered. Barbara Bush used to joke that since Election Day often fell around the same time that hunting season opened, Baker picked shooting over voting. He later swore that was not true, but it seemed a fair reflection of his priorities.

FOR BAKER, the late 1950s and 1960s were about starting a family and building his law career. With his father's firm closed to him, Baker ended up at Andrews, Kurth, Campbell & Bradley, another blue-chip corporate litigation firm and the fifth largest in Texas at the time. Founded in Houston in 1902, the firm had always been close to Baker Botts. In fact, Captain Baker and its co-founder Frank Andrews had originally worked just down the hall from one another and the two firms often sent business to each other if they could not take a case because of a conflict of interest.

Like Baker Botts, Andrews Kurth made itself into a player representing railroads and energy interests in the boom years in Texas. It helped Howard Hughes Sr. found the Hughes Tool Company after he patented a revolutionary oil drill. And it helped his son, Howard Hughes Jr., the eccentric billionaire, with a variety of matters, including the congressional investigation into the Spruce Goose, his massive, taxpayer-financed wooden airplane that flew just once.

As a new associate, Baker was paid just $400 a month, which meant he was still dependent on his father as he and Mary Stuart settled down. His father put up the money so that they could buy their first house in 1957 at 9321 Oakford Court for $45,000. The rest of the family was chagrined at the location of the new house, considerably away from the center of Houston. "Jimmy," Baker's dad added, "why are you going so far out?"

At work, Baker was given an office with a frosted-glass door on the twenty-first floor of the Gulf Building. His neighbor was Robert Weatherall, a law school friend. When the sign painter came to put names on their new offices, Weatherall was away so Baker told the man to put "Mr. Toad" on the door. But moments of levity were balanced by long hours and intense pressure. The firm demanded hard work; the senior partner told newcomers that Saturday was a workday, with hours from 8 a.m. to 1 p.m., and "anyone that doesn't come in on Saturday, don't bother to come in on Monday," as Weatherall recalled.

Baker reported to Harry R. Jones, a partner who became his mentor. From Jones, he learned to be thorough and careful, and never to submit a briefing memo that he was not sure was accurate and complete. "It's fair to say that back in those days the older guys rode the young guys pretty hard—rode hard and put up wet," Baker said, falling back on a Texas horseman's aphorism. In his first year as a lawyer, he dealt with wills and trusts, property disputes and business mergers. He worked on a proposed purchase of natural gas fields by Con Edison and a right-of-way dispute involving Petro-Tex Chemical Corp. He helped write the bylaws of a paper mill.

One of the first legal questions Harry Jones threw his way involved Hollywood portrayals of A. H. "Shanghai" Pierce, a legendary Texas figure who arrived in the state as a stowaway on a boat and ultimately became a powerhouse cattle baron after the Civil War. Shanghai was portrayed in two different productions in 1957, in the big-screen film *Gunfight at the O.K. Corral* and in an episode of the television series *The Life and Legend of Wyatt Earp*. In the movie, Shanghai and his gang shoot up a dance hall in Dodge City and are confronted by Wyatt Earp and Doc Holliday. "You better start praying, Earp," Shanghai snarls, before the heroes get the better of him and march him away to jail.

Shanghai's heirs owned large oil and gas deposits and were important clients of Baker's firm. Upset at the portrayals of their ancestor, they wanted to explore defamation and breach of privacy claims. Baker researched the law and concluded that the heirs would have "an almost impossible burden of proof." Their only options, he told his clients, were to convince state officials to criminally prosecute the filmmakers, sue for libel in a court that would apply the laws of France, Quebec, Queensland, or Tasmania, "assuming there was publication in these areas," or sue for breach of privacy in Utah, citing local law. The message was clear: It was not practical—a standard that would become Baker's benchmark for life. The family dropped the matter.

At first, Baker thought he wanted to be a trial lawyer, much like his father initially aspired to be, so he was given a couple of assignments to sit second chair in defense cases involving railroads and insurance companies. He quickly became turned off, and his work turned into the same sort of corporate deals and bank boards that had dominated the Warden's career. "I became very disillusioned because people would lie and there was no recourse really," Baker said decades later. "It was just a given and witnesses would lie and I became very calloused about trial work and got out of it. I concluded a little bit later on that that's not where the money is in a big firm practice anyway."

It took Baker ten years to become partner, which was relatively standard at the old-school Andrews Kurth. By that point, he was making $18,000 a year. Even as a successful lawyer, Baker depended on the family fortune to finance his growing brood. His father regularly passed along money for various purchases—to send the boys to summer camp, to reupholster the furniture, to buy new suits, to repair the fence in the backyard, to purchase a new station wagon, to finance a vacation and a trip to a Princeton reunion, even to pay the doctor's fee for the delivery of one of their sons. When Baker bought Mary Stuart a mink coat in 1963 for $1,800, more than 10 percent of his salary, his father volunteered to pay half. When they decided to build a new home, Baker's father paid for part of the cost of the architect.

Accompanying the various checks were often letters that sounded more like a lawyer's memos to a colleague than notes from a father to a son. They were dry and impersonal. Even when attempting to be heartfelt, the Warden came across as stern. On Baker's twenty-ninth birthday, his father sent a check for $50 and a typewritten note. "You have always been a very satisfactory son and given both of us much pleasure over the span of your life," he wrote, signing it, "Devotedly, Daddy."

His father drew the line, however, when Baker wanted to buy a hardscrabble ranch in Pearsall in South Texas in 1968. There was not much to the property, not even a house on it. But it appealed to Baker's hunger for the outdoors, the love for roughing it he first developed on that childhood trip to Wyoming. The Warden did not see the allure and refused to help finance the purchase. "Jimmy, I survived the Great Depression," he said, according to family lore. "I had a lot of friends who were land poor. The last thing I need to own is a pile of rocks somewhere out in South Texas."

By then, his father was increasingly in failing health with Parkinson's disease. So Baker's mother quietly overruled the patriarch and allowed her son to use the proceeds from some bonds to buy the ranch. Baker loaded his own boys into the station wagon and drove down for weekends, sleeping in a large canvas tent they pitched on the undeveloped land. It eventually would produce five oil plays and pay for itself. In honor of the Warden, Baker named the property Rockpile Ranch.

THE POLITICS OF THE ERA seemed to largely escape Baker. His father scorned Lyndon Johnson just as he had Franklin Roosevelt, but the tumultuous events of the period left little mark on his son. The Cuban Missile Crisis, the assassination of John F. Kennedy, the Vietnam War, the civil rights movement—Baker's letters from the time refer to none of them, nor would he summon strong memories of the time later in life.

His only real involvement in politics was tangential. He contributed money to Waggoner Carr, a Democrat who ran for state attorney general, but mainly because that was what lawyers in Texas who might have business with the attorney general did. When George H. W. Bush took over as Republican Party chairman in Harris County, which included Houston, Baker wished him good luck with little more interest. But Bush had plans and Baker would fit into them eventually. "George had an eye for people that were bright and coming and promising, friends that do not just say, 'How do you do?' but could be involved in things down the road," his brother, Jonathan Bush, remembered.

For the time being, Baker's sideline was not politics but hunting. He took every opportunity to get away with his guns. Sometimes, he and George Bush would go quail hunting, and he still loved the Eagle Lake Rod & Gun Club that his father had taken him to as a boy. One of his best friends was James O. Winston III, who went by the nickname Jimbo and was a great-nephew of William Marsh Rice, the tycoon whose death had figured so profoundly in Captain Baker's career. Winston was married to the product of another long-standing Texas family, Susan Blackshear Garrett. The Bakers spent New Year's 1962 at the ranch owned by Jimbo's parents. "I have never hunted turkey before and can honestly say I have never enjoyed hunting any game as much," Baker later wrote to them in a thank-you note. A year later, he decided to go hunting with Jimbo in

Mexico. A year after that, the two headed to a place in Colorado called the Faraway Ranch. "The country up there makes a new man out of you, mentally as well as physically," Baker wrote to another friend.

The Bakers and Winstons were close. When Jimbo was arrested for illegally transporting beer, Baker helped get the charge dismissed. When Susan got into a dispute with a landlord who rented her a place in California for the summer, Baker jumped in to represent her. He sponsored Jimbo for membership in the Houston Country Club, noting that the Winstons "both come from families prominent in Houston's past." What Baker did not realize was how much the Winstons' marriage was fraying due to Jimbo's heavy drinking.

Baker was hardly a teetotaler, but Mary Stuart had imposed a new discipline on him. She was a devoted Episcopalian and she pressed her husband to join her and the children at church on Sundays, although he was generally in the habit of working. By 1958, five years after their wedding, he started going with them to St. Martin's, the same Episcopal church the Bushes would join.

"I could not at the last make a final decision to leave the Presbyterian Church," he wrote Rev. J. T. Bagby, the rector at St. Martin's. "However, my wife is a better Episcopalian than I am a Presbyterian and the more I attend St. Martin's, the more I feel that I should probably be confirmed. I imagine that it is only a matter of time before I can make the decision to do so without looking back."

Like his father and grandfather before him, though, Baker made work his first commitment. He was not the disciplinarian the Warden was. He did not like to repeat himself and he would spank a boy for lying or being disrespectful, but his heart was not in it. His son John believed Baker did not want to be like his own father. "Did I ever get my butt whipped?" he said. "Absolutely. But I probably had it coming. But he was not splash-water-in-your-face like his dad. I'm sure he learned a little bit about 'I'm not going to do that with my kids.'"

Baker made a point of regularly taking his sons hunting and fishing, the outdoor escapes that had been the times that he cherished with his father. Each boy was allowed to shoot his first deer at age eleven. If there was anything Baker truly loved, it was those trips in the wilderness. "I remember him talking to me about why he likes turkey hunting so much, just being out there in the middle of this place, calling them in, the beauty of the turkeys, the solitude," George W. Bush recalled. Baker was no romantic, but as the future president remembered him talking about his love of the hunt, it was almost "poetic."

Baker had decided to embrace the family legacy. Soon, he even decreed that his son Jamie—the fifth James Addison Baker—would go north to the Hill School. Baker warned Jamie that being from Texas would make him different on the East Coast. But he also reminded him that his own father had gone to the Hill School and so had his grandfather and his uncles. "That was really the first time I got from him the family line," Jamie recalled years later.

Like his father before him, Baker found himself irritated at the lack of communication from his son after being sent away to boarding school. "Well, here is the letter you wanted so much," Jamie wrote one fall day. "I get so damn mad when I think of that phone call that I want to write this letter like an application sheet with a bunch of vital statistics like: Yesterday I watched T.V. Tonight I have homework. I have a test Wed. etc."

"I am glad that you finally wrote us a one page letter," Baker wrote back in his best impression of the Warden, "but am sorry that you chose to be so sarcastic. All we ask is that you occasionally drop us a line to let us know how you are getting along and how things are going."

The truth was Baker was growing to have a greater appreciation for his father. The harsh discipline, the distant demeanor, the high expectations—suddenly Baker found himself practicing with his own sons what used to aggravate him as a boy. It was perhaps no coincidence that his attitude toward his father softened in the 1960s as the elder Baker's decline accelerated, rendering the Warden less and less able to assert control over the family.

In a rare moment of reflection, Baker wrote his godson, Wallace Barry Wilson, the son of his friend Wallace Stedman Wilson, about the indelible mark the old man had left on him. "He told me that every young man can make of his life what he himself wants to make of it," Baker wrote. "He pointed out that nothing you ever acquire or achieve means anything to you unless you have worked for it; and that if you *have* worked for it, the sense of satisfaction and achievement which results can carry you through the rough times that every man experiences in one form or another." While he used to think of his father as "set in his ways, tied to the past and unrealistic," he wrote, as he himself grew older "the more meaningful the things he said to me have become."

GEORGE BUSH BEGAN to make his political ascent in 1964 with a campaign for Senate, but he chose an inauspicious year for a Republican in Texas. Lyndon Johnson, the first Texan to serve as president, was running for a full term of his own against Barry Goldwater, the flinty conservative Republican from Arizona, and was almost certainly going to pull in a lot of votes in his home state.

The headwinds could hardly have been stronger against a little-known Houston oilman running on the Republican ticket against Senator Ralph Yarborough, the incumbent. Yarborough was, to be sure, out of place as a committed liberal in a deeply conservative state; he was both a champion of organized labor and the only Southern senator to vote that year for the Civil Rights Act. But Yarborough was still a Democrat at a time of entrenched party loyalty. No Republican had won a statewide race in Texas since Reconstruction until John Tower prevailed in a special election in 1961 to take the Senate seat that Johnson had vacated when he became vice president. Ten times as many voters would cast ballots in the Democratic Senate primary in 1964 as in the Republican primary.

Baker paid little attention to this. As the Republican in the house, Mary Stuart volunteered for Bush's campaign, passing out literature and needlepointing bags along with Barbara Bush and Susan Winston, Jimbo's wife. Bush ran hard to the right, coming out against the Civil Rights Act, a decision he would later regret. But the most promising factor working in his favor was a split in the Texas Democratic Party. Governor John Connally did not care for Yarborough and refused to endorse him; some of the governor's supporters backed Bush outright, as did former governor Allan Shivers, another Democrat. A *Houston Chronicle* poll about a week before Election Day had the race at a virtual tie.

But on election night, Johnson won a landslide and his coattails were enough to pull in Yarborough, who prevailed with a convincing 56 percent of the vote to Bush's 44 percent. Three days later, Baker sent his friend a condolence note. "My dear George," he wrote. "You ran a great race against almost overwhelming odds. The cards were stacked against you from the beginning and the breaks never came your way. Most certainly, you are disappointed, and so am I. You could not, however, possibly have any regrets."

Disappointed, yes. Defeated, no. Bush wasted little time deciding to parlay the prominence from his statewide race into another campaign, this time for the House in 1966. A new district was created in the Houston area as a result of the Supreme Court's landmark one-person, one-vote ruling, meaning there was no incumbent to beat this time. Bush asked his doubles partner for support and Baker agreed, although he still refused to become a Republican or work for the campaign.

Bush was facing Democrat Frank Briscoe, a popular Harris County district attorney whose tough-on-crime record, particularly against black suspects, made him "one of the most vicious prosecutors in Houston's history," as *The Texas Observer* put it. Bush confronted uphill odds in a district where registered Democrats outnumbered Republicans six to one. Still, he energetically campaigned, presenting himself as the face of a new generation. With the help of visiting Republican luminaries such as Richard Nixon and Gerald Ford, Bush came out on top with 57 percent of the vote, making him one of only a handful of Republicans to represent Texas in the House in that century.

Baker began to see his war hero of a tennis partner, the age of the big brother he never had, in a new light. "I was sort of in awe of him for a while," he said.

MARY STUART PRESSED her husband to join her in church and in politics, but it was very much Baker's world in which she lived. She took tennis lessons so she could play with him. She took shooting lessons so she could go hunting with him. They did not share a passion for reading, however. That was hers alone. She used to stay up late into the evening ripping through the latest novel. "I'd get up in the middle of the night, it'd be like two in the morning, and her light would be on," recalled Jamie Baker. "She'd be reading."

School vacations were spent with her family. She would pile the boys into their Pontiac station wagon—also purchased with help from the Warden—and drive them to Florida for spring break and to Thousand Islands in upstate New York during the summer. By all accounts, Baker doted on Mary Stuart. He affectionately called her "Mess." If there was conflict, or resentment, no one saw it. Mary Stuart watched the 1960s unfold around her, but she did not join in. The women's movement was a few years in the future and she played the role of traditional wife for Baker and mother for their four boys. Jim worked; Mary Stuart made their life work. Outsiders saw the picture of 1960s domesticity. "They were a great, great marriage," as Jonathan Bush put it. "They were absolutely perfect for each other."

When Baker made partner in 1967, the two decided to build a new home for their large family. It was Mary Stuart's project and she chose the architect and designed her dream house. In February 1968, however, their idyllic life took a sudden, dark turn. Mary Stuart found a lump in her breast. The doctor who examined her thought it was mastitis, a simple breast infection, and told her it would be fine but if it persisted to come back. For the next six months, everything seemed all right. Then she and Baker went on a trip with a friend from the Hill School and his wife in the Wyoming mountains, back to the place he had loved as a boy. They even camped in the same spot where he and his father had slept decades earlier on their famous elk hunt, at Open Creek, near the headwaters of the Yellowstone. One day they rode twenty-six miles on horseback, but Mary Stuart could hardly manage the exertion. "It damn near killed her," Baker recalled. Something was wrong.

When they returned to Houston, she went back to the doctor, who promptly checked her into a hospital. She was told she would need an operation. She had a medical star on her case: Dr. Denton Cooley, a nationally renowned cardiothoracic surgeon who just a few months earlier had performed the first successful adult human-to-human heart transplant in the United States and would soon go on to implant the first totally artificial heart in a patient. But he would not have as much success with Mary Stuart. "I could tell when he came out," Baker said. The news was not good.

Mary Stuart had breast cancer and it was serious, but the two never revealed to the boys just how serious. Jamie, who turned fourteen years old that fall, was away at boarding school and now they sent the other three children away as well to live with friends. Mike, twelve, was shuffled off to live with Wally Wilson, his godfather, while Johnny, eight, and Doug, seven, went to stay with William Lummis, who was Doug's godfather, and his wife, Frances, who had attended Kinkaid with Baker and was close to Mary Stuart. The boys were gone for months. It was an extreme decision. "They just wanted our lives to be somewhat normal," Doug rationalized years later.

After another operation at the Methodist Hospital, Mary Stuart returned home in February 1969. Baker rented an electric hospital bed for the house and brought the boys home to be with their mother. "I thought the kids had been 'farmed out' long enough, and that it was important that we get them home," he wrote Mary Stuart's mother. "Mary Stuart seems to be improving every day, and in fact we are considering taking the kids down to Pearsall this weekend for a cook out."

Mary Stuart seemed to be improving enough that Baker soon began contemplating a career change that would never have occurred to him just a few years earlier. He was thinking of entering politics. His friend George Bush, having won reelection in 1968 without a challenge, had decided by early 1969 to give up his safe House seat and, at the urging of President Richard Nixon, make another run for the Senate. He planned to take on Ralph Yarborough once again, this time in a 1970 race. As Bush looked around to see who might fill his House seat, he settled on his tennis partner. Surprising himself, Baker found the idea intriguing. He had grown tired of the work at Andrews Kurth, telling his cousin Stewart that he "didn't want to spend his whole life on oil and gas leases." Baker had followed the family path. But now in his late thirties, he was bored.

In typical fashion, Baker began methodically researching what would be involved in taking on such a race. He met with people he trusted as well as political figures in the district to sound them out. Reactions were mixed—"some pro, some con," as he put it at the time. A couple other local Republicans were also considering the race and while Baker concluded that he could raise the money, he was warily watching the top of the ticket to see what impact it might have, most specifically whether Yarborough would draw a strong primary opponent, which Baker thought would bring out conservative voters.

Barbara Bush joined in the sales job, sending a handwritten note to Mary Stuart to reassure her about the prospect of becoming a congressional wife. "I'm really sure that G. has made up his mind to run for the Senate and I am so very sorry!" Barbara wrote. "I love the House and am very happy here." But, she added, "if you really want to build up your ego come to Washington and look over the congressional wives—you're such a star to begin with and need no help."

Baker seemed to be edging toward a race. "This is a big and difficult decision for me, which I know you can appreciate," he said in a handwritten note addressed to "Bushie," as he called his friend. "I have made one decision, however, and that is that if I don't get in—or do and lose in the primary—I would like to take some time off to work in your behalf in any area that you think I might be of help. I've reached a position within my firm where I can do this now with no problem." He went on to thank Bush for suggesting he run for the House. "I have never really had a chance to tell you that I consider your confidence in me or my ability as one of the finest compliments I have ever received."

But a few weeks later, Baker abruptly bowed out. He wrote a note to Bush to explain the decision, which came after four months of careful deliberations. In it, he confided something that he had told no one else. "As I've mentioned before, while I know that in politics one has no control over the timing of events, it appears now that this could not come at a worse time for me as far as my family situation is concerned," he wrote Bush. "It is for this reason, and after much soul-searching, that I have concluded that I should not do it." The date was August 22, 1969, and Baker had something to tell Bush that made clear how far beyond the confines of country-club tennis their relationship had come: Mary Stuart, he announced in the letter, would not make it through her cancer after all.

Although her latest operation seemed to have resulted in a remission, the doctors had told Baker that the average length of such a remission in this type of case was only eight to twelve months. That meant she stood a good chance of becoming sick again just as he was in the final stages of a campaign. He wrote Bush:

> Mary Stuart wants me to run as much as I myself feel that I would like to, and if anything were to have happened to her, or if I could know that she would be well through November or next year, the fact of her illness would not keep me out. I know, however, from the experience of January and February, when she was so very sick, that if she would get sick during the campaign period, I could not do the job properly.

Then he added a bombshell:

> George, Mary Stuart does not know her true prognosis. She knows only that her first operation was for a breast malignancy and believes that her second illness was due to a congenital back problem, with the ovarian removal having been done as a preventative measure, which is quite common in breast cancer cases.
>
> I have not told one person, including my Mother, about her true condition in order that it not get back to her. I think it important to her, the children and me that she not spend whatever time she has left worrying over what's to come.
>
> I hope you understand my problem.
>
> Best to Bar and the kids.
Jim

Baker had not told anyone—not his mother, not his children, not even his wife—what was in store. The one person he told, the only person he trusted enough to confide his awful truth, was George Bush. A secret that big creates a bond as nothing else will.

MARY STUART SPENT part of January 1970 with her parents in Florida, where they had an oceanfront house in Boynton Beach. But she looked forward to returning to Houston to finish the house that she and Baker had been building at 5030 Green Tree Road. She had designed it after the Manor House built by renowned architect John Staub for oilman Lawrence Reed on the grounds of the Houstonian Club, complete with a trendy sunken living room bracketed by fireplaces on both sides. They planned to move in within the next few weeks and invited David Paton, Baker's college friend and best man from their wedding, to visit the new place.

On her last day in Florida, however, Mary Stuart felt sick to her stomach. When she arrived back in Houston, her doctor put her in the hospital and began running tests. "We do not have all of the results yet, but Mom is feeling much, much better and should get to come home soon," Baker wrote Jamie at the Hill School on February 4. "The house is definitely going to be ready to move into February 15, although the driveways will not be finished." Two days later, Baker wrote to Paton. "Mary Stuart is in the hospital now, but we have been assured that she will be out in time for the move," he wrote. "Please do try and come as it would mean a lot to her."

If Baker understood how bad things really were, he did not let on. He tried to move ahead as if all were normal. On his schedule for February 13, he listed at noon, "Bush speech—Introduce him." But Mary Stuart was deteriorating quickly even as Baker had hidden the truth from his boys. The most memorable clue for Doug, the youngest at eight, came when he visited her in the hospital and crawled onto the bed to give her a kiss, but she mistook him for Jamie, who was fifteen and away at school. Baker brought Johnny, then nine, to see her on Valentine's Day and deliver a box of chocolates. When Mike, thirteen, came on the night of February 17, he was stunned to see his strong, powerful father on the edge of devastation.

The family did not end up moving into the new house as planned. "She's not going to make it," Baker finally told his cousin Preston Moore. To David Paton, he wrote, "things are not good."

George and Barbara Bush visited Mary Stuart in the hospital. They would be the last friends to see her alive. "The treatment was so terrible," Barbara remembered. "The medication was barbaric. I don't think the boys knew. I think Jimmy knows that was a huge mistake he made."

Mary Stuart died on February 18 at thirty-eight years old, never having seen the finished home she had built for her family. Baker was at her bedside. He later told Jamie that he was holding her hand and distraught at her pain. "He prayed that she would not suffer and she died a minute later," Jamie said. "And he took that as being an answer to prayer."

It was a Wednesday morning and after Mary Stuart was gone, Baker drove over to Kinkaid School and pulled the three younger boys out of class. He took them on a walk across the lawn at the headmaster's house.

"God came today," he told them.

AS IT TURNED OUT, Baker had not fooled Mary Stuart. He may not have told her what he knew—what he had confided in George Bush—but she understood how dire her condition was. She did not talk about it with her husband to spare him. Each of them was trying to protect the other.

A day or two after her death, Mary Stuart's good friend, Susan Winston, came by the house. She had something to tell Baker. During a trip with two other friends to Florida the previous November, she said, Mary Stuart had told her that she knew she would not live long. She wrote a letter to her husband to be given to him after her death. Mary Stuart had explained where to find it, hidden in a drawer in a built-in chest. Winston now retrieved it and gave it to Baker. He wept as he read it, as he would every time he reread it over the next fifty years.

> My dear sweet loving and loveable Jimmy,
>
> I am suffering so much and cannot get relief. If God would take me now I would be grateful. I am sure he will not for though my time to die may not be far off, it is not now. I am not afraid. The thing that grieves me most is to see you suffer so. . . .
>
> You will have a tough job on your hands with the boys over these next fifteen years. Wherever I am I will be doing everything I can to give you the strength you will need and I will be waiting for you to come to me in the hereafter where we can have peace and joy forever together. . . .
>
> Since the night I kissed you on the beach at Bermuda I have loved you more than anybody could ever love another body. If I have seemed selfish in wanting to be with you constantly it's only that I've lived for the times when I could be close to you and to touch you. The only thing that makes me sad about dying is leaving you and the

boys. I often wonder what they will be like as grown men. Since they are half you, they will have some good qualities in them. . . .

Thank you my love for the best life anyone who has ever walked this earth has had. . . . Don't be sad. Rejoice—and come to me someday.

CHAPTER 4

A Long Dark Night

He was, of course, lost without her, alone with four sons and a new home designed by the wife who would never move in to it. The boys had never seen him cry before. But now they did. When his partners at the law firm offered him a bigger office, he turned it down, unable to muster much interest in the work he had done his whole adult life. "He would go to the window and stand and just stare out of the window," remembered Beatrice Green, his childhood nanny who was still working for his mother. At thirty-nine years old, nothing seemed to make sense anymore.

In a daze, Baker turned to two friends to get him through the funeral and reception and all the details that consume the days after the death of a spouse. "In line with our telephone conversation of this morning, I have agreed to let you and Fran Lummis run my life until I decide to fire you, and you have likewise agreed to fire me should you have the inclination," he wrote Dossy Allday a week after Mary Stuart's death. "I am still swamped trying to clear up my personal affairs, get the kids into a routine, etc.," he wrote his mother a week later.

Few understood what Baker was going through more viscerally than his friend George Bush. The loss of his own three-year-old daughter, Robin, to leukemia had just about destroyed him. He had dealt with it by throwing himself into business. Baker, he decided, needed to do the same.

In this case, the business would be politics. If Baker would not run for Bush's soon-to-be-vacated House seat, then he should help his friend with his campaign for the Senate.

"Bake, you need to take your mind off your grief," Bush told him. "Help me run for the Senate."

"George, that's great, but there are two things," he replied. "Number one, I don't know anything about politics. And number two, I'm a Democrat."

"Well, we can take care of that latter problem," Bush replied.

Baker agreed to serve as chairman for Bush's campaign in Harris County, the sprawling jurisdiction that included the city of Houston. Bush was once again angling for the seat of Ralph Yarborough, who beat him in 1964 and had since become a leader of the antiwar left. With Richard Nixon now in the White House and seeking to consolidate the gains that his so-called Southern Strategy had made for Republicans in the once monolithically Democratic South, Bush had the promise of more help from the national party this time around and anticipated a classic left-right matchup in one of the most conservative states in the nation.

What Bush did not expect was to lose Yarborough as an opponent. In the Democratic primary, the incumbent was beaten by Lloyd Bentsen, a former three-term congressman who was far more conservative than Yarborough. Suddenly, Bush's entire campaign strategy had been rendered inoperative. Instead of running against a firebrand liberal, he now faced a centrist of roughly similar temperament and ideology who carried none of Bush's New England outsider baggage. Bentsen, like Bush, had served as a pilot in World War II and, like Bush, was shot down—in his case, twice. Raised on a ranch, he had married a fashion model and after six years in the House started an insurance business that made him a small fortune. Bentsen was as Texas as they came, with a patrician bearing, a deep baritone voice, and an unmistakably Lone Star drawl.

As Baker dived into his campaign duties for Bush, what engaged him was the competition rather than any struggle of ideas. He had no grand views about policy or politics. He was a conservative but hardly an activist. Given a choice between a safer, more cautious solution to a problem and a bolder, more radical one, he would opt for restraint. In a gauzy sort of way, he thought government should be limited and taxes should be low, just as many Texans did, but that did not translate into a sweeping belief system. If Bush was not especially strong on what he would eventually call "the vision thing," neither was his friend. They seemed more like products of Eisenhower's optimistic America than Nixon's divided, angry nation. When it came to politics, Baker approached it like an engineer, not an architect.

A myth would develop that Baker turned to politics because of Mary Stuart's death. But, tired of his legal work, he had already been exploring the race for Bush's House seat before that. His family tragedy did not propel him into politics; it delayed his entry. Now the Bush campaign provided a welcome escape from the misery at home. In addition to mourning his wife, Baker was grappling with his father's deteriorating health. And his sister Bonner had become increasingly ill herself. A talented painter and writer who had excelled at Smith College, Bonner at some point during her years on campus suffered what was later described as a nervous breakdown. After recovering enough to graduate with honors, she married Donald Moffitt, a reporter for *The Houston Post*, yet continued to experience what were eventually diagnosed as schizophrenic episodes. Shortly after Mary Stuart's death, Bonner and Donald divorced. The accumulation of family struggles wore on Baker.

"Jimmy, dear, it just doesn't seem possible that one person should have to shoulder so much tragedy," one friend wrote him. "I guess we none of us know and appreciate when we are really well off."

Baker moved his family into the new house a couple months after Mary Stuart died and sought to make life as normal as possible. But he found little sustained help. One housekeeper after another quit, adding to the upheaval. Baker did not open up to his sons or to his friends. He plopped down in his chair after work and drank a few more martinis than he used to. "If I was ever going to become an alcoholic, that's when I would have done it," he reflected later. He often visited Mary Stuart's grave. Once he took an out-of-town friend to the cemetery, only to discover that the gate had been locked while they were inside. By chance, they found a hacksaw and cut their way out.

Baker knew his reticence had a cost, and, left alone at night with his grieving boys, he relived his actions from those days of crisis. He felt guilty and defensive. Shortly after her death, Baker tried to explain to Mary Stuart's parents in a letter why he had not told them how grim her condition really was:

> I hope you don't feel that my lack of candor with you concerning Mary Stuart's illness was the wrong approach. As I have said before, my primary concern was that she enjoy whatever time she had, that she have peace of mind, and not have to live under the dreadful cloud that she would have had she known the truth. It was for this reason that I did not discuss with a single person the serious nature of her illness. I was terribly afraid that if I did she might be able to read it in their expressions, attitudes, etc. I believe and hope that it was the right decision and take comfort from the fact that her letter to me indicates that it was.

BAKER THREW HIMSELF into the Senate race, learning the basics of fund-raising, policy positions, scheduling, and voter turnout. It was an education for a rookie operative. He proved a quick study.

Predictably enough, Bush found it hard to gain traction against the courtly Lloyd Bentsen. "Bush and Bentsen seemed so alike they could easily have passed for close relations, right down to mutual memberships in the River Oaks Country Club," *Texas Monthly* observed. "Both candidates presented themselves to the public as Christian family men who took long walks in the park with their children and dogs, and helped their wives with the dishes."

With registered Republicans still far outnumbered in Texas, Bush labored to present an alternative compelling enough to peel off Democrats. Indeed, Bentsen ran slightly to the right of Bush, chiding him over votes for gun control and fair housing, while retaining the Democrats' traditional support among minorities and liberals. A last-minute infusion of cash from Nixon's political operation did not help and neither did Bush's vague program, summed up in his slogan that year: "I can do more for Texas." On Election Day in November 1970, Bentsen prevailed with 53 percent of the vote; with 47 percent, Bush had fared somewhat better than he did in 1964 but still fell short.

A bright spot was his home district of Harris County, which he carried with 60 percent, thanks in part to Baker's help. Baker was disappointed for his friend. "I truly don't know what George's plans are right now, but I would not be surprised to see him take a position in the Executive Branch," he told his in-laws.

For his part, Bush saw elective office in Baker's future. "Right now I can't decide whether to head up the Baker for Mayor Committee or the Baker for Congress Committee," Bush wrote him shortly after the election. "I do hope that you will consider running for something someday. You'd be a great candidate and an even greater public servant."

Soon after the election, Mary Stuart's family came for Christmas and New Year's. Her father seemed distant, perhaps still resentful of Baker's secrecy during the cancer. "How sad I was to leave," Rosemary McHenry, Mary Stuart's mother, wrote Baker afterward. "You looked so alone and lonely when we said good night and good bye. Why doesn't granddaddy understand?"

The first holiday season without Mary Stuart was almost impossibly hard. Baker's sister Bonner, meanwhile, was discharged from the hospital on New Year's Eve, only to have to go back three or four days later. At the same time, his mother developed a clot in a vein, cutting the circulation to her right arm, and she too had to check in to a hospital. And his father continued to head downhill with his Parkinson's. It seemed like 1971 would be another tough year.

The kids were struggling too. Mike, then fourteen, was suspended from school for three days for cutting a science class and being thrown out of an English class on the same day. Then he sneaked out of the house one night. "Needless to say, I am plenty burned up and he is not going to be going anywhere for a long time," Baker told Jamie. Mike then got caught driving the family Honda and was ticketed by the police. He wrote his father a letter because he could not summon the courage to tell him in person. "I don't know why I did it dad," he wrote. "I was crazy I guess. Please don't yell at me Dad! Signed your foolish son, Mike."

Dealing with his own grief, Baker had little idea how to help his boys deal with theirs. They were acting out, constantly getting into trouble, fighting with one another, making life miserable for the housekeeper. Baker found his kids to be worlds apart from what he had been at their age. This was the 1970s and the youth rebellion had found its way into their cloistered country-club world. One day he discovered marijuana in one of the boy's rooms and tried it. He got nothing out of it. "I don't think he really knew any of us very well," Jamie reflected years later. "And I'm pretty sure that we didn't know him very well at that point."

IN THE SUMMER OF 1972, Baker went to the Republican National Convention in Miami with Bush, his first exposure to national politics on one of its biggest stages. As Baker had predicted, Bush had been brought onto the Nixon team after sacrificing his safe House seat to make the Senate campaign. His consolation prize was the ambassadorship to the United Nations, a post that gave him a fire-hose introduction to international diplomacy and a lifelong Rolodex of friends from around the world. Back in Texas, Baker continued to dabble in politics, becoming finance chairman for the Texas Republican Party and taking on the tough assignment of raising money in the state during Nixon's reelection bid ("like pulling teeth," he would later recall of the task).

Reunited in Miami, the two made the rounds of parties and fundraisers and meetings with members of Nixon's cabinet. The gathering was marked by raucous antiwar protests, and Baker was somewhat unnerved by the turbulence. "I had a little trouble at last night's session with demonstrators rocking the car, shouting obscenities, etc and got caught in the tear gas once I left the car," he told Mary Stuart's parents.

After Nixon's landslide reelection victory that fall, Baker began hunting for a political appointment, aided by Bush from his new perch in New York. When a seat opened up on the Fifth United States Circuit Court of Appeals, just one rung below the Supreme Court, Bush urged Senator John Tower to recommend Baker to the president. "He has stature, integrity, great character and conviction and could, in my opinion, end up on the Supreme Court—should you recommend him for the Circuit Bench," Bush wrote. "He's that broad-gauged." Baker was passed over.

Home offered only more frustrations. Without their mother, the boys struggled with school, with drugs, with their father, and with each other. Over the course of a couple years, Mike wrecked three cars. Jamie, who in an act of rebellion voted for George McGovern in 1972 and made sure his father knew it, was sent home from the Hill School two days early for smoking in his room and jeopardized his graduation with poor grades. He was rejected by Princeton and Stanford before being accepted to Claremont College. Twelve-year-old Johnny and a couple of his pals chopped down three trees on someone else's property to create a "commando fort," costing his chagrined father $231.

"Things are about the same around here—bedlam," Baker told Mary Stuart's mother at one point. He lectured the boys about their grades and their behavior, but he recognized that he may have had something to do with their troubles. "He has had a pretty tough teenage due in no small part to the loss of his mother in that critical time in his life," he wrote about Jamie. "In addition, I feel that I may have short-changed him, what with all of the other demands on my time and attention."

The demands were hardly letting up. His sister Bonner's depression worsened and the family found a residential facility for her. "I know I have turned out wrong and it's nobody's fault but mine," she wrote Baker. "I don't know what happened exactly but I got mixed up."

Then on May 21, 1973, Baker got a phone call from St. Anthony Center. His father had had a heart attack and died at age eighty. By the end, the elder Baker had been having trouble recognizing anyone. He thought his wife was his mother. He could not feed himself. A World War I hero who had lived in the shadow of his own father, the patriarchal Captain Baker, James A. Baker Jr. had never veered from the path of duty and obligation that he had been prescribed. In the end, as is often true in such cases, grief mixed with relief. "You are right that his death came as a release from a long and debilitating illness," Baker told one mourner. Still, for Baker, it was another loss, this time of the dominant figure in his life, the man who steered him through every step of his upbringing, his education, and his career. He had hardly even known of his son's burgeoning interest in politics and would not have approved if he had. But Baker would no longer have to answer to his father. The Warden was gone.

AMID ALL THE TURMOIL, Baker began dating again. "I'm pretty sure that every woman in town was aiming at him," Barbara Bush remembered. But as it happened, he found a fresh start close to home: Susan Winston, the wife of his hunting buddy Jimbo Winston and the close friend of Mary Stuart. Susan, of course, had been the one who came to his house to retrieve Mary Stuart's posthumous farewell letter and beyond that had become, as Baker put it, "one of those casserole ladies who would show up" with food for the bereft family in the weeks after the funeral. Since then, Susan and Jimbo had finally divorced over his drinking. Now she and Baker, still young and both left unexpectedly alone with children, found a friendship rooted in mutual tragedy evolving into a midlife romance.

She was the daughter of John Travis "Jack" Garrett, a rancher who grew rice and raised cattle near Danbury, Texas, and Mary Blackshear Farish, a young widow whose first husband died in a plane crash. Jack Garrett was a formidable figure, nicknamed "Whispering Jack" because "his voice was like an amplified foghorn," Susan said, and could be heard in the next county over. Mary Garrett was an inveterate volunteer, starting a clothing center for the needy, serving as chair of a county child welfare unit, and devoting time to other causes.

Susan was the oldest of their four children, all of whom had been put to work on the ranch—hardly an upbringing comparable to Jimmy Baker's pampered youth in Houston. The boys were expected to wake up at 5:30 a.m., the girls at 6:30. They were all sometimes farmed out to neighbors to pick cotton, dragging heavy sacks for 50 cents per hundred pounds. Every year, Pappy, as Susan called her father, gave each child a calf to raise. Susan groomed heifers and bulls, presenting them at cattle shows. Once she made it all the way to the State Fair. Theirs was a religious Catholic household where mass was not to be missed. It was also a Republican family in a Democratic state. Eventually, her parents moved to Houston and she graduated from the Kinkaid School, years after Baker attended, then studied at the University of Texas at Austin.

When she met Jimbo Winston, she had thought he was "a drop-dead handsome dynamo and former Marine who could charm the birds out of the trees." Her friends warned her to stay away. She considered herself a "little church mouse" who was gingerly walking through life. But he opened up different worlds to her. And so they married. Together they had three children: Elizabeth, James IV (nicknamed Bo), and William. Her friends, however, were right. Jimbo was the life of the party—marriage and family did not mean he felt any need to change. His drinking grew worse. Twice, she packed her bags and left, only to return upon promises of change. But he never did change, not for long. One evening when Elizabeth, then eight, upset her, Susan screamed and chased her daughter around the house. Later that night, filled with remorse, she broke down in sobs and prayed. And she left Jimbo for good.

Now, she leaned on Baker and he leaned on her. Soon they were inseparable. "Dad saw someone who could really help him with the four Baker boys, who were devastated by Mary Stuart's death," said Will Winston. "And Mom saw stability in her husband where previously she didn't have any of that." Still, Baker's mother needled him for a year to ask Susan to marry him before he finally did.

They eloped in secret on the morning of August 6, 1973, his mother's birthday. He was forty-three; she was thirty-four. The rector at St. Martin's would not marry them because Susan was divorced, so they found a Presbyterian minister instead. Then they took both of their mothers to lunch and broke the news to them.

Only later did they announce the new marriage to their shocked children. "Guess what we did?" they asked after picking up Johnny and Doug from the airport as they returned home from a visit to Mary Stuart's parents. Then the newlyweds headed off for a Texas-style honeymoon, driving down to Rockpile Ranch, where there was still no house. They stayed two nights in a tent before moving on to the coast to go boating in a sixteen-foot Boston whaler.

Susan and her three children moved into the house on Green Tree Road. With only three bedrooms, it was already crowded enough with Baker and his four boys. Now with seven children, four of them in middle school, the house was beyond jammed. Elizabeth slept on a chaise on the landing on the stairwell for months, while the porch and garage were converted into bedrooms. Those living at home attended four different schools, requiring four different carpools, not to mention myriad trips to doctors, sports games, and social occasions. The kitchen was covered in charts about who was using the station wagon when. The laundry machine seemed to run day and night. Just keeping groceries in the house was a challenge.

As the new bride and groom saw it, the merger of their families made sense. The Baker children and the Winston children were close in age and had grown up together. Baker was Bo's godfather. They hung out at each other's house so much it was "sort of a communal type thing," as Bo recalled. At one point, when they were maybe six years old, Johnny Baker asked Elizabeth Winston to marry him; she turned him down because she wanted to marry his brother Doug.

But while *The Brady Bunch* on television was presenting the happy union of six fictional children from two families in the California suburbs to an ABC prime-time audience in 1973, the union of seven real-life children from two families in Houston that same year was in actuality a dark affair, filled with anger, resentment, conflict, and lots of drugs. "We had been a very happy posse before," Elizabeth recalled. "Maybe the tragedies made it difficult for us to come together right away." Announcing the marriage as a fait accompli only made matters worse. "When you have seven children that had that much trauma," tension was inevitable, Susan later concluded.

No one was more upset than Johnny, by then thirteen years old. He vowed to break up the new marriage. He beat up his new step-siblings, broke a pool cue over his brother Doug's head, and descended into narcotic fugues. Convinced that his father was replacing his dead mother, he felt betrayed. "I asked him, 'You're never going to get married again?' 'No, I'm never going to get married again,'" Johnny recalled. "And then he was married three and a half years later. I was bitter. I was pissed off. I didn't understand what was going on. And I was going to break them up. My drug use was a direct result of that."

He may have been the most extreme case, but not the only one. "My grades suffered. My behavior suffered," said Doug. "And obviously in pure retrospect, it was me just going, 'Help.' It was a marriage that obviously both the parents needed and all the kids needed, but not all the kids realized it or wanted it at that time."

One person who did not object to the new marriage, paradoxically, was Jimbo Winston. Baker had even asked permission to propose to his friend's ex-wife. "Jimbo knew that he was not a good father and he wanted his children to have a good father," Elizabeth Winston said. As her brother Bo put it, "I think Dad was incredibly relieved when he found out that Mom and Jimmy were getting married. Incredibly relieved. Because he knew his kids would be taken care of."

After nearly a year of drama and drugs and family counseling, Jim and Susan Baker decided to escape their "house apes," as Susan called them ruefully, with a once-in-a-lifetime trip to Africa, a getaway they would call their "hunting-moon." Baker had always wanted to try a safari. When he started to plan it, he got the name of a legendary guide and hunting lodge from none other than Jimbo Winston.

On Winston's advice, Baker booked twenty-three nights at the Victoria Falls Hotel in what was then known as Rhodesia and later Zimbabwe. He also secured the services of John Dugmore, who had served as a guide for many big-name tourists, including European royalty, and helped Hollywood make such films as Clark Gable's *Mogambo*, John Wayne's *Hatari!*, and William Holden's *The Lion*. Dugmore offered Baker an exhilarating adventure. Emerging from a clearing one day, they found themselves being charged by a buffalo. Dugmore fired a single shot right between the eyes and took down the animal just seven yards from Baker. Baker shipped home $3,000 worth of trophies and later had a series of heads and horns mounted and skins turned into rugs, including a large carpet made out of wildebeest.

Shortly after they returned to Texas came the devastating, though not entirely surprising, news that Jimbo Winston had suddenly died. Baker had been with him briefly the night before. The cause of death was determined to be acute pancreatitis and cirrhosis. "Whatever it was, of course, was brought on by his refusal to ever admit to his alcoholism or to permit himself to be treated," Baker wrote a friend. "It was such a waste of a life that could have been so productive."

IN THE SPRING OF 1973, Baker flew to Washington for a job interview. He had never spent a single day of his post-military career employed anywhere other than his Texas law firm and he had only Bush's word for what a second act in public service might be like. But with so many things in his life starting over, he finally seemed ready to make the leap to politics.

Prodded by Bush, Baker had been searching for an appointment from Nixon ever since he had begun raising money for the Republican Party during the previous year's presidential campaign. While he had not gotten the federal judgeship, he did get an interview to run the powerful Civil Division at the Justice Department. He flew up from Texas and prepared to meet Richard Kleindienst, the attorney general. But their interview was scheduled for April 30, 1973, the very day of the massive government shakeup in which Nixon fired his lawyer, John Dean, and accepted the resignations of his top two White House advisers, H. R. Haldeman and John Ehrlichman, in hopes of finally containing the damage from the rapidly expanding Watergate scandal. Kleindienst was pushed out too because of his close ties to figures implicated in Watergate. Baker got a call from the

White House telling him his interview had been postponed. He was later offered a consolation prize as assistant administrator of the Environmental Protection Agency. "I said, 'Thank you very much, but that's not what I think I want to do,'" he recalled.

As the full extent of the Watergate cover-up became clear over the next year and a half, Baker was often relieved that he had not chosen to join the imploding government, and he watched with dismay as his friend George Bush was uncomfortably trapped in the middle of it. In 1973, after his reelection, Nixon had tapped Bush to become chairman of the Republican National Committee, a job that Bush had been reluctant to take, given the scandals, although he felt he had no choice but to accept. Caught between his sense of loyalty and his sense of integrity, Bush for months stuck staunchly by Nixon, predicting that the Watergate investigation would not touch the president. But when the so-called "smoking gun" tape that recorded Nixon ordering aides to have the CIA impede the FBI investigation was revealed, Bush knew it was over. At a cabinet meeting where other advisers urged Nixon to stand firm, Bush told the president it was time to resign. On August 9, 1974, he did.

Replacing Nixon was his vice president, Gerald Ford, appointed only a year before to fill the post vacated by Spiro Agnew after his own corruption scandal. Like Bush, Ford hailed from the more moderate wing of the party and the two had competed for the vice presidential appointment when Agnew was forced to leave office. Now, once again, Bush was aiming for vice president, this time hoping Ford would choose him, although he had now been passed over twice by Nixon.

Baker joined others in lobbying the new Ford White House to pick his friend. "Age geography foreign affairs experience admiration of Republican Party officials respect of all who knew him in Congress and above all his reputation for honesty and intergrity [sic] argue for George Bush as your vice president," Baker wrote in a telegram to the White House. Baker was once again working on a Bush campaign, as it were. He spoke to reporters, touting his friend's qualifications, even if he suspected the appointment was not meant to be. On talking points he drafted for an interview with ABC News about Bush, Baker scratched the likely verdict at the bottom of the page: "Always bridesmaid."

Sure enough, Ford passed over Bush and another former congressman, Donald Rumsfeld, in favor of Nelson Rockefeller, the liberal Republican former governor of New York. "Dear Bake—Yesterday was an enormous personal disappointment," Bush wrote Baker. He had made the finals but in some ways, he added, "the defeat was more intense" as a result.

"Too bad about George," Baker wrote Mary Stuart's parents. "I know he was deeply disappointed, but as I told him last night, it's better to have been recognized as the number two choice than not to have been in the running at all, particularly when you are only fifty years old and have been in public life for only eight years."

The two runners-up did well. Rumsfeld became Ford's White House chief of staff and Bush was offered his choice of ambassadorships. He bypassed prominent postings in Britain and France in favor of China, where the United States had just begun opening diplomatic relations in one of Nixon's most significant achievements. Bush and his family picked up and moved to Beijing, then still called Peking in the West, for a seminal experience in his political career.

Even from China, Bush was looking out for Baker, urging the new Ford administration to find a job for him. "In spite of Princeton education he is bright, able community leader from Great Texas family," Bush joked in a cable to Rumsfeld, himself a Princeton graduate. "He has political credentials that would help." The White House wrote an evaluation of Baker, noting in his file that "Geo Bush referred." Baker was given the second-highest rating on personal, professional, and educational qualifications.

Then, one of Bush's political friends in Washington made a well-timed visit to China. Rogers Morton, a towering man well over six and a half feet tall who had befriended Bush when they were both young Republican members of the House, stopped in to see the ambassador. Morton, known universally as Rog, was the younger son of a patrician Kentucky family that dated its lineage back to the Revolutionary War general George Clark. Bitten by the campaign bug early in life, he had moved to Maryland, gone into politics, and preceded Bush as chairman of the Republican National Committee before serving as Nixon's secretary of the interior. Now he had been named Ford's commerce secretary. To find a number two, Morton sought out Bush. Did he know of anyone?

He sure did. Soon, Baker was in Washington again, interviewing with Morton. Writing from China, Bush encouraged Baker, noting that the Commerce post was a "high level job" and pointing out that he would start out with something most Washington newcomers did not—the chance to attend cabinet meetings when the secretary was unavailable. Finally, one day in the spring of 1975, the Bakers were driving back from Rockpile Ranch when Baker stopped on the highway at a Stuckey's restaurant to check in with his office and learned that Morton was trying to reach him. When Baker called him back on the pay phone, Morton came on the line and formally asked Baker to join him in Washington as his undersecretary, the second-highest job at the department. Baker thanked Morton, but asked for time to consult with his wife. When Morton pushed for an answer, Baker said yes.

Morton's decision, however, still had to be cleared by the Ford White House, where Baker, despite Bush's advocacy, was an unknown. Rumsfeld wanted to pick a California ally of Ronald Reagan, the hero of the Republican right, to help defuse a potential primary challenge to Ford in 1976. But Morton pushed back, even going directly to the president to make his case for Baker, and ultimately Rumsfeld backed off. On a Saturday in June, Rumsfeld met with Ford and Dick Cheney, his deputy chief of staff, in the Oval Office and surrendered. "We talked about the Under Secretary of Commerce and indicated that Baker, the lawyer from Houston, probably is the right way to go," Rumsfeld wrote afterward. "Rog Morton likes him, he's a southerner, John Tower's very high on him and he should be a good choice."

From China, Bush congratulated Baker. "I am absolutely *elated*," he said. He quickly suggested two people to hire and proposed the Bakers move into the Bushes' house in Washington. "If you aren't careful I'll try to mastermind your life."

Baker was formally nominated on July 22, 1975. On August 1, he was handed a note: "You were confirmed by Senate 9:05 am Eastern daily time." Ten days later, with his "thundering herd" of children on hand, he was sworn in. At the age of forty-five, Baker did not know it yet, but he was about to begin his life's work.

BAKER WAS NEVER introspective. He kept no diary and left no record that survives of how he felt to be moving on from Houston and the burden of so much family history. Until now, he had been a good Texan and a good son. He had never done anything other than what was expected of him, even when he had chafed at the constraints of a corporate lawyer's life. His escape was hunting and still more work. Now family tragedy, a country-club friendship, and the national disaster of Watergate had combined to offer him a different way out.

Less than a year into his new job, he was asked to address his son Mike's commencement from Northwest Academy in Houston. Much of the speech was boilerplate graduation advice. But at one point, Baker spoke with uncharacteristic sweep about the state of the world after Vietnam and Watergate and the tumult of recent years. It had the ring of a personal truth.

We in this country have been going through a long, dark night of self-criticism. We have been telling ourselves that America has tried to run the world, that it is corrupt, that many of our institutions have failed us and need to be "dismantled" under the guise of "reform." Confession may be good for the soul, but there comes a time when too much confession makes us weaker rather than stronger.

Sure we make mistakes, but who in this world doesn't?

For Baker, the long dark night was coming to an end. He was ready to take the next step.

Part Two

CHAPTER 5

Miracle Man

Henry Kissinger had one question: Just who the hell is James A. Baker III anyway?

It was a fair question. Kissinger, after all, was the geopolitical grand wizard who had helped Richard Nixon open the door to China, bring about détente with the Soviet Union, and end the Vietnam War. He was now Gerald Ford's secretary of state and, other than the president, the most important man in government. He was a global celebrity, recognized everywhere he went; even his romantic life was chronicled in the gossip pages. And Baker was, well, nobody, really.

It was the spring of 1976, less than a year into Baker's time in Washington, when he found himself in the crosshairs of the world's most prominent diplomat. As undersecretary of commerce in an administration heading into an election, Baker had drawn the appropriately low card in campaign assignments, a small fundraiser with Republican donors in remote Oklahoma. As far as Baker knew, no reporters were present when he took questions.

"Will Henry Kissinger be in the second Ford administration?" one of the donors asked as they milled around a swimming pool.

Baker offered a blunt answer. "I can't conceive of that happening," he said.

That was the answer conservatives wanted to hear. For all the rage of the left over the secret bombing of Cambodia and his encouragement of Nixon's dark side, Kissinger at the moment was the bête noire of the Republican right, which saw him as the architect of appeasement to the Communists. As Ford faced a revolt within his own party led by Ronald Reagan, Kissinger was a political liability and it would benefit the incumbent president to establish some distance.

In those days, officials felt comfortable making relatively candid remarks in one part of the country without fear that they would ricochet around the world instantly. There was no internet, no social media. But even in 1976, Baker would discover, offhand comments could still make their way back to Washington, at least eventually. It took a day or so, but Baker's prognostication was reported by the news wires, which then got noticed in the White House—and more importantly on the seventh floor of the State Department.

Kissinger was peeved. He did not know Baker and assumed "he probably was some right-wing Texan who was trying to placate" the conservatives, as Kissinger later put it. Baker quickly learned what happened when he irritated a legend. Kissinger made his unhappiness known to Dick Cheney at the White House. At an event in the Rose Garden soon afterward, the president's secretary approached Baker and asked him to stop by Cheney's office before leaving.

Cheney was thirty-five years old and, following Donald Rumsfeld's promotion to defense secretary, had become the youngest man ever to serve as White House chief of staff. With the demeanor of a cool cowboy from Wyoming, the fierce intellect of a Yale dropout-turned-doctoral-candidate, and the discipline of a recovering drinker, Cheney had established himself as a force to be reckoned with in the White House despite his youth. The son of a New Deal government worker and a diner waitress, Cheney shared with Baker a frontier identity and a love of hunting and the outdoors that would form the basis for a lifelong friendship.

On this day, however, it fell to Cheney to play the disciplinarian. When Baker arrived in the chief of staff's corner office, he found Cheney sitting at his desk. He looked up at Baker with a crooked smile that would eventually become famous.

"I understand you announced Henry's resignation from government," Cheney said.

"What are you talking about?" Baker asked. "I didn't do any such thing."

Cheney held up a dispatch ripped from the wire service machine of the type that sat in offices all around Washington, announcing the news in bursts of noise that formed the staccato backdrop of the city's workday. "I got the wire copy right here," he said.

As it dawned on him what Cheney was talking about, Baker assumed that his short career in public service was over. Kissinger was clearly furious. He would demand Baker's head.

But Cheney was not about to make a capital crime out of the gaffe. "Don't worry about it," he said. "Just go back and make it right with Henry."

One thing Baker had learned in his years in the legal world was how to smooth over disputes and massage sizable egos. After Cheney's remonstration in the White House, Baker went back to his office and called Kissinger. This was not even the first time he had gotten on the bad side of the famously prickly secretary of state. Not long before, the two had squared off over a line in a draft Ford speech complaining about cheap Chinese textile imports. Kissinger wanted the line out for fear of disrupting his diplomatic opening to China, but master infighter that he was, he did not bother arguing the matter during the drafting process and instead waited until Ford was already on Air Force One heading to the speech before calling the plane to convince the president to delete it. Tipped off, Baker then called the plane himself and convinced Cheney to urge the president to keep the sentence. In the end, Ford agreed and Baker had his first real introduction to White House intrigue. "Oh, so you're Textile Baker," Kissinger had grumbled when Baker later introduced himself on a State Department receiving line.

As he got Kissinger on the phone following the reports on the Oklahoma comment, Baker was determined to be contrite. "I am calling for two things," he told the secretary of state. "To apologize for the way the story comes across and it is not my recollection that I ever said anything like that." He added: "I want to make it clear to you that I admire you greatly."

Kissinger brushed it off, but not without betraying a sense of bitterness. "Never mind," he said. "It is getting to be a cottage industry."

Baker noted that he had been asked the question about Kissinger staying in the cabinet several times on his trip. "It is an issue in that part of the country and I did not have the presence of mind nor perhaps the experience," he said.

"Conceivably, some people ask because they want me to *stay*," Kissinger said, although he knew better. "I don't give a damn what any of you say."

"I would like you to stay and I feel honestly about that and I am calling to apologize and get the story corrected," Baker said.

With that, Kissinger let it go, but he never forgot. For Baker, it was an early lesson that politics at the highest levels was studded with land mines—and not all of them involved the opposition.

BAKER HAD ARRIVED in Washington less than a year earlier. The young Marine who had first seen the White House from the outside on a cold Eisenhower inauguration day now was a regular in the building. In a city full of ambition, where everyone saw himself as the next Kissinger or at least the next Bush, the corporate lawyer from Texas had somehow managed the impossible, going from obscure to insider in the blink of an eye.

From the start, Baker seemed to thrive. He and Susan and the kids who had not gone off to boarding school or college had moved into a rented house on leafy Chain Bridge Road and he threw himself in to work at the Commerce Department, a relative backwater but exciting nonetheless for the new guy from Texas.

His first break came with his boss. Rog Morton turned out to be not just a seasoned Washington hand, but a friend and mentor. Morton quickly started sending Baker to the White House for economic strategy meetings. Peter Roussel, an aide on the Ford staff, recalled another official leaning over after one of the policy sessions and saying, "What's the deal with this Baker guy? He's pretty impressive."

Baker earned $40,000 a year, a pretty big comedown given that he had been pulling down more than $140,000 a year in pay and investment income, or something like $800,000 in today's dollars. He arrived at the office before 8 a.m. most days and stayed for twelve hours. But he loved it. "This job is extremely fascinating and very challenging," he told David Paton, his old friend from Princeton. "I had an interesting hour or so in the Oval Office on Russian grain a couple of weeks ago, and I am attending a number of Economic Policy Board meetings at the White House when my boss can't go. Very heavy stuff for a lawyer from Houston, Texas!"

Less than two months after he started, the *Houston Post* was profiling Baker as a "man to watch" in Washington. "He's a guy with an unlimited future," the paper quoted an unnamed senior administration official as saying. At home, Susan saw a revitalized husband after the traumas of the last few years. "He was so excited about the ideas, the policy," she said. "It just totally reenergized him."

Baker had passed on Bush's offer of moving into his house, which was fortuitous since Ford brought Bush back to Washington by the end of the year to take over as director of the CIA. It was not a switch that Baker advised; to win Senate confirmation to head the theoretically apolitical spy agency, Bush was forced by Democrats to disavow any aspirations to run for vice president on Ford's ticket in 1976. "My feeling was that he shouldn't be asked to forswear his political birthright in order to take the job," Baker said. "His view was the president wants me to do it." Bush blamed Rumsfeld, seeing it as a scheme to knock a potential rival out of the running. At least it meant that the Bushes and the Bakers were together in the same city again. They were soon back to weekend barbecues and tennis games.

As part of the same shakeup, Ford tapped the veteran Republican Elliot Richardson to take over as commerce secretary, but it took several months for him to extricate himself from the ambassadorship in London. All of a sudden, Baker was left to run the department in the interim, a de facto member of the cabinet overseeing tens of thousands of employees and key government functions ranging from the National Weather Service to the Patent and Trademark Office to the Census Bureau.

Once he arrived, Richardson soon took a liking to Baker too. An aristocratic New Englander, Richardson was on his fourth cabinet appointment—at the time a modern record—and had a penchant for surrounding himself with smart, hard-driving types, such as Baker and another bright young aide, Richard Darman, whom he brought with him to Commerce. Richardson, who had famously quit as Richard Nixon's attorney general rather than carry out the Saturday Night Massacre to block the Watergate investigation, had a great eye for how to actually get things done in the capital and disdained the preening lightweights who flocked to it. Washington, he said once, was a city full of cocker spaniels who would rather be petted than wield power. "Maybe we hit it off because he knew I would rather wield power," Baker would theorize later.

GERALD RUDOLPH FORD WAS the first president Baker would get to know up close. Down-to-earth and unaffected, Ford was a dutiful public servant who did his homework, played by the rules, and never aspired to the White House. His real ambition after twenty-five years as a congressman from Michigan was to serve as Speaker of the House, but he accepted when Nixon offered him the vice presidency following Spiro Agnew's resignation. Less than one agonizing year later, when Nixon himself resigned in August 1974, Ford became the nation's first commander in chief never to have been elected as either president or vice president.

In 1976, he faced the enormous challenge of selling himself to Americans to earn a four-year term of his own. "A Ford, not a Lincoln," as he described himself, he was a self-effacing man, decent and plainspoken, a seeming antidote to the Machiavellian machinations of the Nixon era. But his decision to pardon Nixon shortly after assuming office had wiped out much of the goodwill that accompanied his ascension and the country's deepening economic troubles erased whatever was left.

From the start, Ford struggled in the campaign. He had never run for anything larger than a House district in Michigan and had few loyalists in the party outside his home state. Ronald Reagan, the charismatic former actor and governor of California who was the champion of the emerging conservative movement, had decided to run in the Republican primaries against him and Ford's team underestimated Reagan. "They thought he was nothing—this was going to be a cake walk," said Stuart Spencer, one of Ford's top strategists. Spencer knew better; he had worked for Reagan before and had a sense of how formidable he was.

Indeed, as the 1976 race began, Ford barely squeaked by Reagan in the crucial New Hampshire primary before rolling to victories in the next several contests, including Florida and Illinois. But with the help of the conservative senator Jesse Helms, Reagan ambushed Ford in North Carolina and suddenly momentum shifted. By spring, with his prospects increasingly in doubt, Ford asked Rog Morton to become campaign chairman and take charge of fending off Reagan. With his former boss running the campaign, Baker was now in the middle of it too.

The upcoming May 1 primary in Texas would be crucial and Baker, one of the few Texans in the administration, warned the White House that it was courting disaster by sending Kissinger out on a foreign tour that would kick off with a news conference that could trigger a Reaganite backlash. "If you want to win Texas," Baker told Cheney in a phone call, "you can't do this." Impressed by Baker's urgency, Cheney invited Baker over to the White House to make his case directly to the president. Shortly thereafter, he sat down in the Oval Office, telling Ford that he should sideline his own secretary of state. Still a novice in Washington, Baker seemed to be either heedless or unaware of how risky it might be to go up against Kissinger for a third time.

"Mr. President," Baker would always remember saying, "I'm talking to you now as a Texan. This would be devastating in the lead-up to the primary."

"Well, Jim," Ford replied, "the *thinking* Republicans will understand my position on this."

"Mr. President," he retorted, "with respect to this issue, there *are* no thinking Republicans in Texas right now."

Nonetheless, Kissinger went on his trip and had his news conference.

Whether that had any political effect on Ford or not, Baker was right about the campaign's precarious state in Texas. When the votes were counted on May 1, Reagan had walloped Ford by a two-to-one margin in the state, seizing all of Texas's delegates. Increasingly, it was looking like Republicans were headed to their convention in Kansas City that summer with no clear nominee.

SHORTLY BEFORE the Texas primary, Ford's close friend Jack Stiles had been killed in a car accident. Stiles had run Ford's first race for Congress back in Grand Rapids, Michigan, and for this presidential campaign he had been given a particularly sensitive job, rounding up delegates for Ford at the upcoming Republican convention. With the race now looking as though it might actually come down to the convention floor, the Ford campaign needed someone to replace him and fast. Morton lobbied for his former deputy. Cheney, impressed with Baker's savvy about campaign politics as well as his performance at the Commerce Department, agreed.

Right before the voting in Texas, Baker accompanied Ford on a campaign swing to his home state, riding on Air Force One for the first time in his life. Partway through the flight back, the president asked Baker to take Stiles's old job at the campaign. Baker felt he had no choice but to accept. Just like that, he had gone from an obscure Texas lawyer to delegate hunter for the president of the United States. Never mind that his only real experience in politics consisted of running a single county in a losing Senate race and raising some money.

That Baker was chosen was a reflection of not just his adept networking in the short time he had been in Washington but how decimated the Republican Party had been by Watergate. An entire generation of up-and-coming operatives had been essentially wiped out by their association with Nixon and the party was left to regroup with a new and untested cadre. "We basically had to build a campaign organization on the fly," Cheney said. "We were all green, including the candidate."

Baker came on board in May, just a week after his Air Force One flight. Reagan and Ford traded victories through the rest of the spring until the president took the last two key contests, in New Jersey and Ohio, on June 8. Ford then turned his attention to the states holding meetings that summer to choose convention delegates, only to embarrass himself by flying to Missouri to make a personal appeal to the state's Republicans, who then handed nearly all of their at-large delegates to Reagan. Ford at that point still led overall with 963 delegates to 879 for Reagan, but he was short of the 1,130 needed to secure the nomination. The whole campaign would come down to how good Baker proved to be at his new job.

Baker loved hunting, but he had never hunted delegates before or done anything connected to the arcane and byzantine politics of a party nomination process. What he quickly found was that blunt force was not as useful as cajolery. Baker asked Ford's aides to set aside twenty to thirty minutes a day for the president to make phone calls to key delegates. Baker had an advantage over the Reagan forces—he had the best-known building in the world, the White House, to use as an asset and he did not hesitate to employ it. He brought eight delegates from Pennsylvania to meet with Ford in the Oval Office. He brought uncommitted delegates from Virginia to see the president in the Blue Room. He gave away seats to state dinners for Australia's visiting leader in July and Finland's leader in August. He saved a particularly coveted invitation to a state dinner for Queen Elizabeth II for Clarke Reed, the head of the Mississippi Republican Party and a prized catch. One county party chairman Baker invited from New York left a ten-minute meeting with Ford with a promise to look into his sewer district funding issues.

But Baker rejected those who asked for jobs in exchange for their votes and set aside a special folder where he saved seventeen of the crassest, most inappropriate requests in case he ever needed to prove that he did not make illicit trades for votes, the start of a career-long habit of filing away documents showing unethical proposals he had rebuffed. When one aide suggested bringing all of the uncommitted delegates for a supper and boat ride with the president, Baker refused—not because it would be trading on the presidency but because it could backfire. "To bring them up here in this fashion would make it almost impossible for them to vote for the president for fear of having been 'bought,'" he wrote. It was a murky distinction Baker was drawing; somehow a state dinner was okay but a boat ride was not.

Beyond the direct approach, Baker recruited allies who could work on the targeted delegates. He also made sure the campaign stayed in touch with the delegates it already had. "The worst thing that can happen to a politician is not to have someone to talk to," he wrote to campaign colleagues. "The next worst thing is not to know what is going on."

But he came to hate the process. It was unseemly and grubby. He may not have been buying votes, but he found plenty of would-be sellers. "You'd have to go to pols of the lowest rank and beg," he said later. "I had a guy ask me for $5,000 for his vote. I'd take people into the Oval

Office to meet the president and they'd lecture him on what he was doing wrong. It was so demeaning." So why, he was asked later, did he take the job then? Baker's answer was simple: "Because the president asked me." It was also not lost on him, newcomer to Washington that he was, that his new assignment came with voluminous time spent in the company of the president. In a city where access to power was a form of power all by itself, Baker suddenly had it.

Baker soon assembled a team of capable lieutenants, including a twenty-seven-year-old Republican operative named Paul Manafort, who managed a clutch of states and would later help run the convention floor. Baker and his team kept methodical lists and it quickly became apparent that theirs was a better, more reliable tally than that kept by the Reagan camp. "Jim was in charge of every detail and knew the precise state of play at any given moment," Cheney remembered. Baker earned credibility with national political reporters when it turned out that his counts were accurate and those released by John Sears, Reagan's campaign manager, were inflated or even fictional. That was another lesson that Baker would internalize for later in his career: Never lie to journalists.

In a contest as close as this, details mattered. So did perception. A little less than a month before the convention, on July 19, Sears claimed that Reagan had secured 1,140 delegates, or ten more than needed for a first-ballot victory, and added that "there is a great degree of softness in Mr. Ford's strength." Baker knew the latter was true; Reagan's supporters were more fervent and committed. But he also knew that Sears's numbers were wrong.

On Baker's schedule for that week, an aide had written, "A substantial portion of Baker's time this week should be spent with the press." And so it was. Four days after Sears's declaration, Baker countered by telling reporters that Ford had picked up fifteen delegates from Hawaii, giving him a total of 1,135—five more than required for victory.

Even with a lead now established, Baker dwelled on all sorts of nightmare scenarios that could snatch away the nomination from the president. He ordered up memos on credential challenges, platform amendment fights, and questions such as whether winning the nomination required an absolute majority or only a majority of those voting. He worried about the order of states announcing their votes in the roll call. If it were alphabetical, as was customary, Reagan's strongest states would be stacked in the beginning and an early lead could cause a stampede to give him the nomination. Imagining another dangerous possibility, Baker asked an aide to examine whether Ford delegates who were secretly for Reagan could abstain or be absent on the first vote so as to force a second vote, when they would be free from their obligation to support the president and could switch to the challenger. "In my judgment," said the memo sent in response, "it could work and deny the nomination to the President."

THE WEATHER WAS glorious as Baker and the rest of the Ford team arrived at Kemper Arena in Kansas City for the start of the convention on August 16. Thanks to Baker, Ford seemed to have the edge. "'Miracle Man' Given Credit for Ford Drive," read the headline of a profile in *The New York Times*, referring to the cheeky call sign the convention team had given Baker for their network of walkie-talkies. But Baker had not yet earned the title. He was anxious to win on the first ballot for fear that Ford would lose if it went beyond that.

"We had the incumbency, which is a plus, a strength, but Reagan in many ways had the heart and soul of the delegates," remembered Stuart Spencer, the Ford strategist who had become a close ally of Baker's on the campaign. "He was their guy." Baker and Spencer were both well aware that many candidates over the years had arrived at conventions as frontrunners only to eventually lose the nomination. But no sitting president had been denied a nomination he actually sought since Chester Arthur in 1884, and Ford was determined not to share his fate.

Desperately seeking the key to the final few delegates he needed, Reagan gambled on a bold gesture before the convention by preemptively naming a running mate, Senator Richard Schweiker of Pennsylvania, even though he had not actually secured the nomination. The hope was to lure away Drew Lewis, the Ford campaign chief in Pennsylvania and a close friend of Schweiker's, with the idea that Lewis in turn would bring with him delegates from his crucial home state. Reagan also hoped to force Ford into naming his own running mate early on the theory that he would pick someone who would be unacceptable to many delegates. Ford had alienated many conservatives when he made the liberal Republican Nelson Rockefeller his vice president in 1974, a mistake he implicitly acknowledged by dumping him from the ticket in 1976 without naming a replacement.

But Reagan's move backfired. Schweiker was also considered a liberal—his rating from the American Conservative Union for 1975 was just 9 percent, the same as that of Senator Walter F. Mondale of Minnesota, a close ally of organized labor. Rather than uniting the wings of the party, Reagan's move turned off conservatives who thought their candidate had just sold them out. Most critically, it helped turn around the crucial Mississippi delegation, previously a Reagan redoubt. Until then, Baker's courtship of Clarke Reed, the Mississippi party chief, had yielded no success, despite the invitation to the state dinner. The fast-talking, silver-haired owner of a Mississippi River barge company, Reed "looked the part" of a Southern gentleman "but didn't act the part," as a Reagan aide put it. Reed had equivocated without actually committing to Ford. Now the situation turned around and Reed's thirty delegates were once more up for grabs. "I was really for Reagan, but I wasn't after that," Reed said of the ill-timed Schweiker choice. "How could you trust him?"

Reagan arrived at the convention still hoping to force Ford to name a running mate and his allies proposed a rule change on the floor requiring candidates to identify their pick for vice president. But Ford's team beat back the effort with a vote of 1,180 to 1,069, proving his strength and all but locking up the nomination. "I think we got it, I think we got it," Baker told his son John, who along with his brothers had come to Kansas City with their father. Baker was "very ecstatic," remembered Doug Baker.

Before Ford could claim his prize, though, the Reagan camp made one more effort to disrupt the proceedings by proposing a "morality in foreign policy" plank in the party platform condemning agreements with the Soviet Union, a direct jab at Henry Kissinger. Angry and hurt, Kissinger insisted that Ford fight it and threatened to resign if he did not. Nelson Rockefeller and Brent Scowcroft, the president's national security adviser, backed him up.

But Baker and Cheney advised Ford to let the measure pass, deeming it a waste of energy to fight a statement that had no binding effect. Noticing a lot of empty seats in the convention hall, Baker mentioned to Ford that Reagan supporters were more likely to be the ones who had stayed to vote, meaning the president could suffer an embarrassing loss if he forced the issue. Risking Kissinger's wrath, Ford agreed with Baker and opted not to contest the plank. Afterward, Baker said the Reagan camp's mistake was writing the policy plank in a way that Ford could swallow, however grudgingly. "I could see a two-word plank—'Fire Kissinger'— and we would have had to fight it," Baker said. "And if we had been beaten, we could have lost the whole thing."

Momentum had finally turned to Ford for good. With Clarke Reed's Mississippi delegation switching sides, Baker felt confident. "Everybody thinks this was the swing," Baker recalled.

The roll call of the states was read and one after another the delegates reported almost exactly as Baker had forecast. Ford won on the first ballot with 1,187 votes to 1,070 for Reagan, in what would end up being the last seriously contested nominating convention. The Miracle Man had delivered.

As he savored the victory, Ford now faced the task of bringing the ruptured party back together. The immediate question was whether to offer the vice presidency to Reagan in a gesture of conciliation. Ford had grown personally embittered toward Reagan over the course of their contest, but he understood the strength that Reagan might add to the ticket. Ford was taken off the hook with word that Reagan did not want to be asked. So the president settled instead on Senator Bob Dole, a World War II hero from Kansas and former Republican Party chairman.

As he finished his acceptance speech in the convention hall, Ford reached out to his defeated rival and invited Reagan to the stage to speak as well. Reagan, in classic form, delivered a semi-spontaneous and enormously eloquent oration that thrilled the crowd. "The guy that comes in second is really the darling of the convention," remembered Spencer. As William F. Buckley Jr., the éminence grise of the emerging conservative movement, put it, "Reagan was the dominating presence of the 1976 campaign, even though Ford was the formal victor."

But for now, the nomination was won, the ticket was set, and Baker's job was done. Or so he thought.

LEAVING THE CONVENTION, the president asked Baker to accompany him and the rest of his senior team to his vacation retreat in Vail, Colorado, where they would begin plotting out the general election campaign. But first there was an awkward piece of business: Rogers Morton, the campaign chairman and Baker's patron, had to be replaced.

Morton was ailing with prostate cancer. He had also angered other Ford advisers with a particularly ill-timed article in *The Washington Post* during the endless primary battle with Reagan. Photographed with a row of liquor bottles behind him, Morton had popped off to reporters. Asked if he planned any strategy change after losing so many primaries to Reagan, Morton had said, "I'm not going to rearrange the furniture on the deck of the *Titanic.*"

Now, Ford's White House team wanted him out. Dick Cheney and Stuart Spencer made the case for Baker to replace his mentor. "I thought he'd be good on *Meet the Press,*" Spencer said later. Ford agreed. "Jim Baker had demonstrated an outstanding organizational capability as our chief delegate hunter," he wrote in his memoir.

Baker was reluctant. Morton had been a friend who had brought him to Washington in the first place and the last thing he wanted to do was to stab him in the back. Morton's wife, Anne, even begged Baker not to take the job. Uncomfortable, Baker told her that if it was not him, it would be someone else, but that did not make it any easier. Eventually, he agreed to the assignment on the condition that Morton be allowed to keep the title of chairman emeritus. "That was one of the toughest things that I ever had to deal with," he said later.

Suddenly, Baker was in charge of the president's campaign. He was sent out for a news conference to announce his own appointment and preview the fall election. "I remember being scared to death," he recalled. Events were moving so fast that Jamie Baker only learned that his father had become part of the Ford inner circle when he saw a newspaper with a picture of a familiar face next to the president at Vail.

But the Miracle Man would have to produce another one to keep Ford in the White House. Having pivoted to the right to fend off Ronald Reagan, Ford needed to repair his image with the broader cross section of American voters turned off by his pardon of Richard Nixon and the economic troubles of his tenure. Shortly after the Democratic National Convention, Ford and Bob Dole trailed the newly nominated ticket of former governor Jimmy Carter of Georgia and the Minnesota senator Walter Mondale by 33 percentage points in a Gallup poll. Ford trimmed the deficit to 13 points by the end of the Republican convention, but there was a long hill still to climb.

This being the first presidential election after the campaign abuses revealed during the Watergate scandal, it was subject to new federal rules enacted to reform the system. Each of the two campaigns could spend $21.8 million. As in the primary, Baker again focused on how to maximize the advantages of incumbency so he did not need to use up as much of his budget building an infrastructure as the challenger did, leaving him able to spend half of Ford's budget on advertising. "The candidate who makes the wisest use of dollars is going to win the election," Baker told reporters in Vail.

Baker's ascension drew largely positive reviews. "Blessed with good looks, wealth and personable manners, Baker, 46, seems almost a political natural," *Newsweek* gushed. The magazine noted that some Republicans "would have preferred a bigger and better-known name at the head of the Ford campaign organization," but quoted Cheney in his defense, saying, "Jim is one of those people who can take a dead organization and turn it around."

ONCE BAKER TOOK OVER, the core group of advisers met at the White House every day at 7 a.m. in Cheney's office. Joining them were Stuart Spencer; Robert Teeter, their pollster; and Doug Bailey or John Deardourff, the two main ad makers. The campaign strategy that Baker developed along with Cheney, Spencer, and the others was to cast the president not as a transformational figure but as a reliable, down-to-earth leader after a tumultuous few years for the country—not unlike Baker himself. The advisers wrote down the adjectives they wanted to stress during the race to November: compassionate, experienced, strong, honest, man of action, decisive.

But the challenge they faced in refashioning Ford's image was enormous. A report by Teeter included ten pages of comments by voters taken from across the country. Only three out of hundreds were positive.

"He's honest, but clumsy."
"He's an honest man, but he doesn't have the capability to be president."
"He's honest compared to Nixon, but I don't think he's favorable to women or equality and I don't think he's for labor."

"And these, remember, were the *positive* comments," said Malcolm MacDougall, who worked for Bailey and Deardourff on the ads. In the negative category, Ford was called a "boob," "inept," "a big Zero," "befuddled," "in over his head," "dopey," or, as one man in his thirties put it, "an oatmeal man."

Worse yet, personal exposure to Ford did not seem to help. Usually, when candidates traveled to a city or town, their approval ratings went up. Ford's went down. "We actually quantified the fact that when he went someplace, he had a negative impact on perceptions of himself," said Mary Lukens, one of the pollsters who worked with Teeter. Out of this finding came a decision to keep Ford at the White House as much as possible, both to avoid undercutting his own campaign and to underscore the view of him as president. This Rose Garden strategy, as it was called, grated on Ford. It was "a little bit insulting to the president," Lukens said, "but hey, you work with what you've got." Spencer was blunter in explaining to Ford why they needed to do it this way. "You're a lousy fucking candidate," he told the president. "You've got to stay here."

Baker worshipped preparation, but no amount of preparation could prevent every potential surprise, especially in politics. Baker saw that firsthand that fall after *Rolling Stone* reported that Agriculture Secretary Earl Butz had made shockingly offensive remarks about black Americans. "I'll tell you what coloreds want," Butz had said. "It's three things: first, a tight pussy; second, loose shoes; and third, a warm place to shit. That's all!"

Butz, a holdover from the Nixon administration who grew up in Indiana guiding horse-drawn plows, had made the comments on an airplane leaving the Republican convention in Kansas City that summer to a small group that included John Dean, the former White House counsel who had turned on Richard Nixon during Watergate. Dean, who had just completed a prison term for his role in Watergate, had been assigned by *Rolling Stone* to write a dispatch from the convention and in it he quoted the remarks without identifying the unnamed cabinet officer who made them. It was quickly clear that Butz was the offending party. Butz apologized but Ford was under pressure to fire him. Baker, Spencer, and Cheney initially leaned toward keeping Butz and riding out the storm, but as the blowback grew worse they concluded that he would have to go. Betty Ford in particular was appalled and ultimately her husband accepted Butz's resignation. "Cheney and I slept in his office that night trying to get the whole thing put together," Spencer said.

While getting their own house in order, Baker and his team prepared to face a Democratic challenger who had already upended the political system. Carter, an obscure peanut farmer and one-term governor of Georgia who would turn fifty-two by Election Day, had come out of nowhere to capture the Democratic nomination by outpacing a field of far better-known national figures. With a wide, toothy grin, a down-home country demeanor, a post-Watergate vow to "never lie to you," and exactly 1 percent in the polls when he kicked off his campaign, Carter planted himself in Iowa for months. The strategy worked and he leveraged a surprise win in the caucuses into enough momentum to roll through the subsequent Democratic primaries.

Ford did not know much about Carter and viewed him warily. While impressed by the challenger's quick mind and ability to articulate, Ford saw Carter "as cold and arrogant, even egotistical, and I was convinced he played fast and loose with the facts." But Carter had the advantage of running as the anti-Nixon. While Ford had restored a sense of decency to the White House, he was still a Republican who had pardoned his tarnished predecessor. The party's post-Watergate brand was so bad that the president's campaign "avoided the word 'Republican' like a disease," as Malcolm MacDougall, the ad man, put it.

Carter was running as the outsider who would clean up Washington.

Just as important, he was a Southerner who could rally a region that had been trending Republican in recent years. "With a Southerner leading the ticket, southern states cannot be counted on to abandon their traditional party," a Ford campaign memo sent to Cheney concluded. "This bloc of electoral votes combined with the northern industrial states, which tend to favor any Democrat, will leave very little left for the Republican nominee." On top of that, Carter was hammering away at Ford over the troubled economy, citing a "misery index" that combined the inflation and unemployment rates to illustrate how much everyday Americans were being left behind. At its peak under Ford, the index reached nearly 20 percent.

Facing a double-digit deficit in the polls, Baker and his team decided to gamble as no president had ever done before. They agreed to meet Carter for three televised debates, the first held in a presidential election since the famed 1960 showdowns between John Kennedy and Richard Nixon and the first ever involving an incumbent. Traditionally, sitting presidents had been reluctant to share a stage for fear of making a costly mistake in front of millions of people and elevating a challenger's stature. But this particular incumbent was heading into Labor Day weekend trailing by 15 percentage points, so it was a risk that seemed worth taking.

All three debates would be gentlemanly encounters, especially by the toxic standards of decades to come. The two candidates addressed each other with respect, disagreed politely, and largely avoided anything that might be considered a low blow. The first of the debates, in Philadelphia on September 23, was notable mainly for an odd snafu when the sound suddenly cut out in the middle of the discussion. It took twenty-seven long minutes to restore while Ford and Carter simply stood unmoving at their podiums, "almost like robots," as Carter later put it, waiting for the debate to resume.

Still, the next day, Baker and the other advisers found themselves satisfied that Ford had won. In a meeting, they reviewed the overnight poll numbers, which showed that 36 percent of Americans thought the president did better compared with 32 percent who chose the challenger. Gallup confirmed a debate bounce; Ford had pared Carter's lead to 8 percentage points.

The key moment of all three debates came in the second face-off, held on October 6 at the Palace of Fine Arts Theatre in San Francisco. Max Frankel of *The New York Times* asked Ford whether the Helsinki human rights accord signed by his administration was effectively "an agreement that the Russians have dominance in Eastern Europe."

Ford bridled at the assertion. "There is no Soviet domination of Eastern Europe and there never will be under a Ford administration," he said.

Frankel, stunned, tried to give Ford a chance to take it back or at least explain it. "Did I understand you to say, sir, that the Russians are not using Eastern Europe as their own sphere of influence and occupying most of the countries there and making sure with their troops that it's a Communist zone?" he asked.

"I don't believe, Mr. Frankel, that the Yugoslavians consider themselves dominated by the Soviet Union," Ford replied. "I don't believe that the Romanians consider themselves dominated by the Soviet Union. I don't believe that the Poles consider themselves dominated by the Soviet Union. Each of those countries is independent, autonomous. It has its own territorial integrity. And the United States does not concede that those countries are under the domination of the Soviet Union."

In the holding room, Brent Scowcroft, the national security adviser, felt queasy as his "heart sank into my shoes." He told Stuart Spencer they had a problem. The Soviet Union had more than 200,000 troops in Poland; it was simply not credible to argue that Moscow did not dominate its neighbor. "Cheney and I were spastic," Spencer recalled. After the debate, they headed back to the house where Ford was staying and found Henry Kissinger already there, praising the president for the "wonderful job" he had done. "Dick and I say, 'Goddamn, what are you talking about, Henry?'" Ford chose to believe Kissinger.

But at the hotel where Baker and Scowcroft were left to handle the media storm, it was instantly clear how bad the situation really was. The first question thrown at them was how many Soviet army divisions were stationed in Poland. Baker and Scowcroft "perspired heavily" as they sought to deflect the growing criticism. If nothing else, it was, as Scowcroft said later, "a bonding experience." On the Carter plane back to Atlanta, Stuart Eizenstat, an aide to the Democratic challenger, recalled, "there was an air of exhilaration."

Ford refused to believe that he had made a mistake and the initial polls backed him up, showing that more viewers thought he had won the debate. But as the networks and newspapers focused on the Poland gaffe, public opinion quickly shifted. "The data had totally flipped," Mary Lukens said. Republican allies called in a panic. On Air Force One, Cheney and Spencer badgered Ford to take back his comment, angering the president. "We came within two inches of getting canned," Spencer said.

Ultimately it would take several clarifications by Ford to put the issue to rest, but the damage had been done. The president looked out of touch and had turned off at least some of the Polish Americans and other immi-grants who were key constituencies in battleground states. For the next five or six days, he lost momentum instead of closing in the polls.

THE ISSUE THAT barely came up at the debates at all was probably just as decisive, if not more so. Ford's pardon of Nixon was mentioned only in passing and Carter made no effort to hang it around the president's neck. Ford was asked just one question about Watergate in all three debates. "We had anticipated more," Baker said. "It was a negative. He pardoned a guy who was a criminal."

Paradoxically, because Carter did not raise Watergate in the most watched moments of the campaign, that made it harder for Ford to address the issue and put it to rest. He and his team did not want to raise it them-selves. "How did we handle it?" asked Spencer. "We ignored it." With good reason, they thought. "To take the pardon issue on is to say, 'Okay, let's everybody talk about the pardon,'" said Doug Bailey. "Well, you're not going to win that discussion. You're just not going to win that debate." But the campaign's polls showed that 7 percent of *Republicans* would not vote for Ford because of the pardon, never mind independents or Demo-crats. It was the "eight-hundred-pound gorilla in the room, always hang-ing over everything," as Baker put it.

Still, the debates helped lift Ford as did a series of ads portraying the president as a likable Everyman who was restoring the country's pride. "We have come from a point where many people in this country were just writing us off," Baker said in late October on *Issues and Answers*, the Sunday talk show on ABC. "We had no chance. It was over and done with back there in late August. We have come from twenty-three points back to a situation now where it is a real horse race and up for grabs."

Even so, Ford was having trouble rallying conservatives to his side and grew increasingly aggravated that Ronald Reagan was not helping out. Reagan made only a perfunctory effort on Ford's behalf and declined to campaign for the president in areas where he was popular. Some of Ford's advisers were convinced that more active campaigning by Reagan might have made the difference in Texas and Mississippi, which by themselves would have been enough to keep Ford in the White House. Spencer, who had worked for Reagan before the 1976 campaign, later faulted himself for not figuring out a way to pressure his old boss into doing more. Ford was bitter afterward. "If he had traveled down to some of the southern states where he had tremendous popularity, I think we would have won,"

Ford said. "It's not his nature to help someone else. He believed in winning on his own."

Then again, Ford was not helping himself as much as he could. Under Baker's direction, the campaign was businesslike but hardly inspirational. He was selling integrity and Midwestern decency without articulating a grander vision that would stir voters. "Not one of the president's speeches had offered a program for the future," concluded Malcolm MacDougall, the ad man. "Not one of our two hundred ads and commercials had so much as hinted at what he might do for America in the next four years."

With time running out, Baker and the Ford team debated a more provocative approach. Doug Bailey made a nearly five-minute commercial called the "Cherry Bomb" ad featuring the ditty that had become the theme song of the campaign—*I'm feeling good about America, I'm feeling good about me*—along with street interviews of voters talking about how Ford had restored their faith in the country. The images shifted to Ford giving a speech when a cherry bomb suddenly went off with a bang; the president flinched but kept going. The ad then showed him riding in a car through Dallas, standing up through a sunroof as bystanders cheered. The unseen narrator made reference to John Kennedy's assassination in the same city thirteen years earlier.

> Neither the cherry bombs of a misguided prankster nor all the memories of recent years can keep the people and their president apart. When a limousine can parade openly through the streets of Dallas, there's a change that's come over America. After a decade of tension, the people and their president are back together again.

Bailey thought it was worth airing. "If you know or are 90 percent certain that you're going to lose and you have a way that is perfectly legitimate to raise the issues—raise the bar—raise the issues in such a dramatic way that it scares people into, 'Wait a minute, what am I about to do with my vote,' do you run such a commercial or don't you?" Bailey recalled.

But when he showed it to the campaign team, Baker objected vigorously. "Just all hell broke loose—'oh, we can't do that, we can't do that,'" Bailey said. Baker called the ad "nutty, absolutely screwy. You can't make a reference to Dallas that way without losing the state of Texas." Bailey thought they were going to lose Texas anyway, but Baker won the argument. The ad never aired.

Still, as Ford scratched for any advantage in those final days, Baker was not above using tough tactics. In Plains, the tiny dust mote of a town Carter hailed from, a ready-made racial controversy provided a small opportunity. An eccentric African American minister, Rev. Clennon King of the nondenominational Divine Mission Church in Albany, Georgia, about thirty miles away, chose the dwindling days of October to try to desegregate the Plains First Baptist Church, the all-white parish where Carter had worshipped for years. King was a complicated character with political aspirations. He had run for president in 1960 on the Afro-American Party ticket, tried to win asylum from Jamaica two years later citing persecution in the United States, was later arrested and spent four years in prison for failing to provide child support, and threatened to run against Carter for governor in 1970 as a Republican.

When Reverend King showed up at the Plains church on Sunday, October 31, just two days before the election, he was turned away and the services were canceled. Carter had previously pushed the church leadership to end its discriminatory policy but now it was being used against him. As Ford's campaign head, Baker signed telegrams to four hundred black ministers around the country assailing Carter. "If the former Georgia Governor and life-long member of the Plains Baptist Church cannot influence the decisions and opinions of his own church, can we expect him to influence the issues and opinions of the United States Congress?"

Carter was incensed and his campaign publicized the telegrams, turning the attack against Ford by energizing black voters. Baker later denied encouraging King to disrupt the church but said it was a mistake to send the telegrams. Carter, convinced the Republicans were behind the whole episode, never forgot it. Years later, after he and Baker had worked together on a number of issues, Carter still brought it up in an interview. "I resented one thing he did," he recalled. "That was the only thing I ever experienced with Baker that was not pleasant."

THE ELECTION ARRIVED on a cool, dry day in Washington as the Ford team gathered to monitor the results. Baker, Cheney, and the others presented Ford with early projections in the Oval Office at 5 p.m., but the election was too close to call. Ford studied the numbers and did not say much. As the aides turned to leave, the president pulled out a cigar and gave it to Baker.

"I quit smoking," Baker announced.

"Well, take it anyway," Ford said.

As the night progressed, Ford looked strong in Michigan, his home state, as well as New Jersey and Connecticut, while Ohio, Pennsylvania, and Illinois were too close to call. Texas and New York were on the edge as well. If Ford lost those two big states, aides asked themselves, was there still a path to victory? Deep into the night, Ford and his team waited. Finally, the president went to bed without knowing for sure whether he would wake up to a full term of his own. Around 3 a.m., it became clear to his advisers gathered at a Washington hotel for the election night party that he would fall achingly short. Baker, who had stopped smoking after Mary Stuart died, lit up the cigar.

By morning, it was over. Ford had staged a remarkable comeback. From 33 percentage points down, he had closed the gap to finish the election with 48 percent of the popular vote to 50 percent for Carter. In the Electoral College, it was even closer—if a little more than nine thousand voters in Ohio and Hawaii had gone the other way, it would have flipped those two states and kept the presidency in Ford's hands.

There were enough irregularities that Ford briefly contemplated seeking recounts in close states. But since he had lost the popular vote nationally, "it would be very hard for me to govern if I won the presidency in the Electoral College through a recount," Ford told his team.

Baker, for one, agreed. "He was right, of course," Baker said. Ford conceded.

Ford's chances of winning the election were probably doomed the day he pardoned Richard Nixon. "If he hadn't pardoned Nixon, we would have won," Baker said. "It was the right thing to do for the country, but we would have won. We saw it in our polling every day."

Two days after the election, Baker wrote Ford a note. "The best man did not win this race, and the American people are the losers for it," he said. Ford wrote a gracious letter back and then hand-scrawled a P.S. at the bottom: "You were superb. Thanks from all the Fords."

At the time, however, some Republicans pointed a finger at Baker after they discovered that the campaign still had nearly $1 million in the bank after the election. Given how close the outcome had been, it seemed like political malpractice not to have spent every dollar. Baker later said the money had been allocated to liaison groups and could not be transferred to, say, television commercials. He attributed his caution on this front to the hangover from Watergate. "I was determined that the investigations that take place after you win or lose a presidential election were not going to find that we overspent the limits," he said. "In those days, there were strict limits."

Not everyone found Baker's reasoning persuasive. "When I found out there was still a million left over, I crawled over his frame," Spencer said.

"He pointed out the penalty and I said, 'You think they're going to put the president in jail if he overspends his damn money? Hell no.' I would have pushed the envelope. He wasn't going to push the envelope."

Even so, Baker came out of the campaign a winner. He had taken a candidate far behind in the polls and brought him within a hair of victory. He had assembled top-flight operatives and forged them into a team that would come to dominate Republican Party politics for years to come. And he had impressed many in the party as a steady, pragmatic hand. "He did one superb job," Ford said afterward. "Jim Baker is a talented, able guy and I would trust him anywhere, under any circumstances."

But Baker had no idea what he would do next. After the election, Ford tried to install him as chairman of the Republican National Committee, only to be blocked by Reagan. Baker had come to Washington, risen like a meteor, and now here he was, barely a year later, just forty-six years old with a desk waiting for him back at his Houston law firm and no desire to take it.

CHAPTER 6

Out of the Back Room

R amrod straight, his hair neatly in place, his suit tailored to his slim
  figure, Baker stood up to address a crowd of business leaders gathered at the Houston Chamber of Commerce.

He had been instructed to keep his introduction brief, he told the audience. And that reminded him of a story. A little girl named Sarah was at
church one Sunday, bored by a long-winded sermon. Her attention drifting, she noticed American flags hanging on the wall with gold plaques
underneath each of them.

"Grandma, what are those flags there for?" Baker quoted her asking.

"Why, Sarah, those flags commemorate those who died in service."

"Oh, really? The 9 o'clock service or the 11 o'clock service?"

As the audience laughed, Baker said, "I hope I'm not going to lose you
in my service this afternoon."

Wry and irreverent if old-school in his humor, Baker in 1978 had
decided to put himself on public display for the first time. A backstage
operative no more, he would try his hand as a politician himself, running
for attorney general of Texas. He was not the most natural candidate in
the world. He was earnest in a corporate sort of way, obviously prepared
on the issues and a steady, hardworking, reassuring presence. But he was
not a born glad-hander like his friend George Bush. He did not rouse an
audience to passion. He talked a little too fast and could be too lawyerly.
He was impressive, not inspiring.

The idea of running for office had appealed to Baker since before
Mary Stuart's death, when he briefly toyed with seeking Bush's seat in
the House. But now, eight years later, the Miracle Man had been "bitten by the bug," as he put it, and ready to try. If Bush could do it, why

couldn't he? "He probably saw it as the next logical step," Doug Baker said.

Susan, however, was anything but enthusiastic. She had hardly seen Baker the entire time they were in Washington and as soon as the Ford campaign was over, she became pregnant with what they called their "reacquainted baby" or "bonus baby." On September 6, 1977, barely a month before turning thirty-nine, Susan gave birth to Mary-Bonner Baker, named for her two grandmothers. Bush was her godfather. Susan had been so worried about how to break the news of the baby to the rest of the troubled family that she hid the truth until she was already seven months pregnant. Now with a combined eight children, her husband was hitting the road again. Asked years later about her feelings about his decision to run, she told an interviewer, "They're not printable." Not that she would try to make him feel guilty. She knew that was a lost cause. "One smart thing about Jim Baker is that he doesn't waste a lot of time on guilt," she observed. "In fact, he doesn't waste any time on it."

Baker's political emergence came at a time of transition for both America in general and Texas in particular. In the White House, Jimmy Carter vowed to turn the page on the past, pardoning Vietnam draft dodgers and promising a new era of honest government. But the country remained troubled. The nation's cities were in deep decline. A twenty-five-hour blackout in New York City in the summer of 1977 touched off looting and resulted in thousands of arrests. Ronald Reagan, shaking off his defeat at the hands of Gerald Ford (and Baker), was finding newfound support as the leader of an emboldened conservative wing of the Republican Party. A television evangelist in Virginia named Jerry Falwell was on his way toward founding a new group called the Moral Majority to promote conservative religious values in American politics.

The Texas of that era was still strongly Democratic, though by tradition more than ideology. No Republican had been elected either governor or attorney general since Reconstruction. Just three of thirty-one state senators and nineteen of 150 members of the Texas House of Representatives were Republicans. But as in much of the South, the historic Democratic grip on courthouses and the statehouse in Texas was beginning to slip. As a fellow Southerner, Carter had won Texas in 1976, but he would be the last Democrat to do so for decades to come. Always conservative, Texans were increasingly disenchanted with the liberalism of national Democrats. That was what Baker, a relatively recent Republican convert himself, was counting on.

Baker was not the only Republican in his circle trying his hand at elective politics for the first time that year. Bush's eldest son, George W. Bush, newly married but struggling with alcohol and the oil business, was running for Congress in a House district in West Texas, while Dick Cheney was seeking the only House seat in Wyoming. (Bush would lose; Cheney would win.)

When Baker sat down to talk with George H. W. Bush about his political ambitions at Bush's house in Houston, his friend urged him to skip the attorney general's race and aim higher with a run for governor of Texas. Baker was skeptical. It seemed a reach for a novice who, despite his experience running Ford's campaign, still had relatively little stature outside the Beltway and no personal experience on the campaign trail. Baker was a cold-eyed, calculating man and as he examined the race, he concluded he could not win.

The incumbent governor, Dolph Briscoe, an understated rancher with a reformer's reputation, was finishing his sixth year in office and seemed in a strong position to win another term. Baker assumed the only way he could win a statewide race would be to run against a more liberal Democrat than Briscoe. Looking down the potential ballot, Baker thought he found such an opportunity with the attorney general's office. Price Daniel Jr., the former speaker of the Texas House and a well-known liberal, was angling for the Democratic nomination. If Baker could run against Daniel, he figured he would have a chance. And it could be a stepping-stone for a bigger race down the road. "Jim Baker's election as Attorney General is an investment in the future," his campaign wrote in a pitch letter to donors that was unusual in its candor about the candidate's ambitions beyond the job he was actually seeking. "If you want to see Jim Baker as Governor, help elect him Attorney General first."

Baker figured his biggest challenge was going to be a man who was not even in the race: Ronald Reagan. Texas had gone strongly for Reagan against Ford in the 1976 primary and few were more associated with the former president than Baker, who now needed to reach out to the right. He called Charlie Black, a young Republican operative who had worked for him on the Ford campaign but was well connected to the conservative wing of the party. He explained his plan—first he would run for attorney general and then, if he won, he would set his sights on the governor's mansion. "He never said, 'and then I'll run for president,' but I think that was kind of what he had in mind," Black recalled.

One thing at a time. "Down here, Reagan routed us, so I've got to make friends with all of the conservatives," Baker told Black. "Is there a good Reagan guy, a good hand, who could be my campaign manager?"

A few days later, Black called back to recommend a political operative named Frank Donatelli.

Donatelli had recently served as head of an advocacy group called Young Americans for Freedom, then one of the bulwarks of the American right, and he would be an important ambassador to conservatives if Baker could convince him to help. When Baker got in touch, Donatelli was "a little suspicious that he was on the other side" of the Republican divide, but he flew to Texas to meet the candidate and ended up impressed. "It's clear he did not have much of a relationship or understanding of what was then the organized conservative movement," Donatelli recalled years later. But "he was certainly a conservative on all of the major issues." Besides, Donatelli was looking for a chance to run a statewide campaign and this seemed like a credible opportunity that would allow him to move up the pecking order in the cutthroat world of political strategists.

He had his work cut out for him with the rookie candidate. "My first impression was very positive as far as his knowledge, his understanding of politics," Donatelli said. "It wasn't very good, quite honestly, as a politician. He was a backroom guy." On his first trip to Texas to meet with Baker, Donatelli accompanied him to a speech. "While it was an okay speech on the facts, you could in no way describe it as inspirational," Donatelli said. The word that came to mind instead? "Ho-hum."

Donatelli set to work teaching Baker how to be a candidate. It did not come naturally. "Keep eye contact at end of sentences!" Baker reminded himself in notes scratched in the margins of one speech. On the left side of his announcement address, he wrote in big block letters, "Look at Camera!"

Always clad in the same uniform—boots, tan pants, and a forest green shirt that his staff eventually threatened to burn—Baker drove around the state in the family's white Chevy Suburban, often accompanied by Susan and sometimes with Mary-Bonner in a portable crib. Baker would joke that he was the "candidate who brings his own baby to kiss." The older kids were told to behave whenever in public. "I can remember their shooting the family commercials and we were all like, 'Okay, no fighting on camera,'" Doug Baker said years later.

No one thought Baker had much of a chance. Bob Bullock, the state comptroller and an emerging Democratic power broker in Texas politics, brushed him off in a television interview in February 1978, faulting the GOP for not concentrating all its effort behind Baker. "If the Republicans had not fielded a group of Republican candidates and concentrated on the office of attorney general, Mr. Baker would've had an excellent chance,"

Bullock said, already speaking of him in the past tense. "He could've probably won it." Indeed, with all the other contests on the ballot, it was hard
for Baker to generate attention. "We were competing with those other
races just trying to get a little ink now and then," said Pete Roussel, a
Ford administration veteran who signed on to serve as the campaign's
communications director. Still, Baker had a reasonable plan to beat Price
Daniel. What he did not count on was that Price Daniel would not be
the only Democrat to enter the race. When Mark White, the Texas secretary of state and an avuncular backslapper with a more moderate reputation, decided to run as well, the contest was no longer what Baker had
anticipated.

Daniel, a slender thirty-six-year-old lawyer with surpassing ambition
and an aloof manner, hailed from Texas political royalty. His father, Price
Daniel Sr., had served three terms as governor and held just about every
other major political job in Texas as well, including speaker of the House,
attorney general, and senator. As 1978 rolled around, he was on the Texas
Supreme Court serving as an associate justice.

The younger Daniel had been elected House speaker after the so-
called Sharpstown scandal involving bribery and corruption rocked the
legislature and he pushed through a raft of reforms. But at a state convention to write a new Texas constitution, conservatives rebelled against him,
dooming the effort. Along the way, Daniel made plenty of enemies. "He's
arrogant, shallow, superficial, overwhelmingly ambitious and deceitful, at
least according to conservative establishment Democrats," Baker's campaign team said in a memo. *Texas Monthly* concluded that "Daniel may
well be the most widely disliked person in Texas politics."

Mark White, on the other hand, was a different kind of candidate,
folksy but tough as a bull, far harder to paint as an out-of-touch liberal.
Where Baker had graduated from the blue-chip University of Texas law
school, White had gone to second-tier Baylor University for bachelor's
and law degrees. White styled himself a man of the people. He had been
around Texas politics for years and considered Baker an entitled upstart. "I
didn't know who the hell he was," White recalled later.

Baker first met White in February at a joint appearance before the
Southeast Texas Press Club. Both were disappointed that Daniel, the one
they were each targeting, did not show, but went ahead and presented
their cases anyway. In reality, they were not that different, a conservative
Democrat and a moderate Republican. Both advocated stronger open-
records laws and more women and minorities on the attorney general's
staff. Both agreed that State Supreme Court judges should be appointed,

not elected, a big issue at that time. Given the similarities, Baker tried to carve out his own identity by boasting that he was not part of the ruling Democratic machine.

"There's not much question about my independence," he told the press club audience, noting his family heritage dating back to the storied Judge Baker.

"I'll bet he was a *Democratic* judge," White interjected.

In the Democratic primary, a low-turnout contest for a low-profile office, Daniel had the advantage of name recognition but White impressed voters as a fighter and on May 6 he won the nomination 52 percent to 48 percent. Suddenly, Baker's whole theory of the race was moot and he found himself in the same position that George Bush had been in during his 1970 campaign for Senate, when he thought he would be running against the liberal Ralph Yarborough, only to see the more moderate Lloyd Bentsen win the Democratic nomination.

The next day, Baker's issues coordinator, Jim Cicconi, sent him an eighteen-page memo, warning that, for all of his down-home affect, White was also a slash-and-burn candidate known as "Switchblade Mark." "By all rights, he *should* try to ignore us and run a low-key effort as long as possible," Cicconi told Baker. "However, I don't think he'll do this because I don't think it's in his makeup—he's always been a gut-fighter and gone for the jugular." Cicconi urged Baker to go after White first, arguing that his record as secretary of state "can be wrapped around his throat."

To gauge his chances, Baker, no spendthrift, choked hard and shelled out $20,000 for a baseline voter survey in May, hiring the Republican pollster Arthur J. Finkelstein from New York. The results were not encouraging. When respondents were asked about eleven public figures, Baker was the only one with both favorable and unfavorable numbers in the single digits—only 8.6 percent of the more than 1,000 Texans contacted had a positive impression of the candidate while 7.9 percent had a negative impression. "Jim Baker," Finkelstein concluded, "is unknown to the majority of voters at this time." When it came to a choice, White led 41 percent to just 12 percent for Baker. "The problem for Baker is obvious," Finkelstein said. "The voting population is just so overwhelmingly Democrat."

Baker was exasperated. *Twelve percent?* "I've been busting my ass for six months!" he complained to the pollster.

Against those odds, some close to Baker wondered why he was making the race in the first place. And was he really busting ass? "One had the feeling that he was running for attorney general just to let people know that he was a real politician or something," said Jonathan Bush, the brother of his friend George. "He didn't really have his heart in it."

George W. Bush, by contrast, really was "running his ass off" for Congress and recalled campaigning at a shopping center one day with Baker. As George W. related the story to his uncle Jonathan, "I plunged out of the car and I'm in there thrashing around shaking hands and looked back and Baker is just sitting in the car." Indeed, Baker seemed to be looking beyond the race to the next one to be waged by George W.'s father. "He was already saying, 'When I come back, we'll do this, that and the other,'" Jonathan remembered.

VOTERS COULD BE forgiven if they did not know who Baker was—even Baker was not entirely sure who Baker was at that point. As a first-time candidate, he was still formulating his positions on some of the key issues of the day. One of the trickier ones was abortion. Just five years after the Supreme Court's *Roe v. Wade* decision, the issue had not yet exploded into the dominant question it would become a few years later with Reagan's ascension to the White House. Baker had worked for George Bush and Gerald Ford, both of whom were trying to straddle the ideological divide when it came to abortion. Baker would try the same. An issues binder assembled by his staff said he could not disregard a Supreme Court ruling but would oppose allowing state funds to be used to pay for abortions except in cases of rape, incest, or threat to the health of the mother. If pressed, the issue book recommended he say, "Personally I oppose abortion. However my personal feelings are just that; *personal*. I won't impose them on someone else who happens to disagree."

On a questionnaire for the National Committee for a Human Life Amendment, Baker's aides outlined what they thought was their boss's position. Question one asked if he would support a constitutional amendment banning abortions. "No," Baker's aides wrote for the candidate. "I personally oppose abortion. However, I feel that this is a personal decision and should remain such as long as it is within the limits set by the U.S. Supreme Court in *Roe v. Wade*. In somewhat broader terms, I oppose government dictating by law what are essentially matters of conscience."

Question two asked about government funding. His staff answered that he opposed the use of taxpayer money to pay for abortions, with the usual rape, incest, and health exceptions.

Question three asked if he opposed the use of public hospitals for abortions. "No," the staff answered, saying that it would not reduce the number of abortions. "While I personally oppose abortion and the use of tax funds to pay for them, I feel we should not endanger the life or health of a mother simply because we disagree with her personal decision that she cannot bear a child."

The questionnaire was sent to Baker for his signature but he balked. "This doesn't square w/ what we've said before on this subj.," he told Frank Donatelli in a note. Donatelli ordered the staff to try again. Reflecting the candidate's instructions, they should say that Baker favored a constitutional amendment "to limit abortion on demand" with exceptions for "rape, incest, or danger to life (not health) of the mother" and did not advocate the use of public hospitals for abortions.

Baker tried to tack to the right of Mark White, supporting the death penalty and the state's right-to-work law. He opposed gun control and the Equal Rights Amendment. On other hot-button matters, he tried to hedge. On gay rights, at a time when Texas still criminalized "homosexual conduct," Baker's issue binder said, "I feel that consenting adults should not be subjected to criminal penalties for actions occurring in the privacy of the home. However, I do not feel that homosexuality should be recognized by the state as socially acceptable conduct." On immigration, he said, "I would be very concerned that any crackdown on illegal aliens by the Federal government not result in discrimination against Texas citizens of Mexican heritage. (There is no place for racism in Texas.)"

Baker did not want to run on any of these topics. He was no culture warrior. Social issues such as abortion made him uncomfortable. Instead, he opted to concentrate on crime and present himself as a law-and-order candidate. It was, he knew, disingenuous. Baker understood perfectly well that the state attorney general had very little to do with criminal justice; the position was more akin to the general counsel for the state, representing Texas in court in disputes over the legality of its laws and regulations. The attorney general prosecuted no one and the office's only real involvement in criminal justice was defending the state in appeals of capital cases. Of the office's 14,922 pending cases at the start of 1978, nearly two thirds of them were about defaulted student loans.

But Baker also understood that voters did not want to hear about banking regulations and the like. While crime in Texas was still low by national standards, it was on the rise. Over the previous fifteen years, the number of murders in Texas had more than doubled and there were five times as many reported rapes. Overall, violent crime had tripled. One poll showed that only 5 percent of Texans felt that the problem with crime was improving while 46 percent felt it was worsening and 53 percent felt they would be a victim of crime in the next year. Baker knew good politics when he saw it.

Soon after kicking off his campaign, Baker held a news conference to call for a system of "determinate sentences" for criminals, which would take away some of the flexibility of prosecutors and judges in deciding penalties. Even as he positioned himself as a hard-liner, Baker rejected the type of mandatory sentencing that California had adopted, calling that "much too rigid." But he said there needed to be more uniformity. "I believe the fundamental problem in our present system of criminal justice is the wide disparity in punishments which all too often makes a mockery of justice by being either too lenient or too severe."

Baker was so pleased with the event that the next day he told aides he wanted eight to ten "specific instances where innocent victims of crime have suffered at the hands of one who was a repeat offender and either paroled too soon or let off the first time with minor penalty." Aides came back with the case of Robert Winn, a forty-three-year-old who had just been convicted of his tenth felony and sentenced to life in prison. His previous convictions had resulted in sentences totaling 136 years plus three life terms and yet somehow he had gotten out on parole.

After Labor Day, Baker released a thirty-seven-page position paper detailing five proposals to combat crime, including stiffer sentences for repeat offenders such as Winn, more resources to fight drugs, and a reorganization of juvenile justice. In the campaign's closing weeks, he went on the air with a television commercial titled "Had Enough" that bet his campaign's remaining funds on his crime-fighting message. "My opponent, Mark White, says we don't need to change our criminal justice system," Baker said into the camera stiffly, as if he were an actor auditioning for a part he did not think he would get. "Here are the facts. A man convicted of murder gets probation—he's free. A criminal sexually abuses young children—no jail time. A drug pusher sentenced to six years serves one, gets out and repeats the crime. Had enough? I have." Unable to afford prime time, the campaign placed the ad on soap operas such as *The Young and the Restless* and game shows such as *Family Feud* as well as syndicated repeats of older shows like *Gilligan's Island* and *Gunsmoke*.

Baker also made a play for minority voters at a time when the Republican Party was going the opposite direction. At a meeting with the League of United Latin American Citizens, known as LULAC, he argued that Hispanic voters would get more by standing with him than with the Democrats. "If you write me off as a candidate, I owe you nothing," he told the group. "And Mark White owes you nothing because he already has you sewed up. He will take you for granted. Let's not take each other for granted."

Baker's outreach to minorities concerned Bill Clements, the colorful oil executive and former deputy defense secretary who topped the Republican ticket that year as nominee for governor. "You should be aware that Jim Baker and Bill Clements are developing differences in their policies," an adviser to Clements wrote in a memo on August 7. "Mr. Clements has come out against a state civil rights act and at the LULAC convention in San Antonio a week ago, Baker came out in favor of it."

Baker may not have had much experience on the stage himself, but his legal training gave him an advantage in debates. After one particularly rough face-off in San Antonio, Mark White called his campaign staff. "Hey, no more debates with Jim Baker," he recalled telling aides. "This son of a gun knows as much about this business as I do and there's no need for us exposing ourselves. No more debates."

White then found himself at a joint appearance with Baker the very next day. Livid, he called his staff to complain, only to be told it had already been on the schedule. "Well, you cancel the schedule," he replied. "Tell them I'm sick. I don't want any more debates with him. He's damn good."

BAKER ENLISTED a lot of national star power to help. Bush, of course, was there for him from the start. A host of other Republican luminaries also trekked to Texas to campaign for Baker, including Gerald Ford and Bob Dole. Baker even made a point of flying out to Los Angeles to ask Ronald Reagan to headline a fundraiser for him, which Reagan agreed to do. "That was, sort of, the beginning of the relationship between Ronald Reagan and Jim Baker," the Reagan adviser Michael Deaver would later say.

The Republican stars were not looking at Baker as a future Texas attorney general, however. They were angling for the services of practically the only living Republican who had run a national presidential campaign at that point without being sent to jail. During their appearances for him, Reagan and former governor John Connally of Texas each asked Baker to run his next presidential campaign in 1980. Baker turned them both down. "George Bush is my friend," he recalled telling Connally moments before heading into a fundraiser for Baker, "and if he runs I'm going to be with him." Connally did not hide his pique. "You're never going to amount to much," Connally told him, according to an account Baker later gave one of his sons.

White took advantage of the influx of outsiders to paint Baker as a tool of national interests. "Most of the problems for Texas are generated by the Northeast," White said at one news conference, "and they are supporting my opponent." At another point, he called Baker a federal bureaucrat looking for work. "He's come down here from Washington because he's unemployed," White said.

Another line of attack got under Baker's skin. One of the biggest cases being handled by the Texas attorney general's office involved the massive estate of the eccentric mogul and philanthropist Howard Hughes, who had died in April 1976 while on a flight from Acapulco, Mexico, to Houston for medical treatment. A cousin and aunt who stood to gain from Hughes's will wanted him declared a resident of Nevada, where there was no inheritance tax, but Hughes had listed Texas as his residence in federal income tax forms for decades. At stake was $100 million or more in taxes.

The problem for Baker was that his law firm represented Hughes, which meant that he would have to recuse himself if he were elected attorney general. While Baker himself was not involved in the case at the firm, as a candidate he had frozen his participation in earnings from the Hughes estate, which ultimately would cost him a lot of money. In his memo analyzing the coming campaign, Baker's aide, Jim Cicconi, had identified the Hughes case as "our chief vulnerability" and advised the candidate to emphasize that the issue would probably be resolved by the time a new attorney general was sworn in. But White poked his opponent about it, to Baker's fury. "He went through the roof," White recalled. "Oh my God."

Baker had no compunction about going negative against his opponent either. But when it came down to it, he passed on what could have been a devastating attack on White. In Texas, the secretary of state was in charge of extradition of criminals to other states. Cicconi dug up a case where White had refused to extradite a man wanted by New York for a violent felony after being convinced he would not get a fair trial. The man later went on to murder two people in Texas. Cicconi thought it was "a killer issue" against White, but Baker refused to use it. "He was worried about his own personal reputation," Cicconi said. "It was a very nasty accusation to level against someone, very different than a policy difference—this is like, 'These guys are dead because you didn't do your job.'"

For Baker, it was a moment of truth. "I think he viewed this as whether you're going to take the high road or take the low road," Cicconi said. At this juncture, Baker chose the high road.

MORE IMPORTANT THAN any specific issue were the political realities of Texas. Campaigning one day, Baker ran across a voter and told him he was running for attorney general.

"May I ask which party?" the man asked.

"Republican," Baker answered.

"Oh," the man said.

As a reporter witnessing the exchange wrote, it was "almost as if Baker had just admitted to residing at the state hospital."

Baker had simply never developed the touch of a candidate. "He was the worst retail politician I've ever seen," Jim Barlow, who covered the campaign for the *Houston Chronicle*, reflected years later. "It's not that he was a snob. He didn't feel right in forcing himself on people." Baker was so uncomfortable with small talk that when the two of them were alone on long flights around the state in a tiny campaign airplane, Barlow taught him gin rummy to avoid awkward silences.

In many ways, Barlow concluded, Baker's social background held him back. "We would be walking through a fair or one of these little festivals that every small town in Texas has and he would walk along and there would be people walking toward him and he would smile at them, but he wouldn't stop them and say, 'Hi, I'm Jim Baker and I'm running for attorney general and I'd like your vote.' He'd just slide through the crowd." By contrast, Barlow said, "He was very good at talking with the county judge or the Republican chairman and seeking their support. He was very good at figuring out what's going on in the county and what resonates here and that sort of thing. But he just couldn't take that and put it out in a retail way."

Probably no one covered the race as intensively as Barlow. The *Chronicle* at the time was owned by a charitable foundation, the Houston Endowment, and under state law, such organizations were regulated by the attorney general. "The *Chronicle* was protecting its ass," Barlow said. "They didn't want to ignore the race and have the pissed-off guy say, 'You didn't cover me when I was running.' But the *Chronicle* didn't push me in one way or the other about the race. We played it straight."

Still, on the editorial page, the *Chronicle* placed its bet with the candidate it assumed would win, backing White in an endorsement that did not even mention his Republican opponent. Baker was furious. Unlike White, who was born in northeastern Texas, Baker was a native Houstonian; his family had been key in building the city into the modern metropolis that it had become—including providing the land for the *Chronicle*'s own headquarters. How could his hometown paper snub him that way? But he never held it against Barlow, who came away an admirer of Baker's intelligence and integrity. "I've always thought Baker was the best *backroom* politician I ever saw," he said.

On November 7, Baker cast his ballot in Houston and then settled in to wait for the results. The backroom politician knew what was coming, even if he did not want to admit it. In the end, Baker took 999,431 votes to 1,249,846 for White, a respectable showing in heavily Democratic Texas. For the rest of his life, he would argue that his 44 percent was nothing less than a moral victory for a Republican at that time.

But the truth was, Baker had missed the moment. He was right that Texas was changing—1978 would be the year that Texas really began transforming from a solid Democratic state into a solid Republican one. Bill Clements became the first Republican to win the governorship in more than a century—essentially prevailing with Baker's strategy. Governor Dolph Briscoe had been toppled in the Democratic primary from the left by the outgoing attorney general, John Hill. Clements squeezed by Hill in the general election by portraying him as too liberal, just as Baker had expected to slip by Price Daniel. Senator John Tower, for years the state's senior Republican, managed an equally narrow victory for a fourth term and now had company as the party began expanding its hold on the Texas electorate. Tower, however, rued Baker's loss. "Jimmy is the only one of us who deserved to win," he confided to an aide on election night.

Baker had tasted the spotlight and found that he liked it. The idea of running again would linger in the back of his mind for years to come. But it had hardly been an auspicious start. "Baker was a great politician except when he had his own name on the ballot," his friend Dick Cheney would always tease him.

Besides, everyone knew what was coming next. As Barlow wrote in the *Chronicle* after the election, Baker's defeat "does not mean his exit from politics, but moves Baker's aspirations from the state to the national scene."

In Florida, where Jim and Susan Baker fled to recover from the race, the phone rang three days after the election.

George Bush was on the line.

CHAPTER 7

The Asterisk Club

The discussion was to be held at 10:45 a.m. on a Sunday in 1979. The subject: If George Bush ran for president, what were his chances?

In keeping with his father's preparation mantra, Baker had a six-page paper drawn up by aides to guide the conversation, a brutally honest assessment of the prospective candidate's strengths and weaknesses. His plan was to distribute it among the Bush advisers who would attend the meeting, then collect copies back after it was over to prevent leaks.

"Bush cannot look too hungry," the memo argued, and he "should avoid being labeled as 'moderate' or 'Northeastern' or 'Ford' candidate." Reading it over in advance of the meeting, Baker pulled out his black pen and began scrawling his thoughts next to key lines. In the margins, he ticked off his friend's weaknesses with bracing candor:

1. No "base"
2. "Loser" image
3. Substantive lightweight

Harsh, to be sure, but a fair reckoning of how Bush was seen in the months before the next presidential contest, if not the reality of who he was. Baker knew that there was no point in believing your own spin. Better to tell the truth, at least to yourself, and he was right about Bush's challenges. At age fifty-four as 1979 opened, Bush was an unlikely presidential contender—a former congressman who had served just four years in the House and lost two campaigns for the Senate before taking on a series of high-profile but short-lived political appointments. Bush earned respect, not raves. He was everyone's second choice, a résumé candidate, an insider and a moderate at a moment when his party cared nothing about credentials and everything about finding a crusading conservative to turn Jimmy Carter out of the White House.

But Baker still thought there was a path for Bush, or at least little to lose, and as he read through the memo, he wrote out "one strength," which was that Bush was "a national candidate w/a natl. view of problems & solutions." Bush's experience as Gerald Ford's CIA director, on the other hand, presented a more mixed political dilemma for an aspiring president, Baker thought: "Good w/far right wing. Bad—spy as Pres!" And then toward the end, he wrote out his own formula, the one that would set a plodding candidate on the path to national office and remain Baker's strategy for decades of campaigns to come: "Key to winning is: Start early & develop an organization better than any of the opponents. McGovern did it. Nixon did it. Carter did it. Primary elections are won by organization!—almost regardless of candidate." He underlined "organization."

Baker was nothing if not organized. Tapped by his friend to put together a national campaign, he set about the task with typically painstaking preparation—assembling a staff, drafting a budget, developing a fundraising plan, crafting a message. This was a new challenge for Baker. For all the star power he earned in Ford's campaign, he had arrived late, only taking over after the nomination was won. Now it was up to him to build a campaign from scratch.

AS GEORGE HERBERT WALKER BUSH started out the race for the 1980 Republican nomination, he was nobody's front-runner. That title belonged to Ronald Reagan, who had emerged from his near-upset of Ford with increased stature and the power of a growing conservative movement behind him. Early polls found so little support for Bush that he had an asterisk next to his name. His grim-humored campaign staff declared themselves members of the Asterisk Club.

Baker and Bush had begun discussing a possible campaign as early as December 1976, just weeks after Ford's loss to Jimmy Carter. Then the CIA director, Bush had offered to stay on as a nod to the apolitical nature of the job, but Carter rejected the idea. That left Bush more than a little bitter, but it freed him up to pursue his real ambition. Together, Bush and Baker paid visits to Reagan and Ford to disclose their intentions. Ford indicated that he did not expect to run again and gave Baker his blessing to work for Bush. Reagan was noncommittal about his own plans but expressed appreciation to Bush for the gesture of checking in first. Even as Baker was mounting his ill-fated campaign for office in Texas in 1978, he was advising Bush on what would come next. Now that Baker's bid was over, he became chief executive officer of the Asterisk Club.

The strategy Baker developed was to emulate what another asterisk had recently done to capture the presidency. Carter had been the first candidate to really make the Iowa caucuses an important benchmark of presidential politics, devoting enormous time and shoe leather to working the farm state in advance of the 1976 race. The payoff was huge. Baker calculated that Bush could do the same thing. "I had read Hamilton Jordan's book," Baker said, referring to Carter's political guru, "and I had seen what Iowa did for Jimmy Carter." While Reagan enjoyed the star power, Bush would undercut him by virtually moving to Iowa and building an insurgent campaign. Baker's plan may have lacked in originality, but it had the virtue of capitalizing on Bush's natural friend-making skills. Still, Bush was no peanut farmer; the Ivy League–educated, tennis-playing Connecticut preppy turned oilman from Texas could hardly relate as easily as Carter could to Iowa voters. And in Reagan, Bush faced a competitor with deep Midwestern roots. Reagan had even lived and worked in Iowa early in his career, becoming a popular radio broadcaster known as Dutch.

A host of other prominent Republicans were angling for the nomination as well, including Bob Dole; Senator Howard Baker, who had made a name for himself challenging Richard Nixon during Watergate; and two congressmen from Illinois, Philip Crane, a conservative who had led the charge against Carter's plans to relinquish the Panama Canal and sign an arms control treaty with the Soviet Union, and John Anderson, a moderate who had been a vocal critic of the Vietnam War and advocated raising gasoline taxes to pay for new highways. But the candidate who most worried Baker was John Connally, the former Democratic governor of Texas who had been in the car with John Kennedy when he was shot in Dallas and later joined Nixon's cabinet as treasury secretary. Now a Republican, Connally not only drew from the same Texas base as Bush, but with his tall frame, shock of silver hair, and deep gravelly voice, he looked like "central casting's idea of president of the United States," as Baker put it.

Undeterred, Bush formally announced his candidacy on May 1, 1979, taking care to boast that he was a "lifelong Republican," an unmistakable jab at Reagan and Connally, who were not. His speech was not exactly a rousing call to arms. He promised "principled, stable leadership." But he also promised energy as he took on the sixty-eight-year-old front-runner. He made a point of showcasing himself jogging, a not-too-subtle jab at his opponent's age, which burned Reagan to no end. While Reagan stayed above the fray, Bush made himself omnipresent in Iowa, attending all the cattle calls and coffee fundraisers that he could. In the end, he would spend twenty-seven days campaigning in Iowa before the caucuses, compared with just forty-five hours by Reagan.

The political landscape seemed to tilt in Bush's direction. In November 1979, just two months before Iowa Republicans would caucus, Iranian militants stormed the United States embassy in Tehran and seized more than fifty American diplomats, the start of a long, grinding hostage crisis that would badly damage Carter's credibility even as it played to Bush's foreign policy credentials in his battle with Reagan and Connally. The Soviet invasion of Afghanistan the next month further reinforced the likelihood that the Republican contest would play out against the backdrop of national security challenges.

Still, as he hosted "Ask George Bush" forums, he was neither a polished nor an exciting candidate. He would show up for an event and draw only a single radio reporter. He would sit for an interview with socks that no longer had any elastic, exposing his bare legs to questioners who struggled to avert their eyes. He told audiences that his father "inculcated in me a sense of public service," a line that struck Baker as so awkward that he finally intervened. *Inculcated!* "George, you've got to stop saying that," Baker told him. "It sounds like a venereal disease."

Baker set about building a team of relatively younger aides; many like him had served in Ford's short-lived administration. His meteoric rise in post-Watergate Washington had left Baker with what would become a lifelong network of Republicans. One of the first in the door was Margaret Tutwiler, an Alabama debutante whose family owned much of Birmingham and who had worked under Baker in the 1976 campaign. Another early enlistee was Karl Rove, a young veteran of George W. Bush's failed congressional campaign in 1978. Both of them remained in the Bush family orbit for many years to come.

Robert Mosbacher, a gregarious Texas oil mogul who handled fundraising for Bush's 1970 Senate campaign and served as finance chairman for Ford's 1976 race, was the obvious choice to run the money operation. Baker had become friends with Mosbacher in 1970, when both of them lost their wives to cancer. Baker also brought on two other Ford veterans: Robert Teeter, the pollster, and David Gergen, who had served as White House communications director. From his Texas campaign, Baker recruited Pete Teeley, but he could not convince Frank Donatelli, a diehard Reaganite, to join the Bush team. When he heard that David Keene, a conservative operative working for Reagan, had run afoul of the campaign manager, John Sears, Baker happily summoned him to Texas and convinced him to jump to Bush's team as national political director. Keene then recruited a couple more rising operatives: Rich Bond and Vic Gold. "We didn't have a big gang of people," Teeley said.

Baker did not bring a strong political imagination to the campaign. His asset beyond his close friendship with the candidate was a ruthless pragmatism that allowed him to pick talented staff members and give them the room to perform. "He doesn't pretend to be the great creative genius or anything like that," Keene observed. "That's rare in politics. He knows who he is. He knows what he can do and he does it as well or better than anybody. But he also knows what he doesn't do."

While most top strategists sought to stay close to the candidate, Baker had no need to establish his relationship with Bush and no interest in packing his bags to spend the next few months on the road. "He didn't want to be the candidate's buddy," Keene said. Instead, Baker tried to get Keene to travel with Bush. Keene also said no, and suggested Gold, a former Spiro Agnew aide and one of the party's best speechwriters. "George Bush is a wonderful guy and has no political instincts at all and his reaction time is weeks," Keene said. "So we figured it would be a good mix because Vic's reaction time is nanoseconds." Then again, Gold, once described as the "Mount Vesuvius of press secretaries," also had a habit of getting so worked up that he would quit in a huff before coming back to a campaign. He was known for shouting at press van drivers who fell behind a motorcade and pounding an assistant over the head with a rolled-up newspaper. "Vic was a sideshow in himself," Teeley said.

A BIGGER CHALLENGE for Baker was managing the sprawling and sometimes unruly Bush clan. He would need this skill more than once in the coming years.

Jonathan Bush was a successful investment executive in New Haven, now assigned to his brother's fundraising team, an effective backwater for keeping troublesome relatives out of strategy or messaging. But Jonathan's constant efforts to assert more control over the operation drove Robert Mosbacher to distraction and conflicted with Fred Bush, the finance director (and no relation to the family). Baker was regularly brought in to mediate.

The tension finally blew up into what Baker later characterized as a "shouting match" on the evening of February 12, 1980, when Jonathan laid out a series of grievances over an upcoming Los Angeles fundraiser, complaining that he should "honcho" the dinner instead of Jerry Weintraub, the Hollywood producer and friend of the candidate, who was being named to chair it simply because he was a "big deal late-comer." Baker snapped and told Jonathan to stop being petty.

The next day, Baker put it in writing. "I am sick and tired of getting caught in the middle of your pissing match with Mosbacher and Fred B.," Baker wrote to the candidate's brother. "I am not doing my job for GB when I spend time arguing with you."

Baker even raised the matter with George Bush. But after a night's sleep, he thought better of it. "Forget about my comment about Johnny," Baker wrote to Bush the next day. "You don't need to worry about those things. I am tired of getting caught in the middle of disputes between people in finance, but the situation can be handled without your involvement."

Then he fired off another memo to Jonathan, Mosbacher, and Fred Bush. "I have refereed my last argument over the timing and announcement of fund raising events," he wrote. Unfortunately for Baker, he was wrong.

Finally, in April, Jonathan tried to smooth over the latest dispute. "Let's put our differences aside and bury the hatchet," he wrote Baker.

"The hatchet is buried," Baker wrote back. "But I simply do not have time to argue with you about scheduling decisions."

Jonathan was not the only Bush who got on Baker's nerves. Prescott Bush Jr., another brother of the candidate, called at one point to ask for money because he was convinced George could win a lot of African American votes in the New York contest. Exasperated, Baker replied, "Pres, that's not what we're concentrating on. We're focused on Iowa and New Hampshire." Baker stood his ground, assuming that George would back him up. ("There are no amateurs in politics," Baker sighed years later when asked about this. "Everybody is an expert.")

If handling the family were not awkward enough, there was also the matter of the candidate's longtime personal assistant, Jennifer Fitzgerald, who was quickly making enemies on the campaign staff. Fitzgerald, an attractive young divorcée, first met Bush while working at the Republican National Committee a few years earlier. Neither spoke of it publicly but it was clear a personal relationship of some closeness developed. Bush even called Fitzgerald regularly one summer at the beach house in North Carolina she was sharing, according to a housemate later contacted by the reporter Susan Page. He brought her to China as his personal secretary and then to the CIA. Many who worked for him over the years wondered about their relationship. Bush, a flirt with a habit of bottom-squeezing attractive women he encountered, repeatedly sought out Fitzgerald despite the questions it raised and any pain it caused Barbara. Colleagues often interpreted Fitzgerald's airs as a sign that she was the boss's secret girlfriend. Whether they actually had an affair was never clear; one person in Bush's inner circle told Page that they had a romantic relationship for a dozen years. Both denied it to Bush's biographer, Jon Meacham. Baker always professed not to know—but did not rule it out.

Either way, Fitzgerald caused great consternation for Baker. After Baker arrived to run the campaign, she trashed him during after-hours drinks with other members of the staff. "He's a loser, two-time loser, lost for Ford and then lost for attorney general," she said. Karl Rove reported the comment to Baker, who told Bush about it. But Bush continued to empower Fitzgerald and she was able to get away with behavior that no one else could. She blocked access to the candidate and disregarded instructions. Indeed, she had laid out the campaign headquarters in such a way that Baker had to go through her office to reach Bush. Baker ordered Rove to have a door cut in the wall between his office and Bush's so he could speak with the candidate without having to go through her. "She thought she was in charge of things," said David Keene. "She was a pain in the ass."

Baker thought so too. He considered her rude, presumptuous, and impossible to deal with. She added events to Bush's schedule without consulting Baker, she was slow going through files, she could not delegate efficiently, and she often did not answer the phones. The breaking point came when she told David Gergen to send a speech for the candidate to her rather than to Baker. After he found out, Baker angrily told her to fax him the speech in Washington, but the night passed and it never came. She later claimed that Bush had told her not to send it but when Baker asked the candidate, he denied it.

In frustration, Baker grabbed an envelope and scrawled out a list of complaints about Fitzgerald. "Have worst of all worlds because she didn't do as I asked & she said she would," he wrote. "Responsibility vs. Auth. My pol judg. may not be best but it's better than hers." He was so aggravated that after filling one side, he turned the envelope over to keep going. "If I ask janitor to tell her to do something—she has to do it. Otherwise org. will never function smoothly. To even have to go thru this is stupid. Conspiratorial. Play games."

On another occasion, he wrote more about her in an angry note to himself that he kept for years. "She wants to run the campaign," he complained. Another time, he scratched out a list of people Fitzgerald had offended, including "Barbara Bush!" he added with an exclamation point. "Now—'me' & I get along w/everybody."

One night, Baker groused about the situation with his wife. He did not know what to do, he said. Fitzgerald was only hurting Bush by disrupting the operation.

"Honey, you have to talk to him," Susan told him.

"No," he said. "I can't."

Baker could not bring himself to confront his friend about Fitzgerald. It was too sensitive. Finally, he had an idea. He asked Susan to talk with Bush and tell him that her husband would quit if the situation did not change. It was an extraordinary act of deflection—threatening to resign through his wife.

Nonetheless, Susan could see how upset her husband was and agreed to do it. She dialed Bush from the phone in the kitchen of their Houston house while, unknown to the candidate, Baker stood next to her listening to the conversation. After she explained the problem, she outlined the stakes.

"George," Susan said in her honeyed Texas accent, "you're going to lose Jimmy because he can't operate this way."

Bush seemed surprised. "Oh, really?"

Bush agreed to make a change. He would not fire Fitzgerald—he was too attached to her for that—but he sent her to New York to work on fundraising with Jonathan Bush. For Baker, it lumped two of his problems together. He considered it the perfect solution.

The episode said much about Baker's relationship with Bush. He cherished their friendship and was determined to do everything he could to put him in the White House. But he was no longer the rookie he was when Bush assigned him to run Harris County during his Senate race a decade earlier. Baker was now a seasoned political hand, managing his second presidential campaign, and he was not going to stand for the likes of Jennifer Fitzgerald or Jonathan Bush getting in the way. Some of his aides thought Baker lost a little respect for Bush in the process. Yet for the first time, he was acutely conscious of the fact that he was no longer Bush's peer but his subordinate. And he found direct conflict with his friend and boss intolerable.

BAKER'S BET ON Iowa, meanwhile, seemed as though it might actually pay off. Sticking to the plan Baker had formulated in 1979, Bush attended every fair and every forum in Iowa he could, even as Reagan stayed away. In Iowa, showing up mattered. And Bush had showed up, again and again. When Bush, who had trailed Reagan by 36 percentage points in Iowa seven weeks before the caucuses, suddenly won a straw poll of Republicans in Ames, the victory, although technically meaningless, generated favorable attention and a whole new set of expectations. By the time the frigid day of the caucuses arrived on January 21, 1980, with the temperature dipping to 24 degrees, Bush was surprisingly hot. He now felt he at least had to come in second to Reagan. When reporters asked him the morning of the caucus how he would react to a third-place showing, he said, "I'll make it sound like a victory, but you won't let me get away with it."

As the early results began trickling in that evening, Bush found himself actually leading. The margin held up. Somehow, against all odds, he had pulled off the upset of the year, toppling Reagan, the conservative darling and prohibitive front-runner, with 31.6 percent to 29.5 percent. Bush exulted. "The impossible dream, the asterisk on all these polls just four months ago!" he exclaimed at his victory party.

Bush and Baker had accomplished what they were looking for—they had set themselves up as the clear alternative to Reagan heading into the primaries. None of the other candidates had come close. "I suppose I am out of the pack," Bush said on television after his win, "but they will be after me, howling and yowling at my heels. What we will have is momentum. We will look forward to 'Big Mo' being on our side, as they say in athletics."

Baker grimaced at the "Big Mo" phrase. It sounded too cocky, too premature. It raised expectations too high. And it went against the strategy he had developed. Baker, backed by David Keene and Robert Teeter, urged Bush to talk about the issues that animated his campaign, not his political prospects. They had gotten the attention of voters, but now the candidate needed to tell them what he stood for. Republicans in New Hampshire needed a reason to vote for him other than the fact that he had won in Iowa. "In Iowa, we defined the George Who," Baker said, "but we never had figured out the George Why."

Flush with victory, Bush brushed off Baker and the others. No longer the asterisk, Bush got carried away by success and figured that what worked in Iowa would work again in New Hampshire, where he had also erased a huge deficit in the polls. "You're not out there," he told his team back at headquarters. "You haven't seen what it's like."

Now the trick was to draw out Reagan, who was scrambling after the surprising Iowa debacle. Invariably the contest would boil down to Reagan, still the favorite of conservative insurgents, and a single establish-ment rival. Bush was determined to be that lone alternative. "The clean fingernail Republican," as William Loeb, the publisher of the conservative *Manchester Union Leader* and a Reagan supporter, described Bush.

On February 11, Baker and the Bush campaign team received a letter from Jon Breen, executive editor of the *Nashua Telegraph* in New Hampshire, offering to host a "public meeting" between Reagan and Bush on February 23 at 7:30 p.m. in the gymnasium of Nashua High School, just three days before the all-important primary. "We propose this one-on-one encounter," Breen wrote, "given the prevalent wisdom that Mr. Reagan and Mr. Bush are the front-runners in the campaign for the Republican nomination."

Baker and Bush were ecstatic. *One on one!* They had what they wanted—a two-man race.

DESPITE THE THRILL of the Iowa win, the campaign was a grueling slog for Baker. When the campaign started, "Jim soon became an asterisk at home," Susan recalled. "As punishment for his long and frequent absences, our baby would refuse to hug him for hours after he returned." She added, "He was not in my good graces either." She was left to deal with the troublesome older children as they struggled with drugs and alcohol, all with Dad out of town much of the time.

Baker had rented a house at 718 S. Royal Street in Alexandria, Virginia, just outside Washington and a little over a mile from the campaign head-quarters, living there by himself for months until Susan and Mary-Bonner moved up from Houston. A creature of habit, Baker ate dinner nearly every night at the same restaurant in Alexandria, ordering the same kidney pie before smoking a cheap cigar. "I complained to him once—a guy with your money ought to buy a good one," David Keene said.

Alone in his rental, Baker's thoughts turned toward the strange twist in his life that had brought him into politics—and left him with a rebellious, unhappy brood of kids back in Texas. He sent a note to all four of his sons, enclosing a pamphlet on the health dangers of smoking too much pot. "I hope you each know that I do this only because I deeply love each and every one of you," he wrote. "I haven't lectured any of you for a number of years about this, so I hope you will forgive me this one time."

He added a line designed to weigh on the boys. "It was ten years ago yesterday that Mom left us," he wrote. "I know she's been up there keeping track of us and is proud that each and every one of you are making it in spite of losing her. I know I'm proud, and I'm sending you this material also because I know she would want you to read it."

For Baker, the reference to Mary Stuart was a painful one. She was the one who had been a Republican. She had been the one who had volunteered on campaigns. Imagine what she would have thought had she seen her Democratic husband at the head of a surging Republican campaign for president.

ON THE NIGHT of February 23, Baker and Bush arrived at Nashua High School in New Hampshire only to find a surprise waiting. John Sears, the Reagan campaign manager, sent word to David Keene that he wanted to see Bush. Keene was offended at the presumption. "It doesn't work that way," he said. Campaign managers don't summon candidates. If Sears wanted to see someone, it would be his counterpart. So Baker met with Sears, who told him that Reagan wanted to open up the debate to all the candidates, not just the two of them.

"It's important that we have everybody included," Sears said.

"Well, the ambassador is pretty dead set against it," Baker replied, referring to Bush, "but I'll take the message back."

As he turned to go, Baker noticed the door to an adjacent room was ajar. Inside were Reagan and four other candidates who had not been invited—Bob Dole, Howard Baker, Philip Crane, and John Anderson. At that point, Baker realized it was an ambush.

Baker told Bush what was happening but the candidate, as predicted, remained adamant that they had agreed to a two-man debate. "None of us tried to talk him out of it," Baker said. Only two chairs had been set up onstage, but Reagan marched on with the four excluded candidates. The Reagan campaign had agreed to foot the bill for the debate to get around a complaint that the newspaper was violating federal election law by making what amounted to an illegal campaign contribution to the two candidates it had invited, but now Reagan was pushing to include the entire slate. Jon Breen, the *Telegraph* editor who was serving as moderator, tried to cut him off.

"Turn Mr. Reagan's microphone off," Breen directed the technical staff.

"I am *paying* for this microphone, Mr. Green," Reagan replied sharply, mangling the editor's name but drawing a burst of applause from the audience.

It was a moment of drama that would resonate long after the evening had ended. Reagan appeared confident and decisive, while Bush seemed peevish and unwilling to confront his fellow candidates.

Dole, for one, was livid. As the barred candidates filed off the stage, he whispered to Bush, "I'll get you someday, you fucking Nazi." Descending from the platform, Dole encountered Baker and poked him in the chest. The two had worked together in 1976 when Dole was the vice presidential nominee and Baker the campaign chairman. Now Dole hissed at him. "You're never going to forget this," he snarled.

Bush's handling of the flap did not impress many others either, least of all Reagan. "After the debate in New Hampshire, he thought Bush was a wimp," said Lyn Nofziger, a longtime Reagan aide. With the surprise ambush, Reagan had effectively thwarted the one-on-one moment Bush had sought—while the debate proceeded with just the two candidates, it was thoroughly overshadowed by the confrontation over the other four. Later that night, Baker ran into David Broder, the venerable political reporter from *The Washington Post*, who told him that they had screwed up big-time. "I don't think any of us appreciated the downside that was going to take place as a result of our saying no," Baker said.

Three days later, Reagan roared to a convincing victory in New Hampshire, taking 50 percent of the vote to 23 percent for Bush. It was a devastating defeat for Bush and Baker. The Big Mo was gone. A week later, Bush bounced back with a much narrower win in Massachusetts, but Reagan was still far and away the leader in national polling. The best news for Bush was that at least he had consolidated for himself the role of the main challenger to Reagan. By April, Dole, Baker, Crane, Anderson, and John Connally had all dropped out.

Bush was the last man standing, the last one who had the chance to stop the insurgent conservative movement from capturing the party. But he was fighting the tides. Reagan had harnessed the strength of the newly emerging religious right and vowed to ban abortion, while taking on the Soviet Union and taming a federal government that had grown out of control. Bush offered no particular ideology beyond a conventional country-club Republicanism. While he too talked tough about the Russians and said he personally opposed abortion, he was not as much of a saber-rattler and he did not support a constitutional amendment to overturn *Roe v. Wade*. Rather than attack government, his argument, essentially, was that he would run it better than the other guy.

The establishment rallied behind Bush, even if the political class was never convinced of his capacity for pulling off an upset, and the two candidates raced around the country seeking advantage. Reagan swept most of the succeeding primaries, although Bush squeaked by in Connecticut, where he was born.

Bush made a stand in Pennsylvania, where he thought he had a good chance to pick up a major state with many delegates, and he continued to pound Reagan. In a speech at Carnegie Mellon University in Pittsburgh on April 10, he ridiculed Reagan's supply-side economic theory, the notion that if he cut taxes deeply, it would set off an explosion of growth so powerful that it would produce enough new tax revenue to keep the deficit from ballooning. Reagan had been promising not just to cut taxes but also to dramatically increase defense spending while still reducing budgetary red ink.

"What I'm saying is that it just isn't going to work," Bush said at Carnegie Mellon. Reagan's plan was "what I call a voodoo economic policy."

The phrase was catchy and it stuck. Pete Teeley had come up with it after reading an editorial that criticized Jimmy Carter by calling his policy the product of "witch doctors." Teeley kept the metaphor but switched the target, adapting it to fit the emerging critique of Reagan.

But Baker was not amused. By this point, he had concluded that Bush was not going to win the nomination and he was already thinking ahead. His goal now was to do well enough that Bush would earn his way onto the ticket as the vice presidential running mate. The way to do that was to demonstrate strength but not to alienate Reagan. To that end, Baker had already come up with a list of banned words that Bush's team was never to use about Reagan, including "jingoistic," "extremist," and "irresponsible." Baker even rejected a commercial that the media team had developed showing a picture of Carter with a voice talking about the danger of a former governor with no national experience who could not get the job done. As the announcer warned against making "the same mistake again," Reagan's picture came onto the screen. "It was a very good negative ad," Baker said later. "But if we'd run it, I can promise you, George Bush would never have been put on the ticket."

Now there was Teeley and his "voodoo economics." Baker got on the phone. "Pete, you've got to be goddamn careful in terms of what he's saying out there, because if it goes too far, there will be no way that he's going to get on the ticket," Baker scolded.

Then he called Bush and said much the same thing. "Make sure Teeley doesn't push you too far," Baker said.

But as Bush saw it, he was still running for president not vice president, and he defended Teeley. "Jim, he's the only one here who wants to win other than me," Bush said.

Bush was right about that. A memo sent to Baker from Rich Bond a few days later outlined the prospects in the remaining states, declaring five of them "hopeless" and the rest difficult. "Even with a Pennsylvania win, there will be no significant change in GB's fortunes in the above mentioned states," the memo said.

Bush did go on to beat Reagan in Pennsylvania on April 22 and came close in Texas, but as predicted, Reagan then racked up a string of victories. Baker commissioned a twenty-page memo dated May 1 and titled "Assessing the Value of Campaign Survival Until the Republican Convention," which listed the advantages and disadvantages of staying in. "Bush's major objectives are best met by remaining an active candidate until the convention" as long as he focused on Carter and didn't tear down Reagan, the memo concluded. "One Bush objective perhaps threatened by his campaign's longevity is the Vice Presidential nomination, but there is also no good evidence that his chances are actually improved by his campaign's demise." Staying in, the memo argued, would preserve Bush's visibility and allow him to "lay claim to future leadership" in the party.

Even so, Baker was coming under pressure from Bush allies to press the candidate to call it quits. "I have never wanted to discourage him, so I have not raised the question of withdrawing to George," Representative Bill Frenzel of Minnesota wrote Baker on May 14. "However, it's time for you, or somebody, to do so. In my judgement [*sic*], we are well past the time when we are able to do him any good." It was hard to argue with the math. By the campaign's count, Reagan had secured 870 delegates to 272 for Bush. A memo sent to Baker predicted Reagan would have enough to clinch the nomination before the big June 3 primaries in California, Ohio, and New Jersey.

It turned out not to take even that long. On May 20, the day after the memo, Bush prevailed in Michigan, a big state and a big win. But even as he and his team celebrated, ABC News and CBS News focused on Reagan's victory that same night in Oregon, reporting that it would put him over the top for the nomination. That may have been premature. There were a dozen contests left and different counts had Reagan still a bit short, but Baker could read a map and an accounting ledger. They were running out of money—if they kept up the same burn rate, they would reach the federal spending cap by May 31.

Bush's allies in Congress headed to the Alexandria campaign headquarters to meet with Baker and urge the candidate to withdraw. The time had come, they argued. There was no realistic chance of winning the nomination, so staying in served only to damage Reagan, the inevitable nominee.

Baker was increasingly coming to the same conclusion and struggling to find a way to convince Bush. "Jim turned off the phones in California and closed the headquarters without telling him," David Keene said. That "was like a two-by-four and it got his attention."

When the *Post*'s David Broder called, Baker admitted that the campaign did not have enough money to compete in California, Reagan's home state. "If you can't do California," Baker told Broder, "then you can't argue to people that you still have a shot in terms of the numbers. And once you concede that, why do you stay in?"

It was the question of the hour, but not one that Bush had expected to read in the newspaper. Even though Baker's quote was in the eleventh paragraph of a story on page A3, it exploded with the force of a bomb. Broder interpreted it to mean that Bush would not contest the biggest prize of June 3. "Bush All But Abandons California Race, Plans Think Session," the headline read.

Reporters following Bush in New Jersey peppered him with questions about Baker's comment. "Baker says you don't have anything going in California. Does this mean you're dropping out?"

Bush was furious. From a Holiday Inn in New Jersey, he phoned Baker back at campaign headquarters.

"What in the hell are you doing?" Bush demanded.

"All I did was be truthful," Baker replied. "We don't have the money."

Baker had violated his own cardinal rule about not saying anything publicly that would cause problems for his candidate and he admitted to Bush that he should not have. He would always insist that he had not intended to send a message to the candidate through the media. But the point was still valid.

"George, I think it's time to get out of the race," he said.

Bush was flatly against it. "No, Jimmy," he said. "If we can only get to California, we'll be able to turn this thing around."

"We just don't have the money," Baker said. "I wish to hell we did, but we don't and I don't see how we can get it."

Bush was in denial, but he planned to meet with Baker and other advisers back at his home in Houston over the upcoming Memorial Day weekend. On the plane heading south, Bush remained defiant. "I WILL NEVER GIVE UP. NEVER. NEVER," he wrote out on a notepad. Bush felt that pulling out would be a betrayal of the people working for his campaign in the upcoming states. And he could not stomach the idea of surrendering. Bush was the only person Baker knew who was as preternaturally driven as he was. "He is the most competitive guy you ever met," Baker said. Now Bush was pretty incensed at Baker, thinking of him sitting comfortably back in campaign headquarters. "Jimmy wasn't on the road with us all the time," said Susan Morrison, a press aide, reflecting the way Bush viewed it. "His lack of passion we didn't want to hear. We wanted him to bleed a little."

In the sunroom of his house in Houston, Bush sat down with Baker as well as David Keene and Vic Gold. Barbara Bush and other family members were reinforcing the candidate's instinct to stay in, making Baker's job that much tougher. Some advisers, such as Nick Brady, an investment banker who was close to Bush and running the New Jersey campaign, insisted he could rack up delegates there and elsewhere on June 3. But Baker, Keene, and Teeter agreed that they were done. There was no point to staying in the race. Baker argued that there was still a chance of becoming vice president but not if Bush aggravated Reagan.

"We still have a shot at it," Bush responded.

"George, you've got to know when to hold 'em and know when to fold 'em," Baker replied. "Take a look at these numbers."

Baker took a sheaf of papers and spread them out on the coffee table.

"Jim, I've never quit anything until it was finished," Bush said. "This is no time to start."

"But the campaign *is* finished, George," Baker insisted. "You're the only one who doesn't seem to know it."

Baker made the case for Bush's vice presidential prospects but the candidate was skeptical that Reagan would want him. Baker argued that Reagan would come around. Bush would be the only one at the convention other than Reagan with delegates. "That gives you one hell of a leg up because to solidify the party, he really ought to pick you," Baker said. "You're seen to be a moderate. He's seen to be a conservative. You're the last man standing."

The debate continued over the course of the holiday weekend. It was a brutal task for Baker, pushing his best friend to acknowledge that he had lost. "He had a hell of a tough job convincing the candidate that now was the time to fold," Nick Brady said.

Finally, Bush gave in, telling Baker and the staff to draft a statement for him to look at. "The fat lady may not have sung yet," Bush sighed, "but she's warming up in the back room."

Baker and his team headed back to the local Marriott where they were staying to script Bush's exit. They ended up with a realist's lament that very much sounded like the pragmatic lawyer who had run the campaign with an unsparing eye for his candidate's weaknesses from the start. "My instinct was to keep fighting," Baker had Bush say in his withdrawal statement, adding, "I see the world not as I wish it were, but as it is."

The episode left some raw feelings. Barbara Bush was furious with Baker and would remain upset about it for decades. "I may have been mad at Jimmy Baker at the time for saying that he wanted to get out," she told her biographer, Susan Page.

"I think Baker's point was, if you want to be considered for vice president—" Page began.

Barbara interrupted. "Baker wanted to be considered as chief of staff," she said sharply. "He ran for that."

At that point, of course, Baker had no clue that he might end up running a future Reagan White House, but the comment indicated just how deeply Barbara felt that her husband's best friend had been out for himself first. Yet even if that were true, Baker saw clearly what the family could not. In the end, Bush could not overtake Reagan at a moment when the party was turning sharply to the right.

Still, with Baker's guidance, Bush the asterisk had done better than anyone had a right to expect. He won seven contests and piled up 3 million votes to Reagan's forty-four wins and 7.7 million votes. In the process of pulling the plug on Bush's ambitions, Baker very well may have saved them—and his own.

BAKER RETURNED HOME to find that at least one voter was perfectly happy that the campaign was over. For Susan, it was not just the eighteen months since Bush's phone call interrupted their Florida vacation. It was the Texas attorney general's race. It was the Gerald Ford campaign. It was the Commerce Department and the move to Washington and the merger of two unhappy families.

By the time Bush dropped out in May 1980, Susan was exhausted and ready for her husband to spend time with her and their young bonus baby. "I was so relieved. I was so tired I was cross-eyed," Susan said. "We had been married seven years and I want to tell you it felt like seventy because he was gone all the time."

But Baker was not done. While one campaign was now shutting down, a different one, more subtle, more complicated, was just getting under way, and this one had an electorate of just one. Baker was determined to get Bush onto the 1980 ticket, if not in the number one slot then in the number two position. And he had less than two months to do it.

Bush was right that Reagan was not at all inclined to pick him. Reagan was still raw over Bush the jogger's unspoken but obvious emphasis on the age difference, not to mention the "voodoo economics" comment. The former governor made clear to his own advisers that he wanted someone other than Bush. The search for a running mate soon had an acronym— ABB, for Anybody But Bush.

Baker's argument was a simple one—putting Bush onto the ticket would bring the party together, uniting moderates and conservatives. He began talking up the possibility in interviews and he sent signals in private to the Reagan camp about Bush's willingness.

But Baker found an obstacle he had not anticipated—his old boss, Gerald Ford. In the days leading up to the opening of the Republican National Convention in Detroit on July 14, Reagan contemplated asking his onetime rival to join his ticket. The idea was almost unthinkable, even absurd—a former president serving as vice president? How would that work? What would Ford be called, "Mr. President" in deference to his old position or "Mr. Vice President" in keeping with his new one? Yet as implausible as it seemed, Baker discovered that onetime colleagues like Henry Kissinger and Alan Greenspan, a former Ford economic adviser, were lobbying the former president to do it.

As the convention opened at Detroit's Joe Louis Arena, the delegates were abuzz with the possibility. Intermediaries shuttled between Reagan and Ford to see whether it might work. Ford had conditions—he wanted to chair National Security Council meetings, exercise veto power over certain appointments, and bring Kissinger along with him as secretary of state and Greenspan as secretary of the treasury. Then Ford made a fateful and curious decision to visit the CBS News anchor booth overlooking the convention floor to give an interview to Walter Cronkite. As the delegates stared up at the booth, the Reagan team watched on television with astonishment.

What Ford described was more than the typical vice president's role. Cronkite noted that it sounded like more of a "co-presidency." Ford did not disavow the term. Back in his suite listening, Reagan looked appalled. "No, that's not right," he said.

With that, the Ford boomlet was over. Reagan could not accept an arrangement that diminished his authority as president.

"Who else is there?" he asked.

"There's Bush," said Richard Allen, an adviser to Reagan, circling back to the most obvious alternative.

"I can't take him," Reagan said. "That voodoo economic policy charge and his stand on abortion are wrong."

Allen did not consider that an absolute rejection. He handed the candidate a copy of the Republican platform, which included a strong anti-abortion plank. "If you could be assured that George Bush would support this platform in every detail, would you reconsider Bush?" he asked.

Reagan thought for a moment. "Well, if you put it that way, I would agree to reconsider."

At the Hotel Pontchartrain, Baker and the rest of the Bush team, not knowing any of this, had all but given up on his chances. Baker told Pete Teeley to give a "lid" to the reporters waiting for Bush in the lobby, meaning that there would be no more news for the day. But while Teeley was in the elevator heading down, Baker got a call from someone in the Reagan camp.

"Hold everything," Baker told Bush. "This thing's about to come apart. Somebody's having second thoughts."

Baker ordered another aide to intercept Teeley in the lobby to stop him from dismissing the reporters. "It's not over yet," he said.

Even so, no one in the Bush suite thought he was about to be selected. The candidate, dressed in a red sports shirt, drank a Stroh's beer with his advisers and watched television as the hours drifted by without any further news. Finally, at 11:37 p.m., the phone in Room 1912 rang. Baker picked it up.

"Is Ambassador Bush there?" he heard.

"Who's calling?" Baker asked.

"Governor Reagan."

Baker handed the phone to Bush. Nick Brady went to fetch Barbara Bush, who had gone to rest. Despite the tip to Baker, everyone figured this was the end of the line for George Bush and Reagan was calling to let him down easy. As Bush pressed the receiver against his ear, Baker could only hear his side of the conversation.

"Hello. Yes sir, how are you? Yes sir."

After a pause, Bush suddenly turned, grinned and flashed a thumbs-up signal.

"Why, yes sir," Bush said into the phone. "I think you can say I support the platform wholeheartedly."

With that, George Bush found himself on the Republican ticket as the vice presidential candidate, voodoo economics and his position on abortion readily cast aside in the name of ambition and party unity. Baker's conviction had been right—after proving himself in the primaries, Bush got out just in time to keep from alienating Reagan.

"George's exodus was timely," Senator Paul Laxalt of Nevada, one of Reagan's best friends, said later. "Had he held out much longer, George might well have been vetoed as vice president."

BAKER HAD SUCCEEDED in getting his friend onto the ticket, but now the question was what to do himself. Reagan's advisers asked him to manage the Bush vice presidential campaign, but having already run the general election race for an incumbent president, it did not appeal to him. He dismissed a suggestion to be political director for the same reason. William Casey, who had taken over for John Sears as Reagan's campaign chairman, wanted Baker to come on board as his deputy chairman, but Ed Meese, a longtime Reagan hand from California, already had that title and objected.

Baker had breakfast with David Keene near the Reagan-Bush headquarters in Arlington, Virginia, just outside Washington, to talk over the options.

"What should I ask for?" Baker wondered.

Keene had an idea. "You should volunteer to be the guy that takes care of the debates," he said.

Baker seemed intrigued. Keene noted that the Reagan camp was reluctant to debate, worried that he might not match up to Jimmy Carter. Keene harbored no such doubts.

"If there is a debate, Jim, have you seen Reagan lose one?" he said. "So it's a win-win deal and you're not getting yourself into the day-to-day business and so you don't get into a fight."

Baker took the amorphous title of "senior adviser" and agreed to be in charge of debate negotiations for a campaign that wanted no debates. He moved into an office on the third floor of the Reagan headquarters and brought with him a core team from the Bush campaign, including Margaret Tutwiler and David Gergen. Soon enough, he was asked to attend strategy meetings that went beyond debates. Still, "the Reagan team was in charge," Tutwiler remembered. Baker and his entourage were the outsiders.

Not everyone in the Reagan camp was happy about Baker's arrival, foreshadowing years of internal wars to come. Baker was either a Bush loyalist, or out for himself, not for the cause. In meetings, the self-appointed Reagan loyalists would take on the newcomer. "Jim Baker is the biggest phony who ever lived," said Max Hugel, a Reagan campaign aide who would go on to serve as a deputy CIA director under Bill Casey. "One day we were in a budget meeting and I said, 'I need $3 million for my voters groups.' Baker turned to me and asked, 'Why do you need all that money?' I said, 'I'll tell you why. I studied the campaign you ran for Ford in 1976 and if you had used the three million you had left wisely, you would have won.'"

The 1980 general election battle took place in a country in crisis. With Iran still holding fifty-two American hostages and the Soviets rampaging through Afghanistan, the United States appeared to be in retreat. At home, the country was bogged down in a debilitating recession exacerbated by fuel shortages and high interest rates. Reagan deployed Carter's own "misery index" formulation from 1976 against him—adding unemployment and inflation figures that fall produced a combined rate reaching about 20 percent. Americans were having trouble finding jobs, buying homes, and even filling their cars with gasoline. For Baker, the idea of turning the misery index around on Carter seemed like sweet revenge.

More broadly, the nation was still struggling to find its footing after the twin nightmares of Vietnam and Watergate. Ford and Carter had not restored America's faith in itself—the pardon of Nixon, the energy crisis, a shrinking manufacturing sector, decaying inner cities, waves of crime, a meltdown at the Three Mile Island nuclear plant, and culture clashes over race, sex, and drugs had all taken their toll. National will had been so sapped that Carter ultimately gave a lecturing speech bemoaning what came to be called "malaise," even though he never actually used that word.

Reagan was the anti-malaise candidate, unabashedly patriotic and optimistic, celebrating the United States as a "shining city on the hill," a vision that had been missing in American politics for years. His great appeal came not in his sometimes fuzzy, even muddled, policy prescriptions or his chest-beating anti-Soviet rhetoric, but in his own indomitable belief in American exceptionalism. Contrasted with Carter's Sunday-school-teacher approach to politics, Reagan seemed even to many Democrats to be a breath of fresh air. But his history of unconventional ideas and divisive statements caused trepidation. He had called unemployment insurance "a prepaid vacation plan for freeloaders" and asserted that trees were responsible for 80 percent of air pollution. His strident Cold War rhetoric raised fears of nuclear confrontation. Carter's strategy was to paint him as a dangerous lightweight and warmonger.

When it came to debates, Keene turned out to be right. Managing a candidate with a shaky command of facts and a disconcerting penchant for confusing movie tales with real life, Reagan's team feared putting him onstage without a script for an hour or more, unsure if he would be nimble enough to parry a sitting president far better schooled in the nuances of policy. Nancy Reagan, among others, totally opposed debates. But as the fall wore on, Baker pressed Reagan to take on the president and the California advisers increasingly came to the conclusion that they had to accept at least one or two forums, if only because polls suggested that Reagan still needed to close the deal with the public. "We can't run out the clock when we don't have the football," said Drew Lewis, who ran Reagan's campaign in Pennsylvania.

As Reagan moved toward agreeing to a debate, he was confronted with the question of what to do about John Anderson. The Republican congressman, "a stubborn man who does not suffer fools lightly," as *The Washington Post* described him, had lost the party nomination fight, but filed as an independent in the general election. Running as an earnest if pedantic truth teller, Anderson was polling a distant third, but Reagan took the position that it would not be fair to debate without him also onstage—a way of pumping up the independent's candidacy on the theory that he would draw more voters from Carter. The president, understandably, refused. Ultimately, Baker negotiated two debates, one featuring just Reagan and Anderson and another between the two major party candidates.

Michael Deaver later credited Baker with convincing Reagan to debate Anderson. Either way, Baker thought the visual would work to Reagan's benefit—Carter would look afraid by not showing up. And he counted on Reagan's winning personality to shine against Anderson's dour persona. On the night of the debate in Baltimore on September 21, Baker gave Reagan a card just before he went onstage with one word of advice: "Chuckle." As it turned out, Anderson proved a good sparring partner for Reagan to warm up against. "It sort of wiped Anderson out," Baker said. "He was, after all, a Republican, and he was a terrible debater and he was a colorless guy."

To negotiate the showdown with Carter, the two campaigns met at the office of the sponsoring organization, the League of Women Voters. But the talks bogged down. Baker excused himself to go to the men's room and a minute later so did his Democratic counterpart, Robert Strauss, who happened to be a friend and fellow Texan. Within fifteen minutes, the two lawyers returned with a deal, a dozen details spelled out on the back of a Reagan-Bush campaign envelope that Baker happened to have in his pocket.

The last unsettled issues were time and place. Reagan's team wanted a date as late as possible, figuring that the closer to the election, the better. Baker went so far as to propose that the debate be held on the night before the election. Carter rejected that, assuming that Reagan would make a blunder and wanting more time for any gaffe to sink in with the public. They settled on October 28 at the Cleveland Convention Center—still late enough in the campaign that it played in Reagan's favor. "We were outfoxed by Jim Baker in agreeing to it so close to the election," Stuart Eizenstat, a top Carter adviser, later concluded. More importantly, in Eizenstat's view, Baker's ability to convince Reagan to debate in the first place proved decisive. "His confidence in his candidate may have assured his election," he said. Carter also came to believe that Baker had gotten the better of him. "He out-traded the people who were representing me at the time," he said years later.

Baker would have more than just confidence. Just a few days before the debate, he found himself with a black loose-leaf binder that turned out to be Carter's debate briefing book. Baker remembered receiving it from Bill Casey, the campaign chairman, although Casey would later deny it. Either way, Baker did not ask where it originally came from. He did not want to know. A lawyer who prided himself on his rectitude chose to turn a blind eye to whatever nefariousness had delivered the briefing book into his hands, a rare lapse in judgment for someone who would become famous for seeing potential trouble around corners. But at this point, early in his political career, he suddenly found himself with the road map that Carter's campaign had prepared for the president's showdown with Reagan.

Baker thumbed through it for an hour or two before passing it along to the aides helping to prepare Reagan for the debate. The book outlined Carter's strategy for presenting himself as a seasoned, tested, and mainstream president challenged by an unproven and radical opponent: "You are moderate, he's extreme; you are cautious, he's a hip-shooter; you are trained for the job, he's inexperienced; you understand complexities; he's simplistic." It outlined some snappy lines for Carter to use, such as denouncing Reagan's economic plan as a "rich man's tax cut which would flood the country with dollars as fast as the printing presses could print them." And it repeatedly urged Carter to paint Reagan as a risky choice for America, someone who could only "offer uncertainty for the future."

Baker would later say that the briefing book was not all that helpful, given that many of the themes and arguments contained in it had been used publicly during the campaign already. But at the very least, it provided a certain comfort for Reagan's team that it could anticipate what was to come. What Baker did not anticipate is what the clandestinely obtained briefing book would come to mean for his own life when it was later revealed that he had it.

As for Reagan's own briefing book, David Gergen was in charge of preparing it. The first version was "quite thick" and when he presented it, he noticed "Nancy looking daggers," Gergen said. "I made sure the next book was drastically shorter." The actor in Reagan could always master his lines and articulate his larger themes, but he was hardly a wizard of policy details and Nancy did not want him lost in the weeds.

Either way, Reagan brought his top game to the stage in Cleveland, outflanking the incumbent with a genial performance that defused fears that he was a reckless, trigger-happy cowboy. As Hamilton Jordan, Carter's longtime right-hand man, described it, "Reagan looked relaxed, smiling, robust; the president, erect, lips tight, looking like a coiled spring, ready to pounce, an overtrained boxer, too ready for the bout." Carter pressed his case, portraying himself as a careful student of government while depicting Reagan as a radical right-winger who would gut Medicare and Social Security. "There you go again," Reagan chided Carter for supposedly misrepresenting the Republican's positions, a line that Baker later said was not pre-scripted. Carter was mocked for saying that he had asked his twelve-year-old daughter, Amy, what the most important issue in the campaign was and she answered nuclear nonproliferation. Reagan avoided the gaffes Carter's team had counted on and closed his case with the simple, devastating question that would become a staple for future campaigns: "Are you better off than you were four years ago?"

Stuart Spencer, who had returned to the Reagan fold after his work for Ford in 1976, conceded that Carter may have won on substance, but not on overall presentation. "Carter on the issues did a pretty good job," he said, "but he had a totally different style than Reagan." For Reagan, the debate was a chance to show the public that he was not the scary extremist or bumbling actor that Carter had portrayed, in effect reassuring voters who might have been nervous about turning over the presidency to him. Some of the skeptics were on his own team.

After the debate, Baker called Margaret Tutwiler and asked what she had thought of the showdown. Although she had already voted for Reagan by absentee ballot in her home state, she had been among the strongest loyalists for Bush and had remained dubious of the Republican nominee. But she told Baker she no longer questioned her vote.

"Are you serious?" Baker asked.

Dead serious, she answered.

Baker had already grown to trust Tutwiler's political instincts. If she was now fully on board, he concluded, then they had accomplished what they needed.

"We have won this election," Baker told her.

CHAPTER 8

Troika

O ne day late in the fall of 1980, as the campaign headed toward a climactic Election Day, Baker got a call from Stuart Spencer. Get to the
airport, Spencer said.

"What are you getting me into?" Baker asked.

"Something you'd like," Spencer replied cryptically.

Baker packed and went to the airport to join Ronald Reagan's traveling
party. Spencer and his co-conspirator, Michael Deaver, Reagan's longtime
confidant, wanted Baker to get some face time with the candidate so the
two could get to know each other.

The secret plan was to convince Reagan that he should make Baker his
White House chief of staff if he won. It was more than a little presumptuous, of course, to begin handing out West Wing offices before anyone
had even cast a ballot, but Spencer and Deaver were looking beyond the
election in hopes of averting what they thought would be a disaster. The
intramural feuds of Reagan's advisers were just as vicious, if not more so,
than the institutionalized conflicts with the Democrats, as Washington—
and Baker—would soon see firsthand.

In the inner circle of Californians surrounding the candidate, the
widespread assumption had long been that Ed Meese would be Reagan's
presidential chief of staff, just as he had been in the governor's office in
Sacramento. Avuncular, jowly, and deeply conservative, Meese was a predictable but not entirely plausible choice for the job. Born in Oakland,
Meese went away to study at Yale University, where he became chairman
of the Yale Debating Association, then served two years in the Army. He
finally returned west to earn a law degree at the University of California at
Berkeley, where he was a moot court champion, then went on to serve as
a local prosecutor. He loved wildlife paintings and old ship models and he

had a sense of humor too, collecting pigs from around the world, cheekily embracing the term for police used by 1960s radicals. After Reagan's 1966 election as governor, Meese joined his staff as legal affairs secretary before moving up to run the office for five years. He became so adept at mapping the governor's conservative philosophy that the biographer Lou Cannon dubbed him "Reagan's geographer."

But Meese had no Washington experience and was famously disorganized. Those around Reagan joked that any piece of paper that found its way into Meese's briefcase would never be seen again. "Ed Meese couldn't organize a two-car funeral," Spencer said. "You walked into his office and there would be papers on his chair, on his floor, everywhere." Deaver had an even harsher view. He considered Meese "a bumbling idiot" and felt aggrieved that Meese treated him as "the guy who carried the suitcases," as a friend put it. Spencer and Deaver both resolved to save Reagan from his own worst instincts. And they both had an idea about who should actually be chief of staff instead of Meese.

Spencer, who had grown close to Baker on the Ford campaign, and Deaver, who had admired his performance managing Bush's effort and gotten to know him during the fall campaign sprint, believed that Baker's methodical organizational skills and relatively nonideological approach would suit Reagan well in the White House. Spencer and Deaver each later claimed credit for torpedoing Meese's chances and putting the idea of Baker in Reagan's head. Deaver remembered sitting down with Reagan alone for a drink on the terrace of a borrowed country estate in Middleburg, Virginia, outside Washington, before the election. When the question of who would serve as chief of staff came up, Reagan indicated that he had always figured it would be Meese. Deaver gently steered him away from that, suggesting that Meese could serve in another valuable role and that a new president might want a more seasoned Washington figure.

Do you have anyone in mind, Reagan asked.

"Yes," Deaver answered. "Jim Baker."

"Jim Baker," Reagan repeated, intrigued. "That's an interesting thought."

Deaver left it at that but realized something had to be done to keep Meese happy or Reagan might not go along with the plan. So he called William Clark, another of the Californians in Reagan's retinue, and asked for advice. Clark suggested making Meese counselor to the president. Deaver liked it. Meese could be in charge of policymaking, which would play to his strengths, while Baker actually ran the White House.

Deaver also conspired with Nancy Reagan. No one was more critical to personnel choices in Reagan's world. Fiercely devoted to her Ronnie, Nancy had a finely tuned loyalty detector and was a far more astute judge of staff than her conflict-averse husband. "Dad looks at half a glass of water and says, 'Look at this! It's half full,'" said Michael Reagan, his son from his first marriage. "Nancy is always trying to figure out: 'Who stole the other half from my husband?'"

When Deaver asked her about Meese, she dismissed him as a "jump-off-the-cliff-with-the-flag-flying conservative" and was open to alternatives. Baker made a good impression; he was handsome, debonair, and carried himself well. He struck Nancy as what a chief of staff should seem like. "He was well mannered," said Fred Ryan, a young Reagan aide who would go on to spend much time with Nancy after the White House as president of the Reagan Foundation. "Baker met her image of the man Hollywood would cast for the role," said Ed Rollins, another Reagan adviser. And perhaps most important, Baker had deeply impressed both the candidate and his wife by pressing for debates and demonstrating his faith in Reagan's ability to win them when they themselves had doubts.

With Deaver already on the case, Spencer brought up the matter with both Reagans in their hotel suite in Dallas the day after the debate with Carter, the same forum that Baker had helped to orchestrate. When Spencer noted that many expected Meese to be chief of staff, both Reagans to his surprise responded the same way: "Oh no, no, no." After running through several alternatives, Spencer mentioned Baker.

"You'll guarantee he'll work from Ronnie's agenda and not his own?" Nancy Reagan asked.

"That's an easy one," Spencer replied. "He understands that."

Spencer suggested that he put Baker on the campaign plane so the candidate could get to know him. No one else would know the purpose.

Reagan was soon convinced. Unaware of the machinations behind his back, Meese still expected to be chief of staff and indeed had already mapped out an organizational chart showing himself at the top. As votes began to roll in on Election Day, he headed to Reagan's house in Pacific Palisades for lunch with the candidate and Deaver. Over tunafish salad, Reagan shocked Meese by saying he wanted Baker as his chief of staff. Meese, he said, would be counselor to the president in charge of policy. "If you become burdened with all the details of the White House, you're not going to have time," Reagan told him.

Meese was devastated. Deaver thought he looked like someone had punched him in the stomach. "I don't know whether I can accept this," Meese told Deaver as they left lunch.

That night, at the Century Plaza Hotel in Los Angeles, Baker and the rest of the Reagan team celebrated a landmark election victory. Reagan swamped Carter with 51 percent of the popular vote to 41 percent for the incumbent, with John Anderson taking most of the rest, the first time an elected president had been beaten at the ballot box since 1932. Reagan's landslide in the Electoral College was even more impressive. He won forty-four states and collected ten times as many electoral votes as Carter, shaking up the old political order by reaching deep into working-class and suburban communities that had traditionally gone for the other party. In the end, Reagan won 27 percent of self-identified Democrats, crossover voters who became known as Reagan Democrats. His coattails were long—Republicans captured twelve additional Senate seats to take control of the upper chamber for the first time since Dwight Eisenhower was president and picked up thirty-five seats in the House to narrow the still-sizable Democratic majority. Reagan had capitalized on broad public disenchantment with Washington and the economy to lead a fresh conservative movement to power with the slogan "Let's Make America Great Again." Now Reagan needed someone to help translate his slogan into political reality.

SUSAN BAKER FIRST REALIZED what was about to happen at the election night victory party when she overheard Deaver talking with Spencer about making her Jimmy chief of staff. Baker had known of their plot, but had never even mentioned the possibility to her. She was distraught. That night, she slept fitfully. "I woke up and I just cried and cried and cried," she remembered.

She confronted her husband. "Honey, I can't do this," she told him. "I am wiped out. I'm exhausted. We have all these kids, we have all these problems. I can't do it. I can't live in a fishbowl and do what I need to do for our family."

He tried to mollify her, saying they should just see what would happen. She knew better than to believe his reassurances. Still, she would not stand in his way. She never had.

The morning after the election, Baker returned to the Century Plaza for breakfast with Meese, which was predictably awkward. Baker did not know for sure whether he would be offered the job, nor was he sure what Meese knew.

"The president's going to talk to you about some things that will involve us working together down the line," Meese told him elliptically.

He did not elaborate and Baker decided not to delve any further until he had talked with Reagan.

"I'm sure we can, Ed," he replied simply.

From there, Baker met with the president-elect, who promptly offered him the job of chief of staff. But Reagan made clear he wanted Meese taken care of. "I want you to be my chief of staff, but I hope you'll work it out with Ed," Reagan said.

Finding a way to satisfy Meese would be Baker's first priority. So he did what lawyers do. He sat down with Meese and the two drafted a contract—in this case, a one-page list of duties split between them so there would be no misunderstandings later. It turned out that his negotiating skills translated from law to politics as Baker crafted a way for a rival to swallow a defeat by making it look like it was not one. "He really believes in saving face," said Margaret Tutwiler. "He has this saying that Reagan always used to say—pay attention when you have somebody behind an eight ball that you let them leave the table saving face because next week you could be behind the eight ball."

He took what he and Meese agreed to and had it typed up. Playing to his counterpart's ego, Baker listed Meese's column and his proposed title of counselor to the president first. He sweetened the package by suggesting that Meese have cabinet rank, while Baker would not. Meese would also belong to a "Super Cabinet Executive Committee" and chair it in Reagan's absence. In addition, he would coordinate the work of the National Security Council and the domestic policy office.

Baker, for his part, would be chief of staff and would belong to the same cabinet committee. He would "control all in and out paper flow" to the president as well as his schedule and appointments, preside over White House staff meetings, manage legislative affairs, and operate from the southwest corner office in the West Wing customarily occupied by the chief of staff. Baker and Meese would share oversight of the budget office, economic and environmental councils, and trade negotiator.

To seal the deal, Baker asked to see Reagan and Meese together to show them his power-sharing agreement. Deaver started to join them. "Mike," Baker told him, "I don't want you in the room." Deaver was shocked. "I had never been out of the room of any discussion," he recalled, not to mention that he was the one who had just helped seal Baker's ascension. But Baker wanted to smooth it over with Meese without anyone else around other than the president-elect. He was adamant.

Reagan had no problem with the division of labor. Baker did add one final provision during the meeting, however, after Meese asked for full walk-in privileges to the Oval Office. In the Meese column, Baker scribbled beneath the neatly typewritten column, "Attend any meeting which Pres. attends—w/his consent." Then he wrote the same words under his own column to keep on par. Without realizing it, Meese had given up the right to see Reagan alone.

But the contract worked to assuage Meese, at least temporarily. Meese was satisfied that his would be a prestigious role. "I thought it over, particularly the fact that I would be a member of the cabinet, which had a lot of attraction," he said later. And so he and Baker scratched their initials at the bottom of the page on November 17, not quite two weeks after the election. "*OK—JAB III*," and right below it: "*OK—EM*." Baker slipped the contract into his desk drawer in case he ever needed it to remind Meese of the terms of their deal.

Meese and his team believed he would be the top man in the White House, or at least tried to spin it that way. "It will become obvious that there is one Number 1 and that is Ed Meese," an ally boasted to *The New York Times* the day that Reagan announced their appointments. But what Meese and other newcomers to Washington did not understand was that Baker had kept control of all the levers of power that mattered most. Meese had the status of a cabinet member, but Baker knew that provided little beyond bragging rights. "In the White House, cabinet rank doesn't mean a thing," he said years later. What mattered was that "you have the power, whether you have the rank or not," Baker said. And Baker had the power.

He would be in charge of the paper, the schedule, the hiring and firing, the press and legislative affairs offices—in other words, the parts of a White House that really shaped a presidency. Nothing would get to Reagan without Baker seeing it first and no one would work for the president without Baker signing off. Even the matter of the West Wing corner office, so carefully noted on the contract, was a critical victory for Baker. By operating out of the same space that the chief of staff had in the past, Baker would be perceived as the man in charge. Meese would occupy the northwest corner office previously used by Henry Kissinger, but pedigree could not make up for location and all the meetings that mattered would be held in Baker's office. In Washington, real estate is power. Baker had conducted his first negotiation of the Reagan presidency, and he had won.

JUST AS IMPORTANT as the division of labor was the third member of the trio that would run the Reagan White House, which ultimately came to be called the Troika. Michael Deaver would serve as deputy White House chief of staff in charge of Reagan himself, the body man who would look after the care and feeding of the president and his public image.

Deaver was the perfect choice. Close enough to Reagan to be like a son, Deaver was now forty-two years old and he had already worked for the new president long enough that he could judge his moods and interpret his needs. A native of Bakersfield, California, Deaver at one point during college thought about becoming an Episcopal priest but ended up enrolling in a sales training program at IBM before dropping out to indulge his passion for the piano. Trolling for tips in cocktail lounges proved unsustainable and he eventually went into politics, working for William Clark in Reagan's administration in Sacramento. As Clark moved his way up, he took Deaver with him.

Uncomfortable with Nancy Reagan, Clark assigned Deaver to deal with her and the two forged a strong, personal bond, making him practically a member of the family. Now, Baker hoped Deaver would carry his almost-family status with him to the White House. Baker and Deaver had found themselves in sync since the campaign and quickly grew close. "Mike and Jim Baker hit it off beautifully," Margaret Tutwiler said. Baker recognized that in any power trio, it was essential to be part of the two and not the one; he had every intention of making sure that he and Deaver were the two. No one was going to make Baker the odd man out.

But it was hard to deny that the Troika was ill conceived, a prescription for perpetual dysfunction, with no clear chain of command and three titans wrestling for power. "I went ballistic," said Spencer. "I said, 'That's idiotic. You can't run the place like that.' I lost that one. I blame a lot of it on Baker because he put all this down in writing like a lawyer and Meese is a lawyer. There's two lawyers negotiating over who's going to run the bathrooms."

The vice president–elect, meanwhile, was little more than an afterthought as Baker scrapped for maximum authority in the nascent Reagan White House. Some of Bush's other loyalists thought it all a little self-serving, even disloyal of Baker—among them Barbara Bush. "Now that did piss off Barbara Bush, big-time," recalled Pete Teeley. "She thought he used George Bush in some way to ingratiate himself to the Reagan people."

She had reason to be astonished by the swift change in fortunes. Baker, after all, had spent much of the past five years trying to keep Reagan out of the Oval Office. Now Reagan was staking the success of his presidency on Baker, the campaign manager for the last politician who beat him (Ford in

1976) and the most stubborn rival he had in the most recent primary campaign (Bush in 1980). It said something about Reagan's pragmatism that he wanted someone who was not an ideologue to run his White House and something about his nature that he held no grudges.

But others did. The notion of Baker overseeing the Reagan White House outraged many of the new president's conservative supporters. They had worked for years to take over the party and then the White House, only to have the victory undercut when Reagan handed the keys to a man they considered an unreliable Republican. To them, Baker was everything that was wrong with the GOP, an accommodationist who did not care about scaling back the size and scope of government. "Baker had a very different agenda," concluded Richard Viguerie, a conservative direct mail pioneer who was among the leading voices of the right. "He had a Bush-like agenda."

Baker knew they were bitching about him. During the transition, Pete Teeley informed Baker that an aide had run into Donald "Buz" Lukens, a former Republican congressman who was "bad-mouthing JAB in an incredible fashion all over town," according to a memo about the conversation. "JAB is nothing more than a representative of the Eastern Liberal Establishment," Lukens told the aide, and Reagan would end up governing with a Bush administration "comprised of re-treads" from the Nixon and Ford administrations. Lukens, the memo added, vowed to "make life miserable" for the new gang and Teeley predicted that Baker would see more negative press "directed at you by the right wing."

Baker tried to shore up his position by recruiting a few prominent Reaganites to serve in visible positions in hopes of buying off his critics. He created a new Office of Political Affairs and offered the job of running it to Lyn Nofziger, a crusty, pudgy, rumpled, and unfiltered former reporter with a goatee who had worked as communications director for Reagan in the governor's office and considered himself a keeper of the flame. Nofziger accepted and assumed his appointment meant that Reagan's conservatives really would have influence in the new White House. But rather than give him an office in the West Wing, Baker installed Nofziger across the street in the Old Executive Office Building far from the Oval Office, and the Californian soon came to doubt Baker's intentions. "I was a sop to the conservatives who had fought and bled with and for Reagan right through to his presidency and who now were feeling a tiny bit betrayed. And a lot ignored," Nofziger wrote later. "He was later to throw the 'I-hired-you' in my face as if I were supposed to be grateful. In fact, my presence did more for him than he could, or would, do for me."

Indeed, with Nofziger on board, Baker felt free to do exactly what Buz Lukens feared, bringing in colleagues from the Ford and Bush campaigns and elsewhere in the Republican establishment. He hired David Gergen to handle communications, Max Friedersdorf to run legislative affairs, and John Rogers to handle administrative matters. Margaret Tutwiler wanted to come along too. "Can't I just be, until we figure out what it is, your jack-of-all-trades, your Indian?" she asked. He readily agreed, and she would serve that same role for Baker, with different titles, for a dozen years. "Reagan pretty much gave me free rein and I brought in a lot of non-Reaganite Republicans," Baker said. They were the Baker Republicans, a powerful and fiercely loyal cadre for him in the internal fights to come. "Baker had all these lieutenants and we all swore by him and thought the world of him," Gergen said.

Most important was Baker's selection of Dick Darman as his top deputy. Widely considered brilliant if prickly, Darman had been a protégé of the legendary Elliot Richardson, quitting the Nixon Administration along with him in the Saturday Night Massacre before returning to government as an assistant commerce secretary in the Ford administration, where his new boss turned out to be Baker. A pragmatic technocrat and almost the polar opposite of the movement conservatives who had boosted Reagan politically, Darman was a one-man policy generator who had spent his interregnum out of government at Harvard's Kennedy School of Government; unlike most of Reagan's top aides, he had a sense of how to translate vague goals into concrete programs. He would prove to be Baker's most critical alter ego for the next eight years, forming what Bob Schieffer, the CBS News correspondent, called "one of the most powerful alliances of the Reagan era."

Conservatives watched what was happening with alarm. "The worst thing Baker did was personnel," said Viguerie. "He staffed the personnel office with Bush types. Not entirely, of course. But for the most part, the people who came into the administration were Bush-ites, not Reaganites. He populated the Reagan administration with people like himself."

They were right to be worried. Ideologically, Baker was not in fact on the same page with his new boss, as he acknowledged in a conversation with a political scientist during the transition that winter before Reagan's inauguration. In it, Baker showed he already had a plan for the president's first year that was markedly different from what some key supporters had expected, a Reagan rollout that emphasized the importance of getting the economy back on track even if it meant postponing action on social issues important to the conservative base. And, Baker added, should it prove necessary to walk away from the new president's cherished tax cut proposal, then he would not hesitate to do so.

If Baker was not exactly keeping the right happy, he was not doing much better at home. He had mentioned Susan's discontent to the president. On the day that Baker's appointment was announced, Reagan tried to reassure Susan that it would work out. He put his hands on both of her shoulders and said, "Let me tell you something, Susan, your man is going to be home every night at five."

She appreciated the gesture, but she knew that would never be true. Over the next year, whenever she saw him, Reagan would bring up the subject. "Is your guy coming home on time?" he would ask.

"No," she would answer honestly. Eventually, she told him, "Mr. President, I've given him a dispensation."

EVERY SUCCESSFUL PRESIDENT had relied on someone like Baker to help steer his administration. Abraham Lincoln had two young secretaries, John Nicolay and John Hay. Woodrow Wilson had Colonel Edward House, who was practically his alter ego. In tapping his campaign manager, the former New Hampshire governor Sherman Adams, to guide his White House, Dwight Eisenhower became the first to use the title chief of staff, adopting the term from the military. Adams eventually resigned in a scandal over an expensive vicuña fur coat and Oriental rug he accepted from a businessman under investigation. But the title endured and so did Adams's expansive definition of the job. A famous joke of the era had one Democrat musing to another, "What if Sherman Adams died and Eisenhower became president?" With a White House staff roughly two-thirds bigger than Adams's, a Cold War to run, an economy in free fall, and an outsider president to train, Baker would have an even tougher assignment.

He was well aware of the challenges. "This is a tough job where you make lots of enemies and not many friends," he wrote to Mark White a month after the election. Baker noted tongue in cheek that had White not been such a good candidate during their 1978 contest for Texas attorney general, he might not be in this position now. "I've seen in the press some very nice statements you've made about me," Baker added. "You're still a damn good liar."

The next morning, Baker picked up *The Washington Post* and noticed a column by Richard Cohen about Hamilton Jordan, who served as Jimmy Carter's chief of staff until the middle of 1980. Jordan had been accused of snorting cocaine and exhibiting boorish behavior in a nightclub, although he was later exonerated by an investigation.

"What happened to Jordan has got to give others pause before they would enter high government service," Cohen wrote. "He came in strutting and got knocked silly for his pretensions. He got investigated by the government and the press, his private life went public and anyone with anything mean to say about him had a choice of either going to the newspapers or to the special prosecutor." It was a cautionary tale, and Baker's assistant scratched out a note on the column indicating he wanted to keep it: "Per JAB: clip & save."

Baker was determined not to let anything like that happen to him. He had seen how Washington chewed up and spit out would-be power brokers. It was a tough city. Hubris was an occupational hazard. The media was always ready to pounce. One day you were the man next to the president of the United States, the next you were cast aside, no longer relevant, perhaps even humiliated. This was why Captain Baker always told his grandson to stay away from politics.

But his father taught preparation. To get ready for his new role, Baker turned to Dick Cheney. As the two sat down, Baker pulled out a yellow legal pad and took notes. None of Cheney's advice was brilliant or original, but it amounted to a catechism of Washington's collective wisdom. Many chiefs, before and after Baker, would fail to heed one or all of Cheney's precepts and find themselves in trouble because of it:

> Restore power and authority to the executive branch.
> Orderly schedules and orderly paper flow way you protect the president.
> Most valuable asset in D.C. is time of Ronald Reagan.
> Keep a low profile. Talk to press always on background. If you become
>   a major public figure you lose credibility, feathering your own nest
>   rather than serving the president.

Baker also sat down with other former chiefs, Republican and Democrat. Jack Watson, who held the job for Carter after Jordan, advised him to be an "honest broker" and to "resolve disputes that don't need to go to the Pres," which struck Baker enough that he jotted it down on his legal pad. Donald Rumsfeld gave Baker a twelve-page guide he titled "Rumsfeld's Rules for 'The Assistant to the President.'" It started with "Don't play President" and ended with "Don't play President." In between were a number of useful maxims, including "Assume that everything you say and do will be on the front page of the Washington Post the next morning and conduct yourself accordingly, it may well be."

For Baker, much of this came intuitively, which was a good thing given that he was in fact quite inexperienced in actually governing, having only served barely a year as undersecretary of commerce, hardly one of the capital's power positions. For all the talk about his Washington experience, the truth was that Baker had an innate gift for determining what mattered to others and how to use those motivations to get what he wanted. "He had one of the best antenna for where possibilities lay and how to get to move people in that direction of anybody I've met in contemporary American life," David Gergen remembered.

His cousin Preston Moore told a reporter from *The Christian Science Monitor* trying to figure out Baker at the advent of the Reagan presidency that Washington's new man would be a "velvet hammer" in the White House. The phrase would stick.

CHAPTER 9

Shit Detector

Twenty-eight years after his first Inauguration Day, Baker would end up inside the mansion, not just watching from the outside. The morning of January 20, 1981, dawned with atypical warmth in Washington. The temperature climbed to 56 degrees as Ronald Reagan, dressed in a charcoal gray coat, striped trousers, and dove gray vest and tie, took the oath of office as the fortieth president at 11:57 a.m. on the West Front of the United States Capitol. With Baker sitting a few rows behind him, Reagan became the first president to start his tenure on the side of the building facing west, a nod to his roots on the country's frontier. In his inaugural address, Reagan spoke of big dreams, but also declared war on the government he was about to take over. "In the present crisis," he said, "government is not the solution to our problem; government *is* the problem."

William Safire, the former Nixon speechwriter turned *New York Times* columnist, gave the speech "a respectable seven" on a scale of ten. But the real drama took place halfway around the world just as Reagan finished speaking. At 12:25 p.m., an Algerian Boeing 727 lifted off from Tehran with the remaining fifty-two American hostages bound for freedom, ending the 444-day ordeal that had humiliated a superpower and crippled Jimmy Carter's presidency. The Iranians had reached terms with Carter's envoys during the twilight hours of his administration and then, in one final affront, timed the release to deny him the satisfaction of securing the release before his term officially expired. Still, it unleashed a wave of national relief.

Baker was relieved too. As he listened to Reagan announce the news at a congressional luncheon that followed the inaugural ceremony, he knew that the new presidency had been given a clean slate. "No brilliant Hollywood producer," wrote James Reston in the next day's *Times*, "could have dared to imagine so reckless a script for Reagan on his Inauguration Day." Even so, Baker was not about to dwell on good news. There was plenty of grim reality. "About to inherit worst economic mess of any Pres. in 50 years," he wrote on a legal pad before the ceremony. "So first order of business—get a handle on the economy!" Inflation was running at 13.5 percent and unemployment at 7.5 percent. As the Federal Reserve tried to tame rising costs, Reagan inherited a prime interest rate of 20.5 percent, making it hard to start a new business or buy a new home or car. The top marginal income tax rate stood at 70 percent.

Baker was not wrong about the mess. It was the reason Reagan had won. But Baker still was not sure how to fix it—or how to get his new boss to do what he wanted. Baker's friend George Bush, his Houston companion of a thousand sweaty tennis sets, moved in to the vice president's mansion on Massachusetts Avenue with a prestigious new title but an uncertain portfolio. Baker, though, would be just down the hall from the Oval Office, closer in reality if not in the Constitution to running the country than Bush had yet achieved. He had just turned fifty years old and was surrounded by internal enemies. His own family was unhappy with him. Bush and his clan were still more than a bit bruised by Baker's swift ascension in the service of the recent enemy. He had little relevant experience to guide him in figuring out how to turn around a flailing economy. He had hardly ever worked with lawmakers and certainly never shepherded a major piece of legislation through an opposition-controlled Congress. The Velvet Hammer, already formidable in reputation, had not yet seen real action.

The first challenge would be Reagan himself. To start, Baker had to get to know him, to somehow penetrate the amiable facade of celebrity that had guarded the new president since his B-movie days. The son of an alcoholic shoe salesman, Reagan grew up in Illinois and parlayed a middling career as a radio announcer and film actor into political stardom with his campaign speech promoting Barry Goldwater for president in 1964. A New Deal Democrat and former Screen Actors Guild president who grew disenchanted with the left, Reagan became a hero to conservatives and served two terms as governor of California.

Baker had never been much of a fan of the movie actor. He vaguely recalled seeing *Hellcats of the Navy*, the 1957 film in which Reagan played a World War II submarine commander opposite his wife, then still going by Nancy Davis professionally—the only time the two appeared on-screen together. But if Baker ever saw *Bedtime for Bonzo*, the Reagan movie about a lovable chimpanzee often used as a shorthand for the future president's less-than-monumental contribution to the arts, he did not remember it. Like his friends on the Bush campaign and in the country clubs, he remained dubious about Hollywood as the proper training ground for the leader of the free world.

Baker had first met the future president during Richard Nixon's 1972 campaign when Reagan came to Houston to speak at an event at the new local campaign headquarters. He was impressed with the California governor's political skills, but for years viewed Reagan warily. "We thought he was a nut," Baker said later. "I didn't necessarily think that," he added, "but that was the line on him. Everybody said that he was." Reagan's bellicose rhetoric had fueled the impression of a trigger-happy Cold Warrior. "We honestly thought he was going to start a nuclear war and we were petrified," Baker said.

After Stuart Spencer and Michael Deaver put him on the campaign plane, Baker came to see Reagan as a more complex figure than he had assumed—not an intellectual by any means, but someone with core values and more common sense than he was given credit for. Reagan had managed something neither of Baker's previous two candidates had done, to inspire a nation and run the treacherous gauntlet of a national campaign to the presidency. He was a winner and Baker liked winning. "Jim had tremendous respect for the fact of how he got to the White House, the fact that he got there, the fact that he looked at what he wanted to achieve and could make that decision," said John Rogers, who handled administrative matters for Baker.

Reagan's easygoing exterior, of course, masked a man of driving ambition and more calculation than his public image suggested. "He was the most warmly ruthless man I've ever seen," observed Martin Anderson, his domestic policy adviser. Reagan was intensely impersonal, distant not only from staff but also from his own children, in ways that resonated with Baker. "He wasn't buddy-buddy with anybody," said Meese. Deaver thought Reagan could be elegant and self-mocking "but he does not give back much introspection." Baker was not much for reflection or emotional bonding either. "Neither one of them let a lot of people in," Rogers said. "The only people who got in were the loves of their life. There was a veneer and you cannot get beyond the veneer."

They also shared a love of the outdoors—Reagan preferred to ride horses while Baker loved hunting, but both men relished the solitude. "How many people do you know can sit in a turkey blind and enjoy it?" asked Margaret Tutwiler. "Some people cannot spend time by themselves.

They have to always have this motion and people." Like Reagan, Baker "definitely is social. But he also can spend time with himself."

Their differences, however, would come to matter almost as much. In many ways, it would be Baker's job to compensate for Reagan's weaknesses. The new president, as Baker soon learned, cared little for detail or rigorous analysis. Early on, Baker and his team would prepare ferociously for a briefing, outlining every word they wanted to impart to Reagan and thinking through every question he might ask. Then after they sat down with him to go through the briefing and the time for questions arrived, Reagan would blithely end with a cheery, "Sounds great" or "Go to it." No questions.

As chief of staff, Baker had to make himself the president's alter ego, wielding power on his behalf without overstepping his bounds. Some of it was about proving himself to Reagan. "I ran the campaign that called it voodoo economics," Baker noted. "Reagan never let me forget that." At the same time, Baker was not a yes-man. Some people have the knack for disagreeing with a president; others never learn it. Baker was seemingly born with it. "Jimmy didn't kiss his ass," said Stuart Spencer. "If he disagreed with him, he told him where and why and how."

Each morning at 7:30 a.m., Baker hosted Meese and Deaver for a breakfast of bacon and eggs in his office to prepare for the day. Then, when Reagan arrived at the Oval Office at 9 a.m., the president's secretary called Baker to let him know and the three members of the Troika headed down the hall to brief the president on overnight events around the world, go over the day's schedule, and talk through issues that could not wait. Baker quickly realized that Reagan liked to start these meetings with a joke—and so Baker made a point of bringing his own each morning. They often would not meet the standards of appropriate public discourse, or private discourse, for that matter. "He could have a wicked tongue," said Karen Morgan, a longtime Baker aide. "Mr. Baker could be a boy's boy." So could the president. One of Reagan's favorites was about an aging Arab at an Israeli retirement home who was delighted that everyone seemed to think he was still sexually active. How did he know they thought that? Because everyone kept calling him "that fucking Arab."

A FEW DAYS AFTER THE INAUGURATION, Baker and Meese appeared together for a joint interview on PBS's *MacNeil/Lehrer Report*. They were grilled about their unusual arrangement.

"What is the difference in your two jobs?" the interviewer asked.

Meese handled policy, they explained, while Baker handled the political side. "It's a fairly logical division of functions, really," Baker answered. "There's so much over here to say grace over that one person can hardly do it."

But even as they gave a chummy performance, Baker slipped in the caveat that really mattered. All paper and appointments crossed his desk. "Ultimately," he said, "everything goes through one central point, though, in my office."

From his new corner office, Baker was careful not to assert himself so much in meetings that it would scrape up against Meese and the other power players. Indeed, many inside and outside the administration mistakenly concluded that Meese had actually secured the dominant position in the power-sharing structure. Baker had kept a low profile during the transition, allowing Meese to run it unhindered. Larry Speakes, who had been selected as deputy press secretary, watched the transition with growing alarm and warned Baker that Meese was trying to box him out. Baker "didn't seem too worried," Speakes noticed.

In early meetings in the White House, Meese was more vocal while Baker sat back and deferred to him. Baker still had a lot to learn. Just after the inauguration, he gathered the hundreds of members of the White House staff in an auditorium in the executive office building next door to address the new team. "It was terrible," John Rogers said. "I remember being there and thinking this is the worst speech I ever heard. He was totally inarticulate and disconnected."

Meese appeared "very sure of his authority" while Baker and Deaver "seemed to be lesser players, hanging back a bit," remembered Alexander Haig, the new secretary of state. While Meese offered frank views on issues, Haig said, Baker remained elusive, "reluctant to reveal his opinions and hardly ever expressed a strong preference in clear terms."

In the opening weeks of the administration, Meese was sometimes referred to as "the prime minister" running the country for the king. *The Washington Post* called him "the second most important person in Washington," saying that Reagan had established a system in which the government is "managed by and reports through Meese." But while Meese appeared on the Sunday shows and spoke for Reagan with the confidence of a longtime consigliere, Baker was methodically building his authority. "Every single day Ed Meese was in that White House he lost power or gave up power," Ed Rollins said. "Every single day Jim Baker was in that White House he accumulated power—or Dick Darman accumulated power." For one thing, Meese's staff was simply outclassed by Baker's team in the internal bureaucratic wars that dominated the initial days of the Reagan White House. A key example was a turf masterstroke dreamed up by Darman, who got Baker to form a Legislative Strategy Group to coordinate the approach to Congress, headed, of course, by them. Meese was formally in charge of policy, but there was no real policy if it could not get through the bureaucracy or Congress, so Baker's control over execution gave him de facto control over policy too. "One by one, Baker gathered the levers of power to himself," Haig observed in a memoir, "and as Meese receded from the news and from his early predominance, Baker, in closer and closer collaboration with Deaver, became more and more the puissant figure next to the president."

One of those Baker wrestled with in those early months was Haig, who had occupied the same office where Baker now sat as Richard Nixon's last White House chief of staff. Gruff, driven, manipulative, and supremely self-assured, Haig was raised in a middle-class family in Philadelphia, lost his father to cancer, and joined the Army. He served in Korea and Vietnam, earning various commendations for courage, including a Distinguished Service Cross, but it was his service on the White House front that put stars on his shoulder. Landing on the National Security Council staff, Haig had proved a masterful infighter, outmaneuvering Nixon White House rivals—including his boss, Henry Kissinger—to earn the trust of an embattled president as the Watergate investigation closed in. Haig rose from colonel to four-star general in three years, one of the most remarkable ascents for a deskbound officer in modern times. More importantly, he became Nixon's last man standing, serving as virtual president while the real one melted down and steering Nixon into resigning rather than subjecting the nation to an all-out impeachment battle.

If Haig had seemed something of a cool head guarding the nation's interests during Nixon's final days, he had succumbed to his own considerable ambition ever since. By 1980, having once served as an unelected quasi-president, he imagined he could do the job for real and flirted with a campaign for the White House against Ronald Reagan and George Bush. Although he did not run, he had not given up his goal. So when Reagan considered him for secretary of state at Nixon's urging, the incoming president and his close friend, Paul Laxalt, first wanted to make sure Haig kept his own aspirations in check. After the election, Reagan specifically asked Baker and Laxalt "to go talk to Haig and we met with him in one of the hotels in Washington, I remember that, and he denied having any ambition to run for president," Baker recalled. "So Reagan said, 'That's who I want,' and he picked him."

But the denial hardly meant that Haig could be contained; he saw his own role at the State Department as expansive. No White House staffer like Baker was going to stop him. "He just had contempt for anyone except himself," said Richard Allen, the new national security adviser. Haig was determined to have decisive control over foreign policy and produced a directive to codify that. On Inauguration Day, hours after Reagan was sworn in, while everyone was still in their ceremonial morning coats, Haig swept into the Oval Office with the draft order in hand and passed it to Reagan. Baker and other critics were astonished at what they saw as an ill-advised maneuver to get Reagan to sign such a document on the spot. "That didn't go down real well with a lot of people, particularly Meese and me and Reagan," Baker said. "It was a sort of power play by the secretary of state to be the head of crisis management without working it out collegially with everybody. He just asked the president to sign this document, which the president didn't do." Haig later denied that he intended for the president to approve it immediately, but the damage was done.

Meese pulled Haig, Baker, and Allen into his new office to go over the paper that Haig had brought. "Baker's a quicker study than Meese and Jim Baker looked up and said, 'By this document, you'd have control of everything outside the United States,'" recalled Allen. Meese conducted his own "dogged critique of the paper" and put it in his briefcase, from which it would never emerge. Haig, bristling at the notion of mere aides blocking him, felt that his understandings with Reagan "were disappearing in a haze of nitpicking."

Undaunted, Haig publicly pronounced himself "the vicar of American foreign policy" when he was sworn in two days later, choosing a term of religious pretension that would be used against him in the months to come. He also did not give up his power play, reworking his document and resubmitting it weeks later, only to find himself again ignored. Instead, Baker, Meese, and Allen came up with a plan of their own, one that would define who would be in charge of "crisis management" in case the president himself was not available. They decided to put the vice president in command in such a circumstance and convinced Reagan to sign. Haig was furious and made little effort to hide it. He told a congressional subcommittee that he viewed the decision with "a lack of enthusiasm." His aides put out the word that he had pounded the table in exasperation during internal meetings on the subject.

Everything about the new White House seemed to offend Haig's sensibilities. When he arrived for the first cabinet meeting, he was stunned to find Baker and Meese sitting at the table, rather than in seats on the back wall where aides belonged. In the Nixon White House, H. R. Haldeman and John Ehrlichman "would never have dared" to sit at the table during a cabinet meeting, Haig said. In the weeks and months to come, Haig took offense at what he considered the "schoolboyish habit of scribbling and passing notes" by Baker and some of the others. If he suspected they were commenting on him, he was right—Baker indeed was passing notes about Haig. During one meeting, where Haig's tone had turned especially bellicose, Meese scribbled a few words and passed them to Baker.

"How did we get to WW III while I was out?" he asked Baker.

"We are not at WW III," Baker wrote back. Citing a favorite Haig phrase, he added: "We are only at the fucking disaster stage!"

Baker enjoyed the exchange at Haig's expense so much he saved it in his files. On another occasion, Baker passed a colleague a note titled "A. Haig's Relative Degrees of Crises." In the first column, he wrote Haig's favorite phrases and in the second column what they meant. "Crisis" was code for "Alert," he wrote. "Disaster" was code for "Battle Stations." And "Fucking Disaster" was code for "Take Cover."

It was not just a matter of a blowhard colleague. Washington, after all, was filled with them. Baker and Bush worried that Haig's bluster might have real-world consequences, and they were especially concerned that he would find a way to expand the guerrilla wars in Central America that had become proxy battles in the Cold War superpower contest. In public, Haig had decried arms shipments to leftist fighters in El Salvador and suggested the United States might "go to the source," meaning Fidel Castro's regime in Havana. He advocated a naval blockade of Cuba and, according to Michael Deaver, once during a meeting suggested going even further. "Give me the word and I'll make that island a fucking parking lot," Haig erupted. Would he push Reagan to war in Cuba?

Baker called Haig after the go-to-the-source threat. "In essence, he said, 'Al, we agree with you that this gun-running is dangerous, and we wish you well. But would you please get the hell off television?'" recalled David Gergen. The actual words, Gergen said, were hardly that polite. The reply was unprintable too. Baker, though, could do little about Haig's performance off camera in the Situation Room other than shake his head. "He just thought he was crazy," Richard Allen said.

BAKER WANTED Haig off television not just because threatening military action against Cuba would risk blowing up into a war, but because he wanted to maintain "message discipline," a two-word phrase that would come to be uttered more than just about any other by Reagan's White House team. With jobs still hard to find and inflation still out of control, Baker told aides that they should have three priorities at the opening stage of the presidency and all three of them were the economy. In a practical sense, that meant the administration should concentrate its energies on the president's tax and spending program, and only on that.

Less than a week into Reagan's tenure, Baker visited Deaver's office to make a pact to stop the hard-liners from taking the presidency off course into some Cold War misadventure. He pulled a chair up next to Deaver's, behind his desk so that their knees were practically touching. It was so early in their tenure that Deaver could barely find the men's room. But Baker had identified his chief concern about the term to come.

"Let me tell you something," Baker informed him. "Here's your job and my job for the next four years. Those bastards in the NSC want to get us in a war in Central America. And you and I have got to keep them out of it."

"What do you mean, a war in Central America?" Deaver asked.

"I'm telling you, if we get enmeshed in a war, this guy is never going to get reelected. And we've got to get this economic situation straightened out before we get into all this foreign policy bullshit."

"Well, what do you want me to do?"

"I want you to report everything you hear. When you're in the Oval Office, you hear the president. Anything. You and I have to be a team on this."

Deaver agreed.

Even without any foreign policy distractions, Baker knew it would be an uphill fight to convince a Democratic House to approve the Reagan economic plan. Under the president's proposal, income tax rates would be cut by 10 percent each year for three years, a dramatic reduction that would be hard to sell even in the short window of public goodwill granted new presidents at the beginning of their tenure.

Baker's insistence on controlling the agenda also had the benefit of allowing him to dispense with Reagan's more extreme, impractical, or divisive campaign promises, such as abolishing the Department of Education or working to ban abortion. Baker was personally more conservative than his detractors on the right suspected, but he saw only political peril in engaging in quixotic ideological battles. To that end, he kept Reagan from addressing in person the annual anti-abortion rally on the anniversary of the Supreme Court's *Roe v. Wade* decision; instead, Reagan welcomed a few of the activists to the Oval Office. He also made sure the president's copy of *Human Events,* the conservative journal, was diverted to prevent Reagan from getting some crazy idea into his head. "Baker was constantly keeping him away from that kind of trouble and yet somehow doing it in a way where they couldn't really complain," said Hedrick Smith, who had been assigned the White House beat by *The New York Times.*

As he settled into his job, Baker came to understand pretty quickly what his real role was. When Smith asked him one day what was the most important skill for a White House chief of staff, Baker did not use any of the phrases his predecessors had offered up. He did not mention high-minded concepts like loyalty or being an honest broker.

"Shit detector," Baker answered. "It's my job to keep the president from getting into trouble—and when he gets into trouble to get him out of it."

CHAPTER 10

Big Leagues

On the afternoon of March 30, the seventieth day of the new administration, Baker was in his corner office in the West Wing with no idea that there might not be a seventy-first. Then he looked up to find a rattled David Gergen bursting in.

"Do you know what's happened?" he asked. "Somebody's tried to shoot the president—and Brady's been hit."

Reagan had been at the Washington Hilton Hotel just two miles up Connecticut Avenue from the White House addressing a national conference of the AFL-CIO's Building Construction Trades Department, accompanied by his press secretary, Jim Brady. Baker had been supposed to go too but had begged off, sending Michael Deaver in his place. Reagan was leaving the Hilton on a dreary, drizzly afternoon when a disturbed young man trying to impress a Hollywood actress opened fire.

As Baker tried to absorb Gergen's news, the telephone rang. Margaret Tutwiler picked it up. It was 2:38 p.m., eleven minutes after the shooting, and Deaver was on the line from George Washington University Hospital, where Reagan had been rushed. Deaver told her to keep the line open and put Baker on. Deaver told Baker what had happened—how a bullet had whizzed right past him, how Brady and at least one Secret Service agent had been hit, how the president had been thrown roughly into a limousine by another agent and seemed to have been hurt, perhaps with a bruised or broken rib.

"We don't know what the problem is," Deaver said. "It may be a heart attack."

Ed Meese rushed into Baker's office. He had just seen on the electronic board that displayed the president's location that he was en route to the hospital.

Tutwiler announced that Deaver had come back on the open line. Meese picked up another extension to listen.

"He's taken a shot in the back," Deaver reported.

"Shit," exclaimed Baker.

"Jesus," said Meese.

Just then, Jim Brady, his skull pierced by a bullet, was wheeled past a horrified Deaver. "It doesn't look good for Jim," he reported back to Baker and Meese.

Deaver passed the telephone to Daniel Ruge, the White House physician, who was with him at the hospital. The president was losing blood, the doctor explained. He was in serious danger. Baker pulled out his black felt pen and took notes as he listened. "P hit/fighting," he scrawled as other aides looked over his shoulder in shock.

Just like that, Baker's world seemed to have stopped. Not quite eighteen years after the murder of John Kennedy, another president had been hit by a would-be assassin's bullet. Once again, the country was thrown into turmoil. Who was behind it? Was it the work of America's enemies? Did the threat extend beyond this shooting? Most important, would the president make it?

For Baker, this would be the true opening test of his time in the White House. He had quarreled with Al Haig about crisis management, but no one had really considered a scenario like this and no one had had a serious conversation about presidential succession despite Reagan's advanced age. While Baker had prevailed over Haig in making sure that George Bush would be in charge in a crisis, the vice president at the moment was in Texas, where he had just given a speech to a cattlemen's convention. It was up to Baker to decide what to do. For all of his fixation with the Five Ps, nothing in his experience practicing law in Texas or running political campaigns had prepared him for such a moment. All he could do was keep calm and, just as crucially, *appear* calm. He knew that everyone would be looking to him.

Meese announced that he would go to the hospital and Baker decided to go too, but before they left, the phone rang again. Haig was on the line and had heard the news but was still under the impression that Reagan had not been hit. Baker filled him in.

"It looks quite serious," Baker said. "I'm going right to the hospital."

Haig, the general, kicked into command mode. "I will move immediately to the White House," he said. He would gather cabinet secretaries and call Bush.

Lacking a better option, Baker concurred. "You will be my point of contact," he said.

Moments later, Baker, Meese, Lyn Nofziger, the political director, and Larry Speakes, the deputy press secretary, piled into a White House car and raced the few blocks to the hospital with sirens blaring and lights flashing. As they hurried into the emergency room, they found Reagan on a gurney, his shirt off, an oxygen mask on his face. Baker was shocked by his appearance. Normally, Reagan had a ruddy color. "Now, he was ghostly pale," Baker recalled.

He had not lost his sense of humor. Reagan had already joked with Nancy that he "forgot to duck" and asked his doctors if they were Republicans. Now seeing his top aides, the president winked at Baker and, spotting Meese too, asked, "Who's minding the store?"

But the situation was serious. Speakes took notes as the doctors briefed Baker and the others. "Doctors believe bleeding to death," he wrote. "Can't find a wound. Think we're going to lose him. Touch and go."

Eventually the doctors found an entry wound under Reagan's left arm and concluded that the .22 caliber bullet had lodged in his lung. They whisked him off to surgery. Baker and the others headed to a small hospital chapel, where they were joined by Nancy. Baker dropped to his knees to pray.

At this point, Baker was presented with the most important decision of the crisis. The president had been shot and was undergoing surgery. Should Reagan's powers be transferred temporarily to the vice president? Under the Twenty-fifth Amendment to the Constitution, ratified three years after Kennedy's assassination, if the vice president and a majority of the cabinet judged "that the President is unable to discharge the powers and duties of his office, the Vice President shall immediately assume the powers and duties of the office as Acting President." The provision had never been invoked before. Reagan was clearly not able to discharge his duties.

But Baker was reluctant to take action that would put his best friend in the Oval Office, even temporarily. He knew that Reagan's conservative coterie remained suspicious of his loyalties. "I didn't want people thinking—and I knew George Bush didn't want people thinking—that there would be a power play by the vice president's office," Baker said later. Baker, Meese, and Nofziger ducked into a broom closet at the hospital to discuss the matter. They decided by themselves that they would not declare Bush the acting president, justifying it because the doctors told them Reagan would not be unconscious for long. Bush himself was not part of the discussion. Pete Teeley, by then the vice president's press secretary, had called him in Texas to inform him about the shooting and Haig later reached Bush on Air Force Two to tell him to come home. But Baker did not ask his friend about the pressing question; there had not been time. "I never talked to him about that," Baker said later. "We made that decision at the hospital."

On the open line back to the White House, though, Baker was told that Fred Fielding, the White House counsel, had gone ahead and drafted letters to Congress that would trigger the temporary transfer of power to Bush just in case. Dick Darman, Baker's right-hand man, had found Haig, Fielding, and others going over the papers and grew alarmed. Never shy, Darman broke into their conversation and said it was premature. He snatched the documents and took them to his office, where he hid them in a safe. On the phone with Baker, he asked for permission to do what he had already done. Baker, miffed that Fielding had presumed to draft such critical documents without consulting him first, authorized Darman's actions after the fact.

The afternoon was a blur of misinformation and miscalculation. At one point, television networks reported that Brady had died, when in fact he was still alive. "This thing is out of control," Deaver told Baker. Baker had Nofziger brief reporters at the hospital and sent Speakes back to the White House to deal with the media there. But watching on television from the White House basement, Haig grew agitated by Speakes's uncertain performance at the podium and before anyone knew what was happening, the headstrong secretary of state was marching upstairs to set the record straight.

Just a year removed from triple bypass surgery, Haig was in such a hurry racing up the stairs that he overexerted himself. He burst into the briefing room, sweaty and out of breath, his voice quavering. As cameras transmitted the scene to a jittery nation, Haig came across as the opposite of calm. Asked by reporters who was in charge, Haig said he was.

"Constitutionally, gentlemen, you have the president, the vice president and the secretary of state, in that order, and should the president decide he wants to transfer the helm to the vice president, he will do so," Haig declared. "As of now, I am in control here in the White House, pending return of the vice president and am in close touch with him. If something came up, I would check with him, of course."

In fairness, Haig was trying to be reassuring, but he was wrong on more than one point. The order of presidential succession beyond the vice president was determined by statute, not the Constitution, and according to the statute, the speaker of the House and the president pro tempore of the Senate came after the vice president and before the secretary of state. Moreover, absent the president and vice president, the law put the secretary of defense in charge of emergency military commands. More troubling than his legal misinformation, Haig gave the impression of someone eager to seize power, provoking derision and mockery, including within the White House.

Baker returned to the White House at 6:15 p.m. and briefed everyone in the Situation Room on the latest from the hospital. He was exhausted but, unlike Haig, unflappable and in command. Others noticed that his suit remained creased and his tie firmly in place.

"The president is in good shape," he reported. During two hours of surgery, the doctors had opened Reagan's chest and stopped the bleeding. The doctors' prognosis, Baker added, was "better than good, but they wouldn't say very good." Jim Brady, however, had been shot in the head and would survive only with brain damage. Two others were hit, but would live—Tim McCarthy, a Secret Service agent who turned into the line of fire to shield the president, and Thomas Delahanty, a Washington police officer who was struck in the neck and suffered nerve damage.

Richard Allen, the national security adviser, recommended that Bush take over some of Reagan's tasks the next day, including leading a cabinet meeting.

"I think that's fine," Baker said. But they should not get "involved in questions of succession and incapacity and that sort of thing."

Air Force Two landed at Andrews Air Force Base outside Washington at 6:30 p.m. but instead of having his helicopter take him directly to the White House, Bush ordered it to fly to the vice president's mansion on the grounds of the Naval Observatory, where he would board a motorcade and ride to the White House. Sensitive to creating the wrong impression, Bush reasoned that only the president landed on the South Lawn. He arrived in the Situation Room at 7 p.m. Neither Baker nor Bush would do anything to give their conservative critics any ammunition, even at the risk of making the wrong decision on transferring power. "I got criticized roundly" for not invoking the Twenty-fifth Amendment, Baker said years later, "maybe justifiably." But the Washington logic of the situation dictated exactly the course that Baker had taken. He and Bush were untarnished. Reagan's hold on his office was unquestioned. His bureaucratic rival Haig looked like an unstable and power-hungry fool. No wonder Baker maintained that "it turned out to be absolutely the right decision."

What's more, Baker had firmly established himself as a steady leader in a crisis, cementing his place in charge of the White House without ever needing to actually declare it. Even Ed Meese was impressed.

"I want to tell you, it's a pleasure doing business with you," Meese told him as the terrifying day came to an end.

"Same here, Ed," Baker replied.

ACCOMPANIED BY MEESE and Michael Deaver, Baker arrived at Reagan's hospital room the next morning at 7:15 a.m. The president had had a breathing tube in his throat over the previous night, making it difficult to talk, and had been peppering the nurses with notes scribbled out on pink and white hospital forms. "I am aren't alive aren't I?" he wrote, woozily mixing up the words. He later said he had woken up in a white room with a white ceiling and a pretty nurse staring down at him so he thought he might be in heaven. Over the course of the next few hours, he dashed off a flurry of other notes, some in black felt pen, others in pencil.

"Could we rewrite this scene beginning about the time I left the hotel?"

"What happened to the guy with the gun?"

"Was anyone hurt?"

"All in all I'd rather be in Phil," meaning Philadelphia, reprising the famous W. C. Fields line.

The notes were reassuring. His sense of humor intact, Reagan seemed aware of what had happened to him and was asking the right questions. Now with the tube removed, he was able to make wan jokes out loud.

"I should have known I wasn't going to avoid a staff meeting," he said as he noticed Baker and the rest of the Troika entering the room.

When the aides told him not to worry, that the government was still functioning, Reagan quipped, "What makes you think I'd be happy about that?"

Baker had brought with him a bill to be signed, a measure on milk price supports whose importance at this point was mainly to show that the president was still in charge. Reagan borrowed Baker's pen and summoned enough strength to scratch his signature across the bottom, making it law. They told him a little about his assailant, John W. Hinckley Jr., a twenty-five-year-old drifter who grew up in Texas and became obsessed with the actress Jodie Foster, resolving to win her favor by killing the president. Reagan feigned disappointment. "I had hoped it was a KGB agent. On second thought, he wouldn't have missed then."

Baker was happy to see the president in relatively good humor, but it was clear he was still in rough shape. Reagan was a seventy-year-old man who had been shot in the chest. The episode was generating enormous national sympathy for the president, but Baker worried that a long recovery and any demonstrable weakness could revive questions about his age. Baker and the others explicitly resolved to convince the country that Reagan was better off than he really was. Aides throughout American history have labored to hide presidential maladies, from Woodrow Wilson's virtual incapacitation late in his tenure to John Kennedy's Addison's disease, and while this did not compare to those cover-ups, the Baker team would not be fully forthcoming with the public either.

Signing the dairy legislation was a first step in projecting the image of a president still capable of carrying out his duties. But Reagan was in no shape to make decisions and it was Baker who was really in charge. The aftermath of the assassination attempt reinforced a truth that was counterintuitive—even with Bush holding the number two constitutional position, his friend was the one actually running the White House in Reagan's name, even when the president was well. "The vice president is not a powerful position and the chief of staff is an extraordinarily powerful position," Baker reflected later. Baker made a point of stopping by Bush's office next door to keep him updated on events, but he was not taking direction from Bush anymore.

In the days after the shooting, Baker labored to shield Reagan from scrutiny, fearing visitors would surely notice his diminished capacity. After Senator Strom Thurmond, the Republican from South Carolina, somehow made it past the Secret Service and talked his way into Reagan's hospital room, Nancy Reagan was livid. Baker summoned Max Friedersdorf, the president's legislative director. "Max," Baker told him when he arrived at the hospital, "I want you to stay here until I tell you to leave." He was to let in no member of Congress. An exception was made for Tip O'Neill, the Democratic House speaker from Massachusetts, who would be critical to Reagan's legislative agenda. Bringing a book of Irish humor as a gift, O'Neill arrived in the hospital room, grabbed Reagan's hands, and kissed his head. "God bless you, Mr. President," a teary O'Neill said, and then got on his knees to pray for Reagan, choosing the Twenty-third Psalm. He left shocked at the president's condition, concluding that he had come "closer to death than most of us realized."

O'Neill's visit helped cement the beginning of an unlikely friendship between the two men. From the start, Baker had recognized that it would be in Reagan's interest to reach out to O'Neill. The president faced a House dominated by Democrats and the only way he would get his agenda through would be to forge a coalition that included at least some in the opposition party. A bulky old-school pol with a bulbous nose, a thick mass of white hair, and a jovial style that belied his legislative savvy, O'Neill was a backscratching ward heeler who operated on the theory that all politics was local. He was as liberal as Reagan was conservative, a creature of Cambridge and Washington who was skeptical of the outsider from California. But they were both Irish storytellers of roughly the same age who enjoyed a good joke and a hearty laugh. Richard Williamson, a White House aide, had prepared a memo during the transition identifying O'Neill as an important target for Reagan's charm offensive.

"Speaker O'Neill will never be an enthusiastic supporter of Ronald Reagan's programs," the memo said. "However, he could become a valuable ally, just as Democratic Senate Majority Leader Lyndon Johnson was often a valuable ally to President Eisenhower in the 50's and Republican Senate Minority Leader Ev Dirksen was often a valuable help to Presidents Kennedy and Johnson in the 60's." The memo urged Reagan to invite O'Neill to the White House regularly. "As they get to know one another, they will like each other. Speaker O'Neill sincerely wants what is best for America. And while he will often disagree with Reagan's substantive proposals, he sincerely will want President Reagan to succeed." The same memo recommended that Reagan make a gesture to Jimmy Carter in his early months in office, such as inviting him to a White House dinner. "Ultimately, while the American people overwhelmingly rejected President Carter, they continue to like Jimmy Carter personally," it said.

In a later generation, the idea of reaching out to leaders of the other party would be anathema, but to Baker it was only common sense. It suited Reagan too. He never did have Carter for dinner and essentially stiffed his predecessor for eight years, but he made a point of reaching out to O'Neill. During the transition, the incoming president had visited the speaker on Capitol Hill. At their meeting, Reagan predicted he would get along well with the Democrats in Congress since he had had good relations with the California legislature. O'Neill could not help thinking that a little naive. "That was the minor leagues," he told Reagan. "You're in the big leagues now." Still, soon after the inauguration, the Reagans invited O'Neill and his wife, Millie, to the White House residence for a private dinner along with Baker and Susan, Baker's staff making sure to obtain the speaker's favorite cigar for the occasion. Reagan and O'Neill talked movies and swapped Irish tales. O'Neill was struck by how little Reagan seemed conversant with or even interested in the details of policy. But like so many others, O'Neill found it hard not to like the new president, deeming him "an exceptionally congenial and charming man."

After a week with the president in the hospital, Baker resolved to return the White House to action. "We need to get back on substance this week; news play on President's health largely over," said an agenda written for Baker for the staff meeting on April 6. Reagan, wearing a red cardigan and a wide grin, returned to the White House five days later and appeared in a series of carefully staged photographs. The country rallied behind him; his approval rating in the Gallup poll rose from 55 percent to 66 percent and pundits praised his unflappable response to the near-death experience. "The honeymoon has ended and a new legend has been born," David Broder wrote in *The Washington Post*. On April 28, just under a month after the shooting, a vigorous-looking Reagan rode up to Capitol Hill to address a joint session of Congress, which gave him a hero's welcome.

With Reagan now out of danger, Baker resolved to capitalize on it. He knew that poll numbers drove legislation and that any Congress, even one controlled by the opposition, could not resist a president with so much support.

BY NOW, Baker was picking up on the ways of Washington. Through a combination of instinct and intense experience, he had learned a lot about how the capital worked and how he could make it work for him. Some of his methods were simple common sense. He had assembled an inner circle deeply loyal to him and highly competent. Baker turned their efficiency into a political calling card. It was then that he adopted his habit of returning any call from a member of Congress by the end of the day—to be sure, he might not return the call until the evening when he could be reasonably sure the lawmaker had gone home, but it generally still earned him credit with the members. "Nobody was ever better at dealing with Congress," said Larry Speakes.

Baker was careful, too, to make sure that rivals within the White House, such as Ed Meese, felt included and informed as much as possible. He had Michael Deaver tend to Nancy Reagan, who had clearly emerged as the critical unseen player in the White House. But the surface comity masked deeper fault lines. "It didn't matter how much Meese and Baker and Deaver would all hug," said Ed Rogers, a White House aide at the time. "At the staff level, there was always tension and banana peels being thrown in front of each other." The Meese faction, dominated by the California conservatives who had been with Reagan for years, resented Baker, the Washington usurper. "Deaver and Baker had the attitude that they had to protect the president from himself," observed William Clark, the longtime California adviser who came to Washington first as deputy secretary of state. "Meese had the attitude: Let's let Reagan be Reagan, number one, and secondly, let's advance what we know to be his vision and his innermost philosophy and thoughts."

For his part, Baker could be scornful of Meese, whom he privately called "Poppin' Fresh, the doughboy," after the famous Pillsbury commercial of the time. Meese's ideological purity was never going to get anything done, Baker believed, nor did he understand how actions would play with the public. When two Navy F-14s shot down a pair of Libyan jets that opened fire on them in the Gulf of Sidra in August, Meese was in charge while Baker was off in Texas and Deaver was away on vacation. Meese chose not to wake Reagan until hours later. Baker and Deaver "were furious," Bob Schieffer of CBS News recalled. "They feared that once the story was discovered by the press, Reagan would be portrayed as a president who was not in command of a tense situation that easily could have escalated into a crisis." Baker and Deaver resolved afterward that they had to take foreign policy out of Meese's portfolio; one way to do that was to push out Richard Allen and replace him as national security adviser, which would take time but reflected the emerging power dynamics in the administration. Meese had no idea what was coming and did not recognize the danger he faced as Baker gradually surpassed him as the most important force in Reagan's White House. "It isn't really undercutting Meese," said Hedrick Smith, the *New York Times* White House correspondent. "It's just outdistancing Meese."

Baker exuded competence, which drew people toward him and enhanced his position within the West Wing. "Jim Baker looked like the efficient production foreman, with a pencil behind his ear," recalled David Stockman, the budget director. "He cussed a blue streak and told off-color jokes. He was tall, trim and self-confident. He had a way of moving things along, of pointing to the ceiling and spinning his arm around in a 360-degree circle, saying, 'Let's go, let's move it.' He struck me as the one who really knew what he was doing."

As important as any factor in Baker's rise was his assiduous courtship of journalists. Baker recognized, as Meese and others did not, that power in Washington was driven in part by the *perception* of power and that no one did more to create or preserve that perception than the media—especially the national television broadcasters, who still dominated an era when millions of Americans stopped everything to watch one of the three nightly newscasts. Like other Republicans, Baker assumed most reporters skewed liberal, but unlike many of the Reaganites, he did not view them as the enemy. He understood that what they really wanted more than anything was a good story. If he kept them supplied, they would be happy—and less likely to come after him. If he got his version of events out, the stories were more likely to reflect his point of view. And he used journalists as an early warning system. "You'd walk into his office and he'd greet you with, 'Smith, what are you up to today?'" Hedrick Smith said. "He's so canny about sensing where trouble is coming from."

Baker started each day trying to shape the coverage that would come. "Okay, what's our story today?" he asked in the morning staff meeting. As with senators and representatives, Baker tried to return any call from a reporter by the end of the same day and, if he could not, made sure that Margaret Tutwiler did on his behalf. Larry Speakes estimated that Baker spent as much as 50 percent of his time with reporters and editors, probably an exaggeration but a revealing one. The media, at least the part of it that really mattered, was still small enough that it could be managed; aside from ABC, CBS, and NBC, there were the wire services, *The New York Times*, *The Washington Post*, *The Wall Street Journal*, and the weekly newsmagazines *Time*, *Newsweek*, and *U.S. News & World Report*. Baker, as chief of staff, became an expert in their care and feeding.

Baker was acutely aware of reporters' deadlines and knew that if he called a broadcast journalist shortly before the evening news went on the air, he could shape the resulting report. If Tutwiler popped her head into his office in the late afternoon to say that ABC's Sam Donaldson was on the phone and wanted something fresh for the broadcast, Baker would come up with a new tidbit and have her pass it along to him. He would then stop whatever meeting he was in at 6:30 p.m. to turn on the television and watch the top of the network shows. Each Friday, he invited reporters from the newsmagazines to his office before their issues were put to bed so that he could dole out the insider nuggets that they craved to distinguish their stories from those in the daily newspapers. He fed the egos of reporters who loved nothing more than boasting of their inside sources at the White House. Reporters knew that his version of events could be self-serving or incomplete, but they also knew that Baker was always accurate with whatever he chose to share. "You could pretty well take it to the bank; he was a straight shooter," said the *Post*'s Lou Cannon, the premier chronicler of the Reagan era. "I think the press corps was willing to be spun by Baker because he was so accessible and because he was basically honest."

Baker was the master of the strategic leak. If he wanted to bury a bad story that was bound to come out anyway, he might give it to the wire services late on a Friday afternoon so it would get less notice as the town emptied out for the weekend. If he wanted to highlight a positive story or float a new initiative, he arranged for it to land in the Monday morning newspapers, when it could set the agenda for the week. He routinely used such trial balloons to test a policy proposal or a personnel appointment before actually approving it; if the leak generated fierce opposition, he could drop the idea without ever assuming authorship. He often used cutouts. "Darman and I were sometimes the designated leakers and Baker would expect us to put certain things out," said David Gergen.

When Baker personally ventured out on the Sunday television talk shows, he invited a large coterie of advisers to go over every possible question he might be asked and script out answers. He scribbled notes on his typical yellow legal pad. "He would say, 'That's a good answer on that, now let me get that down,'" Larry Speakes recalled. "And then someone, most likely Darman, would say, 'Wait a minute, maybe you ought to couch that in a different way.' And Baker would say, 'Well, let's see how this sounds now.'" The sessions dragged on so long that Speakes began making excuses to avoid attending, citing his son's Little League games or other reasons. "It was a tortured process that took hours longer than it should have, tying up Baker, me and several other top-level White House staffers," Speakes groused.

For the most part, though, Baker preferred speaking with journalists "on background," meaning that he would be quoted only as an anonymous senior White House official. In doing so, he gave reporters the sense of being on the inside. "Candor and gentle persuasion are the fish Baker peddles," Deaver said. By providing the narrative through his own eyes, of course, Baker ended up as the protagonist of many stories.

Baker always insisted that he did this in service of Reagan's agenda and indeed his careful cultivation of the press did advance the president's interests. "Almost all the other great leakers I'd known had this crying need for publicity for themselves or recognition or praise—the Kissinger approach, which whenever he leaked something, he really wanted everyone to know who put it out," said Marlin Fitzwater, who served in the White House under both Reagan and George Bush. "Baker never did that. He was the honest broker in that sense. When he chose to deal with the press, it was for a reason and the reason was for the success of the presidency."

Even so, Baker understood that his own interests were served if the presidency's were. And he considered tending journalists necessary for survival in a cutthroat White House. "I got the reputation in the Reagan administration for being an extraordinarily prolific leaker," he told a ghostwriter on one of his memoirs after leaving office in comments that were never published. "I was. In that milieu, it was rat fuck. If you didn't leak, you didn't live." He had freedom others did not. "I had a license to operate; sometimes I went too far," he admitted, without elaborating.

The drawback for Baker was that everyone in the White House knew he leaked. His fingerprints were seen on every story—even those in which he actually had no part. "Baker is one of the great leakers of our time," complained Lyn Nofziger. "You could tell every time something came out that was needling Meese or me or one of us. You knew exactly where it came from." Some even began to suspect Baker of leaking information masked in a way that was intended to be blamed on his rivals, a Washington skill that has had many White House practitioners over the years. "The Baker team were masters of the black art of using someone else's phrases with reporters so somebody else got fingered for their leaks," remembered Ed Rollins. Meese, by contrast, was not much of a leaker and his team was not particularly adept at it. All they could do was complain. "I would say that generally the leaking was to the disservice of the president, from whoever it might have come from," Meese later said mildly. He was sharper in his memoir, complaining about "backstabbing by leak."

The relationship between politicians and journalists was different in those days, adversarial during the day but clubby at night. They could socialize together or even play pranks on one another without it being publicized. Once, at Deaver's request, Lesley Stahl, the CBS reporter, taped a fake broadcast reporting that Baker had fallen out of favor with Reagan, who was supposedly planning to ask for his resignation. Moreover, Stahl reported, Baker was secretly suffering from anorexia. Deaver edited the "report" into a tape of the evening news and showed it to Baker, who was flabbergasted until he got the joke.

Not one to take a prank like that lying down, Baker exacted his revenge by getting Tom Wyman, the CBS chairman, to call Stahl at her White House booth the next day and pretend to dress her down for unprofessional behavior.

"It's inappropriate for you to be cavorting like that with the White House staff," he lectured.

Then Wyman relented. "Baker's put me up to this. Don't tell him I told you."

BAKER KEPT a ferocious schedule. He woke at 6:00 each morning in the house that he and Susan had bought at 2415 Foxhall Road in the woodsy Spring Valley area of Washington, just across the street from Nelson Rockefeller's old estate, and arrived at his office about an hour later. At 7:30, he hosted the Troika for breakfast served in his office by Filipino stewards. Each of the three presidential advisers brought notes but Baker tended to dominate the discussion. "He always had the longer checklist," Deaver said. They reviewed overnight developments overseas, went through the morning news, and plotted out the day's agenda. At 8:00, Baker hosted the morning meeting of the senior staff, collecting more information and issuing instructions. It was a disciplined session but Baker was open to dissent. "His staff would tell him he was nuts or blow up at him in meetings and he would tolerate it," Deaver said. "He had no problem with their form of communication."

Around 9:00, Reagan arrived at the Oval Office and his secretary would then summon Baker, Deaver, and Meese. The rest of the day was filled with additional meetings, phone calls, and brushfires, with Baker sneaking a quick lunch of tunafish on toast and a glass of buttermilk or, on Thursdays, the Mexican special from the White House Mess. Baker was relentless about following through, constantly making notes on his yellow legal pads and ensuring that tasks had been completed. "He was absolutely tenacious, at times to the point of driving me nearly bonkers," Deaver said. "Jim would call ten or twelve times in a morning, checking to be sure I had done something he had mentioned at breakfast." Baker would return home around 8 or 9 p.m. Weekends were just two more workdays until Monday. "He doesn't ask you to come in on Saturday," remembered Margaret Tutwiler. "But he's in, so you're there."

It would require a fanatical work ethic to push through Reagan's proposed 30 percent tax cut as his first major initiative. To coordinate the effort, Baker relied on the Legislative Strategy Group that Dick Darman had set up inside the White House. Meeting several times a week, the group allowed Baker to control the most important elements of the Reagan presidency through a handful of aides put in charge of strategy and priorities. "It was the main policymaking and governing institution inside the White House, short of the Oval Office," said Kenneth Duberstein, then a legislative aide. To keep Meese happy, Baker made him a regular member along with Max Friedersdorf, David Gergen, and Craig Fuller, the vice president's chief of staff. Others would sometimes attend as well, including Donald Regan, the treasury secretary; David Stockman, the budget director; and Martin Anderson, the president's domestic policy adviser. But Baker put Darman in charge and Darman reported to him.

Darman was a force unto himself in the White House. Born into a family of New England textile mill owners, he had a fierce intellect and knew it. He was still irritated that he got a 790 on one part of his SAT for college instead of a perfect 800. He earned undergraduate and business degrees from Harvard before going into government, where he worked in the Nixon administration for Elliot Richardson in three cabinet departments: Health, Education, and Welfare; Defense; and finally Justice. At the latter, he was involved in reaching the plea agreement that resulted in Spiro Agnew's resignation, although the Watergate turmoil soon had him and Richardson quitting in the Saturday Night Massacre. Richardson was his first mentor; they lived near each other in the Virginia suburbs and Richardson was godfather to one of Darman's sons.

For Darman, government was an instrument to be tamed and used to advance the country; he was "a creature of the center," in his own words, not a revolutionary. He favored markets and pluralism, but he was fundamentally a technocrat who did not care much for ideology. By the time he arrived at Reagan's White House, he had added a fourth cabinet department to his résumé. "That gives my dad something that was really pretty rare among Republicans, which was an understanding of how government works," his son, Jonathan Darman, observed. Which is why when Baker allowed him to write his own job description, he crafted it in such a way that he would handle all the paper that went through the White House. Darman understood that paper was power and it was one of the things that Baker came to appreciate most about him. "Reagan's in-box was my out-box and vice versa," Darman once said. At the same time, it made him a control freak. "He screams and throws paper when he is not happy," said Marlin Fitzwater. "And he's not happy when he's not in total control."

Darman was a policy innovator who found ways of achieving the president's goals that others had not imagined. He understood the numbers and pored through briefing books that often went ignored. "He was the only guy in the Reagan White House who knew where every piece of paper was and what was on it on policy," said Stuart Spencer. "That's the kind of animal he is." But Darman's willingness to cut ideological corners to make deals generated great animosity from conservatives like Ed Rollins, who described him as "a man whose talents were as prodigious as his ego." Darman's sharp elbows and derisive manner won him few friends even among those who might agree with him politically. "Dick was somewhat insecure so anybody who threatened his shadow, he would react very strongly," said David Gergen. "He thought I did that. I thought he did that." Martin Anderson called him "easily the most disliked man in the White House," concluding that "even his boss, Baker, didn't seem to care for him very much." But Baker was no sentimentalist and he was in the White House to win, not to make friends. He understood that Darman's bedside manner rubbed some colleagues the wrong way, but considered him too valuable for it to matter.

The task for Baker and Darman was translating Reagan's grand design into reality. In his first few weeks in office, Reagan had outlined a program of tax cuts, spending reductions, and military expansion, but the package had stalled until the assassination attempt. Just days before John Hinckley opened fire, *Newsweek* published a story under the headline "Is the Big Tax Cut Dead?"

The president's courageous recovery from the shooting changed the political dynamics and Baker intended to capitalize on it. He understood that Reagan's economic plan would require bipartisan agreement. While the Senate was in Republican hands, Democrats still held a strong majority in the House, led by Tip O'Neill, the old-style liberal who, as David Stockman saw him, "was a fly in New Deal amber." But Baker's team gambled that there were enough conservative Southern Democrats, known as Boll Weevils, to build a coalition with the Republican minority. Darman identified sixty-seven "potentially gettable Democrats" as their targets.

Baker sought to pave the way for the tax drive through careful orchestration. Republicans started with a bipartisan budget-cutting plan known as Gramm-Latta, named for its sponsors, Representatives Phil Gramm, a conservative Democrat from Texas, and Delbert Latta, a Republican from Ohio. The budget was meant to bring the government under control and eliminate the federal deficit by 1984, when Reagan would presumably be running for reelection. But it proved harder than Reagan's team had imagined—every program they wanted to cut had a constituency, it seemed, often including fellow Republicans. By the time they came up with their blueprint, the Reagan plan was $44 billion short of wiping out the deficit. In a bit of budgetary legerdemain, Stockman simply designated the shortfall as cuts that would be identified later. He came to call it the "magic asterisk."

Despite this fundamental flaw, Baker and the White House peeled away enough of O'Neill's caucus to pass it handily. On Reagan's behalf,

Baker had figured out how to wield power on Capitol Hill; as much as anyone at that point, he seemed to be clearly in command of the capital. Back in his district the next day, a dispirited O'Neill was asked by a constituent what was happening in Washington. "What's happening to me in Washington?" O'Neill replied. "What's happening to me is I'm getting the shit whaled out of me."

Even before the budget vote, Baker's team drafted a plan for the next stage, a plan that would surely have made headlines had it been revealed at the time. The memo outlining it showed how calculated Baker was with the media, gaming out leaks and story lines in advance to make it look as though Reagan was working with the opposition when, in fact, he was manipulating it. "Leak story that White House has been approached by several key members of Congress (including Democrats) about coming up with a tax accommodation," read one memo from Baker's team. "'The White House' would be said to be 'intrigued' by the possibility." If not an outright lie, Baker was certainly willing to stretch the truth to shape the narrative in ways that were advantageous.

But then Baker was thrown off by an issue he did not expect. Franklin Roosevelt's popular Social Security program, now more than four decades old and embedded in American society, turned out to be confronting both short-term financial instability and long-term demographic trends. The immediate crisis stemmed from lower-than-expected payroll tax revenues due to higher-than-expected unemployment in recent years and cost-of-living increases automatically tied to inflation. In the longer term, the program would be threatened when the first of the post–World War II baby boom generation began to retire at the end of the century. With recipients living longer and fewer new workers to pay into the system, Social Security would eventually face bankruptcy.

David Stockman developed a plan for about $100 billion in cuts to make the program solvent for decades, including postponing the next cost-of-living increase for current retirees and trimming benefits significantly for future retirees. Early retirees who began collecting checks at sixty-two would find their benefits slashed by about 30 percent. Stockman understood his proposed cutbacks would be controversial, so to outmaneuver potential opponents, he circulated the plan around the West Wing on a Saturday and then presented it to Reagan on the following Monday along with Martin Anderson, the domestic policy adviser, and Richard Schweiker, the former senator and onetime putative running mate for Reagan in 1976 who was now serving as health and human services secretary.

Reagan had a history as a critic of Social Security. In his breakthrough moment in politics, delivering his 1964 speech on behalf of Barry Goldwater, Reagan had declared that paying into and collecting Social Security should be "voluntary" for those who could provide for their own retirements, a position that opponents had hung around his neck ever since. In 1976, Gerald Ford hammered him on Social Security before the Florida primary, going on to win the delegate-rich state, a victory that arguably helped the incumbent secure the nomination. So raising the issue now risked reviving questions about Reagan's commitment to the politically popular program. Darman warned Baker that it "could well ignite an inferno on the Hill," as Stockman later put it. But the president surprised Baker and Darman by signing off on Stockman's plan on the spot.

Baker was too late to stop the president from approving the proposal, but he could control how it would be presented and sold. Within hours, he convened the Legislative Strategy Group and outsourced the plan away from the White House. "They wanted the president to announce it and I said, 'Wait a minute, that's the third rail, we're not going to do it,'" Baker recalled. "And it wasn't easy to get Reagan to agree not to do it, to be very honest with you." Instead, Baker insisted that it be announced by Schweiker; Darman even suggested that it be announced in Baltimore, the home of the Social Security Administration—and far from the capital. Schweiker objected. "If there's *any* doubt as to where the president stands, this'll be dead on arrival when it gets to the Hill," he argued. "By damn, I've spent twenty years on the Hill and I know when something will fly. So let's not start on the defensive." Baker refused to give in; Schweiker would be the front man. "I was furious," Stockman said later. "But there was nothing I could do. Baker was chief of staff."

He was also right. Switchboards on Capitol Hill lit up with calls of protest and the plan quickly flopped. Handed a political weapon, Tip O'Neill and the Democrats bludgeoned Republicans for shafting older Americans. Republicans in Congress wanted nothing to do with the plan and within a week of Schweiker's announcement, the Senate voted 96 to 0 to oppose its major elements. Baker had learned his lesson. Never again would he let Reagan walk into such a trap. "Jim Baker carried around a bazooka, firing first and asking questions later of anyone who mentioned the words 'Social Security,'" Stockman said.

The damage done, Baker quickly pivoted back to the tax cuts. O'Neill and other Democratic leaders opposed them, arguing that they would balloon the deficit, benefit the rich, and be used to justify more cuts to programs for the poor. Like George Bush during the Republican primaries, they derided what would come to be known as Reaganomics, mocking the idea that Washington could cut taxes, increase defense spending, and still balance the budget. But O'Neill recognized there was no way to thwart a popular new president on such a voter-friendly initiative, especially amid the national outpouring of sympathy after the assassination attempt. So even as he publicly skewered the tax cuts as mean-spirited, he made no effort to keep the legislation from coming to the House floor.

Representative Dan Rostenkowski of Illinois, the powerful Democratic chairman of the House Ways and Means Committee, suggested smaller rate cuts phased in over time. Baker was holding a strong hand, though, and unwilling to give in to Rostenkowski. Instead, he recruited other Democrats. For Baker, congressional maneuvering was like playing a game of pinball, as Darman put it, with the ball ricocheting from one bumper to another. The player had to make sure the flippers hit at just the right moment. This was Baker's great skill. He recognized when the time had come to make a deal. "He knew you were never going to come to a table and get everything you wanted," said Karen Morgan, his long-time aide. "That just wasn't realistic. And so he would always look for the elements where you could give a little bit because he's a realist and he's a diplomat and he's a negotiator." He also understood how far he could go without pushing too hard. Reagan agreed to delay the first year of the tax cuts and reduce the total to 25 percent, but that was as low as he would go. "Jim Baker made a few private runs at the president," Stockman said. "But Baker knew a Rock of Gibraltar when he saw one and nothing was to be gained by running his boat up against it."

On June 4, Reagan appeared in the Rose Garden to announce a bipartisan tax-cutting program that included concessions intended to lure Democrats without acceding entirely to Rostenkowski's demands. The plan would cut rates across the board by 5 percent in 1981, another 10 percent in 1982, and a final 10 percent in 1983, instead of 10 percent each year. The top rate would come down from 70 percent to 50 percent and tax breaks would be expanded for married couples, retirement accounts, capital gains, and estates, while some of the business breaks originally envisioned would be trimmed. Joining the president for the event were several Democrats, including Senators David Boren of Oklahoma and Lloyd Bentsen of Texas, and the Democrat-turned-independent Harry Byrd of Virginia.

While O'Neill remained opposed, Baker set about wooing other Democrats. "We stroked and we stroked and we stroked and we stroked and we stroked and we traded, and the president was very good at that and willing to do it all day and all night," Baker said. So was Baker. "Jim kept saying to me, 'Give me more members to call,' " said Kenneth Duberstein, the White House lobbyist. Baker told Boll Weevil Democrats that Reagan would not campaign against them in 1982 if they supported the tax cuts, effectively trading away the party's chances in the next election in order to secure a more immediate victory.

On July 29, both houses of Congress passed versions of the tax measure. Reagan won the key vote in the House 238 to 195, with forty-eight Democrats joining a nearly unanimous Republican caucus; even more jumped on the bandwagon for the final vote. After the two bills were reconciled into a final measure, Reagan, wearing faded jeans, a denim jacket, and cowboy boots, signed it into law on August 13 in front of his white-stucco ranch house in California.

O'Neill grudgingly appreciated Baker's skill. "They put only one legislative ball in play at a time," he said years later, "and they kept their eye on it all the way through."

A young James A. Baker III with his grandfather and father, the dominant figures of his early life. He and his friends nicknamed his strict dad "the Warden."

His grandfather, later known as Captain Baker, was one of the prime forces in the development of modern Houston but warned his grandson to stay out of politics.

Baker's parents, James and Bonner, visiting Hawaii in 1929. After thirteen childless years, his mother discovered she was pregnant on the return trip.

Born in Houston in 1930, months into the Depression but isolated from its effects, Baker was "the hero son," expected "to succeed in a grand way."

Baker's mother, Bonner Means Baker, shown with his sister, Bonner, told him, "You have quite a legacy to live up to."

At Princeton, half a continent away from the Warden, "I just went nuts having so much fun, I damn near flunked out."

On spring break of sophomore year, Baker met and got "the screaming A-bomb hots" for Mary Stuart McHenry of Ohio. The two were married in 1953.

By 1961, they had four young sons: Mike, Jamie, Doug, and John. Tragically, Mary Stuart died of cancer in 1970.

Baker and George H. W. Bush became best friends and doubles partners in the 1960s. In 1970, when Bush ran for Senate, he enlisted the grieving Baker, previously a Democrat who steered clear of politics, to run the campaign in Harris County.

Baker came to Washington in 1975 and within a year had become President Gerald Ford's campaign chairman, riding with him on Air Force One.

After Mary Stuart died, Baker married her close friend, Susan Garrett Winston, in 1973. Between them, they had seven children, a complicated real-life "Brady Bunch."

With Baker's help, Ford beat Ronald Reagan for the Republican nomination in the 1976 campaign, but the president's pardon of Richard Nixon was the "eight-hundred-pound gorilla in the room, always hanging over everything" and helped cost him the election in the fall to Democrat Jimmy Carter.

Despite running two Republican campaigns against Ronald Reagan, Baker became his White House chief of staff in 1981 and, as Brent Scowcroft put it, "co-president in a way."

Baker still loved to play tennis with now-Vice President Bush, although Bush joked that his friend had a "powder puff serve."

Reagan's more conservative allies never trusted Baker, but the president defended him to critics. "Jim, if ever there was a Reaganite, you're it."
Courtesy of David Hume Kennerly/Getty Images

Baker was first among equals in the famously feuding Troika that included Michael Deaver, left, and Ed Meese. "Every single day Jim Baker was in that White House he accumulated power," a rival lamented.

A pragmatist amid the Reagan Revolution, Baker urged the president to work with Tip O'Neill, left, the Democratic speaker of the House.

Baker and Susan had a "bonus baby," Mary-Bonner, their eighth child, after Baker's ill-fated run for attorney general in Texas, and she became a favorite of the Reagans.

Baker used to quote Reagan as saying, "I'd rather get 80 percent of what I want than go over the cliff with my flag flying." Baker was in charge of the getting. Exhausted after four years, he engineered a shift to become Reagan's second-term treasury secretary.

Part Three

The Witches' Brew

The letter was harsh. The fact that it came from his home state made it personal. Never mind that Baker did not really know Clymer L. Wright Jr., who had been the Texas finance chairman of Ronald Reagan's campaign in 1980. Wright felt he knew Baker and, with a three-page bill of particulars sent to fellow Republicans in May 1982, he made it his mission to expose the chief of staff as an enemy within, a traitor intent on destroying Reagan's presidency.

Baker had heard this ever since he took the job, of course. To some of Reagan's most fervent supporters, Baker was an apostate, a sellout, a moderate, a liberal even. He was a country-club Republican. A Bush guy. A Ford man. Worse, he was a manipulator, steering an overly trusting true conservative of a president to the mushy middle, ever willing to sacrifice principle in the name of pragmatism. Baker found this indictment endlessly aggravating. When pressed, he insisted he was every bit as conservative as any other Reagan adviser. He was from Texas after all. But unlike the purists, he understood how to get things done.

To be sure, he had successfully kept Reagan out of what Baker considered losing fights over pointless ideology. By focusing on tax cuts as the main priority in the opening months of the administration, Baker had effectively sidelined some of Reagan's more radical campaign promises. When Reagan made his first appointment to the Supreme Court in July 1981, Baker helped direct him to Sandra Day O'Connor, a state judge from Arizona and the first woman in American history to become a justice.

The subsequent fight over her confirmation taught conservatives, if they did not know already, that Baker was no ally and they learned to their fury that the chief of staff was a roadblock to their access to Reagan. Paul Weyrich, one of the founders of the modern political right, was agitated over O'Connor, viewing her as a suspect figure who would come to the court with little fidelity to conservative judicial philosophy. But when he went to Baker seeking a meeting with the president, the chief of staff kept him out of the Oval Office. Others were convinced, with some justification, that Baker was disdainful of them behind closed doors. John Lofton, a conservative columnist, told people that Baker had called the activists opposing O'Connor "kooks," according to the scuttlebutt passed along to Baker by Richard Williamson, a White House aide. ("Not helpful," Williamson added, "whether accurate or not.") O'Connor went on to be confirmed by the Senate with no opposition just two months later—and Weyrich's fears proved well founded, as she evolved into a centrist figure on the court on issues such as abortion and affirmative action.

The columnists Rowland Evans and Robert Novak, well-connected conservative insiders who often signaled where the new right was headed, wrote that the O'Connor nomination showed that "Reagan shares the view of Jim Baker and his other aides that the Moral Majority is not vital to his political coalition." Baker resented the column and Novak later said it ruined their relationship. "With this, I burned bridges to the White House, Baker, and maybe the president," Novak recalled. But he kept the flames blazing. Every week, it seemed, Evans and Novak targeted Baker in their column. At a Washington party in May 1982, "the air crackled" when Novak approached Baker, as Sara Fritz, a writer for *U.S. News & World Report*, recorded in an internal memo to colleagues the next day. "How come you didn't write anything bad about me today?" Baker asked Novak with more than a little edge. The columnist insisted that he actually admired Baker. "This was followed by a stiff silence that caused everybody to feel uncomfortable," Fritz wrote.

Just eleven days later, Clymer Wright sent his letter assailing Baker to fellow Republicans. "Dear Friend of Ronald Reagan," he wrote. "Our beloved President today stands alone under siege. His economic program is being undermined by White House Chief of Staff James Baker." Calling him a "usurper," Wright enclosed a story from the *New York Post* and one of those columns by Evans and Novak. He also noted that Baker had run losing campaigns for Gerald Ford and George Bush:

> Now is the time for Ronald Reagan to ask James Baker for his resignation. Now is the time to replace James Baker with someone who is loyal to Ronald Reagan personally and to his programs. Now is the time for the man we elected to assume command of his own administration. It is essential

that his key staff be philosophically in tune with the President; Mr. Baker obviously is not.

The attack got under Baker's skin. Reagan personally responded with a tough "Dear Clymer" letter that Baker allowed years later was likely sent at his instigation. "Yes, there is undermining of my efforts going on and, yes, there is sabotage of all I'm trying to accomplish," Reagan wrote. "But it's being done by the people who write these articles and columns, not by any White House staff member and certainly not by Jim Baker." He added that he resented the notion that he was "led around by the nose" by Baker:

Clymer, I'm in charge and my people are helping to carry out the policies I set. No, we don't get everything we want and, yes, we have to compromise to get 75% or 80% of our programs. We try to see that the 75% or 80% is more than worth the compromise we have to accept. So far it has been. There has not been one single instance of Jim Baker doing anything but what I've settled on as our policy. He goes all out to help bring that about.

Reagan's testimonial notwithstanding, Baker remained a target. A song composed to the tune of Jim Croce's "You Don't Mess Around with Jim" and distributed among Baker's enemies captured the moment.

> *Well—outa oily south Texas*
> *Came this Princeton dude*
> *He's slicker than a lib'ral snake*
> *Bamboozled Jerry Ford*
> *Switched to Bush and got bored*
> *Now Reagan's a-payin' this fake*
>
> *So us right-wingers gotta save the country*
> *Jim Baker's stabbin' us in the back*
> *Side-trackin' all our guys, hirin' Bush-men on the sly*
> *We may never get school prayer back.*

The attacks found their target. "The ceaseless sniping from the far right took its toll on Baker, more than it did on me," Michael Deaver remembered. But only those close to Baker could really see it. Peggy Noonan, who rose to fame as a speechwriter for Reagan later in his tenure, did not realize it until long after the White House during a flight she shared with Baker when he opened up about the old wounds. "I never knew until just a few years ago how he, Jim Baker, suffered through those days," she said. Noonan never bought the notion that Baker had "delusions of grandeur" that he was going to make Reagan a moderate. "Reagan was going to be a conservative and Baker was going to be the conservative's chief of staff," she said. "I don't think he tried to change his boss but when he thought an issue was not going to be a fruitful area for Reagan I think he would tell him." Stuart Spencer considered the line of attack ludicrous. "The accusation used to drive me crazy," he said. "I'd say, 'This guy is a Republican Texan! They are conservative!' But he's a pragmatist too, just like Reagan was."

David Stockman believed Baker was, at heart, instinctively conservative but driven more by success than ideology or details. "On matters of policy and substance," he said, "Baker was a 'leaner'; that is, given the choice between more central government and bureaucracy versus greater emphasis on private markets and local governments, he inclined strongly toward the latter. But Baker was, deep down, neither very versed on matters of policy nor intensely interested in them. As long as it was directionally sound, he was satisfied."

Baker came under fire in large part because conservatives did not dare criticize the president himself. "Frankly, we weren't in a position to be out there attacking Reagan," Richard Viguerie said years later. "He was too popular with the grass roots. It was easier to go after Dick Darman, Baker, Mike Deaver and all of them. So we directed our anger, disappointment, frustration toward those people. But truth be known, Reagan knew what he was doing." Viguerie acknowledged Baker's value to Reagan. "Every president needs a Jim Baker," he said. "Jim Baker made his trains run on time. He did the hiring and firing and he just made life much easier for Reagan than it would have been otherwise. I just wish he had chosen someone more ideologically akin to him."

NOT ALL OF the rivalries in the Reagan White House were about ideology. Baker was already emerging as an unusually powerful chief of staff, but the staff itself was a dysfunctional mess of the more conventional kind, torn by intrigue, backbiting, rival power centers, personal feuds, and shameless posturing. The rule of thumb, as Peggy Noonan later put it, was that "we would have not been stabbing each other in the back, we would have been stabbing each other in the front."

Larry Speakes, for instance, detested David Gergen, deeming him a

Baker spy and a rival for the top media role in Reagan's White House, so he gave the six-foot-five communications director the nickname "the Tall Man," a phrase that he meant to be derogatory and later shortened to just "Tall." When Gergen addressed reporters, Speakes had his staff lower the lectern in the White House briefing room so that he would "tower over it like Ichabod Crane." As Speakes later admitted, "we threw virtually every booby trap in his way that we could, planted every story, egged the press on to get down on him."

Speakes, who took over the press operation after the assassination attempt but never assumed the title of press secretary out of deference to Jim Brady, also ran afoul of Baker at times. When Speakes described for a *Washington Post* reporter how the staff prepared Reagan for a news conference, it resulted in a story that made the president look like he simply delivered scripted answers. After the article appeared, Baker took Speakes aside. "I want you to go into the Oval Office and apologize to the president," he ordered. Speakes did. Reagan was forgiving but clearly wounded. "That's all right," the president told Speakes, "but you made me look like Charlie McCarthy," the ventriloquist's dummy.

That was a tried-and-true technique for Baker, sending rogue staffers into the Oval Office, where he knew they would be pardoned by a softhearted president. When Ed Rollins, the White House political director, was quoted as telling a reporter that Maureen Reagan, the president's oldest daughter, who was running for Senate in California, had "the highest negatives of any candidate I've seen," he was summoned to Baker's office. Deaver was there, waving a copy of a wire service news story with the quote and fuming with anger. Baker let Rollins stew about it over the weekend and then on the following Monday morning told him he would not be fired but would have to apologize to the president. "You've gotta go to the woodshed and he'll kick your ass good," Baker told him, "but I saved your ass." As with Speakes, Reagan went easy on him. After all, the president himself had said publicly that he wished that Maureen would not run. Baker did not take Rollins's relief well, seemingly miffed that he was not acting chastened enough. "Now goddamnit, you walk out of here like a guy who's been to the woodshed," Baker demanded. "I don't care how good you feel. You're a mighty lucky man." Baker again claimed responsibility for the outcome. "Just remember who your friend was," he lectured, although Rollins later concluded that Baker had taken credit for saving him when in fact he had not.

No one, however, demonstrated greater indiscipline in the first year of Reagan's presidency than David Stockman. Brilliant more than wise, too candid for his own good, the thirty-four-year-old former congress-man was a onetime Marxist who was turned off by antiwar violence and concluded that "the left was inherently totalitarian." He had joined the Reagan White House with a zealous sense of mission, determined to tame big government and make it "a spare and stingy creature, which offered even-handed public justice, but no more." But as Reagan's presidency pro-gressed, Stockman grew disenchanted with the forces of status quo he called the Second Republic, and came to the belated realization that even fellow conservatives were not fully committed to radically scaling back the scope of government if it involved political pain.

Stockman secretly confided these frustrations and experiences to Wil-liam Greider, a *Washington Post* editor who was writing a long article for *The Atlantic Monthly*. In eighteen tape-recorded sessions over the course of his first year, Stockman exhibited a cynical view of Reagan's economic program, saying that supply-side theory was just a disguised version of "trickle-down" policy and that the tax cut legislation was just a "Trojan horse to bring down the top rate" on the wealthiest. He revealed to Grei-der the "magic asterisk" that the White House had used to disguise future deficits with illusory unspecified spending cuts.

When the article was published under the headline "The Education of David Stockman" in November 1981, Baker faced the fallout. Deaver, Ed Meese, Lyn Nofziger, and others wanted Stockman fired. "David Stock-man stuck a knife between the president's ribs," Deaver complained. Baker still valued Stockman's skill and wanted to keep him, making the case "in that deliberate, dispassionate, almost lulling way," as Reagan's long-time aide, Helene Von Damm, put it. Fortunately for Stockman, Reagan agreed. "He didn't like to fire people," Meese said later, "largely, I think, because his father had been fired and he always remembered that."

But Baker knew a public price had to be paid and orchestrated a ritual punishment for Stockman. Summoned to the chief of staff's corner office, Stockman found a different Baker than he was used to—no off-color jokes, no casual waltz around his office, no jump shot sending a wad of paper into the wastebasket.

"My friend," Baker started, "I want you to listen up good. Your ass is in a sling. All of the rest of them want you shit-canned right now. Immedi-ately. This afternoon. If it weren't for me, you'd be a goner already. But I got you one last chance to save yourself. So you're going to do it precisely and exactly like I tell you. Otherwise, you're finished around here."

Baker told Stockman that he was to have lunch with the president. "The menu is humble pie," Baker said. "You're going to eat every last mother fucking spoonful of it. You're going to be the most contrite son of a bitch this world has ever seen."

Baker stood to end the meeting. "Let me repeat something, just in case you didn't get the point," he added sternly. "When you go through the Oval Office door, I want to see that sorry ass of yours dragging on the carpet."

Stockman was stunned. Never in his life had anyone talked to him in such a humiliating way. But he realized that Baker was trying to shock him into understanding that the shark feed was on. Baker played the disciplinarian because he knew Reagan would not. Indeed, when Stockman went in for his "woodshed" session, the president said he was disappointed but readily forgave him over soup and tuna salad, just as he would with other transgressors. The grateful miscreants were meant to thank Reagan—and Baker—for saving them.

AS POWERFUL AS he was becoming in Reagan's White House, Baker largely played a secondary role when it came to foreign policy in his early years as chief of staff. His pact with Deaver to keep an eye on the Central America hard-liners was largely defensive. He considered himself a Cold War conservative but he was not interested in provoking another turf war, nor did he have enough mastery of the issues to play a major role in shaping policy. To a large extent, he ceded the territory to Ed Meese, who wrested control in their initial power-sharing negotiation and made sure that the national security adviser Richard Allen reported to him.

The exception was when Congress got involved. Then it usually fell to Baker to make lawmakers fall in line, a task sometimes easier defined than achieved with the House in opposition hands. Baker's main involvement with international affairs in his first year came with the sale of sophisticated aircraft to Saudi Arabia. Jimmy Carter had favored the arms sale and, as he left office, one of the few things he asked of Reagan was to follow through on it. The incoming president agreed. When Baker heard that would be one of the top priorities for the White House, he "was politically disappointed because he did not see that as anywhere near the priority of other things that they wanted to move on," said Robert Kimmitt, then a young military officer working on the National Security Council staff. Baker managed to put off the fight for months, under his economy-first dictum, but by the late summer of 1981 he could wait no longer. It became a test of Reagan's clout, a test that Baker had to pass.

The $8.5 billion arms sale would provide Saudi Arabia with, among other weapons, five Airborne Warning and Control System planes, commonly known as AWACS, used to give early warning against enemy attack and to manage air-to-air combat. Israel strongly opposed the sale, fearing it would empower an Arab adversary. A strong supporter of Israel, Reagan was reluctant to disappoint a friend but he saw value in building relationships with key Arab allies. Moreover, Reagan grew annoyed by Israeli lobbying. Hosting Prime Minister Menachem Begin for a State Dinner in September, Reagan thought the Israeli leader had promised not to fight the sale, only to grow perturbed when he learned that Begin was in fact rallying opposition on Capitol Hill. When he formally announced plans to proceed with the sale, Reagan made his irritation plain. "It is not the business of other nations to make American foreign policy," the president said.

Under the arcane rules of arms sales, the deal would go through unless both houses voted against it, which meant Baker only had to prevail in the Republican-controlled Senate. When President Anwar Sadat of Egypt, who courageously made peace with Begin in Camp David talks hosted by Carter, was assassinated just days after Reagan's announcement, Baker brought key lawmakers to the White House to meet with the president and hear him talk about the need to bolster the forces of moderation in the region. Nonetheless, the House voted overwhelmingly, 301 to 111, to block the sale. Baker understood that Reagan's credibility, both at home and abroad, was at stake. "We knew we had to win this fight," said Kimmitt.

Baker sat down with several Republican senators who wanted conditions in exchange for their votes. Ultimately, Baker and his team adopted some of their proposed language and crafted a letter with six conditions that the president promised to meet before executing the sale. Among them, he would obtain an agreement from the Saudis that would prevent use of the aircraft against Israel and certify that the Saudis were making efforts to encourage peace between the Israelis and Arabs. It was a classic Baker solution to the problem. As a negotiator, he always looked for ways to satisfy his counterparts' concerns—or more precisely, ways to let his counterparts publicly demonstrate that their concerns had been addressed—without giving up the substance of what he was trying to secure.

When the day of the vote arrived, eight original sponsors of the resolution of disapproval voted against their own motion, giving the White House a 52 to 48 victory. Senator John Glenn, an Ohio Democrat leading the opposition, groused that Baker's team had bought and strong-armed votes, declaring that the president was "ill served by a staff that uses methods like that."

The AWACS fight completed Baker's disenchantment with Richard Allen and ultimately helped accelerate the end of his tour as national security adviser. A hawk on Vietnam and a skeptic of détente with the Soviet Union, Allen had served as a deputy to Henry Kissinger in the Nixon White House before becoming Reagan's foreign policy adviser in the years leading up to his election. Allen was close enough to the future president that he was the one who suggested George Bush as the backup choice for running mate when the misguided negotiations with Gerald Ford collapsed.

But even though he was named national security adviser, Allen had not been given the same stature and authority that Kissinger had. Ed Meese took the northwest corner office that Kissinger and other national security advisers had occupied while Allen was consigned to the White House basement. Rather than report directly to the president, as his predecessors had, Allen answered to Meese. Allen's briefings to the president were eventually cut out altogether in the name of efficiency. He was, in the words of David Rothkopf, a historian of the National Security Council, the "not-quite-national-security adviser." According to Al Haig, Allen was "regarded by his colleagues as being irrelevant. In time, I am sorry to say, I came to regard him in that light too."

So Allen was already standing in quicksand when he got in trouble for accepting $1,000 from a Japanese magazine intended for Nancy Reagan as a gratuity for granting an interview on the day after her husband's inauguration. This was in keeping with the custom of Japanese media. Allen explained that he had been given an envelope with ten $100 bills but instructed an aide to figure out what to do about it, whereupon the cash was stored in his office safe. He forgot about it until colleagues came across it. The Japanese journalists had also given him two wristwatches. When the matter went public, Allen took a leave while the Justice Department investigated. He was cleared, but when Allen arrived in the White House expecting to return to his job, he discovered that Reagan was not prepared to have him back. "I could see he had been gotten to by others," Allen said later. Did he suspect Baker's hand? "No," Allen said. "I just think he didn't help. He wasn't the hatchet in that respect."

To replace him, Reagan tapped William Clark, the Californian serving as Haig's deputy. Ideologically, there was little difference between Allen and Clark. They were both conservatives favoring a hawkish approach to the Soviet Union. But Clark had the closer relationship with Reagan and had in fact been Meese's superior in California, and he was not about to become his subordinate now; instead of reporting to Meese, he would report directly to the president. As a result, Clark's arrival had the added benefit from Baker's perspective of further diminishing Meese's power.

Reagan saw foreign policy in Cold War terms and, as Baker had antici-pated, the president and his more conservative advisers were fixated on Nicaragua as the latest battleground in the long-running proxy war with the Soviet Union. The Somoza dynasty, a brutal, pro-American govern-ment that ruled Nicaragua for forty-three years, had fallen in July 1979 amid widespread public discontent. By the next year, power was consoli-dated in the hands of the Marxist opposition force known as the San-dinista National Liberation Front, named after General Augusto César Sandino, an iconic figure who had opposed American policy in the region until his assassination in 1934.

The Sandinistas, led by Daniel Ortega, a fiery guerrilla leader with a bushy mustache and designer sunglasses, signed agreements with the Soviet Union for military aid while Cuban advisers streamed into the country. Nicaragua also started actively aiding the leftist rebellion against the pro-Washington military government in neighboring El Salvador. To Reagan and some of his advisers, this was the old domino theory all over again, playing out in America's backyard. To stop it, they decided to embrace a motley assemblage of resistance fighters known as the contras, or counterrevolutionaries, a mix of former Somoza national guardsmen, disaffected Sandinistas, and Nicaraguans unaffiliated with either side. On December 1, 1981, Reagan signed an order known as an intelligence find-ing authorizing a covert CIA program to arm, train, and supply the con-tras with about $19 million. The stated goal at that point was to stop the flow of arms from Nicaragua to El Salvador.

To Baker, this could be the first step down the slippery slope that he had feared from the earliest days of the administration. Reagan saw it as a noble venture, part of his broader assault on the Soviet empire. Addressing both houses of Britain's Parliament in Westminster Palace in June 1982, Reagan gave one of the defining speeches of the Cold War, presciently diagnosing the "decay of the Soviet experiment" and vowing to promote democracy around the world. "What I am describing now is a plan and a hope for the long term—the march of freedom and democracy, which will leave Marxism-Leninism on the ash heap of history."

By that summer of 1982, Baker's most pressing foreign policy problem, however, was in Washington. The foreign policy team was, he believed, a "witches' brew of intrigue, elbows, egos, and separate agendas." The chief intriguer, in his mind, was Al Haig, whose tenure in the cabinet had gone from bad to worse to simply untenable as far as the chief of staff was concerned. Since the first day of the administration, Baker had struggled to keep Haig in line, only to find the willful secretary of state virtually unmanageable. "What an ego!" Baker was overheard calling out when he hung up the phone after another testy conversation with the secretary. Baker was not alone. Haig had few allies in the West Wing. "I used to describe Al Haig as a cobra among garter snakes," said Donald Gregg, a White House aide who would become the vice president's national security adviser. "At the cabinet meetings, whereas everybody else would be sort of slithering happily around the table, he was up there, with his lips spread, looking for somebody to bite." Haig had threatened to resign on multiple occasions over the course of Reagan's first year, but Baker and his camp initially feared the damage a public rupture might cause. Michael Deaver, no Haig fan, had argued that they could not afford to let him go, at least not right away. "I was convinced that politically it would be terrible if Reagan lost his secretary of state the first year," Deaver said.

Haig's sense of his own importance was boundless. At Anwar Sadat's funeral in Egypt, he was miffed that the three former American presidents also in the delegation were getting more attention than he was. He ordered the American ambassador in Cairo to threaten the Egyptians with the loss of foreign aid if he did not get more play in the media.

Haig never did figure out the Reagan operation. The man who had expertly maneuvered himself to the highest echelon of the Nixon White House was left scratching his head about this new team. "To me, the White House was as mysterious as a ghost ship; you heard the creak of the rigging and the groan of the timbers and sometimes even glimpsed the crew on deck," he said. "But which of the crew had the helm? Was it Meese, was it Baker, was it someone else? It was impossible to know for sure."

Privately, he saw Baker as the villain, "That son of a bitch is the worst influence I have ever seen in the federal government," Haig told a colleague. Publicly, he complained about what he called a "guerrilla campaign" against him, led presumably by Baker. Amused, Deaver borrowed a gorilla outfit and burst into a cabinet meeting around Baker's birthday.

"Happy birthday Jim, from the White House gorillas," Deaver called out.

"The president broke up," Deaver recalled, "but Haig found no humor in it at all."

By the second year, the situation was unsustainable and Baker and

Deaver, joined by William Clark, no longer seemed reticent to show Haig the door. Larry Speakes thought their plan was a time-honored scheme in Washington, "trying to irritate him enough to make him quit." That seemed a fair surmise when the White House gave Haig a KC-135 retrofitted cargo transport with no windows for a trip to Britain and Argentina and assigned him to a noisy military helicopter open to the wind during a visit to London. Enraged, Haig blamed Baker. "Clark told me that James Baker was in charge of assigning aircraft and that he guarded the prerogative jealously," Haig said. "It was he who had chosen my plane and only he could change the order." Baker later denied that, saying it was really Deaver, acting on behalf of Nancy Reagan, who had "decided that Haig was not serving her husband well."

When Israel invaded Lebanon in June 1982, just a couple days before Reagan's Westminster speech, the war inside the administration reached a climax. Baker and the others grew irritated that Haig sought the limelight in the midst of a grave international crisis "in a manner that seemed to pre-empt the president's authority," as Robert "Bud" McFarlane, then the deputy national security adviser, put it. They were particularly annoyed when Haig gave instructions on how to handle the unfolding crisis to Philip Habib, the administration's special envoy, without approval from Reagan. For his part, Haig was irked during a trip to Europe with the president when he was seated on Air Force One behind the compartment with Baker and Deaver. "At least he's got a window this time," Baker whispered to Deaver. But the trip only widened the rift amid a series of quarrels over a United Nations resolution. Baker and Deaver returned to Washington "with a white-knuckled animus toward Al Haig," McFarlane said.

Haig, feeling undercut once again by the Baker "guerrillas," told the president he would leave unless his status was restored and the incoherent foreign policy lines of communication were clarified once and for all in his favor. This time, Reagan stunned Haig by accepting his secretary's threat to step down. Floored, Haig headed back to the State Department and set about writing a letter of resignation he had not actually expected to submit when he heard his departure announced on television along with the selection of former treasury secretary George Shultz as his replacement. "I assumed that he had been convinced to get rid of me by Baker and Deaver," Haig said. He blamed them for "planting their toxic stories."

Baker thought Haig had used the resignation bluff once too often. "I was in there when the president said, 'Well, Al, you just better let me have that letter. I'm sorry.'" Haig's perceived discourtesy to Nancy Reagan certainly did not help. The news of Haig's fall spread quickly in the West Wing and produced a wave of rejoicing. "I don't think anyone inside the White House on the president's staff was sorry that Secretary of State Haig resigned," said Margaret Tutwiler. Deaver was blunter: "We were all high-fiving inside the Oval Office."

Even Reagan seemed glad to have it finally resolved. As he headed to the White House briefing room to announce Haig's resignation, he cracked a few jokes. Baker, ever worried about the president's public image, cautioned him against levity.

"Whoa there," Baker said. "We better get serious here."

"Oh, don't worry," said Reagan, still very much the actor. "I'll play it somber."

After the announcement, Reagan headed to Camp David and then watched Haig read his resignation letter on television. "He gave only one reason and did say there was a disagreement on foreign policy," Reagan wrote in his diary that night. "Actually the only disagreement was over whether I made policy or the Sec. of State did."

That night, Haig went to a previously scheduled dinner at the home of the plugged-in Saudi diplomat, Prince Bandar bin Sultan. He was overcome with emotion—and blamed Baker and his coterie for his downfall. "I was set up and I was so stupid," he told the dinner guests. "I let them set me up."

BY THE TIME Haig was out, it was increasingly clear that Baker had emerged as the dominant force inside the White House. The Troika was more and more just a fiction for public consumption. Craig Fuller admitted as much one day in a background interview with Sara Fritz from *U.S. News & World Report.* "Baker is solely in charge," she wrote in her notes, summarizing their conversation. When she wrote up an item in the next week's magazine to that effect, without naming Fuller as her source, Meese erupted and stormed into Deaver's office demanding to know what he would do about it. But there was nothing to do. The reality was what it was. Baker had won.

The question was what Baker could do with the influence. Deep into the administration's second year, the country was back in recession and, after the tax cuts of Reagan's early months and the unrealized spending cuts of the "magic asterisk," the government was swimming in red ink. Baker felt increasing pressure to do more to reverse the trends, but negotiations seeking more budget cuts with Democrats on Capitol Hill resulted in stalemate. Reagan's approval rating had fallen from 68 percent several weeks after the assassination attempt to 43 percent in the spring of 1982. For months, David Stockman had been trying to get the White House to back more serious spending restraints but kept running into roadblocks. Baker deep-sixed another run at Social Security. Defense Secretary Caspar Weinberger refused to pare back his hard-won military spending increases. And Donald Regan objected to any delay in the tax cuts.

But Baker concluded that something needed to be done. As much as he hated to admit it, perhaps they had gone too far in slashing taxes the year before. Knowing that such a course correction would be a hard sell with the president, Baker set about gathering allies, convincing Deaver, Ed Meese, and even Nancy Reagan that raising taxes was inevitable. When they made their case to Reagan, Baker tried to make it more acceptable by telling him that they would cut spending three dollars for every dollar of taxes raised.

Reagan never really understood the economic theories or the complicated numbers involved. He was a big-picture guy and depended on Baker and the others to fill it in. Instead, he kept telling the same old musty anecdotes about how he saved money as California governor by printing forms on smaller paper so they would not have to be folded and the state could buy fewer file cabinets.

Finally, against his instincts, Reagan gave in. Angry, the normally laid-back president threw his glasses down on the table. "All right, goddamn it, I'm going to do it," he snapped. "But it's wrong."

Reagan authorized Baker to negotiate a deficit reduction plan that would include tax increases and cuts in the new military spending Reagan had already gotten passed. Reagan rebuffed Democratic pressure to cancel the third year of his original income tax rate cuts, so Baker and his team brokered a deal with Speaker Tip O'Neill to raise $98 billion over three years by closing loopholes, raising corporate tax rates, and adopting other measures. Conservatives howled at the apostasy. To them, it was the ultimate proof that Baker was leading Reagan down the wrong path. Baker was "extraordinarily cunning and manipulative, a man for whom making the deal is more important than what's in it," said Ed Rollins.

Among the critics was Lyn Nofziger, the scruffy political director who had left the White House by then as a committed enemy of Baker. The two had not gotten along from the start. To Nofziger, Baker was "among the slickest of political operators in a town where slick operators came a dime a dozen, or cheaper." There was no commitment to Reagan or the Reagan cause, Nofziger believed. "His best buddy is himself, James A. Baker III."

The two sniped over even the pettiest issues. When Baker ordered staff members to wear their White House passes at all times while in the building, Nofziger ostentatiously refused. He came to regret accepting the post of political director, declaring that he had made three mistakes after Reagan's election. "The first was taking the job and the second and third were trusting Jim Baker." The feeling was mutual. "I did make a mistake doing that," Baker said later of his decision to hire Nofziger. He had hoped that would win him points with conservatives. "That's how naive I was; I thought this would be good cover for me."

So when Reagan agreed to support tax increases, an outraged Nofziger met with conservative allies to map out opposition to the plan, including Martin Anderson, the president's onetime domestic policy adviser who had also left the White House. When Reagan learned about the meeting, he summoned Nofziger and Anderson to the White House and, with Baker, Deaver, and Meese sitting nearby, expressed disappointment that his former aides were organizing against him. Before Nofziger could plead their case, Baker interrupted.

"Why don't you ask Lyn to come down and help us pass the bill?" he asked Reagan.

The president seemed dumbfounded. So was Nofziger.

"Would you?" Reagan asked.

Nofziger asked to think about it.

Baker had sandbagged him. He knew Nofziger could hardly refuse Reagan and thought that putting a prominent conservative in charge of passing a tax increase would potentially moot some of the opposition—or, at the very least, put the blame on a rival if it failed. Nofziger grudgingly agreed to come back to the White House later that day to meet with Baker to discuss the idea, but when he arrived at the gate and showed the Secret Service his old, expired pass, the officer refused to let him in and seized the badge. Swearing, Nofziger stormed off, blaming Baker. Back at his office, Nofziger grabbed a picture of Baker off the wall, threw it on the floor, and stomped on it. He refused to take Baker's call.

The next morning, Baker and Deaver personally showed up at Nofziger's office to ask him to take the assignment. Baker tossed Nofziger's pass on the coffee table.

"There's your pass," he said. "I didn't tell them to confiscate it, but next time make arrangements to keep it."

"It seemed clear to me that you didn't want me very badly if you were going to take my pass," Nofziger said.

"We want you," Baker insisted. "The president needs you."

Between them, Baker and Nofziger pushed the tax plan through Congress, overcoming conservative resistance and cajoling 103 House Republicans to support it. In years to come, many would cite Reagan's willingness to forgo his natural instincts on taxes as proof that he was more pragmatic than commonly assumed. And they would credit, or blame, Baker for being the one to lead him there—or manipulate him, depending on the point of view. The tax increases helped offset some of the lost revenue from the original tax cuts. But Baker came to regret the move. "He was right and we were wrong," he said of Reagan. They had overreacted, Baker concluded in retirement. "I'm a reformed drunk when it comes to supply-side economics."

WITH HIS ELEVATED PROFILE, some Texas Republicans began wooing Baker to return home and run for office. Senator Lloyd Bentsen, the Democrat who had beat his friend George Bush in 1970, was up for reelection and some thought Reagan's popularity could help Baker unseat him. Baker was sent poll numbers intended to entice him, showing that he had the most support of five possible candidates in a Republican primary with 18 percent; of the five, he tested second-best against Bentsen. If there was a temptation to take down the Democrat who defeated Bush, however, Baker resisted the urge. He knew how tough Bentsen would be to beat even in a good election year. In red ink, he scribbled at the top of the memo with the poll results: "(1) I'm not running. (2) We don't get involved in primaries."

He even resisted encouragement on the home front. "Dad, why don't you run for that?" his son Doug asked one day.

"I don't really want to be a freshman senator," he answered. "I'm White House chief of staff."

Baker was a political realist and he knew that even with Reagan as the party's titular head, the Republicans were looking ahead to a tough campaign season. Despite Baker's success at mastering the politics of Capitol Hill and convincing a Congress partly controlled by the opposition to follow Reagan's lead, the country was mired in a dark mood in the administration's second year. History would later obscure this period amid gauzy revisionist narratives of the Reagan era, but that's not how it looked at the time. The recession was the worst economic contraction since the Great

Depression to that point and the comparisons were certainly not helping Reagan politically.

With the Federal Reserve raising interest rates to try to tame inflation, jobs were vanishing and businesses shuttering their doors. By November 1982, unemployment had reached 10.8 percent, far worse than anything during Jimmy Carter's presidency and the highest rate since the Depression. More than seventeen thousand businesses failed, the second highest since 1933. Farms were foreclosed on, home sales fell. Reagan's once sky-high approval ratings continued sinking as polls showed most Americans blaming his policies.

The economy hit bottom just as voters went to the polls in the midterm elections. As predicted, they exacted punishment on Reagan's Republicans. On November 2, the president's team joined him in the White House residence for a buffet dinner to watch the returns. The GOP lost twenty-six seats in the House that night, effectively ending the conservative coalition that Reagan had built with conservative Democrats and giving Tip O'Neill firm control over the body. "Had to expect that & it could have been worse," Reagan dictated to his diary. Republicans did better in the Senate, holding on to their majority and even adding a seat.

But Reagan was politically damaged. His approval rating dropped to 35 percent in January 1983, the lowest of his presidency. Only a third of Americans even wanted him to run for reelection in two years. If Baker was to turn things around and win a second term for his president, he would have to live up to his 1976 nickname, the Miracle Man.

CHAPTER 12

The Ratfuck

One day just a few weeks after the disastrous 1982 midterm elections, Baker got a call. His son John had been arrested on drug charges back in Texas. The private troubles that had been afflicting Baker's family for the past decade were about to spill over into public view.

Baker had made a name for himself at this point as the buttoned-down lawyer who ran the White House efficiently and effectively. What few around him knew was that he struggled to run his own home efficiently and effectively. With the children mostly grown or away in school, the tensions had subsided, but each day brought the risk of another meltdown.

In John's case, it came in the form of a sting operation by the sheriff's department in Pearsall, where he had recently moved. Now twenty-two years old, the only one of the Baker children not to go to college, John had been bouncing around without much purpose, officially managing the family's Rockpile Ranch but more interested in smoking another joint than finding a real job. Baker understood what his son was up to. When John moved to Pearsall, his father had warned him that Frio County was a Democratic jurisdiction with a Democratic sheriff. "Without saying it, he knew I was doing drugs and he was trying to tell me, without telling me, 'Don't do that, you need to be careful who you're with,'" John said years later. "And I was like, 'I know what the hell I'm doing.'"

Except, of course, he did not. Undercover agents came to him asking to buy some pot and he sold it to them. They later arrested him on a felony charge of delivering less than an ounce of marijuana. John was positive it was a political attack on his father. "They clearly knew who I was," he said. "It was a raw deal." Not that he denied the crime. Later in life, after years of rehabilitation, he would admit the fault was his. But he also knew he had put his father in a terrible position, and that added to the emotional turmoil. After spending just thirty minutes in jail on that day in December 1982, John was released on a $10,000 bond, but faced a maximum penalty of ten years in prison and a $5,000 fine. Baker reached his son by telephone and tried to console him. Baker then put Larry Speakes, the White House spokesman, on the line to advise him how to handle any reporter inquiries. Baker felt miserable. "It was a BS thing," he concluded. "If he hadn't been my son, he would never have had" all the attention. "Poor kid. I felt really sorry for him."

The episode with John came as Baker was working for a president who had made "the war on drugs" a centerpiece of his domestic agenda. Just two months before the arrest, Reagan had declared in a speech at the Justice Department that illegal drugs now constituted a threat to the national security of the United States. Nancy Reagan picked up on the issue too. During a stop at Longfellow Elementary School in Oakland, California, she urged youngsters to stay away from drugs. When a fourth-grade girl asked what they should do if someone offered them drugs, the first lady replied, "Just say no." With that, a slogan was born, one that she would transform into the signature of her time in the White House. Eventually, Just Say No clubs would form and Nancy Reagan would record public service announcements, write guest articles, and appear on popular television shows like *Diff'rent Strokes* and *Dynasty* to promote an antidrug message.

Little did she realize that her husband's top aide was struggling with the issue in his own family. Baker later recalled no conversations with the first lady about it, an indication of just how much he kept his private life private. The Reagans were surely aware of what had happened—John's arrest had been reported in the media and other staff members knew about it—but they were no likelier to inquire than Baker was to volunteer. If it was awkward for Baker to be running the just-say-no White House while his children were just saying yes, he did not let on. And it was a sign of the times that reporters, while publishing short notices about John's arrest, did not make a big story of it. Baker's friends in the mainstream press were sympathetic and, in that era at least, largely stayed away from reporting on the families of the people they covered.

But the Baker family's ordeal was one that defined the era. Thirty-four percent of high school students in the United States reported using illicit drugs in 1982, a huge proportion of the nation's emerging adults and only slightly off its peak in 1979. Eleven percent reported using cocaine, double the proportion in the middle of the previous decade. In Mexico and Colombia, a whole deadly new industry had arisen around cocaine as drug cartels led by shadowy figures like the soon-to-be notorious Pablo

Escobar made millions catering to the tastes of wealthy North Americans. The explosion of the derivative crack cocaine later in the 1980s would wreak havoc on inner cities and fuel a surge of violence.

Baker sat in policy meetings discussing what to do about the drug crisis during the day and then confronted it at home at night. "He had to balance his professional career at the White House with his personal life," said Doug Baker. "Susan could handle most of it but he needed to get involved in the real diplomacy, father-son moments, to sort of say, 'Look, I get where you're coming from, but this is unacceptable and you've got to get a handle on it and if that means going somewhere and family being involved in these sessions, I'm willing to do it.' "

John ultimately reached a plea bargain, admitting guilt on a misdemeanor charge and paying a $2,000 fine. After his arrest, he flew to New York to check in to a drug rehabilitation clinic. At the airport, he found his father, trailed by Secret Service agents, waiting to take him. "When I saw my dad and I saw the look on his face, I burst into tears," John said. "He just put his arms around me and told me, you know, 'You're going to get through this. I'm very proud of you. We've got a hiccup. We've just got to get through this.' "

Eventually, they would, but not without more pain and heartache. For Baker, it was a defining challenge of his personal life. "I think every one of our kids, with the possible exception of Bo and Mary-Bonner, tried drugs at one time," he said years later. "Maybe not Doug."

Susan, sitting next to him, shook her head at her husband's naïveté. "Honey," she said indulgently, "Bo was the *ringleader*."

"But MB never did, right?" Baker asked almost plaintively, referring to Mary-Bonner. "She did?"

Susan smiled. "Shall I burst the bubble?"

AFTER TWO YEARS, Baker had built a relationship with Reagan and come to dominate the White House, but his growing influence had made him even more of a target. The brawling at this point was endemic. Baker came to call it *the ratfuck*, an old Texas term for "people stabbing you in the back, always fighting." He saw secret trapdoors everywhere and he knew his rivals were eagerly playing the president in hopes of securing advantage. After the midterm election, for instance, Reagan offered Baker the job of secretary of transportation—an idea that other White House aides believed was planted by Ed Meese to get rid of his foe. Baker turned it down.

With the election behind them, Baker took on the third rail that had singed him back in the early months of the administration: Social Security. Following the debacle of David Stockman's original proposal to stabilize the retirement program's finances, Reagan and congressional leaders had appointed a fifteen-member bipartisan commission to study the issue, headed by Alan Greenspan, the widely respected former economic adviser to Gerald Ford, and including prominent appointees from both parties. Baker was "*the* conduit, it was his commission," Greenspan recalled. "He set it up so that both Tip O'Neill and Reagan were brought along from the very early stages." The commission was due to report back after the 1982 election but stalled amid disagreement over how to spread the pain. The issue was urgent—the Social Security trust fund was projected to run out by the middle of 1983, meaning that 36 million recipients were at risk of having their checks held up. So finally, a handful of commission members formed what was called a "sub-group" to work out a plan with Baker.

On January 5, 1983, the chief of staff invited the negotiators to his house on Foxhall Road, where no one would know they were meeting. They proceeded downstairs to the basement with its large picture window facing out on the woods, big-game trophy heads mounted on the wall, and a zebra skin covering the floor. While the group included senators, congressmen, and other White House aides, it ultimately fell to Baker and Robert Ball, a former Social Security commissioner who was O'Neill's appointee, to hammer out an agreement. For Baker, it was a characteristically pragmatic negotiation, just hardheaded bargaining over what was doable and what was not. Baker came in proposing a three-year delay in cost-of-living increases. Ball resisted and eventually they compromised on a six-month postponement that would permanently change the date that future increases took effect each year. When Ball pushed for more revenues, Baker ultimately agreed to move up already scheduled tax increases so they would take effect sooner.

The talks continued largely in secret over the next ten days, with little more than a break to watch the Washington Redskins beat the Detroit Lions to advance in the playoffs. When the press caught on to what was happening, they staked out Ball's house in hopes of following him to wherever the clandestine talks were taking place. Ball had to call Baker for help and then slip out the back and down a hill to a White House car that the chief of staff sent for him. By the end of the negotiations, they moved the group to Blair House across the street from the White House, so that Baker could easily shuttle back and forth while consulting with Reagan.

Ultimately, Baker and Ball came up with a formula that both their bosses could live with, a mix of measures that would spread the pain. In addition to the cost-of-living and tax schedule changes, their plan would tax the benefits of higher-income recipients, expand the pool of contributors by bringing in all new federal employees, require the self-employed to pay the employer share of payroll taxes in addition to the employee share, and transfer money from the general government fund to cover the cost of benefits for military veterans. Altogether, it would raise $168 billion to get the fund through the 1980s and into the 1990s, when for a time the program would be in better health because of the increased contributions of the maturing baby boomers. The commission adopted the plan with twelve Republicans and Democrats voting yes and three conservatives voting no. But it came close to falling apart when Baker insisted that Reagan and O'Neill issue a joint statement endorsing the plan, evidently afraid that the president could be left holding the bag if the speaker sounded any less supportive than Reagan did. O'Neill refused but he sent over a copy of the statement he would make, which allowed Baker to calibrate Reagan's so they were roughly parallel. The two leaders worked together to fend off attacks in Congress, although lawmakers did change it in one major respect by adding another provision gradually increasing the full retirement age to sixty-seven by the year 2027.

The joint commitment by Reagan and O'Neill was key to success. They each had to swallow provisions they disdained, but they agreed that compromise was better than conflict. Reagan and O'Neill were neither buddies nor soul mates yet they shared a love for a funny anecdote and an incentive to make deals with the opposition. The two showed on Social Security that they were willing to do just that, even as they bashed each other freely about other issues. The legislation that Reagan signed in April 1983 became known as a model for bipartisan cooperation to solve a critical national problem, one that when it came to Social Security at least would not be repeated again for decades. "This bill demonstrates for all time our nation's ironclad commitment to Social Security," Reagan, whose own commitment to the program until then had been something less than ironclad, said as he put his signature on the bill with O'Neill at his side.

It also was a model for how Baker approached issues. Rather than unilaterally propose unpopular plans that had no chance of success, the way David Stockman had done in 1981, the lesson of Social Security reform in 1983 was to bring all the parties together, keep the principals such as Reagan and O'Neill informed and committed to the process, define the problem as precisely as possible, and agree to stand behind the final product even against members of one's own party. This was all vintage Baker. "The commission he built was a virtuoso demonstration of how to get things done in Washington," Greenspan reflected. Ball pointed out that the commission itself was a bust but agreed that Baker's intervention showed that bipartisan progress was possible. "In our negotiations he was able to put ideology aside and focus on the substance of what had to be done to get an agreement that would meet the needs of both sides," Ball said. "He was also very clearly in charge on his side of the table." As a result, Baker took the issue out of the next election.

Reagan was happy to leave the details to Baker. Strong on his core principles, Reagan was not one for the intricacies of the policies he was ostensibly pursuing. At the Group of 7, or G7, meeting in Williamsburg, Virginia, in spring 1983, Baker gave Reagan a briefing book. The next morning, Reagan arrived late for a meeting with his staff, his eyes puffy and gait slow, looking "as if he had been run over by a Mack truck," as David Gergen recalled. After about twenty minutes, Reagan finally pleaded guilty. "Fellas, I've got a confession to make," he said. Rather than go through the briefing book, he had flipped on the television and found *The Sound of Music*, one of his favorite movies, so he stayed up late watching that instead.

"Reagan really needed a chief of staff," observed Brent Scowcroft. "He wasn't interested in much of the work of the president. So Baker really was co-president in a way." That did not go over well with everyone. Some Reagan stalwarts thought Baker presumed too much. Baker and Deaver treated the president "rather like a grandfather whom one humors but does not take very seriously," observed Richard Pipes, a hawkish historian from Harvard who served on the National Security Council staff.

Baker had more than one Reagan to manage, of course. Nancy was always looming in the background, a force to be reckoned with. She routinely passed judgment on the people who worked for her husband and she was regularly consulted on his schedule. If there was a news conference or a trip or speech, Baker would pass along the proposed date to Deaver, who would check it with the first lady and come back to say whether it looked okay or not.

At some point in his third year as chief of staff, Baker finally learned the secret: Nancy was consulting with an astrologer to determine the best timing for her husband's major events. After the assassination attempt, she got back in touch with Joan Quigley, who read horoscopes in California, and explained that she was scared every time Reagan left the White House.

From that point onward, she would check with Quigley about dates and times for everything from the State of the Union address to foreign visits to medical procedures. "Nancy felt terribly guilty that she hadn't been with Dad when the assassination attempt happened," said Michael Reagan. "She thought somehow that if she had been there, it never would have happened. So she reached out to try to find any way that she could stop this from happening again."

Baker was flabbergasted, but he never objected. If that was what the first lady wanted, then so be it. She did not weigh in on policy or political decisions, just scheduling. Baker never did know whether the president realized what his wife was up to and he was not going to ask. "I was just trying to keep the trains running on time," he said later. "I had a massive workload and I didn't sit there and think, 'Well, wait a minute now, you ought not to schedule a presidential speech on the basis of a horoscope.' I didn't worry about that. My job was to get things done."

Baker kept the secret close and did not even share it with his closest aides. When the traveling press complained at one point about a predawn departure from Andrews Air Force Base that had been necessitated by one of the astrological signs, Margaret Tutwiler confronted Baker and asked why they had to leave that early.

"Why don't you go talk to Mike about this," he suggested.

So she did. And she was stunned when Deaver explained. "It was *insane*," she recalled. She went back to Baker's office. He turned around to face her.

"Do you understand *now*?" he asked.

Baker recognized that part of his job was keeping the first lady happy, which he did with Deaver's help. Nancy respected Baker's skill in running the White House and came to value his counsel. She thought he was more willing than Reagan to compromise, but unlike Baker's conservative critics she considered him loyal to the president. Still, she recognized that he was a Washington operator. "He also cultivated the press assiduously— perhaps too much, because he leaked constantly," she wrote in her memoir. "Although Jim did a lot for Ronnie, I always felt that his main interest was Jim Baker."

BAKER FOUND HIMSELF increasingly under fire from the right. In December 1982, someone slipped him a copy of a letter that Lyn Nofziger had written to several veterans of Reagan's 1980 campaign, summoning them to a breakfast meeting the following morning to discuss the prospective reelection bid in 1984. "I think it is important that the next presidential election be a Reagan-Bush campaign, not a Bush-Reagan campaign," Nofziger wrote in the letter, a clear jab at Baker. Nofziger went on to say that the true conservatives had to win control of the campaign apparatus from the start. "Frankly, while I'm confident that the President is going to run," he wrote, "I'm not confident that the campaign will be run by Reaganites."

Fuming, Baker showed the letter to Reagan. "How long do I have to work for you before I'm a Reaganite?" he asked, according to an account he later gave a colleague.

Reagan assured him that he was one.

Baker called Nofziger from Air Force One as he and the president returned from South America. Nofziger later described Baker as "out of control, screaming and shouting about my letter and threatening dire circumstances." Nofziger interrupted and said they were not on a secure line and told him to call back when the plane landed. He then hung up.

The phone rang again three minutes later. This time it was Reagan. "Lynwood," he started, referring to Nofziger's full first name like the parent of a teenager who had gone astray. "What are we going to do about this?" he asked, more calmly than Baker, but clearly responding to his angry chief of staff's entreaty to intervene.

Nofziger, unwilling to challenge Reagan, said he would never deliberately embarrass the president and backed off. He promised to tell any reporters who called that he had misspoken. He later sent a letter of apology to Bush. But Baker was not mollified. Still livid, he sent a message to all of Nofziger's invitees who worked in the administration ordering them not to attend the breakfast.

A few weeks later, Baker boasted that he had put Nofziger in his place. "I think we did what we should have done," he told a reporter for *The Dallas Morning News* while hunting wild turkey back in Texas during the holiday break. "We cut him off at the knees." Baker, dressed in military fatigues, went on to complain that Nofziger had stepped out of bounds. "How in the world, if you're in charge of politics at the White House, can you let some damn guy announce he's having a meeting planning the '84 campaign and he hasn't even told you about it?" he fumed. He acknowledged, however, that Nofziger reflected a wider disgruntlement on the right. "Are there a bunch of them out there who'd love to have my scalp? Yeah," he said. "But they know they're not going to get it."

The outburst was a rare instance of Baker being quoted on the record discussing his internal feuds, probably a result of assuming the old rules of speaking on background applied with a reporter who was not one of his usual Washington contacts, and he caught flak for it once it was published. The Nofziger put-down, though, was overshadowed by another comment Baker made during the turkey hunt when he said that Labor Secretary Raymond Donovan should step down. Donovan had been investigated for reputed mafia ties while in business before joining the cabinet, but the special prosecutor determined there was not enough evidence to bring charges. "Ray Donovan shouldn't be in here," Baker told the Dallas reporter. The labor secretary was vindicated, he noted. However, he added, "Now he ought to do what's right for the president." After the story appeared, Reagan was forced to issue a statement expressing full confidence in Donovan and calling Baker's comment "inadvertent and regrettable."

All of this took a toll on Baker, who was finishing his second year running the White House with an eye on the exit. He and Bush remained close and he confided some of his troubles to the friend who had gotten him into politics in the first place. The vice president was not always a day-to-day player in Baker's hectic new life, but he remained a confidant, an ally and a counselor. "Jimmy Baker at year end is tired and would like to transfer," Bush dictated to his taped diary on New Year's Day as 1983 opened. "He would love to be CIA or Defense or certainly Attorney General; but there is no indication that the president is going to make any changes of this nature." Bush doubted that Reagan would let Baker go. A few weeks later, Baker stopped by to see the vice president at his office and asked what his friend thought about the United Nations post. Jeane Kirkpatrick, the ambassador to the UN, evidently was interested in moving on and Baker wondered whether he should consider replacing her. Bush, who had held the job himself during the Nixon administration, encouraged him to consider it.

"I think he should get out," Bush later recorded in his diary. "He's my friend and a loyal friend, but I think it would be good for him to be on about his business and doing something else. You get destroyed in there." Bush suggested that maybe Bill Casey should go to the United Nations and Baker could take over the CIA, another of the vice president's former stomping grounds. "He was thrilled and went charging out of the office," Bush told his diary, "but what he did with that brilliant idea of mine, I don't know."

Reagan was not eager for a change, though, and so Baker remained in the corner office, the crosshairs tattooed on his forehead. On January 20, 1983, at a reunion of administration officials at the DAR Constitution Hall celebrating the second anniversary of Reagan's inauguration, James Watt, a conservative firebrand serving as interior secretary, drew roaring approval with a chant aimed squarely at Baker, who was sitting in the hall. "Let Reagan be Reagan!" Watt shouted as the room erupted in cheers. "Let Reagan be Reagan!"

Allies of Bush and Baker in the room chafed, correctly interpreting it as a dig at them. The refrain, in fact, was such a hit that it became an instant favorite slogan on the right, often repeated at rallies. "This always struck me as odd, for these supposed Reagan devotees were in effect saying the same thing as his most vicious foes, namely that Reagan was a witless actor who merely recited lines others had written for him," reflected Chase Untermeyer, a fellow Houston Republican serving as Bush's executive assistant.

But it was enough to keep Baker and Bush on edge. *Human Events*, the conservative journal that Baker hid from Reagan, blamed the chief of staff for the defeat of a new defense spending increase. Mocking his supposed "legislative wizardry," the journal said that "Mickey Mouse could probably do as well as Baker." As for Bush, he worried about his own place on the coming reelection ticket. When *Conservative Digest* surveyed leaders on the right and found that 64 percent wanted Bush replaced as Reagan's running mate, Bush sent a copy to Baker. "Light reading," he scribbled on a cover sheet along with a frowning face.

Baker's troubles stemmed not just from ideological differences with the ascendant right but from a conviction that he was too smooth for his own good and, as Nancy Reagan said, always out for Jim Baker. Even his friends and admirers acknowledged that he could be cynical and manipulative.

One day in April 1983, Baker summoned Ed Rollins, the White House political director, to his corner office. Burly, balding, and bearded, Rollins was a contrarian figure in the White House, a onetime teenage boxer who grew up in California as a self-described "blue-collar Democrat" before converting for Reagan. Along with Lyn Nofziger, he considered himself one of the keepers of the Reagan flame against the likes of Baker.

"Rollins," Baker told him, "I want you to know that I'm going to give you a place in history and you damn well better remember who did it for you. I've been in there fighting for the last two hours to make you Reagan's campaign manager. It's not a done deal, but if you get it, it's because of me."

Rollins was surprised but pleased and when Baker called again later in the day to tell him the decision was final, he figured the chief of staff must really have gone to bat for him. Paul Laxalt, the senator who was close to Reagan and would serve as chairman of the campaign, called Rollins to congratulate him.

Rollins said he figured he must owe thanks to Baker. Laxalt asked where he got that idea and Rollins told him about his conversation with Baker.

"So *that's* where he went when he snuck out of the meeting," Laxalt said, in Rollins's account. "Ed, you need to know Jim was fighting against you all the way." Baker, in fact, had floated two other candidates for the job: Drew Lewis or Paul Manafort, two operatives he knew from the 1976 Ford campaign. But no one viewed as close to Baker was going to be acceptable to the Reaganites. Rollins became the fallback. Indeed, Laxalt added, Baker assumed that Rollins would not last in the job. His last words to Laxalt were supposedly: "He'll never survive and then I get my pick." That was Rollins's version anyway.

Stuart Spencer remembered the episode differently. In his version, Baker did favor Rollins becoming campaign manager, over Spencer's objection. "I got in this big argument with Baker and Deaver," Spencer said years later. "So finally, I said, 'Okay, I'll take Rollins, but he's got to take Atwater with him.' That's exactly what happened at that meeting." Lee Atwater, a talented young operative in the White House political affairs office, did in fact end up going with Rollins to the campaign. Spencer was clear about the reason too—by tapping him to run the campaign, Baker and Deaver were pushing Rollins out of the White House. "He was dumping on them, he was leaking crap on them, he was saying negative things on Baker," Spencer explained. "They were trying to get rid of him."

Baker in later years made no effort to hide the motivation. "We wanted to get Rollins offline and the way to do that was to make him the campaign manager, where he could go out and be a face card and do some interviews for the campaign, but not have any real serious input," Baker said. "The '84 reelect was run out of my office and Rollins, we gave him the title campaign manager, moved him out of the political job at the White House over to the campaign."

One way or the other, the episode spoke volumes about how Baker operated. Either he cunningly took credit for something he actually opposed in order to pocket a chit or he contemptuously arranged for a fake promotion to rid himself of a troublesome aide who was never to be genuinely allowed to perform the duties assigned.

ON THE MORNING of June 9, Baker woke to find his worst nightmare in *The Washington Post*. It was just a 246-word item buried on page fifteen, hardly a banner story, but the newspaper's White House correspondent, David Hoffman, reported that during the 1980 campaign, the Reagan team had secretly obtained a copy of Jimmy Carter's briefing book before the candidates' only debate. The article also pointed out that Baker had been in charge of debate preparations.

The story was based on *Gambling with History*, a new book by Laurence I. Barrett, a *Time* magazine correspondent, and while the briefing book episode occupied no more space in the text than Hoffman's article, it would quickly transform into perhaps the most threatening and stressful time of Baker's life in politics. The book said that "a Reagan mole in the Carter camp" had stolen the briefing material and that while Baker did not personally know how the Reagan team happened to obtain it, "he looked the other way when a dirty trick was perpetrated on Carter."

For Baker, who cherished his reputation for scruples more than almost anything else, those few words were a body blow. "Baker was really torn apart by that," recalled David Keene. "It's like they're ripping off his merit badge." Having entered politics in the unsettling aftermath of the scandal that forced out a Republican president, Baker had been a stickler for the rules in every campaign and government job he had had, sometimes to a fault. "I came up through Watergate," he said later. "I'm a lawyer and I'm cautious by nature. I'm a cross-the-Ts and dot-the-Is person." It mattered to him that he be seen as a straight arrow. The son of the Warden, the grandson of the Captain, and the great-grandson of the Judge had no intention of being viewed as just another slippery pol. "You build a reputation in the private sector, spend a whole lifetime doing it, go to Washington and one little thing like that could kill you," he said.

Worse, what quickly became dubbed Debategate opened yet another rift within the Reagan team, one that would pit Baker against one of the senior members of the president's circle. Soon after the book's publication, Representative Donald Albosta of Michigan, a little-known Democratic chairman of a minor subcommittee, decided to investigate, prompting a series of conflicting statements from Reagan's administration. Baker dictated a letter to Albosta, but left out the critical information at first. "It is my recollection that I was given the book by"—and here the secretary left a blank space with "(don't know)" in parentheses before continuing—"with the suggestion that it might be of use to the debate briefing team."

He left out the name at first to avoid it leaking, but filled it in for the final draft sent to the committee—Bill Casey, the campaign chairman who had become CIA director.

"I did not know then, nor do I know now, how that book was obtained by the Reagan campaign," Baker wrote in the letter. "I never, directly or indirectly, asked anyone in or out of our campaign, or in the Carter campaign or White House, to provide or acquire that book from the Carter campaign or White House." He added: "It is correct that, after seeing the book, I did not undertake to find out how our campaign had obtained it. There was nothing on its face that suggested it may have been an official document or a document sufficiently sensitive to have been controlled or closely held." He said he "had no reason to believe that the book was illegally acquired."

But Casey denied giving Baker the briefing book or ever having seen it himself. Baker was beside himself. How could Casey deny it? They met on a Sunday to try to reconcile their memories. "Say you saw it," Baker pleaded, assuring Casey that it would not get him into trouble. Casey refused. He insisted he had not seen it.

Soon the *Post* broached the idea of lie detector tests to see who was telling the truth. "It put the fear of God in me because Casey was CIA director and I figured he'll game it and I'm telling the truth and I'll get screwed," Baker said later.

Casey was a formidable adversary. Hunched over with disheveled clothes, thick glasses, a barely decipherable mumble, and a penchant for secrecy, Casey seemed at times like not just America's spy chief but a character out of an espionage novel. A Queens-born lawyer, Casey served during World War II in the Office of Strategic Services, or OSS, the precursor to the CIA, becoming head of secret intelligence in Europe. He returned to the private sector after the war, making millions as a venture capitalist, then bounced around Republican politics for years before Richard Nixon named him chairman of the Securities and Exchange Commission. He later served as an undersecretary of state, chairman of the Export-Import Bank, and a member of the President's Foreign Intelligence Advisory Board before leading Reagan's campaign in 1980.

For his reward, Casey wanted to be secretary of state. But instead he was sent to Langley to head the CIA. "He wasn't quite suave enough" for the world of diplomacy, Nofziger said. "When he talked, he chewed on the end of his tie; food would get caught in his teeth and in the middle of the meal he'd reach around and get it out." Some Reagan confidants thought it was not a good idea to pick Casey for the CIA either. "It was a double mistake, because he put an embittered, brilliant Casey in charge of the CIA, and that led to problems," said Martin Anderson. By the end of his first year in office, Casey was running a secret war in Nicaragua to counter what he viewed as a Communist beachhead in North America.

Since the beginning, when he warned Michael Deaver that Central America could be dangerous to Reagan's presidency, Baker had sensed that Casey was one of those figures whose adventurism could mean trouble. He instructed Dick Darman to set up a system to ensure that Casey would never see Reagan without the chief of staff knowing about it. Anytime Casey did get in to see the president, Baker urged Michael Deaver to casually "drop by" or, at the least, he would personally head over to the Oval Office afterward to debrief Reagan. "Baker was convinced from day one that the hard-right people—Casey, Clark and Haig—would try to move the president into some kind of military action in Central America and would destroy his presidency," Deaver said. "So he would use me, because I could go into a meeting since I wasn't thought of as a player, as far as policy was concerned."

Even when Baker was in the room, it was never totally clear what Casey was up to. The CIA chief would sit next to Reagan and mutter at length until finally the president would nod as if he were following, even though everyone else in the room was convinced that Reagan did not understand what Casey was saying any better than they did. "God knows what he just approved," Baker would lean over and whisper to other advisers afterward.

Casey pushed back against Baker, regularly sending what became known as "zingers" to the chief of staff, usually news stories with notes attached like, "Stop these leaks" or "They are coming from the White House." Baker would show the notes to Larry Speakes, who took offense. "We should turn this right back around and send it back to CIA," Speakes would say. "This is where the leaks are coming from."

After the revelations about the briefing book, months of investigation ensued. Baker's carefully constructed reputation and his cultivation of Democrats and the media paid off. Robert Strauss, the former Democratic National Committee chairman from Texas who guided Carter's campaign in 1976 while Baker ran Gerald Ford's, attested to his former adversary's integrity. "Anything Jim Baker says, I would judge to be true," Strauss said publicly. "There isn't anyone in American politics whose ethics I place higher than Jim Baker's."

Even Donald Albosta, the Democrat running the congressional probe, did not wait for the investigation to be over to indicate that he was inclined to believe Baker over Casey, and the chief of staff never did have to take a polygraph. "I term Jim Baker an honest person," Albosta told the media. "I term him a friend. I'd feel very badly if anything came up that reflected badly on Jim Baker. If it does, it's a loss to the country." He added, "As for the others, I don't take any position."

Just how helpful the purloined briefing book was for the Reagan camp was never clear. Although Reagan said he had never seen it himself, David Stockman, who played Carter in the debate rehearsals, had a copy. "It wasn't worth a damn," Baker insisted. But the *Post* examined it against the transcript of the 1980 debate and found that at various points, Reagan seemed to anticipate Carter attacks that had been outlined in the briefing book with ready responses. At one point, the paper noted, Reagan even rebutted Carter's statistical attacks before Carter used them. For years to come, Carter was convinced that the briefing book made a difference. "Reagan was quite well briefed before I got there," he said. But Carter accepted Baker's account. "If Baker said he didn't know it, I believe that would be the truth."

Baker was so intensely focused on the matter that when Margaret Tutwiler mentioned almost in passing one day in the West Wing that she recalled him telling her in 1980 that he had received Carter campaign material from Casey, he instantly picked up a telephone and barked at an aide to summon Fred Fielding, the White House counsel. When Fielding arrived, Baker ordered Tutwiler to repeat what she had told him, then told her to instantly write a memo recording her recollection. Her memory corroborated him in his fight with Casey. Baker privately told an associate that Casey would "rue the day" if their conflicting accounts were ever tested in a legal setting.

The months of inquiry weighed on Baker. "It ate away at him," said Jim Cicconi, his aide. A poll showed that 70 percent of Americans believed that the president should fire Baker, Casey, and Stockman if they were shown to have committed improper acts. "It ain't fun to see your name dragged through the crud every day," Baker confided privately to a reporter. One night, Baker took Tutwiler and Darman across the street from the White House to Maison Blanche, a favored Reagan administration hangout where reporters liked to meet presidential aides for expense-account dinners ("the hot shots' hot spot," owner Tony Greco boasted to *People* magazine). Baker told his aides over the meal that he was thinking about resigning. But when Baker went to Reagan and offered to step down, the only time he would do so during eight years in the administration, the president refused to accept. "He had months of hell over this," said Susan

Baker. Even in his rare moments at home, he was obsessing over it. "Dick Darman had to come over and hold his hand any number of times."

Eventually, the Justice Department determined that there was no criminal wrongdoing to investigate and the 2,400-page report produced by Albosta's subcommittee concluded in 1984 that Baker's account was more believable than Casey's. The subcommittee was told that Casey had received the briefing book from Paul Corbin, a longtime Kennedy family retainer who was paid $1,500 by Casey three days before the debate and another $1,360 a week later for "professional services." Corbin denied it to the subcommittee in a sworn statement, but he had privately told a Republican friend, Timothy Wyngaard, that he delivered the briefing book to Casey, and Wyngaard told his boss, Dick Cheney, Baker's old Ford colleague. "I was able to call Jim and say, 'Jim, here's what happened,'" Cheney said later. Craig Shirley, a Republican consultant who went on to become a prominent Reagan biographer, later investigated and concluded that there was "little doubt" of Corbin's involvement.

Casey never did let go of the dispute. Nearly a year after the Albosta subcommittee's report, Baker made light of the controversy at the Gridiron Dinner, the annual white-tie gala that brought together the president and top Washington figures with journalists for a night of awkward skits. When his turn came to speak, Baker joked about the briefing papers episode, saying he would challenge Casey to a duel—lie detectors at ten paces. Casey was livid and scratched out an angry six-page typed letter to Baker. He rewrote it over and over again, making it a virtual indictment of Baker. "Jim, you succeeded in reviving my interest in finding some way to get to the bottom of this matter," Casey wrote. "Your credibility was put at stake again when you raised this matter again last Saturday night."

But Casey equivocated over sending the letter. On a separate piece of paper, he wrote out four pros and seven cons. On the plus side, it "gets record straight" and "lets individual and others know depth of feelings," he wrote. But on the negative side, it would "cause a public dispute within the Administration family" and might provoke Baker to call for a special prosecutor and "reopen case with possibility of a criminal investigation or at least lead to the calling for polygraph examinations." In the end, the cons outweighed the pros in Casey's mind. On a draft in his files was written, "No version apparently sent."

Just as Casey never let go, neither did Baker. Even decades later, he mustered deep outrage over what had happened. Susan Baker equated the trauma of the briefing book flap to the death of a granddaughter as "the two most awful things" her husband had endured during the time they had been married. The Warden's son did not like attacks on his integrity. He did not like questions about his credibility. And he was not about to sully the Baker name. "Baker cared a great deal about doing no harm to his family's heritage," Tutwiler observed. "That's very important to him."

CHAPTER 13

The Dark Side

Baker was in an official car one day in the fall of 1983 on the way to lunch at the Madison Hotel, a favorite venue just a few blocks from the White House and across the street from *The Washington Post*, when Michael Deaver mentioned almost offhandedly that the president had ordered a leak investigation. With lie detector tests for everyone. Including Baker.

"I'll be goddamned!" Baker erupted. Lie detectors? Again? How had that happened without him knowing about it? Baker realized that Reagan had been upset about stories in the *Post* and other outlets reporting about a secret order he had just given to American forces in Lebanon, but no one had mentioned lie detector tests. Baker was the chief of staff but someone had clearly pulled an end run around him and gotten to the old man.

Deeply agitated both at being circumvented and at the prospect of strapping members of the White House staff to polygraph machines, Baker ordered the driver to turn the car around and rush back to the White House. When they arrived just a few minutes later, Baker raced through the corridors of the West Wing with Deaver hot on his heels and burst into the Oval Office, where he found Reagan in the small adjacent dining room having lunch with George Bush and George Shultz, who had succeeded Al Haig as secretary of state. The usually deferential Baker confronted Reagan.

"Mr. President, Mike tells me you just signed an order for a leaks investigation," Baker said.

"Yeah," Reagan confirmed. "That was a terrible leak."

"But he also said you've ordered polygraphs on everybody at the NSC meeting," Baker said.

"That's right."

"With all due respect, sir, I'm not sure you can polygraph a constitutional officer," Baker said, referring to the vice president, who was sitting at the table, taking this all in.

At that point, Shultz, who was hearing about the leak probe for the first time, spoke up in full umbrage. His honor was being besmirched. "Mr. President, you'll only polygraph me one time," he said, "and then you'll get yourself another secretary of state."

Baker's objections were both principled and practical, recognizing that even if he was not guilty of this leak, a lie detector test could open the door to all sorts of questions he would just as soon not answer. Eventually, Reagan backed down on the polygraphs rather than face the scandal of his secretary of state resigning in protest, but the leak investigation would proceed through other means. Despite his tactical victory, Baker still felt in danger. He was well known as a leaker and understood that suspicions would fall on him despite his denials. Once again, the tribal rivalries of Reagan's White House were consuming Baker and placing him at grave risk.

The rupture inside the West Wing came as the president struggled to deal with the ongoing civil war in Lebanon, a benighted corner of the Middle East ripped apart by competing factions and trammeled by unforgiving neighbors. After Israel invaded in the summer of 1982, Reagan had sent eight hundred Marines to Beirut to serve as peacekeepers and oversee the departure of Palestinian forces, in what was the first significant overseas military deployment of his presidency. The Marines soon left, but after Lebanon's president-elect Bashir Gemayel was assassinated and attacks by pro-Gemayel forces resulted in the slaughter of hundreds of civilians in Palestinian refugee camps, Reagan sent them back to stop the country from spiraling out of control. It was never clear, however, how much he or his team were really committed to the mission. Baker looked at it more from a political standpoint than a geopolitical one. "It's easy to start a war," he said years later. "It's hard to end it. And a lot of presidents get in trouble with foreign adventures, wars of choice particularly."

Sure enough, a car bomb in April 1983 devastated the American embassy in Beirut, killing sixty-three people, including seventeen Americans. By that fall, the situation had deteriorated even further. Dispatched to Lebanon to scope out the situation, Robert McFarlane, the deputy national security adviser, sent back a grim report. In a memo marked "SECRET" and "NODIS" (for No Distribution), he warned the White House on September 10 that events on the ground raised the concern that Lebanese armed forces could be defeated and the government could topple. "In short," he wrote, "tonight we could be behind enemy lines." In another cable, McFarlane recommended that United States forces use tactical air strikes to support the Lebanese or risk a partial "Syrian takeover of this country."

Reagan discussed the matter in the Situation Room for much of Sunday, September 11, with his top advisers, including Baker; Bill Casey; William Clark, the national security adviser; Jeane Kirkpatrick, the United Nations ambassador; Caspar Weinberger, the defense secretary; and others. Baker and most of the other aides argued against an escalation of force or took no position, but Reagan agreed to authorize air power, justifying it as backing up the Marines on the ground even at the risk of becoming further entangled in the civil war. He signed a secret order giving the Marine commander permission to call in naval gunfire from the USS *New Jersey* offshore in the Mediterranean as well as tactical air strikes by American warplanes. By the next day, however, the secret was blown. No fewer than eight news organizations, including *The Washington Post* and *The New York Times*, reported the decision. In Lebanon, McFarlane was furious and threatened to resign, complaining that his diplomacy and even his safety had been jeopardized. The leak roiled the administration and, at the behest of Clark and Ed Meese, Reagan ordered Attorney General William French Smith to investigate. "I ask you to use all legitimate means in your interviews including use of the polygraph," Reagan told Smith. If anyone failed to cooperate or was discovered to have leaked, he added, "I will expect that person to resign."

Baker's lunchtime intervention had stopped the polygraphing before it started, but he felt exposed nonetheless. After all, he had actually talked with Lou Cannon, one of the reporters who wrote the *Post* story. Baker maintained that he and Cannon had only discussed a nonsecret element of the story, the White House strategy to get congressional backing for its troop presence in Lebanon. "We're seeking bipartisan support, not a Tonkin Gulf resolution," an unnamed White House official had told Cannon. On a copy of the article, Baker scratched next to that quote, "Me." But he insisted he had not been the one to divulge the order to fire.

Anxious, Baker called Cannon. According to notes Baker took of the call, he did not tell the reporter that an investigation had been launched but he did say that questions had been raised about whether he had been a source on the air strike part of the story. Cannon agreed to provide Baker a letter affirming that the chief of staff had not told him about the president's order. Baker then met with FBI agents and denied being the source. But he was still worked up about the possibility of lie detector tests. On the back of a piece of White House stationery, he summed up his concerns: "(1) only if *all* are; and (2) only if BC will take re: the articles in my file." By that, he meant William Clark, whom he blamed for hostile leaks in other news stories. "Bad idea tho'—distrust, etc."

Journalists rarely agree to discuss their sources for a story, even to rule any out, since doing so could point leak hunters to the right target, but Cannon gave Baker the letter exonerating him anyway, underscoring the chief of staff's close relationship with reporters. "We did not talk about matters relating to Lebanon except War Powers," Cannon wrote in the letter. "My recollection on this is clear." No one was ever held responsible for the Lebanon leak. David Gergen, who wrote a seven-page memo analyzing the news stories for clues, noted that military affairs reporters had bylines on several of the articles and pointed out that after the decision was made, Pentagon officials began giving instructions, which widened the circle of people who knew about it. "There was no leak but a gush," Gergen wrote.

Baker had escaped blame, but the tension within the national security team would only grow.

BAKER HAD initially favored William Clark's appointment as national security adviser. Judge Clark, as he was called because of his previous service as a Reagan appointee on the California Supreme Court, had seemed far preferable to the ineffective Richard Allen. A fellow rancher as close to Reagan as a "brother," as the United Nations ambassador Jeane Kirkpatrick once put it, Clark went all the way back to the beginning with the president, to his first campaign for governor in 1966. He had been Reagan's chief of staff, executive secretary, and cabinet secretary in Sacramento. He had personally recruited both Ed Meese and Michael Deaver. He would not be pushed around by them or anyone else. But that clout carried a price for Baker. The first sign of trouble came when Clark had insisted on reporting directly to the president, not through Baker or Meese. "That's how we're going to get into a war," Baker complained to Deaver. But Clark's long relationship with Reagan had made it impossible for Baker to block the arrangement.

Soon enough, Baker and Clark found themselves at odds, the embodiment of the *ratfuck* that had so worn down the chief of staff. He seethed when he found out that Clark had secretly tried to open a back channel to the Soviet Union. And he swung into action after learning that Clark had brought Kirkpatrick to the Oval Office to convince the president to send her to Central America without telling George Shultz. "Mr. President, don't you think that your secretary of state should be made aware?" Baker asked, effectively killing that end run.

For his part, Clark objected to what he considered a campaign of leaks by Baker's team to undercut him. Clark was convinced that Baker's staff began its morning meetings asking, "How do we roll Clark today?" He saw Dick Darman as the prime culprit and eventually had the code changed on the electronic lock to the national security suite to keep him out. Darman retaliated by having a coded entry installed on his own office door. At one point, angry at negative media references to Faith Whittlesey, one of the conservatives on his staff, Clark brought his complaint directly to Reagan in the Oval Office. While a stunned Baker looked on, Clark accused the chief of staff's team of "brutalizing" Whittlesey. Livid at the ambush, Baker later called Clark and lit into him. "It was the only time Baker lost his temper with me," Clark said.

This was about more than turf and ego. The struggle had its roots in a broader philosophical divide within the Reagan administration. Clark, a staunch Cold Warrior, thought Baker was too soft on the Soviet Union and had poisoned Nancy Reagan against him and the equally hawkish Caspar Weinberger at the Pentagon. "Baker tried to convince her that Cap and I were too aggressive with the Soviets, that we were too hard-line, that our conservative postures could start World War III, that we were irresponsible for convincing the president to double the defense budget," Clark said. He was more than a little right. Whether due to Baker or not, Nancy saw Clark as "a user" who claimed to represent Reagan even when he did not. As for Baker, he considered Clark "not the brightest bulb in the chandelier," a "rogue NSC adviser" who despite a lack of command of foreign policy was playing to Reagan's ideological convictions in order to push for dangerously confrontational policies. "We never knew where Clark was going and he always appealed to the dark side of the old man," Baker said years later.

The fall of 1983 was a grim time in the Cold War. On September 1, a Soviet warplane shot down a Korean Air Lines civilian passenger jet that had wandered into Russian airspace, killing all 269 people on board—including an American congressman, Larry McDonald, a Democrat from Georgia. The Soviets initially denied involvement and only later admitted destroying KAL Flight 007, while asserting that it had actually been an American spy plane. Reagan was furious and publicly denounced the incident as a "crime against humanity," an "act of barbarism," and "inhuman brutality," but he did not retaliate in a meaningful way.

Reagan's restraint earned him praise from his usual critics and much of the mainstream media, but engendered frustration among his conservative allies. "If the best this president can do is shout 'barbarism' and order a few mild sanctions in the wake of Moscow's murderous attack on the South Korean airliner, there should be dancing tonight in the Kremlin," *The Detroit News* said in an editorial that David Gergen highlighted in yellow and sent to Baker. "Even Jimmy Carter did better than that."

The Cold War had reached one of its lowest moments. Reagan had written a personal letter to the longtime Soviet leader Leonid Brezhnev after the assassination attempt two years earlier, but that had not yielded any change in the relationship and then Brezhnev died, handing power to Yuri Andropov, the KGB chief, who soon fell ill too. By then, the war against the Sandinista government in Nicaragua was raging and the Reagan administration was looking for better ways to counter the Soviets in Afghanistan. Reagan's defense buildup was changing the balance of power, but his insistence on deploying Pershing II nuclear missiles in Europe had provoked mass protests in the streets of Western capitals and driven a wedge among the allies. Popular support for a nuclear freeze was fueled in the United States with the airing that fall of an ABC television movie called *The Day After*, depicting an apocalyptic America reeling from the devastation of a nuclear war. Reaction to the movie was so powerful that a nervous White House dispatched officials and surrogates to make dozens of public and media appearances to calm nerves and explain administration policy.

Amid all the geopolitical tension, the atmosphere inside the West Wing among Reagan's feuding advisers grew so toxic that Deaver tried to get Reagan to intervene. "It just became almost intolerable," Deaver said. After discussing the matter with Reagan, Deaver brought Baker, Meese, and Clark to the Oval Office, but the president, ever conflict averse, meandered around without bringing up the purpose of the meeting. "Everybody sat there and nobody would say anything," Deaver recalled. Finally, Deaver raised the elephant in the room. "We can't operate this way anymore," he told Reagan, asking him to direct the combatants to craft a compromise that would restore order. Reagan agreed, but no one ever followed up. So Deaver tried again by inviting Baker and the two others to Blair House for drinks one night, hoping they might lubricate their way to a peace accord. It was not to be. At the end of the night, Baker and Meese agreed to shake hands but Clark refused even that, leading to more recriminations.

By October, Clark, who found himself suffering painful headaches at night, finally gave in. Recognizing the forces stacked against him, he decided to call it quits. By happenstance, James Watt, the controversial interior secretary whose tenure had generated fierce criticism from environmentalists, had just imploded with an ill-considered crack about the diversity of a coal advisory commission. "I have a black, I have a woman, two Jews and a cripple," he told a breakfast of lobbyists. Under pressure from Baker, Watt resigned, which solved two problems for the chief of staff by creating an opening that Baker could slide Clark into.

With Clark's nomination as interior secretary, Baker saw a way out of his own crushing workload. Hoping to finally move beyond the role of fixer, he came up with the perfect replacement for Clark as national security adviser—himself. He would gain experience at foreign policy and would be dealing with issues of great import rather than trying to keep the bumper cars of the West Wing from crashing into each other every day. Dick Darman would come along as his deputy.

To make the switch, Baker knew that he would have to find a new chief of staff who would be acceptable to Reagan, as well as to Nancy, so he set his sights on Deaver. Never mind that Deaver was actually thinking about leaving the White House. Baker convinced him that he had to take over the big corner office. "Baker knew just how much arm to twist—'I'll be right downstairs, we'll have the same team and it will be good for the president,'" Deaver remembered him saying. Deaver agreed and the two presented the idea to Reagan, who signed off on it without seeming to give much thought to such a momentous personnel shift.

The plan had the support of George Shultz, who thought Baker had run the White House "with brilliance" and a "deft touch." "Baker was by miles the most competent person over there and would be good to work with," Shultz later wrote in his memoir. But Baker knew his appointment would run into opposition among the conservatives, so he conspired to keep them in the dark. Clark's departure for Interior was announced on October 13. Baker planned to have his own new assignment announced the next day and Reagan agreed. Baker had a news release drafted and ready to go. When Baker went to the Oval Office to go over the final details, he and Reagan discussed whether the president should go immediately to the press briefing room to make the announcement or first tell the rest of the national security team at a meeting that was about to start down in the Situation Room. Baker said Reagan should tell the national security team first and, in a rare miscalculation, decided not to attend the meeting himself for fear of tipping off his rivals, who would wonder why he was there.

But the debate about how to announce the decision had made the president late for the meeting and William Clark came up to the Oval Office to find him and bring him down to the Situation Room. In the hallway heading down to the meeting, Reagan showed Clark the news release announcing Baker as his successor.

Clark was flabbergasted. *Baker as national security adviser?* He appealed to the president to first "roundtable" the decision, using a favorite Reagan term for consulting his team, and so, reluctantly, the president did not announce the move when he joined his advisers in the Situation Room, giving Clark a chance to rally opposition. As the group discussed Lebanon, Clark passed a note around the table tipping off his allies, Meese, Weinberger, and Casey, who were equally outraged at the prospect of Baker running national security.

After the meeting, the four conservatives huddled and agreed to throw themselves at the president as a unifed front. They pulled Reagan into Clark's basement office and told him that they could not accept Baker in that job. He had no foreign policy experience. He would not be able to serve as an honest broker since he was already seen as aligned with Shultz. And he could not keep a secret. "Mr. President," said Casey, still burning from his scrap with Baker over Debategate, "you can't have the biggest leaker in Washington as your national security adviser."

Meese also objected to Deaver as chief of staff, bitter that his old colleague from California had effectively betrayed him to tip the balance of the Troika to Baker. He had come to see Deaver as power crazy and now took the opportunity to exact retribution by torpedoing his promotion.

Reagan was shocked at the virulence of the objections to both men and agreed not to move forward with the appointments. Reversing the decision would be a painful exercise. He knew he would be upsetting two close advisers who had been loyal to him. "I'm not sure that Mike Deaver will speak to me after this," the president said as he left the room. Once he was gone, Clark found Robert McFarlane and filled him in. "That was a close call," Clark told him.

Upstairs, Reagan summoned Baker and Deaver to the Oval Office. "Fellas, I got a revolt on my hands," he explained. He was right about Deaver's reaction. Deaver had not really wanted to be chief of staff in the first place and had to be talked into it by Baker, but now hearing that Reagan was abandoning him, he erupted. "How could you do this?" he demanded. One report even had him cursing the president and saying, "This is the second time you've done this to me," referring to a split the two had back in their campaign days, although he later denied it. "I would never say that," Deaver insisted. "I may have been *thinking* it, but I wouldn't have said it." Either way, there were angry words from someone who had been close to an adopted son to Reagan. "I was getting mad," he conceded later. "I was thinking, you know, Come on, I've been around here for 20 years."

Baker, by contrast, accepted defeat graciously. "Mr. President, when I came here, I said I'd do whatever you wanted me to do," he said. "Don't you worry about it. I don't have to do this. I'll be whatever you want me to be for as long as you want me to be."

Deaver felt chagrined. "God, what kind of jerk am I?" he remembered thinking. "Here's Baker, he's only been here three years, and he's being what an American is supposed to be. He's loyal. I've never forgotten that."

Reagan noticed too. He hated personal conflict and Deaver's hurt feelings were painful to confront. He was grateful to Baker for not making it worse. "Jim took it well but Mike was pretty upset," Reagan wrote in his diary that night. "It was an unhappy day all around."

That did not mean Baker was not devastated. He was just better at hiding his feelings. He had thought that he would serve as chief of staff for two years—that was about the typical run and for good reason. It was such a burnout job. Baker felt the weight of the presidency on his shoulders. The best days of Reagan's tenure might be behind him; with the economy on tenterhooks and an election coming the following year, Baker was ready for a new challenge. And he had literally come within five minutes of getting it. As Robert Kimmitt, who was then the executive secretary of the National Security Council, observed, had Baker and the others not lingered in the Oval Office to discuss how to make the announcement and Reagan just showed up in the Situation Room without encountering Clark first, the president would have disclosed his decision to the assembled team. It would have been done, and the dissenters would have had to accept it. "If they hadn't had that debate and he had just come down on time," Kimmitt said, "history would have been very different."

Baker might have been thwarted in his personal ambition. But he had not been routed entirely and he set about making sure that Meese, Casey, and their camp would not be able to install one of their own at the NSC. As Reagan retreated to Camp David for the weekend to consider other choices for national security adviser, the conservatives lobbied for Jeane Kirkpatrick. Baker, along with Shultz and Deaver, considered her too hard-line and managed to block that idea—to Baker's own detriment, in a way, since Reagan was thinking about sending him to the United Nations to replace Kirkpatrick if she did get the job. Kirkpatrick never forgave

Baker. She saw him and Deaver as sexist, devious manipulators of a good-hearted president. "One thing I didn't understand was why Reagan didn't see how objectionable Baker and Deaver were," she wrote in an unpublished autobiography. "Like Iago. Why didn't Othello see who he really was?"

Instead of Kirkpatrick, Reagan settled on Clark's low-key, self-effacing deputy, Robert McFarlane, a Marine veteran who had served in Vietnam and worked on Henry Kissinger's staff. Casey was not happy with the selection, fearing that it would still give Baker too much sway, but overall McFarlane was seen as a safe choice, unobjectionable to most camps, probably because each side thought it could manage him. But it was a fateful decision. McFarlane's ambition to help free American hostages held in Lebanon by dealing with Iran and to keep money flowing to the contras in Nicaragua despite congressional restrictions would have profound consequences in Reagan's second term. Had Baker been national security adviser instead, Deaver concluded, "Iran-contra wouldn't have happened, that's for sure."

Reagan too came to regret the outcome. "My decision not to appoint Jim Baker as national security adviser, I suppose, was a turning point for my administration," he wrote in his memoir, "although I had no idea at the time how significant it would prove to be."

AS BAKER HAD FEARED, the Lebanon mission took a deadly turn just six days after McFarlane's appointment was announced. The escalation of force had indeed drawn the United States deeper into the country's bloody war and made the American peacekeepers even more important targets.

On October 23, Hezbollah terrorists slammed a truck filled with explosives into the Marine barracks in Beirut, collapsing the four-story concrete building in a cloud of dust and debris and killing 241 American military personnel, mainly Marines. It was the largest single-day loss of life for the Marines since the Battle of Iwo Jima during World War II.

Reagan, who was staying at the Augusta National Golf Club at the time, was shaken when McFarlane woke him up and told him the news. "How could this happen?" the president asked, looking as if all the air had been sucked out of him. Many Americans were distraught as well, wondering why their troops were there in the first place. Among those who shared that view was Baker. While he had failed to become national security adviser, he began weighing in on the Lebanon venture.

"Bud, what is the light at the end of the tunnel here?" he began asking McFarlane at regular intervals.

"There really isn't any," McFarlane acknowledged.

In the immediate aftermath, Reagan vowed firmness and scorned Democrats who called for him to pull the Marines out, saying that would amount to "surrender." But in fact, he took little action in response, much like the aftermath of the Korean airliner shoot-down. Influenced by Baker and others, he quietly ordered the withdrawal of the Marines several months later. To Baker, it was a wise pivot to avoid another Vietnam; if Lyndon Johnson had resisted the instinct to keep doubling down, America would never have been caught in the devastating spiral of escalation in Southeast Asia. But the decision would nonetheless have its own consequences. In years to come, other Islamic terrorists in the Middle East, including a radical named Osama bin Laden, would point to the episode as evidence that Americans were paper tigers who could be bloodied and forced to retreat for just the cost of a truck, a few tons of explosives, and a single suicide bomber.

As the country was reeling from the Beirut bombing, Reagan and his team were headed to military action in a more unlikely place far closer to home. In mid-October, a military junta had seized control of the tiny Caribbean island of Grenada. Within six days, Reagan decided to send in American troops. He was ostensibly responding to a request for intervention by several other Caribbean islands and acting to protect and evacuate 1,100 Americans studying at a medical school in St. George's, the capital. But in reality, Grenada had become an unlikely Cold War battleground and Reagan determined to make a show of force close to home, a warning to the Soviets and anyone else who might be testing Reagan's resolve. As tests go, it was a pretty minor one. There was little risk of major resistance. But as Baker helped manage the preparations, he was acutely aware that, while the goal in Lebanon was to maintain peace, this would be the first time the United States was sending its forces into actual combat since Vietnam.

Baker knew it would be important to get Congress on Reagan's side for the operation, or at least mute any opposition. Shortly before the troops were to land, he snuck over to the Capitol using back staircases and little-known doors to slip into Tip O'Neill's office. He asked the House Speaker to come to the White House that night for a secret meeting with Reagan. When O'Neill and other congressional leaders arrived a few hours later, they were shepherded into the mansion through a roundabout way to avoid reporters and taken upstairs to the residence. Reagan disclosed his intention to invade Grenada and then had Caspar Weinberger and General John Vessey, chairman of the Joint Chiefs of Staff, present detailed maps. O'Neill was miffed at being presented with a fait accompli. "This is not a consultation," he complained. "This is a notification." Getting up to walk out, O'Neill told Reagan, "Good luck." Baker interpreted that to mean, *You're on your own.*

The other challenge for Baker was figuring out how to keep the operation secret from the White House press corps. No one had told Larry Speakes what was going on, so when Bill Plante of CBS News heard rumors of American forces assembling for an invasion, the spokesman checked with Rear Admiral John Poindexter, who had just taken McFarlane's job as deputy national security adviser. "Preposterous, knock it down hard," Poindexter responded through a staff aide. Speakes used the same word with Plante. But later that night, after Plante called again with more information, Speakes feared that he had been misled and called Baker, who was at a dinner party.

Baker judged that he could not disclose the operation to Speakes, but unlike Poindexter was careful enough not to get trapped in a lie or to let the White House spokesman get caught in one either. On the phone from the dinner, Baker simply cautioned Speakes not to make definitive statements.

"Larry," he said, "be careful what you say. There is something going on."

He instructed Speakes to show up early the next morning and meet him at the White House mess at 5:45. When Speakes arrived at the appointed hour, Baker handed him an inch-thick packet of documents on Grenada and told him to announce the invasion at 7 a.m.

Furious at Poindexter for lying to him, Speakes was not much happier with Baker for leaving him in the dark until hours after troops had actually gone ashore. He had been given just an hour to get up to speed before briefing the press corps. "That was treatment about as unfair as I had ever received," Speakes said later. "I had never been so mad in my life, but I knew there was nothing I could do except to choke it down and head out there in front of the press and try to do my job." The episode badly damaged his credibility with the reporters he had to face every day. Baker regretted that. "I may have made a mistake," he said later, "but we were so afraid that there might be a leak that would cost lives and in the back of our minds, that Vietnam syndrome was very, very big."

In the end, United States forces had no trouble seizing Grenada, installing a friendlier government, and routing a unit of Cuban troops, with eighteen American troops killed in the fighting. The medical students had never been in as much danger nor the Cubans as involved in the island as the Reagan White House had claimed, but it was a relatively quick and efficient operation, especially compared to the mess in Lebanon. Some suspected that was the point—to flex muscles in the Caribbean to distract from the failure in the Middle East. Baker insisted the students really were a concern, albeit an exaggerated one. "It wasn't *just* manufactured," he said. "But it was important to knock down this little tyrant who had appeared there; it was of the same ilk as the Sandinistas and the Cubans. We made it clear that this was not something we were going to permit."

AFTER NEARLY THREE YEARS in what he considered the worst job in Washington other than his friend George's role as vice president, Baker was still eager to find a way out. With the national security adviser post now unavailable, he was intrigued when he was approached about becoming commissioner of Major League Baseball. Baker was eventually one of two finalists along with Peter Ueberroth, president of the Los Angeles Olympic Organizing Committee, to replace Bowie Kuhn, who had failed to muster enough votes for a third term. George Will, the *Washington Post* columnist who had a passion for baseball, wrote that if Baker wanted to run for president someday, he should take the job because it would give him far higher name recognition.

Baker was not exactly a big baseball fan and had no particular history with the sport, but he took the prospect seriously enough that he had the league headquarters send over documents about how the organization worked and he wrote out questions, including everything from the size of the staff to the powers of the office to the state of the collective bargaining agreement. His kids loved the idea. "When I found out, I was ecstatic," said Doug Baker. "Commissioner of baseball over chief of staff any day."

Exhausted and stressed out, Baker claimed to be seriously considering the job. But of course he could not just step away from running the country. "Baseball commissioner?" Margaret Tutwiler yelled at him. "What kind of a nothing job is that? You don't even know anything about baseball." Finally, the reality came home when Baker spoke with Edward Bennett Williams, the legendary Washington lawyer and owner of the Baltimore Orioles. Williams was the original man to see in Washington, a counselor to presidents and the first person to call when someone powerful got in trouble. He told Baker that the baseball owners would love to have him as commissioner, but there was no way he could leave the government because Reagan was eventually going to put him in the cabinet. That was not so clear to Baker, but he bowed to the inevitability that Williams had sensed and, once again, deferred to Reagan.

Looking for the cabinet position that Williams had foreseen, Baker set his sights on the Justice Department. But when William French Smith prepared to step down, Baker once again found himself at odds with Ed Meese, who also had his hopes set on becoming attorney general. Meese had been fascinated with law enforcement for years and Reagan accommodated him by nominating him in January 1984. "This is his life long dream," Reagan wrote in his diary.

Frustrated, Baker made clear publicly that he would not stay in his corner office beyond the 1984 election. "I think the president would be better served by someone else in this job in a second term," he told the *Fort Worth Star-Telegram*.

But the music was coming to a stop and there were no empty chairs for Baker. When Bill Casey told the White House that he did not want to run the CIA in a second term, Baker once again topped the list of possible replacements. An ally broached the topic with Casey one evening as they enjoyed an after-hours drink.

"So Jim Baker's going to get your job," the ally ventured.

"He's the last fucker that will get that job," Casey growled.

Casey ended up remaining at Langley deep into the second term. No way would he hand over his job to Baker.

Through all of the ordeals, the family crises and the conflicts in the White House, through all of the *ratfuck*, Baker turned to his faith. Unlike so many religious conservatives who loudly supported Reagan, Baker kept his devotion private, but thanks to Susan he had become a more committed believer. Few around him realized just how religious he really was, but it was a regular part of his day. While chief of staff, he increasingly found himself reading a well-thumbed edition of *The Runner's Bible*, a collection of more than one thousand Bible passages and commentaries first assembled by Nora Holm in 1910 for a busy seventeen-year-old daughter. Meant as "spiritual guidance for people on the run," it would become a standard resource for many Christians.

One day in the summer of 1984, with the election looming and his future on the line, Baker recommended the book in a letter to a woman who had been ill. "I want to call your attention to The Runners Bible, which has been a source of great comfort to me through trials and tribulations, both in this office and elsewhere," he wrote her. "My mother gave me one when I was much younger, and every day I try to read the chapters entitled 'Fear Not Only Believe' and 'I Will Help Thee.' It is small, easily read and I carry it with me. Perhaps you will find it as comforting as I do."

CHAPTER 14

Morning in America

Baker got to know Ronald Reagan long before the myth of Ronald Reagan was created. In fact, he helped create the myth. But he never fooled himself into believing it. In the years and decades that followed Reagan's time in office, his admirers would transform him from a successful president to a political saint, reimagining him as an ideal leader, the Republican answer to Reagan's childhood idol Franklin Roosevelt. His promoters spent years waging a campaign to attach his name to all sorts of public institutions, from Washington's National Airport to a large new federal office building to schools and roads across the country. It was not enough that he be an admirable president; he had to be a venerated one.

In reality, of course, Reagan was no saint. He was a politician with extraordinary talents and clear weaknesses. He sometimes dozed off in meetings. He confused scenes from movies with real-life events and once mistook his own housing secretary for a visiting mayor. He stoked racial division with his talk of "welfare queens" and widened America's income gap. He told the same stories again and again as metaphors for his beliefs, no matter how sketchy the facts. His mastery of policy was hazy at best. David Stockman tore his hair out trying to get Reagan to understand the consequences of his own financial policies, to no avail. Clark Clifford, the Democratic elder statesman who had seen presidents up close since Harry Truman, privately referred to Reagan as an "amiable dunce."

Reagan was at the very least a diligent student of his lines, carrying around four-by-six cards in his breast pocket to refresh his memory, but he put in light hours at the office and favored afternoon naps. "It's true that hard work never killed anybody," he liked to joke, "but I figure why take the chance?" As congenial as he was, he charmed people rather than connected with them, rarely letting others in. Not particularly social beyond a tight circle of friends, he preferred retiring to the White House residence after a day at the office, changing into his pajamas, and eating dinner with Nancy on trays in front of the television set. He hated personal conflict and let disputes within his team fester, to the detriment of his own agenda. He was personally generous when he came across a hard-luck case, secretly sending checks to help individuals whose stories of trouble he learned from a letter or on the news, but he expressed little empathy for the needy in the aggregate as he urged cuts to social programs. An indifferent manager, he tolerated a degree of scandal within his administration that a more assertive president would have shut down.

What made Reagan special was his boundless sense of optimism at a time when America desperately needed it. Despite the economic hardship he inherited and the "crisis of confidence" that his predecessor had identified, Reagan managed through sheer force of personality to infuse the nation with his belief in a better tomorrow. One of his favorite anecdotes was the story of two children at Christmas; the pessimist was given a roomful of toys and suspected that there had to be a catch while the optimist got a roomful of manure and giddily plunged his hands into the pile, reasoning that if there was this much dung, there must be a pony in there somewhere. After years of unrest through Vietnam, Watergate, recession, and the Iran hostage crisis, Reagan reversed a sense of national decline and replaced it with a renewed confidence. He was devoted to the new conservative catechism of lower taxes, a strong military, and anti-Communism, but not so wedded to the details that it stopped him from reaching across the aisle to achieve many of his priorities with bipartisan support. To Reagan, compromise was acceptable and course corrections necessary at times. He did not practice the politics of personal destruction; he fought hard but treated his opponents with dignity and respect.

Working at his side every day, Baker had come to understand Reagan in a way that few others did. Reagan's most fervent supporters had a vision of what they thought he was—or what they thought he ought to be—but it often did not comport with what his chief of staff saw day in and day out in the Oval Office. Baker did not delude himself into thinking that Reagan was smarter than he was. He knew the president was neither oracle nor sage. Yet he had come to respect Reagan's horse sense and political instincts. He had learned how to manage Reagan the way any good chief of staff must manage a president—by listening to what really mattered to him and what did not.

Baker also recognized that while Reagan talked in black and white, he governed in gray. For all of the conservative chanting about "let Reagan be Reagan," Baker saw time and again a president who was more prag-matic than some of his supporters assumed. "I'd rather get 80 percent of what I want than go over the cliff with my flag flying," Reagan told Baker repeatedly. Holding out for some pure version of policy or principle was not Reagan's way. He was willing to take what he could get, then come back and get more the next time. Sometimes he even took a few steps backward in the interest of moving ahead another day. "That was Ronald Reagan," said Jim Cicconi, a White House aide to Baker. "He was the labor negotiator and he was a very principled conservative but he believed in getting things done and he recognized that in a democracy you can't have your way 100 percent all the time."

While widely hailed as the man who made Reagan's presidency effec-tive, Baker had a remarkable talent for distancing himself from its failings. In that, he was like his boss, who was dubbed the "Teflon president" by Representative Patricia Schroeder, a Democrat from Colorado, because nothing stuck to him. There were plenty of ethical lapses that might have tarnished a different president or chief of staff. By the spring of 1984, the press and opposition Democrats had already coined the phrase "sleaze factor" to cover the administration's growing roster of scandals. In addi-tion to Richard Allen and the Japanese money in the safe, other senior officials found themselves in trouble, including Bill Casey, whose stock dealings were called into question; William French Smith, who was forced to give back a $50,000 severance payment from his old company; and Anne Gorsuch Burford, who resigned as head of the Environmental Pro-tection Agency after being cited for contempt by Congress for refusing to turn over papers related to suspected favoritism to industry. On top of that, the head of the Small Business Administration resigned after investigations into grants, a deputy CIA director resigned amid allega-tions of irregular stock transactions, the deputy defense secretary resigned after being accused of insider trading, and an assistant EPA administrator was convicted of perjury.

The latest questions involved Baker's rival, Ed Meese. After Reagan selected Meese for attorney general, allegations surfaced about his deal-ings with a San Diego savings and loan and subsequent federal jobs for some of those who helped him with financial matters. In April, a special prosecutor was appointed to look into the situation, holding up his confir-mation. By one count, six high-ranking administration officials had been indicted on criminal charges and twenty-five had resigned, been fired, or had their nominations withdrawn under fire. Baker, as alert as he was to his own reputation and rigorous about avoiding any issues that could impugn his own integrity, had clearly not been able to impose comparable discipline on the government that he effectively ran from that corner office in the West Wing. Yet, as smelly as the administration got at times, Baker was able to keep away from the stench.

Likewise, he was rarely cited when critics assailed some of the more controversial aspects of Reagan's first-term record, from the accumulating deficits and the budget cuts affecting the most vulnerable to the ideological warfare that seemed to leave the United States on the same side as death squads in Central America and a brutally racist apartheid regime in South Africa. Ever close to the press, Baker was always associated with the victories and rarely if ever the defeats.

AS THE 1984 ELECTION year opened, the United States was a different place than it had been the last time voters were asked to pick a president. Reagan's America had moved beyond the 1960s and 1970s, and it was beginning to recover its strength economically and reassert itself on the world stage. The social movements of the previous decade pushing for expanded rights for women, minorities, and gay Americans had ebbed; the deadline for the Equal Rights Amendment expired during Reagan's first term, falling three states short of the thirty-eight it needed for ratification. Instead, Christian conservatives had gained momentum, preaching against the feminism, casual premarital sex, open homosexuality, widespread drug use, and other cultural changes that had alienated many traditionalists. The culture war was on, especially in the South and West.

American lifestyles were changing dramatically as technological innovation disrupted workplaces and homes. The spread of cable television transformed the entertainment landscape and the emergence of Cable News Network, or CNN, brought a new twenty-four-hour-a-day urgency to the latest developments in Washington, around the country, and overseas. The first Apple Macintosh personal computer went on sale in January 1984. Hewlett-Packard followed later in the year with the first home ink jet printer. Motorola had just released a massive brick of a mobile phone.

Under Reagan, not only innovation but capitalism itself seemed back—and so, many argued, was greed, which became a running theme of the decade's cultural and political debates. "Once more acquisition of wealth had been given a moral rationale," Haynes Johnson wrote in his account of those years, *Sleepwalking Through History*. A new show debuted in early 1984 called *Lifestyles of the Rich and Famous* celebrating Reagan-era extravagance. It would be a few more years before Michael Douglas's Gordon Gekko in the movie *Wall Street* would popularize the phrase "greed is good," but the conversation had already turned.

Overall, the economy was indeed booming, expanding by 7.2 percent in 1984, the highest growth rate in three decades and higher than any year in the three decades that would follow. No one was talking about the "misery index" anymore. Although the federal deficit had doubled on Reagan's watch, inflation and gas prices had fallen dramatically since he took office, which had more direct impact on many Americans' daily lives. Unemployment stood at 8 percent as the election year opened, higher than it had been at any point during Jimmy Carter's presidency but it was falling, down from 10.8 percent at the end of 1982 and heading toward 7.2 percent by Election Day. If the country was still struggling, the trend lines at least seemed to be pointing in the right direction.

The benefits of Reaganomics, however, skewed to the rich. Average annual income rose by 3.5 percent in Reagan's first term, according to a study by the Urban Institute released in 1984, but by just one percent for typical middle-class families compared with 9 percent for the top one fifth of earners. The poor, those in the lowest one fifth economically, actually saw their income fall by 8 percent, according to the study. For black families of all economic strata, income fell by 3.7 percent.

Many parts of the country did not feel the boom. Steel mills and factories in places such as Pittsburgh, Cleveland, and Detroit were trimming workforces or closing altogether. The term Rust Belt describing the sinking industrial Midwest was popularized. In Los Angeles, crack cocaine was introduced to the streets and with it came a spasm of violence that signaled a deadly new phase of the illegal drug crisis. Across the country, homelessness was on the rise. And scientists were grappling with an emerging virus called acquired immune deficiency syndrome, or AIDS, that was devastating the gay community, an epidemic that Reagan was slow to recognize or confront.

But Reagan had changed public expectations for what government would or could do about the ills of society. The idea that the state would help the disadvantaged and aggressively move to end discrimination had given way to the belief that government had gone too far. "The debate in the last four years has been over which federal aid programs to cut rather than which to expand, over which civil rights rules to limit rather than which to enlarge, and over which natural resources to develop rather than which to protect," noted David Rosenbaum of *The New York Times*.

For all of that, the public perceived the country to be heading toward a better future in a way that it had not for many years. Fifty percent of

Americans said they were satisfied with the way things were going in the United States, twice as many as felt that way before the 1982 midterm elections and up from just 12 percent during the worst moment of the Carter presidency in 1979. Reagan may have advanced a divisive ideology, but he wrapped it in a warm and grandfatherly package that resonated. "President Reagan has made a mockery of the conventional wisdom that the country was ungovernable," the author and historian Richard Reeves wrote as the election year began.

THAT OWED TO BAKER as much as anyone. It was his job to translate Reagan's vision into concrete action. He was the negotiator, the implementer, the enforcer. It fell to him to deal with the problems, and the problem people, that Reagan preferred to avoid.

When David Stockman made another run at raising taxes to bring down the deficit, Reagan slammed the door hard, insisting that the problem was spending not taxes. The next day, Stockman told Baker that he was going to resign. He would have nothing more to do with what he considered fiscal know-nothingism and he did not want to be associated with deficits that over the course of five years would top $1 trillion.

"I can't make a fool of myself any longer, Jim," he said. "This budget is so bad, it's beyond the pale."

Baker responded with icy coldness. "You do that and you'll stab the president right in the back," he said. "The Democrats will have a field day in the 1984 campaign. Let me remind you of something, my friend. He stuck by you. Now you stick by him. You've made as many mistakes as the rest of us around here. So stick that unwarranted pride of yours right up your ass and get back in the trenches with the rest of us." Stockman stayed.

Central to Baker's mission, as he saw it, was helping Reagan avoid mistakes, particularly the kind that could cripple his presidency. At the top of his list was the proxy battle with the Soviets that kept escalating in Nicaragua. Reagan was in a constant struggle with Congress for enough money to keep the ragtag contras fighting, and Democratic lawmakers were increasingly restless. Sensing the danger to Reagan, Baker "was like a dog with a bone" about Central America, Michael Deaver said, convinced that "the crazies want to get us into war."

If Baker needed any further proof, he got it with the revelation early in 1984 that the CIA had placed magnetic mines in three of Nicaragua's harbors in hopes of sinking a transport ship carrying weapons, an operation that was clearly an act of war. Disclosure of the mining alienated one of the president's chief allies on Capitol Hill, Senator Barry Goldwater, chairman of the Senate Intelligence Committee and the conservative icon who had given Reagan his start in national politics back in 1964. Goldwater had just assured another member of his committee that the administration was not mining the harbors. Now he felt betrayed. "Dear Bill," Goldwater wrote in a letter to Bill Casey. "All this past weekend, I've been trying to figure out how I can most easily tell you my feelings about the discovery of the president having approved mining some of the harbors of Central America. It gets down to one, little, simple phrase: I am pissed off!"

Equally upset was the top Democrat on the committee, Senator Daniel Patrick Moynihan of New York, who resigned from the panel in protest. Only after Casey apologized and promised to do a better job of keeping the lawmakers informed did Goldwater cool down and Moynihan rescind his resignation. But in hindsight, Moynihan would see this as a pivotal moment for Reagan's administration and for the country, the "first acts of deception that gradually mutated into a policy of deceit."

Congress had been seeking to limit American involvement in the region for two years and the Reagan team had been laboring just as hard to figure ways around the restrictions to get more money for the contras. Lawmakers passed the first Boland Amendment, named after its Democratic sponsor, Representative Edward Boland of Massachusetts, in late 1982, barring the CIA from financing any group in Nicaragua with the goal of toppling the government. The CIA bypassed that by claiming its support for the contras was not for regime change but to stop Nicaragua's efforts to destabilize El Salvador. Congress, however, limited the funds available even for that purpose and finally the money ran out in May.

Among the ideas to circumvent the limits was soliciting third countries to contribute, a suggestion that Baker quickly rejected. In June, Robert McFarlane called a meeting of the National Security Planning Group to discuss the options. Baker was not there, but he was much invoked as Reagan's most senior officials tried to figure out how they could get the money without illegally defying Congress.

"I would like to get money for the contras also, but another lawyer, Jim Baker, said that if we go out and try to get money from third countries, it is an impeachable offense," George Shultz said in a discussion that would be transcribed and later studied by investigators.

Casey pushed back. "Jim Baker said that if we tried to get money from third countries without notifying the oversight committees, it could be a problem and he was informed that the finding does provide for the participation and cooperation of third countries. Once he learned that the finding does encourage cooperation from third countries, Jim Baker immediately dropped his view that this could be an impeachable offense, and you heard him say that, George."

Shultz refused to back off. "Jim Baker's argument is that the U.S. government may raise and spend funds only through an appropriation of the Congress," he said.

"I am another lawyer who isn't practicing law," Caspar Weinberger chimed in, "but Jim Baker should realize that the United States would not be spending the money for the anti-Sandinista program; it is merely helping the anti-Sandinistas obtain the money from other sources."

Even Baker's close friend George Bush seemed open to the idea of soliciting foreign countries for money for the contras. "How can anyone object to the U.S. encouraging third parties to provide help to the anti-Sandinistas under the finding?" the vice president asked. "The only problem that might come up is if the United States were to promise to give these third parties something in return so that some people could interpret this as some kind of an exchange."

The discussion ended inconclusively. McFarlane said that no one should be authorized to seek financial help for the contras until they had more information. "And I certainly hope none of this discussion will be made public in any way," he warned.

Reagan agreed. "If such a story gets out," he said, "we'll all be hanging by our thumbs in front of the White House until we find out who did it."

In years to come, investigators would look back at this meeting as a key milestone on a path that would deeply damage Reagan's administration. That Baker was not present is telling, as he had wanted to keep clear of any shenanigans that the "crazies" were up to. But not only was he aware of the debate then raging over how far the White House could push traditional boundaries, he had weighed in on it. Baker later told investigators that he did not remember using the phrase "impeachable offense" but did advise that "we should take a very close look at the question of legality" of such solicitations and argued that "we could not do indirectly what we couldn't do directly."

WITH THE COLD WAR still raging and the Sandinistas still in power and the economy still fragile, Reagan had to decide whether to seek a second term. At seventy-three, he was already the oldest man to serve in the presidency. Was he really up for another four years? Did he have the vigor for the ordeals of the world's most pressure-filled job?

One person who never seemed to doubt that Reagan would run for a second term was Baker. When a colleague wrote out a series of notes on a legal pad seeking Baker's guidance, number thirteen on the list was "If Reagan not run, what." Baker dismissed the question out of hand. "Going to run!" he wrote next to it on the legal pad. "I'm certain." In speaking with reporters on background, without allowing his name to be used, he assured them that he was "99 percent" confident that Reagan would run. He bet so many of them that Reagan would run, he eventually had $225 on the line.

Whether Reagan could win was another matter. In the aftermath of the midterm defeat, he was at the nadir of his presidency, his approval rating sliding to a dismal 35 percent. Hypothetical matchups against leading Democrats showed him losing. The outsider in 1980 was now the incumbent, an insurgent no more, and if he could not turn things around, someone could do to him what he had done to Jimmy Carter.

Baker's political team looked for ways to rehabilitate Reagan's image, especially among his own base. One of the most important keys to success for a president seeking a second term is first knitting up his own party; three of Reagan's four most recent predecessors faced primary challenges that cost them. Baker and the other strategists were determined to avoid that. A few months after the midterm elections, aides drafted a proposal for "concrete steps we can take to improve our standing with the populists." Among the suggestions: Have Reagan do play-by-play for a baseball or football game, reprising his days as a sportscaster; invite retired athletes or rodeo champions to the White House; visit a national park; and give a speech to the National Rifle Association. In his own memo, Ed Rollins argued that Reagan needed to reconnect with the nation. "Ronald Reagan has always expressed the best aspect of populism, which is optimism about people," he wrote. "He has always scorned the elitist view of mankind, which is pessimism about people."

Baker made sure that the planning for the reelection campaign began long before Reagan decided whether he would run again. Lee Atwater, the young political operative, drafted a sixty-three-page memo for Baker and the rest of the team analyzing the nation's shifting politics. The balance of power for Republicans, he noted, had been moving to the Sun Belt, a band of states stretching from the Old South to the Pacific coast that now controlled 266 electoral votes, just four shy of the majority necessary to secure the presidency. That worked to the advantage of Reagan, a character straight out of the American West who was most popular in that part of the country.

But Baker had multiple contests to run and win in 1984, and not all of them were with the voters. With Reagan stalwarts like Ed Rollins and Lyn Nofziger making noise about Baker's leadership and plotting against him, the challenge was to stay on top of what would become a massive campaign apparatus from his West Wing office. History showed that incumbent presidents had no choice but to run their reelection campaigns from the White House, which meant that Baker would be in charge. He held a meeting at 7 a.m. each day with Michael Deaver, Stuart Spencer, and Bob Teeter. They studied the latest data from the president's pollster Richard Wirthlin—or "Numbers," as Baker called him—and made the strategic decisions that were passed along to Rollins at campaign headquarters, located near Capitol Hill in offices with all the charm of an insurance company.

To keep tabs on Rollins, Baker assigned Margaret Tutwiler to serve as his liaison to the campaign, playing bad cop when necessary. After years of working for Baker, she had long since expanded her role beyond her early years as a glorified personal assistant. Increasingly, she was known as Baker's right hand and alter ego, the person who most understood his mind-set at any given moment and who could speak for him authoritatively without even checking first. Lee Atwater came to see her as a power player. Once when Rollins failed to come through on a routine request, she laid down the law with Atwater. "Let me give you a bit of advice," she said. "If Baker asks you what's the weather like today, you'd better send over a weather map."

Like Baker, Tutwiler hailed from Southern aristocracy, in her case two of Birmingham's oldest and most prominent families, the Tutwilers and the DeBardelebens. An early Tutwiler helped bring the first railroad to the state and the family made its fortune in minerals and real estate. Her father jumped with the Eighty-second Airborne Division on D-Day and was shot, but survived to become an investment banker. "When her parents married it was not so much a wedding as the merging of two coal and iron fortunes," Elisabeth Bumiller wrote in *The Washington Post.* Tutwiler was educated her first few years in a one-room schoolhouse where she and a friend made up the entire fourth grade, but hers was also a childhood of country clubs and coming-out balls. She went to Finch College, the same New York finishing school that Mary Stuart Baker had attended, before returning home to study at the University of Alabama.

In the Reagan White House, Tutwiler was often the only woman in the room and the only supporter of abortion rights. She was known to deeply admire and even worship her boss, always referring to him deferentially, even in private, as "Mr. Baker." But she had a deliciously sharp tongue and, at age thirty-three, could talk back to him like no one else could. When he would ask her to do something he found too unpleasant to do himself, like discipline a wayward aide, she would say, "You're fifty-four years old. Why can't you?" She often chided "Mr. Caution" for his restraint. For his birthday that election year, she gave him a book titled *The Wimp*. In an era and a profession where women were not major players, Tutwiler proved herself to be indispensable to Baker—"tough and smarter than a shithouse rat," as Richard Nixon once described her.

Rollins, the campaign manager, however, resisted the Baker-Tutwiler leash. At one point, Rollins complained to Paul Laxalt, who had been given the title of campaign chairman, that he had been told to report to Baker at the White House. Laxalt called up Baker to demand to see Reagan. Baker asked what he wanted to talk about.

"I've known Ronald Reagan a lot longer than you," Laxalt snapped, according to an account he later gave Rollins. "I don't have to tell you what I want to see him about."

When Laxalt arrived in the Oval Office, Baker was there waiting. "Mr. President," the senator said, "I just want to know who's running your campaign, me or Jim."

"You are," Baker interjected.

"I didn't ask you, Jim," Laxalt said.

Reagan told Laxalt he was in charge of the campaign.

Laxalt then turned to Baker. "Jim, leave Rollins alone," he said. "He reports to me. I'll report to the president and keep you informed."

Baker was livid and called Rollins afterward. "Why the hell are you sandbagging me?" he demanded.

"I'm not sandbagging you," Rollins said with faux innocence. "I'm just trying to get the pecking order straight."

IF IT WERE NOT clear already, the pecking order ended at Baker's desk. "Baker might have been in the White House but we were all working for him," said Charlie Black, the political strategist. Even as Baker managed the tribal conflicts inside his party, he kept a close eye on the other side of the aisle to anticipate Reagan's fall opponent. After the poor GOP showing in the 1982 midterm elections, a strong field of Democrats had been drawn into the race, sensing an opportunity to take down a weakened Republican incumbent.

Walter Mondale, the former vice president, started as the favorite of most of the party's institutional elite. A classic, old-school liberal from Minnesota, Mondale, however, was confronted by a variety of challengers, including Senators John Glenn of Ohio, Alan Cranston of California, Ernest Hollings of South Carolina, and Gary Hart of Colorado; former senator George McGovern of South Dakota, the party's 1972 nominee; former governor Reubin Askew of Florida; and the Reverend Jesse Jackson, the fiery civil rights leader.

Like everyone else, Baker assumed that Mondale was likely to win the nomination once Senator Ted Kennedy decided not to join the race and figured they could simply rerun Reagan's 1980 playbook. Baker joked with colleagues that they could print up bumper stickers that said, "Mondale— What If He's Worse Than Carter?" Glenn was the Democrat Baker worried most about. The first American astronaut to orbit the earth, Glenn could match Reagan on patriotism and family values. Adding to Glenn's heroic sheen was the conveniently timed release of the big-screen movie *The Right Stuff* in the fall of 1983 in which the lookalike actor Ed Harris portrayed Glenn as a young Boy Scout–like astronaut during his heady Mercury Seven days. But as Glenn positioned himself in the political center, he struggled to build an effective organization and never caught fire with liberal primary voters. Most of the other candidates did not even get that far. Cranston marginalized himself as a one-note nuclear-freeze candidate, Askew excited exactly no one outside Florida, and McGovern was quickly relegated to the also-ran category, a ghost from a failed past.

Instead, Mondale found himself pressed on two sides by Hart, a wavy-haired Westerner with Kennedy-esque good looks presenting himself as a new-generation Democrat, and Jackson, a charismatic, media-savvy preacher rallying the party's all-important African American constituency and its most fervent liberal activists. With his traditional organization, Mondale easily won the Iowa caucuses but lost in a stunning upset to Hart in the New Hampshire primary. Suddenly, Hart was the fresh face, the candidate with "splash, dash and glitter," as he wryly put it.

Mondale slugged it out with Hart over the next several months trading primary wins. Hart, who ran McGovern's 1972 campaign, hammered away at the former vice president as a creature of special interests and a Great Society throwback. Mondale finally confronted Hart during a Democratic debate when he mocked the young senator's so-called "new ideas" by borrowing a line from a Wendy's fast food hamburger chain advertisement then playing on television. "Where's the beef?" Mondale demanded. While Hart had arguably put out more substantive policy ideas than Mondale, he struggled to respond. He was not helped by subsequent news reports that as a young man he had changed his name, his signature, and even his date of birth.

Jackson was never a threat to take the nomination away from Mondale but as he mounted the most serious presidential campaign ever waged by an African American candidate, he drained the front-runner of left-leaning voters who otherwise might have sided with him against Hart. Jackson had a talent for grabbing the limelight with his catchy campaign rhetoric—"hands that once picked cotton can now pick presidents," he declared—and he was determined to make the Democratic Party take both him and his African American base seriously. "We are going from the guttermost to the uppermost," he vowed. Jackson even upstaged Reagan with a freelance diplomatic mission to Syria where he secured the release of an American Navy navigator who had been shot down over Lebanon.

Still, Mondale had all the institutional advantages of a former vice president—the finances, the organization, the endorsements, everything except the energy. Bereft of passion as it was, Mondale Inc., as his campaign came to be called, finally outpaced Hart to secure the nomination at the Democratic National Convention in San Francisco in July. Hoping to energize his campaign and bring his party together after the fractious battle, Mondale looked past Hart and Jackson to pick a running mate, selecting instead Representative Geraldine Ferraro of New York, the first woman ever to have a place on a major party's national ticket.

PIVOTING TO THE GENERAL ELECTION, Mondale now faced the daunting task of taking on an incumbent who was now recovering much of his strength. As the economy rebounded in 1983 and 1984, so did Reagan's standing with the public. The president's approval rating, mired in the mid-30s a year earlier, shot up to 55 percent by the beginning of the election year and he looked like a far more formidable opponent than when Mondale first decided to run.

Mondale chose to hit the president on the high deficits Reagan had racked up, perhaps his starkest failure. Rather than balance the budget by 1984, as he had promised, Reagan had widened the gap between revenues and expenses exponentially, from $74 billion in Jimmy Carter's last full year in office to $208 billion at the end of 1983, the largest deficit since World War II, both in raw dollars and as a share of the economy. Promising to cut the deficit by two thirds in four years, Mondale made the case that spending cuts alone would not solve the problem—and that Reagan knew it. "Let's tell the truth," Mondale said in his nationally televised acceptance speech at the convention. "It must be done. It must be done. Mr. Reagan will raise taxes and so will I. He won't tell you. I just did."

The idea was to position himself as the candidate of candor, but Mondale also opened himself up to the predictable attacks from Republicans. Never mind that just the day before Mondale's speech, Reagan had signed a budget bill into law raising taxes by $50 billion over four years while cutting spending by $11 billion. Reagan was seen as the tax cutter and he would run on that for the rest of the campaign. Moreover, Mondale's choice of Ferraro, another Northern liberal, for his running mate seemed to play right into Lee Atwater's Sun Belt electoral strategy. "In a very real sense, the election is over," Atwater wrote in a memo four days after the Democratic convention. "What we do now will determine the shape and size of our victory—but barring a major catastrophe, President Reagan is assured of reelection."

Still, Baker's responsibility gene meant that he understood that Mondale might be right and he argued that Reagan could not—or at least should not—categorically rule out raising taxes in his next term. He also suspected that the Democrats were trying to trap Reagan into making a definitive vow ruling out new taxes so that they could then accuse him of preparing to cut Social Security and Medicare to balance the books. So Baker and others on the pragmatist side of the Reagan camp argued for what they called "wiggle room." On a sheet of talking points, Baker scratched out his recommendation for how the president should approach the issue: "(a.) Don't say *will* balance budget—Want to, but need tools—line item veto, Balanced Budget Amendment. (b.) Don't say NEVER on tax ques—Say: I want to cut, not raise."

Baker took a jaundiced view of the difference between campaigning and governing. A memo prepared for him anticipated the possibility of a flip-flop on taxes, noting that three other presidents in the last century had made major promises during the campaign that they would not keep after taking office—Woodrow Wilson, Franklin Roosevelt, and Lyndon Johnson. The memo singled out in particular Wilson, who campaigned for reelection in 1916 on the slogan of "he kept us out of war," then just weeks after being inaugurated took the United States into World War I. "The exigencies of the election force us to solemnly swear that Walter Mondale is the tax-increase candidate and Ronald Reagan is the no-tax-increase candidate," the memo said. "We need to hold that posture through November 6. After that we can always do as Wilson, Roosevelt and Johnson did."

Reagan accepted Baker's advice. In his initial response to Mondale, the president insisted that he had "no plans" to raise taxes—Washington code for keeping his options open—and said he would do so only if the government, after cutting everything possible, was still spending more than it was taking in. A few days later, he hit on the phrasing that would preserve his flexibility while drawing the distinction with Mondale. "My opponent has spent his political life supporting more taxes and more spending," he said. "For him, raising taxes is a first resort. For me, it is a last resort."

That effectively settled the matter and underscored another rule of politics. Candidates or elected officials are given the benefit of the doubt on issues where they are associated with taking a strong ideological stance. Because Reagan was seen as a tax cutter, voters forgave him when he raised taxes, as he did in 1982 and again right before the Democratic convention, assuming he must have had no choice.

None of that would matter if the economy took a downward turn again. As chief of staff running a reelection campaign for an incumbent president, Baker had one top priority: keeping the good times rolling at any cost. And so one day that summer, he summoned Paul Volcker, chairman of the Federal Reserve Bank, to the White House to meet with the president.

The Fed controls the money supply and interest rates, giving it the power to stimulate growth or strangle it. For the entirety of Reagan's presidency to this point, the bank had been led by Volcker, a six-foot-seven giant of a man, who dominated intellectually as well as physically. Originally appointed by Jimmy Carter, Volcker had been given a second term by Reagan out of a desire to maintain continuity and he had largely conquered the extreme inflation that had afflicted the country in the 1970s. But the Fed was supposed to be an independent entity, isolated from political machinations.

When Volcker arrived at the White House, he was taken not to the Oval Office but the more informal library. Reagan was there but seemed uncomfortable to Volcker and uttered not a word. Instead, he left the business to Baker, who delivered his message to the central banker with characteristic Texan bluntness.

"The president is ordering you not to raise interest rates before the election," Baker declared.

Volcker was stunned; it was clearly overstepping a president's authority to try to order a Fed chairman what to do.

Unsure how to respond to such an egregious violation of norms, Volcker said nothing and just walked out. As it happened, he had not been planning an interest rate increase anyway and so the matter never came to a head. But it showed how far Baker was willing to go to preserve power.

With the economy in good shape, Baker envisioned a stay-the-course, feel-good campaign with little in the way of new policy pronouncements or specific campaign promises. Instead, Reagan capitalized on a summer of patriotism, fusing himself with the national identity. He traveled to Normandy to commemorate the fortieth anniversary of the D-Day landings, delivering a stirring speech from Pointe du Hoc. The next month Reagan flew to Los Angeles to attend the opening ceremony of the Summer Olympic Games, the first American president to do so. With the Soviet Union and the rest of the eastern bloc boycotting in retaliation for the American boycott of the Moscow Olympics in 1980, the United States won eighty-three gold medals, the most ever by any country in any Summer Games. Two weeks of crowds chanting "U-S-A, U-S-A!" on national television reinforced Reagan's election-year message that "America is back." When the Republican National Convention opened in Dallas barely a week after the closing ceremony, the delegates who gathered to renominate Reagan were chanting, "U-S-A, U-S-A!" too. At a rally in Orange County, California, that followed the convention, one woman in the audience told a reporter, "First, the Olympics, now this. I'm just OD-ing on pride in America."

That was the goal for Baker and the Tuesday Team, as the campaign's media squad was called. In what would become the most iconic advertisement of the year, the team produced a sixty-second spot that radiated sentimentality. "It's morning again in America," the fatherly narrator said. "Today, more men and women will go to work than ever before in our country's history." Featuring images of a paperboy and a farm tractor and a church wedding, the ad evoked a nostalgic return to the seeming simplicity of the 1950s after decades of social upheaval, economic dislocation, political crises, and overseas conflicts. "Under the leadership of President Reagan, our country is prouder, and stronger, and better," it concluded. "Why would we ever want to return to where we were less than four short years ago?"

The campaign was selling a narrative of rebirth and renewal, even if it was selective. Mondale complained about the sugary theme of the Reagan campaign. "It's all picket fences and puppy dogs," he said on the campaign trail. "No one's hurting. No one's alone. No one's hungry. No one's unemployed. No one gets old. Everybody's happy." But if Reagan's version of reality was a little rosy, it was a version that many Americans were ready to embrace. *Time* magazine ran a cover that fall with the headline "I ♥ U.S." and the overline "America's Upbeat Mood."

INDEED, REAGAN APPEARED to be cruising to an easy victory when he showed up for the first debate with Mondale in Louisville on October 7. Richard Wirthlin's polls had him up by 55 percent to 37 percent on the morning of the encounter, a whopping 18-point lead that would be hard for the Democrat to erase in just four weeks. All Reagan had to do was not make any big mistakes in either of the two face-offs that had been scheduled.

But there were warning signs during the rehearsals leading up to the debate. Baker told David Stockman, who was playing Reagan's Democratic opponent, to push hard in hopes of shaking the president out of what seemed to be an incumbent's complacency. While Reagan was better versed on policy details now that he had been in office dealing with them every day, it had been four years since he had debated anyone. He was not used to being challenged frontally.

Stockman took up his assignment with relish, pressing Reagan relentlessly to the point that the president finally blew up at him. "Shut up!" Reagan yelled during a discussion of Social Security.

Afterward, an unsettled Reagan shook Stockman's hand. "You better send me some flowers because you've been nasty to me," Reagan said.

Stockman blanched. "Baker made me do it," he said.

Even from afar, Mondale's team sensed an opening. Patrick Caddell, a strategist for the candidate, sent him a memo before the debate urging him to be aggressive yet gracious with the president. "Reagan has been so cocooned that the public may not realize that Reagan is having more difficulty hearing, following arguments, etc., than he did several years ago," Caddell wrote.

Caddell had a point. Reagan was clearly not as sharp as he was four years earlier and while he probably had not yet developed the Alzheimer's disease that would eventually take his life after leaving office, he had moments when he seemed out of it. When a reporter asked him during his summer retreat to his California ranch what the United States could do to bring the Soviets to the bargaining table, Reagan stared blankly for a few moments without answering. Nancy whispered to him, "Doing everything we can." He then faithfully repeated that out loud: "Doing everything we can."

As the president and his challenger greeted each other onstage at Louisville's Center for the Performing Arts on that evening in October, Mondale sensed that something was wrong with Reagan. "He didn't seem alert—not tired exactly, but not all there," Mondale wrote later. Mondale followed Caddell's advice and Reagan quickly fell on the defensive. He stumbled over words, mangled his own familiar stories, repeated mind-numbing statistics, rambled through his closing statement, and seemed to lose track of the rules at one point. "I'm all confused now," he admitted.

When Mondale pushed him on taxes, the president retreated to an old favorite. "There you go again," Reagan said.

This time, though, Mondale was ready. He noted that when Reagan used that line against Jimmy Carter in 1980, he was denying that he would cut Medicare. But in fact, Mondale said, Reagan then proceeded to do just that as president.

"And so when you say, 'there you go again,' people remember this, you know," Mondale said.

That was something of an exaggeration; Reagan really had not made much of a push to scale back Medicare, unlike other programs. But the rejoinder worked for Mondale. Suddenly, Reagan appeared old, a befuddled septuagenarian well past his prime. A race that was supposed to be a runaway now looked competitive. While Reagan still had a sizable lead after the debate, Mondale was declared the winner of the debate by 66 percent to 17 percent. If Reagan could not dispense with the age question, it seemed conceivable that Mondale could overtake him. Reagan knew he did badly. "I stunk," he told Stuart Spencer afterward.

Baker was on edge in the aftermath. Nancy Reagan was furious. "What have you done to my husband?" she demanded of Michael Deaver. She was looking for someone to blame and her candidates were Baker and Dick Darman, who was in charge of debate preparations. It had not escaped her attention that Baker seemed to take credit for her husband's achievements, so he should take blame for his setbacks.

Baker knew that Reagan's poor performance was not Darman's fault and did not think it was his own either. Reagan simply had not put in the work needed. Spencer had gone to Camp David with the Reagans the weekend before. "I had the briefing books with me," Spencer said. "Put them on that table and he and I watched movies for two days. Every morning when I'd come over, I'd look at the books and they hadn't moved."

But Nancy and Paul Laxalt decided that the problem was that Reagan had been *over*-prepared, his head stuffed with too many facts and figures. "He was brutalized by a briefing process that didn't make any sense," Laxalt told reporters, a public repudiation of Baker and Darman. Baker was too important to the White House to toss overboard, but Darman was seen as arrogant and neither Nancy nor Laxalt would miss him terribly if he were gone. Baker and Darman felt aggrieved; they both knew that the reason October 7 had been picked as the date for the debate was because Nancy had insisted on it after consulting with her astrologer.

Baker wanted to keep Darman if at all possible. While Baker knew how much his aide could grate on colleagues, he had come to depend on Darman. But Baker could not—or would not—stop Nancy from sending Spencer to tell Darman to resign.

At 5 p.m. one day after the debate, Darman dropped by Baker's office. Instead of his usual welcome, Baker turned away from Darman, staring out the window onto the patio outside the West Wing.

"What's up?" Darman asked.

"What's your reaction?"

"My reaction to what?"

"Didn't Stu talk to you?"

"No," Darman said. "He stopped by my office. But I wasn't there. And when I came back, I couldn't find him."

Baker said nothing, seemingly uncomfortable.

"What did Spencer want?" Darman asked.

Baker stared at him grimly. "He was going to tell you that you had to resign."

Darman felt he had been hit in the stomach. As he put it in his memoir, "When Spencer was commissioned as the angel of death, there weren't many victims who survived."

Reeling, Darman ventured with a lightness he did not feel that he was glad he had not been there when Spencer stopped by. "What is the supposed reason I'm to resign?"

"The first lady wants you out."

"Have you talked with her?"

"No. But a job's been done on you. Spencer says she's dead serious. I argued with him. And I want you to know I told Spencer that I would have to get the message from the president."

"You mean you didn't say, 'If he goes, I go'?"

Darman meant it half jokingly, but Baker did not take it that way. Instead, Baker pointed out that Darman had always said that if he ever became a liability he would go. Darman knew that Baker, while a friend, was habitually careful about putting himself in danger. The two discussed the matter further and agreed that Darman should go see the president himself.

In the end, Darman appealed to Deaver, who agreed to fix the matter with Nancy. Darman was spared, but it was a close call. It was also a revealing moment about Baker. No matter how much he relied on an adviser, even one as close as Darman, Baker would only go so far for someone else. By insisting that any order to dismiss Darman had to come from the president, Baker did protect Darman, because he knew that Reagan would never fire a member of his staff in such a circumstance. But Baker was not willing to take on Nancy directly. He did not stop Spencer from trying to convey Nancy's edict nor did he even warn Darman that it was coming. Indeed, Spencer later denied that he told Baker that Darman had to go, saying that he had only "cautioned him about Darman." So when Darman showed up at his office unawares, Baker's first question was to ask his reaction to a resignation demand that may never have been made—in other words, testing to see if Darman might voluntarily fall on his sword, thus relieving Baker of the pressure. Ultimately, it was Deaver, not Baker, who saved Darman.

Darman emerged from the episode scarred. He told one friend that Nancy was "insane." More important, it soured Darman on his mentor Baker. As one person close to Darman said, he "took that very personally when he got blamed for that and he was upset that Baker didn't stick up for him."

ON THE DEFENSIVE, Baker and the campaign team decided to shift the advertising to something a little closer to a policy argument—although not much closer. A new ad produced by the Tuesday Team began airing after the debate that returned to the Cold War, invoking Reagan's peace-through-strength approach to national security, albeit without any specifics of any kind. "There's a bear in the woods," the narrator said as the screen showed a lumbering beast with a hunter standing watch nearby. "Some people say the bear is tame. Others say it's vicious and dangerous. Since no one can really be sure who's right, isn't it smart to be as strong as the bear?" It was the scary metaphorical counterpoint to "Morning in America."

If Baker was hoping that his friend George Bush would right the ship during his own vice presidential debate just four days after Reagan's, he was destined to be disappointed. Bush was wary of facing off against

Geraldine Ferraro. Never before had male and female candidates gone head to head on a national stage like this and Bush was uncertain how to strike the right balance—he needed to attack the other ticket to stanch its momentum following the Louisville debate, but he did not want to look like he was beating up a woman. Ferraro had been on the defensive in recent weeks because of financial questions about her husband, John Zaccaro, who ran a real estate holding company and initially refused to release his tax returns. But Bush knew if he pounded too hard, it might generate sympathy for her.

The balance he sought eluded him as they met for their debate in Philadelphia on October 11. When he pushed back against Ferraro's comparison of Reagan's policy in Lebanon with Jimmy Carter's record in Iran, Bush came across as condescending.

"Let me help you with the difference, Mrs. Ferraro, between Iran and the embassy in Lebanon," he said.

"Let me just say, first of all," Ferraro replied, "that I almost resent, Vice President Bush, your patronizing attitude that you have to teach me about foreign policy."

Bush did not dig out of that hole when he was caught on a live microphone the day after the debate awkwardly boasting about his performance to a group of longshoremen. "We tried to kick a little ass last night," he was overheard saying.

Not so much. It would fall to Reagan, who had one last chance in Kansas City on October 21. Rather than worry as much about briefing books or critiquing his last debate, Baker and the campaign team focused on building up the president's confidence for the next one. They brought in Roger Ailes, a longtime Republican strategist whose habit of pumping up Reagan earned him the nickname "Dr. Feelgood."

The writer Garry Wills compared Reagan's performance in the first debate to the legendary actor Laurence Olivier experiencing stage fright late in his career. Olivier overcame that by having a fellow actor always in sight; Reagan's team adopted the technique by making sure that Nancy would always be in the president's view when he took on Mondale. They wanted him loose, not worried. Just before Reagan went onstage at the Kansas City Municipal Auditorium, Baker handed him a note alluding to the one he had given him back in 1980. "Chuckle again," it said, "and have fun out there."

He did. The debate was in theory about foreign policy, but about a third of the way through, the inevitable age question came up. Henry Trewhitt of the Baltimore *Sun* couched the question in polite terms, recalling that during the Cuban Missile Crisis John Kennedy had to go with little sleep for days.

"Is there any doubt in your mind that you would be able to function in such circumstances?" he asked Reagan.

"Not at all, Mr. Trewhitt," Reagan answered. "And I want you to know that also I will not make age an issue of this campaign," he went on, adding with mock seriousness, "I am not going to exploit for political purposes my opponent's youth and inexperience."

Even Mondale burst out laughing. And the reporter acknowledged that Reagan had hit a home run.

"Mr. President, I'd like to head for the fence and try to catch that one before it goes over, but I'll go on to another question," Trewhitt said.

Indeed, from that moment on, the age question was essentially settled. Baker later insisted that the line had not been scripted ahead of time. Reagan did not use the response that his advisers had actually prepared for him: "Yes, age is an issue in this campaign—my opponent's ideas are too old." But at some point before the first debate, Baker recalled, Reagan had tried out something similar during a ride in a White House limousine. "Well, I might just say, if I'm asked, 'If he doesn't question my age, I won't raise questions about his youth and inexperience,'" Reagan had told him. The next time Baker heard Reagan use it was on the debate stage.

Mondale never had a real chance after that. Reagan probably would have won no matter what, but with the second debate he had quelled the most serious concern the public had about keeping him in office. He had an 11-point lead in Wirthlin's poll on the morning of the debate, which ballooned to 17 points by the following day. "You'll see that I was smiling," Mondale said, remembering the moment years later. "But I think if you come in close, you'll see some tears coming down because I knew he had gotten me there. That was really the end of my campaign that night, I think." Afterward, he said, "I walked off and I was almost certain the campaign was over, and it was."

Two weeks later, on November 6, Reagan won in a landslide, capturing forty-nine states, losing only Mondale's home of Minnesota and the District of Columbia. He took a resounding 59 percent of the popular vote and 525 electoral votes, the most ever in American history. He prevailed in nearly every income group and drew especially strong support among younger voters who had been skeptical of him four years earlier. He cemented the South as the party's new base and held on to the Reagan Democrats who crossed lines during his first election.

His coattails, however, were not particularly long. While Republicans picked up fifteen seats in the House, Democrats retained a strong majority, and in the Senate, Reagan's party actually lost two seats. The victory was more about Reagan than Republicans.

Either way, the president and Baker's team savored the success at an election night party at the Century Plaza hotel where Susan had first learned of Reagan's plans to conscript her husband four years earlier.

"Four more years!" the crowd chanted. "Four more years!"

"I think," Reagan said, "that's just been arranged."

AFTER THE VOTE, Baker met with reporters for breakfast. The election was a great victory, he said, but he acknowledged that it did not add up to much of a mandate. They had run on a gauzy cloud of patriotism but did little to define an agenda for a second term beyond not raising taxes and limiting the scope of government. They would not be able to point back to any particular policy that was effectively ratified by voters. And because they did not carry Congress with them, there would be limits on how much they could muscle through anyway.

One of the reporters later mentioned the conversation to Ed Rollins, who interpreted it in the most objectionable way and confronted Baker about it.

"We *have* to play down the mandate talk," Baker said, according to Rollins. "We didn't get the congressional seats we needed. Tip is still in charge and we don't want to antagonize him."

"Jim, that's bullshit," Rollins remembered replying. "The president just won forty-nine states and 59 percent of the vote and that's a mandate in anybody's book."

"The campaign is over," Baker said. "Now we've got to govern."

For Baker, campaigning was what you did to get the chance to govern. You said what you had to say but the true test was what came afterward. To some critics, the Reagan campaign of 1984 signaled the triumph of image over reality, of "large lies told through the calculated repetition of soothing imagery and potent symbolism," as William Greider, the same journalist who had played confessor to David Stockman, wrote in *Rolling Stone*. "If the politics of 1984 describes the future," he added, "then Americans are being reduced to a nation of befogged sheep, beguiled by false images and manipulated ruthlessly."

Baker did not see it that way, or at least he did not admit to seeing it that way. The reelection represented a validation—of Reagan, yes, but of Baker too. And it had turned out better than even he had hoped it might.

A month after the vote, Baker sent $250 to the columnist Joseph Alsop to pay off a bet made before the election over a dinner of stone crabs at a party with a bunch of journalists at the home of Meg Greenfield, the editorial page editor at *The Washington Post.* "As I remember it," Baker wrote to Alsop, "you felt that we would win in excess of 58% of the popular vote in the Presidential election, and I expected it to be something less than that." He also sent a copy to Greenfield. "Meg," he wrote, "I bet you didn't know your guests were running a bookie operation at your dinner parties. JAB III."

After four years in the White House, Baker was a full-fledged member of the club. It did not matter that Reagan was a conservative and the *Post's* editorial page editor was a liberal. They were part of the same ruling establishment. The Reagans loved Greenfield's boss, Katharine Graham, and went to her Georgetown home for dinner from time to time. Baker did too. This was when Washingtonians from opposing parties could share a meal without being accused of selling out their principles.

Baker had steered Reagan through the worst moments of the first term and helped transform him from a muddled, gaffe-prone former actor struggling with a miserable economy to the most successful president of a generation. Baker had lashed Reagan's story to the country's, making him the essential leader of his time. The seeds of the myth that would later develop had been planted.

Now, Baker hoped, he might finally be liberated himself.

CHAPTER 15

Fencing Master

For Baker, the escape route presented itself, oddly enough, in the form of a hung-up telephone. It was 7:50 in the morning, ten days after the election, and Baker was dealing with a red-hot treasury secretary. Donald Regan shouted at him with all the lusty profanity of the Marine he had once been. "Fuck yourself and the horse you rode in on," Regan snapped and then slammed down the receiver.

Regan was upset that his remarks on the economy at a cabinet meeting the day before had been leaked to *The Washington Post* even though he had gone on the warpath about leaks. He should not have been surprised. But Regan took the matter so seriously that after hanging up on Baker he drafted a letter of resignation. Baker told Reagan what had happened, then volunteered to go mollify the fuming cabinet secretary.

By the time Baker arrived at the Treasury Building, next door to the White House, Regan had cooled down but he still had the letter of resignation ready. Baker told Regan that the president might refuse to accept it, not knowing if that was really true or not. Regan suggested that the two of them have lunch and they shared their mutual frustrations. Regan could not help noticing that Baker seemed worn out and distracted. When the harried White House aide collapsed in a chair, sighed loudly, shook his head, and smiled ruefully, Regan asked what was wrong. Baker described a litany of aggravations—budget battles, hostile press coverage, campaign pressures, and so forth.

"You're tired, aren't you?" Regan said.

"You're damn right I am," Baker said. "Don, nobody's ever held this job as long as I have that hadn't either been fired or gone to jail."

"You know what we should do, Jim?" Regan suddenly said. "We should swap jobs."

Rather than laughing away the offhand comment, Baker looked like a drowning man who had just been thrown a life vest.

"Do you mean that?" Baker asked.

Regan paused. "I guess I do."

Baker stood to leave, looking less harried. "Watch out," he said. "I may take you up on that."

As Regan described it later, the words just popped out of his mouth. It was less a carefully considered plan than a reaction to the moment. Regan was ready for a change too. As much as Baker was eager to break out of the hothouse center of the action, Regan found himself drawn to it.

Spontaneous or not, Baker took the idea of a switch seriously. Running the Treasury had not been his first choice. He had thought about secretary of state, but there seemed little chance that George Shultz would move on. He also would have liked to be attorney general, but Ed Meese had endured a year of delay amid questions about his ethics and now finally seemed headed toward confirmation. Baker had no special preparation for the job of treasury secretary—indeed, he had flunked at least one economics exam in college—but it was the second-ranking cabinet position and a chance to finally break out of the job that had been wearing him down.

In classic Baker fashion, he spent the following days methodically weighing the pros and cons, and carefully saved the arguments in his file. On the positive side, he wrote:

> Both parties are tired of their current jobs and have spent a fair amount of personal political capital in them.

> Both have completed a natural cycle—and the State of the Union would be a natural point for a shift.

> Both would be re-invigorated by the shift—as would the Administration, thereby.

Dick Darman prepared another list of factors for Baker to consider under two columns, "Stay" and "Treas," with each having two subheads, "Upside" and "Downside." The upsides for taking the position included "Serious, substantive job—back to professional image (not just pol.); better positioning for later." Another was "Can make own agenda—and stay a 'winner.'" The downsides included "'leaving a sinking ship' stories" and "not as good as State (but: bird in hand vs. bush)." The notion that treasury secretary would be a stepping-stone "positioning for later" spoke to the extent of Baker's ambitions even then—what could be better than treasury secretary? Secretary of state? Yes, and beyond that only vice president and president.

Baker talked it over with Michael Deaver, who was planning at last to leave the White House himself. Deaver liked the idea. Baker invited him to his Foxhall Road house in December for lunch with Regan to discuss it. As Baker and Regan outlined their proposed swap, the treasury secretary realized that Deaver already seemed to know about it. With Christmas nearly upon them, the three decided to wait to approach the president until after the holiday.

When they finally broached it with Reagan in January, Deaver recalled introducing the idea of Regan moving to the West Wing with a joke. "Mr. President," he said, "I've brought you a playmate of your own age."

The idea met with no resistance from the president, who was about to turn seventy-four. Reagan "nodded affably," recalled Regan, then sixty-six. Asking no questions, Reagan promptly signed off on the switch.

Just like that, the president agreed to a job trade that would stun Washington and reorder his whole administration. With no extended evaluation of whether Baker would make a good treasury secretary or Regan a good chief of staff, Reagan had just staked his second term on a personnel decision that had been presented to him as all but a fait accompli.

In later years, Baker would insist that he genuinely thought Regan would run an effective White House, but others doubted that, even at the time. Stuart Spencer learned about the swap from the radio and assumed that Baker had not asked his advice because he knew what it would have been. "I'd have flipped out," Spencer said. The longtime chairman and chief executive officer of Merrill Lynch, Regan was used to running things his way. He could be imperious and impatient. He cared a little too much about the perquisites of power. Baker's maxim about his job was to focus more on the "staff" than the "chief"; Regan looked at it the other way around. And so in his desire to move on and move up, Baker left Regan with a partner manifestly ill-suited for the job, arguably a disservice to the president he had worked so hard to make successful. One confidant said Baker did not want Regan to fail, but was so eager to get out that he did not focus on what would happen to the White House after he left. "If I was totally honest," the confidant said, "I don't think he cared."

The day after Reagan signed off on the swap, the White House promptly announced it to a shocked capital—once made, Baker was not going to let the decision linger lest it start to draw fire the way his abortive appointment as national security adviser had. His confirmation hearing before the Senate Finance Committee on January 23 turned out to be a "friendly session," as Senator Bob Packwood of Oregon, the Republican chairman, put it, a serious, sedate affair that Baker navigated readily enough. Susan was in the audience to show support along with three of their eight children. None of the senators expressed doubt about Baker's qualifications for the job or challenged his judgment. No one questioned his decisions as chief of staff or mentioned his lack of a financial policy background. Instead, they tried to pin him down on tax reform, questions that he dodged with practiced ease. The Senate followed up six days later by voting 95 to 0 to confirm Baker as the nation's sixty-seventh secretary of the treasury.

Baker was sworn in twice, the first time in the basement of his home on February 3 with Mary-Bonner, now seven years old, holding his mother's Bible for a quick installation so he could get to work, and then again five days later in more ceremonial fashion in the Oval Office with Reagan presiding. George Bush was out of town, so Barbara Bush came to represent the family at the White House ceremony. Baker introduced his children to Reagan one at a time, nervous enough at one point that he misidentified one of the boys and had to be corrected by Susan. "Isn't it something to have so many children you get mixed up?" she joked as Reagan greeted her with a kiss on the cheek.

In taking the oath, Baker assumed the same position once held by the likes of Alexander Hamilton, Andrew Mellon, and Henry Morgenthau. The Secret Service, which was part of his department, gave him the code name "Fencing Master" and his distinctive James A. Baker III signature was put on the next printing of the United States dollar. Susan bought him a green tie from Neiman Marcus representing the color of the currency, a fashion choice that would soon become a trademark for the rest of his career. Finally, he had transcended his role of fixer. Finally, he was no longer staff. He was, in Washington terms, a Principal. "He couldn't have been more thrilled," said Margaret Tutwiler.

Baker's mandate was set by the president in his State of the Union address to Congress on February 6 when Reagan called for historic reform. "Tonight," Reagan added, "I am instructing Treasury Secretary James Baker"—and here he paused to joke, "I have to get used to saying that"—before continuing, "to begin working with congressional authors and committees for bipartisan legislation conforming to these principles." The deadline he set was soon—a bill by the end of 1985. "Together, we can pass, this year, a tax bill for fairness, simplicity and growth, making this economy the engine of our dreams and America the investment capital of the world. So let us begin."

WHAT REAGAN WAS assigning Baker to do was both monumental and politically fraught. Cutting taxes, as they had done in the first term, was easy and popular enough. This was different and much, much harder, rewriting the tax code from top to bottom to make it more rational. Any efforts to clean out the system had routinely fallen short over the years. But this time, the stars seemed to be aligned.

In the Reagan era, nearly everyone agreed that the tax code was a disaster. It was pockmarked with lucrative breaks for industries whose lobbyists had adeptly worked the halls of the Capitol, reflecting the power of special interests to game the system. Even tax provisions with more altruistic goals, such as the deduction for charitable contributions, were a reflection of policymakers using the code to drive favored policies, often layered upon each other in piecemeal fashion rather than a comprehensive statement of national priorities. Polls found that Americans no longer considered the federal system fairer than their state or local tax systems.

In 1983, about thirty thousand taxpayers making more than $250,000 a year—including three thousand millionaires—paid less than 5 percent of their income in taxes, according to a Treasury Department study. Corporate America was shouldering a smaller and smaller share of the overall tax burden, just 6 percent in 1983 compared with 25 percent when Dwight Eisenhower was president, a trend accelerated by Reagan's original tax cut legislation. Another study found that since that bill was passed, 128 large, profitable companies paid no federal income taxes at all in at least one year while collectively earning profits of $57.1 billion, including such corporate giants as General Electric, Boeing, Dow Chemical, Tenneco, General Dynamics, and Lockheed.

All of this was no accident. Business had invested huge amounts of cash in the two political parties. By the time Baker set his sights on the issue, political action committees were contributing eight times as much money to congressional candidates as they were a decade earlier, with a sizable share devoted to the lawmakers who sat on the tax-writing committees in the House and Senate. Every major industry, it seemed, had a champion on the panels and every major tax break had someone who stood to lose and would fight to protect their interests. The status quo was held in place by powerful political gravity. "I sort of like the tax code the way it is," said Bob Packwood, the Republican whose Senate Finance Committee would have to approve any changes.

The plan produced by Donald Regan's Treasury Department in November 1984 and left for Baker when he arrived at the beginning of 1985 was a dud from the start. It proposed reducing tax rates by abolishing nearly all deductions, including popular ones favored by many taxpayers and businesses. In effect, it was the way a theoretician, freed of any political considerations, might have designed the tax code. "It was a very apolitical, idealized version of what the Treasury Department believed was appropriate to tax reform," said Ronald Pearlman, who served as assistant secretary for tax policy under Regan and stayed on under Baker. "It was very controversial. Everyone had criticisms because with few exceptions it went after everything." When Baker showed up at the Treasury Department, he "was quite hostile" to the plan, Pearlman recalled, less because of its substantive provisions than out of "his political judgment" about its viability. The plan, Baker said later, was developed with "a tin ear for politics." Baker, who had immersed himself in the politics of Capitol Hill as Reagan's chief of staff, decided to scrap the proposal and start again.

Settling into his new third-floor office in the Classical Revival building that had housed treasury secretaries for more than 140 years, Baker essentially imported his old White House team to help him do it. Dick Darman would be his deputy secretary and Margaret Tutwiler would be assistant secretary for public affairs and public liaison, his chief policy and political lieutenants respectively. John Rogers would be another assistant secretary. Robert Kimmitt would be general counsel.

Darman, Baker knew, came with baggage. He was brilliant, the brains behind many key policies of the last four years. He was a conceptual thinker in a way that Baker was not, and he was an instinctive contrarian, the one who, if everyone else in the room agreed that something was true, would say, "Don't be too sure." But even though Baker had long defended him, there were times when he grew aggravated with Darman as well. On the day that Reagan announced his appointment as treasury secretary, Baker scribbled out some rules of the road:

> I've got to be the Sect.—can't take away a "Baker/Darman." All public pronouncements—JAB III. (Don't need a "Baker/Darman" situation developing at Treas. like here at W.H.) Dick likes to foster image of "<u>power behind the throne</u>." Limit total charge of an issue area. Dick should have no "own agenda" w/J Kemp or otherwise. Manage the Dept—R.G.D. Managing RGD is going to continue to be a prob. Be my dep'ty not <u>own</u> persona. If you want to go on this basis—OK. Otherwise something else.

Darman agreed. He was ready for a bigger role and eager to take on tax reform. In a memo he had written before Baker's job swap, Darman had already identified an overhaul of the tax code as a possible domestic initiative for the second term. For a policy wonk, getting the chance to design and enact it was the opportunity of a lifetime.

But the tension with Baker during this transition reflected the reality of their complicated relationship. Darman despised the idea of being just an "aide." In private, he groused that Baker would never have been Baker if not for Darman. His resentment at being Baker's glorified sidekick was so palpable that for Reagan's second swearing-in ceremony, Margaret Tutwiler and John Rogers teasingly had a special inaugural license plate made for Darman that read: "BAKER AIDE." They slipped it to one of Darman's assistants to have it put on his car so they would have plausible deniability. Darman angrily bent the license plate in half. "Dad *hated* that," his son, Jonathan Darman, said of the gag plate.

Now was Darman's chance to transcend his staffer past. As deputy treasury secretary, he would be a Senate-confirmed senior official, more than just an assistant. And so he and Baker put aside the strain and set out to remake the tax code. To develop their own tax reform plan, Baker and Darman reprised their approach to Social Security in 1983, picking out a few key negotiators from both parties and both houses of Congress and inviting them to Baker's Foxhall Road house to haggle over details in secret.

The players gathered on Saturdays in the den in the basement. But Baker quickly discovered that he could not start from scratch with so many large personalities in one room. Representative Dan Rostenkowski, the Chicago ward-heeling pol who headed the House Ways and Means Committee and would be key to any tax legislation, resisted sitting down with junior members such as Representative Dick Gephardt of Missouri, a Democrat who had been pushing for reform. While Rostenkowski was fond of Baker, he resisted the secretary's charms. "Jimmy boy, you're massaging me," Rostenkowski told Baker. "I have been handled by better than you and your hands are cold."

Baker and Darman then shifted gears, deciding to write their own plan without Democrats and take their chances by sending it to Rostenkowski and Congress. Baker began holding Saturday meetings with his staff at the Treasury Building to map out a palatable plan, showing up with trademark cowboy boots on his feet and Red Man tobacco in his jaw as they chewed over ideas. Philosophy was out. Politics was in. The question Baker kept asking in one form or another was not *Is this the best way to do this?* but *Can this pass?* The challenge was all the more daunting because the plan not only had to lower rates while closing loopholes, but Reagan had made clear that it could not change the bottom line amount of money brought into government coffers. The total tax revenues would have to remain the same. In the vernacular of Washington, this was called "revenue neutral" and it would be the major challenge in crafting a final plan—every decision keeping one tax break would require a tradeoff to make up for the lost revenue.

As Baker had anticipated, Darman's cantankerous demeanor caused headaches. When congressmen involved in the tax debate wanted to have a principals-only meeting and insisted that he leave the room because he was "staff," Darman erupted, declaring that he was the deputy secretary of treasury confirmed by the United States Senate, *not staff.* And as a self-perceived principal, Darman felt little need to confide in subordinates what he was up to. Ron Pearlman, the assistant secretary who was supposed to be in charge of tax policy, would find out from friends on Capitol Hill that Darman had been up there negotiating without telling him.

"There were times of stress and strain between him and me," Pearlman said. Baker sought to calm him. "The secretary at times would tell me, 'Cool down, don't take it seriously, he's a brilliant guy, I'm the decision maker here, don't get too uptight.'" Pearlman came to believe that Baker had made a devil's bargain in bringing Darman to Treasury, accepting his deputy's volatile nature and dismissive side as the price for his intellect and policy creativity. "Baker knew that he brought a lot to the table," Pearlman said of Darman. "There were times he would go too far, he would alienate someone, he would take a position that didn't make a great deal of substantive sense. But Baker could deal with that."

Baker and his team presented their plan to Reagan, with Donald Regan, author of the version they had scrapped, sitting in Baker's old chair as chief of staff. Over the course of several meetings, the president approved all the major provisions. But suddenly the Treasury Department's revenue estimates shifted so that the plan would bring in $150 billion less over five years than originally projected. When the Treasury team arrived at the White House to explain to Reagan what had happened, an irritated Baker felt no urge to take the blame.

"Ron, *you* describe this to the president," he instructed Pearlman, whose office had been responsible.

Pearlman years later recalled Baker saying it jokingly, but with a real edge. "It was a jab," he said. "He clearly wanted to communicate to the president this was something he wasn't involved in."

After adjustments were made to eliminate the new revenue gap, Reagan finally unveiled the plan in a nationally televised address to the nation from the Oval Office on May 28. "Death and taxes may be inevitable, but unjust taxes are not," he said as Baker watched. "The first American Revolution was sparked by an unshakable conviction—taxation without representation is tyranny. Two centuries later, a second American revolution for hope and opportunity is gathering force again—a peaceful revolution, but born of popular resentment against a tax system that is unwise, unwanted and unfair."

Dan Rostenkowski gave the Democrats' televised reply and he welcomed Reagan's initiative. "If the president's plan is everything he says it is, he'll have a great deal of Democratic support," Rostenkowski said. "That's the real difference this time. A Republican president has joined the Democrats in Congress to try to redeem this long-standing commitment to a tax system that's simple and fair. If we work together with good faith and determination, this time the people may win. This time, I really think we can get tax reform."

Rostenkowski's response sent a powerful signal to the nation and spoke volumes about the credibility of Baker's efforts across the aisle. In later years, with different presidents and treasury secretaries and congressional leaders, tax proposals would be cause for immediate and relentless partisan battling. In this case, Baker was seeking nothing less than a wholesale revision of the tax code, affecting nearly every taxpayer and business in the country, and he was trying to do it in tandem with the opposition party. Rostenkowski had just made clear that he was ready to give it a shot, embracing Baker in a high-stakes venture.

FOR BAKER, the drive to rewrite the tax code was only part of the mission in his new role. One of the challenges he found when he arrived at the Treasury Building was the strength of the dollar, which, odd as it must have sounded to his political team, was not necessarily a good thing for the country.

While there were advantages, a strong dollar meant that American exports became more expensive for foreign customers to buy and therefore domestic firms found themselves all but shut out of overseas markets, especially industries producing steel, textiles, aircraft, automobiles, and agriculture. The dollar had appreciated by 28 percent after inflation between 1980 and 1982 and, after a temporary decline, rose another 14 percent from 1983 to 1984.

As a result, the country was flooded with cheap imports and the trade deficit ballooned to an all-time record of $109 billion in 1984, more than four times as high as when Reagan took office, while West Germany and Japan developed large trade surpluses. This came at a time when Japan's soaring economic growth was leading to grim prognostications of American decline. The Japanese were conquering world markets with their automobiles, computers, cameras, and video recorders. They were investing their surplus cash buying up American government debt. One prominent economist compared the United States to the husband who spends too much and Japan to the wife who saves. Americans were reading headlines like "The Japanning of America Today."

In keeping with his free market philosophy, Reagan had taken a hands-off approach to the dollar for most of the first term but as the situation worsened, he faced threats of protectionist legislation in Congress. Finally, in mid-1984, Donald Regan negotiated an agreement with Japan intended to liberalize its financial system and strengthen the yen against the dollar. But it had the opposite effect. Between mid-1984 and February 1985, the dollar appreciated another 20 percent.

Now it fell to Baker to fix the problem. Never ones to let ideology stand in the way, Baker and Darman opted to put aside the first-term laissez-faire policy altogether and intervene more aggressively to weaken the dollar to improve conditions for American exporters and make it easier to pay down American debt. In a memo to Reagan, Baker argued that his effort could be useful in "diffusing protectionist pressures in Congress."

What Baker wanted to try was something no American official had pulled off before—he set out to secretly craft an agreement with the world's other leading economic powers to coordinate their currencies. To do so, he had to keep the whole effort hidden from the public, lest a leak set off furious market speculation. So he furtively invited his counterparts and top central bankers from four allies known, together with the United States, as the Group of 5, or G5—Britain, Japan, France, and West Germany—to the landmark Plaza Hotel in New York to negotiate an agreement on exchange rates. On a Sunday in September 1985, when the markets were closed, he snuck them into the hotel without anyone noticing and only allowed aides to notify reporters about the meeting after it was already under way. Needless to say, this was not how finance ministers typically rolled.

Baker convinced the other officials to go along with his plan by scaring them with the prospect of new trade barriers being threatened by populist members of Congress. Sitting together in the Plaza's ornate Gold Room, Baker and the finance ministers set a mutual goal of depreciating the dollar by 10 percent to 12 percent. The other nations would begin selling dollars in international currency markets to increase the supply and bring down the value of the dollar. The five powers also agreed on specific adjustments to their macroeconomic policies. Japan committed to opening its markets to more foreign goods. West Germany agreed to cut taxes to stimulate economic growth. The United States, for its part, vowed to rein in its out-of-control budget deficits.

The full scope of what was agreed to was profound and largely without precedent. It was the first time individual countries had agreed to change their economic policies to achieve an international goal and the first time that the world's top central bankers had agreed to intervene in currency markets. The Plaza Accord, as it came to be known, was a key step en route to the globalization of financial markets. Not all of this was publicly announced when Baker and other ministers emerged from the secret talks, however, and it would have caused a big stir if it had been. Still, the communiqué released to reporters, while cryptic, signaled clearly that a significant move had been taken. In it, Baker and the other ministers declared that a weaker dollar "is desirable" and added that "they stand ready to cooperate more closely to encourage this when to do so would be helpful." Baker followed up in person with the media to hail the agreement. "What's new is that we're all here together," he told reporters.

He was not entirely together with his colleagues in the Reagan administration, though. Baker's fixation on secrecy meant that some key American officials were caught off guard, not least George Shultz, who as secretary of state (and a former treasury secretary) felt blindsided about major negotiations with top allies, even if they were on Baker's turf. "Shultz got livid at me," Baker recalled.

But Baker was determined to keep others out of his lane. Just two days after the Plaza Accord, Commerce Secretary Malcolm Baldrige said at a breakfast for reporters that the United States did not plan a massive intervention in currency markets to reduce the value of the dollar but that in his personal opinion, the dollar would need a 25 percent decrease to make it competitive once again. "I don't think we would get into massive intervention," Baldrige said. Which of course was what Baker had just agreed to do with the world's other leading powers.

Baker slapped him down hard. In a two-sentence memo sent the same day and marked "EXTREMELY URGENT," he wrote Baldrige: "This is killing us. Please get out a correction saying that you were misinterpreted and that the United States does not and will not comment on intervention." Baker cracked the whip on Baldrige publicly a few days later when a reporter asked about the commerce secretary's comments. Baldrige, Baker said, "doesn't speak for the administration on the subject of exchange rates." He claimed that "we do not have a target" but added that "a moderate, gradual decline in the dollar would not displease us."

The agreement worked. By the next day, the dollar slid by about 5 percent and reached its lowest level against the Japanese yen in nearly four years. Between 1985 and 1987, the dollar depreciated by 40 percent. The plan worked so well that just seventeen months later, Baker and his counterparts got together again to apply the brakes. Some of the other powers, especially Japan, were buffeted by the fall of the dollar. Meeting in February 1987, this time at the iconic Louvre Museum in Paris, and joined by the finance ministers from Canada and Italy, Baker and his counterparts agreed to stabilize the dollar at its current, much lower rate by purchasing dollars in international currency markets, thus reducing the supply and bolstering the dollar's value, and by tightening American monetary policy, thus reducing inflation. As part of the Louvre Accord, Baker also agreed to stop talking down the dollar, which he had done in the past to convince international markets that it would continue to decrease in value.

But in some ways, all these interventions may have worked too well. By weakening the dollar and then locking in a lower rate, the accords had strengthened the yen, enabling the Japanese to embark on an epic buying spree in the United States. In the four years following the Plaza Accord, Japanese investors bought a series of American landmarks, from Columbia Pictures to Rockefeller Center in New York, triggering a political backlash among American politicians and public figures who competed in their Japan-bashing.

Among the bashers was a brash New York real estate developer named Donald Trump. A showman and tabloid magnet who opened his signature Trump Tower on Fifth Avenue in 1983 and his namesake Atlantic City casino in 1984, Trump had lately decided to take his New York brand of notoriety national, making splashy acquisitions and commenting on politics. "A lot of people are tired of watching other countries ripping off the United States," he said in 1987. "They laugh at us behind our backs. They laugh at us because of our own stupidity." Trump took out a full-page ad in newspapers including *The New York Times* arguing that the United States should charge countries such as Japan for protecting oil tankers traveling through the Persian Gulf, an ad developed by the same public relations executives who had been part of Reagan's Tuesday Team in 1984.

Trump even signaled that he might run for president in 1988. "I think I'd win," Trump told the talk show host Oprah Winfrey. "I'll tell you what: I wouldn't go in to lose."

NEGOTIATING WITH the Japanese was one thing. Negotiating with Dan Rostenkowski was another. With Baker's plan for tax reform now being considered by Congress, it was time to reach out again to the powerful committee chairman to see if they could reach the deal they could not in the spring.

Rostenkowski was an archetypal figure on Capitol Hill, physically imposing and gruff, an old-school wheeler and dealer who maintained tight control over his committee, dispensed favors to friends, punished enemies, and savored the perks of power as he held court on the lobbyists' dime at the new Morton's Steakhouse in Georgetown. The son of a Chicago alderman, Rostenkowski grew up in the machine of Mayor Richard Daley. As a young man, he played baseball well enough to earn a tryout with the Philadelphia Athletics and served in the Army during the Korean War but was already on the road to a life in politics like his father.

He won a seat in the House in 1958 at age thirty, making him the youngest member of the House at the time. He went on to build a power base, helping to write the law that created Medicare and many other pieces of financial legislation. Blunt spoken, with a girth as expansive as his back-slapping personality, Rostenkowski became chairman of Ways and Means in 1981, as Reagan was being sworn in, and he was determined to keep the exclusive panel "the Cadillac of committees," as one of his young protégés, Representative Tom Downey of New York, remembered him calling it. To do so, he had no problem working with Republicans. "Rosty," as he was universally known, had compromised with Baker on tax cuts and Social Security in the first term and was ready to do so again.

"Rostenkowski and Baker both really wanted to get the deal done and neither of them was obsessed with precisely what was in it," said Jim Jaffe, a longtime aide to Rostenkowski. "They shared that. They shared a friendship going in." That did not make it easy sailing. In the months after Reagan unveiled Baker's plan, the secretary and the chairman engaged in their share of shouting matches. They quarreled over details and strategy. But Baker understood how to manage the relationship.

"Baker really played Rostenkowski like a cello," Jaffe remembered. Rostenkowski was still eager to show that he could be a power broker like those who had previously held the Ways and Means chairmanship, such as his mentor, the legendary Wilbur Mills. "This is Rostenkowski's first opportunity to prove he's the capital-C chairman and Baker's going to enable him to do this." Rostenkowski was "still sort of awed by people who wear $800 suits and have a lot of money like Jim Baker. Baker plays him by saying, 'You are the chairman, you're the guy who can get this done.' Baker comes in and says, 'You're the man, you know how to get things done, we're going to get this done together, you tell me what you need me to do and I'll do it.'" The two also bonded over the seeming impossibility of the task they were taking on. "The whole it-can't-be-done thing made it even more appealing to both Baker and Rostenkowski," Jaffe said. "They both puffed up their chest and said, 'You say this can't be done, but we'll show you.'"

The relationship sometimes left others feeling resentful. Dick Gephardt, one of the early promoters of tax reform, bristled at being shut out. "I have heard more about what the president plans to do on this issue from the press than I have from the president's representatives who were supposedly consulting with me," Gephardt griped in a statement to reporters. Baker marked that sentence on a copy of the statement. "Cheap shot," he wrote. "Politics—just trying to get ink."

The politics of putting together the bill were treacherous. Baker set four bedrock conditions on behalf of the president—in addition to being revenue neutral, any final measure had to reduce the top income tax rate for individuals to no higher than 35 percent, remove millions of lower-income families from the tax rolls, and retain the popular mortgage interest deduction. That left plenty to fight about. An army of lobbyists in designer loafers mobilized, nervously trolling outside the committee chambers in the Longworth House Office Building as they tried to figure out how to protect the favored treatment of various industries. This would provide the title of the classic book on the legislative battle by the *Wall Street Journal* reporters who covered it, Jeffrey Birnbaum and Alan Murray: *Showdown at Gucci Gulch.*

It was perhaps the most complicated legislation considered by Congress in a generation. One lawmaker's boondoggle was another's must-have provision. Those from states with high taxes were determined not to let the deduction for such levies be repealed. Every member had a local industry to protect. And every industry had a special pleading. Manufacturers wanted to make sure they could still write off the depreciation from their expensive equipment. Retail businesses could not care less about that but eagerly pushed to lower the corporate tax rate. Baker the Fencing Master was jousting with all sorts of adversaries at once; the challenge was figuring out which lawmakers and interests he could afford to brush off. "Tax reform gets tougher and tougher, and a lot of the press are ready to write us off," Baker wrote his son Will Winston in September. "But that's premature, and we still have a chance of getting there—if not this year, certainly during the first part of next."

Among those who objected to what Baker was doing was Donald Trump who this time was complaining about a matter of more immediate concern to his bottom line. When he arrived in Baker's office at the Treasury Building for a 4:45 p.m. appointment with the secretary on July 9, he raised hell about the impact of the tax reform legislation on real estate. "He came in there like a stormtrooper," Baker recalled. Baker finally pointed out the window to the White House. "Look," he said, "you're at the wrong building. This building right across the street here, a guy that wants to do this is in that building and you need to go over there."

The bill Rostenkowski ultimately came up with did not meet all of Reagan's conditions, much less Trump's. It lowered the top rate only to 38 percent, included a less generous personal exemption for taxpayers who did not itemize, and raised taxes on corporations more than the administration's plan. Baker concluded it was better to pass the bill, flawed as it was, and get it to the Senate, where it could still be adjusted. But that was not an argument that worked with Republicans, who balked at voting for what they considered a Democratic measure. Leading the revolt, in fact, was Baker's old friend Dick Cheney, now a congressman from Wyoming. "We're going to oppose you on this and we're going to beat you," Cheney told Baker. Much as he had with Donald Trump, Baker told Cheney that he should take it up with the man next door. But Cheney was not so easily dissuaded. "It was garbage, it was not a good bill," Cheney said later. "We didn't want to have to vote on a bad bill."

Cheney teamed up with Representative Trent Lott of Mississippi, another conservative leader, and rallied the Republicans. Not wanting to vote directly against Reagan, they decided to vote against the procedural rule necessary for the bill to come to the floor in the first place. Baker tried to get Reagan to issue a statement accepting the bill with the promise that he would keep working to make it better, but his importuning generated no response from the West Wing and Washington began to suspect the White House was preparing to abandon the effort.

Baker appealed directly to Reagan. "Tax reform is one of your top two domestic priorities—and it will likely die if you do not support moving the Ways and Means bill forward," he wrote the president on December 2. "The bill can be improved in the Senate." If it is not, "you can veto it." When that did not work either, the savvy former chief of staff went to Nancy Reagan, sending her a copy of a Baltimore *Sun* editorial and underlining several sentences that warned that if her husband did not get involved, he would "suffer the worst defeat of his presidency"—and at the hands of fellow Republicans. "Nancy," Baker wrote, by now close enough to use her first name, "I think this editorial is right on the mark. The President 'wants the process to go forward'—but there is a real risk that it won't, because of G.O.P. votes, if he isn't active early next week in calls & letters to Republicans. JABIII."

Still, the message did not register. Baker had spent four years running the White House and now could not get it to respond. He was furious. On December 11, his warnings came true and Cheney fulfilled his vow to beat Baker as the House voted down the procedural rule by a vote of 223 to 202. Only fourteen Republicans sided with Reagan and Baker, a stunning rebuke. "Goddamnit," Rostenkowski shouted into the phone when he reached the stunned treasury secretary. "The rule is going down." As Baker recalled it later, "that was a very dark day."

Tip O'Neill announced after the vote that he would only try to salvage the legislation if Reagan personally informed him that he had a list of fifty to seventy-five Republicans who would vote for final passage, a number Baker did not have. He appealed to O'Neill instead with pure emotion.

"Mr. Speaker, when in your lifetime will you have the chance again to take 6 million poor Americans off the tax rolls?" Baker asked.

But O'Neill would not budge. "You know, this is your bill, this was your idea," he told Baker. "Now you've got to produce the votes for it."

With the biggest domestic initiative of his second term hanging in the balance, Reagan finally engaged in the battle and arrived on Capitol Hill on the afternoon of December 16. Just that morning, Reagan had flown to Fort Campbell, Kentucky, to preside over a memorial service for 248 members of the 101st Airborne Division who had been killed in a plane crash in Gander, Newfoundland. As he addressed the House Republican caucus, he was in an emotional mood. "He got up and talked about sacrifice and patriotism and what it meant to be American and it was pure Reagan—off the cuff, very well done, touched every heart in the room, people in tears," Cheney recalled. "He got all through and he said, 'Now, gentlemen, about that tax bill.' That's all he said. Henry Hyde jumped up and said, 'I'm with you, Mr. President, you can count on me,'" he added, referring to a widely respected Illinois congressman.

That broke the dam. Baker then spent the afternoon calling Republicans and securing commitments. *The president really needs you*, he told them. By the end of the day, Baker had Reagan call O'Neill to say that he had the fifty votes. O'Neill then allowed a face-saving amendment, a non-binding call to change the effective date of the legislation, so that Republicans could say they were voting on a different rule. It passed the next day, 258 to 168, with seventy Republicans siding with Reagan and Baker.

Cheney assumed that Baker had cleverly timed Reagan's meeting with the House Republicans for right after the memorial service, knowing that the president would maximize the emotional patriotism of the moment. "Obviously, a big part of that was Reagan's natural talent," Cheney said, "but you can bet your bottom dollar that Jim had a hand in scheduling the session." Whether Baker really did manipulate the timing with that in mind, it says a lot that his friend believed that he did.

Either way, it had been a near-death experience. Now Baker had to convince the Senate to get on board.

THE KEY WOULD BE Bob Packwood, the Finance Committee chairman, who had admitted that he kind of liked the tax code the way it was—no doubt at least in part due to the fact that he and his colleagues had helped make it that way. A native of Oregon who studied law at New York University, Packwood had worked his way up in politics in his home state, first in Republican Party organizations and then the state legislature before winning his Senate seat in 1968. In Oregon tradition, he was far more moderate than most of his caucus, supporting abortion rights and gun control. He was the first Senate Republican to come out for impeachment of Richard Nixon. He was also known as one of those senators who took advantage of women who worked for him or lobbied him, a predilection that would later come back to haunt him.

Irascible and self-assured, Packwood had little patience for Baker. He was scornful of the treasury secretary, viewing him as a pain who was interfering in legislative affairs that were Packwood's to manage. While the two were both Republicans predisposed to pragmatic politics, they would never forge the bond that Baker had across the aisle with Rostenkowski. Instead, the secretary had to try to manage the prickly senator without alienating him altogether.

Other senators found Baker refreshing and welcomed his determination to get something done. "He had a great way of communicating," remembered Bill Bradley, a New Jersey Democrat who had made tax reform his personal project. "If you're in a legislative situation, you communicate a lot with your eyes and your head and that kind of thing. Your lips are saying, 'No, no, no,' but your eyes are saying, 'yes, yes, yes.' Any number of times when somebody was saying something, even if they're Republican, that was totally idiotic, he would look at me and raise an eyebrow as if to say, 'I'm not really with this guy.' And that makes you feel a part of all this."

If Bradley was a willing partner, some in Baker's own party were not, including Jack Kemp, the New York congressman and the Republican Party's most prominent tax cutter other than Reagan himself. Kemp, a driving force behind the first-term tax-cutting legislation, intervened when he became concerned that Baker was selling out. In March, he wrote Baker a letter taking issue with the secretary's embrace of the latest plan from the Senate. "I was astonished to read in yesterday's paper that, in your judgment, the current Senate Finance Committee proposal meets the President's goals for tax reform," Kemp wrote.

Baker bridled at the congressman's tone, interpreting the letter as classic Washington ass-covering, a way for Kemp to create a document trail that he could later point to in order to prove that he had spoken out against a flawed final product. "If you are again 'astonished' by what you read in the newspaper, please just pick up the phone," Baker wrote back. "We'll only get from here to where we both want to go if we talk directly—not as if we are merely trying to establish a written record."

Baker seemed even more miffed when Bill Archer, a Republican congressman from Houston and a friend going back to their days as children at Camp Rio Vista, took what Baker considered a "cheap shot" by seeming to accuse Baker of misrepresenting the Senate bill. "I've got to tell you its [*sic*] damn disappointing to me to be insulted by my own Congressman, with whom I grew up and who over the last five and one-half years has frequently requested (and received) my cooperation on various matters," Baker wrote. "Cooperation and common courtesy are two-way streets."

Kemp and Archer were not the only ones dissatisfied with what was coming out of the Senate. So was Bob Packwood. The proposal was too measly, not ambitious enough, and it was being pecked to death by different senators. Among those with personal interests was Baker himself, the product of an oil-producing state and a family that had made its fortune in part from the energy industry. Throughout the process, from the Saturday meetings at his home to the back rooms of the House, Baker had been protective to some degree of the oil and gas industry, which was fighting to preserve tax breaks it said were needed to encourage exploration and offset dependence on foreign suppliers. The original plan that Baker developed for Reagan did trim tax advantages for energy companies but not by as much as others had proposed. By the time the House bill reached the Senate, Baker was seen as a guard against deeper cuts in the industry's benefits. "He acted like he was an elected representative from Texas," observed Jeffrey Birnbaum, coauthor of the definitive history of the reform fight. Still, Bill Bradley, who made an effort to slash subsidies for oil and gas firms, only to lose an 11 to 9 vote, said Baker was not the industry's main protector, naming Senator Russell Long, the Democrat from Louisiana, another oil state, as his main adversary.

Baker had one other personal interest in the bill that received little attention at the time. Amid the complicated negotiations, Baker found a way to finally exact revenge against the *Houston Chronicle* for endorsing Mark White over him in the 1978 attorney general's race. The *Chronicle's* decision not to back Baker had bothered him for nearly a decade and now he had the opportunity for retribution by using the tax bill to force the publisher to give up control of the newspaper. The *Chronicle* was owned by the Houston Endowment, a charitable trust set up by Jesse Jones, the Houston magnate who had worked with Captain Baker decades earlier. Under a 1969 federal law, nonprofit organizations were required to sell newspapers on the theory that it was unfair competition for profit-or-loss businesses. Publishers such as the Houston Endowment were given twenty years to divest themselves of their newspapers.

Ever since then, Senator Lloyd Bentsen, the Texas Democrat who beat George Bush in 1970 and served on the Finance Committee, had been inserting provisions into bills to protect the Houston Endowment from the requirement, provisions that were passed by the Senate only to die in the House. But when the provision was inserted into the tax reform bill, Baker stepped in and had it eliminated. As a result, the Houston Endowment was forced to sell the *Chronicle* in 1987 for $400 million.

In retirement, Baker owned up to this heavyhanded use of power to settle a grudge, acknowledging that it was "payback" that might look "vindictive" for partisan or personal reasons. But he was content not contrite. "Did I get them back or what?" he responded when asked about it. "I don't believe in getting mad. I believe in getting even."

ONCE AGAIN the bill looked to be on the brink of failure. With all the lobbying and special riders, the overall legislation was mired in the same complex swamp that had defeated all previous efforts at comprehensive reform. Finally, Bob Packwood pulled the bill rather than let it come to a vote and be defeated. Baker was frustrated. So was Packwood.

The chairman took his staff director, Bill Diefenderfer, over to the Irish Times, a bar near the Capitol, where the two began downing beer after beer even though it was lunchtime. After two pitchers, Packwood's confidence, or perhaps his cockiness, had risen several levels and the tipsy senator declared that the problem was that they were not being ambitious enough. They should force the top bracket all the way down to 25 percent, which would give them leverage to be much more aggressive in wiping out special interest loopholes because everyone would appreciate the lower rate. "To hell with it," he declared. "If they want tax reform, I'll give 'em tax reform."

It was an audacious idea, but Baker agreed to go along. Packwood handpicked six other members of his committee from both parties and convened them in secret to work it out, telling reporters—and other senators—that the panel was done with business for the weekend while in fact meeting surreptitiously with the select negotiators. The seven agreed that any issue decided by four of them would be binding on all of them. Packwood and Diefenderfer basically told Baker to butt out.

"Bill and I in essence said, 'Oh, Jim, shut up,'" he recorded in his diary. "Here we are talking to the Treasury secretary—'shut up, here you've got a plan. All we need you to say is "we think it is wonderful." We'll get it to the president. Jim, we're going to wrap this up by Sunday. Don't fuck it up.'" As if addressing Baker, Packwood went on: "'You put in one pro forma appearance before the Senate Finance Committee Republicans and get your little tail out to Tokyo or wherever it is the president is going to be meeting. And leave Darman here to take care of the strategy and the details and we'll have this done before you get back, but don't start niggling and quibbling over miniscule details.'"

One of the keys to Baker's success over the years was knowing when to back off. In a feat of legislative wizardry, Packwood delivered on his promise after eleven secret meetings over seven days, producing a radical plan along the lines he had outlined in his beer-fueled haze at the Irish Times. He even passed it out of his previously gridlocked committee on a unanimous 20 to 0 vote one night after midnight. The lawmakers celebrated with champagne while Darman called Baker in Tokyo, where he was accompanying Reagan at a Group of 7 summit meeting.

"Jim, tell him to shut up," Packwood heard Darman tell Baker. The senator could only hear Darman's side of the conversation but it seemed that he was trying to get the secretary to reassure the president. "He's going to like this bill, but he's got friends who aren't going to like a lot of this bill. Don't let them get to him before I have a chance to get to you and explain everything that has happened. Let me emphasize again—he is going to like this bill."

So did most members of the Senate. On June 24, the upper chamber approved the bill by a stunning 97 to 3 vote, one of the few times in the modern era when such sweeping legislation passed with so little opposition on the final tally. The issue then went to a conference committee with members from both House and Senate who would reconcile the different bills passed by the two bodies. Packwood, leading the Senate team, and Dan Rostenkowski, leading the House team, found common ground on the general principles they wanted in the final bill, but they knew there would be obstacles. "After Danny and I agreed, it became very clear to me that the real problem in this conference wasn't going to be between the House and the Senate," Packwood told his diary. "It will be Baker who is pro-energy, pro-Texas and pro-depreciation."

Baker, however, was not about to let any details get in the way of final passage. Among other things, he was not above playing a little fast with the numbers to get to a bill that, on paper at least, met the revenue neutral goal. One gimmick stipulated that a research and development tax credit that was popular with businesses would expire one year before the end of the period covered by the tax bill, in theory raising money that would no longer go back to businesses for that last year. But everyone understood that Congress would never actually let it expire and, before the deadline, would certainly pass new legislation extending it. Likewise, Baker pressed the IRS commissioner to commit to bringing in an extra $17 billion through better enforcement, a theoretical revenue raiser at best.

Still, Baker was feeling more confident about the bill's chances. One day in September, he showed up on Capitol Hill dressed in what one congressional aide called a "Nathan Detroit suit," a pinstripe with wide lapels seemingly borrowed from the wardrobe of *Guys and Dolls*. He then performed for a group of lawmakers, aides, and reporters a rap number he called the Tax Reform Shuffle, modeled on the Super Bowl Shuffle of that year's champion Chicago Bears.

> *They said tax reform was dead. But now it's alive.*
> *Here's its story. It began in '85.*
> *We drew up a plan and sent it out in May*
> *But the special interests said, "Ain't no way."*
>
> *Rosty started hearings before the fall.*
> *They were Gucci to Gucci out in the hall.*

December came, reform was off track.
So to the Hill rode the Gipper, to bring it back.

All along it's been a big tussle.
But we keep doing the Tax Reform Shuffle.

Even Bob had his doubts, but then he saw the light.
For tax reform, he'd fight the good fight.
The Senate came close to stopping this bill.
But low rates and a broad base made it too hard to kill.

The conference met and everybody asked,
"Who can give the most to the middle class?"
Revenues got short; reform was in the red.
So "shoot the estimator," somebody said.

Rosty and Bob finally agreed.
Let's take it from those who aren't in any need.

All along it's been a big tussle.
But we keep doing the Tax Reform Shuffle.

So tax reform will pass, probably this September.
But there's just one thing for us to remember.
From the goals of reform there can be no defections.
Not even in a bill of technical corrections!

Tax reform would never be in this position
But for the hard work of your coalition.
We're pushing this bill, we're not gonna rest.
When tax reform is law, it will be America's best.

All along it's been a big tussle.
But we keep doing the Tax Reform Shuffle.

Ironically, Baker had never even seen the hit Bears video. But he knew a clever idea when he saw it and he had gamely agreed to play along once an aide explained. It was a big hit. "This is this stick-up-his-ass, high-priced Texas lawyer who's shucking and jiving with the brothers," remembered Jim Jaffe, the Rostenkowski aide. "It's very humanizing. For me, that was typical of Baker. This was a guy of many faces, who could play many roles."

In the end, Packwood and Rostenkowski snuck off to an anteroom and sealed the deal themselves. "Jim is a relatively little part of it," Packwood said years later, overlooking the fact that he himself had no interest in changing the tax code until Baker mustered political momentum behind the idea. Either way, Baker was elated; all the hard work had paid off. But the White House seemed oddly tepid about one of the most important achievements of Reagan's presidency. The draft statement about the plan sent over for Baker's review ended with an equivocal line: "We look forward to studying it in detail." Baker asked that the line be deleted, and Dick Darman scratched out his own much grander substitute on a piece of paper: "This is a triumph for the American people and the American system." After the votes, Baker and Darman headed back to the Treasury Building. It was almost midnight. Baker reached into the small refrigerator in his office, pulled out two cans of Budweiser, and popped the tops. The two men clinked the cans together in celebration.

The Tax Reform Act of 1986 collapsed fourteen tax brackets for individuals to two and lowered the top rate from 50 percent to 28 percent, although a surtax would bring that up to 33 percent on the wealthiest. The personal exemption was nearly doubled to $2,000 and more than 4 million working-poor Americans were freed from paying income taxes at all, but deductions for state sales taxes were eliminated, disproportionately affecting many others with lower incomes. For corporations, the top rate was brought down from 46 percent to 34 percent, offset by $300 billion raised over five years by closing loopholes. Overall, the measure raised corporate taxes by a net $120 billion, the biggest tax increase on businesses in history, while cutting taxes for individuals the same amount. Large, profitable firms would no longer be able to avoid paying any taxes.

The House passed the measure by a lopsided and bipartisan 292 to 136 vote on September 25, followed two days later by the Senate 74 to 23. More than 1,500 people gathered on the South Lawn of the White House to watch Reagan sign the bill into law on October 22. "All of us here today know what a herculean effort it took to get this landmark bill to my desk," Reagan said, singling out the "incomparable" Baker for his leadership.

The Fencing Master had proved the naysayers wrong. "For years to come," David Rosenbaum wrote in *The New York Times*, "students of politics will look to the odyssey of the new tax law as a prime example of how the American system of government gets things done."

CHAPTER 16

Black Monday

On Friday, November 14, 1986, Baker was getting ready to head off on an early morning hunting trip the next day on Maryland's Eastern Shore, but he took time out to write a note to his old friend and ally, Michael Deaver.

In the two years since both of them had left the White House, Deaver had formed a public affairs firm but succumbed to a long-standing drinking problem. He was also under investigation for his lobbying. On top of that, barely ten days earlier, Republicans lost control of the Senate in another bad midterm election.

But Baker had something else on his mind as he scrawled out a few lines to Deaver on a card emblazoned "The Secretary of the Treasury" that day. "Can you believe this arms to Iran stuff?" Baker wrote in his characteristic slanted cursive. "I like to think it wouldn't have happened if either one of us had been consulted."

From his corner office in the Treasury Building, Baker had been watching as the biggest scandal of the Reagan administration began engulfing the place that he and Deaver once ran. The day before the midterm election, a Lebanese magazine reported that the United States had sold missiles to Iran and that Robert McFarlane, who had stepped down the year before as national security adviser, had even visited Tehran as part of a far-fetched scheme to win the freedom of seven Americans held hostage by Hezbollah terrorists backed by Iran's theocratic rulers. In the days that followed, more details emerged, none of them exculpatory. Ed Meese, now the attorney general, was investigating.

But the worst was yet to come. The dealings with Iran were only part of the secret machinations orchestrated from the White House basement by a Marine lieutenant colonel named Oliver North serving on the staff of the National Security Council, first under McFarlane and then under his successor, John Poindexter, who had been promoted to vice admiral. Baker got a hint of what else was going on during a conversation over the weekend of November 22–23 with George Shultz, who told him that he had just been interviewed by Meese and that there was a chance money from the weapons sales had gone to the contras fighting in Nicaragua. Such a link would turn an already explosive story into a crisis that had the potential to bring down Reagan's presidency. Suddenly, Baker's fears from the start of the administration about the "crazies" and their adventures in Central America seemed to be coming true.

On the Monday after his conversation with Shultz, Baker showed up at the White House for a previously scheduled meeting with Donald Regan about the deficit, but he was kept cooling his heels in the outer office. A series of people cycled in and out of Regan's office, including Meese and Peter Wallison, the White House counsel. The deficit was clearly not the dominant issue of the day. After a half hour of waiting, Baker was finally shown in. Regan was clearly perturbed, shaking his head.

"We've got big problems," Regan told Baker. "You don't want to know."

Baker ventured a guess. "Does it have anything to do with money from the Iranian arms sales going to the contras?"

"You got it," Regan said. "And the problem is three people knew about it—Poindexter, North and McFarlane. I'm just going to have to ask John to resign." He realized he should have kept that to himself. "Please don't tell anyone. Let the president announce it."

Baker agreed. By his later account, the two went on to their deficit meeting without any further discussion about the scandal that was about to consume the White House like no other since Watergate. But it would not be the last time it would come up.

The next morning, Baker was invited to a meeting on the matter in the Oval Office with Reagan, Regan, Meese, Shultz, George Bush, Bill Casey, and Caspar Weinberger. They were told that Poindexter and North were out and that no one else knew anything about the operation except McFarlane, who was no longer in government. Casey, according to a memo Baker dictated afterward for his file, mumbled something about having been approached three or four weeks earlier by someone who told him something like this was going on. He said he mentioned it to Poindexter, but seemed to indicate the matter went nowhere. Baker's only contribution at the meeting was to suggest that the president not take questions when he appeared before reporters to make a statement because "we're dealing here with illegality and possible criminality."

Baker was happy to escape Washington the next day—in the era before security lines, his schedule had him arriving at National Airport at 9:20 a.m. to catch a 9:30 a.m. flight. He, Susan, and Mary-Bonner flew to Houston and then, after a day at home, headed to Rockpile Ranch, where the family celebrated Thanksgiving and he gave thanks that he had not been included in the deliberations that led to the secret operations. When he got back to the capital, Poindexter apologized for keeping him in the dark. "John," Baker replied, "that was the biggest favor you could have done for me."

What would quickly be dubbed the Iran-contra affair soon consumed the Reagan administration. The notion that the government, or rogue operators within it, had siphoned off blood money from Iranian mullahs and used it to finance the Nicaraguan rebels despite congressional restrictions shocked the nation and even Reagan's friends. Investigations ensued, hearings were held, lawyers were hired, and the capital once again was asking the question that animated the Watergate proceedings a dozen years earlier: What did the president know and when did he know it?

Reagan, improbably, kept insisting that he was not trading arms for hostages until the evidence mounted and he was forced to reluctantly concede that the evidence made plain that that was indeed the goal of the initiative. Reagan also denied knowing about the diversion of funds to the contras, which seemed more plausible. But even if that were the case, it raised questions about an out-of-control White House and the aging, inattentive president at its helm. A leader who had seemingly restored faith in the presidency now appeared damaged, possibly beyond repair. And for what?

As a matter of foreign policy, the two-pronged initiative itself had been a bust. There was no strategic change in the relationship with Iran, as Reagan had been promised, no "moderates" that he had been told he was dealing with, only shady middlemen. While three hostages were released, another three were later seized. The contras got money that Congress had refused to provide but were still unable to win the war against the Sandinistas, leaving Nicaragua and the rest of Central America trapped in stalemate.

When he was chief of staff, Baker had met North whenever funding for the contras came up at meetings of the Legislative Strategy Group. Baker later told investigators that he was aware of North's fervent commitment to the cause. Otherwise, their only interaction came when North asked Baker, as a onetime Marine, to give a speech to Marines at the base in Quantico, Virginia. North was not Baker's kind of player—too ideologically driven, too willing to dissemble and skirt the rules. Soon enough, Baker's nemesis, Bill Casey, was caught up in the scandal as well.

By February 1987, Donald Regan was shown the door, a sacrifice to demonstrate that Reagan took the breakdown of his White House seriously. Among the lessons Regan failed to learn from Baker was how to manage the first lady. The two had engaged in a running feud, culminating one day with the chief of staff hanging up on the president's wife. "You don't hang up on the first lady," Baker said later in disbelief. Once again, Baker came out looking good compared to his successor, who had let the president down. "If, by some miracle, I could take back one decision in Ronnie's presidency, it would be his agreement in January 1985 that Jim Baker and Donald Regan should swap jobs," Nancy wrote in her memoir. "It seemed like a good idea at the time," she added, and neither she nor the president had any "reason to expect that this new arrangement would lead to a political disaster." But that is what had happened.

With Regan now out, Washington wondered whether Baker might come back, take over his old office, and put the White House in order again. Baker later said he would have had to do it if the president had asked, but Reagan knew that he did not want to do so and never broached the subject. Instead, the president brought in another Baker to be chief of staff—Howard Baker, the former Senate Republican leader from Tennessee and veteran of the Watergate investigation who had some of the same traits of dignified moderation and political pragmatism.

Regan had been sacrificed, but the investigations surrounding Iran-contra continued—one by an independent counsel, Lawrence Walsh, and the other by a commission led by John Tower, who had retired from the Senate. Baker watched as friends from the Ford years became immersed in the inquiries; Brent Scowcroft ran the Tower Commission, while Dick Cheney sat on the House committee that investigated. But Baker was barely touched directly. In December, FBI agents showed up at his office for a brief interview on a very narrow aspect of the story, asking if Meese had ever mentioned an issue involving the customs agency, which fell under the Treasury Department's purview, and retired Major General Richard Secord or Southern Air Transport. Secord had been an ally of North's on the outside helping to keep the contras afloat and Southern Air Transport was a CIA front used to ship arms to Iran and the Nicaraguan rebels. Baker told the agents that Meese once said something about "some overzealous investigation on the part of some of" the customs agents, but did not recall him mentioning Southern Air Transport specifically. The agents departed Baker's office after just fifteen minutes.

The furor left Baker unsure whether there would still be enough political capital to accomplish anything during the last two years of the administration. He was angry about it, and the tarnishing of a legacy he had worked hard to build. "It's the one lasting blot on the Reagan presidency and it didn't have to happen," he said later. "It shouldn't have happened." He also worried about whether it would undercut his friend's chances of winning the presidency in 1988. George Bush, like Reagan, may not have been aware that proceeds from the arms sales had been sent to the contras but there was reasonable evidence that he knew more than he admitted about the scheme to win the release of the hostages. Bush acknowledged being generally aware of the Iran initiative but added a new phrase to the Washington scandal lexicon by claiming to be "out of the loop" on the details and unaware of the strong objections lodged by George Shultz and Caspar Weinberger. Records and testimony, however, indicated that the vice president was present for key meetings. Shultz later said that he expressed his own vehement opposition to the Iran deal at a session attended by the vice president.

So did Bush know? "I didn't know the answer to that," Baker said years later. "I didn't know how much he knew or didn't know. He indicated to me that he didn't know and I believed him. I think there was a difference of opinion between Shultz and Bush about what he knew. When George told me he didn't have anything to do with it, I believed him." But even as Baker was vouching for his friend, the way he said it seemed to suggest doubt. He was attributing the denial, not adopting it.

At the time, Baker had seemed curious about how deep Bush's role really was. After the scandal broke, he called Robert McFarlane and invited him to his office at the Treasury Building. McFarlane was feeling deeply remorseful over what had happened.

"I think I let the president down," he told Baker.

"No, you didn't," Baker consoled him, although McFarlane knew he was just being generous.

After leaving Baker's office, McFarlane pondered what the meeting was really all about. "I have wondered whether Jim just looking to '88 was wondering how bad the exposure to the vice president was," McFarlane said years later. "But he didn't say that overtly." At one point, he recalled, Baker mentioned the vice president in passing, in what McFarlane took to be an attempt to nudge him to talk about Bush's role. But he did not—

and Baker would not have liked what he had to say if he had. "The vice president was party to every single meeting on the Iran initiative," McFarlane said years after the fact. Bush presumably did not know about the diversion of funds to the contras, but McFarlane, Shultz, and others were certain he knew about the dealings with Iran and supported them over the objections of the secretaries of state and defense.

It was a season of scandal. While more Iran-contra revelations rocked the administration—a Bible and a cake in the shape of a key delivered to the Iranians, shredded documents, papers that a secretary named Fawn Hall hid in her brassiere—Michael Deaver's problems had worsened too. In spring 1986, Deaver had invited trouble by posing for a *Time* magazine cover sitting in the back of a limousine talking on a car telephone, with the Capitol in view out the window. "Who's This Man Calling? Influence Peddling in Washington," read the headline. Even Nancy Reagan chided him for that one, telling him, "Mike, you've made a big mistake. I think you're going to regret it." So when Congress summoned Deaver to testify, Baker warned him to watch out because he could be charged if he was caught lying. He did and he was. Eventually, Deaver was convicted of three counts of lying under oath, given a suspended three-year prison sentence, and fined $100,000. "I think he's had the fastest rise and the fastest fall ever in this town," gloated Ed Rollins, who had quarreled with both Baker and Deaver in the first term.

WHILE BAKER FOCUSED on his work in the cabinet, Susan found herself in a new, more public role as well. Until then, she had been the model of an old-school political spouse, a stay-at-home Texas transplant to the capital who handled the enormous load of their combined eight children while Baker immersed himself in politics and government. She had never wanted to become a public figure, but after an unsettling conversation with Mary-Bonner sometime in 1984, she came to believe she had no choice.

"Mama," Mary-Bonner asked her mother one day, "what's a virgin?"

"What do you mean?" Susan asked.

"Well, Madonna sings this song, 'Like a virgin, touched for the very first time.' What's a virgin?"

Susan was shaken. Her daughter was seven years old and still playing with Cabbage Patch dolls but was listening to songs with sexually suggestive lyrics? Susan began talking with other mothers and discovered that they were also worried about the music their children were listening to.

From that innocent question about a loss-of-innocence song came a new cause for Susan Baker that would eventually produce one of Washington's iconic confrontations of the 1980s. It would pit the idea of a parent's right to shield children from mature themes against traditions of free speech and artistic independence. And it would make Susan an unlikely leader in the culture wars of the decade while defining her image as either a righteous crusader against an increasingly coarse society or an uptight prude moralizing to a younger generation.

Neither stereotype really fit. Susan was deeply religious—Jim liked to joke that the first sound he heard each morning was the thump on the floor as she got on her knees to pray. But she was not, at heart, a Moral Majority, fire-and-brimstone type. She did not hide her faith as if it were unfashionable the way many in Washington did, but neither did she preach to others. She would always insist she did not set out to ban dirty lyrics but to warn other parents who might not be aware of what their children were hearing. "We were just mad mamas who wanted our friends and, particularly, educators to know what kind of trash our children were buying," she said.

She started out with two friends who also had powerful husbands, Pam Howar, married to a prominent realtor, and Sally Nevius, married to the chairman of Washington's City Council. They soon realized that to have any real impact they needed a prominent Democrat to join them, so they approached Tipper Gore, whose husband, Al, was a senator from Tennessee with bigger ambitions. Together, they founded the Parents Music Resource Center and began campaigning for warning labels on record albums. Starting with their extensive Christmas card lists, they sent letters, held public meetings, called journalists, and published research about provocative lyrics. They lobbied the Recording Industry Association of America and contacted more than fifty record labels.

Eventually, they decided to illustrate their concerns by issuing a list of fifteen songs that they argued should be kept off the radio, a list that became known as the "Filthy Fifteen." Madonna's "Like a Virgin" was on it, as well as Prince's "Darling Nikki" (*"I met her in a hotel lobby, masturbating with a magazine"*). Cyndi Lauper, Twisted Sister, Venom, and others were targeted too. Soon the "Washington Wives," as they were called, were making their case on *Good Morning America* and Oprah Winfrey's talk show.

Rock stars and their fans were apoplectic. Joanne McDuffie, a singer for Mary Jane Girls, which made the Filthy Fifteen list, called it a "modern-day witch hunt." Conrad Lant, the singer for Venom known as Cronos,

said he originally thought the whole thing was a prank. "I couldn't understand how supposedly intelligent people could be so ignorant," he recalled.
"Of course, rock and roll has all of the subject matter they accused it of
having. It's rock and roll! It's supposed to be hard core and edgy."

On September 19, 1985, Susan arrived on Capitol Hill along with Tipper Gore to testify before the Senate Commerce Committee, a panel that
included Al Gore, in a nationally televised hearing watched assiduously
by teenagers who had probably never seen a congressional proceeding
before. Also testifying were three stars, Frank Zappa, Dee Snider, and,
incongruously, John Denver, the clean-as-a-whistle country singer, all of
whom decried any restrictions on their music. It was a showdown, the
prim mothers versus the vulgar rockers, and it drew outsized attention as
a cultural moment.

"We don't question their right to have their own music," Susan Baker
told the senators. What bothered them, she said, was "the proliferation of
songs glorifying rape, sadomasochism, incest, the occult and suicide."

Zappa, who cut his hair and wore a white shirt, red tie, and dark suit for
the occasion, denounced the proposed warning labels as "an ill-conceived
piece of nonsense which fails to deliver any real benefits to children,
infringes the civil liberties of people who are not children and promises to
keep the courts busy for years."

Whether any minds were changed, it proved to be good television.
While the rockers were not intimidated, the record labels were feeling the
heat. The National PTA, with 6.5 million members, had joined the cause.
In November, the Recording Industry Association of America agreed to
a voluntary labeling system. It was no panacea—and indeed, the warning labels were so small as to be ineffective until a few years later when
the industry agreed to larger, standardized warning notices. But it generated a national debate and fostered greater awareness among parents
that they had to take an active role in monitoring what their children were
listening to.

Not all of Susan Baker's causes were quite so controversial. She began
taking an interest in homelessness in America and made a point of educat-
ing herself. She lobbied Reagan cabinet members to recycle food returned
by military commissaries so it could go to the poor and she pressed the
administration to establish a task force on the homeless. When Mitch
Snyder, a well-known activist for the homeless living on the streets of
Washington, embarked on a hunger strike to press the federal government to fix up a shelter not far from the Capitol, Susan went to pray at

his bedside a half dozen times. Finally, her husband interceded. On the weekend before the 1984 election, Baker, still White House chief of staff, called his wife from Air Force One and asked what it would take to save Snyder's life. Baker came up with the money. Susan's interest in the issue led her to found a nonprofit group called the Committee for Food and Shelter, later becoming the National Alliance to End Homelessness, which she would help lead for decades to come.

Susan also befriended people in crisis. After speaking at a Christian prayer breakfast, she received a letter from Lucille Levin, whose husband, Jeremy, a CNN reporter, was one of the seven hostages in Lebanon that Oliver North's Iran venture was intended to liberate. Susan knew nothing about that, but she responded to Lucille's letter and the two struck up a relationship over dinner and prayer sessions at the Baker home. Lucille later credited Susan with helping her endure the months until her husband managed to escape.

"I'm sure there are a lot of people who think I'm nuts but I couldn't care less," Susan told Maureen Dowd of *The New York Times*. "God really calls me to be his instrument. And there are an awful lot of people in this town that have very deep problems."

Her faith was not partisan. She belonged to a women's prayer group that included Democrats and Republicans. Just a month after her husband left office for the last time in 1993, Susan's group welcomed a new member, Hillary Clinton. She and Susan became friendly over the years and forged a relationship unaffected by the politics of their spouses, or their own. "Susan Baker visited and wrote me, offering encouragement and empathy about events ranging from the loss of my father to the political storms surrounding Bill's presidency," Clinton later wrote in her first memoir.

Susan knew something about storms. More than a decade after she and Baker brought their wounded clans together, they were still weathering the uneasy merger. Drugs and resentment remained dominant forces within the family and no matter how much Jim and Susan struggled to get ahold of the problem, they had yet to fully do so.

The family's private pain was telegraphed in a surprising way when *The Washington Post* set out to write a profile of the treasury secretary. Encouraged by Margaret Tutwiler to talk to the reporter, Jamie Baker was open about the distance between his father and himself and his brothers. He pointed out that Baker had a photograph of Mary Stuart in his office in the Treasury Building. "But there are none of us," Jamie said. "That in itself should be telling. I'm sure it's just an oversight and I don't want to sound like I'm jealous. But I am." The reporter, Lois Romano, asked if he had ever told his father how he felt. "I'm doing that now," Jamie responded.

Baker was stunned when he read the story, taking it as a wakeup call about how much his own children were still hurting. Tutwiler felt terrible having set up the interview, not realizing the familial Pandora's box she was opening. A few months later, Mike Baker went to Arizona for a month of drug rehabilitation. And a few months after that, John went to Four Winds Hospital in Katonah, New York, for his own treatment. "We love you and we're proud of you," Baker wrote John, underlining the two phrases.

THE SECRETARY OF THE TREASURY may have the most prominent leadership role when it comes to the nation's economy, but he shares influence with the chairman of the Federal Reserve, usually a figure of little prominence with the general public despite his enormous power to shape the fate of the country. Paul Volcker had been a powerful force in keeping the economy going. But he was not on the team as far as Baker was concerned. The two had that fractious encounter during the 1984 campaign when Baker pressured Volcker not to raise interest rates. The Fed chairman had also been a skeptic of the Plaza Accord and later refused to sign a communiqué that Baker had negotiated with other finance ministers hinting at monetary easing. Baker thought it was time that Reagan got a Fed chairman of his own—one who would be more sensitive to the administration's economic policies, especially heading into election season.

Unwilling to force Volcker out, Baker knew they would have to wait until his term expired in 1987. But in the meantime, he could effectively take over the Fed board through Reagan's appointees. To fill vacancies, two more choices, Manuel Johnson and Wayne Angell, joined the seven-member board on February 7, 1986, which along with previous appointees effectively gave Baker's allies a majority. They wasted little time seeking to use that newfound power. On February 24, they ambushed Volcker at a Fed board meeting. At the end of the session, the Reagan appointees led by Preston Martin, the vice chairman of the board, suddenly moved to lower the discount interest rate, which would make borrowing easier and presumably keep the economy humming. Assuming he was still in control, Volcker allowed a vote, only to find himself on the losing end of a 4 to 3 tally. After nearly seven years in the chairman's seat, it was the first time Volcker had ever lost and he was furious at the temerity of the rebels.

"You can do what you want from now on—but without me," he snapped before storming out of the room.

Volcker returned to his office, where he wrote out a letter of resignation by hand on a pad of yellow lined paper and gave it to his secretary to type up.

As it happened, he was already scheduled to have lunch with Baker and the visiting finance minister of Mexico. After the minister departed, Volcker confronted Baker about the revolt.

"I'm resigning," Volcker declared.

Baker was taken aback and told him he was overreacting. "You can't do that," he said. "You lost a vote, you don't resign."

"Maybe you don't," Volcker shot back, "but I do."

Baker asked what was wrong with the board expressing its will, but Volcker made clear that if he was no longer in control, there was no point in staying. Suddenly, Baker faced a possible disaster. He wanted the rate cut and the dollar weakened but an abrupt resignation in protest could cause a huge backlash given Volcker's credibility with the markets.

By 2 p.m., Baker's appointees retreated. Wayne Angell, one of the Baker allies named to the board barely two weeks earlier, visited Volcker in his office and told him that he would be willing to rethink their move. Angell expressed understanding for Volcker's position that any decision should be coordinated first with the West Germans and Japanese and he suggested a delay.

"Mr. Chairman, if you need more time, that's not a problem," Angell said. "We can just call the board into your office and we'll have a stand-up meeting in your office and do it. I'll move to reconsider."

In short order, the other members of the board were summoned to Volcker's office, where they did just that, standing around the chairman's desk. Volcker put away the resignation letter and within a couple weeks the West Germans and Japanese agreed to coordinate a move, whereupon the Fed board went ahead with the rate cut on a unanimous vote.

Baker's team had executed a power play but Volcker pulled one of his own in response. In retirement, Volcker said he never knew for sure if Baker had been behind the vote against him but it was hard not to notice that Martin, the leader of the move, was a Reagan appointee and presumably wanted to be chairman. "I don't know if he was in cahoots with Jim Baker or not," Volcker said. "I suspect he might have been." Another of the Reagan rebels, Manuel Johnson, a former assistant treasury secretary under Baker who was the other new member installed shortly before the confrontation, told Volcker that he had promised Baker that he would vote to lower the discount rate, suggesting a deal in effect for his appointment.

Wayne Angell said years later that he moved to reverse the vote after learning that Volcker had threatened to resign and while he did not talk with Baker, he presumed that Johnson had. "The only conversation Baker had was with Manny Johnson and Manny and I were so together that everybody knew that talking with one was talking with the other one," Angell said. Baker, for his part, said he knew Johnson agreed with the need to lower rates to juice the economy but was not sure whether there was an explicit commitment to vote that way. "I don't remember getting Manny to promise specifically that he would lower the discount rate," Baker said. "I remember him saying that he thought the economy needed some stimulus." That was enough. "It's fair to say that I wanted to see us appoint people who would be more attentive to helping the economy," he said. As for whether he called off the revolt to prevent the resignation, his memory was also unclear. "I may have talked to one of them," he said.

It would take another year, but Baker would ultimately win the power struggle. In March 1987, Volcker called Howard Baker at the White House and said he wanted to step down before his term ended. He had been running out of money and had promised his wife that he would resign; he would have done it earlier but did not want to bail on Reagan in the heat of the Iran-contra disclosures. Howard Baker told him to think about it over the weekend.

But Jim Baker welcomed the opportunity. "Volcker is not cooperating with us," he said later. "That's when we dumped him." Baker told Reagan it was time to put a Republican in the chairman's seat. "Mr. President," he said, "Paul's been a good Fed chairman, we've cooperated with him when he squeezed inflation out of the economy. It worked for you, worked for the country. We've reappointed him. But you deserve to have your own Fed chairman at some time during your presidency. You should not leave office without ever having appointed your own Fed chairman." Reagan asked if he had anyone in mind. Baker had one name: Alan Greenspan.

Baker had known Greenspan from his days as Gerald Ford's economic adviser and the two had worked together well during the Social Security negotiations that led to the reform legislation in 1983. He called Greenspan and asked him to come over to the Foxhall Road house the next morning. When Greenspan showed up, he found both Bakers, Jim and Howard, waiting for him. Volcker may be leaving, Howard Baker said. If he did, would you be interested? Greenspan said yes.

Reagan announced Greenspan's nomination on June 2 and the Senate confirmed him on August 11. He would go on to serve nearly nineteen years and become one of the most consequential economic players in modern American history. His opening months, though, would not be quiet.

AMID ALL THE TUMULT of the second term, Baker remained a utility player for Reagan, one of the few able to push through policy ideas despite the challenges of a damaged administration. One of Reagan's key initiatives was a free trade agreement with Canada but when negotiations stalled in the fall of 1987, Brian Mulroney, the prime minister of Canada, decided that the only way to salvage a possible deal was to bring in Baker. He called Reagan.

"You know, Ron, this thing is going to go down the tubes and the reason will be benign neglect on your part," he told Reagan.

"What do you think I should do?" Reagan asked.

"I think you should put Jim Baker in charge right now," Mulroney said. "He's the only person in Washington who can save this."

"Leave it with me," Reagan said.

It was no easy assignment for Baker. The United States and Canada had been trying to forge an economic agreement for a century without success. One of the first attempts came in 1888 with the drafting of a special economic arrangement, but the Senate rejected the treaty. The two sides got close again in 1911, only to have Canada pull back. By the time 1986 rolled around, the two countries were doing more than $113 billion in trade a year across the most open border in the world without a rational trade agreement.

Trade talks were not usually the domain of the treasury secretary, but as with the Federal Reserve, Baker's influence was wide and deep. Reagan's trade representative, Clayton Yeutter, had been unable to hammer out a deal and lost credibility with his counterparts when he professed to know about Canadian culture because he had gone to Niagara Falls on his honeymoon.

Baker, knowing the pact was a top priority for the president, jumped in with a mix of power politics, smooth diplomacy, and locker room talk that broke the ice. The good-old-boy persona he sometimes pulled out for such moments perplexed his Canadian interlocutors, who nicknamed him Texas Crude for his sharp tongue. But they recognized Baker was someone who could get things done. "He was very much at ease representing the raw power of the United States," observed Derek Burney, Mulroney's chief of staff.

With Baker steering the talks, the two sides eventually came to agreement on most of the contentious issues like subsidies and anti-dumping rules but the whole thing almost fell apart over establishing a process for the two sides to resolve future trade disputes. The mechanism favored by the Canadians ran into trouble with the American attorneys and lawmakers, who complained about its legality. Neither side was willing to budge. The talks seemed headed for collapse before a congressionally imposed deadline of October 4. With time running out, each side drafted its own statement announcing failure.

But Baker was not ready to accept defeat. He met alone with Burney in a small office across from his own in the Treasury Building on a Saturday morning, the day before the deadline, to see if they could still reach consensus. Burney told Baker he could make concessions on the American priorities of investment and financial services but only if the dispute settlement issue was resolved. That was the deal-breaker, he told Baker.

The day wore on with no movement and Burney called Mulroney at 7 p.m. to tell him it was over. Mulroney instructed Burney to inform Baker that the prime minister wanted to call Reagan to confirm the negotiations were finished. Burney passed along the message to Baker, who played for time by asking that Reagan not be disturbed for a while because he was watching a movie at Camp David. Finally, Baker got on the phone directly with Mulroney and quarreled over the dispute resolution provision.

"The congressional people are arguing that this would be a dilution of their sovereignty, the constitutional sovereignty that they have in terms of international trade," Baker said.

"Look, Jim," Mulroney said, "when you joined NATO, you surrendered a little sovereignty. When you join the U.N.—we all surrender a little sovereignty for the greater good."

"I'm arguing with them because I'd like this to go through," Baker said, "but I'm not getting very far."

"Well, I'll tell you Jim, if that's the case I'm going to call President Reagan," Mulroney said. "He's at Camp David and I just have one question to ask him."

"What's that?"

"I'm going to say, 'Now Ron, how is it that the United States can agree to a nuclear reduction deal with their worst enemy, the Soviet Union, and they can't agree to a free trade agreement with their best friend, the Canadians?'"

Baker did not like the sound of that. "Prime Minister, can you give me twenty minutes?" he asked.

"Sure."

Finally, at 9 p.m., Baker burst into the office where Burney had been waiting and tossed a piece of paper on the table.

"All right," he said, "you can have your goddamn dispute settlement mechanism. Now can we send the report to Congress?"

They had a deal. Baker had overpowered the lawyers and lawmakers to get what he needed. The pact was America's first bilateral free trade agreement with another country other than Israel and a top goal for Reagan, one that might have slipped away had it been left in anyone else's hands. In the end, it paved the road for the broader North American Free Trade Agreement, or NAFTA, that brought in Mexico, negotiated under President George Bush and approved by Congress under President Bill Clinton. And it provided a template for a whole generation of free trade agreements that would follow.

"Had it not been for Jim," said Mulroney, "we would have had no Canada-U.S. Free Trade agreement, which was really the model for the world." It also led to a lasting friendship with Mulroney that would endure long after both left office.

TWO WEEKS LATER, Baker rewarded himself with a rare boondoggle. He flew to Sweden, where the king had invited him to go elk hunting. Baker generally did not accept such offers, but he figured this one time would be okay. When his plane landed, however, he found an anxious Swedish finance minister waiting for him at the bottom of the stairs, his face "as white as these walls," as Baker later put it. The minister told Baker that while he had been in the air, there had been a frightening economic development.

"The market dropped five," he said.

Baker was not alarmed. "The market drops five, the market goes up five."

"No," the minister said, "I mean *five hundred*."

"What?" Baker replied.

It was Monday, October 19, 1987, and markets around the world were devastated by a financial tidal wave that started in Asia, washed through

London, and then slammed into Wall Street. The Dow Jones Industrial Average plunged by 508 points to 1738.74, a breathtaking drop of 22.6 percent, the largest single-day plummet as a percentage in the market's history—worse even than the crash of 1929. In the space of a few hours, some $500 billion of wealth was wiped out, the equivalent of more than $1.1 trillion in today's dollars.

Baker was caught out of position, far from the nerve centers of the American economic system, for the most terrifying twenty-hour hours of the post-Depression era. He raced to a hotel, where he planted himself on the telephone, calling his staff back in Washington and his counterparts from Japan, Britain, West Germany, France, and other major economic powers to get a handle on what was happening and figure out what to do about it. The next morning he flew home on the Concorde, racing back toward a crisis whose end was not at all clear. "I never saw an elk and never even saw the king of Sweden," he said.

On Wall Street, Black Monday sent tremors through investors suddenly worried that the country was facing another economic collapse. "PANIC!" said the giant headline on the cover of the New York *Daily News*. Not to be outdone, the *New York Post* went with "CRASH!" Underneath the double-banner headline on the next day's *New York Times* was a news analysis that asked the chilling question, "Does 1987 Equal 1929?" From the White House, Howard Baker put in a desperate call to Alan Greenspan, barely two months into his new job. "I said, 'Put him on,'" Greenspan recalled, "and there's a little silence and all I could hear is—'Help!'"

Neither Jim Baker nor Greenspan fully saw the crisis coming, but some critics were quick to blame the treasury secretary for helping to touch it off. The sell-off capped two months of weakness in the markets that further deteriorated in the days before the crash on fears of a trade war and slower growth. In his opening bid as the new chairman of the Federal Reserve, Greenspan in September raised the discount rate by a half percentage point, the first increase in three years and a move that made borrowing more expensive for businesses. Defying American pressure, the West German Bundesbank signaled on October 6 that it would also raise interest rates, which would diminish demand for American goods rather than increase it, as Baker had been seeking. Japanese officials followed suit a few days later. Markets fell on the news. Higher-than-expected trade deficit numbers released on October 14 only exacerbated the concern over American exports, sending the Dow down 3.8 percent and then another 2.4 percent the next day.

Baker was upset. The only way to reduce the trade deficit was if America's biggest trading partners stimulated demand, but they were heading in the opposite direction. On October 15, Baker warned that the United States would not support the dollar, which would have the effect of undercutting its value at the expense of the West Germans and Japanese. The Dow fell again, closing Friday 9.5 percent down for the week, at that time the largest weekly decrease since World War II. Reagan was worried that Greenspan's rate increase was choking the economy and told him and Baker so in a meeting on Friday. "I'm concerned about money supply—has Fed been too tight," the president recorded in his diary that night. "Alan doesn't agree & believes this is only an overdue correction."

Baker then doubled down on his remarks about the dollar in an interview with CNN the next day, resulting in a story that led the Sunday edition of *The New York Times*. Wall Street took notice. West Germany "should not expect us to sit back here and accept" interest rate increases, Baker said. He added that "we will have to reexamine the scope and basis" of economic agreements between the United States, West Germany, and other major powers made just weeks earlier. The comments were taken as a vow of retribution that could have dramatic consequences. By the time markets opened the next day, investors were dumping stocks on the anticipation that the dollar would fall and growth would shrink.

Reagan, distracted because Nancy had a mastectomy over that weekend, projected an air of unconcern about the market. "There is nothing wrong with the economy," he told reporters. So why had the market collapsed? he was asked. "Maybe some people seeing a chance to grab a profit, I don't know," he said.

When he landed back in Washington, Baker, operating on little sleep, headed straight to his office, where he met with Greenspan and Howard Baker. They agreed that Reagan had sounded too optimistic by delivering what Greenspan later called "a Herbert Hoover type of response." They went to the White House to meet with the president and convinced him to publicly offer to work with Congress to cut the federal deficit, a statement intended to reassure the markets that the government would get its fiscal house in order. Baker's long experience in figuring out how to sell Reagan on an approach paid off. "The way Jim set the thing up, Reagan just essentially said, 'Sounds good to me,' or something like that," Greenspan said. At the same time, Greenspan pumped more money into the system to stimulate confidence and John Phelan, chairman of the New York Stock Exchange, placed new limits on computerized automated trading that was seen as accelerating the collapse.

The intervention succeeded enough that the market began ticking back up again in succeeding days. By the time Reagan left office, the market had essentially recovered what it lost on that day. Eventually, instead of Reagan and Baker being remembered for presiding over the greatest crash in American history and the start of a new depression, Black Monday would be forgotten by later generations. By the time Reagan got around to writing his memoir, the crash occupied just a few sentences, mainly as a counterpoint to his wife's medical crisis. "Stock market or no stock market," he wrote, "it was mainly Nancy, not Wall Street, I was worried about."

Baker's comments about West Germany were, at most, only part of what triggered the crash. The market was already overvalued judging by the price-to-earnings ratio, and investors were spooked by the Fed's rate increase, the trade deficit numbers, reports of congressional efforts to eliminate tax breaks that encouraged corporate buyouts, and an Iranian missile attack on an American tanker that raised fears of a larger conflict. The selling was magnified by the computerized program trading system known as portfolio insurance that ordered stocks to be automatically liquidated as prices fell, which only sent them further down. Each drop in values prompted another round of frantic selling, a self-perpetuating spiral that got out of control. What might have been a relatively normal market reverse became a global meltdown instead.

The Brady Commission, appointed by Reagan to determine what caused the crash, focused mainly on the program trading, mentioning Baker's comments only in passing. Robert Shiller, an economist at Yale University who would later win the Nobel Prize, dismissed the emphasis on mechanical sell orders, concluding that the commission underestimated the human factor of trader panic. In the end, he attributed the crash more to market psychology than market technology. But he likewise saw only a modest connection to Baker. In response to a questionnaire he sent to more than three thousand investors four days after the crash, Shiller found that Baker's comments were cited as a factor but not a dominant one. Asked to rank the issues that motivated their decisions on a scale of one to seven, the investors judged the comments a four, right in the middle. "If you're looking at the biggest stock market move ever, a good chance is it's a confluence of many factors at once, not just one," Shiller said. "It's a perfect storm."

Baker rejected any suggestion that his veiled threat to West Germany was the cause. "It conceivably could have made a little contribution to the noise," he said later, "but I don't believe it was a proximate cause of the crash, I really don't. On the other hand, would it probably have been better if I hadn't said it? Yeah, probably. But they were giving us an awful hard time."

AS REAGAN'S PRESIDENCY HEADED into its twilight, Baker was confronted with the choice he did not want to make. George Bush was gearing up his campaign to succeed Reagan and the person he most wanted to run it, of course, was his friend. But his friend had little interest. Baker had already run three campaigns—Gerald Ford's in 1976, George Bush's in 1980, and Ronald Reagan's in 1984—and even if two of them were not successful, he had come out a winner anyway.

Baker had since transcended the role of fixer, or so he hoped. "I didn't want to be the most famous political operative," he said. And why should he? His name was on the dollar bill. He sat in the cabinet and ran his own department. He was fifth in line for the presidency. His mere utterances were enough to move markets. He was receiving dozens of letters from everyday Americans urging *him* to run for president in 1988, letters that he meticulously forwarded to Margaret Tutwiler, with sentences urging him to mount a campaign underlined. "People used to ask me at Treasury, 'Why don't you run for president?'" he later recalled in an unpublished interview with his ghostwriter. But Bush was his friend, his daughter's godfather. "It was never a question of my going out and running against my friend," he said. "Never."

Yet he kept those letters in his files for more than three decades, random missives from random people he did not know. Of course he was tempted. Of course he thought he could be president. Some thought he already *had* been during his four years as chief of staff to a sometimes befuddled, generally hands-off chief executive. Brent Scowcroft, who knew a thing or two about the White House, had referred to him as the co-president. Arguably Baker had more preparation for being president as chief of staff than Bush did as vice president. Loyalty meant everything to Baker. Bush meant everything to him. Still, Baker could hardly be blamed for sizing himself up next to his friend and wondering why he was the one who was being asked to run the campaign for president.

The pull of gravity would eventually draw him into Bush's campaign anyway; the only question was how long he could resist. Unwilling to impose on Baker to give up the Treasury Department sooner than necessary, Bush set about building a team that would at least carry him through the early stages of the 1988 race. He tapped Lee Atwater to run the campaign, joined by five other top advisers who each had their own fiefdoms and came to be known as the Group of 6, or G-6—Nick Brady, the president's friend who served briefly as a senator; Robert Mosbacher, the fund-raiser; Robert Teeter, the pollster; Craig Fuller, the vice presidential chief of staff; and Roger Ailes, the media consultant. They would be in charge of winning the Republican nomination for Bush while Baker stayed on the sidelines, kibitzing without fully taking ownership of the effort until the general election campaign.

Reagan had pulled out of the pit of Iran-contra to rebuild his credibility with the American people, who grew increasingly fond of him again. With the emergence in Moscow of a new, younger, reformist leader named Mikhail Gorbachev, Reagan spent his last years in office seeking to make peace with the crumbling Soviet Union. Reagan's approval ratings floated back up into the 50s on the way toward 60 percent in his final weeks. All of which made the challenge for Bush that much more complicated. Bush needed to establish himself as the rightful heir to Reagan even as he showed he was his own man. The phenomenal loyalty he had demonstrated through two terms as vice president meant that the president had come to like and trust him, but it did not make him another Reagan. The Republican Party was not about to automatically anoint him as its next standard-bearer.

Where Reagan was inspirational and invoked the rugged romanticism of the Republican Party's base in the frontier West, Bush was still a preppy New Englander with a reedy voice, quirky affectations, and an unfortunate penchant for phrases like "deep doo-doo." Never mind that he was also a war hero and a Texas transplant who made his way in the hardscrabble oil patch, Bush seemed less than a political titan. His fealty to Reagan could come across as obsequiousness and his essential decency was too often mistaken for weakness. The comic strip *Doonesbury* portrayed a Bush who put his manhood into a blind trust. George Will, the conservative columnist who was close with the Reagans, derided the vice president's speeches for resembling "a thin, tinny 'arf'—the sound of a lapdog." When *Newsweek* famously put Bush on its cover driving his cigarette boat with the headline "Fighting the 'Wimp Factor'" on the day he announced his candidacy, the vice president erupted in righteous indignation and ordered his staff not to give any more special treatment to the magazine.

The cold war with *Newsweek* stretched for a year and it finally fell to Baker to broker peace. Tom DeFrank, the widely respected *Newsweek* correspondent, who had worked with Baker since 1975, complained about being cut off for the magazine's campaign book that would run after the election and that depended on extra access. In an angry phone call with Margaret Tutwiler, he snapped something "along the lines of 'with friends like this, I don't need enemies.'" The barb stung. DeFrank also sent a hand-delivered letter to Bush, who wrote a long, gracious note back promising to have Baker look into it. Tutwiler called a few days later to suggest the two have lunch to talk it out. When the assigned day came, the *Newsweek* receptionist told DeFrank his guest had arrived. He headed out to the lobby to find not Tutwiler but Baker, who had engaged in the subterfuge to personally patch up the rift.

TO WIN THE NOMINATION, Bush would have to prove himself against a phalanx of accomplished challengers, most notably Bob Dole, the confident and acerbic Senate Republican leader who ran on Gerald Ford's ticket in 1976 and fought Reagan and Bush for the nomination in 1980. Others unwilling to simply hand the crown to Bush included three Republicans Baker had crossed swords with—Jack Kemp, Al Haig, and Paul Laxalt—as well as former governor Pete du Pont of Delaware. The televangelist Pat Robertson jumped into the race as a wild-card candidate, a favorite of an important constituency within the party who had no chance of winning the nomination but could scramble the race and force more conventional candidates to tilt further to the ideological extremes.

Bush's contest against Dole felt more about whose turn it was than about any particular issue; they shared a pragmatic, center-right philosophy and a long record in the Washington establishment. But in Dole, Bush faced a competitor whose Great Plains roots and plainspoken style stood in contrast to his WASP pedigree. Theirs was a contest of Kansas versus Kennebunkport, Washburn Law School versus Yale University. Bush's father was an investment banker turned senator. Dole's father ran the town creamery and later the grain elevator. With his gravelly voice, dark hair, and confident demeanor, Dole had plenty of admirers and could not only match Bush's war record but exceed it with his experience charging a machine gun nest in Italy that cost him the use of his right arm. Dole was a legislative engineer, not a policy innovator, and he articulated no greater vision for the country than Bush did. But he had a sharp tongue and biting wit that delighted audiences even as he struck some as mean-spirited.

Hungry for a victory after two previous flops on the national stage, Dole upset Bush in the Iowa caucuses, doing to him what Bush had done to Reagan eight years earlier. Bush did not just lose, he suffered the humiliation of finishing third behind Robertson. But like Reagan, Bush came back to win a convincing victory in the New Hampshire primary thanks to his competitive hustle, a devastating attack ad by Lee Atwater painting Dole as a serial tax increaser, and an army of volunteers commanded by John Sununu, the state's governor. Dole was not a good loser. Asked on live television by Tom Brokaw of NBC News if he had a message for the victor, he growled, "Yeah, stop lying about my record." Bush went on to crush Dole in South Carolina and sweep Super Tuesday, outpacing the Kansas senator with organization, resources, and the relentless momentum of the front-runner. Even though Dole's wife, Elizabeth Hanford Dole, served as Reagan's secretary of transportation, the senator lamented that Bush had effectively seized the mantle of the outgoing president. "I'm sort of running against the ghost of Ronald Reagan," Dole complained at one point. Bush clinched the nomination when Dole dropped out at the end of March.

From the Treasury Building, Baker had been helping in his own way. He talked with Bush most days and when New Hampshire looked problematic suggested that he buy a block of television time to show one of his "Ask George Bush" forums the way he had in 1980. Baker also had Bush's back inside the administration, supporting the vice president during a national security meeting called to discuss whether to cut a deal with Manuel Noriega, the dictator of Panama who was under indictment in the United States for drug-running. Bush resisted dropping the charges as part of any agreement and when he lost the argument publicly signaled his disagreement, his first real break with Reagan. Baker urged him to make another one by publicly calling on Ed Meese, caught up in a web of ethics questions, to resign as attorney general, but Bush equivocated so long that Meese finally stepped aside on his own.

As Bush wrapped up the nomination and turned his attention to the fall, the question became whether it was time to finally call in Baker full-time. Bush was trailing the Democratic nominee, Governor Michael Dukakis of Massachusetts, and anxiety was rising at the Republican headquarters. If anyone could turn around the situation, it was Baker. "We've got to get him over here," George W. Bush, the candidate's oldest son, told Pete Teeley, the longtime aide to his father.

Teeley went to see Baker to make the case.

"I don't want to do that," Baker said. "Can Atwater do this?"

"Yeah, he can do this," Teeley said, "but he can't do it the way you can do it and the campaign needs you."

But Baker was still reluctant to give up his cabinet post. "You *know* I really don't want to do it," he told Kenneth Duberstein, who had succeeded Howard Baker as White House chief of staff. Ever protective of his reputation, Jim Baker found the prospect of another campaign even less enticing with Bush falling behind in the polls; taking over an operation on the path to defeat was hardly appealing.

Baker waged a quiet but not-so-subtle campaign against the draft that was building. He fed a line to Hugh Sidey, the renowned writer for *Time* magazine, about how he might actually be more useful to Bush by sticking it out at the Treasury Department and ensuring that the economy remained healthy through the election. "The best thing I can do for now is stay right here," Sidey quoted Baker as telling "inquiring pols," fudging whether he had said it directly to the columnist or not. Sidey embraced the argument. "How Baker tunes the economy will, more than any other factor besides the nature of Bush himself, determine the Republican future," he wrote.

Others advised Bush against it for different reasons, seeing a call to the Baker cavalry as a sign of Bush's weakness. "On reflection I think it would be a serious mistake for Jim to take a leave of absence," Richard Nixon told Bush in May. "The antis in the media would seize on it as a lack of confidence in your ability to win and too much deference to Reagan."

But with his fortunes slipping, Bush waved aside the caution. "I'm really going to need you in the campaign," Bush told Baker. At Bush's behest, a reluctant Baker went to Reagan to sound him out.

The president repeated the line that Baker had been peddling. "Well, Jim, I think you'd be more valuable to George staying where you are and running the economy," Reagan told Baker, or so he reported back to Bush afterward.

"Let me tell you something, pal, if this is going to happen, *you're* going to have to make it happen," Baker told Bush. He was putting the onus on the vice president, clearly still hoping that his friend might just drop the idea.

Each week for the next few weeks, Bush told Baker he would raise the issue at his regular Wednesday lunch with Reagan. But after each lunch, Duberstein asked the president if the matter had come up and Reagan said no. Baker, on the other hand, reported that Bush had told him that he *had* raised it and did not think there would be a problem. "He did it so softly that it didn't register really," Duberstein said.

Finally, Bush went to see Reagan in the White House residence, bringing Baker with him. Nancy joined them too. The vice president made the case that he needed Baker to win, which would be the most important thing for Reagan's legacy.

Nancy echoed Baker's argument. "I'm sure he would be better running the economy," she said.

But Bush pressed and Reagan acceded to his wishes. "Well, George, if that's the way you want it, that's the way it will be," he said.

The decision was made. Baker would give up his cabinet post to become a fixer again, if only for a few months. On August 5, Reagan appeared with Baker in the White House briefing room to announce the change. He was typically gracious in praising his outgoing treasury secretary. But then he gave the validation that meant the most to Baker given the suspicions from Reagan's most fervent supporters. "He's taken his licks and earned his stripes," the president said. Turning to Baker, he added, "Jim, if there ever was a Reaganite, you're it."

BY THE TIME Baker left the Treasury Department, the economy had reached a reasonable cruising velocity. Unemployment had fallen on his watch from 7.3 percent to 5.6 percent. The economy was growing by a healthy 4 percent a year. Interest rates were down, inflation was holding around 4 percent. After peaking in his first couple years, both the budget deficit and the trade deficit had declined to slightly less than when Baker took office, although both were still high and ultimately would continue to rise in years to come.

There were, however, economic dangers ahead that Baker did not fully recognize. Most worrisome was the increasing number of savings and loan institutions that were failing. Scores of S&Ls, as they were known, had collapsed or been closed by the federal government during Baker's tenure—most infamously the Silverado Savings and Loan, whose board included Neil Bush, one of the vice president's sons, and whose collapse cost taxpayers $1.3 billion. Baker left office before the full price tag for the flailing industry would come due.

Baker later argued that it was not his responsibility because the industry was regulated by an independent federal bank board, not by the Treasury Department. "I can promise you, there was never one second spent discussing whether or not we would deal with the savings and loan crisis before the '88 election or after," he said. "We didn't have the authority to deal with it. You had to get changes in the law and we were dealing with a whole lot of other things."

The other things were significant. Baker had rewritten the tax code with support from both parties, brokered two significant currency agreements with other major economic powers, sealed a free trade pact with one of America's largest trading partners, and stared down a financial crash that could have sent the country into an economic tailspin. Bush faced plenty of political headwinds approaching the general election but the economy would not be one of them.

Or so Baker thought until just days before the Republican convention. As he was busy preparing to move over to the campaign headquarters on Fifteenth Street, just a few blocks from the White House, Alan Greenspan arrived at Baker's office in the Treasury Building to let him know that the Federal Reserve had just decided to raise the main interest rate from 6 percent to 6.5 percent—not even just the usual quarter-point increment but a full half point. The Fed was determined to wring inflation out of the system, but the increase would presumably dampen economic growth heading into the crucial fall campaign, hurting the incumbent party.

"I'm sure you're not going to be happy about this," Greenspan said, in a bit of understatement.

Baker curled up his fist and punched himself in the midsection. "You've hit me right here," he complained.

"I'm sorry, Jim."

Baker then vented frustration at a Federal Reserve out of touch with the needs of the country. Greenspan let him get it out of his system. "I knew this tirade was just an act," he said later.

Finally, the two men smiled at each other and Baker laughed.

"I know you had to do it," Baker conceded, ever the pragmatist.

Now Baker would have to do what he had to do, even if it felt like another punch in the gut.

CHAPTER 17

The Handler

They shared a tent in the wilds near Cody, Wyoming, the vice president and the secretary of the treasury, far away from the noise and the polls and the naysayers. For four days, they rode horses and fished for trout as if they were still just a couple of old friends from Texas, never mind the Secret Service agents who formed a perimeter around their encampment.

A backcountry camping trip in the Shoshone National Forest seemed like the right way for Baker and Bush to get away during the Democratic National Convention that nominated Michael Dukakis in July 1988. Tradition stipulated that a candidate stay out of public view during the other party's quadrennial conclave. Baker was in his last days before resigning from the cabinet to take over the campaign for the fall election. Wyoming had always been his place to escape, the place where he felt most himself, ever since that long-ago adventure with his father. This time, Baker had planned to go fly-fishing there with Dick Cheney, but the Wyoming congressman was sidelined with a quadruple bypass heart operation. Baker decided to take the trip anyway, inviting Bush instead. It was, he thought, the perfect way for them to reconnect.

In the tent, they did not hear Bush mocked at the convention in Atlanta as a child of privilege, "born with a silver foot in his mouth," as Ann Richards, the tart-tongued, silver-haired state treasurer of Texas put it. They did not hear Jim Hightower, the caustic Texas agriculture commissioner, call Bush "a man who was born on third base and thinks he hit a triple." They did not hear Tony Coelho, the House majority whip, joke that Bush took Baker along on his fishing trip "in case George is too squeamish to bait his own hook." They did not hear Ted Kennedy skewer the vice president for failing to stop major mistakes made by the Reagan administration like Iran-contra, leading the assembled Democrats in a chant, "Where was George?" After emerging from the forest, Bush told reporters, "The good thing about the absolute wilderness is you don't have to listen to Ted Kennedy."

Bush and Baker may have tuned out, but the Democratic convention was a success and Baker knew that he was about to take over a dysfunctional campaign in deep trouble. Bush had dispatched his Republican rivals and was heading toward his own convention. He had yet to persuade the American public, however, that he was the right man for the job. In anointing Dukakis, the son of Greek immigrants and the third-term governor of Massachusetts, the Democrats had selected a standard-bearer with an inspiring story rooted in the American Dream. While he was a cool, even stoic character, not burdened with an excess of either emotion or charisma, Dukakis boasted a record of economic revival in his state that had been dubbed the "Massachusetts Miracle." He projected steady assurance, a mows-his-own-lawn integrity. "This election is not about ideology, it's about competence," he declared at the convention.

In the months leading up to Atlanta, Dukakis had emerged from a pack of well-credentialed but little-known Democrats to win the nomination after more celebrated figures flamed out, like Gary Hart once his overnight rendezvous with a model named Donna Rice was exposed, or chose not to run, like the liberal icon, Governor Mario Cuomo of New York. Although he was a stolid technocrat, Dukakis had no trouble outpacing Jesse Jackson, Al Gore, Dick Gephardt, former governor Bruce Babbitt of Arizona and Senators Joseph Biden of Delaware and Paul Simon of Illinois. It was an uninspired race despite the party's frustrations after eight years of Reagan. For a while, Representative Patricia Schroeder of Colorado considered a campaign, leading pundits to describe the field as Snow White and the Seven Dwarfs. Dukakis relied on superior organization and finances as he piled up enough delegates to claim the nomination. To pull the party together, Dukakis selected as his running mate Lloyd Bentsen, Bush's old Texas adversary, a choice hailed as a canny reprise of the Boston-Austin axis that propelled John Kennedy and Lyndon Johnson to the White House in 1960. Dukakis emerged from the convention with a commanding 17-point lead over the incumbent vice president.

Not only was Bush trailing badly in the polls, he had an organization that was riven by infighting, turf wars, and competing theories of the case for Bush. It was the early Reagan White House all over again. The G-6 led by Lee Atwater that was supposed to seamlessly lead a transition from one Republican presidency to the next had degenerated into a politburo of rivals. As Baker began focusing on his new mission, he received a memo from Gary MacDougal, an assistant campaign manager who came to Bush from a successful career in the business world, laying out in the stark terms of the Harvard MBA and McKinsey consultant he had once been just how messed up the campaign really was. The link between Lee Atwater, Bob Teeter, and Craig Fuller, the top strategists, and the actual campaign staff was "weak and intermittent," the MacDougal memo said, resulting in Bush "largely getting the short-term thinking of three people, and not enough product of the campaign organization."

"There is tremendous confusion and considerable animosity" between the two sides, MacDougal told Baker, "with key members of each referring to the other as a 'black hole.'" There was more: Speeches were not creative. There was no agreement on policies. Coordination between the Republican National Committee and the White House was poor. Leaks were endemic. There was too much last-minute event planning and not enough preparation for important meetings. "This all adds up to the fact that the Vice President is not being served with the best possible product in a timely fashion—in speeches, events, or policy," MacDougal concluded.

Baker's arrival temporarily made it even worse, stirring up the team's barely suppressed stew of resentments and insecurities. When he resigned as treasury secretary to take over as campaign chairman, the only person as unhappy as Baker was Atwater, who feared the arrival of the vice president's close friend. "Lee was running on paranoia all the time," Fuller recalled, and thought he was being supplanted by someone with far greater influence over the candidate. He was "nervous about getting layered," said Ed Rogers, his deputy. "There was a time when it was, 'Are we out of here? Is there going to be a new team? Are we getting flushed?'"

Baker had no interest in flushing Atwater. After seeing Atwater in action during the 1980 and 1984 campaigns, he had a healthy respect for the operative's talents. More importantly, he did not want to be Lee Atwater. He wanted to be the treasury secretary—or the secretary of state in waiting. If he was going to pilot the campaign, he planned to fly at a far higher altitude than Atwater did. "He was very upset," Baker remembered. "I said, 'Look, Lee, this isn't going to diminish you. It's going to enhance your role and you don't need to worry about it.' . . . What he didn't understand was I didn't want to be the chief political operator." Like the candidate himself, Baker still saw politics as a dirty business. The campaign was a necessary if unseemly way station in between jobs that were *important*.

In many ways, Baker and Atwater were as opposite as could be. "They were very different personalities," said Frank Donatelli, who was White House political director for Reagan at the time and coordinating with the Bush campaign. Baker "was a buttoned-down lawyer and Lee was a wild man." At thirty-seven years old, Atwater was full of twitchy, manic energy, "an insecure kid who got to play in the big leagues," as his onetime boss, Ed Rollins, put it. The son of an insurance adjuster and a high school Spanish teacher, Atwater led his own rock band in school called the Upsetters Revue and cut his teeth on Republican campaigns in the New South immediately after college. Working on one race after another before joining Reagan's White House, he had a reputation for no-holds-barred politics, a dirty trickster who, according to legend that he denied, encouraged an anti-Semitic fringe candidate to go after a mutual opponent and arranged for an operative of a competing campaign selling a fundraising ticket to be arrested for scalping. Atwater reread Machiavelli every year, or at least wanted people to think he did, and kept a likeness of Stonewall Jackson on his wall next to a photograph of Reagan. When it came time for a biography to be written about Atwater, it was, naturally, titled *Bad Boy*.

To assuage Atwater's concerns, Baker let him keep his prime corner office at campaign headquarters and took another one across the hall instead. Baker heaped praise on him at an early staff meeting, boasting that Atwater was the first person he hired when he became Reagan's chief of staff. That, Rogers said, was the "Southern pol" in Baker, telling a "preacher's story" that might not hew exactly to the facts but was intended to stroke its subject. "Baker didn't know for some weeks after I was hired that I was working there," Atwater told colleagues.

Baker also enlisted the candidate's son George W. to reassure the jumpy campaign manager. The younger Bush had been suspicious of Atwater at first, challenging him during an early campaign strategy session with the family at Camp David in 1985. "How do we know we can trust you?" George W. asked then. If he had doubts, Atwater replied, then he should move to Washington and work in the campaign to keep an eye on him, a dare that the brash son accepted. When David Remnick profiled Atwater in *Esquire* magazine as a ruthless, conscience-free operator—"all blood on the floor and don't look back"—who was so crude that he pulled down his pants and urinated in front of the writer, it fell to the younger George to reprimand him. "You need to earn your spurs through performance, not interviews," he told Atwater.

Atwater got the message and, by the time Baker arrived, he and George W. had come to trust each other, making the candidate's son the right emissary. "He was nervous about Baker, which meant that his priorities might not have been 100 percent correct," George W. recalled later.

"He knew Baker, how close he was to Dad, and he didn't want to get cut out of the mix."

Atwater was not the only one wary of Baker's arrival. When he convened an introductory meeting, Baker told the staff that he was not planning to make major changes, that he was just a superstructure coming in on top. But he noticed a young woman in the corner staring at him with a look of resentment. "We'd just come through this campaign," the woman, Janet Mullins, recalled later, referring to the primaries. "We'd won. What do we need this guy for?" Several people had to move offices in order to accommodate Baker and his portable team, she remembered, "so that had everybody—at least it had me—in a snit."

Baker had his assistant Caron Jackson summon Mullins to his new office to meet one-on-one. Mullins, who had come from the informal culture on Capitol Hill, where she had been an aide to Senator Mitch McConnell of Kentucky, was in the habit of walking around the campaign headquarters without shoes. Now, she felt defiant as she headed down the corridor. "I had my jacket off, my suit jacket off, and I'm barefoot, and I walk down to the other end of the hall barefoot and walk in and stick out my hand and say, 'Hey, Jim, nice to meet you,'" she said. "*Nobody* calls him Jim, nobody. I thought Caron was going to faint on the spot." Baker, though, laughed. "It was kind of an instant bonding moment," Mullins said.

In the end, Atwater, Mullins, and the others came to appreciate that Baker was not mounting a hostile takeover. If anything, Baker's arrival meant the end of the campaign by committee that had been paralyzing Bush's effort. Finally, there was a boss. "It was chaos," said Robert Zoellick, who accompanied Baker from the Treasury Department. "Baker brought order." He had unquestioned authority. No one would dare go around Baker to appeal one of his rulings, because he spoke with Bush's proxy in a way that Atwater simply could not. A decision was now a decision. Atwater had been running "a pretty loose ship," as Donatelli put it, and the ship was all but lost in the fog. Not only was Michael Dukakis far ahead on the eve of the Republican National Convention, he was leading in twenty-four states with a total of 353 electoral votes, far more than the 270 needed to win the presidency.

BAKER'S PROBLEMS WERE NOT just with his staff. Bush himself turned out to have an end run in mind and it was about as big a maneuver as a candidate could make without consulting his own campaign chief. On their fishing trip in Wyoming, the two men had talked about the looming choice of a vice presidential running mate and Bush had offered a quick handicapping of some of the possibilities. But the only actual decision he told Baker about in the tent that night was that he had reluctantly ruled out his good friend Alan Simpson, the state's abortion-rights-supporting Republican senator. Now that it came time to actually pick a candidate to join the Republican ticket, Baker was entirely in the dark. Bush had made the selection without telling anyone. Baker had arranged for vetting to be handled by one of his own advisers, Robert Kimmitt, his general counsel at the Treasury Department. But while Bush had Kimmitt vet a variety of possible choices, the vice president did not share his thoughts on what Kimmitt turned up. "I wanted it totally kept to myself," Bush said years later.

In a way, it seemed like an act of rebellion against Baker. Like many politicians, Bush had never liked the idea of being handled and resented the portrayal of Baker as the wise man behind the bumbling leader. Reporters were already writing that Baker would be a sort of "deputy president" in a putative Bush White House. "If you're Bush, you don't like this perception that somehow Baker's the puppet master," said Janet Mullins. "You can certainly draw a conclusion that that was Bush asserting his independence and authority. He was going to make that decision on his own." Bush may also have reckoned that Baker would not like his choice. "There's a side of me that also thought Bush didn't consult with Baker because he knew Baker wasn't going to agree with him," Mullins said.

With Simpson ruled out, the finalists included both Bob and Elizabeth Dole; Jack Kemp; Senator Pete Domenici of New Mexico; and a little-known junior senator from Indiana named Dan Quayle, talked up by conservatives as a fresh face at age forty-one. Quayle would be a reassuringly hard-line presence on a ticket with Bush, who had never really overcome their doubts despite eight years as Reagan's loyal sidekick. (Donald Trump, the media-hungry developer who had groused about Baker's economic policies, sent word through Lee Atwater that he would be willing to serve as vice president, an offer that Bush dismissed as "strange and unbelievable.")

At a meeting the Friday before the convention, Baker and other Bush advisers met to discuss the list of finalists. Bob Teeter asked everyone for their first, second, and third choices. Only Roger Ailes and Craig Fuller named Quayle as their first choice (Fuller also made Quayle his second and third choice). If Baker gave his preference, it has never been reported. He was widely believed to favor Bob Dole, a safe, conventional choice. Years later, Baker denied having a favorite, Dole or anyone else.

Shortly after the meeting, Bush advisers leaked the finalists to *The New York Times* and suggested that while Dole was the front-runner, Quayle had "surprisingly strong support." It was an old Washington trick to leak the prospect of a decision you disagreed with in hopes that public disclosure would generate enough vocal opposition to kill it. At least some savvy readers of the *Times* assumed the leak was Baker's way of trying to sink Quayle. But if so, it did not work, perhaps because few in Washington took the idea of a Quayle selection all that seriously.

Quayle himself was bewildered by the story, unsure what to make of it, so he called Baker on Sunday night to find out what was going on.

"I don't know who leaked that," Baker told Quayle.

Quayle said fine, but if it was true, preparations needed to be made.

"Don't worry," he remembered Baker answering. "I've got a great team if you're the nominee."

But that was a big if. Baker did not think Quayle's selection was likely and despite his mantra about the Five Ps did nothing more to prepare for it.

ON TUESDAY, AUGUST 16, the second day of the Republican National Convention, Bush was in the White House. He held his regular intelligence briefing, then prepared to leave for the gathering in New Orleans that would officially designate him as Reagan's successor. To Baker, the focus should be establishing Bush as his own man finally, not Reagan's shadow. But there was another disaster brewing. After the briefer left, Craig Fuller asked Bush if he had made his decision about his vice presidential choice; it was supposed to be announced Thursday, the final day of the convention, with much fanfare, and advisers were still in the dark. Instead of answering, Bush shrugged and headed to Marine Two to fly to Andrews Air Force Base, where he would board Air Force Two for the flight to New Orleans. Alarmed, Fuller grabbed Baker at the first moment he could pull him aside.

"There may be a problem," Fuller said.

Fuller explained his conversation with Bush. "There was only one answer to the question that's acceptable—have you made your decision?—but I didn't get it," he said.

"You're kidding," Baker said.

"No, I'm not."

"I'll deal with it."

After Air Force Two took off, Baker met privately in the plane's cabin with the vice president. Bush had grown agitated the night before watching television images of reporters stalking some of his prospective running mates and he listened to Dole grouse publicly about the indignity of the process. Baker and Bush talked about moving up his plan and announcing his choice once he landed in New Orleans. Why wait? Bush agreed. "He thought it was unfair to them so he decided to accelerate the pick," George W. Bush said of his father. Some Bush advisers suspected that Dole's televised complaining may have killed any remaining chance that he would be picked for the ticket. Either way, just like that, the whole rollout plan was upended.

Everyone was hanging on Bush's decision. During the flight, aides wrote out their guesses on scraps of paper. "None of us were right," Fuller said. As Air Force Two began its descent for landing, Bush finally confided in Baker. Dan Quayle was his choice. Any doubts Baker harbored were put aside. "By the time Bush said, 'I'm going with Quayle,' Jim wasn't going to argue with him," said Charlie Black, the political strategist.

Even George W. Bush was out of the loop, waiting for his father in New Orleans with a puckish sign that said, "Dad you can tell me!" Also eager to find out was Reagan, who had addressed the convention the night before. Baker had arranged with Kenneth Duberstein, the chief of staff, for Reagan to meet Bush on the tarmac at Belle Chasse Naval Air Station outside New Orleans when Air Force Two landed. They shook hands and then Reagan boarded Air Force One to leave, a symbolic passing of the torch. During their brief encounter, Bush leaned over and whispered his decision in Reagan's ear. Once airborne, curious aides asked Reagan: Who had Bush selected? But the hard-of-hearing president had gotten only that it was the senator from Indiana, so some of his staff assumed that meant Richard Lugar, the state's senior lawmaker. Even at this late hour, the idea of Quayle still seemed implausible.

After Reagan's departure, Bush and his entourage were taken to the house of the naval station's commandant, where sandwiches were waiting for them. Bush and Baker huddled again in another room, then Baker came out to break the news to the rest of the team that Quayle would be the running mate. Aides raced to notify the losing candidates and track down the winner in a hotel room in New Orleans.

Baker got Quayle on the phone. "I thought, 'Oh crap, I lost,'" Quayle recalled, since he assumed that Bush would call the winner himself and leave the runners-up to Baker.

But Baker surprised him. "Hang on for the veep," he said.

Bush picked up. Would you join me on the ticket? he asked Quayle.

Excited, Quayle instantly said yes.

Bush was pleased. Quayle had been *his* choice and he had made it, unswayed by Baker or anyone else. In his mind, it was bold, it was confident. He was picking the next generation of political leadership. He was not being handled. To Bush, the blond-haired, blue-eyed senator came straight out of central casting as the embodiment of the future, a youthful rebuttal to all those stories dinging Bush as the exemplar of the status quo. He was putting next in line to the presidency someone he really did not know, with a scant record and a thin reputation, but that did not seem to bother Bush.

The vice president told Quayle they would announce the decision shortly at the Spanish Plaza boat pier. Baker then came back on the line to manage the logistics and the Bush team's slapdash, even reckless, approach to one of the campaign's key decisions quickly became apparent. When Quayle expressed concern about navigating his way to the announcement given the thousands of people who had gathered, Baker told Quayle that was his first assignment—to figure out how to get there.

Don't blow it, Baker said. "Remember," he added in an edgy joke, "this decision is revocable."

They both laughed, but as Quayle later put it, "it was the last laugh I would have for a long, long time."

QUAYLE WAS an unlikely choice for a conventional thinker like Bush. The scion of a newspaper empire, Quayle was born in Indiana, lived most of his childhood in Arizona, and then returned to Indiana for high school, college, and law school. His mother's father, Eugene Pulliam, owned more than a dozen medium-sized newspapers, including *The Arizona Republic* and *The Indianapolis Star*. Quayle joined the Indiana National Guard during Vietnam, a decision that spared him combat overseas but would soon prove problematic back home. He worked in the family business and in state government before winning a seat in Congress in 1976. Four years later, at the age of thirty-three, he defeated Senator Birch Bayh to become the youngest person ever elected to the Senate from Indiana.

Conservative and friendly, with movie-star looks and a boyish grin, Quayle impressed some of the older Republicans in the Senate but hardly cut a wide swath on Capitol Hill. His one claim to major legislation was a bipartisan worker training bill co-sponsored with Ted Kennedy. Baker knew Quayle but not well. He had little regard for him. A son of privilege himself, Baker could hardly be offended by Quayle's family background. But for a lawyer with an exacting eye and a serious sensibility, Baker clearly found something about Quayle off-putting, the sense perhaps of a callow youth without the heft to justify the exalted position he was being given.

His first teasing line to Quayle—*this decision is revocable*—would set the terms for the relationship. Bush might have offered the job, but now Baker would tell him how to handle it. This was direction, not deference, as if Baker wanted Quayle to understand who would be calling the shots from the very start. What other staff member—and despite his time in the cabinet, that was what Baker was now again—would feel so uninhibited in joking about punishing a prospective vice president?

What came next would be the antithesis of Baker's famous Five Ps. As Bush rode the *Natchez*, a paddleboat on the Mississippi, up to New Orleans, Quayle was left to find his way to the Spanish Plaza without help. "Nothing!" he remembered with undiminished exasperation twenty-five years later. "I have to get there on my own!" When he did get there, he was winded and frazzled, unprepared for his worldwide television debut.

The scene was chaotic. Two Secret Service agents making their way through the crowd called out, "Where's Quayle? Where's Quayle?"

Finally, the senator got to the stage and Bush happily introduced him as "a young man born in the middle of this century and from the middle of this country."

Quayle had trouble containing his enthusiasm. "Hot" and "pumped up," as Craig Fuller remembered him, Quayle came across like a cheerleader at a high school football game, grabbing Bush's arm and shoulders again and again, telling the crowd, "Let's go get 'em! All right? You got it?"

The awkward scene only presaged the pandemonium that would follow. Unfamiliar to many in the national media, Quayle suddenly confronted questions about his background: Did his family use its money or influence to buy his way into the National Guard to avoid military service in Vietnam? What did he do during a Florida golfing weekend with two other members of Congress and a lobbyist named Paula Parkinson, who later posed for *Playboy* after an investigation into whether sex was traded for votes? Was he a lightweight not up to the job? Robert Kimmitt had vetted Quayle, but at Bush's instruction had shared his research with no one other than the candidate.

Now Baker, uncharacteristically unprepared for the media storm over Quayle, jotted down notes on his yellow legal paper to try to get hold of the story. He came up with phrases to describe Quayle: "A Leader for the Future!" and "Bold Reach Across Generations." Quayle was indeed young, Baker thought, but that should be turned into an advantage. "JFK Pres at 42," he wrote, a comparison that Quayle would later pick up on to his eternal regret. Next to the initials "P.P.," for Paula Parkinson, Baker wrote, "Absolutely nothing to it, checked out."

As day turned to night, Baker huddled in Room 3820 of the Marriott with his close aides trying to figure out damage control. "It was not a happy group," Dick Darman remembered. They were trying to squelch any talk of dumping Quayle, but several top campaign officials understood that was the unspoken option on the table. "It seemed obvious that if—if—there were to be any change of candidate, it would have to be done by Thursday, before the acceptance speeches," Darman said.

Baker called Quayle. "Look," he said, "there's a total meltdown on this National Guard thing. It's absolutely coming unglued. We've got to talk to you. I'm sending over Kimmitt and Darman."

Quayle objected. It was already midnight. "This is totally ridiculous," he said. He would just go out in the morning and answer questions.

"How are you going to answer the questions when you don't know what happened twenty years ago?" Baker asked sharply.

"I'll give my version of it."

"What if your version is different from somebody else's version?"

"Well, that's life, isn't it?"

No, that was not how it would be done, not in a Baker operation. Darman and Kimmitt slipped over to Quayle's hotel room and found the senator in his underwear and his wife, Marilyn, in bed. For the next two hours, until 2 a.m., they went over the questions with Quayle in detail.

Returning to Baker's suite, Kimmitt and Darman reported that while Quayle could not remember everything, he was probably being honest in his denials of wrongdoing. The mad scramble continued throughout the night, with Baker's team even calling and waking up Quayle's father to ask what he remembered.

The staff typed up two pages of questions that Quayle might face and some suggested answers. Baker reviewed it and circled three about the National Guard that he thought were most troublesome:

Do you think you got preferential treatment?
Do you think it proper to move some people ahead of others?
Do you think it was fair for you to get in when others didn't?

Predictably, those were some of the many questions Quayle was pummeled with by reporters the next day and the senator, alone and hardly prepared, quickly grew resentful at Baker's efforts to take control. Amid the press frenzy, Baker went to the ABC News booth at the convention to offer public support for Quayle. But when Quayle came into the hall for the news conference at which he intended to clear the air, he noticed Baker pulling out a piece of paper and previewing for gathered reporters "almost verbatim" what Quayle was about to tell them. "The intended effect," Quayle said later, "was to show them that he was in charge of me. Baker wanted to signal to the media that I was not really his choice, and that he was making the best of a bad situation. He was putting himself in a win-win position. If I sank the ticket, it was somebody else's fault, not Baker's. If I didn't, it was because Baker had taken charge of me."

In the heat of the moment, Baker was not sure about the path forward. Talking points delivered to him for the last day of the convention included this line, to be used only if asked: "There has been no serious discussion or consideration of replacing Dan Quayle on the ticket." Baker hedged his bets. "Did he lie?" he wrote next to the typed talking points. "To the best of my knowledge—No." And then he added in parentheses: "Based on everything I know now—No!"

There was plenty of finger-pointing afterward. Still furious after New Orleans, Baker asked Kimmitt to explain why he had not done more to vet Quayle. Why, for instance, had he not interviewed Paula Parkinson? Kimmitt explained that Bush had asked him not to contact outsiders to preserve the secrecy of the process. And in any case, Kimmitt said, he would not have approached Parkinson. "Through conversations with those who know her," he told Baker in a memo the next week recounting what had happened, "we believe her to be deceitful, opportunistic and unbalanced, and the mere fact of interviewing her would have given her more standing and credibility than she deserves." Kimmitt also rejected assertions that he had not examined Quayle's military service. "I did discuss the Guard issue, both in my first interview of Quayle and in my report to the Vice President," he wrote to Baker. "It would therefore be inaccurate for either of them to indicate the matter was not discussed before the selection or that the issue of favoritism (my term, as opposed to 'preferential treatment') was not raised in those discussions."

But no one on the campaign was mollified. They knew that the introduction of Quayle was a model of how not to announce a running mate. They could have used careful leaks over a couple weeks to prepare the ground for a Quayle nomination and draw out vulnerabilities well before-hand. They could have known their candidate better and been ready to address the criticism. But Bush had not trusted his own team, or even his own best friend, enough to make that happen. "It was Dad who changed the timing, not Baker," George W. Bush said later. "The problem was you either make the decision to announce the guy a week ahead of time or you wait for the last minute so that there's not time for the shark tank to start feeding on the blood." Somehow, his father let himself get caught in the middle, with terrible results. "It was my decision, and I blew it," the elder Bush dictated to his diary after the convention, "but I'm not about to say that I blew it." He seemed to be referring to the *way* the choice was announced, not the choice itself, but Baker thought both were true. "How dumb," Baker said later. "We spent the first week of the campaign answer-ing questions about Quayle's background." Baker was mad—at both Bush and himself.

WHILE BAKER STRUGGLED with the Quayle contretemps, he hardly even touched another internal battle within the Bush campaign that would arguably have greater consequences. Peggy Noonan, the speechwriter for Ronald Reagan, already famous for her soaring words, had been assigned to draft Bush's convention speech accepting the nomination, probably the single best chance for the vice president to step out of Reagan's shadow and frame his message for the fall.

It had been, up until now, an empty campaign. Bush's argument for the presidency had essentially amounted to a recitation of all the impres-sive jobs he had held. The ultimate résumé candidate, Bush had never touched a chord with the public the way Reagan had nor articulated a larger idea that animated his drive for public office beyond the sense of noblesse oblige he inherited from his father. Indeed, he dismissed all the talk about "the vision thing," as he put it derisively.

And so it fell to Noonan to make the case for a candidate who had not done so himself. The unofficial lyricist of the Reagan Revolution, she crafted an address that would give voice to what she saw as Bush's best qualities, while making sure he embraced Reagan's conservative causes. It was a tricky balance. The speech was meant to be Bush's declaration of independence after nearly eight years at Reagan's side. With Noonan as his muse, Bush would define his mission as more inclusive than that of the outgoing president, who was often criticized for indifference to the plight of disadvantaged Americans. "I want a kinder and gentler nation,"

Bush would say. The speech would have him call for a nation where private groups and citizens, not government, stepped up to address society's issues, "like a thousand points of light in a broad and peaceful sky."

As Noonan drafted the speech, though, the other important goal was to dispel the wimp charge once and for all. The best place to do that was the section where Bush would pledge opposition to tax hikes, a surefire applause line. Noonan was aiming for something maximally memorable. Channeling the tough-guy movie hero Dirty Harry played by Clint Eastwood, she wrote in the line: "My opponent won't rule out raising taxes, but I will, and the Congress will push me to raise taxes and I'll say no, and they'll push and I'll say no, and they'll push again and I'll say to them, 'Read my lips: No new taxes.'"

Dick Darman and Craig Fuller were aghast when they saw her draft. The policy advisers, more moderate than Noonan, fretted that it was unrealistic for Bush to tie his own hands so tightly. Darman deleted the line. When the draft speech was returned to Noonan, she noticed it was missing and put it back in. The next time it came back to her with more edits, the line was gone again. "We all knew it was a good line," Fuller said. "We just didn't know in governing you could stick with it."

In her memoir, Noonan said she thought Bush's aides did not like the personal imagery because "lips are organs" and "there is no history of presidential candidates making personal-organ references in acceptance speeches." But, she said, "I kept putting it back in. Why? Because it's definite. It's not subject to misinterpretation. It means, I mean this."

Noonan showed the speech to Baker, who offered no objection to the line. His only instructions were to put in more good economic news. Baker, just arriving on the campaign, had given Darman his proxy to review and scrub the convention speech. If Baker had intervened and backed up Darman and Fuller, he presumably would have succeeded in excising the flamboyant language. But he did not get involved in the debate and without him, Darman and Fuller failed to persuade Roger Ailes, who thought it would work. "We got overruled," Fuller said.

A WEEK AFTER the convention, Baker convened an all-day meeting of the campaign team to evaluate just how bad things were for Bush's candidacy. The first of four planned sessions was, according to the agenda, supposed to address "the nature of the problem." Baker's diagnosis was as crisp as it was cutting. "Seen as weak," he scribbled on the written schedule for the day.

At least Bush had emerged from the convention finally on a positive trajectory. He had picked up support from Catholics, ticket splitters, and independents. But he still faced a 12-point gender gap among women. He was ahead in the South, behind in the Mid-Atlantic and California, and roughly tied in the Midwest battleground states such as Ohio, Illinois, and Michigan. An analysis prepared for the meeting concluded that Bush had 126 electoral votes in his base plus marginal leads in states with another 168 electoral votes. He had to win nearly all of them to cobble together a 270-vote majority in the Electoral College. Bush was in trouble and Baker harbored few illusions about what it would take to get him elected.

"Our biggest prob.—need to have Bush seen as a strong leader," Baker wrote. "Bush's negatives due to perception of him as weak." He listed four main objectives: establishing Bush as his own man, controlling the agenda, staying on offense, and, perhaps most significant for the final campaign sprint to come, tearing down Dukakis. "He's out of mainstream of trad. Am. Values," Baker wrote. Next to that, he scribbled, "Prison Furlough, Pledge. Veto of mandatory sen. for drug dealers. Death penalty for drug kingpins."

In the end, Baker concluded that Bush was better on offense than defense. "Anytime GB has been on attack he has gained in polls," Baker wrote. "Whenever he gets ahead and stops attacking—his standing declines."

So the answer was clear: Keep attacking. The kinder and gentler Bush would have to wait.

When Baker first arrived on the campaign, Atwater had feared that "Baker would oversee a very punctual, orderly, on- or under-budget state funeral." He need not have worried. Just because Baker carried himself in a more formal, cabinet secretary kind of way did not mean he eschewed Atwater's scorched-earth campaign tactics. Baker was more than willing to give him latitude to run the campaign largely as he saw fit. Bush and Baker knew exactly what they were getting in their aggressive campaign manager. Atwater was the high priest of the negative campaign and this was the era when attack ads created by poll-driven campaign consultants like the relentless young South Carolinian ruled American politics more than ever before. With Americans glued to their television sets watching a proliferating array of cable television channels, they were a captive audience to be bombarded with marketing messages. Atwater had figured out early in his career that sometimes it was harder to sell your candidate than to attack the other guy (he called it "driving up the opposition's negatives"), and Bush was proving to be a hard sell.

Still, Atwater now had to convince Baker to go along with a slash-and-burn fall campaign tougher than any in recent memory. "Lee, who was plenty happy to do negative campaigning, was shaking his head and saying, 'How in the hell are we going to get Baker and Bush to go along with this?'" recalled Charlie Black. "Jim was always looking at everything to make sure we weren't crossing the line on things," Black remembered, but it soon turned out that Baker rarely vetoed tough attacks. "Sometimes we might want to hit a little harder on something and Baker said, 'No, you've got to put that in Bush's words,' or something like that," Black said. "But when you had to go strong on the offense there, Baker was better able to get Bush to do it."

Although Baker would long cultivate a reputation for civility in an uncivil era, the post-convention strategy sessions convinced him that there was no other way to win but attacking and he signed off on an unrelenting, flag-waving campaign to paint Dukakis, the son of Greek immigrants, as an unpatriotic leftist out of touch with old-fashioned American values. While he may not have conceived the attacks, Baker did not object to hitting Dukakis on the full array of opposition-research-driven, culture-war "wedge" issues that Atwater and Roger Ailes proposed to use, such as harping on Dukakis's decision, back in 1977, to veto a Massachusetts bill to require teachers to lead students in the Pledge of Allegiance. "What is it about the Pledge of Allegiance that upsets him so much?" the mild-mannered Bush was soon shouting at campaign rallies. Nor did Baker complain about Atwater and Ailes going after Dukakis on a prison furlough program in Massachusetts that released a black convict named Willie Horton who then raped a white Maryland woman and bound and stabbed her boyfriend. The program was part of an effort to help ease convicts' eventual reintegration back into society and most states had similar programs at that point before the tough-on-crime wave of legislation of the 1990s. But Massachusetts was the only one that included first-degree murderers serving life sentences without the possibility of parole. The program had been started by a Republican governor, but Dukakis defended it and refused to sign legislation exempting first-degree murderers serving life sentences and imposing other restrictions.

Al Gore was the first to weaponize the Willie Horton case against Dukakis, during the Democratic primaries. James Pinkerton, a Bush campaign researcher, noticed and included it among seven possible attacks on Dukakis that he gave Atwater. Bush began citing the case during speeches through the summer. How much had changed for Baker over the last ten years—the same candidate for Texas attorney general who had refused to go after an opponent in 1978 for not extraditing a suspect who then later went on to kill two people was now leading a national campaign eagerly exploiting an eerily similar case. Baker had lost that campaign; he did not plan to lose this one.

By fall, the Baker-run operation began airing a television ad attacking the Massachusetts furlough program, showing a series of inmates walking through the revolving door of a prison. Nearly all of the prisoners in the video were white; just one was black, although he was the only one who glanced up at the camera with a sinister look. This was a long way from the sunny campaign optimism of Reagan's "Morning in America."

The Willie Horton commercial that would go down in history, however, was a different ad produced by an operative named Larry McCarthy, working for an ostensibly independent group called the National Security Political Action Committee. In that ad, called "Weekend Passes," Horton was singled out, a picture of his scowling killer's face shown as the narrator described his torture and rape of the Maryland couple. In the end, the ad was only shown sporadically on cable television, but its impact was magnified by repeated coverage on newscasts, giving it far more distribution than it otherwise would have had.

Baker had no quarrel with the ad at first, but when Democrats and media commentators criticized it for brazenly appealing to racial fears, he tried to distance the campaign by writing the committee that aired it and asking that it be withdrawn. The letter, however, hardly seemed the act of someone genuinely disturbed by the ad. The day it first aired for the start of a planned twenty-eight-day run, McCarthy's committee had hand-delivered an offer to Baker to take it down if he objected. Baker did not write his letter in response until twenty-five days later, when the commercial was just about finished with its programmed schedule. And while Baker did not control the committee that made the ad, many found that implausible. "Anybody who believes that believes in the tooth fairy," Dukakis said later.

In any case, the record was clear that the Bush campaign had long focused on Horton as a major vulnerability for Dukakis. "If I can make Willie Horton a household name, we'll win the election," Atwater had told a breakfast of Republican activists back in June. A month later, in a speech, Atwater referred to Horton, "who for all I know may end up being Dukakis's running mate." Roger Ailes told *Time* magazine in August that "the only question is whether we depict Willie Horton with a knife in his hand or without it."

Dukakis later called his failure to respond more effectively to the Willie Horton attack "the biggest mistake of my political career." By the time it aired, Bush had already pulled ahead of Dukakis and polls suggested that his widening lead coincided as much with the fall debates as the controversy over the ad. Still, Willie Horton would be associated with Bush—and Baker—for years to come, a metaphor for racially coded campaign tactics aimed at dividing Americans for political benefit.

When it was all over, Dukakis the bland technocrat had been remade into a dangerous and practically un-American figure, a foolish liberal who favored criminals over their victims, who would watch you get mugged in a dark alley and do nothing. Baker, who prided himself on working across the aisle to get things done, had no hesitation about employing bare-knuckled tactics to win office. The campaign he walked into was losing and he wanted to win. This, he thought then and still thought years later, was what it took.

BAKER USED his reputation for rectitude as a negotiating tool. As he haggled with the Dukakis camp over debates, he brought along a useful foil in Roger Ailes, who was so well known for his hardball politics that *Time* magazine later that year called him "the dark prince of political advertising." As Ailes put it, "Baker and I would do good cop, bad cop. They thought I was crazy and Baker was sane." Both men played their roles with gusto. "Every once in a while I'd go crazy and say something half-obscene and Baker would calm me down," Ailes said. "Then he'd say, 'I've got to leave, got to get back to the White House. I'll leave you with Ailes.' And, of course, they'd immediately say, 'No, no, no. That's okay. Don't leave us with Ailes.'"

Baker, as usual, got what he wanted out of the negotiations—in this case, two presidential debates instead of the four Dukakis demanded and the last one more than three weeks before the election, so there would be time to recover from any stumbles. Even the little things mattered. Ailes kept pushing for a taller podium that would emphasize Dukakis's short stature; the Democrat was just five-foot-eight to Bush's six-foot-two and Americans had an almost unbroken record in the television era of electing the taller presidential candidate. But Bush was still nervous headed into the debates. He was far more schooled in the details of policy than Reagan had been, but he had none of the president's deft touch when it came to translating his views for a mass audience. And then there was Bush's "transcendent dorkiness," as *Newsweek* called it—his fractured syntax, refusal to use the first person, and propensity for odd locutions and verbal stumbles, such as when he declared September 7 to be Pearl Harbor Day or referred to the "successful Reagan White House" as the "sexy Reagan White House."

Baker scheduled three mock debates to prepare. Dick Darman played Dukakis. Advisers gave Bush a seven-page strategy memo urging him to be aggressive. "You cannot afford to lie back or be defensive," it said. He should focus on "furloughs and pardons, tax increases, spending" and bad judgment by Dukakis. By hand, Baker added his suggestion that Bush emphasize Dukakis's membership in the American Civil Liberties Union, outlining for Bush arguments he could use to claim the group should be considered radical: "Prohibit nativity scenes and menoras. Elim. movie ratings. Take In God We Trust off money. Opposed to death penalty. De-crim. some drugs. And on and on!"

Baker tried setting public expectations low for Bush by emphasizing to reporters that Dukakis was a master debater. But he did not set the bar low enough. When Bush first met Dukakis onstage at Wake Forest University in Winston-Salem, North Carolina, on September 25, the vice president trotted out his anticipated attack lines to little effect. Instead, Dukakis put him on the defensive about abortion, asserting that Bush's position in favor of outlawing the procedure would "brand a woman a criminal" and threaten her with prison.

Bush came offstage feeling down. He had dutifully mocked Dukakis for calling himself a "card-carrying member of the ACLU," as Baker sug-gested, and run down the list of the group's controversial legal positions in one of the night's more memorable attacks, but he did not think he had done well and neither did the media. "I'm going to do a heck of a lot better the next time," he promised Baker.

Baker thought part of the problem was poor management of the can-didate. Bush had become too anxious about the debate and his team was not giving him enough time to rest. His speeches for the next day were coming in too late each night and Bush had trouble sleeping if he did not get them before going to bed. "Energy Level: Slower to recover from fatigue than 1 month ago," Baker wrote by hand. "He's tired. (Loosen up on schedule)."

Bush's wobbly first debate performance was quickly followed by another headache for Baker. At the vice presidential debate with Lloyd Bentsen at the Omaha Civic Auditorium on October 5, Quayle could hardly compete with the white-haired Texan with the rich accent and the wise-man gravitas. The debate produced perhaps the most devastating line in modern American politics. Under fire for his youth, Quayle noted that he had as much experience as John Kennedy had when he ran for president, a comparison Baker had made. Bentsen looked like a coyote ready to pounce.

"Senator," he drawled, "I served with Jack Kennedy. I knew Jack Kennedy. Jack Kennedy was a friend of mine." Then, with a practiced pause, he added, "Senator, you're no Jack Kennedy."

Quayle refused even to look at Bentsen during the exchange. "That was really uncalled for, senator," he responded, tight-lipped and fuming.

Bentsen, with a sly smile, seemed to enjoy the moment. "You're the one that was making the comparison, senator," he said, nearly snorting the word *senator*, "and I'm one who knew him well."

Bush stood by his running mate, dutifully claiming that Quayle had "knocked it right out of the park." Reagan weighed in to brand Bentsen's Kennedy line a "cheap shot." But if it was cheap, it was certainly effective. Baker understood that Bentsen had turned Quayle into a punch line and made little effort to pretend otherwise. "When you think about what might have happened, we have to be pretty happy," Baker told CNN, damning Quayle with faint praise. Quayle and his wife, Marilyn, who had come to especially dislike Baker, fumed as they saw the campaign chairman tell reporters that both candidates did well during the debate.

After stewing for a couple days, Quayle finally erupted, telling reporters that he had reached a "snapping point" with the campaign trying to control him—and no one doubted that he meant Baker. Given the code name "Supervisor" by the Secret Service, Quayle declared that he would no longer be supervised. He had had it with the campaign trying to script his every word and every move, right down to when he should wave at crowds. He had not been getting along with Stuart Spencer, whom Baker had placed on the running mate's plane to watch over him.

"I am my own handler," Quayle declared. "I've done it their way this far and now it's my turn."

After hearing about the candidate's outburst, Baker tracked him down on the road. In no uncertain terms, Baker warned him against rejecting the campaign's advice. It was the only time since Bush and Baker together had called to offer him the vice presidential nomination that Quayle remembered hearing directly from Baker, but the running mate was in no mood to back down.

"I've had all the advice I can take," Quayle complained, "and none of it has been any good."

Baker, trying to contain the damage, put out word that he understood Quayle's frustration, saying the candidate was "justified at being steamed" over anonymous sniping by Bush aides and adding that "if I could find out who it was who criticized him, they would be fired." But few took that seriously. *Newsweek* noted that Baker "threatens to dismiss any Bush aide who trashes Quayle." Then the magazine asked, cheekily, "Will he fire himself?"

THE FINAL DEBATE between Bush and Dukakis on October 13 proved a turning point—and Bush never even had to say anything. In a crowded auditorium at the University of California at Los Angeles, Bernard Shaw, the CNN anchor and lead moderator of the debate, opened right from the start with a question stemming from Bush's attacks on Dukakis for being soft on crime.

"Governor, if Kitty Dukakis were raped and murdered, would you favor an irrevocable death penalty for the killer?" Shaw asked.

It was a shocking question, envisioning the brutal killing of a candidate's wife. Murmurs of disbelief rippled through the press room, where reporters were watching. But Dukakis, who in the days leading up to the debate had been feverish as he battled a virus, gave an answer that conveyed no sense of outrage.

"No, I don't, Bernard," he said. "And I think you know that I've opposed the death penalty during all of my life. I don't see any evidence that it's a deterrent and I think there are better and more effective ways to deal with violent crime." In his typically cool, bloodless manner, Dukakis then went on to give an exposition on the best way to approach drugs and crime.

It was, arguably, a principled response sticking closely to a position Dukakis had long taken, one he was unwilling to modify even if his own family was theoretically involved. But his lifeless rendition made him seem hardly human. This was his wife, after all, that Shaw was talking about. No one needed to tell Baker that Bush had come out the winner of that encounter. The rest of the ninety-minute debate might as well have been called off. By the next day, Dukakis's support in the polls had fallen from 49 percent to 42 percent. The 17-point lead of late summer had turned into a decided Bush advantage.

"Well, this debate's gone so good, I guess we can pull all the negatives," Baker said with a wink as the team celebrated in a nearby hotel afterward. Lee Atwater missed the wink and immediately panicked. Baker calmed him down. "Don't be shakin' your knee," he teased.

Baker had no intention of letting up. The attack ads would continue.

After Dukakis made the mistake of riding in a sixty-eight-ton M1A1 Abrams Main Battle Tank wearing an ill-fitting helmet in the vain hope of reinforcing his national security credibility, the Bush operation pounced. Sig Rogich, a media consultant who had been part of the Tuesday Team that made Reagan's "Morning in America" commercial in 1984, saw news coverage of the event and wrote a script at his home the same night. In short order, he put together an ad using the images to ridicule the diminutive Democrat and portray him as weak on defense.

But Rogich had second thoughts. He began to worry that it might be too cruel, overkill for a campaign that was already well ahead. He called Baker at campaign headquarters to suggest running a more positive ad instead. Baker was having none of it.

"We're all sitting around the table and we're taking a vote," Baker told him, "and you lost."

Rogich should not have been surprised. To Baker, campaigns were not about charity. As he often told Rogich, "Let's not forget, it's about winning."

The ad debuted on October 18 during Game 3 of the World Series and the impact was devastating. Dukakis looked ludicrous, grinning in the tank as if he were a kid on a ride at Disney World, his head all but swallowed by the wide helmet. Dukakis filmed a response, lambasting Bush for his negative barrage. "I'm fed up with it," the governor said. But it was too late. The indelible image of Dukakis in the tank not only stuck with the public, it would become a metaphor for years to come, a cautionary lesson for generations of new candidates about the photo op that backfired. Never would future candidates in either party let themselves pose with something silly on their head. Dukakis in a tank would become a byword for failure, the worst presidential public relations stunt since Calvin Coolidge cavorted in a Native American headdress back in 1927.

The Bush attack ads were so successful that coverage of his campaign's relentless negativity became the primary topic of the race's final days, and Baker took a drubbing for it during an appearance on *Face the Nation* on CBS.

"How much lower will this campaign sink?" Lesley Stahl asked in her introduction to the program. "We'll ask the Bush-Quayle campaign chairman Jim Baker. Is this the meanest, dirtiest campaign ever?"

Stahl had known Baker for years and been one of his regular contacts in the media, not to mention his conspirator in practical jokes on each other. But as soon as the camera turned to Baker, she went right after him.

"I want to show you something," she said, holding up a flyer distributed by the Maryland Republican Party highlighting what it called the "Dukakis-Willie Horton team."

"They suggest that if you vote for Michael Dukakis, Willie Horton is going to come pay you a visit," Stahl said. "Now, come on."

"That is totally out of bounds, totally unauthorized," Baker agreed. "It was not authorized by our campaign."

Baker came prepared to turn the tables. He pulled out another set of flyers, including one with a squirrel portraying Bush as nuts. He quoted Dick Gephardt as saying that "Adolf Hitler would love these people," adding, "Now, *that's* an outrageous statement." The real negativity, he added, began with "the absolute savaging" of Bush at the Democratic convention.

But Stahl did not back off. She cited a furlough ad run by the Bush campaign that featured an announcer saying that Dukakis had let out first-degree murderers even as the words "268 escaped" flashed on the screen. "Now, the words and the sign are very misleading," she said, "because 268 murderers did not escape."

"I don't admit that it's misleading and I don't admit that it's incorrect," Baker replied.

"I'll tell you something," Stahl chided, "it's my business and in my business as a television reporter, if I say something and put some words up on the screen that conflict, that's inaccurate."

BAKER MAY HAVE BEEN defensive, but with a comfortable lead, the Bush team's main fear in the final days of the campaign was appearing to look overconfident. A few weeks out, Bush held a news conference at which he was peppered with questions about what his presidency would look like and whom he would appoint to key positions. "I just cannot let myself get distracted into thinking about that," he insisted. "Nobody in this room believes me. But I am telling you the truth—the whole truth. . . . There are no names or lists."

By Saturday morning, October 22, more than two weeks before Election Day, that was no longer the case and Bush interrupted the last-minute campaign prep to talk to Baker about becoming his secretary of state. Baker had already had some of Washington's most powerful jobs, but this was the one he had long coveted. "I am assuming that Jim said yes," Barbara Bush recorded in her diary. "Ridiculous to talk about jobs when you haven't won, but very necessary."

On the same day he talked with Baker about taking over the State

Department, Bush asked John Sununu to be his White House chief of staff if he won. Sununu, the bulldozer governor of New Hampshire, had arguably saved Bush's candidacy during his state's primary. But he was an acquired taste, an imperial force with none of Baker's finesse or appreciation for the subtleties of the corner West Wing office. "Baker doesn't like it at all," Craig Fuller recalled. As with the Quayle nomination, though, Bush pointedly did not ask Baker's opinion, another act of rebellion against the man he had brought in to save his campaign. Bush's resentment of Baker's reputation was only enhanced by a *Time* magazine cover story in the final weeks of the race featuring Baker and John Sasso, Dukakis's adviser, with the headline, "Battle of the Handlers." Baker hated it too, but for a different reason: it was a reminder that he was not secretary of state yet, that for all his glorified status and glowing reviews, he was still just a staffer, down in the muck with Lee Atwater, slinging negative ads. Years later, he would remember the *Time* cover and wince. "That just cut me to the quick," he said.

Baker made a halting attempt to counter Bush's decision on Sununu, quietly tasking an emissary to reach out to Fuller to implore him to stay in the White House as deputy chief of staff. Fuller rebuffed the suggestion; he had already decided to leave government and, besides, it would do no good for Sununu to have a staff that was not his own, nor would it work if Bush did not want it. Baker later raised the matter with Fuller directly.

"You need to think about this," he said.

"I have," Fuller said. "Jim, it's not what he wants."

Resigned to a decision that he considered a mistake, the Handler from Houston flew home the day before Election Day. On the morning of the vote on November 8, he and Susan went to cast their ballots, then went out for some Mexican food. Baker was too nervous to talk much about the State Department. Instead, he and Susan talked about escaping to the new ranch in Wyoming that they had just managed to buy after years of on-again, off-again looking. Wyoming was where he had gone with Bush at the start of the long, stressful campaign summer and it had been on his mind at the New Orleans convention a few weeks later when he had run into Donald Kendall, the chief executive officer of PepsiCo. Kendall told Baker he was just back from his own ranch in Wyoming. "I'm a jealous wreck," Baker had responded, mentioning how much he wished that he too could find a place there. A couple weeks later, Kendall unexpectedly called back with news of a ranch that had just become available. Baker, mid-campaign, could not go see it, but Susan flew out and fell in love with the remote old homestead called the Silver Creek Ranch. It covered

1,555 acres in the Wind River range of the Rocky Mountains on the other side of Yellowstone from Baker's first Wyoming elk hunt with his father more than four decades earlier. He and Susan would buy it for $625,000 as soon as the campaign was over.

But first they had an election night to get through and, later that evening, as returns began to come in, they joined the Bushes at the home of Charles and Sally Neblett, two longtime friends of both families. The early results were surprisingly worrisome. "We walked into the Nebletts' feeling pretty shaky," Barbara Bush recalled. "All our friends thought we had it in the bag."

Baker, feeling cautious, bet Lee Atwater that Bush would get under 53 percent of the popular vote. Atwater would later pay him off halfway through the evening. Even as the numbers improved later that night, Baker resisted accepting victory. "We need to wait on Michigan," he said at one point. At another, someone ribbed him that he was the last holdout: "NBC, ABC and CBS have called it but Baker's still out."

By the time the evening was over, Bush had won. He would be the nation's forty-first president. In the end, he swept forty states to take 426 electoral votes and mustered 53 percent of the popular vote, becoming the first sitting vice president since Martin Van Buren in 1836 to earn a promotion. Bush's win did not match Reagan's landslide of four years earlier, but it was a smashing comeback for a candidate who had appeared a sure loser as recently as Labor Day.

The next day, Bush announced his first appointment as president-elect, surprising exactly no one by choosing as his secretary of state James Addison Baker III.

Part Four

———

CHAPTER 18

Jigsaw Puzzle

Baker's career as an international diplomat began, as many things in Washington do, at a dinner party. He had never loved the compulsive schmoozing that was so much a part of the capital's life, although he had always seen the utility of it in a city that drew little distinction between working and socializing. In the early 1980s, when he ran Ronald Reagan's White House, he was invited to everything but dreaded the red-carpet glitz that Nancy brought to entertaining, seeing it as an interruption to his endless piles of work. He would sneak out of even the most dazzling State Dinner after the food was served to go back to his office, while the other A-listers were still watching the entertainment.

Still, he made sure to show up when it counted and he and Susan had become regulars at the famous Sunday-night suppers of the hawkish old columnist Joseph Alsop in Georgetown, a bipartisan tradition of the city's ruling class going back decades. When Katharine Graham, the Washington Post Company chairwoman and the city's ruling social power, celebrated her seventieth birthday in 1987 with a black-tie soiree for six hundred, the Bakers were there and he grew friendly enough with Graham to play mixed doubles tennis against her and George Shultz, another of her favorites.

Robert Strauss was one of those whose invitations Baker would accept. Fellow Texans, the two had been friends since their days facing off during the 1976 presidential election, when one was the Republican campaign chief and the other the chairman of the Democratic National Committee. Both subscribed to the school of thinking in Washington that did not let differences in political parties get in the way of either dinner parties or problem solving. Although Strauss held no official title beyond law firm partner at that point, *The New York Times* had dubbed him "the capital's leading wise man" and he was so well connected on both sides of the aisle that Jim Wright, the Democratic House speaker and another Texan, once offered a toast, calling him "a close friend of the next president of the United States—whoever the hell he may be." In fact, just a year earlier, Strauss had tried to bring Wright together with Shultz to settle the great foreign policy feud of 1980s Washington, the years-long debate over Nicaragua and the contras. "I'm terribly partisan," Strauss told *The Times*, "but I think people trust me."

The effort fizzled, but Baker's ascension to Foggy Bottom offered another chance. "I want to get you and Jim Wright together," Strauss told the incoming secretary of state. "I think Wright would like to work with you, he thinks he can work with you, and maybe the two of you can find a way to take Central American policy off the domestic political agenda." Wright had become one of the most vocal opponents of Reagan's contra war, going much further than past speakers by intervening directly in foreign policy. Baker, for his part, had watched as the Reagan administration's fixation on Nicaragua led to a debilitating misjudgment that nearly wrecked an otherwise successful presidency.

On the evening of December 8, 1988, Jim and Susan Baker arrived at Strauss's top-floor Watergate apartment, where they joined Wright and his wife, Betty, as well as Nick Brady and his wife, Kitty. After the main course, with chairs pushed back to savor the expansive view over the Potomac River, the dinner table talk turned to Central America, as it had for years in Washington.

Baker told Wright that the new president was ready to talk. He wanted to take Nicaragua off the table, Baker said, and would not ask Congress for any more military aid for the contras.

Wright brightened up. If so, he replied, then there was a real chance for a bipartisan ending to a dispute that had divided the capital for a decade.

That was just what Baker wanted to hear and he resolved that his first big negotiation as secretary of state would be not with a foreign power but with the Congress of the United States.

The goal was both audacious and unlikely, in that it would require Democrats still furious with Baker for running what they considered the nastiest, most superficial presidential campaign to date to make a deal that would extricate America (and Bush) from a guerrilla war that had caused Republicans nothing but political problems. The conservatives who had long questioned Baker's fidelity to their cause would howl, but he believed that if he did not find a way to end the war in America's backyard, he would never have a chance to achieve bigger things elsewhere. "That was the holy grail of the political left in this country and the political right," Baker said. He would be the statesman who would finally settle it—and allow the country to move on.

ON JANUARY 25, 1989, late in the afternoon on the third full workday of the Bush presidency, the Senate unanimously confirmed Baker as the nation's sixty-first secretary of state. Shortly thereafter, Baker raised his right hand and was sworn in by a White House clerk, with no fanfare or guests. He had a pile of urgent work and big plans, as his opening to Wright signaled. The new president might still call him Jimmy in private moments, but Baker believed that he had finally shed the burden of being merely his best friend's aide. The State Department would give him the platform and the stature. Eight years at the upper levels of the Washington power structure had taught him how to use it.

A natural deal-maker, he had already negotiated tax reform with Democrats on Capitol Hill and currency policy with other world powers. In Baker's Washington, bipartisanship was not a synonym for selling out, it was the way to get things done now that the election was over. He had little in the way of direct foreign policy experience, but he had observed Reagan wage the closing battles of the Cold War. The press, usually favorable, would now be even more explicitly Baker's instrument. So would that forever friendship with Bush, although he would have to carefully tend it. As the bruising campaign they had just been through together showed Baker, Bush could be insecure too. Foreign policy was his first interest and now it would be Baker's turf. Conflict was almost inevitable. The sharp-edged Washington player that Baker had become was nothing if not zealous about guarding his territory. Baker was, as Bush confided to his diary early in the new administration, "very, very sensitive about his prerogatives." Even before either of them was sworn in, coverage of his secretary of state rankled the incoming president. One narrative in the press predicted that Baker would be so powerful in the new administration that he would essentially act as "the alternate president." Bush knew he should ignore it, but he just could not. "Nonsense," he grumbled in his diary even as he made a point of mentioning it.

None of this, of course, stopped Bush from throwing a grand party in the White House for the ceremonial swearing-in of his secretary of state (new Secret Service code name: "Foxtail"), two days after his confirmation. The doubles team from the Houston Country Club had made it big and both Bush and Baker shed their usual preppy reserve for the East

Room celebration, an invitation-only affair presided over by Chief Justice William Rehnquist. Baker's large blended family was present, including all eight children, everyone except his mother, who, unable to travel at age ninety-four, had received a congratulatory phone call from Bush earlier in the day. Baker's youngest daughter, their bonus baby Mary-Bonner, was not yet twelve years old; her godfather was now president. Standing in the back were Baker's loyal aides Dick Darman, now about to become Bush's budget director, Margaret Tutwiler, and Robert Kimmitt. Brent Scowcroft, the elfin former national security adviser to Ford who was returning to the same post for Bush, almost did not get a seat when a guard said he was not on the guest list.

"This is a very special occasion for me," Bush told the audience, "because as you all know, Jim and I have been friends for a long time, going back perhaps more years than either of us would care to admit— long, really, before our public lives began." Baker was savvy, sensitive, and tough, Bush said, and he "will be my principal foreign policy adviser" dealing with "a world that demands new strategies and new solutions." Seeming to forget about the harsh campaign that had just gotten them into the White House, Bush also vowed that he and Baker would "restore bipartisanship to foreign policy," bringing back something that had been lost in the epic battles of the Reagan era. Baker, he concluded, "will be a great secretary of state."

Baker took the microphone next. "As you mentioned, Mr. President, you and I have come a long distance together," he said in his Texas twang. "I hope to continue to merit your confidence. I know I will continue to enjoy our friendship. One other thing—I hope that in foreign policy, we're going to make a better team than we oftentimes did on the tennis courts in Texas." He smiled. It was the sort of teasing comment only a friend could make—and one that for the room and the larger international audience reinforced a message Baker wanted to send, that the two of them were more than just commander in chief and secretary of state, that when he spoke he was speaking for them both. Baker finished with a nod to the hard days that might lie ahead. "It's been my experience for eight years here now in Washington," he said, "that after the swearing in, sooner or later, comes the swearing at."

Baker had long aspired to the State Department, an ambition born of a success so rapid that it was easy to forget how quickly it had all happened. He was fifty-eight years old and only ten years earlier he had been a between-jobs Houston lawyer who had just lost a campaign for the only political office he ever tried to win. It was a mark of his convincing rise that Baker's appointment now was not the least bit controversial. No one mentioned it, but the new secretary of state had never been to Moscow. He did not speak any foreign languages. He had no international relations philosophy. Washington simply expected him to succeed in this, as he had succeeded at every challenge the city had thrown at him. Baker, relentlessly competitive and, by this point, more than a little bit cocky, would surely find a way to win at this too.

It was one of those accidents of history that Bush and Baker would get their chance to lead America on the world stage at such a moment. Both were profoundly cautious men, believers in words like "prudence" and "restraint" at a time when a revolution was actually happening. "The totalitarian era is passing," Bush had said in his inaugural address a few days earlier as he was sworn in as the nation's forty-first president. "A new breeze is blowing." Usually such rhetoric from presidents is overblown. But not this time. The rapprochement with the Soviet Union, unthinkable just a few years earlier, was for real, and old Cold War certainties were unraveling along with it. In nearly four years in the Kremlin, Mikhail Gorbachev had steered America's greatest enemy in a new direction, introducing market reforms, opening up democratic discourse, and making arms control breakthroughs with Reagan. Now, unrest in the outer reaches of Moscow's empire hinted at the possibility of a dramatic transformation of the European order, while the proxy wars of the superpower confrontation in places such as Afghanistan and Angola as well as Nicaragua and El Salvador might also finally be coming to an end.

This was the main event and Baker knew it. Baker had learned at the White House and Treasury Department how to be strategic and disciplined about picking priorities, leaving other matters, even very pressing ones, to the people who worked for him. As he surveyed this "moment rich with promise," in Peggy Noonan's grand phrasing for the Bush inaugural address, Baker had no intention of letting himself get bogged down by the daily crises that could easily consume a secretary of state's time. Baker had little interest in Asia, Africa, or South America, nor did he want to become embroiled in the turmoil in South Africa as its system of racial apartheid unraveled in the face of international protests and sanctions. He especially wanted to stay away from the Middle East and the endless failed quest for peace between Israel and the Arabs. Baker was determined not to get sidetracked on a fool's errand. "Now is *not the time* to come up with a high visibility initiative," a memo prepared for Baker stated about the Middle East. Baker picked up a pen and underlined the phrase "not the time." The end of the Cold War was too big, too all-consuming. He and Bush did not exactly know yet what they would do about it, but of its overriding importance they were sure.

WHEN HE SHOWED up on the seventh floor of the State Department's blocky headquarters in Foggy Bottom, he was determined to clean house. Those who had worked for the Reagan administration would not automatically be staying. "This is *not* a friendly takeover," Baker told associates. Other secretaries had become captive to the building, he felt, and therefore worked at cross-purposes to the presidents they were supposed to serve. Although he did not say so explicitly, this was at least partially what Baker thought about his immediate predecessor and friend from the Reagan administration, George Shultz, who was beloved by the career diplomats even as many of them took issue with Reagan's foreign policy. "I'm going to be the White House's man at the State Department," Baker said again and again, "not the State Department's man at the White House."

Scarred by the turf wars between Shultz at the State Department and Caspar Weinberger at the Pentagon, well aware of how Shultz had often lost out, not only to Weinberger but also to the brash, ideological White House staffers who had gravitated to Reagan's National Security Council, Baker had resolved to stay tight with Bush and his other top advisers, no matter what. "Nothing comes between me and my president" became his mantra and if it was sometimes honored in the breach, it was, at least, a constant reminder to Baker of where his true power derived. Baker well remembered the troubles that had plagued the Reagan national security team. One way to avoid that was to work closely with Brent Scowcroft. Baker had known him since the Ford administration and while their relationship to that point had been "mostly a bantering one," as Scowcroft put it, they shared a certain pragmatic sensibility about international affairs. Baker appointed one of Scowcroft's closest friends, Lawrence Eagleburger, a career diplomat, as deputy secretary of state, giving himself a sounding board about how the national security adviser might view certain issues and effectively ensuring that there would be no secrets between the State Department and the White House. It was a relief to Scowcroft too, who saw Eagleburger "like an arm right into the Baker camp." The two had worked together on Kissinger's National Security Council staff and were "soul mates," as Scowcroft put it.

For his own deputy, Scowcroft picked Robert Gates, a career CIA officer who had risen to deputy director of the agency and was known as a hard-liner on the Soviet Union. But in a nod to Baker, Scowcroft promised that the secretary of state would be the primary foreign policy voice for the administration. Scowcroft said he would do no television interviews and give no public speeches without clearing them first with Baker, a deference that few if any of his predecessors had shown and one that soon became unnecessary because Baker trusted Scowcroft implicitly. Needless to say, that was not the case with all of Bush's men. Baker remained especially suspicious of Dan Quayle. When Bush told Baker right before the inauguration that he was thinking of sending Quayle on an early European visit to meet with foreign leaders, Baker intervened. How about sending Quayle on a tour of South America instead? Bush readily agreed.

On key appointments, especially those that concerned foreign policy, Baker did not hesitate to make his views heard. When John Tower, the former Texas senator who was Bush's initial choice for defense secretary, was rejected by the Senate amid allegations of drinking and groping women, Bush was bombarded with names of possible replacements. He toyed with moving Scowcroft over to the Pentagon, but could not bear to part with his national security adviser. So Baker got behind Scowcroft's idea of turning to their mutual friend, Dick Cheney, who had been rising in the ranks of the House Republican leadership. Now Republican whip, Cheney was poised to become the House minority leader when Representative Robert Michel, a genial moderate from Illinois who had led the caucus for eight years, retired. On a Friday afternoon in March, however, Bush upended those plans. Baker sat with Bush in the residential part of the White House when the new president called to offer Cheney the defense appointment. That night, Baker called Cheney's house in Virginia to make sure he was in. "Dick, damn it, I hope you'll take this job," he said. Cheney was more of a hard-liner than Baker was, especially when it came to the Soviet Union and the contras, but Baker, who had established a tradition of fly-fishing trips with Cheney in the Wyoming backcountry, also considered him a reasonable voice who would be a team player.

The tandem of Baker, Cheney, and Scowcroft in the three most important national security positions would over the next four years guarantee a close collaboration unheard of in modern administrations. From the start, the three decided to have breakfast once a week without staff in Scowcroft's West Wing office, where they could hash over the big issues without becoming ensnared in the politics of their separate institutions. It was a striking change from the Reaganite past when the top national security officials were barely on speaking terms. "We all knew each other," Cheney said. "We all trusted each other."

For the career diplomats at the State Department, however, Baker was already proving an intimidating figure. Staffers were told that he had exacting preferences for the way memos should be formatted, down to the font size and margins. Rumors even ran around the building that he had fired not one but two assistants in prior stops in government because of typos, the sort of mythology that cements a reputation, whether it was true or not. "He was so tightly wound and focused," said Lorne Craner, a legislative aide to the new secretary. No matter how distinguished their careers or urgent their problems, the permanent foreign service staff learned quickly that Baker would rely heavily—at times, almost exclusively—on the small coterie of advisers he brought with him.

Unlike George Shultz, who famously showed up in Foggy Bottom without a single aide of his own, Baker brought his "plug-in unit" with him to the State Department, "Baker's dozen," as some career officials took to calling them, although the real inner circle was not even that big. Robert Kimmitt came as undersecretary of state and Robert Zoellick as Baker's counselor. Janet Mullins moved over from the campaign to serve as legislative liaison. Margaret Tutwiler would come too, of course, although she had to be convinced to take on the very visible role of assistant secretary for public affairs because she was nervous about briefing reporters every day when she was not yet a master of the details and jargon of foreign affairs. She turned down the job four times before giving in. Karen Groomes and Caron Jackson would also make the move with Baker.

Baker and his team "came to the State Department with a certain animus against the career Foreign Service," said David Mack, a Middle East specialist in the department. That was not entirely true; there were some assistant secretaries who would penetrate the circle. But by and large, Baker brought with him the approach that had worked for him at the White House, Treasury Department, and several presidential campaigns. "Jim Baker ran policy cabalistically, with a small group of insiders who were not well connected to the building and who, in fact, attempted to discourage the bubbling up of ideas from the building and who really had no guiding overall strategic sense," said Chas Freeman Jr., who was soon tapped by Bush to be ambassador to Saudi Arabia.

Among the few newcomers to the tight Baker circle was a smart young Soviet specialist named Dennis Ross, who had served on the National Security Council staff under Reagan and then joined the Bush campaign even though he was a Democrat who had once worked on the campaigns of Robert F. Kennedy and George McGovern. After the election, Scowcroft asked Ross to be his deputy national security adviser, but Ross took an offer from Baker instead to be the State Department director of policy planning, the job that the storied Sovietologist George Kennan, architect of containment, had invented for himself in the momentous years when the Cold War was just beginning. In theory, it was a less powerful position than the White House job Ross turned down, but given the new secretary's forceful persona and unique relationship with the incoming president, Ross "felt the action would be with Baker."

THE ACTION WOULD indeed be with Baker, but not right away. Bush came out of the box intent on slowing down and rethinking the nation's foreign policy, especially when it came to the Soviet Union.

Bush first met Mikhail Gorbachev in 1985 at the funeral of his predecessor Konstantin Chernenko and thought the new Soviet leader, up until then a relatively unknown former party boss from Stavropol in southern Russia, was just a slicker sort of apparatchik with "a disarming smile, warm eyes and an engaging way of making an unpleasant point," as he put it in a cable to Reagan. But Bush wanted to maintain good relations. In December 1987, as he was gearing up to run for president, Bush told Gorbachev during a Washington visit not to pay attention to the "empty cannons of rhetoric" he would hear in the upcoming campaign. After the election, in December 1988, Bush joined Reagan for another meeting with Gorbachev on Governors Island in New York.

But while publicly supportive of Reagan, Bush had no plans to simply pick up where the outgoing president left off. He privately believed Reagan had become too accommodating to Gorbachev, as did many Republican hard-liners throughout Reagan's administration. Baker shared Bush's assessment. While he had a lot of respect for Shultz, privately he thought his predecessor had not been a tough enough negotiator and gave up too much to the Soviets. "Don't you think you all went too far?" Baker asked Rozanne Ridgway, an assistant secretary under Shultz and top negotiator for Reagan's summits with Gorbachev. Ridgway would be eased out within a year.

Bush wanted to recalibrate. So instead of action, his first move toward the Soviet Union was to order a strategic policy review that would come to be known as The Pause. It took months, maddening allies and adversaries alike, and ultimately resolving little at all. But Gorbachev was not planning to wait. He used that December 1988 visit to New York to deliver a speech at the United Nations announcing that he would withdraw 500,000 troops from Eastern Europe, a splashy move that caught Reagan and Bush off guard and established once again that the Soviet leader was the driving force in a changing world.

When Bush and Baker met during the transition with Henry Kissinger to talk about the Soviets, the old intriguer first insulted them by implying that they did not have an overarching strategy, then suggested one of his own design: a secret understanding with the Kremlin in which the Soviets would agree not to use force to stop reform movements in Eastern Europe while the West would promise not to take advantage of the situation at the expense of Moscow's security interests. Kissinger called it the "Finlandization" of Eastern Europe, suggesting that the region would be nominally independent but dominated by the Soviets—a concession that, had it gotten out, would have caused the new administration no end of trouble with conservatives who would consider it a sellout. To convey the idea, Kissinger proposed that a back channel be established with the Soviets, clearly seeing himself as the go-between and eager for one more chance to get in on the action. Bush and Baker had little time for that.

But the incoming president did use Kissinger to take a letter to Gorbachev on a forthcoming trip to Moscow, repeating his assurances of goodwill and urging him not to see anything nefarious in The Pause. "Our purpose is to assure a sound and coherent American approach," Bush wrote. "It is in no way an attempt to delay or reverse the positive progress that has marked the past year or two."

Kissinger met with Gorbachev in Moscow on January 17, 1989, three days before Bush's inauguration, and faxed a memo back to Scowcroft summing up the encounter. Gorbachev told Kissinger that changes were afoot in Eastern Europe that no one could stop, but warned that both sides should be careful not to threaten each other's security. When Kissinger was getting up to leave, Gorbachev grew pensive. "I lead a strange country," he told Kissinger. "I am trying to take my people in a direction they do not understand and many do not want to go." His economic reforms had taken longer than he thought. What he needed, he said, was "a long period of peace." That gave Bush room to maneuver, Kissinger thought. "In my view Gorbachev is treading water with perestroika," he wrote in his memo to Scowcroft. "He is looking to foreign policy as a way out. He will pay a reasonable price to that end."

Kissinger again offered himself as a secret conduit when he showed up later that month to personally brief Bush and Baker on his meetings in Moscow. Baker and Kissinger had a complicated relationship, not just because of the tense way they first encountered each other in the 1976 campaign, when Baker, an obscure Ford political appointee, assured Republicans that the controversial secretary of state would not be retained in a new term. Beyond the personal friction, there was a genuine gulf in the experience and self-conception of these two secretaries of state. Kissinger saw himself as a geopolitical strategist and a grand architect of history, a latter-day Metternich shaping the forces that guided the world. Baker, by contrast, gave little thought to the Treaty of Westphalia or the historical context of great-power competition. He was no professor. He would seek to cut diplomatic deals as a corporate lawyer would. He was a problem solver, animated by the challenge of finding ways to get things done. "For Baker, the world was like a giant jigsaw puzzle, unassembled on the living room floor," said Aaron David Miller, who worked on Middle East issues for the new secretary.

Baker and Kissinger might both be considered realists and both were perfectly comfortable negotiating with the nation's enemies and making concessions to get a better deal. But Kissinger had a hard time seeing Baker as a worthy successor. To him, Baker was still a fixer, not a statesman. "He has a less complicated approach to international order," Kissinger would say archly of Baker in years to come. The sense of competition was palpable between the two men, who would end up as the two most important secretaries of state of the last half century.

IF HE WAS GOING to fix something, Baker had determined that it would be the futile war in Nicaragua. The conflict had ground on for years without a clear victory. A preliminary peace accord had halted much of the fighting but failed to advance a permanent resolution. Baker's dinner conversation with Jim Wright that night at Robert Strauss's apartment had convinced him that he could make the issue finally go away once and for all with the right kind of bipartisan deal. "He knew the time was right to come in and do this in the afterglow of having won the election," said Janet Mullins.

To help make it happen, Baker decided to hire a point person from outside of his party altogether, asking Bernard Aronson to become his assistant secretary of state for inter-American affairs. Aronson was a little stunned. A proud Democrat who had served as policy director for the Democratic National Committee, he hailed from a family with roots in the civil rights movement and he got into politics himself through trade unions. But Aronson also supported the contras and thought theirs was a worthy cause. He was friendly with congressional Republicans such as John McCain and Henry Hyde and, at one point, even wrote a speech on the subject for Reagan.

For Baker, hiring a Democrat, albeit one philosophically in tune with himself, was a clever gambit. Dan Quayle was not too pleased and neither was Senator Jesse Helms, the crotchety conservative Republican from North Carolina who served on the Senate Foreign Relations Committee, but Baker got Aronson confirmed nonetheless. The only way to accomplish what he wanted, Baker calculated, was to forge a consensus with lawmakers, and that meant Democrats. "Work w/Congress," he wrote on notes for the administration's first cabinet meeting. He underlined it, twice.

Baker knew he would never get Democrats to agree to any more military aid but he and Bush could not let the contras languish in the field either and humanitarian aid was due to expire on March 31. "They couldn't just walk away because of the politics and the geopolitics," said Aronson. "And yet they didn't want to refight the Central American wars starting out their presidency." If Baker could get lawmakers to approve funds for food, clothing, and shelter just for a year, that would tide over the fighters until elections scheduled for February 1990. The administration would commit to respecting the results of the vote as long as it was deemed free and fair. Baker knew that might mean accepting the Moscow-backed Sandinistas in power since they were likely to win, but he reckoned that was better than keeping up a flailing war.

He met with Republican leaders on Capitol Hill to sell the idea. To make it work, though, Baker focused most of his energy on Democrats whose buy-in was crucial. Part of the strategy was setting himself up as a reasonable interlocutor, holding off the conservative flank of his own party. "It has now turned into a negotiation between me and the Democrats in the House and Senate," he wrote in talking points in preparation for a call with Senator George Mitchell of Maine, the Democratic majority leader. "My own party is excluded from that process and I am beginning to catch hell for that. Jesse Helms wants to introduce a military aid package right now and I am trying to hold them off."

No Democrat in Congress had been more outspoken in opposition to the contras—and more of a thorn in the side of the Reagan administration—than Jim Wright. For years, the speaker had inveighed against the American-sponsored war and inserted himself into negotiations in the region, much to the consternation of the Reagan White House. But he too seemed ready to move on. Wright told that to Bush himself as well as to Baker; over steak and salad at an early lunch in his congressional office with the incoming president, Bush had asked him to work with Baker on a deal and Wright agreed. In early March, Baker went to see Wright on Capitol Hill.

"We want to wind this thing down," Baker told him. "We're willing to substitute negotiations for military action. But the president is getting some flak from the right wing. They're already accusing him of abandoning the contras. That's the one thing he promised in the campaign never to do."

Wright was struck that Baker did not use the favored Reagan-era term "freedom fighters" to describe the contras. For Baker, the contra cause was not some article of religious faith. He was willing to cut deals.

For eleven days in a row, Baker and Aronson shuttled back and forth between Republicans and Democrats. "This was to be the pattern of his diplomacy during the next few weeks," Wright later wrote. "He would meet with each faction privately, hear its complaints, weigh its demands. Then he would go to the other side and present the opposition's wish as its 'bottom line.' Baker would tell Democrats how intractable Republicans were being. I had no doubt he was telling them how unreasonably we were behaving." With so much at stake, Baker sweated the details. He personally called the president of Honduras to pin down an extension on the amount of time exiled contra fighters could remain in camps in his country, then haggled with Wright over which Democrats to invite to a meeting. When he brought a detailed, two-page single-spaced proposal stamped "SECRET" across the top to a session with Democratic leaders, Baker personally collected every copy except the one he left with Wright.

All the talking, all the horse-trading came down to sniffing out what the many players needed to come to terms, a process that was Baker at his strongest. He was at heart a canny pol who knew Congress well, knew who could deliver, knew how to play them off each other just enough to get them to give a little, knew he needed to give enough himself so that everyone could come out of the negotiation feeling they had won. Baker had a talent for connection. He could be whatever he needed to be at the moment it was necessary. The young man who slid back and forth from Texas to Princeton, from the Ivy Club in the spring to the wildcatter's rig in the summer, now applied the same skills on Capitol Hill.

Lorne Craner, the legislative aide, recalled Baker during the contra talks moving from office to office, conservative to liberal and back again. For Craner, it was a master class in deal-making. One day, he accompanied Baker to meet with Jesse Helms and other hard-line Republicans, watching the secretary of state softening up the North Carolina senator by talking about duck hunting. When that ended, Baker went next door to meet with Senator Chris Dodd, the Connecticut Democrat who was outspoken on Central America, and the two bonded over opera. It worked in part because it was genuine. "Baker would tell a dirty joke or talk about hunting or ask John Dingell if he'd been out shooting birds. That was how he related to these guys," Janet Mullins remembered, referring to an old bull Democratic congressman. "When he wanted something and was up against somebody who didn't want to give him what he wanted, he'd bring 'em in and give them that squinty-eyed look and talk pretty straight with people. And he was always more briefed than anybody else, so you weren't going to outwit him."

Baker's smooth charm masked his driving ambition. There was always an agenda, sometimes hidden. "He has a compelling presence," Maureen Dowd and Thomas Friedman wrote in *The New York Times Magazine*, "but he is such a fox that you feel the impulse to check your wallet when you leave his office." Yet Baker believed there were rarely permanent enemies. There was nowhere he would not go if he thought he could make progress. As he sought bipartisan support for a resolution of the Nicaragua war, another Democrat he wanted to enlist was Jimmy Carter. Never mind that Baker had worked on two campaigns against Carter—Ford's in 1976 and Reagan's in 1980—he knew that Carter had taken a strong interest in Central America and had a lot of friends there on the other side of the ideological divide. If he could collaborate with Carter, it would defuse a lot of the potential opposition, both in Washington and in the region.

Baker made a point of flying to Atlanta shortly after Bush's election for a public appearance at the Carter Center and sat down privately with the former president. Ostracized over the eight years of Reagan's tenure, Carter was happy to finally be consulted again, given the due he felt a former president deserved. "I'm one of the few Republicans who has a high regard for Carter," Baker would say later. It helped that, like Wright, they shared a friendship with Robert Strauss. And Carter knew that Baker carried weight that his predecessors did not, thanks to his friendship with Bush. "They were probably as close together as any president and secretary of state that I remember with the possible exception of Nixon and Kissinger," Carter said. "I knew he spoke for President Bush when he came down to Georgia."

On Capitol Hill, the Democrats eventually agreed to go along with Baker's plan, authorizing $4.5 million a month in humanitarian aid to the contras until the following February. But Representative Dave Obey of

Wisconsin, who chaired a key appropriations subcommittee, insisted that the humanitarian aid be authorized for only part of the year, so that Congress could review what was happening on the ground. Baker agreed to stop aid at the end of November if the top four congressional leaders did not send letters approving its continuation, in effect handing lawmakers a veto if they chose to use it. "Baker knew we had a losing hand and he was very open to reshuffling the cards and trying to both defuse the bitterness so that he could start his tenure, and the president's tenure, with a good relationship with the Democratic Congress," Aronson said. "It was a chance to live to fight another day, but on very different terms."

Bush signed the agreement on March 24 in the Cabinet Room of the White House with Baker and legislative leaders from both parties by his side, a far cry from the Reagan days when Democrats wanted nothing to do with his Central American adventures. "Today, for the first time in many years, the president and Congress, the Democratic and Republican leadership in the House and Senate, are speaking with one voice about Central America," Bush said.

Baker later went to the White House briefing room, where he acknowledged that he was cleaning up the mess left by his former administration. "We all have to admit that the policy basically failed to some extent because we were not united," he told reporters. "We had an executive branch going in one direction and a legislative branch going in another."

"Does it mean an end to the war?" he added. "Let's hope so."

Not everyone in the administration was happy with Baker. Although he had purged many of the Reagan true believers at the State Department, Dan Quayle and other conservatives thought the secretary of state was selling out the contras. Acutely aware of the pockets of opposition, Baker had negotiated the deal himself and while keeping in touch with Bush and Scowcroft, he did not feel the need to shop it around to other players.

As a result, C. Boyden Gray, the White House counsel, was miffed not to have a chance to review the agreement, as he normally would with nearly any other deal. He spoke out when he received a call while on vacation in Florida from Robert Pear, a *New York Times* reporter. The agreement, he told Pear, could have constitutional issues if it effectively gave a single house of Congress veto power over actions of the executive branch. Baker's position was that it presented no such problems because it was a political "gentleman's agreement," not binding legislation.

Caught off guard by the reporter's call, Gray did not think through how his comments would be received. By the time the next day's *Times* arrived with the front-page headline "Unease Is Voiced on Contra Accord," Gray knew he was in trouble. "Within minutes," Gray remembered, "Bush called me and said we have a very unhappy secretary of state who's about to go on *Meet the Press* and this is going to mess up what he was trying to say or what he wanted to say. It's just awful. He said come in and talk, we've got to figure out what happened."

Baker was indeed a very unhappy secretary of state. Robert Zoellick called Margaret Tutwiler to let her know about the story and she reached Baker in Houston. "Baker was absolutely livid," Bernard Aronson remembered. Baker was already upset at Gray over the White House counsel's insistence a few weeks earlier that the secretary sell some bank stock that could pose ethical questions. In fact, he had been so mad about it he had actually gone to the Oval Office to tell Bush to his face that he did not think the new president's chief lawyer was "up to the job." Now Gray was inserting himself into Baker's policy lane too. "This was the first foreign policy achievement of our administration and the White House counsel is saying it might not be," Baker said. "That was because we didn't bring him into the loop—and had we brought him into the loop, we may never have gotten the deal."

Gray called Baker to apologize and got an earful. "He was mad," Gray said. "He was very mad. He has this Southern graciousness so he did accept my apology, but you could tell it was not a happy acceptance."

In public, Baker tried to restrain his pique, but he held firm on the larger point, going on television that Sunday as planned to reinforce it. "Basically, it's a restoration of presidential power and not any diminution of it," he said on ABC's *This Week*. In private, the feud went on for days. By Tuesday, Bush himself had to intervene, calling first Gray and then Baker to urge them to settle their differences.

Baker's deal, meanwhile, stuck. The wars in Central America, which had so dominated Reagan's foreign policy, disappeared from the front pages.

CHAPTER 19

Fly-Fishing with Shevy

I guess we bombed out there today, didn't we?"
It was early March 1989 and the new secretary of state had just finished his debut speech in Vienna at the opening session of a key round of negotiations over how many conventional military forces the Cold War rivals would keep in Europe now that the conflict was winding down.

Counterparts from dozens of countries around Europe were present, but with the administration's foreign policy toward the Soviet Union still under review, Baker did not really have much new to offer. He felt the room go flat. The Pause was not playing well. Once again, the Soviets were seen as driving the discussion.

Dennis Ross tried to reassure the secretary that he had not bombed. "Not really," he said. "If you look at the substance of what's happening, the Soviets are accepting our position."

"I'm talking about the *politics* of it all," Baker replied. He had just come off the campaign trail. He knew when he had lost a crowd. "Look who's getting the big cheers. Then look at who's getting the big yawns."

An accord with Congress was one thing—Baker was a seasoned master at that—but now he was playing on a much bigger stage as the chief diplomat of the United States at a time when the Soviet Union was roiling with change. Baker had come to Vienna less because of the conventional forces talks than for a first chance to sit down for an extended meeting with his counterpart from Moscow, the man who would be his partner in ending the Cold War.

Eduard Shevardnadze, the Soviet foreign minister, was hardly the archetypal Moscow diplomat. Shorter, stockier, and two years older than Baker, with a winning smile and a head of flowing white hair, Shevardnadze cut a far different figure than his longtime predecessor, the dour and imposing Andrei Gromyko, nicknamed "Mr. Nyet" for his gruff approach to the West. Shevardnadze's real distinction was that he was a provincial upstart with no prior international experience when Gorbachev installed him at the Foreign Ministry. The son of a teacher, Shevardnadze grew up in Soviet Georgia, working his way up the Communist apparatus, becoming head of the region's interior ministry and then the local party's first secretary before being plucked to join the Central Committee in Moscow and later the Politburo. He and Gorbachev had been friends since the 1950s, secretly bonding over their disdain for the creaking Soviet system. "Everything is rotten," Shevardnadze had once confided to the future general secretary during a walk at a Black Sea resort.

If anything, it would soon turn out that Shevardnadze was even more committed to breaking up the old system than Gorbachev, sympathetic to the nationalist aspirations of his fellow Georgians and scarred by the Stalinist repressions that had claimed his wife's father, executed as an "enemy of the people," and also swept up his cousin, a famous artist. At the time, Shevardnadze's true leanings were not yet entirely clear to the Americans, although intelligence analysts had correctly pegged him as a key Gorbachev ally on the Politburo and a fellow believer in what Russians called the "new thinking." Just as importantly, in his first few years at the Foreign Ministry, Shevardnadze had impressed his Reagan counterparts as serious and reliable; George Shultz assured Baker that he could do business with Shevardnadze. Bush called in from Camp David before the meeting in Vienna too, "giving Jimmy a few suggestions based on my own personal contacts with Gorbachev that will show Shevardnadze how close Jim and I are," he told his diary. This might be a new team, Bush wanted Baker to tell the Soviets, but it is "a team that knows what it's doing."

It did not necessarily seem that way. In Vienna, Shevardnadze proposed dramatic reductions in conventional troops in Europe by both NATO and the Warsaw Pact, leaving Baker, held hostage to The Pause, with nothing concrete to counter. The absence of a proposal left the Soviets worried and Shevardnadze feared that Baker was taking a harder line than Shultz had. The Soviet translator, Pavel Palazchenko, thought Baker's speech was laying out what "sounds like an imperious demand" on the Soviets for further concessions.

Baker and Shevardnadze met the next day in the same American ambassador's residence where John Kennedy was by his own reckoning "savaged" by Nikita Khrushchev during their first encounter in 1961. The Baker-Shevardnadze meeting was far more cordial, with the one-on-one part of the session in the ambassador's study lasting an hour and seven minutes rather than the twenty minutes allotted. The Soviets were struck that the new secretary of state was willing to get more into the details of arms control than Shultz had been, but also noticed that he needed to rely on his briefing book and aides more than his predecessor. Either way, they were frustrated by Baker's larger message that Bush was not yet ready to engage. "What were they waiting for?" Gorbachev asked later. "Some of the signals we were receiving were quite alarming." Hard-liners in Moscow thought The Pause was "evidence that Washington was plotting against the Soviet Union, or at least had no intention of improving relations."

To prepare for his first session with Baker, Shevardnadze had his government produce a dossier on the new secretary of state. It concluded that Baker was a "pragmatist," not a "zoological anti-Communist," a dealmaker with whom the Soviets could work. But when they met, Shevardnadze came away with a mixed impression of Baker. He seemed like a "cold fellow," he told Gorbachev, with none of the humanity that he had found in Shultz. For his part, Baker had immediately liked Shevardnadze but was struck by the stress that Soviet reformers were under to deliver. "Can't help but get impression of the pressure Shevardnadze and Gorbachev feel to make perestroika succeed quickly," Baker wrote in six pages of typed notes from the trip. "They're leaders in a great hurry, possessing a sense of urgency, but lacking a plan."

Baker returned to Washington looking for a plan too. The Pause was not wearing well at home, and Baker hated being assailed for what the conservative *National Review* magazine called his "decidedly listless debut" on the international stage. The strategic reviews that the new president had ordered were disappointing, just "mush," as Baker put it, with the bureaucracy sending up warmed-over versions of past ideas. Aides came to call the proposals they were getting the "status quo plus" option and thought there was little plus about it. But the career diplomats were growing as impatient as the Soviets. Jack Matlock, the ambassador to Moscow, bitterly told colleagues that the marching orders from Washington amounted to: "Don't just do something, *stand there!*"

Bush was increasingly ready to pick a course, but there was still no consensus within his inner circle about Gorbachev and what he was really up to. Baker was the most optimistic that the Soviet reform effort was real. Dick Cheney, Robert Gates, Dan Quayle, and Brent Scowcroft remained skeptical. At a meeting on March 30, Bush told his team that Gorbachev had eroded American leadership in Europe and that it was time to seize the initiative again. With the president's prearranged approval, Scowcroft then proposed that the United States and the Soviet Union set a goal of withdrawing all of their ground troops from Europe by the turn of the century. "Cheney looked at Scowcroft as if he'd lost his mind," Gates remembered. Cheney countered by suggesting that they push Gorbachev to release more information about the Soviet military, an idea that hardly satisfied Bush's grand ambition. Baker, always looking for a deal, tried coming in somewhere in the middle, proposing that both sides get rid of all of their tanks in Europe. But Scowcroft thought that missed the point—he wanted to get rid of troops because that would take the Soviet boot off Eastern Europe. Bush ended the meeting dissatisfied. "If we don't regain leadership, things are going to fall apart," he warned.

As the Bush team dithered, events were barreling ahead. In April, Poland legalized the Solidarity labor movement that had challenged the Soviet-backed regime and set elections in which the opposition could compete, ending the Communist Party's forty-five-year monopoly on power. Eastern Europe was not waiting for The Pause. Bush decided to deliver a speech in Hamtramck, Michigan, home to many Polish Americans, promising his support. But the tangible offerings were meager and unimpressive—tariff relief, possible debt rescheduling, modest new loans. Even these ideas provoked a debate. Nick Brady, the onetime Bush campaign lieutenant who had succeeded Baker as treasury secretary, resisted financial aid, arguing that it should be given only for economic reform, not political changes. Baker disagreed.

The Bush team was an unusually collaborative group, especially compared with its predecessors. But that did not stop Baker from pushing back when he thought other cabinet officials wandered too far into his diplomatic lane. In late April, Cheney went on CNN and expressed doubts about Gorbachev's capacity. "If I had to guess today, I would guess that he would ultimately fail," Cheney told Robert Novak and Rowland Evans on their talk show. "That is to say that he will not be able to reform the Soviet economy to turn it into an efficient, modern society. And when that happens, he's likely to be replaced by somebody who will be far more hostile than he's been in terms of his attitude towards the West."

When Baker heard about the interview, he erupted. That was not the message he wanted to send—Cheney made it sound as if Bush had no faith in Gorbachev's staying power. Aggravated, Baker called Cheney.

"Cheney, you're off the reservation," the defense secretary remembered Baker telling him.

Cheney offered a mea culpa. "I got it," he said. "Won't happen again."

But Baker was not done. He wanted to make sure Cheney's view would not represent the administration's position. He called Bush as well as Scowcroft and told them that the White House should distance itself from Cheney's remarks.

"Dump on Dick with all possible alacrity," Baker told Scowcroft.

The White House did just that. At his daily briefing, Marlin Fitzwater, the White House press secretary, dismissed Cheney's comments as merely "his personal observations." In a speech later the same day, Bush, without mentioning Cheney by name, noted that he had told Gorbachev that "we wanted to see perestroika succeed in the Soviet Union."

In case anyone missed the point, Baker piled on a few days later in a speech of his own. "The president has said and I have said that we have absolutely no wish to see perestroika fail," he said. "To the contrary, we would very much like it to succeed." He added that they had been "so encouraged by the words and the concepts of what General Secretary Gorbachev refers to as the 'new thinking.' And in a number of places, I think it's fair to say that words have turned into realities."

ON MAY 10, 1989, Baker's government Boeing 707 touched down outside Moscow in the clearing of a birch forest just outside the capital at Vnukovo-2, the strictly off-limits airport reserved for Communist Party leaders and visiting foreign dignitaries. It was Baker's first big trip as secretary of state and his first time in the Soviet Union. The plane had been on historic missions before, even if Baker had not—the legendary Air Force jetliner with the blue-and-white United States of America paint job had ferried Henry Kissinger to Paris for secret talks with the North Vietnamese and taken three former American presidents to the 1981 funeral of Egypt's assassinated leader Anwar Sadat.

Its first assignment, when it rolled off the line back in 1962, was to serve as Air Force One for John Kennedy. It took the young president to Berlin in 1963 and, later that year, to Dallas. His body was brought back to Washington on board that terrible November day and it was on the plane that Lyndon Johnson took the oath of office. The plane was handed over to secretaries of state in the 1970s and Baker would make constant use of it over the next few years, treating the small stateroom up front as an airborne office when it was not a bedroom, with faxes flying back and forth to Washington and secure voice communications that usually worked. The plane was ancient by then, rattling and shaking every time it took off. Once, over Guam, the stabilizer went out, and "we damn near tanked," Baker remembered, plunging to just a few hundred feet over the water before the Air Force pilots got the plane under control again.

While Baker had written his junior thesis on Russia at Princeton, he had never before visited Moscow and the Russian capital he landed in that spring day was a city unlike anything the secretary of state had encountered before. May was just about the best time to visit Moscow, when temperatures were moderate and the sun got up early and stayed up late. Yet Baker was stunned to see how drab and shabby the capital of the world's other nuclear superpower really was. A country with enough military power to wipe out half the planet looked like a run-down vestige of a nineteenth-century power, with peeling paint and empty roads. He was struck that at night the few drivers on the streets only flipped on their headlights at busy intersections and, when it rained, pulled over to reattach windshield wipers that were otherwise kept hidden away lest they be stolen. It reminded Baker of a trip to Mexico City when he was a child. As treasury secretary, he had dealt with a number of developing countries, but when a reporter asked him if Moscow resembled those, Baker said no—this was worse.

Baker had come to test Gorbachev to see if he was for real. Just a few days before Baker's departure from Washington, the Soviet leader had sent a secret letter that, among other things, mentioned almost offhandedly that Moscow had cut off arms shipments to the Sandinistas in Nicaragua and in fact had not delivered any weapons to them since 1988. None of America's intelligence agencies had detected an arms cutoff, but if it were true, it would represent an important step as Baker sought to defuse the regional conflict.

Baker arrived at the Kremlin the day after landing in Moscow and was ushered through a series of reception rooms to St. Catherine Hall. In contrast to the grimy streets, he and his entourage noticed the massive, gold-leafed doors and tsarist splendor left intact by the Communist bosses. The two delegations sat at a long blond-wood table. In addition to Gorbachev and Shevardnadze, the Soviet side included Marshal Sergei Akhromeyev, chief of the General Staff, in full-dress uniform. (Baker aides counted twelve rows of ribbons on his chest.)

Gorbachev opened with a forty-five-minute disquisition on perestroika. Baker's visit had come right in the middle of an extraordinary experiment in democracy unleashed by Gorbachev's reforms. A new party congress had just been chosen in a partially competitive election across the Soviet Union, a landmark first, and later that month the new legislature, including Gorbachev rivals such as Boris Yeltsin, the renegade Moscow party boss, and Andrei Sakharov, the Nobel Prize–winning physicist turned dissident, would convene in Moscow. The Communist Party, much to the dismay of some of the hard-liners sitting around the table with Gorbachev and Baker that day, was starting to surrender its monopoly on power. "You have to stay the course," Baker told Gorbachev, pointing out that that was Reagan's campaign slogan in 1984. They took a lot of criticism for it, he noted, but they won.

Still, Gorbachev was on edge. At such a delicate political moment inside the Soviet Union, he needed to prove that his opening to the West was yielding results, results that Bush had not yet delivered. Gorbachev was well briefed on what was happening in Washington. He made a point of mentioning Cheney's televised comments and took note of the fact that Baker had brought with him Robert Gates, suggesting that the deputy national security adviser was the head of a secret cell within the American government intent on discrediting perestroika. Baker assured Gorbachev that Cheney's remarks did not reflect American policy and defended Gates by saying that everyone in the American government wanted perestroika to succeed. It was not entirely true, as Baker well knew—in fact, Gates was both influential and deeply skeptical of Gorbachev, "the Eeyore of Sovietology," as David Ignatius wrote that month in *The Washington Post*, "someone capable of finding a dark lining in even the brightest cloud." For years, Gates and his colleagues at the CIA had taken the position that Gorbachev's reforms would fail and that the United States should remain extremely cautious in dealing with him. Gates saw no reason to change his mind now. Those views were well known and many believed that Gates was, as Ignatius put it, the "main architect of the Bush administration's cautious, sensible and utterly uninspiring response to Gorbachev."

Gorbachev could not afford to wait for Baker and sprung a surprise on him during the Moscow visit, publicly announcing that he would unilaterally withdraw five hundred short-range nuclear weapons from Europe. The Americans were not impressed on the merits—their intelligence said that would still leave the Soviets with ten times as many as the United States. What they did not realize was that the Soviets actually had far fewer such weapons than American intelligence agencies believed, making the cut a much greater share than it seemed at the time. Even more important than the numbers, as a matter of political symbolism, Gorbachev had once again gotten the jump on them.

The reviews of Baker's visit were not glowing. "Baker is one of the foxiest of inside operators dealing with Congress and in American politics," wrote Robert Novak, who accompanied the secretary on the trip. "But he is the new boy in the global high-stakes game, and Gorbachev left him sprawled in the dust." Baker understood that he had been embarrassed. On the flight home, he "invented reasons to come back to the press area of his plane three times," according to Don Oberdorfer of *The Washington Post*, talking off the record in hopes at least of swaying his own department's press corps. He left a clear impression that he did not intend to let Gorbachev upstage him again.

Instead, it was Cheney who almost did so. As Baker made his way back to Washington, Bush was scheduled to give three commencement addresses over the course of two weeks to discuss his emerging approach to the Soviet Union, at Texas A&M University, Boston University, and the Coast Guard Academy. The day before Bush was to deliver the first of them, however, Cheney was planning to give his own speech, reflecting his distinctly darker view, right after Baker had insisted to Gorbachev that Cheney did not speak for the administration. "We hope the Soviet changes are sincere and permanent," the draft of Cheney's speech read. But "it would be dangerous—extremely dangerous—to believe we should abandon a policy that works, just because we have some reason to hope." In fact, that was just what Bush was about to do—favor hope over long-standing policy. Getting word of the speech, the White House ordered Cheney not to give it, the second time in a month he had to be reined in.

Bush proceeded with his own addresses, which attracted only modest attention given the paucity of concrete initiatives in them. During one of the speeches, he resurrected Dwight Eisenhower's never-approved idea of an "open skies" agreement allowing the superpowers to fly reconnaissance flights over each other's territory to reduce suspicion of arms buildups, but while that may have been momentous in the 1950s, it was less meaningful in the age of spy satellites. Still, Bush offered a telling phrase coined by his Soviet adviser, a young Ph.D. named Condoleezza Rice, to describe where he was headed—"beyond containment," meaning the United States was finished with George Kennan's signature approach to the Cold War and now intended to engage the Soviet Union on another level. "Containment worked," Bush said at College Station, Texas. But it was time to move on. "We seek the integration of the Soviet Union into the community of nations," he said, adding: "Ultimately, our objective is to welcome the Soviet Union back into the world order."

Yet his administration kept speaking with multiple voices. While Cheney had been shut down, just four days after Bush's "beyond containment" speech Marlin Fitzwater referred to Gorbachev from the White House briefing room podium as a "drugstore cowboy," selling arms control proposals that did not actually add up to that much. A few days after that, Dan Quayle defended Fitzwater and echoed the assessment, calling Gorbachev "a bit of a phony." Baker stewed over the disconnect.

Bush was tired of being outplayed by Gorbachev and sidelined by the bureaucratic infighters of his own team. He summoned advisers to his family's oceanfront estate in Kennebunkport, Maine, on May 19 to explore options for getting out in front of the Soviet leader. Adopting an idea from Baker, Bush advanced a proposal to slash American forces in Europe by 25 percent, which would involve withdrawing 75,000 of the more than 300,000 troops stationed on the continent. Under his plan, the Soviets would pull down to the same bottom-line number, which would be a more radical reduction for them because they far outnumbered the Americans in the theater. Still, Cheney and Admiral William Crowe, chairman of the Joint Chiefs of Staff, reacted with alarm, arguing that that was drawing down too much. Crowe "fought virtually every proposal tooth and nail," Baker recalled. Cheney's point was that Gorbachev was moving in their direction already, so they should not make concessions to get what he would probably give them anyway.

Frustrated, Bush snapped that he wanted to be bold. History was watching and he did not want to be on the wrong side. "Don't keep telling me why it *can't* be done," he demanded. "Tell me how it *can* be done."

Eventually, the plan was cut by more than half, to a proposed 10 percent reduction in United States forces in Europe, or 30,000 troops. If the Soviets were to come down to the same level, by contrast, they would have to pull out 325,000. Bush's proposal also called for moving up the deadline for withdrawal by five years to 1992.

That was intended to help make it easier for Baker to smooth over a rift that had developed within NATO over short-range nuclear weapons. The Intermediate-Range Nuclear Forces Treaty, or INF, signed by Reagan and Gorbachev in 1987, had eliminated a whole class of weapons, but small, tactical nuclear bombs that could be delivered at a range of hundreds of miles and wipe out tens of thousands of people were not covered. The United States and Britain had been advocating the modernization of these weapons, while German leaders were opposed, recognizing that if any of them were ever used, it would be on their territory. "The shorter the missile, the deader the Germans," became their mantra. But if conventional forces were cut dramatically, it would reduce the need for such weapons, which were intended mainly to counter the overwhelming Soviet advantage in ground troops in Europe.

Baker flew to Brussels in advance of the NATO summit to sell the wary allies on the initiative. Baker sat down with the other foreign ministers at 5 p.m. on May 28 for what would prove to be a marathon negotiation. The British, acting on the views of Prime Minister Margaret Thatcher, were still pressing for modernization of the tactical nuclear weapons, while the Germans were resisting. The group canceled a dinner planned at a nearby castle and instead brought in sandwiches and cookies while they kept haggling.

At some point, Robert Zoellick wearied of the British intransigence and told Baker they did not have to put up with it. But Baker said the time was not yet right. "Sometime very late tonight or tomorrow morning, my friend George Bush is going to have to make a decision—who is running this alliance, him or Margaret Thatcher?" Baker told him. "I watched Margaret Thatcher wrap Ronald Reagan around her little finger. And when the moment comes, I want to make it as easy as possible for my friend to do the right thing."

Baker had no intention of caving to the British demands; his patience was aimed at making sure that Bush could tell Thatcher that his secretary of state had stuck by the British every step of the way and they had gotten what they could so it was time to move on. Zoellick was struck by Baker's three-dimensional chess. "I thought, 'Holy shit, I'm working at this level; he's playing about six steps ahead.'"

In the end, Bush never had to make the alpha move with Thatcher because Baker, consulting with him by telephone throughout the long night, got the British to cave first. They settled for a face-saving announcement about the troop cuts, and by 12:50 a.m. Baker signed off on the final language as long as the word "partial" was used before "reductions"—and that "partial" be underlined. That shattered the deadlock and the meeting finally broke up at 1:04 a.m. Baker, feeling pumped up at what amounted to his first overseas deal as secretary of state, returned to his hotel to drink a celebratory beer with his team.

That set the stage for Bush's arrival in Brussels for the meeting with other NATO leaders. His announcement of the proposed troop cuts drew rave reviews and finally put the Americans back into a leadership role. In a speech after the summit in the medieval West German city of Mainz on the Rhine River, Bush articulated a vision of a new order without an Iron Curtain, of a Soviet sphere integrated into the rest of the world and not isolated from it. "Let Europe be whole and free," he declared, a phrase that would come to define success for American policy for more than a quarter century to come. The Pause was finally over.

ON THE FIRST WEEKEND of June, Baker looked forward to a rare opportunity to relax after the trips to Moscow and Brussels. With the president at Kennebunkport, Baker figured he could escape for a few hours, so he called his son Jamie to propose a round of golf.

"Grab your sticks and come over right now," Baker said.

For a moment, Jamie did not reply. "I don't think you are going to be playing any golf today," he said finally. "I'm sitting here watching tanks roll through Tiananmen Square on CNN."

"You're kidding me," Baker said.

At that moment, the other phone in the house rang, the secure line connected to the State Department's operations center. When Baker picked up, he was told that protests in Beijing had turned violent and the Chinese military was firing into the crowds. There were heavy casualties and great uncertainty.

Golf was definitely out. And so was the equilibrium that Baker and the rest of the Bush administration had sought in the relationship with China since taking office barely four months earlier. The bloody crackdown on June 4 in Beijing's monumental Tiananmen Square would present Baker and Bush with their first real foreign policy crisis, one that would test the lines between moral values and the national interest.

Pressure had been building for weeks as nearly a million Chinese flooded into the center of Beijing demanding change. With the movement for democracy sweeping Communist-dominated Eastern Europe, younger Chinese responded by challenging their own repressive government, pushing for the resignation of Communist Party officials and embracing Western values. Occupying Tiananmen Square, they erected a thirty-three-foot-tall statue made of foam, papier-mâché, plaster, and metal framing that they called the Goddess of Democracy. That it bore a striking resemblance to the Statue of Liberty hardly went unnoticed in Washington.

Viewing the protesters as an existential threat to their grip on power, China's Communist Party leaders chose a different course than Gorbachev in Moscow. Rather than reforms, they opted for a brutal crackdown. When the troops were mobilized that June weekend, they opened fire indiscriminately, killing hundreds and perhaps thousands of protesters. Pictures of the slaughter were beamed around the world, including the unforgettable image of a lone protester standing in front of a tank and refusing to move out of the way.

The massacre put Bush in an awkward position. As a former envoy to China, he had a long-standing predilection for building and maintaining strong relations. China was one area of the world where Baker would play only a supporting role. "President Bush was the desk officer on China," Baker liked to say. The last thing the president wanted was a rupture. But he could hardly fail to object to the butchery in Tiananmen. Complicating matters even further, Fang Lizhi, a noted astrophysicist and China's best-known dissident, showed up at the American embassy in Beijing asking for refuge amid the crackdown; he was taken in, unavoidably inserting the United States into the middle of the already volatile situation.

Bush flew back from Maine the next day and consulted with Baker and Brent Scowcroft. "We deplore the decision to use force," the president told reporters. He suspended arms sales and military contacts while promising a sympathetic review of requests by Chinese students in the United States to extend their stays. But he imposed no sanctions nor did he recall his ambassador or take stronger measures. He immediately came under fire from both liberals and conservatives. "While angry rhetoric might be temporarily satisfying to some, I believed it would deeply hurt our efforts in the long term," Bush wrote in his foreign policy memoir.

Baker concurred with Bush's instincts. As shocked as anyone by the violence, he nonetheless worried that an excessive reaction would unravel all of the progress made since Richard Nixon's diplomatic opening. So did Nixon, who called Bush to urge restraint. When it came to balancing human rights concerns against what he perceived to be the national interest, Baker could be unsentimental. China was not the only such case confronting him in that first spring at Foggy Bottom. The white-minority regime in South Africa, whose system of apartheid had drawn worldwide condemnation, appeared on the edge of collapse. Just a week before the Tiananmen Square massacre, Baker had met with South Africa's foreign minister and pressed him to end apartheid and release the country's most famous political prisoner, Nelson Mandela. At the same time, he made clear that there were limits to how far the administration would go. Baker told the visiting minister that he "would like to not increase economic sanctions because we think they are counterproductive," but he had "to work with Congress," and South Africa should understand "how strongly Congress views their practice of apartheid."

The reaction in Congress also loomed large for Baker in handling this crisis with China. Although Bush had served in the House for four years, Baker was actually more attuned to the politics of Capitol Hill from his Reagan-era tax reform and other deal-making and he urged the president to issue tougher statements to head off any measures that would go further than Bush wanted. This realpolitik response to Tiananmen Square did not go over well with everyone on Baker's team. He was coming under considerable pressure from Margaret Tutwiler, who was devastated by the pictures of innocents trammeled by tanks and gunned down in the street. She had a friend in China she was not able to reach and she was taking the situation personally. She kept pressing Baker to speak out more strongly, to take more action. And for the first time, she refused to go out to the State Department podium and publicly deliver the company line.

"I'm not briefing," she told Baker. "I can't do this."

He looked at her with an even stare. "Well, you *are*," he said.

"No, no, no, I'm sending Richard," she replied, referring to her deputy, Richard Boucher. "I can't do this."

Baker would not budge. "Well, you *are*."

She did, unhappily, but did not let up her private importuning of Baker as the crackdown continued. Dozens of Chinese students were peremptorily executed and when Baker met with the Chinese ambassador to Washington to lodge protests, he was told in no uncertain terms that this was an internal matter and the United States should keep out of it. Baker then gave voice to the administration's criticism in an appearance before the House Foreign Affairs Committee. "They may be able to clear the square," he said. "They won't be able to clear their conscience."

Still, Bush refused to take harsher actions urged by lawmakers on both sides of the aisle. The president tried to personally call Chinese leader Deng Xiaoping and, when he could not get through, wrote a letter emphasizing that he did not want a break in relations and offering to secretly send a personal envoy. Deng sent word back that he would receive an emissary from Bush.

The president called Baker and told him it should not be the secretary of state because the trip had to be under the radar. "Jim Baker does not want to be undermined, so I thought of a lot of alternatives," Bush later recorded in his diary. "Kissinger and Nixon—too high profile, and too much propensity for leakage, though both would be very good," he added. He considered several ambassadors or diplomats, "but I don't want to undermine Baker's running foreign policy." So he settled on Scowcroft, who would be close enough to the president to be taken seriously but low-profile enough to slip in and out without notice. Baker agreed but suggested that his own deputy, Larry Eagleburger, go along too. In fact, Baker did not seem all that unhappy about being supplanted. His keen instinct for self-preservation kicked in. "Baker dropped China like a hot potato right after Tiananmen," observed Richard Solomon, the assistant secretary for East Asia and the Pacific. "Baker didn't want to get sullied by this nasty issue."

Scowcroft and Eagleburger flew to Beijing in July and returned to Washington without anyone noticing. They delivered Bush's message, that China had to find a way to come to terms with the dissenters without further violence, only to be rebuffed by party leaders who told them that it was none of America's business. The situation remained stalemated for months as Congress agitated for more sanctions while Bush and Baker resisted in the name of preserving relations.

When Baker sat down with China's foreign minister, Qian Qichen, in September, he made clear that the administration's approach was driven more by political pressure than moral outrage. "I believe that the domestic situation in the United States may now be a little bit better with regard to the U.S.-China relationship," he told Qian at the Waldorf-Astoria in New York during a break from the United Nations General Assembly. "I hope we can continue our dialogue so as to find a way to put the relationship back on track."

Qian suggested one way to do that would be to proceed with a previous agreement to have Chinese rockets put American satellites into orbit. Baker concurred, but again stressed the political pressures on him. "This is a very sensitive issue in the U.S. and if it became publicized, I fear Congress would require us to prohibit it or refuse to go ahead," he said. "Therefore, we need to be very careful about timing, when to move forward."

This was classic Baker—more focused on how to keep the relationship stable than expressing indignation over China's actions, while using Congress as a prod to induce better behavior by Beijing. Scowcroft made a return visit to China that winter, this time publicly, and there was much outrage back in Washington when the national security adviser was shown toasting Chinese leaders by candlelight, "as friends, to resume our important dialogue," a mere six months after the massacre. But the administration's political calculation was correct. The heat over Tiananmen faded with time. A year after the slaughter, the Chinese finally allowed Fang Lizhi to leave the country for exile in the United States while Bush moved the relationship back onto a more normal track. The Chinese had not only succeeded in their crackdown, they had made a definitive choice that would redound in the international system for decades to come, opting for economic liberalization without easing up politically. There would be no glasnost in Beijing.

IN EARLY JULY, Baker and Bush turned their attention back to Europe and the Soviet Union. The president traveled to Poland and Hungary to see for himself the rapid changes in Eastern Europe. As with China, their mutual instinct skewed toward stability. While Solidarity led by Lech Wałęsa had just swept parliamentary elections in Poland in a stunning victory over the old regime, Bush nonetheless urged General Wojciech Jaruzelski to run for president to manage the transition to a more democratic system in a steady fashion. Jaruzelski, the dour Communist leader who ordered tanks to crush Solidarity in 1981, had in recent months opened the door to a new, freer society and allowed his onetime opponents to move into power. Bush sought to show support for change with a package of economic assistance for Poland, but it was so small that Scowcroft privately considered it "embarrassingly meager." The package Bush offered in Hungary was even less significant.

From there, Bush headed to Paris for the annual Group of 7 meeting. At one point, he sat on the steps of the terrace at the American embassy with Baker and Scowcroft, brooding over how to move forward with the Soviets. Both Bush and Baker prodded Scowcroft into conceding that it was finally time for a meeting with Gorbachev. Still wary of the Soviet leader, Scowcroft had resisted getting together until they knew what could come of it, but Bush had grown impatient. It did not have to be a full summit, he said, just an informal get-to-know-you session. Scowcroft gave in. On Air Force One leaving Paris, Bush wrote Gorbachev a letter proposing the meeting, an invitation the Soviet leader would quickly accept.

Baker found himself back in Paris just ten days later after receiving a surprising inquiry from Eduard Shevardnadze asking if he had planned to attend an international conference on Cambodia in the French capital. Baker had not yet decided to go, but he took the question as a summons. Shevardnadze would not have asked if he was not eager to meet. And so once more Baker boarded his plane and jetted across the ocean. During a break in the Cambodia conference, the two met for three hours and Shevardnadze unloaded about the troubles at home—worker strikes, regional restlessness, economic stagnation. It was a remarkably frank and disquieting performance. No other Soviet official, Baker thought, would have opened up like this. The foreign minister was unburdening himself in a way that made it even clearer that if Baker and Bush were going to invest in Gorbachev, they had to figure out how to deliver for him. The public platitudes would not suffice, a reality that was even more urgent after Tiananmen, which had stiffened the resolve of Soviet hard-liners who were eager to send their tanks into the streets too.

Once again, Baker came away from meeting with Shevardnadze with a sense of him as a heroic figure racing against time. At Margaret Tutwiler's suggestion, Baker invited Shevardnadze to travel with him in the fall to Wyoming, where he had recently bought his new ranch, pitching it as a chance for them to further build their relationship. Staring at panoramic photographs that Baker had brought with him of the mountain homestead, Shevardnadze accepted right away. Baker sent a long account back to Bush for his private reading. "My day in Paris," he called it.

Baker and Shevardnadze would have to figure out how to get Bush and Gorbachev together—and how to give them each something to show for the encounter. Even just making it happen was proving to be both a political and logistical headache. Finding a venue and date was not easy. Finally, after Bush learned that Gorbachev would be traveling in December to Italy, someone proposed Malta. Bush's younger brother, William, who went by Bucky, had just been to the Mediterranean island and raved about how lovely it was. Scowcroft, meanwhile, had mentioned that Franklin Roosevelt had met during World War II with Winston Churchill aboard a Navy ship off Newfoundland, an idea that appealed to Bush's desire to downplay the meeting and have an excuse to keep the media at arm's length. They set the dates for December 2 and 3. Bush told everyone: Do not call it a summit.

While the Malta non-summit was being arranged in secret, the administration came under fire back home for not taking a more energetic approach to the Soviets. Senator George Mitchell, the Democratic majority leader, assailed the Bush team's "timidity" and "almost passive stance," suggesting that it seemed practically "nostalgic about the Cold War." Irritated, Baker fired back the next day at a news conference, his first since becoming secretary. "When the president of the United States is rocking along with a 70 percent approval rating on his handling of foreign policy, and I were the leader of the opposition party, I might have something similar to say," Baker said.

It was a blatantly partisan comment for a secretary of state, underscoring how much Baker still saw statecraft through the lens of domestic politics. Some of his administration colleagues were privately uncomfortable not only about the tenor of Baker's response but the validity of Mitchell's criticism. Even Scowcroft, who had resisted a presidential meeting and recognized that Mitchell was motivated by partisanship, would later say,

"I also believed we should be doing more." But could the two foreign ministers deliver it?

Shevardnadze arrived in Washington in September for the trip to Wyoming. Baker invited the Soviet minister to join him on an Air Force DC-9 for the flight west. Shevardnadze usually traveled on his own plane, but when Baker aides said the secretary wanted to use the four-and-a-half-hour trip for an unstructured discussion, he agreed to fly on the American aircraft. Baker, his coat and tie off, sat with Shevardnadze, wearing a white shirt and black vest, across a table in the front of the plane. They tucked into a dinner of chicken parmesan and a Robert Mondavi 1987 sauvignon blanc served by Air Force stewards, then settled in for a long conversation. In addition to the interpreters, Dennis Ross sat uncomfortably on a State Department attaché case next to Baker taking notes, while a Soviet aide did the same for Shevardnadze. Jack Matlock, the American ambassador to Moscow, and his Soviet counterpart listened intently.

Baker and Shevardnadze talked for nearly two hours, with the Soviet minister going even further than he had in Paris describing the dysfunction back home. The republics were increasingly pulling away from Moscow, he said, and he personally favored "total autonomy" for them even while hoping to maintain some semblance of a union. He described a deteriorating economy and public discontent. For Baker, it was an eye-opening conversation. Ross thought the secretary and foreign minister had "crossed a threshold" during the flight, forging a personal connection that went beyond typical diplomatic cordiality.

Once on the ground in Wyoming, the two stayed at the Jackson Lake Lodge in Jackson Hole—Baker's new ranch was far too rustic and off the grid—and continued their talks in a log cabin built in the 1930s with a breathtaking view of Jackson Lake in the Grand Teton National Park. At one point when the two ministers were having their picture taken, a pair of moose appeared behind them. At night they could hear coyotes howl.

Shevardnadze came bearing two major concessions. In an effort to break the deadlock over nuclear arms control, he said the Soviets would no longer link a new treaty to their concerns over the Strategic Defense Initiative missile defense program that had so divided Reagan and Gorbachev. And he announced that Moscow would dismantle its phased array radar facility in Krasnoyarsk that the United States had long considered a violation of the Anti-Ballistic Missile Treaty, or ABM. Those policy shifts cleared the way for Baker and Shevardnadze to sign seven bilateral accords and announce progress on the Strategic Arms Reduction Treaty, or START.

Before leaving, Baker wanted to show Shevardnadze one of the things he loved about Wyoming by taking him fishing. That proved a bit of a nightmare for his staff. ("Can I tell you how difficult it is to translate 'waders' into Russian?" said Karen Groomes, the aide who handled the logistics. "They were like, 'What do you mean?'") When the two eventually went angling for trout on the Snake River, Shevardnadze, a novice, unsurprisingly failed to catch anything. "We almost had major crisis in US-USSR relations—he'd never fished before—at all!" Baker wrote afterward in a note to Tom Brokaw of NBC News, a fellow outdoorsman. As a parting gift, Baker presented Shevardnadze with black cowboy boots with his initials on them, made specially in Houston.

Baker and his team saw the visit as a turning point; he and "Shevy," as he now called the foreign minister, were to be partners going forward as much as interlocutors. "That was a real bonding experience with Shevardnadze and Baker," Robert Gates, who was on the trip, remembered years later. "That relationship in some ways may have been more important than the president's relationship with Gorbachev."

Yet at the time, Gates was not sure where it would lead. In the weeks after Wyoming, the deputy national security adviser wrote out a speech giving voice to his doubts. The twenty-nine-page text he drafted for a security conference at Georgetown University concluded that Gorbachev's economic program "is likely to fall far short" and he forecast the reassertion of "Stalinist controls over the economy." Gorbachev's policies, he wrote, "are likely to lead in the foreseeable future to major instability" and, perhaps thinking of the recent events in Tiananmen, Gates predicted "a growing likelihood of the broad use of force at home." When it came to ongoing Soviet support for regimes in North Korea, Cuba, and Nicaragua, Gates added, Gorbachev's "new thinking" actually "seems to well serve old goals."

When Baker saw the draft, he grew incensed. It was Cheney all over again. Scowcroft tried to mollify Baker by having Gates rewrite the speech. But Gates kept the thrust of his remarks, choosing instead to add about a half dozen references to Baker's past speeches in an effort to make it seem as if the two were on the same page. "I believe his text as revised basically is a complement to your speeches, and provides a useful perspective in the current environment in a way that is helpful to the President," Scowcroft wrote Baker as he sent the amended text to the State Department. Baker was not assuaged. He certainly was not going to fall for such a transparent Washington ploy. He underlined the phrase "complement to your speeches" in Scowcroft's cover memo. "No way," he scribbled next to it. Then he marked up the latest Gates draft with acerbic comments.

The next day, Baker handed Bush a one-page memo outlining his grievances about the speech in eight bullet points. His pique radiated off the page. Gates's speech "in some places directly contradicts the policy I announced" and "would be a major mistake and create the view that there are two schools of thought in the Administration." Few had dared publicly to challenge Baker's lack of foreign policy gravitas or academic experience. But he knew the critique existed anyway. "I don't understand why the Deputy Director of the NSC—a staff position—feels the need to be visibly on the record in articulating US-Soviet policy," he wrote, asserting his foreign policy primacy as secretary of state.

Baker succeeded in killing the speech but not without leaving some scars. "You're breaking a lot of china over here," Bush told him. Invariably, the conflict found its way into *The New York Times* when its well-sourced diplomatic correspondent Thomas Friedman heard about it. With the flap now exposed, Gates sent an apologetic note to the secretary. "It is most unfortunate that our private exchanges on this became public," he wrote to Baker. "As I think you know, Friedman did not get the story from here— nor will any other journalist." He tried to repair the damage with flattery. "For what it's worth, I am a big admirer and booster of yours and would not want to do anything to cause you (or the President, about whom I care very deeply) a problem."

In reality, Gates was less remorseful than angry at being steamrollered. He had sent the original draft of the speech to the State Department and it had been signed off on by Robert Kimmitt. "I felt I'd played by the rules in getting it cleared and everything and then all of a sudden, I'm told to stuff it," Gates recalled years later. Still, with the passage of time, Gates was ready to concede that Baker had read the changes in the Soviet Union better than he had. "At the end of the day, Jim was right and I was wrong. But I was very pouty for a day or two."

The episode was not just a process foul or a doctrinal difference about Soviet policy. It was also, significantly, a marker of Baker's sensitivity about his relationship with Bush. The Gates speech, he worried, would encourage some to question whether he and the president were on the same page; even asking the question, Baker believed, would be a direct threat to his power. When Baker spoke, senators and foreign leaders had to assume that it was the same thing as Bush speaking. His clout in Washington and around the world stemmed not just from his friendship with Bush, but from the perception of it.

A master leaker himself, Baker hated when others leaked about him. Just days after the Gates flap, the columnist Morton Kondracke wrote in *The Washington Times* about Baker's periodic feuding with Dan Quayle, quoting unnamed advisers to the vice president who had called the secretary's support for Gorbachev's reform efforts "appeasement." They had also speculated that the secretary of state was positioning himself to run for president in 1996 after a second Bush term instead of Quayle. Kondracke cited Margaret Tutwiler who quoted Baker saying, "No, I don't want to be president." But Baker again chafed at being publicly undercut. Pulling out his black felt pen, he scribbled in the margin of the column: "Mr. P—We have successfully avoided this kind of crap for 9 months! We won't be able to continue if these people keep it up. Please have it knocked off." He then sent it to the Oval Office.

Bush understood Baker's sensitivity as well as anyone. He too bristled under the barrage of criticism of their shared approach. While Quayle and Gates worried about going soft on Gorbachev, Bush was just as peeved by the outsiders who thought he was letting an opportunity slip away.

"I keep hearing the critics saying we're not doing enough on Eastern Europe," Bush recorded in his diary. But, he added, "if we mishandle it, get way out looking like an American project, you would invite crackdown." And that, he said, "could result in bloodshed."

The date was November 8, 1989.

CHAPTER 20

The Curtain Falls

The next day, Baker was hosting a luncheon in the ornate Benjamin Franklin Room at the State Department in honor of President Corazon Aquino of the Philippines, the popular hero of a "people power" revolution that had toppled the dictator Ferdinand Marcos a few years earlier. About 150 diplomats, officials, and business leaders were seated at tables around the room, including Baker's Democratic superlawyer pal Robert Strauss, as well as Dick Cheney and General Colin Powell, the chairman of the Joint Chiefs of Staff.

Baker had just returned from an eight-day trip to Australia, where he attended an Asia-Pacific summit meeting, and he was understandably tired from the twenty-five-hour flight home. But the memo handed to him in the midst of the meal provided a jolt that would have woken up anyone. In careful, restrained language, the typed note from his special assistant, J. Stapleton Roy, let Baker know that the world had changed while he was at lunch.

> Mr. Secretary:
> The East German Government has just announced that it is fully opening its borders to the West. The implication from the announcement is full freedom of travel via current East German/West German links between borders. We are asking EUR to give you an analysis.
>
> Stape

Baker stared at the page. He did not need an analysis from the State Department's European Bureau to know this was momentous. Twenty-eight years after the Berlin Wall was erected, the forbidding barrier that had divided Germany and, by extension, Europe itself was coming down. Baker called for attention around the room, read the note to the assembled group, and offered a toast to a day that would go down in history.

After escorting Aquino out, Baker spoke briefly to reporters, for once not prepared by extensive talking points. If the reports were true, he said, still cautious, the United States would welcome the East German decision after so many years of waiting. But he begged off saying more, then hopped in a car and rushed over to the White House. On the back of a news summary, he scrawled out his first thoughts: "Something we've wanted for 40 years. Eur. that's whole & free." And then, looking ahead to the implications, to the diplomatic haggling he knew would inevitably follow, he added: "Premature to deal w/issue of reunification. Reunification 'on basis of Western values.'"

At the White House, Bush was at his desk when Brent Scowcroft rushed in to tell him the news. There was no plan for this. They would, like the rest of the world, watch and react. The two went to the study off the Oval Office and turned on a television to find images of jubilant crowds gathering in Berlin. Baker arrived. Soon, the president summoned reporters to hail the breakthrough, but even as he did, he remained deliberately reserved, wary of looking triumphal lest he be seen as taunting Mikhail Gorbachev or, worse, provoking hard-liners in Moscow to take action to stop what was happening. The last thing Bush wanted was to inadvertently goad the Soviets into a Tiananmen Square solution in East Germany.

"Of course, I welcome the decision by the East German leadership to open the borders to those wishing to emigrate or travel," Bush said tepidly to the reporters hurriedly gathered around his desk in the Oval Office. "I am very pleased with this development."

The reporters were mystified at his restrained, even bland reaction. Exuberant Germans were breaking through the wall that had represented the worst of the Cold War and the most expressive word the president of the United States could come up with was "pleased"?

Lesley Stahl of CBS News pressed him on it. "This is a sort of great victory for our side in the big East-West battle, but you don't seem elated," she pointed out.

"I am not an emotional kind of guy," Bush said.

"Well, how elated are you?"

"I'm very pleased."

It hardly seemed equal to the moment. Even as Bush spoke, tens of thousands of East Germans who until recently would have been shot merely for approaching the wall now fearlessly climbed on top of it and headed west. Some took ice picks to crack away at it. Others danced in the streets. Tom Brokaw, the NBC News anchor who by chance had picked that week to broadcast from Berlin, beamed the revelry to the rest of the world, pronouncing it "a historic moment, a moment that will live forever."

Taking his cue from Bush, Baker remained undemonstrative even as he went on ABC and CBS to talk about the remarkable changes. Then he headed off to the State Dinner for Aquino, still jet-lagged from the long flight from Australia but exhilarated by the day's events and already calculating in his mind what might come next.

After letting the moment sink in, Baker the next day called Hans-Dietrich Genscher, the West German foreign minister. As Baker waited for him to come on the line, the West German phone operator spoke up.

"God bless America," she told Baker. "Thanks for everything, sir."

BERLIN SAT UNEASILY at the center of the Cold War from the start. Located within East Germany, but divided by the four victorious powers at the end of World War II, the city remained a camp filled with hostile parties living uneasily next to each other, part capitalist and democratic, part Communist and totalitarian.

When Joseph Stalin cut off West Berlin from the rest of West Germany in 1948, Harry Truman ordered an airlift to keep its citizens fed and supplied until the Soviets finally backed down nearly a year later. By 1961, the Communist leadership had grown so aggravated by citizens of the eastern part of the city traveling to the West that one night under cover of darkness, it erected barbed wire fences to stop them. What became known as the Berlin Wall was in reality a series of fortified barriers over twenty-seven miles, a mix of concrete walls, ditches, fences, and tank traps. It was a physical manifestation of the Iron Curtain that Winston Churchill had so memorably described dividing Europe. Over the course of its history, East Germans tried to escape by tunneling under, flying over, or crashing through the barricades. Some hid in trunks or falsified documents. At least 140 people were shot or died of accidents or suicide at the wall and, by some estimates, significantly more. As late as February 1989, a twenty-year-old waiter became the last wall jumper shot and killed by East German border guards, cut down by a hail of ten bullets.

American presidents saw the wall as the front line in the ideological struggle with Communism. In 1963, two years after the wall went up, John Kennedy traveled to West Berlin to show solidarity with the enclosed city, famously proclaiming *"Ich bin ein Berliner."* Ronald Reagan came in 1987 to insist that it was time to end the division, using a memorable phrase added to his speech over the objections of nervous advisers. "Mr. Gorbachev," he declared, "tear down this wall."

Neither they nor any other American leader, however, did anything tangible to make it happen. The East German people did that themselves. Throughout 1989, unrest grew throughout the country as it did across Eastern Europe. Hungary was the first to open its border to the West via Austria and, disabling the electric alarm system and cutting through barbed wire, thousands of East Germans made their way to West Germany via the circuitous route. Demonstrations broke out not just in East Berlin but in places like Dresden, where a KGB officer named Vladimir Putin personally confronted protesters with a pistol outside the tan, two-story villa that served as the local headquarters for the Soviet spy agency, brandishing the gun to keep the mob from breaking in as his KGB colleagues frantically burned papers inside.

Erich Honecker, the aged, iron-fisted Communist ruler of East Germany, was forced out on October 18 and replaced by his protégé, Egon Krenz, who promised reforms. In the first week of November, at least a half million people and perhaps twice as many poured into the streets of East Berlin demanding free speech, open elections, and elimination of the Communist monopoly on power. The fall of the wall a few days later was, in reality, an accident, the result of a string of misunderstandings and miscalculations. The days leading up to the event had been marked by East Germans trying to transit to the West through Czechoslovakia. Hoping to ease the situation, Krenz and the Politburo decided to issue a new temporary travel regulation meant to allow East Germans to cross the border into West Germany at a single transit point in the countryside, creating in effect a hole that would let off steam. But it did not turn out that way; once television erroneously broadcast the decree as if it were an unconditional opening, it in effect became one. There was no way to undo the rapturous night of November 9, 1989.

Soon, the unforgettable scenes in Berlin were followed by a cascade of uprisings throughout Eastern Europe. On the day after the wall fell, Bulgaria's president, Todor Zhivkov, stepped down, ending thirty-five years in power. Two weeks later, amid massive demonstrations in Prague's Wenceslaus Square, Miloš Jakeš, the Communist Party boss in Czechoslovakia, resigned. Barely a month after that, the dissident playwright Václav Havel was elected president, the climax of the country's Velvet Revolution. On Christmas Day, Romania's brutal leader Nicolae Ceaușescu and his wife were convicted by a military court and summarily executed by firing squad as tears streamed down the dictator's face. By spring, Hungary would hold its first direct presidential election and by the end of that year the Solidarity leader Lech Wałęsa would be elected president of Poland.

For Baker, the series of earth-shattering events cut through all the months of pointless bureaucratic wavering and Washington infighting about Soviet policy. They would have to act. But Baker was not wired for revolution. He was not the type to jump on a wall, figuratively or literally. His first instinct was for stability. As a young man, he was so wedded to order that he did whatever the Warden told him, even after graduating college and serving in the Marines. So Baker watched what was happening in Berlin and Prague and Warsaw with a sober eye, wondering how to harness the revolutionary energies now unleashed and channel them to a secure outcome with a minimum of damage.

By his own account, Bush had "given little thought to reunification" when he took office. Few imagined the two Germanys would merge into one quickly, or even on Bush's watch. "Virtually no West German expects German reunification to happen in this century," Philip Zelikow and Robert Blackwill, two National Security Council officials, wrote in a memo sent to Bush on March 20, 1989, two months after his inauguration, although "there is no German of any age who does not dream of it in his soul."

But events were moving swiftly. In a May 15 memo to Baker ahead of the NATO summit, Robert Zoellick thought there was more of a chance to finally end the division of Germany and he urged the secretary of state to embrace the goal. "This is the real opportunity to get ahead of the curve and to exceed expectations," he wrote. "The real question is whether Gorbachev will grab it first. (Or else the Germans will grab it, especially after Honecker passes from the scene.)" Zoellick recommended that the Bush administration advocate for "normalization," not "reunification," and make clear that any future Germany be firmly anchored in the West.

When the wall finally fell that November, no one could say for sure what would happen next. The East German government could have reacted by cracking down. So could Gorbachev, as his predecessors did during brief moments of reform in Hungary in 1956 and Czechoslovakia in 1968. With some 380,000 Soviet troops stationed in East Germany, the Kremlin still held the real power to decide. But Gorbachev opted not to intervene, letting East Germany go its own way, a decision that effectively set free all of the Warsaw Pact countries. It might not have been obvious in the moment, but Gorbachev's action—or lack thereof—would become perhaps the most critical turning point on the path toward the end of the Cold War.

The sense of jubilation was hard to overstate. Nine million East Germans visited the West just in the first week alone after the wall fell, which was more than half of the country's population, and while most returned home it was clear that no wall could keep Germans apart any longer. Reunification was not only possible now, it appeared to be happening. But after four decades of division, no one knew how to proceed with making the two Germanys one nation again, whose interests that would serve, or what that would mean for the superpowers whose nuclear-armed forces confronted each other across Europe's dividing line. "We were all caught off guard," said Dieter Kastrup, a top adviser to the West German foreign minister. "That meant we had no blueprint or master plan in our drawers."

Four days after the fall of the wall, Baker joined Bush and Brent Scowcroft for dinner with Henry Kissinger at the White House residence. The former secretary of state, who had been born to a Jewish famly in Bavaria and fled Hitler's Germany as a boy in 1938, believed that reunification was now inevitable. Yet even with millions of people streaming across the open border, a merger still seemed daunting. In one of their first conversations after the wall fell, Chancellor Helmut Kohl of West Germany predicted to Bush that reunification would probably take five years. Within weeks, he was talking about as quickly as three years. Not long after that, the time frame accelerated even further and it was clear that Kohl would press for the fastest possible merger. Every day, facts on the ground were outpacing political leaders struggling to adjust to a reality that seemed increasingly beyond their control.

On November 28, Kohl announced a ten-point plan for closer ties with East Germany, although he did not yet propose negotiations for reunification. "When Helmut Kohl gave his ten-point speech, we thought it would take five to ten years to unify Germany," said Horst Teltschik, the chancellor's national security adviser. "The high speed just came from the people of the GDR," as the German Democratic Republic, or East Germany, was called.

While peeved at the lack of advance warning, Bush broadly supported Kohl's approach. Inside Baker's State Department, a fight had been raging since almost the minute the wall was breached. The cautious careerists in his European bureau had produced a paper counseling Baker to avoid being "stampeded" into premature diplomatic initiatives. Zoellick and Dennis Ross vehemently disagreed, and Zoellick kept a copy of the memo on his desk for years afterward, often pulling it out to remind diplomats about the overly cautious mind-set of their profession. Ross set his policy planning staff to work on ideas for Baker to put America into the center of the conversation and by mid-November a brilliant young academic who had recently become his deputy, Francis Fukuyama, proposed that the secretary seize the initiative by announcing a series of principles to guide the reunification process.

Fukuyama, whose wonkish cover story in that summer's *National Interest* proclaiming "the end of history" had made him an unlikely celebrity, had written a memo back in May arguing with the career experts that a revolution in East Germany was imminent. Days before the fall of the wall, he had been in Berlin to meet with Ross's counterpart in the West German Foreign Office, who confidently assured Fukuyama once again that he was wrong. "Germany will not unify in my lifetime," the diplomat told Fukuyama. Now Fukuyama would have the chance to write his own script for "the triumph of the West" his article had envisioned. He suggested four main points for the secretary, and the day after Kohl's speech Baker rolled them out publicly, saying that any move toward unity should be gradual and peaceful; based on the self-determination of the German people, not the dictates of outsiders; ensure that a single Germany remain in NATO; and guarantee that current borders with Germany's neighbors remain inviolate.

Not everyone was as supportive of an integrated Germany. After two devastating world wars sparked by German militarism, other European powers remained understandably nervous. Gorbachev was hardly more enthusiastic than the hard-liners in the Soviet security agencies about a powerful German neighbor, much less one still anchored in NATO. Poland worried that a new Germany would seek to reclaim territory it lost to its eastern neighbor in the aftermath of World War II. President François Mitterrand of France was wary. Britain's Margaret Thatcher was downright hostile. "Mitterrand was not the problem," Teltschik recalled. "The problem was Margaret Thatcher." At a dinner of European leaders ten days after Kohl's speech, Thatcher stunned him by telling the heads of state, "We beat the Germans twice and now they're back." Mitterrand encouraged her, warning in a private lunch at the Élysée Palace memorialized by a British note taker that a reunited Germany could give the country more influence even than it had under Adolf Hitler.

NEVER MIND HIS STINT afloat in the Mediterranean as a Marine; Baker was not much of a sailor. He had a habit of getting violently seasick, so the much-anticipated meetings with Mikhail Gorbachev scheduled aboard American and Soviet ships docked at Malta would have been a challenge for Baker no matter what. But when they arrived for the non-summit, the weather was treacherous. The waters off the island republic were roiling and the ships were pitching back and forth like plastic toys in a bathtub. Baker never did throw up, contrary to subsequent rumor, but he felt like it and headed for the sick bay, where doctors gave him a patch to put behind his ear to settle his queasy stomach.

No one had anticipated the storm that hit Malta just as the leaders of the world's two nuclear superpowers arrived for their first official meeting since Bush became president. It was less than a month since the fall of the Berlin Wall and the rain came down in sheets as Bush and Baker stepped off Air Force One to find a drenched military band welcoming them. After a courtesy call on Malta's prime minister, they took off by helicopter for the aircraft carrier USS *Forrestal*. Getting off the choppers onto the slippery deck was hazardous enough but the howling winds and backwash from the rotor blades prompted some Baker aides to worry about getting blown out to sea.

Baker was brought to the admiral's loft to watch as nineteen aircraft took off in a demonstration of American might—F-14 fighter planes, E-2 Hawkeyes, A-7 bombers, and more. After Bush addressed the crew, he and Baker headed by helicopter to the USS *Belknap*, a guided missile cruiser that would be their headquarters for the summit. Baker then went ashore for dinner with Brent Scowcroft, John Sununu, and Margaret Tutwiler. The Maltese capital of Valletta, known for its narrow avenues and limestone palaces dating as far back as the sixteenth century, was eerie amid the storm—there were no streetlights, traffic was light, and the shops were nearly empty. At the end of the evening, the owner of the restaurant asked Baker to sign the menu.

For a non-summit with no formal agenda, Baker and Bush spent a lot of time coming up with a formal agenda. Gorbachev had repeatedly gotten the better of them over the year since Bush's election, presenting headline-grabbing initiatives that left the Americans looking unimaginative. Advice streamed in on how Bush could turn the tables. Nixon sent a six-page letter with ideas. Bush zeroed in on one suggestion on page five that suggested "a possible PR ploy" for the president, specifically a Bush-Gorbachev Mediterranean Charter, modeled after Franklin Roosevelt's Atlantic Charter with Winston Churchill. It would endorse Western values like free elections, free speech, and self-determination. "He won't abide by such an agreement, just as Stalin did not abide by his agreement at Yalta for elections in Poland," Nixon wrote. "But it would be very useful to nail him down." He added: "The greatest PR danger is that the nuts on the right will try to make the case that Malta was simply a second Yalta. The answer to that is that Yalta divided Europe. Malta laid the groundwork for uniting it through agreement on and adherence to the great values which the United States and our Western European allies have always cherished."

Baker had another thought. He recommended that Bush come up with as many initiatives as he could in all sorts of areas—not grand bargains, not historic advances, but a collection of ideas that, by sheer volume, would give the impression of Bush as a man of action. Since Gorbachev had been told this was just a get-to-know-you meeting, it was possible that he would not have anything to put on the table, but if he did, Bush at least would be ready. Brent Scowcroft did not think much of Baker's idea, deeming it "unprofessional at best and corny at worst," but Bush liked it and the national security team assembled seventeen proposals on issues like arms control, human rights, Central America, and the environment for him to present. It was diplomacy by ambush, not the way Baker usually liked to operate, but he was determined not to be outplayed again by the drugstore cowboy from Moscow.

On the morning of December 2, winds roared at practically gale force intensity and ocean waves reached as high as sixteen feet. The weather was so rough that the meeting could not be held on the Soviet ship *Slava* as originally planned, so Baker and Bush agreed to meet Gorbachev instead on the *Maxim Gorky*, where he was staying. Just getting onto the launch was a challenge for the president and secretary of state. The captain of the *Belknap* told the president that in a quarter century in the Navy he had never experienced such turbulent seas in harbor. At one point, Margaret Tutwiler tried for fifty minutes to reach Baker from shore before giving up and talking with him over an open radio.

As the two leaders and their teams sat across from each other on the *Maxim Gorky*, Bush opened by rolling out his seventeen initiatives, one after the other, clearly taking Gorbachev by surprise. He spoke for a long time before finally yielding the floor. "This is the end of my non-agenda," Bush said lightly. For once, he and Baker had the advantage.

Perhaps more important, though, Bush made a point of reassuring Gorbachev that he had no interest in trumpeting the changes in Eastern Europe.

"I have been called cautious or timid," Bush noted. "I *am* cautious, but not timid. But I have conducted myself in ways not to complicate your life. That's why I have not jumped up and down on the Berlin Wall."

"Yes, we have seen that and appreciate that," Gorbachev said.

Gorbachev expressed reservations about German reunification. "Unlike they—and you—I am saying there are two states, mandated by history," he said. "So let history decide the outcome."

Bush nodded. "We will do nothing to recklessly try to speed up reunification," he promised.

After four and a half hours, Bush and Baker and their advisers left the Soviet ship, but as swells lifted and dropped their barge fifteen feet in a second, they had a hard time even getting back on board the *Belknap*. Their barge smashed the starboard landing platform to pieces, keeping them lurching around the harbor longer as the barge made its way, with great difficulty, to the port platform instead. Gorbachev never made it at all. He was supposed to visit the *Belknap* himself for dinner that evening, but when he could not get there, Bush and Baker feasted on swordfish and lobster without him. They were bunkmates in the captain's quarters as Tom Brokaw said on NBC News that the Soviet-American get-together should be called the "seasick summit."

Back on shore, Margaret Tutwiler realized that the treacherous weather was becoming the story and desperately called Baker. "Mr. Baker, this is a drowning rat calling for help," she shouted over the winds. "I know you and the president are out there all by yourselves, sipping champagne or whatever, and you can't know what's going on here on the mainland. But I'm going to tell you, we're getting crucified. We're getting absolutely stomped."

Baker understood immediately and instinctively came up with a plan to recapture the public relations initiative. Rather than wait until the end of the summit to unveil the seventeen proposals Bush had brought for Gorbachev, Baker told Tutwiler to announce them right away. "Dump!" he yelled into the phone.

With the reporters fed a fresh story, Bush and Baker returned to the *Maxim Gorky* the next morning to talk with Gorbachev about the Baltic states, which were straining for independence from the Soviet Union. The United States had never recognized the Soviet absorption of Latvia, Lithuania, and Estonia during World War II, so Bush could hardly fail to back their efforts now to finally break away from Moscow. At the same time, he worried about encouraging a violent revolt that the United States would not be able to support, much as happened in Hungary in 1956 when Dwight Eisenhower sat on the sidelines. Bush used the meeting to press Gorbachev not to use force with the restless Balts.

Gorbachev did not take to lecturing, however. At one point, when Bush said the division of Europe could only be overcome on the basis of "Western values," Gorbachev bristled at the phrase.

"We share the values of democracy, individual liberty and freedom," he insisted.

Hoping to smooth over the matter, Baker offered alternative wording. "What about calling them *democratic* values?" he asked.

"That's good!" Gorbachev agreed.

While they were still at odds over important issues, Bush and Gorbachev had begun to develop the kind of partnership that Baker and Shevardnadze already had, and all four of them thought this would be key to managing the forces of change that were just then washing over Europe. Baker believed Gorbachev at Malta had made concessions to the evolving reality that other Soviet leaders never would have. "Gorby went out of his way to emphasize importance of U.S. staying in Eur.—even talked about importance of U.S. troop presence," Baker wrote by hand on a cable sent to the American consulate in Leningrad summing up the meetings.

After nearly a year on the defensive, Baker felt the administration was finally on the right track. Gorbachev characteristically pressed them for even more. Why not get rid of NATO and the Warsaw Pact altogether? he asked in Malta. This was still too fanciful, almost unimaginable. Baker and company were fighting their own wars back in Washington, with anti-Communist hard-liners who wanted to talk about how to get the Soviets out of Nicaragua and Cuba and all the rest. But for the first time, Baker believed that Gorbachev was no longer looking to show up the Americans.

BAKER FLEW the next day to Brussels, where he had dinner with Hans-Dietrich Genscher to fill in the West German foreign minister. Over venison steak and potatoes, the two spent most of their time talking about what was happening in the two Germanys. Genscher would be a key figure for Baker in the months to come. Genscher noted that he "inherited my tendency for harmony" from his father, a lawyer like Baker's dad, who died when the boy was just nine. As a teenager, Genscher was pressed into service in Hitler's Wehrmacht during the last months of World War II and became an American prisoner of war. After the war, Genscher joined a liberal party in East Germany until he fled to the West in 1952. He became leader of the Free Democratic Party in West Germany and led it into a coalition government first with one dominant party and then with another, taking on the role of foreign minister in 1974, a post he still occupied when the Berlin Wall came down.

Jowly with receding dark hair, a favorite yellow pullover sweater, and a crafty flair for politics, Genscher served in Helmut Kohl's cabinet, in an uneasy alliance always strained by their political differences. After years of working together, they had come to despise each other personally as well as politically and were famously not on speaking terms much of the time. For Baker this meant negotiating not only with two different Germanys but with two different parties within one of those Germanys. Indeed, the situation was so complicated that Baker deliberately took Genscher to dinner in Brussels rather than attend Bush's meeting with Kohl so as to keep the foreign minister away and allow the chancellor to speak more frankly with the president. Baker would find in the months to come that Kohl did not always clear his plans with Genscher or vice versa. "What Baker learned very fast was that he had to take care what Genscher said and what Helmut Kohl said because there was not always full agreement," remembered Horst Teltschik, the Kohl adviser. Teltschik regularly received calls from Baker after a Genscher meeting to confirm the chancellor's position.

Even as American, Soviet, and West German leaders conferred in Malta and Brussels, the situation on the ground in East Germany was evolving by the hour. Egon Krenz resigned as the country's last Communist chief, as did the Politburo, and several of its members were arrested. A warrant was issued for Erich Honecker, the previously deposed leader. Baker and his aides became increasingly nervous about the pace of change. The place seemed on the brink of anarchy. Baker's team heard reports about Soviet troops being put on a higher level of alert. It was not hard to imagine a conflagration set off by a wrong move. Baker was heading next to West Berlin and for several weeks had been considering a trip into East Germany as well. Dan Quayle had wanted to be the first American official to visit following the fall of the wall, but Baker objected and got Bush to block it. "If I'd been in Baker's position, I would have done the same thing," Quayle later acknowledged.

The night before Baker arrived in West Berlin, the American ambassador, Vernon Walters, met with his counterparts from the three other victorious World War II powers at their insistence, a way of flexing muscle by London, Paris, and Moscow to make clear that they had not surrendered their rights to help determine the fate of Germany. Baker had instructed Walters to keep the meeting low-key to avoid antagonizing the Germans and grew angry when he saw pictures on the news of Walters posing with the other diplomats. As Baker had feared, the Germans were furious. "We were in fact appalled and up in arms about that," said Dieter Kastrup, Genscher's adviser.

When he landed, Baker met in his hotel room with Walters and Richard Barkley, the American ambassador to East Germany, and discussed his idea of taking a secret journey across the line into East Germany. Two previous secretaries of state had visited East Berlin but none had ventured into East Germany beyond the city and Baker was entranced by the idea of going where his predecessors had never gone, especially at such a historic moment. Barkley strongly supported it, urging Baker to come push the teetering East German government to reaffirm its commitment to holding new elections, the country's first shot at a free and fair vote. But Walters opposed a visit, telling Baker flatly, "If you come, you will support the Communists." Also opposed was James Dobbins, a top Europe official at the State Department. With Egon Krenz now out, East Germany was on its third leader in seven weeks. A visit by the American secretary of state, Dobbins argued, "would enhance the stature of a regime that was on its last legs."

Baker was not one to forgive and forget. His discussion about venturing into East Germany would be his last substantive conversation with his ambassador to West Germany despite the intense focus on the country over the next year. Jovial and self-confident, Walters, a retired lieutenant general and former deputy CIA director who spoke a half-dozen languages, grated on Baker, who found him too willing to speak out of school, rather than stick to the company line. The two were opposites who did not attract. As Dobbins noted, "Baker's mind was quick and analytical; Walters's the polar opposite: ruminative, loquacious and anecdotal." From then on, the American embassy in Bonn would essentially be excluded from the biggest issue on its turf. When Bush later hosted Helmut Kohl at Camp David, Baker gave orders that Walters not be allowed on the helicopter to join them. Walters, who twice threatened to resign, later attributed his troubles to the fact that he had publicly, and correctly, predicted German reunification more than six months before the wall fell. "Baker seemed not to forgive me for being right about German unity," he wrote in a memoir. Either way, the freeze-out of America's ambassador on the ground underscored Baker's reliance on his own close advisers even at the expense of the rest of the State Department.

On December 12, Baker arrived at the Berlin Wall. He could see where people had chiseled holes through the graffiti-covered barrier and he could see the river where a young man had not so long ago had tried to swim across only to be captured. Baker's motorcade then headed to the Glienicke Bridge, the famed site of prisoner exchanges during the Cold War, including the transfer of the downed American U-2 pilot Francis Gary Powers and the Soviet Jewish dissident Natan Sharansky. Once Baker's car reached the bridge, his West German police escort, an imposing phalanx of several dozen motorcycles and cruisers, stopped and turned Baker's entourage over to their East German counterparts, a much more modest group. The transition to dilapidated East Berlin was stark. Baker's extra-large six-passenger Mercedes drove to Potsdam at a slow pace, past tiny cars, empty streets, decaying buildings. "It was terrible," he said later. "Everything was run-down. Lights were not bright. Just totally different."

In Potsdam, site of the final Big Three summit near the end of World War II, Baker met with Hans Modrow, the new East German prime minister. Modrow updated him on the disarray in his country. The pull of the two Germanys toward each other was accelerating. "The process here is irreversible," Modrow said. Afterward, arriving in the fading light of dusk, Baker visited St. Nicholas Church, a center of opposition to the old order. "A lot of people wish reunification to take place," one of the church leaders told Baker. "We have a right to the same way of life as in the West."

Baker returned to West Berlin that night increasingly convinced that reunification was coming—sooner than anyone had originally expected. And it was not going to be a merger. It was going to be a takeover.

IT WAS NOT EXACTLY the ideal moment for a war back home in the Western Hemisphere. Baker returned from Berlin jolted by the revolution in Eastern Europe and increasingly aware that, if the United States did not figure out something fast, the whole post–World War II order on the continent was about to unravel without any agreement on what would replace it. With that on his mind, the last thing he wanted to have to think about was Manuel Noriega. But it was not his choice.

Tensions with Panama had been growing throughout the year. In May, Noriega, the dictator who remained under indictment in the United States, had annulled a presidential election won by opposition leader Guillermo Endara, who was then attacked and beaten by a government-organized paramilitary squad. Noriega's continuing provocations against American troops in the Panama Canal Zone were exacerbating long-standing antagonism with Washington. Having targeted Noriega during the 1988 presidential campaign, to the point of breaking with Reagan, Bush had little choice but to take him seriously now. In Bob Woodward's *The Com-*

manders, Baker was quoted telling colleagues, "If we had known we would win the election by so much, we would not have dug such a deep hole for ourselves." Baker later disputed the quote, but the sentiment rang true. By elevating Noriega as a signal enemy of the United States, Bush and Baker now had no choice but to confront him.

They resolved to push Noriega out of power but when a group of Panamanian military officers made an amateurish attempt to oust him in October, Bush and his team hesitated and what Baker later called a "comic-opera coup" collapsed. Bush and Baker resolved to take advantage when the next opportunity came, which it did soon enough. On December 16, an off-duty American Marine was shot to death at a Panamanian Defense Forces roadblock. The next day, Baker joined a meeting with other national security officials in the White House residence to discuss what to do. The Pentagon had an invasion plan called Operation Blue Spoon ready to go if the president so ordered.

"I think we ought to go," Baker said. "As you know, the State Department has been for this for a long time." He then launched into "the downsides of doing it," which would include criticism by the Soviet Union and a protest by the Organization of American States. But Baker predicted that, whatever was said publicly, no major country would be genuinely upset if Noriega were dislodged.

Bush agreed and gave the order. Three days later, 12,000 American troops already stationed in Panama, joined by another 9,000 shipped in to help, launched what was now renamed Operation Just Cause aimed at toppling Noriega's government and bringing him to justice. Baker and his team remained at the State Department and ordered in Chinese food as they waited for the invasion to begin. Baker lay down on the sofa in his office to rest. Shortly after midnight, Army Rangers parachuted in and the operation began. Baker called and woke up congressional leaders and the secretaries-general of the United Nations and the Organization of American States.

American troops routed the Panamanian Defense Forces in short order, and Endara was sworn in as president at the American military base. But Noriega could not be found. By 3 a.m., there was a rumor that he was dead. Then came another report that he was alive. "No news on #1—i.e. Noriega," Baker wrote on notes during a 3 a.m. call with his ambassador in Panama City. "Emb has taken a few rounds but no one hurt."

By December 24, the United States military had overwhelmed the organized resistance, with twenty-three American soldiers and three American civilians killed along with hundreds of Panamanian troops and civilians. Noriega eluded capture, moving from one hideout to another, before arriving with a gun and a knife on Christmas Eve at the door of the papal nunciature in Panama City. The Vatican refused to hand him over to the Americans.

In Houston for the holiday, Baker called Agostino Cardinal Casaroli, the Vatican secretary of state, catching the church official on his way to mass. "You must understand that, having lost twenty-five American lives to help restore democracy in Panama, we cannot allow Noriega to go to any other country than the United States," Baker told him.

Noriega had been indicted for international drug trafficking, but Baker assured the cardinal that none of the charges would subject him to the death penalty, a prime concern for the church. "It's not a political matter," Baker said. "He's a common criminal."

For ten days, Noriega remained holed up at the nunciature until finally being told that his refuge would expire at noon on January 4, 1990. Given a choice of facing justice in his own country or taking his chances in a United States court, Noriega surrendered to the Americans. Bush had made his point. If the United States gave the impression of a superpower flexing its muscles to impose its will on a smaller country, it also sent a message that it still planned to exercise a dominant role in what the president would later call the New World Order.

Another conflict in Central America came to a resolution of its own a few weeks later. On February 25, Nicaraguans went to the polls in the election that was key to Baker's strategy to end the contra war. Just days before the vote, Daniel Ortega, the Sandinista revolutionary turned president, had boasted that his opponent did not have "even a hypothetical possibility" of winning. But Violeta Chamorro, the widow of the opposition newspaper publisher whose assassination fueled the rebellion that brought the Sandinistas to power, ran away with the election, outpacing Ortega with 55 percent of the vote to 41 percent. Ortega had miscalculated.

The result surprised Baker, who all along had assumed that the Sandinistas would win and that Washington would have to accept their government. Indeed, just a few weeks earlier, Baker and Bush had argued in the Oval Office about it. Reading out loud from a secret cable on Nicaragua filled with critical reports about the Sandinistas, Bush had chided Baker for betting too heavily on the Soviets' horse. When Baker heatedly objected, Bush admitted, as he later dictated to his diary, that "the intelligence was given to me by Quayle's office." Baker had been feuding with the hard-line conservatives on Quayle's staff for months and he seized on this as the latest example. They are "poisoning the well," he told the president. They "keep trying to push for outdated, kind of right-wing reactionary positions." This time, though, Bush was more or less on their side, even if he had exposed the Quayle team's backdoor attacks on his secretary of state.

When Nicaraguans went to the polls, Jimmy Carter was on the ground as an election observer and his presence proved critical. The Sandinistas initially refused to admit that they had lost until the former American president forced Ortega to face reality and personally took him over to Chamorro to concede defeat. Around 4:15 a.m., Carter finally called Baker in Washington to tell him the news and urged him to welcome the results without gloating.

"I hope that you'll make a statement along those lines," Carter said.

"I really don't know what to say," Baker replied.

"Do you have pencil and paper?"

"Yes."

So Carter dictated the outlines of a statement, the gist of which Baker would later polish and release. It was an extraordinary collaboration between a Democratic former president and a Republican secretary of state who had twice worked to defeat him at the polls.

Around 4:30 a.m., Baker called Bush to update him and they savored the moment, Baker in particular given all that he had gambled on the election and even argued with Bush about it. "They were like sky high," remembered Bernard Aronson, the assistant secretary of state, who had been the target of Quayle's backdoor complaining to Bush about the State Department's supposedly weak policy. When Baker called Aronson, "we sort of high-fived over the phone."

Baker had shown what could be accomplished through negotiation, achieving through diplomacy what Ronald Reagan and his band of Cold Warriors had not through military action. Baker had eased out a Communist dictatorship in America's backyard by democratic means, albeit after years of war increased the pressure for an open election. "It was a much more important defeat of the Sandinistas than if we had overthrown them through military aid," Aronson reckoned. "Then their supporters would always say it was imperialism and they were popular." Instead, "we demobilized the contras, we had a democratic government, and everybody could claim victory." In the United States, "the right could say we defeated the Sandinistas; we got them out. The left could say we ended the contra war."

It was not a permanent solution. In 2006, long after Baker left office, Ortega mounted a comeback and won back the presidency. But for America, at least, the war was over.

AS BAKER PREPARED to head back on the road to negotiate the fate of Germany, he had an advantage that no secretary of state before him ever had. Everyone knew that he was Bush's good friend and that when Baker spoke, he was speaking with the authority of the president of the United States. No one could go around him or over his head. Quayle and others had already tried and Baker invariably shut them down, often by directly intervening with Bush. If Baker declared a position on behalf of America, his interlocutors knew it would stick. And if he made a promise, they knew he could deliver. For nearly four years, it was almost as if the country had a second president to send overseas to negotiate and lay down the law.

The relationship between Bush and Baker was forged in personal friendship and deepened by Mary Stuart's untimely death. "Very close friend—probably closest," Bush recalled years later. "And I think they knew it. The closeness was evident to all." That was unlike any president and secretary of state before or since. Some secretaries were chosen because of their expertise in foreign affairs like Dean Acheson, John Foster Dulles, or Henry Kissinger. Others were political allies or even adversaries of the president like William Jennings Bryan in the early twentieth century. Many were clearly subordinates, not equals. Probably not since James Madison served Thomas Jefferson had a president and secretary of state enjoyed a genuine friendship before entering office.

For Baker, the relationship with Bush was an asset, invaluable political capital that he knew how to spend. "That empowered him in Washington during tough troubles," said Aaron David Miller, who saw it up close as a Middle East negotiator for Baker. "It empowered him abroad. When you showed up, when you landed in capital X and got off that plane, I saw the difference in the way people reacted to Baker and the others. I mean, it was like mounting a small invasion of a foreign country. People were on edge. They were nervous. They were worried. They were sitting on the edge of their chairs in meetings wondering, 'What's he going to ask me to do? Can I do what he wants me to do? Is he going to get mad at me?' And a lot of that mystique was certainly deliberately cultivated. But it reflected a reality that everyone understood—there was no daylight, zero, between the two institutions and the two individuals."

Baker talked with Bush nearly every day and made a point of haunting the halls of the West Wing as often as possible. "Baker seemed to spend almost as much time in the White House as at State," noticed James Dobbins, the Europe adviser. To Dobbins and other State Department institutionalists, that was not necessarily a compliment. But they did not deny that their boss had clout where it mattered. Baker had two private, thirty-minute meetings with Bush in the Oval Office each week, on Wednesdays and Fridays, when they were in town. Wherever he was in the world, Baker also sent Bush a one-page overnight summary each day called the "Secretary's Night Letter to the President" covering at least three topics. "He'd tell it like it was," Bush recalled. "He didn't shield any bad stuff for fear or worry about him. It's great. Having someone there that you totally trusted was a good thing for me."

If he needed to, Baker would call late at night or come by the executive mansion on a Sunday afternoon. When they traveled together, Bush and Baker would share quarters, as they had on the storm-tossed Navy cruiser during the Malta summit. Sometimes, they would conjure up the other part of their life together, getting back on the tennis court or dreaming up a hunting trip. When they flew in a helicopter over Barranquilla, Colombia, in February for a summit, Baker looked out the window at the landscape below and said to Bush, "This is a place where you and I could shoot some quail."

Baker made a point of calling Bush "Mr. President" in front of others, but in more relaxed moments, Bush called his friend "Bake" and the secretary called the president *El Jefe*, Spanish for "the chief," or *Jef* for short. Robert Kimmitt noticed that there was "a visible lightness, almost jocularity in the relationship between" the two. By protocol, the secretary of state sat to the president's right during cabinet and National Security Council meetings, and before the formalities began, Baker and Bush would often poke each other over, for instance, who got to bed earlier the night before. "Bush would say, 'Oh, I had to meet with this group or that group,'" Kimmitt said, "and Baker said, 'Well, that's why you're the social butterfly and I'm not.'" Sometimes their poking had an edge to it. During a meeting with Eduard Shevardnadze, Bush said that his approach to arms control was not due to a love of power. "Well, I'm not sure about Jim!" Bush joked.

If they were like brothers, it was a relationship shadowed by sibling rivalry. "They're good friends, but there was always that little bit of competition," Dan Quayle observed. "Baker, he ran for office, didn't succeed, his buddy Bush did and he's president and I think Baker always thought he could have been president. However, it didn't work out that way." Bush no doubt sensed that. When Baker pushed too hard, Bush would push back. "If you're so smart, how come you're not vice president?" he would say during the Reagan years. That was modified after Bush won the White House. "If you're so smart, how come you're not president?"

Whenever it got to that stage, Baker knew it was time to ease up. "Like most siblings, we've been known to argue and holler at one another in private," Baker reflected, "and there's a healthy measure of friendly competition between us."

The imbalance in their partnership grated from time to time. No matter how far back they went, Bush was now president and Baker was not. When the two returned from a trip together to Andrews Air Force Base outside Washington, Bush boarded Marine One and flew to the White House in a matter of minutes. Baker had to return home via a half-hour car ride; to add insult to injury, by security protocol, he had to wait until the president's helicopter was safely away before he could even leave the base.

Baker was not above using his friendship with Bush to swat away nuisances. After one too many times cooling his heels on the tarmac at Andrews, Baker personally appealed to the director of the Secret Service. "I hope that you can find a way to grant the Secretary of State an exemption," he said. "What I am really requesting is that my limo and a follow-up car be permitted to leave the tarmac upon arrival rather than having to wait until the actual lift-off of Marine One, which on our last visit was some 12–15 minutes after arrival." He even had the president of the United States personally endorse the request. "Let's do this," Bush wrote by hand on the top of the letter. "GB." Baker did not hesitate to go directly to the president on more significant turf battles either and there were regular feuds with not only Quayle, but also the two men now filling posts that Baker had held during the Reagan administration: John Sununu, the White House chief of staff, and Nick Brady, the treasury secretary.

When dealing with Brent Scowcroft, Baker was usually careful not to flaunt the relationship with Bush, keenly aware that the national security adviser had his own equities and was in the White House every day. If Baker called Bush personally to brief him on a development or consult on a decision, he usually made sure that Scowcroft knew it. Yet he was acutely sensitive to any slights from the other direction. "Brent and Jim did get moderately crosswise, but very rarely," Bush said after leaving office. "Jim worried that he might be excluded from a decision that affected his department. As a former chief of staff, Baker knew how a strong-willed presidential advisor, if backed by the president, can easily isolate a cabinet member." And in some ways, Scowcroft was growing closer to the president than even Baker. The son of a wholesale grocer who became an air force pilot, Scowcroft, like Bush, flew in World War II. After the war, he crashed his P-51B Mustang in a New Hampshire forest, breaking his back and leaving him in a hospital for two years. After years of government service, he had learned to be the ultimate staff man and had become Bush's alter ego inside the White House. It was Scowcroft, not Baker, who would later coauthor a book on foreign policy with Bush.

In status-conscious Washington, Baker's high visibility was in and of itself a form of power and even many of his colleagues in the administration believed Baker's priority was looking out for himself at the expense of his friend. "He demanded more loyalty of the president than he gave in return," Robert Gates said years later. "When Baker would go beyond his brief, get in a jam, or get the president in hot water, he would call Scowcroft to insist that the president stand behind him. On the other hand, when convenient, he would at times take credit that in fact belonged to the president—or occasionally, in difficult circumstances, distance himself from the president." Quayle concluded that Baker used his ties to the president as both sword and shield in internal fights but, in fact, was insecure about it. "Baker's frequent invoking his 'thirty-five-year friendship' with Bush was taken as a sign of weakness by some," Quayle wrote in his memoir.

The tensions were real and the next few months of intensive negotiations with the Soviets would test their friendship like never before. But if Baker pushed the limits at times with Bush, it was because the president let him. Baker was not only Bush's friend. Bush would not have been in the White House without him.

CHAPTER 21

Winners and Losers

Within a couple of months of the fall of the Berlin Wall, it was clear to Bush and Baker that, as the president dictated to his diary, "reunification appears inevitable." But that did not mean they had any real plan yet for making it happen, other than assuming it was too important a matter to leave to others. Both the president and secretary of state took it for granted that the United States had to set the course. "We've got to lead," Bush told Baker and Brent Scowcroft after one particularly nerve-wracking round of conversations over a weekend in February 1990 with Helmut Kohl at Camp David and then Margaret Thatcher by telephone. The formidable British prime minister was still extremely wary of a reunified Germany, telling the Americans she was more worried about it now than about the Soviet threat.

At the same time, Baker realized how sensitive the Germans were to the notion that their future would be determined by the Four Powers who still held some measure of authority by virtue of their victory in World War II. In the past, meetings of the representatives of the Four Powers with the two Germanys had come across as demeaning to the Germans, as if the four grown-ups were at one table and the two Germans were at a small side table. "We called it the cat table," said Horst Teltschik. When Vernon Walters seemed to be repeating that with his meeting on the eve of Baker's Berlin visit, Hans-Dietrich Genscher quickly complained to Baker. The American secretary reassured the foreign minister. "Hans-Dietrich, we understand you," he said.

Baker knew that the Soviets also had to be assuaged and made to feel as if they still had some sway over what was to come. Having lost 27 million people in World War II fighting the Germans, the Soviets did not consider Germany's status some abstract historical curiosity. Practically no Russian family had been spared from devastating loss. Even if Mikhail Gorbachev and Eduard Shevardnadze were privately willing to accede to German unity, they had complicated domestic politics to navigate, both with hard-liners in the security agencies and with the broader population. Baker was searching for a diplomatic approach that would, at the very least, give Moscow some face-saving role in the coming negotiation.

The solution he seized on was a formula cooked up by his advisers at the State Department called Two Plus Four, meaning the two Germanys plus the four World War II victors. Over time, a debate would develop over who exactly first conceived the idea—Frank Fukuyama and other members of the policy planning team had worked all through the Christmas holiday on the proposal and Dennis Ross sent their plan on to Baker by late January. Baker had no pride of authorship on this one; his practice was not to come up with ideas so much as to recognize the good ones and run with them. Under the plan, the two Germanys would take on the central task of negotiating between themselves with the four others playing a subsidiary role confined to issues dealing with external security. This would give the Soviets cover, to make it look like they were a part of the process rather than having it imposed on them. "You had to make it appear that this wasn't a total defeat for them," said Ross. Brent Scowcroft, however, was dubious. He thought the Two Plus Four concept would add too many players to the process and, ultimately, slow it down. Still, he was willing to defer while Baker tested the idea with the other parties.

Genscher reacted favorably as long as it really was "Two Plus Four and not Four Plus Two," which Baker understood. Baker also adopted an idea that Genscher had advanced in a meeting in Washington that would reassure the Soviets by agreeing that NATO territory would not move eastward with a united Germany and that the alliance would not advance its forces beyond the old lines. Baker then flew to Moscow to try out his concept on the Soviets. Along the way, he met with Roland Dumas, the French foreign minister, during a 2 a.m. refueling stop in Shannon, Ireland, and secured his support. From there, Baker stopped in a foggy Prague, where he met with Václav Havel, the leader of Czechoslovakia's Velvet Revolution.

By the time Baker made it to Moscow, the Soviet capital was consumed by its own political tumult. On February 7, just as he was arriving, the Central Committee of the Communist Party agreed to the latest Gorbachev reform proposal and voted to give up its monopoly on political power. Other parties, banned since the days of Lenin, would now be allowed. The world seemed to be spinning so quickly that neither Baker nor anyone else could keep up. As he traveled, a debate broke out among his staff about whether he should stop in Bulgaria after Moscow, a decision complicated by uncertainty over whether the government in Sofia would still be in office by the time he got there. In case that were not enough, in South Africa, the anti-apartheid leader Nelson Mandela was released from prison after twenty-seven years of captivity, presaging the eventual collapse of white minority rule.

In Moscow, Baker rolled out his Two Plus Four proposal to Shevardnadze, offering what he called "iron-clad guarantees that NATO's jurisdiction or forces would not move eastward." Baker met with Gorbachev in St. Catherine Hall in the Kremlin on February 9. The Soviet leader exuded self-confidence and strode into the hall as if he did not have a care.

"Events are moving rapidly in the world since Malta, more rapidly than any of us would have thought," Baker told him. But "for what it's worth, our relationship has moved from competition to cooperation."

"Those are my feelings," Gorbachev replied. "I have to tell you, there are one or two persons in your country who still regard us as the enemy. Let's face it. That's reality."

"There are fewer of those," Baker said, although in fact back home he and Bush were getting more and more fed up with the "right-wingers," as Bush called them, who seemed increasingly out of step with the rapid warming of relations with the Soviets.

Baker and Gorbachev discussed the status of ongoing nuclear arms talks as well as Bush's latest plan for a cap on conventional forces in Europe. Then they moved on to possible agreements on chemical weapons and a nuclear test ban. "I saw our negotiator yesterday in the men's room," Baker said, "and he told me he was making progress."

"All important business is always done in men's rooms and smoking rooms," Gorbachev joked.

But the electric question of the moment remained Germany. Baker explained his Two Plus Four concept to Gorbachev, who said he had been thinking about a six-power forum himself.

"I say Four Plus Two, you say Two Plus Four," Gorbachev said. "How do you look at this formula?"

"Two Plus Four is a better way," Baker said. It put the German states first.

To reassure Gorbachev, Baker brought up Genscher's idea and took it a step further. "There would be no extension of NATO's jurisdiction for forces of NATO one inch to the east," he told Gorbachev, coming back to the formula three times in the course of the conversation. The addition of the word "jurisdiction" was a mistake, a careless change in vocabulary of the sort that the lawyerly Baker usually avoided. It would come back to haunt him.

Gorbachev seemed resigned to the merger of East and West. "There is nothing terrifying in the prospect of a unified Germany," he said. But he insisted it should not be part of NATO, as Bush and Baker wanted, and broached the idea of a neutral Germany, belonging to neither Eastern nor Western alliance.

"A neutral Germany does not necessarily mean a demilitarized Germany," Baker cautioned, as he reverted to the official line, arguing that Europe would be better off with a reconstituted Germany firmly anchored in NATO. He asked Gorbachev if he would rather see an independent Germany outside NATO with no American forces present or a united Germany tied to NATO with the stabilizing presence of the United States.

Gorbachev said he would think about that. But, he quickly added, "Any extension of the zone of NATO is unacceptable."

"I agree," Baker said.

Back in Washington, Scowcroft's staff was alarmed when it learned about Baker's language. The word "jurisdiction" could imply that the NATO doctrine of collective defense, encapsulated in Article 5 of the North Atlantic Treaty, would apply only to part of German territory. That would unacceptably limit German sovereignty. It was one thing to agree not to move troops into the East right away, but all of Germany had to be part of NATO. "The NSC got to him pretty quickly and said that language might be misinterpreted," remembered Condoleezza Rice, then a Soviet adviser to Bush. At Baker's next stop, in Sofia, Bulgaria, he got a call from Scowcroft and his own deputy, Larry Eagleburger, expressing concern that he had shown too much flexibility on the issue of a reunited Germany in NATO. On the call, Baker maintained that he really had been insistent with the Russians, stressing "membership, membership, membership," as Bush recorded in his diary. But Baker heard the White House message and, without conceding a mistake, began walking back his words by ditching the term "jurisdiction" from all future discussions.

After Moscow and Bulgaria, Baker flew on to Romania, touring the outer reaches of the rapidly fraying Soviet empire. In Sofia, he had addressed a crowd of opposition activists chanting, "Bye-bye, Commies!" In Bucharest, he passed the palace where Nicolae Ceauşescu had ruled for nearly twenty-five years and saw smashed windows and hundreds of bullet marks on the exterior of the building.

Baker next flew to Ottawa, where envoys from twenty-three nations were gathering for a conference on an open-skies initiative intended to lead to a treaty allowing the United States, the Soviet Union, and other signatories to launch unarmed aerial observation flights over one another's territories on the theory that transparency would reduce the chances of conflict. Baker effectively commandeered the gathering in Ottawa's grand converted central railway station, turning the Beaux-Arts hallways into his personal venue for securing approval of his Two Plus Four approach. He hoped to strike quickly and announce it right away. Baker met with Shevardnadze and Hans-Dietrich Genscher separately at least five times in a single day as well as France's Roland Dumas and Douglas Hurd, the British foreign minister. Shevardnadze and Genscher also met without Baker, arguing for two hours over the terms "unity" versus "unification." The negotiations, Baker's speechwriter Andrew Carpendale said later, were "wild and wooly."

Shevardnadze was not happy with what he saw as the hijacking of the open-skies conference to discuss Germany, telling an aide it was a "stupid situation" and, when Baker pressed him, he refused to specify what Moscow's conditions for reunification really were. Still, Baker clinched a conventional forces agreement with Shevardnadze, codifying the massive withdrawal of troops from Europe that Bush had been seeking. Under the deal, each side would station no more than 195,000 troops in Central Europe, while the United States could keep another 30,000 elsewhere in Europe, primarily in Britain and Italy. That would force the Soviets to pull far more troops out of the middle of Europe than the United States would have to because Moscow had so many more there to begin with.

But back in Washington, Scowcroft was disturbed by how quickly all of this was coming together. He had thought Baker was merely going to test the viability of the Two Plus Four idea, not race ahead and make it a reality. And Scowcroft thought the conventional forces limits would be flexible, allowing the United States an aggregate 225,000, rather than committing to rigid, geographically specific sublimits. "Hit the roof twice," a Baker aide wrote of Scowcroft in notes from the day.

For once, Baker found himself at a real disconnect with the White House. Bush had not come up with a proposal of his own, but neither was he fully committed to Baker's idea and he wondered whether Helmut Kohl really was on board with the Two Plus Four concept, which was exactly what Kohl wondered about Bush. To clear things up, Bush got Kohl on the phone to confirm his position, a call that unintentionally had sent the signal that Bush was himself ambivalent. Did that mean Baker was freelancing? When Genscher told Baker that the chancellor's office had doubts about the White House commitment to the strategy, the secretary firmly assured him that the president did in fact support the plan. According to Dennis Ross, an aggravated Baker then headed back to his suite and called Bush, complaining that he had been undercut. "If I'm ever put in that position again," Baker snapped, "you'll be looking for a new secretary of state."

But Bush needed reassurance himself. While Genscher had told Baker that West Germany would go along with the Two Plus Four structure, Bush was not sure Kohl had really agreed. So Baker quickly found Genscher and told him to have Kohl call Bush to reassure him. Kohl did, but even then their conversation was vague enough that Bush felt compelled to call back to get a more explicit assurance. Finally, Bush conceded. "I had a long talk with Helmut Kohl," Bush recorded in his diary. "He wanted to go with what Jim Baker proposed and so we have."

It was hardly a ringing endorsement. Scowcroft was still not happy with all this uncertainty. He thought Baker was playing Bush. "He believed that Baker had presented Bush with a fait accompli and the president had been obliged, with some hesitation, to accept it," Condoleezza Rice and Philip Zelikow later wrote in their history of German reunification.

Baker was not above such maneuvering—and he pushed harder on Bush in this case than in almost any other. Here was an opening, *his* opening. In Ottawa, he seized it.

IT TURNED OUT that even Mikhail Gorbachev considered Baker a leaker. After the Ottawa summit, Gorbachev evidently saw a news account quoting an unnamed American official bragging that the Soviets had blinked. Gorbachev groused about it to Admiral William Crowe, the former chairman of the Joint Chiefs of Staff, who was visiting Moscow, and blamed it on Baker. Crowe duly reported back to the secretary.

Chagrined, Baker dashed off a handwritten note to Gorbachev saying that Crowe had told him about the conversation. "He said you had said that you thought the remarks came from me," Baker wrote. "They did not. Nor did I authorize them, although they could have been said by a member of our delegation." He added that he and Bush understood the pressures Gorbachev faced and wanted to help him, not make his task more difficult. "I am sorry if this statement was made," he added, and then repeated, "It was not authorized."

For German reunification to work, Baker knew that he had to find a way to keep Gorbachev on board. The danger of a rupture over Germany loomed large. If Gorbachev were provoked, he could use Soviet troops in East Germany to stop any merger and impose a new, Moscow-friendly government in East Berlin. He could also reverse his laissez-faire approach to the rest of Eastern Europe and reassert Soviet dominance, squelching the nascent democratic movement. Even worse, perhaps, the hard-liners in Moscow could turn on Gorbachev as a sellout to the West and topple him to form a revanchist regime that would roll back all of the gains of the last few years. The Cold War might be ending, but it was not over yet.

"We must find a solution where there won't be any winners and losers but where everybody wins," Baker told Shevardnadze at one point. At another, he plumbed Shevardnadze's bottom line. "Tell us what you need to make what is happening more acceptable to you," he said. "Tell us what you need and we'll see what we can do."

But this approach ran up against hard realities. Just weeks after Ottawa, in fact, Shevardnadze passed an urgent message to Baker through his ambassador in Moscow, warning that the situation for Gorbachev was now "critical" because of unrest in the three Baltic republics. The Soviet hold over the Baltics after a half century of Soviet rule seemed more tenuous than ever and mass protests practically defied the Kremlin to crack down. Baker was so worried about Shevardnadze's warning that he personally brought it to Bush at the White House on the morning of March 7.

Shevardnadze was right. On March 11, the crisis hit in full as Lithuania declared its independence, becoming the first Soviet republic to do so. Gorbachev responded by imposing an oil embargo and economic blockade against the tiny republic. For Washington, any response promised to create further problems as the United States was officially on record supporting Baltic independence, yet Bush and Baker were reluctant to push Gorbachev too hard for fear of triggering a backlash. The only way Lithuania and the other Baltic states could actually achieve independence was by convincing Gorbachev to let them go. So while Baker pressed Shevardnadze not to use force, critics in Washington were assailing the administration for not taking a stronger stand on behalf of Lithuanian national aspirations.

At a national security team meeting one early evening in April, Bush and Scowcroft looked for ways to toughen the American response to the Soviet embargo on Lithuania and discussed imposing sanctions against Moscow. Baker urged caution, suggesting that their two goals should be to protect the overall relationship with the Soviet Union and to avoid a fight with America's allies in Europe. Bush agreed, deciding to forgo sanctions and proceed with a summit with Gorbachev in Washington in the spring. This did not go over well on Capitol Hill or among the Baltic dissidents making a revolution against Moscow. Vytautas Landsbergis, the fifty-seven-year-old music professor in a worn suit who was leading the independence movement and had been named head of the new Lithuanian state, complained of "another Munich," while the United States Senate voted overwhelmingly against proceeding with a new trade agreement that Bush was negotiating with the Soviet Union until the embargo was lifted.

For Baker, Germany was the bigger priority, one that he was not willing to sacrifice in favor of the Baltic states. He remained determined to help Shevardnadze, his friend and negotiating partner. But he and Bush were feeling the political heat at home and looking for a way out. At one point, Baker even inserted himself into this Soviet internal dispute. What if, he asked Shevardnadze, Landsbergis agreed to "suspend" Lithuania's independence decree to pursue talks with the Kremlin? Shevardnadze was unmoved, but Bush at least was relieved that Baker seemed determined to get them out of what was starting to feel like an increasingly untenable situation. "After the Baker conversation, I felt like a kettle whose steam had been drained off a little bit," the president told his diary.

East Germans, meanwhile, were not waiting for the superpowers to sort things out. They went to the polls in March and elected a parliament controlled by allies of Helmut Kohl's party in the West, delivering an overwhelming mandate for reunification. But Kohl and Genscher were sending conflicting signals about the future of a merged German state in NATO. Genscher suggested that it might be reasonable to leave the former East German territory out of NATO, which Kohl quickly rejected. The first meeting of the Two Plus Four ministers, held in the World Room of the West German Foreign Ministry in Bonn, did not resolve the matter and Shevardnadze laid down an uncompromising Soviet position against NATO membership for the future German state.

BAKER ARRIVED in Moscow in May hoping to break the impasse. He offered what came to be called the nine reassurances, including a commitment to allow Soviet troops in East Germany to remain for a transition period and not to extend NATO forces into that territory until they left. This was hardly the promise not to extend the alliance east at all that he had once floated too casually. But he now insisted to the Soviets that this was the best the United States could do. Baker recorded his overall message to Gorbachev in notes: "Anchor Germany to West. Unless we do instability. History will repeat!" Gorbachev was not convinced. Reflecting increasing pressure from his security services, Gorbachev told Baker, "we cannot accept a unified Germany as a member of just NATO or the Warsaw Pact."

Gorbachev was not the only one facing rebellious Cold Warriors reluctant to give up the fight. In Washington, Baker's continuing nuclear arms control talks with the Kremlin were taken by some of the same hard-liners suspicious of Baker and Bush since the early days of the Reagan administration as nothing short of an American surrender. "Taking Baker to the Cleaners," was the headline over a *New York Times* column by William Safire, who had an open line to the dissidents inside the Bush team. "The right wing is jumping on us about arms control," Bush lamented privately. Incensed by the column, Baker fingered Bush's special adviser on arms control, a lieutenant general named Edward Rowny, an outspoken hawk who, Baker told the president, had been seen coming out of Safire's office the day before the column appeared.

Bristling at the friendly fire, Baker established a secret back channel to Colin Powell during the negotiations for a reality check on what was actually necessary for the national security and what was not. "Jim would come to me, quietly and surreptitiously, to ask about what was really tolerable," Powell recalled. "'Colin, can we really give up the Tacit Rainbow system?'" Tacit Rainbow was a jet-powered missile designed to suppress enemy air defenses. "I would give him a military opinion, which was, 'Yeah, give it up.'"

During one negotiation in Moscow, the two sides were debating limits on the Tu-22M Soviet bomber, which NATO called the Backfire bomber. First introduced in the 1970s, the Backfire bomber gave headaches to Western militaries because of its ability to penetrate air defenses at low altitudes, which made it harder to track and counter. Western military planners anticipated that in the event of war it would likely be used to attack American aircraft carrier groups in the Atlantic and Mediterranean as well as European ports and airfields, but it could also be sent on intercontinental missions against the United States.

For years, the Russians had argued that the Backfire was a medium-range aircraft that should not be covered by the emerging treaty, but the Pentagon had estimated its range between 2,900 and 3,350 miles, which could be extended even farther with in-air refueling, making it a threat to the American mainland and therefore a weapon that should be restricted under any strategic arms agreement. Even if it were intended mainly for theater combat, leaving it out of the treaty would effectively give the Soviets a loophole so that they could replace what they gave up in long-range capacity with the Backfire. "It became a totem for the conservatives—you had to do something about the Backfire," recalled Richard Burt, who was Baker's arms control negotiator.

When Burt and his Soviet counterpart could not agree on how many Backfire bombers Moscow should be allowed, the issue got kicked upstairs to Baker and Shevardnadze. Rather than split the difference, Baker shifted course and proposed a cap of five hundred bombers, a number even lower than the original American position. Shevardnadze, who was under pressure from his own hawks, appeared as if he were in deep pain. "He looks at Baker with these pleading eyes and Baker just won't give an inch," Burt said. "He just won't give an inch." Burt waited, shifting uncomfortably in his chair, as if watching a game of chicken with two cars racing toward each other for a certain collision. He kept expecting Baker to finally say, fine, he would meet in the middle. "But Baker doesn't do it. Baker does not move. And there's a silence in the room that goes on for, I would say, over a minute or so. And finally, Shevardnadze says, 'Okay, let's move on to the next topic.'"

Baker had gotten a better deal than the American side had originally sought. As he and his team slipped into the car to leave the negotiations, Baker turned to a stunned Burt.

"Rick, you're probably pissed at me, right?" Baker asked. "You have to deal with these guys tomorrow."

"No, I'm not pissed," Burt answered. "You have this relationship with Shevardnadze so I'm surprised you pressed him that hard."

"Let me tell you something," Baker said. "This wasn't really a negotiation between me and Shevardnadze or the U.S. against the Russians. This has more to do with the negotiations *within* the U.S. government."

His adversary, in other words, was not the Soviet Union; it was the Pentagon. When they returned to the embassy, Baker went to report on the results of the talks to a roomful of military officers. He walked through all the other results but left out the Backfire until someone brought it up.

"How many Backfires did they get?" one of the military officers asked, as if to say, *how many did you give away?*

Baker leaned over the table. "Five hundred," he said.

Triumphantly, he added: "Fuck you."

THE POLARIZED POLITICS in both capitals set up a climactic encounter in Washington at the end of May, when Gorbachev visited for his second meeting of the Bush presidency. Unlike Malta, this was meant to be a full-fledged superpower summit, complete with red carpets and monumental agreements to sign. On the morning of May 31, Bush welcomed Gorbachev on the South Lawn with a formal ceremony including a fife and drum corps in Revolutionary garb and a twenty-one-gun salute. In the evening he hosted a glittery State Dinner, serving Maine lobster *en gelée* to the Soviets on a perfect, balmy Washington spring night. But Lithuania complicated what had promised to be a display of the new friendship between longtime adversaries.

When the two presidents sat down in the Oval Office for the first of their meetings over four days, Gorbachev seemed most focused on securing the trade agreement that Bush under pressure from Congress had effectively shelved because of the Lithuania crisis. Baker heard the same from Shevardnadze in a separate meeting in another room. Shevardnadze was unusually passionate, almost beseeching Baker, making clear that Gorbachev's standing at home depended on his leaving Washington with something tangible to justify his outreach to the West.

The afternoon session in the Cabinet Room of the White House brought the presidents and foreign ministers together with their aides and focused intensely on the German question. The two sides ran through their well-rehearsed arguments over German membership in NATO until finally Bush cited the Helsinki Final Act, an accord signed in the Finnish capital in 1975 by thirty-five nations including the Soviet Union to ratify the rights of nations and peoples in postwar Europe.

Given Helsinki, Bush asked Gorbachev, would not a united Germany have the right to decide for itself which alliance it would join?

Gorbachev shrugged. Yes, he said, that was true.

Suddenly, Marshal Sergei Akhromeyev, now Gorbachev's senior military adviser, and other aides on the Soviet side were shifting in their seats uncomfortably as the Americans were waiting for the translation and still not sure what had been said. "It was as if everybody on the other side of the table just heard his mother died," recalled Robert Blackwill, the national security aide. Just like that, the Soviet leader had conceded that the new German state could join NATO if it wanted to. It took a few moments for the Americans to catch up.

Shevardnadze, sitting next to Gorbachev, leaned forward and tried to whisper something to him, but the Soviet president just brushed him off.

Blackwill scribbled out a note and passed it to Bush: *Get him to say it again. Do I understand you right?*

Bush nodded. "I'm gratified that you and I seem to agree that nations can choose their own alliances," he told Gorbachev.

"Do you and I agree that a united Germany has the right to be non-aligned or a member of NATO in a final document?" Gorbachev asked.

"I agree with that," Bush answered, "but the German public wants to be in NATO. But if they want out of NATO, we will respect that. They are a democracy."

"I agree to say so publicly," Gorbachev said, "that the United States and the USSR are in favor of seeing a united Germany with a final settlement leaving it up to where a united Germany can choose."

"I would put it differently," Bush replied. "We support a united Germany in NATO. If they don't want in, we will respect that."

Gorbachev accepted that. His aides, however, were in a quiet frenzy. After the meeting broke up, Akhromeyev "practically assaulted" one of Gorbachev's top foreign policy advisers, Anatoly Chernyaev, on the White House lawn, pressing to know whether the concession had been planned. Chernyaev said it was not; Gorbachev had spoken entirely off the cuff.

Impromptu or not, it was a landmark breakthrough. The Soviet Union had not only agreed to allow Germany to reunify but to do so on Western terms. Months of patient diplomacy had paid off. The challenge for Baker now was to keep hard-liners like Akhromeyev from unraveling the accord. One way to do that was to give Gorbachev a win. As the summit wound down, Baker and Bush came up with an impromptu formula of their own: What if the president signed the trade agreement, but told Gorbachev he would not send it to Congress for final approval until the embargo on Lithuania was lifted? Given the progress on Germany, Bush and Baker wanted to advance the trade agreement even though they knew it would generate considerable criticism at home. Publicly, they made it contingent on the expected Soviet passage of a law liberalizing emigration policy. Privately, they used Baker's formula, letting Gorbachev know they would only send the agreement to Capitol Hill if he ended the Lithuania embargo.

This was a careful balance, reflecting Baker's approach to international relations, taking a hit at home if necessary in order to give the other side something to hold on to. For Baker, the real goal here was a unified Germany anchored in NATO without a Soviet backlash—and to get it, he was willing to make concessions even at the expense of more conservative carping.

As the two leaders and their teams headed to Camp David for addi-tional talks, the mood eased. Gorbachev threw a ringer his first time out at Bush's favorite horseshoe pit and the two shed some of their summit shields. Gorbachev had a ribald, off-color sense of humor. Baker could remember one joke that Gorbachev liked to tell: "They say Mitterrand has 1,000 lovers. One has AIDS, but he doesn't know which one. Bush has 100 bodyguards. One is a terrorist, but he doesn't know which one. Gorbachev has 100 economic advisers. One is smart, but he doesn't know which one." He said it often and it always got a laugh.

When coffee was served at Camp David, Gorbachev was astonished to be offered regular or decaffeinated, which did not exist in the Soviet Union. "Drinking decaffeinated coffee is like licking sugar through glass," he said wryly.

Then he looked around the room. "We're all men here?" he said. "So, having intercourse with a condom is the same thing as licking sugar through glass."

That was the kind of boys' talk that Gorbachev liked to engage in. Baker and Bush did not mind. They had their own bawdy humor and there were no women on either side in the official delegations for the talks. Condoleezza Rice was Bush's top Soviet adviser, a Russian speaker with a doctorate in political science, but she had gotten used to the frater-nity atmosphere that surrounded her.

Rice would play a key role as the Bush team figured out how to con-firm their negotiating breakthrough with Gorbachev at the end of the summit without unduly alarming their Soviet counterparts. In their mind, Gorbachev's acknowledgment that Germany could choose its own alli-ances was the turning point in the struggle over reunification and Baker and Bush wanted to lock it in without calling so much attention to it that it would fuel what Bush later called the "virtually open rebellion" among the Soviet hard-liners. No formal announcement would be made. Instead, American officials decided to include a comment from Bush memorializ-ing Gorbachev's concession in the prepared remarks that he would deliver to open the joint news conference that the two leaders would hold at the end of the summit.

"We are in full agreement that the matter of alliance membership is, in accordance with the Helsinki Final Act, a matter for the Germans to decide," Bush would say, according to the draft they came up with. Rice gave a copy to Alexander Bessmertnykh, the Soviet ambassador to Washington, to see if Gorbachev would protest the characterization. After studying it, the Soviets returned it with no objections, so Bush went ahead with the comment at their session with reporters on June 3, elliptically announcing the deal that for all intents and purposes would end more than four decades of division in the heart of Europe.

Journalists failed to pick up on its significance. The next day's *Washington Post* did not quote Bush's statement until the twenty-third paragraph. The *New York Times* story only mentioned it in the twenty-ninth paragraph, adding that "administration officials said they did not read much significance into the comment." A separate front-page news analysis concluded that the talks produced "no real progress on the German question." Baker, however, knew better.

SEVERAL MONTHS LATER, in early September, Baker was deep asleep in his hotel room around 1 a.m. in Moscow after taking a sleeping pill when the West German foreign minister demanded that he be roused. The treaty sealing German reunification was to be signed in the morning but now it looked like the whole thing was falling apart.

In the eventful summer since Gorbachev's concession in Washington, Checkpoint Charlie, the most infamous crossing point in the old Berlin Wall, had been dismantled and East Germany had adopted the West's deutsche mark as its currency. At points, the Soviets had seemed to backtrack on Gorbachev's position, only to be persuaded to return. And now a formal treaty was ready. Not even Baker, the fanatic for preparation, had anticipated the possible collapse of the whole deal just hours before it was to be finalized.

The last-minute crisis began when Britain's Douglas Hurd insisted that the agreement specifically permit NATO allies to conduct military exercises on the territory of the former East Germany. Over the course of the evening, Hurd's narrow point had turned into a deal killer as Shevardnadze declared that the Soviet Union was canceling the signing ceremony. When Genscher, laughing and ebullient, returned from dinner and learned what was happening, he grew "deeply agitated" and insisted that he had to see Baker immediately.

The Germans called the Americans, who told them that the jet-lagged Baker had had a nightcap, gone to bed, and could not be disturbed.

"Well, *I* will disturb him," Genscher declared and set off for Baker's hotel.

Robert Zoellick and Margaret Tutwiler knocked on Baker's door and woke him to let him know what was happening. Groggy, he put on pajamas and a grayish brown hotel bathrobe, then washed his face. Genscher arrived and explained the dilemma to Baker, who was out of sorts at the late-night disruption. "He was not in the best of moods," conceded Dieter Kastrup, who accompanied Genscher.

But Baker quickly dissected the problem and agreed to finagle it. The treaty stipulated that foreign NATO troops could not be "stationed" or "deployed" in the former East Germany. Hurd wanted that interpreted to mean that short-term exercises involving small numbers of troops could still be held there, while Shevardnadze insisted on a total ban. Baker concluded that they should leave the word "deployed" in the text but agree verbally that there would be no large-scale maneuvers in the east.

In the morning, Baker met the other Western foreign ministers at 8:30 a.m. for what Hurd called "a dour autumnal breakfast" at the French embassy and struck a compromise. An annex to the treaty would make clear that the meaning of "deployed" would be left to the new Germany, which would interpret it responsibly "taking into account the security interests" of the other parties. Hurd thought the Russians and Germans had overreacted. "The late night flurry was unnecessary," he said. "I had no intention of allowing a relatively minor argument to get out of hand."

The signing then went ahead as planned. On September 12, 1990, Baker joined Gorbachev and the other ministers in the same hotel with drooping crystal chandeliers and teal blue cloth on the walls where the Warsaw Pact traditionally met when its leaders were in town, a fitting bit of symbolism. Under the treaty, the Four Powers relinquished their occupying rights over their defeated World War II enemy and Germany regained its complete sovereignty, forty-five years after the conflict. The treaty paved the way for East Germany to be absorbed into West Germany on October 3, with the enlarged state remaining in NATO. Soviet troops would depart by the end of 1994.

"The new Germany is here," Baker declared, signing on behalf of the United States. Champagne was brought out and Baker, Gorbachev, and the others toasted. Ten months earlier, the moment had been unthinkable. Ten months later, it might well have been politically impossible.

The next day, Baker flew off to the Middle East. Iraq had invaded Kuwait only a few weeks before. He had a new crisis to manage.

CHAPTER 22

Desert Diplomacy

This time they went fishing for Siberian grayling. A freshwater cousin of the salmon, the grayling was bigger than Wyoming trout, so Eduard Shevardnadze figured he had a fighting chance. He held the rod with determination, his face marked by tension as he studied the water intently. "He did not want to fail again," his translator remembered. Finally, the foreign minister got a bite and happily reeled in his catch as Baker and their aides expressed delight.

It was the summer of 1990, and Baker had accepted an invitation from Shevardnadze to reciprocate for their Wyoming frontier sojourn. Rather than meet in stolid, forbidding Moscow, Shevardnadze asked Baker to join him in Irkutsk, a Siberian outpost on the shores of Lake Baikal, the world's largest freshwater lake, filled in summertime with melted ice from the mountains.

Baker arrived at 2:20 a.m., recovering from a nasty case of intestinal flu from a prior stop in Singapore. He and Shevardnadze spent most of the next day in meetings and cruising on a hydrofoil around the lake and the Angara River, where they each caught a single fish. In the evening, they gathered in a VIP log cabin built to host Dwight Eisenhower in 1960, before his visit was canceled over the U-2 spy plane incident. In classic Russian fashion, an eight-course meal was then laid on, keeping them up until late at night.

The talks centered on the rapid unwinding of the geopolitical order in Europe, the same issues that had occupied Baker and Shevardnadze over the past year and a half. Only in passing did they even touch on the topic that would consume them for the next half year—the growing instability in the Middle East, where Saddam Hussein, the blustery, mustachioed Arab strongman who ruled Iraq with an iron fist, had been hounding his smaller neighbor in Kuwait for months, coveting its oil fields to add to his own.

Reassured by Middle East allies, including President Hosni Mubarak of Egypt, King Fahd of Saudi Arabia, and King Hussein of Jordan, that Saddam Hussein would never actually invade Kuwait, Baker felt free to focus on other matters. But around midnight, after returning from his marathon day with Shevardnadze, the traveling secretary of state received a call from Robert Kimmitt back in Washington telling him that Iraq was massing troops on the Kuwait border. The CIA's deputy director, Richard Kerr, now thought the chances of an invasion were growing. At 7:45 a.m. Siberian time on August 2, Kimmitt called back with grimmer news, speaking elliptically over the phone, given that the secretary was on Soviet territory on a line that was presumably being monitored.

"Do you recall the subject we talked about before?" Kimmitt asked.

"Yes," Baker said.

"Well, Dick Kerr's people now think it's more likely than not the country we spoke about is going to move."

Baker got the message. After hanging up, he headed to his first meeting of the day with Shevardnadze and repeated what he had just been told.

"It looks bad," Baker told him. "We hope you can restrain them."

Shevardnadze, deeply familiar with Iraq, a Soviet ally and arms customer for decades, expressed skepticism that Hussein would be so brazen. "I can't believe that. What could he possibly gain?"

The minister instructed an aide to check with Soviet intelligence and then reported back to Baker. "Don't worry," Shevardnadze said. "Nothing's going to happen."

As the meeting progressed, Margaret Tutwiler suddenly appeared and slipped Baker a note. "Gentlemen," Baker announced after reading it, "the State Department operations center has received information that Iraqi troops crossed the border of Kuwait." Yet even with this news, neither the American secretary of state nor the Soviet foreign minister fully recognized the opening of a new crisis. Perhaps it was only a feint or a limited incursion that could be reversed. "The Kuwaiti ambassador in Washington does not believe that it is yet a full-scale invasion," Baker reported.

Shevardnadze, too, remained dubious. Iraqi troops had crossed their neighbors' borders before and stayed briefly before turning around. Baghdad could hardly want another fight after its disastrous eight-year war with neighboring Iran, which had practically bankrupted Iraq and led to hundreds of thousands of deaths before ending in an inconclusive stalemate barely two years earlier. "I could not imagine that Saddam Hussein would dare to invade Kuwait," Shevardnadze said later. It seemed "completely irrational." The two went back to their discussions about conventional forces in Europe.

As the official meetings wrapped up, Baker and Shevardnadze were hoping that Iraq might pull back. Still not entirely absorbing the import of the situation he now had to deal with, Baker went ahead to his next scheduled stop in Mongolia, where his real goal was two days of hunting ibex in the Gobi Desert. Rather than accompanying him, several of his aides, including Dennis Ross and Robert Zoellick, were already scheduled to hitch a ride on Shevardnadze's plane back to Moscow, which they did, enjoying generous helpings of caviar during the flight while speculating with the Soviets about what Hussein was up to. Shevardnadze was in an expansive mood with his guests, but just as uninformed as the Americans.

Any hopes that Hussein was bluffing had evaporated by the time Baker landed in Mongolia, where he received word that Iraqi troops were heading to Kuwait City, the capital, and gobbling up the entire country. Seizing Kuwait would give Hussein control of 20 percent of the world's oil reserves; if he continued on to Saudi Arabia, now within easy striking distance, he would become master of nearly half of the petroleum supplies on the planet.

In his hotel room in Ulan Bator, the Mongolian capital, Baker was woken in the middle of the night by Tutwiler, who reported that his team in Moscow was suggesting a joint statement with the Soviets condemning the invasion and that Shevardnadze was willing. At 1:45 a.m., Baker called Bush, who was on Air Force One en route to Aspen, Colorado, for a speech and a meeting with Margaret Thatcher. Bush signed off on the idea.

Baker never got to the ibex hunt. Cutting short his Mongolian visit, he decided to fly to Moscow to stand with Shevardnadze for their joint statement, but while he was in the air, the Soviets kept pulling back from the tough language in the draft. Ross told his Soviet counterpart, Sergei Tarasenko, that the statement had to threaten an arms boycott to have any real bite, but Iraq had been a Soviet client state for years and Russian generals were pushing back. Shevardnadze worried about aggravating Hussein at a time when eight thousand Soviet citizens were still in Iraq and potentially at risk. Ross threatened to tell Baker to turn his plane around and not come to Moscow if the statement was toothless.

What Baker's team guessed but did not fully know was that Shevardnadze was fighting a rearguard battle inside his own government. "For several hours, I had been trying to overcome strong resistance," Shevardnadze acknowledged later. When Baker landed at Vnukovo-2, the VIP airport outside Moscow, Ross came on board his plane to explain the impasse. Shevardnadze then spirited Baker into an airport building and upstairs to a spartan second-floor conference room. Baker quickly detected that Shevardnadze needed to hear that the joint statement was not an automatic green light for an American war. "I gave him the assurance that it was not just an excuse to create a U.S. military presence," Baker said.

After ninety minutes, Baker closed the deal and Shevardnadze agreed to the stronger language, including an arms embargo. "It was one of the most difficult decisions I had ever had to make," Shevardnadze said. Baker learned afterward that the Soviet foreign minister acted without Gorbachev's explicit permission.

Looking tired after a long flight across the Eurasian continent, Baker read the statement to reporters, denouncing the "brutal and illegal invasion of Kuwait by Iraqi military forces." With Shevardnadze at his side, Baker said: "Today, we take the unusual step of jointly calling upon the rest of the international community to join with us in an international cutoff of all arms supplies to Iraq."

The collaboration was a singular moment in Russian-American relations. After forty-five years of jockeying for control of the world, the United States and the Soviet Union were suddenly joining together to enforce common standards of international conduct. The message seemed clear: The days of tyrants like Hussein playing one superpower off the other were coming to an end. If the pending reunification of Germany were not enough indication that the world had changed, the scene of American and Soviet officials standing side by side surely was. As Baker wrote later, "The Cold War breathed its last at an airport terminal on the outskirts of Moscow."

AT THE STATE DEPARTMENT, Baker's team was already calling it "the first post–Cold War crisis." The confrontation in the Persian Gulf would determine the rules of the road for a new age. Bush would soon be speaking of a New World Order, but no one knew yet just what kind of order there would be. And could the United States successfully rally the world to enforce it?

There were plenty of reasons why the Iraqi invasion posed a threat beyond the immediate crisis. Here was a regional power exercising force to redraw national boundaries, oppress a weaker neighbor, violate the human rights of its people, seize control of oil resources, and threaten another even more critical neighbor. But beyond the national and international interests at stake, Bush was simply offended. If the United States was going to be the world's policeman, then Hussein was one street thug who would have to be put in his place.

That Iraq would suddenly become the primary focus of the Bush presidency only underscored how much Baker and his team had missed the warning signs. "We didn't pay any attention to Iraq," Baker admitted later. Absorbed by the negotiations over Germany and managing the jaw-dropping developments in the Soviet Union and Eastern Europe, he had left the Middle East to others to monitor. The professionals at the State Department had done so, observing the run-up to the invasion, but uncertain what to make of it or how hard to push. In the prelude to war, Baker's office had sent cables to the American embassy in Baghdad, and April Glaspie, the ambassador, had forwarded the messages to Hussein.

On July 24, a cable in Baker's name outlined administration policy:

> While we take no position on the border delineation issue raised by Iraq with respect to Kuwait, or on other bilateral disputes, Iraqi statements suggest an intention to resolve outstanding disagreements by the use of force, an approach which is contrary to U.N. charter principles. The implications of having oil production and pricing policy in the gulf determined and enforced by Iraqi guns are disturbing.

Without warning, Hussein summoned Glaspie the next day. Fluent in Arabic, she went to see Hussein alone without a translator or aide. In her rush, Glaspie had no time to seek additional guidance from Washington, so she stuck to the instructions she had already received. She told Hussein that any dispute should be settled by peaceful means, even as she noted that "we have no opinion on the Arab-Arab conflicts, like your border disagreement with Kuwait." She added: "James Baker has directed our official spokesmen to emphasize this instruction." At one point, Hussein was interrupted and left to take a telephone call. When he returned, he told Glaspie that Egypt's Hosni Mubarak had offered to broker talks with the Kuwaitis and he had agreed. "This is good news," Glaspie said. "Congratulations."

Glaspie's message of neutrality in a border dispute was certainly not meant as an endorsement of Iraq's claims against Kuwait, but simply a statement of long-standing American policy that Washington would not meddle in the specifics. Still, while Baker was focused elsewhere, some administration officials like Dennis Ross and Paul Wolfowitz, the undersecretary of defense, worried that Glaspie's tone was not strong enough. They decided to send a letter in Bush's name to Hussein repeating that "differences are best resolved by peaceful means and not by threats."

After the invasion, critics complained that the administration had not done more to stop it from happening, pointing to Glaspie's meeting with Hussein as Exhibit A. Bush, for one, defended Glaspie. "She was lied to by him," he wrote after leaving office, "and she clearly spelled out that we could not condone settlement of disputes by other than peaceful means. It is a total misreading of this conversation to conclude that we were giving Saddam a green light to seize his neighbor."

But Baker seemed more interested in distancing himself. Asked about the episode on NBC's *Meet the Press* a few weeks after the invasion, he all but disavowed any knowledge of the instructions to Glaspie. "What you want me to do is say that those instructions were sent specifically by me on my specific orders," he said. "I'm not going to deny what the policy was, but I'm going to say to you that there are probably 312,000 or so cables that go out under my name as secretary of state." His defense did not impress. In a harsh column headlined "James A. Baker, Please Resign," Michael Kinsley wrote in *The Washington Post* that "Washington's greatest self-positioner" should step down as an act of accountability. "But taking responsibility isn't Jim Baker's style," Kinsley wrote. "He has distanced himself from Glaspie. He also has mounted a damage-control campaign, both contemptible and hilarious, through his favorite medium of self-aggrandizing leaks to the press."

Years after leaving office, Baker chose to deflect blame for deflecting blame. "We were being accused of hanging April Glaspie out to dry and we probably should have," he told his ghostwriter one day while working on his memoir. "What I was *really* doing there, for which I got a lot of grief, was trying to protect her, because she didn't *receive* any instructions." He added that he did not want to say that on *Meet the Press* "and put another nail into her coffin, if you will. So I just kissed it away by saying, 'Well, there are a lot of cables that went out under my name.'" In fact there was no cable, he repeated. "So if I'd been thoroughly honest about it I would have been nailing April Glaspie and I was trying not to."

What Baker meant was that Glaspie had no time to obtain specific instructions after Hussein summoned her. But that was a bit disingenuous; she was, in fact, operating on instructions that she had received in Baker's name, just a day earlier. Later in retirement, long after the heat of the moment had passed, Baker was less sensitive about the matter and more willing to exonerate Glaspie. "She didn't do anything wrong in my opinion," he said. "It all happened very quickly. He hauled her in and she was just parroting what our policy" had been to that point. Did she get a raw deal? "I thought she did. She was blamed for something. She was just articulating what our standard policy was."

Glaspie, for her part, seemed less forgiving of Baker. Asked in an interview with an Arab news outlet nearly eighteen years later what she thought about the "blame from Baker," she pointedly did not say what she thought of the secretary of state, offering praise instead for Bush. The idea that she had given Hussein a green light, she added, "was invented by Tariq Aziz," the Iraqi foreign minister. "Obviously I did not give Saddam any such idea that we would not interfere in a border dispute," she said. "What I did tell him was he must not interfere in Kuwait or anywhere else."

She acknowledged that he might not have taken her message seriously enough. "I am quite happy to take the blame," she said. "Perhaps I was not able to make Saddam believe that we would do what we said we would do, but in all honesty, I don't think anybody in the world could have persuaded him." For his part, Aziz later said he did not take her message as a green light. "She didn't tell us in the sense that we concluded that the Americans will not retaliate," he said.

Then again, even the Americans had no idea whether they would or not. Baker believed in prior preparation, but there was no plan for this. Going to war with Iraq was not then, nor had it ever been, on the agenda.

AT THE TIME, in fact, both Bush and Baker were extremely defensive. Hussein's swift takeover of Kuwait seemed another catastrophe at a moment when the administration was struggling with its worst political crisis yet. Indeed, while Baker was preoccupied with the unraveling of the Soviet empire in Eastern Europe, the president had spent the summer in an escalating Republican feud that Baker had tried to warn him about.

In December 1988, just a month after the election and weeks before Bush would move into the White House, Baker had ridden up Massachusetts Avenue to the vice presidential residence for a meeting of the new domestic policy team, including Dan Quayle, John Sununu, Nick Brady, and Bob Teeter. Dick Darman, taking over as budget director, was scheduled to go over the nation's increasingly precarious finances.

Baker was there mainly in his capacity as Bush's friend and adviser. He suspected that some of the people in the room, including Brady and Teeter, had plans to talk Bush into breaking his read-my-lips vow against new taxes. Even though Darman had harbored deep doubts about the pledge,

Baker understood that now that it was made, it would be politically self-destructive to renounce it right out of the gate.

"Watch these guys," he whispered to Quayle. "They're going to try to get him to raise taxes."

Once the discussion began, Teeter turned to Bush. "In the end, you will have no choice," he said. "You will have to raise taxes."

Baker jumped in, not deferring even though it was no longer his area of responsibility. "We don't need to do that this year," he said.

His response was telling. Baker was not objecting on philosophical grounds. The architect of Reagan's 1982 tax increase was hardly allergic to raising levies if fiscally necessary and politically palatable. Instead, he was protesting the poor timing and the obvious damage to Bush's credibility if he were seen as reversing his most memorable campaign promise so quickly after taking office. But by the summer of 1990, as Baker was jetting around the world negotiating the new boundaries of Europe, the president agreed during budget negotiations with Democrats to consider a tax hike along with spending cuts to bring down the deficit. Sununu tried to cover for the broken campaign promise by arguing that they would only consider tax *revenue* increases, as opposed to tax *rate* increases, which in theory could mean additional money for the treasury generated by economic growth or better enforcement of the existing tax code.

Even Baker, the master of the wordsmithing sleight-of-hand, did not think this would convince the country. Seeing Darman in the White House parking lot after the creative explanation of new taxes, Baker stuck his head in his old deputy's car.

"Too cute by half, Dick," he said. Then he added, "You've bought yourself about ten days."

As Darman later noted, Baker's "prediction was closer to correct than the president's."

By the late summer, the backlash to the shift on taxes was brutal. Bush's approval ratings were plummeting and his own party leaders were close to open rebellion. When headlines on August 2, the day of the Iraq invasion of Kuwait, referenced a "crisis" engulfing the Bush presidency, it had nothing to do with the Middle East. That fall, after days of closed-door talks at Andrews Air Force Base by negotiators for both parties, Bush agreed to a bipartisan budget agreement to bring down the deficit by $500 billion over five years, a deal that included higher taxes on gasoline, alcohol, tobacco, and luxury items such as yachts. "He cut the deal because he was getting ready to go to war with Saddam," Dan Quayle said later. "He had to get a deal. He just felt very uncomfortable not having a budget." But the belligerent House Republican whip Newt Gingrich, after initially signing on, bolted and led the conservative opposition, infuriating Bush and Darman, who saw it as treachery. "He hated Newt after what he saw as the betrayal," recalled Jonathan Darman, the budget director's son. The agreement passed narrowly, with most Republicans abandoning their president.

In the years to come, the agreement would make a considerable difference in reining in the budget deficit, leading to better economic times and contributing to a balanced budget during the presidency of Bush's successor. In the annals of history, it would come to be seen as a mark of Bush's political courage. But at the time, in Baker's suite on the seventh floor of the State Department, it was viewed as a political disaster. "We just saw the train wreck coming," Janet Mullins recalled. "Once it was done, I remember sitting in the inner offices with Baker and just going, 'Fuck, we are dead, this is unexplainable.'"

For Baker, it was another reminder of why he was glad to be secretary of state.

BAKER DID NOT WANT to go to war. Arriving back from Moscow, Baker, by nature cautious, risk-averse, and always wary of pulling the United States into a foreign quagmire, made it to Camp David that August weekend in time to discuss with Bush and his national security team how to respond. Bush had already ordered American warships to head to the Persian Gulf while freezing Iraqi and Kuwaiti money in the United States. He was particularly worried that Iraq would now strike Saudi Arabia.

William Webster, the CIA director, reported that Iraq had 100,000 troops in Kuwait and some of them were massing near the Saudi border. General Norman Schwarzkopf, head of the United States Central Command and a burly, brusque officer straight from central casting, outlined Operations Plan 90-1002 to defend Saudi Arabia, but said it would take seventeen weeks to deploy 250,000 American troops. If they decided to eject Iraq from Kuwait, that would require a far larger force and as much as eight to twelve months to assemble.

At this point, the main goal of what would be called Operation Desert Shield was to guard the Saudi oil fields. No one was ready to commit to reversing the occupation of Kuwait with military force. No one, that is, except for Bush. When he returned from Camp David aboard Marine One, the president landed on the South Lawn to find reporters waiting for him.

"This will not stand," Bush told them, jabbing his finger with emphasis, "this aggression against Kuwait."

Colin Powell, the Joint Chiefs chairman, watching on television at home, was startled. *Will not stand?* That was far more definitive than anything the administration had decided to do. In that moment, Powell felt that Bush had effectively declared war on Iraq. Brent Scowcroft, watching with Dan Quayle in the Cabinet Room of the White House, was also surprised and bothered.

"What's the matter, Brent?" Quayle asked.

"That was a little stronger than I thought," he said.

Bush came in. "How'd I do?" he asked.

"Well," Scowcroft answered, "I could have done without that line."

Baker too realized that Bush had set a new policy with his tough-guy sentence and worried about what it would mean. While later he would call it "arguably the most famous—and courageous—line of his presidency," at the time Baker feared that Bush was committing himself to more than the United States was ready to handle.

When Powell came to see Baker soon after Bush's remarks, he was in a similar frame of mind. Powell respected Baker from their time in the Reagan administration, deeming him "one smart son of a bitch," and the two shared a wariness about the prospect of a major military clash. Iraq had the world's fourth-largest army and much more recent combat experience than America's forces. Moreover, Iraq had used chemical weapons during the Iran war, demonstrating a willingness to violate the international rules of war that would automatically raise the stakes for American troops sent to fight in the desert. Powell wanted to talk about containment, an idea that Baker too was entertaining. For the nation's chief diplomat, this was a chance to prove that diplomacy could resolve a crisis.

Baker did not confine his reservations about the emerging plan to Powell. He was blunt with the president too, even when he saw where Bush was inexorably headed. He had run presidential campaigns for the last four election cycles and he did not want Bush to end up as a one-term president. "I know you're aware of the fact that this has all the ingredients that brought down three of the last five presidents—a hostage crisis, body bags and a full-fledged economic recession caused by forty-dollar oil," he told Bush at one point. Bush got the message. "Jim Baker is worried that we will get bogged down in another Vietnam," he later recorded in his diary, "and lose the support of the people and have the Bush presidency destroyed."

But Bush seemed determined. He was going to make it clear to Hussein that Saudi Arabia would receive American protection. He had already given that message to the kingdom's colorful, wired ambassador to Washington, Prince Bandar bin Sultan. A onetime fighter pilot who spoke colloquial English and loved the Dallas Cowboys, Bandar now embedded himself inside Bush's team, becoming what one historian later called "a de facto member of the National Security Council." The Saudis viewed the Americans skeptically, recalling that Jimmy Carter once sent a squadron of F-15s when the kingdom felt threatened by the Islamic Revolution in Iran in 1979, only for it to be revealed that the fighter jets were unarmed. They also considered Ronald Reagan's withdrawal of the Marines from Beirut in 1983 to have been a sign of America's irresolve. But Bush assured Bandar personally of his commitment to defending the kingdom. By August 7, he decided to send thousands of American soldiers, the biggest gamble of his presidency.

Was America headed toward a full-blown war? Despite Baker's efforts, it sure seemed that way later in August when an Iraqi ship, the *Khanaqin*, was spotted heading to Yemen in violation of United Nations sanctions imposed to cut off Hussein's oil revenue after the invasion. After an American warship fired warning shots, Hussein's government said there would be "grave consequences" if the ship were fired upon again. Baker was at his ranch in Wyoming while Bush was in Kennebunkport as a series of phone calls ensued to figure out what to do. From London, Margaret Thatcher urged Bush to intercept the ship and sink it if necessary. Cheney agreed, as did Scowcroft. "Everybody said you've got to take that ship out or you're going to be seen to be a wimp," Baker recalled.

But Baker had been talking with Eduard Shevardnadze, trying to get the Soviets to sign on to a new United Nations resolution threatening force to enforce the blockade. From Moscow, Shevardnadze pleaded with Baker not to take action against the ship at least for a few days. Otherwise, he feared, Gorbachev might find it politically impossible to go along with the proposed resolution. "We want one fact at our disposal to show Iraq is not complying," Shevardnadze told Baker by phone. From Wyoming, testing the limits of the State Department communications team that had set up a satellite on a rock outside the front porch of his off-the-grid ranch house, Baker pushed Bush strongly to hold off.

Others disagreed, including Thatcher. She did not think much of Baker. She saw him as an operator, someone who cared only about the politics of a situation. She was already at odds with him over German reunification and she blamed him for what she saw as an increasing American tilt away from its old friend Britain. "Jim Baker's many abilities lay in the area of 'fixing,'" she said. "He had a mixed record of this." She considered the Plaza and Louvre Accords on currency rates to be disastrous decisions "with highly deleterious effects," as she put it. "Now at the State Department, Jim Baker and his team brought a similar, allegedly 'pragmatic' problem-solving approach to bear on U.S. foreign policy."

But once again, Baker convinced Bush to follow his advice. Bush decided to hold off firing on the ship so as not to chance disrupting the collaboration with Moscow. He called Thatcher to let her know.

"Well, all right, George," she replied archly, "but this is no time to go wobbly."

The *Khanaqin* made it to port but Hussein never challenged the blockade again and, more important, the Soviets voted for the United Nations resolution authorizing the use of force to stop ships violating the cordon, just as Baker had hoped. For Baker, this was "the crunch point" of the crisis. If he had any chance of resolving it without American kids being sent into combat, he would have to preserve the unique Soviet-American alliance he was forging.

But Bush had already staked his credibility and that of the country on the confrontation with Iraq. He began huddling regularly with what became known as the Gang of Eight—Bush, Baker, Cheney, Powell, Scowcroft, Dan Quayle, John Sununu, and Robert Gates—debating diplomatic and economic options even as more troops kept flooding to the region and the likelihood of military action seemed to grow.

On a cold, rainy fall day during one of the periodic meetings of the Gang of Eight at Camp David, Baker shared a golf cart with a pensive Quayle.

"Jim, what do you really think about it?" Quayle asked.

"I don't know," Baker asked. "It's a big gamble."

Quayle looked at Baker, his mind on the next election. "Would you put your presidency on the line for this?" he asked Baker.

"Neither one of us," Quayle said later, "had an answer to that."

AS WAS SO OFTEN the case, the crisis abroad came amid another crisis at home. This time it was Baker's daughter, Elizabeth Winston, who in the fall of 1990 was living at the Menninger Clinic, the leading specialty psychiatric hospital in Houston, trying to recover from post-traumatic stress.

Twenty-nine years old, Winston had endured a bizarre series of episodes for years that she could never fully explain. During a college debate, she passed out several minutes into the program for no apparent reason.

In law school at the University of Texas at Austin, she blanked out onstage when she got up to read part of a paper, stood there for a few minutes without uttering a word, then simply said thank you very much and walked off. She felt extreme sensitivity to light and sound and found herself regularly "self-medicating" with alcohol and partying.

Susan Baker noticed a troubling disconnect. Winston would talk with her mother about coming up to Washington to visit and then a week later, when asked if she had made arrangements, not remember the original conversation. During a law school exam, Winston heard the bell ring ending the test time and discovered she had not even opened her blue book. "It was at that point I realized something weird was going on," she said. "I went to a friend's house and said, 'I need some help.'" Winston visited a psychoanalyst in Houston and he determined that she was suffering from post-traumatic stress stemming from her chaotic childhood with her alcoholic father, Jimbo Winston. The psychoanalyst recommended she check in to the Menninger Clinic, where she stayed for six months, essentially unlearning all of the defense mechanisms she had created as a child to protect herself. "For the first time in my life, I really had a sense of hope," she said.

Baker did not visit during those six months, nor did anyone from the family. The arrival of the secretary of state would have invariably involved an entourage and ruined any sense of anonymity that Winston had there. But Baker checked in even as he jetted from capital to capital. "He was as supportive as he could be," she said later. "All I felt from him in that situation was unconditional support."

Most of Baker's staff had little idea any of this was going on. Baker did not exactly confide his personal problems in them, nor did he invite aides to confide theirs in him. He could be gregarious and charming, intuitive about other people and their needs in the course of a negotiation, but utterly indifferent to the personal lives of the people he worked with the most. "Jim really is an enigma to anybody who isn't his family," said Colin Powell, who spent lots of time with Baker in the White House Situation Room. In reality, this was true even to some who were in his family. "Look at Baker's relationship with his sons—this is not Mr. Warm and Fuzzy," Robert Zoellick would later point out.

Zoellick was arguably Baker's most important adviser at the State Department and architect of his signature diplomatic ventures. A Harvard-educated lawyer, he was the fastidious "minister without portfolio" who worked so hard he carried his own cheese, crackers, and raisins on the road because there was never enough time for room service. Yet not even he was invited to see the secretary outside of their all-consuming work hours. "I don't think until later he even knew what my home state was; he didn't meet my wife," Zoellick said. "It was all business." Relations even with his closest advisers were formal. "He never said to me, 'Call me Jim,'" Zoellick said. "So I just refer to him as 'Secretary Baker.'" Sometimes people go to friends at work for reassurance, Zoellick noted. "You don't go to Baker for that. You'll get a cold, calculating view," he said. "If you want emotional support, you have a wife or a dog."

Baker's relationship with Susan had evolved since the early days of the Reagan administration when she felt abandoned at home to deal with a tumultuous family life. With all of the children other than Mary-Bonner now grown, Susan often accompanied Baker on his trips around the world. She loved poring through his briefing books and hearing his end of conversations and then talking about them afterward. She sometimes picked up intelligence from her separate meetings with spouses of other ministers.

But when Susan was not around, Baker remained inside his armor. Only occasionally did he let his guard down. During a flight back to Washington from a meeting at Bush's home in Kennebunkport that fall, Baker seemed in an unusually contemplative mood. He turned to Richard Haass, an NSC aide traveling with him, and asked how old he was.

"Thirty-nine," Haass said.

"A good age," Baker mused. "I remember where I was twenty years ago. It was a rough time. My four children had just lost their mother. I didn't know if I could make it. Men just aren't equipped to provide kids what it is they need."

The conversation turned back to Iraq for a few minutes, then Haass brought up a story in that day's newspaper mentioning that Baker had once been considered for baseball commissioner.

Baker confirmed that was true.

Did he regret not taking it?

No, he said, only George Will, the baseball-loving columnist, ever told him that he had made the wrong choice.

"I've been secretary of the treasury and now secretary of state," Baker said. "That's not bad."

AFTER A SWING THROUGH the Middle East building solidarity against Iraq among its Arab neighbors, Baker flew to Helsinki to join Bush for a hurriedly arranged summit with Gorbachev on September 9 to coordinate the response to Saddam Hussein's aggression. The joint statement a month earlier would mean nothing if Moscow now went its own way.

On the plane ride, Baker had Dennis Ross draft a new joint statement, one with more teeth than the last one, to demonstrate that the two superpowers remained united in the face of Hussein's intransigence. While Bush met privately with Gorbachev, Baker sat down with Shevardnadze. Baker quickly gleaned that the Soviets were planning to hold their cooperation in the emerging coalition hostage to their long-standing desire for an international peace conference to work on the Arab-Israeli conflict. Having just come from the region, Baker knew that would infuriate the Saudis and Egyptians because it would, in effect, validate Hussein's actions and make him a hero on the Arab street for forcing the world to confront Israel.

"Eduard, that would be a disaster," Baker protested. "It would look like Saddam had delivered, that he would have gotten something nobody else could have."

Shevardnadze finally acquiesced. "Okay," he said, "but let's talk about peace in some way."

Baker showed him the draft statement that Ross had written and Shevardnadze seemed to accept it. But when Baker then met with Bush, it was clear that Gorbachev had pushed the president even harder on the proposed Middle East peace conference—and that Bush seemed inclined to go along.

Ross, operating on little sleep, interrupted the president with a heated objection, "impassioned almost to the point of intemperance," as Baker put it later.

"You can't do that," Ross told Bush. "This will absolutely undercut what we're trying to do. We'll put the moderate Arabs in a position where Saddam is delivering for the Palestinians and they're not. If we create linkage, he can claim victory. And if he does that, we will have undermined our friends in the area and we are going to face a Middle East that is far more dangerous than we've ever seen."

Bush was startled at the outburst and appeared ready to get angry, but Baker intervened to save Ross. "You are wrong on this and Dennis is right," Baker told his old friend, with a directness that few others would dare employ to a president's face. Baker pointed out that they already had a draft that Shevardnadze had agreed to and he echoed Ross in saying that a statement like the one Gorbachev wanted "would be a big victory" for Hussein.

"Well, I am afraid we're going to find we have to do this," Bush said. "We need a joint statement and Gorbachev is going to want that in there."

"We've already *got* a draft and it's not even mentioned," Baker said. "Don't worry about it."

"Well, I've *got* to worry about it," Bush shot back sharply. "I put all those kids out there. Nobody else did it. *I* did it. And I've got to take every step to be sure that I don't put their lives at risk needlessly. If I can get them out of there without fighting, I'll do it."

The room went quiet. There laid out for all to hear was a president's anguish at the prospect of war. His assembled advisers did not know what to say.

Finally, John Sununu broke the silence. "Well, maybe we can put a reference to an international conference in there," he said.

Baker snapped. "Get off of it, John," he said.

A weary Bush gave in. "Look, Jimmy," he said, "if you can get the statement without it, fine."

The testy back-and-forth in Helsinki captured the dynamics of the Baker-Bush relationship as this latest crisis hit. Baker had long since stopped thinking of himself as Bush's little brother and, while respectful of the president, did not feel the need to be overly deferential. After all, Baker was the one on those long flights crisscrossing the world and he was the one who had a better feel for what the allies could accept and what they could not. Bush, under the pressure of ordering hundreds of thousands of troops to the Middle East for a possible war, was less attuned to the nuances of the coalition that his secretary of state was assembling and more eager to get along with his interlocutor, in this case Gorbachev. But when pressed, Bush was willing to accept Baker's guidance.

Indeed, when the two sat down with Gorbachev and Shevardnadze, Bush all but turned over the discussion of the draft statement to Baker. Aides on the two sides had finessed the issue by including vague language about working together after the Iraq crisis was settled "to resolve all remaining conflicts in the Middle East and the Persian Gulf." Sitting in the meeting, Gorbachev accepted it but had some thoughts about the wording.

Bush called on Baker to address the changes. "Why don't you just do it with Jimmy?" the president told Gorbachev.

Empowered, Baker settled on language with Gorbachev. But before the meeting was over, Ross quietly informed Baker that the proposed Mideast peace conference was no longer their only problem. Soviet hard-liners had prepared another draft of the statement that dropped the demand for an unconditional withdrawal by Hussein and watered down the threat of additional steps if he did not comply.

Baker abruptly interrupted the ongoing meeting to expose the end run. "Mr. President, isn't this what you have agreed to?" Baker asked Gorbachev, reading the draft they had already worked out.

"Da," Gorbachev confirmed.

That finally ended the matter. But as they left Helsinki, Bush and Baker made a private commitment to Gorbachev that, although they would not say so in the public statement, they would work on an Arab-Israeli peace conference after Kuwait was liberated. It was the same type of maneuver that Baker had employed many times on Capitol Hill, a private concession that appears nowhere in the public record. It worked internationally too. And for now, the tactic was enough to keep Gorbachev on the team.

As he flew back to Washington, Bush called Baker from Air Force One. Thank you, he told his secretary of state, for saving him from making a mistake.

BAKER'S OWN MISTAKE came a few weeks later. As American troops continued to pour into the region, the Bush administration was still trying to convince the public why a conflict halfway around the world between two Arab states, neither of them democracies, mattered to them.

During a meeting with Canada's foreign minister in Bermuda, the famously on-message Baker slipped and, rather than repeating the high-minded case that he and Bush had been articulating, reduced the matter to far cruder terms. "To bring it down to the average American citizen, let me say that means jobs," Baker said. "If you want to sum it up in one word, it's jobs. Because an economic recession worldwide, caused by the control of one nation, one dictator, if you will, of the West's economic lifeline will result in the loss of jobs on the part of American citizens."

The explanation, which came to be known as Baker's "jobs, jobs, jobs" news conference, rattled the White House. While he meant that the energy-rich Middle East held the key to the world economy and therefore its fate mattered to the United States, the way he put it came across as an obnoxious combination of greed and crass domestic politics. Brent Scowcroft groaned. "I knew what he was trying to say," Scowcroft said, "but the way he put it sounded like the whole dispute was simply commercialism."

Baker was already in hot water in the West Wing because of a Thomas Friedman article on the front page of *The New York Times* a few days earlier portraying the secretary of state as the mature hand restraining a president too eager for war, "a brake on any immediate impulse to use military force." While making the point that their differences were a matter of degree rather than outright disagreement, Friedman astutely identified Baker's approach to the crisis. "Mr. Baker is a calculating pragmatist, who assesses any particular foreign-policy issue based on a complex equation of what he feels is the national interest, what seems possible, what will serve Mr. Bush's interests, what can be sold to the public, how it will be received on Capitol Hill and finally, how it will affect James Baker." As far as some of Baker's White House colleagues were concerned, Friedman's factors were right, although maybe not always in that order.

The Friedman article and the "jobs, jobs, jobs" comment focused more attention on Baker than he wanted amid the ongoing debate over what to do about Iraq. Mary McGrory, the liberal columnist for *The Washington Post*, who was both despised and avidly read by the president, made matters worse, referring to Baker a couple days after the ill-fated news conference as "the ablest of the president's men" and "the most seductive secretary of state since Henry A. Kissinger." She portrayed him as a formidable spinner of reporters on his official plane who until now had managed to elude responsibility for setbacks with the same Teflon that coated his previous boss. "Some scribes have rudely noted that Baker ducks the blame for dirty campaigns or bad policy—as in the case of the Iraq aggression, which some 500,000 Americans eventually may be committed to stopping," she wrote. "But Baker's job security is the best in the city."

On that, she was right. Bush needed Baker and, while irritated, was hardly about to push him away. Baker was flying around the world creating a coalition against Iraq and soliciting financial contributions from other nations so that the United States would not bear the entire cost of military operations. His "tin cup trip" would ultimately bring in $53.7 billion from other nations to offset costs of $61.1 billion. At one point, administration officials worried that Baker would be too successful and the United States would actually make a profit from the war.

While Washington gossiped over his role in the administration's war council, Baker was racing through Bahrain, Saudi Arabia, Egypt, Turkey, Britain, France, and the Soviet Union to line up support for another United Nations resolution, this time to enforce with military means the previous call on Iraq to withdraw from Kuwait. In effect, the resolution would pave the way for Operation Desert Shield to become Operation Desert Storm if Bush opted to forcibly eject Iraq from Kuwait. It was important that Baker secure votes and pass the resolution by the end of November since the United States occupied the rotating presidency of the Security Council that month—and taking over next would be Yemen, an ally of Iraq.

In London, Margaret Thatcher argued that such a resolution was unnecessary and would set a bad precedent by implying that United Nations member states could not take action on their own moral authority, but Baker maintained that he and Bush needed international approval to convince the American public. The key votes would be the Soviet Union and China, both of which had veto power on the Security Council.

Baker met Qian Qichen, the Chinese foreign minister, during a stop in Cairo and pressed for a yes vote, or failing that at least an abstention. Still subject to international isolation following the Tiananmen Square massacre, China more than anything wanted out of the penalty box. Baker offered a way: if Beijing voted for the resolution, he would invite Qian to Washington for a meeting with Bush, an encounter that would be valuable for the Chinese. If Beijing abstained, Qian could come to Washington for a meeting with Baker. The Chinese promised to think about it.

When he reached Moscow, however, Baker found himself blindsided by an announcement back in Washington that the president had decided to double American forces in the Persian Gulf. Baker was livid, fearing that his careful statecraft was being upstaged by Pentagon deployment schedules and that the Soviets would think his trip to consult with them was a sham since the decision to go to war had clearly already been made. Baker lashed out at Richard Haass, who was on the secretary's plane as a liaison to the White House.

"Why the hell do I have an NSC guy here with me if the White House is going to do things that undermine my trip?" Baker barked.

Haass had also been blindsided by the news, but he was a convenient target for Baker's ire. "He nearly threw me off the plane at 36,000 feet," Haass recalled later. "He dropped about twenty-six F-bombs in the course of about one minute."

Baker sat down with Shevardnadze the next day. Once again, the friendship they had developed would prove crucial to the outcome. While aggravated by Hussein, the Soviets had always been categorically opposed to the United Nations authorizing military action against one of its members, particularly one that had been a Moscow client state for so long. When Baker handed Shevardnadze a draft resolution with the phrase "use of force" in it, the foreign minister said it would never be acceptable.

Baker's years of experience at finding ways around political and diplomatic roadblocks now kicked in. What about some sort of euphemism for force? Would that make it easier to swallow? He pulled out a pen and tried one, two, three, four, five possible alternatives before settling on "all necessary means." That was vague enough that the Soviets could tell their anti-American hard-liners that it could include sanctions or other measures, while Baker, sitting in the chair as president of the United Nations Security Council, could use his prerogative after the vote to make clear for the record that the United States interpreted the phrase to include force. Shevardnadze insisted the resolution include a six-week delay before becoming operative to allow a final attempt at diplomacy. Baker agreed.

Now Baker needed to get Gorbachev on board. Shevardnadze got on the telephone with Gorbachev and pressed him to agree, then raced out to his dacha outside Moscow to lobby further before Baker could get there. "Gorbachev is close but not there yet," Baker cabled back to Washington. By the time Baker arrived at the dacha, Gorbachev was open to the "all necessary means" language.

"The first thing we must do is stick together," he told Baker. "If we let a thug like this get away with what he's done, then there will be no hope for the kind of new international reality that we would like to see."

But they were not fooling themselves about what was coming. "Mr. Secretary, you know you can't back off once you start down the road," Shevardnadze told Baker. "You will have to implement the resolution" if Iraq did not comply.

"I'm afraid you're right," Baker said.

TO SIGNAL the day's importance, Baker flew to New York to personally take the American seat at the Security Council on November 29. By this point, he had finished an extraordinary diplomatic blitz, racing 100,000 miles around the world in ten weeks on the old Boeing 707 and holding more than two hundred meetings with heads of state and foreign ministers to forge a coalition against Iraq. He had coaxed and wheedled and bluffed and intimidated, the tactic depending on the target, then took a Halcion for a few hours of sleep and prepared to do it all over again. He was not above lubricating where necessary—debt forgiveness for Egypt, textile trade concessions for Turkey. This was just the sort of thing Baker knew how to do. He had signed up wavering convention delegates for Gerald Ford in 1976. He had found a way to get tax reform through Congress. A deal was a deal and trading was part of it. Rounding up votes for war was not, in the end, all that different.

As Baker opened the debate over the "all necessary means" resolution, he drew a parallel to the appeasement of Hitler's Germany in the 1930s. This time, he was the one throwing around the Munich references. "History now has given us another chance," Baker said. "With the Cold

War behind us, we now have the chance to build a world which was envisioned by this organization, by the founders of the United Nations." He added: "We must not let the United Nations go the way of the League of Nations."

United Nations Security Council Resolution 678 set a deadline of January 15, 1991, for Iraq to withdraw from Kuwait, and, while the measure did not overtly threaten military force if Iraq refused, Baker made clear that was how the phrase "all necessary means" would be interpreted. "If Iraq does not reverse its course peacefully," he said, "then other necessary measures, including the use of force, should be authorized."

Then he sat back and listened to his fellow foreign ministers make their speeches. The outcome was not in doubt—Baker had seen to that—but he found it hard sitting through the endless orations. Countries had been warned, however; you were either with Baker or against him on this one and if you were against him, he had no intention of letting it slide. When Yemen's ambassador sternly rebuked the United States and declared that he would vote against the resolution, Baker passed a note to Robert Kimmitt suggesting that he would cut off American aid to Yemen in retaliation. "Yemen's perm. rep. just enjoyed about $200 to $250 million worth of applause for that speech," Baker wrote, adding that he would take it up with a couple of aides: "I want to talk to Kelly and Reggie about our aid program to Yemen." It was not an idle threat; Baker later canceled all military cooperation, nonhumanitarian aid, and even the Peace Corps program in Yemen, while slashing development assistance nearly to zero. "Baker would have happily cut off the entire relationship," said David Mack, a deputy assistant secretary of state for the region. "Together with a few other administration officials, I managed, through a little bit of bureaucratic guerrilla warfare, to keep a very shaky, very slim relationship with Yemen."

Speaking for China, Qian Qichen warned against "hasty actions" that could lead to war. Baker scribbled down another observation, this one just for himself. "China can't go for military means—except in case of traffic jams—like the one in Tiananmen Square in June of 1989," he wrote derisively.

But none of that changed the final result. At 5:32 p.m., the council approved the resolution 12 to 2 with one abstention. Cuba joined Yemen in voting no, while China abstained, the first time it had failed to support a measure against Iraq since the invasion of Kuwait. Still, so long as China did not use its veto to block the action, it did not matter. "An historic moment," Kimmitt wrote Baker. "Congratulations!"

Baker savored the victory. He had accomplished what his doubters said he could not, forging an unlikely consensus in the most fractious international forum in the world. Not since the Korean War had the United Nations taken such a momentous step to impose its will on a dangerous rogue state.

In a holding room at the United Nations, Baker received a call from Bush offering congratulations. But the president was already thinking ahead.

"I want to talk to you about an idea I have," he told Baker.

BAKER MET with Bush and Scowcroft in the Oval Office the next day. The president wanted to make a dramatic, last-minute gesture of peace before going to war. The best way to do that was to publicly propose sending Baker to Baghdad to meet with Saddam Hussein sometime between December 15 and January 15 while the president would agree to receive Tariq Aziz, the Iraqi foreign minister, at the White House.

Scowcroft was dubious, but Baker was eager to make the trip, still seeing a chance to get out of the crisis without resorting to force. "He was more willing to reach out, more willing to take a chance than I was," said Scowcroft. Even if Baker could not make the trip happen, the proposal itself was useful. By making such an offer, they would demonstrate to the world that they went the extra mile to avoid bloodshed—and they might be able to win a vote in Congress authorizing force by showcasing Hussein's recalcitrance. Still, the proposal was announced without even Baker's top advisers being informed in advance and many of them thought it was a mistake, a sign of weakness or a chance for Hussein to muddy the waters.

The way forward was not yet clear. War seemed imminent, but not everyone on Bush's team thought he needed a congressional vote to authorize it or that he should seek one. The Constitution gave Congress the sole power to declare war but it had not exercised that authority since World War II. Instead, presidents since then had taken the country to war by relying on their inherent authority as commander in chief or on more general votes by lawmakers. Dick Cheney, among others, urged Bush not to go to Congress despite—or perhaps because of—his own ten years of service in the House. John Sununu thought they should ignore Congress, and Boyden Gray, the White House counsel, maintained that Bush did not need a vote constitutionally. But Baker thought Bush *did* need a vote, not constitutionally but politically. Better to have buy-in by lawmakers before hostilities opened; otherwise they would more readily turn against the president the minute the fighting got tough. "We wanted everybody in the boat in case this thing went bad," said Janet Mullins, Baker's legislative chief. "Baker got it. Bush had to be convinced."

Within hours of announcing his offer to send Baker to Baghdad, the president hosted congressional leaders in the Cabinet Room of the White House to discuss the crisis and seek their support. After an opening statement, Bush turned the meeting over to Baker, who argued that lawmakers would actually help the cause of peace by voting for war.

"The threat of force is not the same as the use of force," Baker said. "You've got to give us the threat as a diplomatic tool."

Democratic leaders pushed the president to stick with sanctions for as long as a year, but Bush and Baker maintained sanctions alone would not work.

Ever looking for the angle, Baker asked the Democrats if Congress would authorize offensive operations so long as they were limited to air power. Senator George Mitchell of Maine, the Democratic majority leader, said no.

Baker was not surprised. He knew better than anyone in the administration that a vote in favor of a war resolution was anything but a given. He had a secret back channel to the Democrats in the Senate: Janet Mullins was quietly dating Mitchell. Baker's legislative liaison was not only getting real-time information from Republican leaders through her day job, she knew what was happening on the Democratic side and she shared her intelligence with her boss.

During a meeting to discuss a possible congressional resolution, she made clear that the odds were against them. "I'm like, guys, we don't have the votes," she recalled. "If we have the vote today, we would lose." Not everyone listened to her. "Sununu was like, 'Oh, bullshit.'"

Mullins's relationship with Mitchell caused consternation in the Oval Office. "Bush did not like Mitchell, and when he found out that we were dating he was not happy and there were a couple conversations about, 'Do you think she can be trusted?'" Mullins recalled. "That never occurred to Baker. Baker knew me better than 4I knew me, and Baker saw the advantages right away." Baker joked about it, but understood when Mitchell was sending messages through Mullins. "He also was perfectly comfortable knowing that I was not going to compromise the administration for the sake of pillow talk," she said.

Mullins's relationship with Mitchell underscored the differences between Baker and Bush. For Bush, it was a question of loyalty; you were either on the team or you were not. For Baker, it was about how this could be turned to his own benefit; any edge was useful. "Bush never got the strategic advantage that could come from that," Mullins said. "Baker got that almost immediately." In the runup to the war vote, her connection to Mitchell was so useful that she could tell Baker when senators were playing both sides. She informed Baker, for example, that while Al Gore had told Bob Dole, the Republican leader, that he would vote for war, he was secretly reassuring Mitchell that he would oppose it. Mitchell's late-night handicapping had convinced Mullins there was more work to be done. "That's part of why I knew how much we didn't have the votes," she said.

While Baker was trying to make a partner out of Mitchell, he lost another partner overseas, one who had been critically important to him. On December 20, Eduard Shevardnadze shocked both Moscow and Washington by abruptly stepping down as foreign minister, warning darkly as he left that "dictatorship is coming." His resignation was meant as a signal to Gorbachev that the Soviet leader was cozying up too much to the hardliners in an effort to save himself.

Shevardnadze had not given Baker a heads-up, so the secretary of state was caught off guard like everyone else. The loss of his friend and fishing partner, the counterpart he had invested so much in and accomplished so much with, was devastating. Baker interpreted it as an ominous sign of what was to come: "Hard-liners are taking over."

CHAPTER 23

Eyes of a Killer

Perennially in command of himself and his surroundings, Baker struck advisers and colleagues as characteristically cool heading into what would be perhaps the most historic meeting of his diplomatic career. Only later did he admit to an aide that it was just a front. "I was shitting in my pants," he confessed.

Baker was in Geneva for a final chance to head off war with Iraq. Saddam Hussein had danced around in response to Bush's invitation, refusing to agree to a Baghdad visit by Baker on any of the dates offered. Finally, Bush issued another invitation, this one for a meeting between Baker and Tariq Aziz on neutral territory in Switzerland. This time, Hussein accepted.

The surprise meeting angered the Saudis, who thought the Bush team had suddenly gotten cold feet on the planned military operation to dislodge Saddam and was looking for a way out. "I had to scrape an incensed Bandar off the ceiling," said Richard Haass, referring to the Saudi ambassador. Other administration officials feared that Hussein was merely seeking to confuse matters after the clarity of the United Nations vote. "I was extremely nervous," said Brent Scowcroft. He worried that "they could maybe sell us a bill of goods and then make any use of force that we might have to resort to harder to get to." Would Baker buy that bill of goods?

Baker understood just how much was riding on the encounter. "The whole world was looking at this meeting," remembered Gamal Helal, Baker's State Department Arabic translator. Baker did not harbor illusions that he would walk out with a deal to prevent armed conflict and in fact had long since resigned himself to it. He knew that the way the war was seen by the world—in effect, its legitimacy—would depend at least in part on this meeting. And he did not completely rule out the long-shot possibility that he could still find a path to peace. "He never forgot that President Bush had hoped to solve this without a war," Colin Powell said. "Any way you can avoid war and achieve your objective, you avoid."

They sat down in the Salon des Nations at the Intercontinental Hotel at 11:15 a.m. on January 9, 1991, just six days before the deadline for Iraq to pull out of Kuwait. The Iraqis were exceedingly tense and no wonder. Baker noticed that sitting next to Aziz was Barzan Ibrahim Hasan al-Tikriti, Hussein's half brother and the former director of Iraq's dreaded Mukhabarat secret police. Barzan was a notoriously brutal figure in Iraq, known for presiding over the executions of opponents at home and the assassination of rivals abroad. With a cold expression and "the eyes of a killer," in the words of Stephen Hadley, who attended the meeting as an aide to Dick Cheney, Barzan was clearly present as the enforcer to keep the foreign minister from drifting away from his instructions. While Baker seemed calm, Aziz seemed nervous, with those killer eyes staring at him from his own side of the table. Aziz spoke fluent English, but Baker ordered that his own words be translated into Arabic for the benefit of the rest of the Iraqis. "We wanted to make sure that the entire Iraqi delegation would understand what Baker was saying," Helal said.

At age fifty-four, Aziz was a physically diminutive figure, belying his role as Hussein's right-hand man. With a dark mustache, gray hair, large, thick glasses, and a wily grin, Aziz had been the mild international face of a ruthless regime for years. Born a Chaldean Christian named Mikhail Yuhanna, he worked as a journalist and joined the revolutionary Ba'ath Party in 1957, changing his name to something more Arabic-sounding. He grew close to Hussein and, after the Ba'athists took power, was appointed deputy prime minister in 1979 and foreign minister in 1983.

Baker first met Aziz in October 1989 when the Americans were still supportive of Hussein's government after years of war with their mutual enemies in Iran. "I remember how urbane and sort of cosmopolitan this foreign minister of Iraq was and how he spoke very good English and seemed to have an excellent command of his brief," Baker said later. "And midway through what seemed to me a fairly friendly and positive meeting, he began to accuse us of interfering in their internal affairs and of conducting clandestine efforts to subvert the government." Nonetheless, a month later, Baker pressed for $1 billion in agricultural credits for Iraq.

Now they were meeting again under radically different circumstances. Baker consciously remembered not to smile as he shook Aziz's hand in front of a throng of international media. "He knew that the pictures from that meeting, that handshake, that starting of that meeting, would set the tone for the stories as they played out of that room, and those pictures would be immortalized as this was the last chance for peace," said Karen Groomes, his aide.

After the journalists were escorted out of the room, Baker opened the meeting with grim candor. "Our purpose ought not, in any sense, to be to pressure each other," Baker began. "However, it should be no surprise that I'm not here to negotiate from the resolutions passed by the" Security Council.

Baker said he had a message to pass along from Bush to Hussein. He slid a sealed envelope across the table to Aziz containing a three-page letter as well as a separate copy translated into Arabic for the foreign minister.

Aziz picked up the copy of the letter. His hands were shaking and the papers flapped noticeably as he began reading. For five minutes, the room remained silent as he underlined several sentences. "Unless you withdraw from Kuwait completely and without condition, you will lose more than Kuwait," the letter said. "What is at issue here is not the future of Kuwait—it will be free, its government will be restored—but rather the future of Iraq. The choice is yours to make."

Finally, Aziz looked up at Baker and dismissed the letter as an insult to his president. "That is why I can't accept the way the letter is worded and I repeat I am going to have to apologize for not receiving it," he told Baker. "I suggest you can publish it in the press or give it to the media."

Aziz put the letter back on the table, but Baker left it untouched. It would end up sitting there for hours, visible to Aziz, "sort of like the sword of Damocles on the table," as Hadley put it later.

Baker told Aziz that the letter was not a threat but simply a frank statement of reality. "The only question is by what path you leave Kuwait— a peaceful withdrawal or withdrawal by force," Baker said sternly. "Clearly, if there is a peaceful settlement and you withdraw, those in power in Iraq today will have a say in Iraq's future. If withdrawal takes place by force, others will determine that future."

In effect, Baker was offering Hussein a deal: *Pull out now and you can continue to rule Iraq. If you make us expel you by force, then you may not.* The message was intended to reach Hussein at his most elemental level, his desire to hold on to power. But it was something of a bluff—the White House had made no decision to remove Hussein and in fact would later rule that out as the explicit goal of the coming military campaign.

Baker went on to enumerate what he called the "catastrophic consequences for Iraq" if the United States were to use its military against Iraq. "We believe these forces will really destroy your ability to run the country," Baker said. Lest the Iraqis misjudge American resolve given its recent past, he made a point of saying: "This will not be another Vietnam."

Then he delivered a warning that Dick Cheney and Colin Powell had specifically urged him to include: any use of weapons of mass destruction would be treated as a regime-ending moment. "If conflict ensues and you use chemical or biological weapons against U.S. forces, the American people will demand vengeance," Baker said. "And we have the means to exact it. Let me say with regard to this part of my presentation, this is not a threat; it is a promise. If there is any use of weapons like that, our objective won't just be the liberation of Kuwait, but the elimination of the current Iraqi regime." America, he added, "will turn Iraq into a weak and backward country." While he never used the words, he intended to leave Aziz with the impression that the United States would even use nuclear weapons in retaliation.

Aziz bridled at what he called the "insults" of Baker's presentation. "The present leadership will continue to lead Iraq now and in the future," Aziz said. "Those who will disappear are not in Iraq but some of your friends in the region." He added that the Iraqi public would not turn on its own leaders, as Baker seemed to imply. "Our people not only support us but they love us," he said. "These are the facts." Aziz went on to lay out a list of grievances, complaining that the Kuwaitis had been the hostile ones by overproducing oil to drive down the price and thus weaken Iraq. Then he brought up the Palestinian dispute with Israel.

Baker dismissed that as "ludicrous" and irrelevant to the issue at hand.

"We have been committed to the Palestinian question for decades," Aziz said.

"That is not the reason you invaded Kuwait," Baker said.

"That's your view."

The two men talked around and around for roughly seven hours, taking only brief breaks to report back to their capitals. As Aziz droned on, Baker rolled his pen in his hand. Finally, at 7 p.m., Baker said he had had enough. He looked at the envelope with Bush's letter to Hussein, still sitting unopened in the middle of the table.

"Mr. Minister," Baker asked, "is it your intention not to take the letter?"

"Yes," Aziz said.

Baker stood up and walked out, while an aide retrieved the letter. Back at the White House, in the little dining room just off the Oval Office, Bush, Cheney, and Scowcroft were watching on television with some congressional leaders. Bush would remember it as "one of the toughest days of my presidency." But they instantly understood the outcome when Baker came on the screen even before he said a word. "You could tell by the look on Jim's face that peace was not going to come out of this process," Cheney recalled. Not everyone was unhappy about it. In his diary, Dan Quayle wrote: "Baker-Aziz meeting. Went as planned. Baker failed."

Meeting the huge throng of journalists waiting in Geneva, Baker sounded glum. "Regrettably," he said, "in over six hours of talks, I heard nothing today that suggested to me any Iraqi flexibility whatsoever on complying with the United Nations Security Council resolutions."

The next morning, Baker headed to the airport. The plane was tense and quiet as it lifted off. "Everyone was, especially him, emotionally raw, psychologically raw," said Karen Groomes. "You could feel the air in the plane."

War, Baker knew, was now inevitable.

THE NEXT DAY, on January 11, Baker climbed onto a camouflage-covered makeshift platform in the hangar of an airbase in Taif, Saudi Arabia, where he had visited American troops the previous fall, to deliver one more warning in case Saddam Hussein had failed to understand the previous ones. The secretary of state's stentorian speech before hundreds of American pilots and other members of the Air Force's Forty-eighth Tactical Fighter Wing was crystal clear. So was the import of the F-111 fighter-bomber, a supersonic killing machine, that was parked behind him.

"When I talked to you four months ago," Baker said, "some of you told me that you were ready. But you also asked how long before you would know whether you would be called into action to undo this terrible aggression. Now, as the clock ticks down to midnight January 15, I cannot give you an absolutely definitive answer. But I can tell you that you will not have to wait much longer for an answer to that question."

The pilots and crews cheered, impatient after months of waiting in the desert. Part of a force that had grown to 500,000, they were ready to move and, after months of trying to avoid it, so was Baker. He had flown directly from his meeting with Aziz in Geneva to the Middle East to meet with King Fahd in Saudi Arabia, the ousted emir of Kuwait, and other regional leaders. He brought with him Lieutenant General Howard Graves, representing the Joint Chiefs of Staff, to outline the military plan. He had resigned himself to the coming war. The young American fighters did not know for sure that it was happening, but Baker did. He found it an emotional moment "because I knew they were going," as he remembered later, "and they didn't know they were going."

The next day, after three days of wrenching, sober-minded, and eloquent debate, Congress voted to authorize Bush to use force. Until two days beforehand, Baker and the rest of the team were not sure they would prevail. But in the end, the House voted for the war resolution 250 to 183, with all but three Republicans siding with Bush joined by eighty-six Democrats. The Senate vote was far closer, 52 to 47, with ten Democrats joining a nearly unanimous Republican caucus in favor of the measure. As Baker expected, George Mitchell voted no despite the relationship with Janet Mullins, while Al Gore did vote yes in the end. They were the most divided congressional votes for military action since the War of 1812, but they were enough, Baker hoped, to send a message of resolve to Baghdad.

Yet it was a message that, like the letter left on the table in Geneva, went unreceived. The United Nations' midnight deadline passed with no action from Hussein. Bush ordered the bombing to begin by the end of the day on January 16, and Baker, finally back in Washington, joined Cheney and Scowcroft at the White House at 7:15 a.m. as they divided up a list of allies and lawmakers to notify when the war began.

A few hours later, Bush asked Baker to come back to the White House for lunch. Bush was dwelling on the casualty projections by the Pentagon, which had shipped twenty thousand body bags to the Middle East.

The president was looking for reassurance not from his secretary of state but from one of his oldest friends. While Baker had served in the Marines, he had never seen combat. Bush had. He had survived the shootdown of his plane in World War II when his crewmates died. That had never left him.

"I'm convinced I've done the right thing," Bush told Baker, perhaps still trying to convince himself.

"I am too," Baker replied.

Around 4:30 p.m. Washington time, the first wave of bombers took off from Saudi Arabia and nearby aircraft carriers, but they would take time to arrive at their targets. From his State Department office, Baker's task was to touch base with as many allies as possible. He summoned ambassadors from Saudi Arabia, Syria, Israel, Kuwait, Germany, and Japan to the State Department, shuffling them in and out for meetings that lasted five minutes or so. He also called the foreign ministers of the Soviet Union, Egypt, the Netherlands, Spain, Italy, and Luxembourg as well as the NATO secretary-general. Baker struggled with his emotions. "You could hear it in his voice," said Zalman Shoval, the Israeli ambassador. "I almost thought I could see it in his eyes."

Baker telephoned Moscow, waking up Alexander Bessmertnykh, who had taken over for Eduard Shevardnadze as Soviet foreign minister. Bessmertnykh asked for a delay in the start of the operation. Mikhail Gorbachev wanted more time "so that I could try to convince Iraq to withdraw its troops," as the general secretary put it later, but Baker sent back word that it was too late. The die was cast.

Baker turned on the television, but there were still no reports of any action. Why hadn't anything happened? CNN's correspondents in Baghdad were reporting that it was all quiet in the Iraqi capital. Baker called out to one of his assistants, John Crowley.

"John, bring me a big martini on the rocks," he said.

The martini arrived, but the war did not.

Finally, around 6:30 p.m., the CNN reporters speaking by telephone from their hotel in Baghdad reported hearing explosions and seeing tracer fire from antiaircraft batteries in the sky. Operation Desert Storm was under way. At 7:08 p.m., Marlin Fitzwater, the press secretary, took the podium at the White House and announced, "The liberation of Kuwait has begun." Baker watched Bush's address to the nation on television two hours later announcing the start of hostilities, then at 9:30 p.m. headed home.

By the next night, as waves of American and allied warplanes rained down powerful bombs on ill-prepared Iraqi troops, Baker and the others were afraid the carefully constructed coalition might still fall apart. Iraq had followed through on a threat to launch Scud missiles at Israel in hopes of drawing it into the war. The Israelis were understandably eager to retaliate, something Baker was equally eager to avoid lest it jeopardize the alliance with Arab states. Although he had secretly obtained reassurances from Arab leaders that they would not back out of the coalition if Israel responded to an attack, he could not be sure they would live up to that. Baker rushed over to the White House and joined the team in Scowcroft's office. As Baker absently fingered his key chain, an aide from the Situation Room arrived to tell the group that nerve gas had supposedly been detected in the debris of one of the missile strikes against Israel.

"If they've been hit with chemicals, Katie bar the door because they're going to do something," an agitated Larry Eagleburger exclaimed.

Baker tried to call Israel through the White House switchboard, only to listen in astonishment as a recording announced that all circuits were busy.

"Holy shit," said Roman Popadiuk, a national security spokesman. "The world's burning down and we can't get a line out?"

Soon, the group learned that the report of chemical gas was false, but there were other reports that dozens of Israeli warplanes had launched into the air. The Israelis had contacted Cheney at the Pentagon to ask for the identification codes necessary for Israeli warplanes to avoid accidentally shooting at or being shot by American or allied planes if they streaked into Iraqi airspace. Baker was working the phones with Arab officials trying to keep everyone calm, but a debate quickly broke out. Cheney and others thought it was hard to ask Israel to restrain itself given that it was under attack. But Baker and Scowcroft insisted that they had to keep Israel out of the fight or risk losing the support of the Arab world.

"We are going after western Iraq full bore, Mr. Prime Minister," Baker assured Yitzhak Shamir when he finally reached the Israeli leader around 10:40 p.m. Washington time. "We've got aircraft over the launch sites." That was something of a bluff. Baker did not know exactly where the American planes were, but figured it was close enough. "There is nothing that your air force can do that we are not doing. If there is, tell us and we'll do it. We appreciate your restraint, but please don't play into Saddam's hands." Shamir was noncommittal.

Through the long hours into the night in what they later dubbed "Scud Thursday," Baker dealt with the tension by writing doggerel poetry, some of it about his friend Scowcroft. He taped his racy limericks to Scowcroft's walls and cabinets. "They were very, very funny," recalled Robert Gates, "and very obscene."

Baker had not been in bed for long that night before Shamir called him at home at 2:03 a.m. and announced that his cabinet had decided to prepare an immediate response. Baker pleaded with him again. "You cannot do this, Prime Minister," he implored.

In the end, the Israelis held off that night as Baker wanted, perhaps due to the simple fact that it was too dangerous militarily to send Israeli planes into hostile territory without the American identification codes. Bush quickly dispatched Eagleburger and Paul Wolfowitz, the undersecretary of defense, to Israel to provide more reassurance and ordered two Patriot batteries operated and guarded by American troops to be deployed to Israel to shoot down any further Iraqi Scud missiles.

The pressure from Tel Aviv only intensified, however. Moshe Arens, Israel's hawkish defense minister, arrived in Washington in the middle of the air war to push again for Israeli retaliation. By that point, thirty-one Scuds had been fired at Israel, resulting in about a dozen deaths.

"We may now have to act," Arens told Baker.

"Our boys are doing the job for you," Baker replied.

Arens grew angry but before he had a chance to reply, an assistant entered with a message that a Scud missile had just landed not far from where he lived. He left the room to call home and reached his wife, who was unhurt, then returned to the discussion and told Baker what had happened. Baker made polite inquiries about his wife and then moved on. "I didn't sense any real sympathy from him," Arens said. "Nothing. It just went on like nothing happened."

AMERICAN WARPLANES JOINED by those from Britain, France, Egypt, Saudi Arabia, and Kuwait pounded the Iraqis from the sky. Although projections presented to Baker and the rest of the national security team had envisioned the loss of as many as 150 American aircraft, in fact the armada of fighters and bombers ruled the skies over Kuwait and Iraq. Saddam Hussein had promised "the mother of all battles," but the war was playing out as a pretty one-sided affair.

For Baker, the major challenge was not the Iraqi military but his partners in Moscow, who kept trying to intervene with one peacemaking venture after another. Mikhail Gorbachev sent Yevgeny Primakov, a Soviet diplomat with deep experience in the Arab world, to talk with Hussein and then advanced ideas for calling off the American-led assault without the complete pullback from Kuwait that Bush had demanded.

Baker's usual judgment failed him two weeks into the war when Shevardnadze's successor as foreign minister, Alexander Bessmertnykh, visited him in Washington. After discussions at the State Department, Bessmertnykh asked if the two could issue a joint statement restating their mutual commitment to finding a resolution to the conflict. Baker reluctantly agreed, deeming the statement a fairly anodyne document that did not break any ground. Indeed, he did not clear it with the White House and just figured it would be left in the State Department press room where reporters would probably not even find it until the next day. What he did not count on was Bessmertnykh encountering a group of reporters when he left the building and eagerly pulling a copy of the statement out of his pocket to read to them. "The Ministers continue to believe that a cessation of hostilities would be possible if Iraq would make an unequivocal commitment to withdraw from Kuwait," the statement said. Dennis Ross had made sure the statement included the word "continue" to emphasize that it did not signal a change in policy.

But in fact, it did. Baker had just suggested that Hussein could win a cease-fire simply by *promising* to pull out, not by actually pulling out. If

Baker was too tired to recognize what he had just done, others were not. Journalists flashed out the news, which quickly reached the White House just as Bush was getting ready to go to the Capitol to deliver his annual State of the Union address. In any administration, the rule was that no one was to make news on the day of a State of the Union to avoid upstaging the president. Baker had just broken the rule.

Brent Scowcroft was conducting a background briefing for reporters when he was asked if Baker was announcing a policy shift on Iraq. Not knowing anything about the statement, Scowcroft mumbled something to the effect that he had not seen it yet.

"Was Baker out of line?" a reporter asked.

Scowcroft said he would have to see the comments.

After the briefing was over, Scowcroft obtained a copy of the statement and went to tell Bush what happened, finding him in the White House basement having makeup applied for his televised address. "His face turned ashen even under the makeup," Scowcroft said. "Then the anger—as sharp as I'd ever seen in him—started to rise." Bush later acknowledged that he "was furious," even though he knew Baker "had not meant to 'blindside' me." Marlin Fitzwater, who recalled showing Bush a wire story about the Baker-Bessmertnykh statement in the limousine returning from the Capitol, said the president "got that steel jaw he gets every once in a while when you know he's not happy."

Baker was so upset at the screwup that he told aides the next morning that he had only slept three hours. He called Bush to apologize. "Sorry about the way it was played," Baker wrote in notes preparing for the conversation. "WH aides say 'trying to upstage'—BS. Saw statement as non-event; breaks no new ground."

Bush forgave his friend, but Baker's critics saw it as a sign that his own sense of self-importance had grown out of control. "He should fire him for this but he won't," Richard Nixon told Monica Crowley, his foreign policy assistant. "Baker took it upon himself to do this. God he's just *dying* to be president."

Even Cheney grumbled about Baker's mistake. As Gorbachev continued trying to play peacemaker, he dispatched an envoy to Baghdad and then sent Bush a letter reporting the results, suggesting that the Americans hold off a ground attack pending further talks. Cheney tied that to the opening provided by the statement with Bessmertnykh. "Baker bends over backward to please the Soviets and now the Soviets are bending over backward to help Saddam," he told associates. "That's just great!"

Three weeks later, Gorbachev came back with a refined peace plan,

In 1989, his best friend became the forty-first president of the United States and Baker became his secretary of state. They were closer than any president and secretary of state in history, but there was also a brotherly rivalry. "If you're so smart, how come you're not president?" Bush would say when he became exasperated.

Baker and Bush plotted strategy for the 1988 race at the vice-presidential mansion. "Let's not forget, it's about winning," Baker used to say.

Bush picked Dan Quayle for vice president without telling Baker, in what some saw as an act of rebellion against the perception that his friend would really be the "deputy president."

To win, Baker would rely on the negative campaigning skills of Lee Atwater, who privately resented Baker. "Lee was running on paranoia all the time," a colleague said.

Every week, Baker had breakfast alone with Dick Cheney, the defense secretary, and Brent Scowcroft, the national security adviser. It was an unusually seamless team.
Baker and Cheney © Bettman via Getty Images

During the Democratic convention in 1988, Baker and Bush went camping in Wyoming, Baker's favorite escape.

Barbara Bush was fond of Baker but she prized loyalty and wasn't above wondering whether his first loyalty was not to her husband but to himself.
Mark Reinstein/Shutterstock.com

Baker worked closely with Mikhail Gorbachev to manage the end of the Cold War and reunification of Germany. When Dick Cheney publicly expressed skepticism about Gorbachev, Baker made the White House disavow him. "Dump on Dick with all possible alacrity."

Margaret Thatcher was a skeptic of German reunification—and of Baker. "He had a mixed record," she thought.

Courtesy of Time *magazine*

After the fall of the Berlin Wall, Baker came to see for himself and became the first secretary of state to venture into East Germany beyond Berlin.

Baker forged a strong relationship with Soviet Foreign Minister Eduard Shevardnadze, even inviting him on a Wyoming fishing trip. "That was a real bonding experience."

After Saddam Hussein invaded Kuwait in 1990, Baker assembled a coalition to oppose him, but worried about another Vietnam.
Greg English / The LIFE *Picture Collection via Getty Images*

After the war, Baker shuttled around the region organizing a Madrid peace conference bringing Israel together with its Arab neighbors and the Palestinians for the first time.

At the conference, he conferred with his close advisers Dennis Ross, left, Ed Djerejian, and Margaret Tutwiler, part of the "plug-in unit" he brought with him to each job.
David Rubinger/The LIFE *Images Collection via Getty Images*

After Bush lost reelection in 1992, he and Baker remained close but other Bush family members were upset at Baker, including George W. Bush.

But when his own election was in trouble in 2000, the younger Bush turned to Baker to manage the recount in Florida, where he overwhelmed his Democratic counterpart, Warren Christopher. "He looked strong, Chris looked weak."
Patrick D. McDermott/UPI

When the younger Bush found his own war with Iraq flailing, Baker oversaw the Iraq Study Group seeking a way out.
Larry Downing /Reuters

In later years, the Bakers and Bushes returned to Houston, the struggles of Washington left behind. When Bush died in 2019, Baker was at his bedside, rubbing his feet. Above, the two families gathered at the 2010 dedication of a bronze statue of Baker set across a Houston park from one of Bush, the two friends facing each other in perpetuity.
Michael Paulsen / Houston Chronicle

reporting that Hussein was open to a withdrawal over three weeks. Returning from Ford's Theatre, where he saw a play called *Black Eagles* about the
Tuskegee airmen, Bush met with the Gang of Eight in his private study
upstairs at 10:20 p.m. on February 21 to consider the latest Soviet move.
Cheney and Quayle were in tuxedoes from an event they had attended.
No one thought Gorbachev's plan was viable, but Baker did not want to
alienate the Soviets either. Cheney thought they should tell Gorbachev to
go to hell. Colin Powell suggested they issue another ultimatum with a
deadline for Iraq to leave Kuwait or face a ground assault. They settled on
noon Saturday, less than two days later. Bush liked it.

"What's it do for you, Jim?" Bush asked.

Baker wondered whether the land operation was still necessary given
the pounding the Iraqis had taken from the air, but Bush and Cheney
wanted to make sure to take out a substantial portion of Hussein's military.

Seeing the direction the decision was going, Baker opted to sign on.
"It's good for me too, but it's a new item that the allies don't know about
and we need to get back to them about it." He returned to the State
Department and began calling foreign ministers late into the night.

The deadline was issued and then ignored, so after six weeks of bom-
bardment, the ground war began on February 24, with American troops
joined by units from some of Baker's coalition, a remarkable collection
of three dozen countries that included not just traditional allies such as
Britain and France but Arab states such as Egypt, Saudi Arabia, Qatar, the
United Arab Emirates, Bahrain, Oman, Kuwait, and even Syria, normally
hostile to the West.

The ground war did not take long. After just three days of pummeling
by American ground forces, it was clear that Iraq had lost and its troops
were fleeing Kuwait. The real question became how long to continue the
fighting. There was a desire to keep going enough to cripple the Iraqi military, ensuring that it would not continue to be a threat to its neighbors.
But there was growing discomfort both inside and outside the administration at the level of the killing. The "highway of death," as the media now
called the road out of Kuwait, was littered with corpses and burned-out
tanks.

Baker's team debated the issue with him before he went to the White
House to discuss it with the president. "Margaret and I were both, 'What
are we doing here?'" recalled Janet Mullins. "The boys were like, 'Yeah,
let's keep killing them.'"

At a meeting in the Oval Office on the afternoon of February 27, Bush
asked whether it was time to call a halt to the war.

Baker said yes. "We have done the job," he said. "We can stop. We have achieved our aims. We have gotten them out of Kuwait."

No one disagreed. Even Cheney concurred. "We were all in agreement that we'd done what we had set out to do, achieved our objectives," he said later. "Nobody argued, 'Let's go to Baghdad.' It wasn't an option."

Powell picked up an Oval Office phone and reached Norman Schwarzkopf to see what he thought. The general agreed it was appropriate to end offensive operations, but asked for time to consult his commanders before giving a final view. The team reconvened at 6 p.m., by which point Schwarzkopf had checked with his team and confirmed his opinion. They agreed to end hostilities at midnight Washington time, when the ground war would be exactly one hundred hours old.

Rather than feeling elated, Bush was somewhat dispirited. "It hasn't been a clean end—there is no battleship *Missouri* surrender," he recorded in his diary. "This is what's missing to make this akin to WWII, to separate Kuwait from Korea and Vietnam." Saddam Hussein remained in power. At cease-fire talks in Safwan, the southern Iraqi town where Schwarzkopf met his Iraqi counterparts, the Americans allowed the dictator continued use of his military helicopters, which he then employed to crush internal opposition.

In later years, Baker and other administration officials would emphasize that their mission had always been to liberate Kuwait, not drive Hussein from power. In fact, there was a growing desire on their part as the war proceeded to do both. On February 15, Bush in a speech urged "the Iraqi military and the Iraqi people to take matters into their own hands to force Saddam Hussein the dictator to step aside." Cheney the next day suggested "there's an incentive for some of the senior commanders to want to replace Saddam." And Baker himself chimed in the day after that, saying in an interview that "there would be no tears shed if the Iraqi people decided to change their leadership."

But the Bush administration was not prepared to do anything to help the people they were encouraging to stand up to Hussein. In the end, the strongman in Baghdad was left with enough military might to destroy uprisings by Shiites in the south and Kurds in the north while American troops stood on the sidelines. Baker feared the "Lebanonization of Iraq," a messy conflict that would fracture the country and drag American forces into a quagmire. "We are not prepared to go down the slippery slope of being sucked into a civil war," he told reporters as he traveled to the region in April. "We cannot police what goes on inside Iraq and we cannot be the arbiters of who shall govern Iraq." Yet just a day later, the cost of that realpolitik decision stared him in the face as he visited a refugee camp in the Kurdistan region of Iraq, where 50,000 people had fled, a fraction of a much larger displacement. Baker was stunned by the misery he witnessed. "We are suffering," one man told him. "Our children are suffering from starvation. We need doctors, we need medicine, we need water." Baker stressed to Bush the scale of the humanitarian disaster and aid was flown in. But not combat troops. While the United States would eventually set up and enforce no-fly zones in the north and south, Hussein remained in charge, a regional menace thumbing his nose at American power.

Still, it was a military victory that achieved its stated aims and avoided the dangers of mission creep. Kuwait was liberated and its government restored. The world had stood as one in declaring that the sort of aggression waged by Hussein would not be tolerated. Thanks to Baker's diplomacy, the United States and the Soviet Union worked in tandem for the first time since World War II to resolve a major regional conflict. The Arab world joined the coalition that Baker forged against one of its own and, however reluctantly, Israel stayed out of the fight, preventing Hussein from transforming the crisis into a confrontation with the Jewish state. One hundred and forty-eight American troops were killed in battle, about a quarter of them due to friendly fire.

Bush felt that the Vietnam syndrome that had hobbled the United States for nearly two decades had been finally purged. America was emerging from the Gulf War a more confident power at a time when it would increasingly assume the responsibility of unchallenged leadership. Bush's own stature was unquestioned. His approval rating shot up to 89 percent in the Gallup poll, at that point higher than any American president had seen since the advent of opinion surveys.

Bush was not the only one to emerge from the war with his public standing enhanced. Baker was enjoying an 84 percent approval rating and some considered him a prospect for higher office. Asked about the 1992 ticket, only 44 percent of Americans said Bush should keep Quayle as his running mate while 41 percent said Bush should replace the vice president with Baker.

On March 6, Bush addressed a joint session of Congress to hail the victory in the Gulf. Baker and Cheney sat side by side. The hall erupted in cheers.

"It doesn't get any better than this," Cheney said.

"No, it doesn't," Baker agreed.

CHAPTER 24

In the Souk

B aker was livid and he did not bother to hide it from the visitor in his seventh-floor office at the State Department. Dispensing with diplomatic niceties, Baker made clear that he would not tolerate what he considered offensive talk even from the ambassador of one of America's closest allies. If it happened again, he said sternly, there would be consequences.

The offending ambassador was Zalman Shoval from Israel and his crime in Baker's eyes was an all-too-candid interview with the Reuters news agency in the dwindling days of the Persian Gulf War. Effectively blocked by America from striking back at Iraq following Scud missile attacks on civilian targets, Israeli officials were frustrated with the Bush administration. Shoval had told Reuters that Israel "has not received one cent in aid" as financial compensation promised for losses in the war and that "we sometimes feel we are being given the runaround" from Washington on $400 million in housing loan guarantees to help resettle Jewish immigrants from the Soviet Union.

Coming just weeks after the Bush administration had dispatched Patriot batteries operated by American soldiers to protect Israel from the Iraqi Scuds, this struck a nerve. "Baker took it personally, that it was questioning our word," said Dennis Ross. Baker's attitude, he said, was "if you have this problem, you come and you see me. Tell me—you don't say it publicly." While other secretaries of state might have let the slight pass or even reached out to reassure a nervous and prickly Israel of America's enduring friendship, an irritated Baker decided to send a message. Not satisfied by the dressing-down he had delivered to Shoval in person at his office, Baker had Bush issue a public statement through his spokesman condemning the comments as "outrageous and outside the bounds of acceptable behavior by the ambassador of any friendly country."

To further drive home the point, Baker also crafted a private letter to Israel's prime minister, Yitzhak Shamir, threatening to expel Shoval from the United States altogether, an action almost never taken against an envoy from an allied nation:

> Yesterday your Ambassador made a series of statements about Israeli-US relations which I found not only inaccurate or misleading but deeply offensive. I must tell you in all frankness that it will be difficult to continue to conduct our diplomatic business through him given the obvious prejudice in his actions. Were the times not so tense and critical as they now are, I would not accept that he continue as your representative in Washington. As it is, Mr. Prime Minister, I will suppress my feelings in recognition of the importance of the fact and the appearance of maintaining close and continuous contact between our two countries in this complex period. However, should there be a repetition of the Ambassador's performance of yesterday, I would have no choice but to ask him to leave.

The Israelis thought Baker was overreacting. Shoval publicly apologized, but later recalled that the vast majority of his comments to Reuters were "very laudatory towards Bush" and the administration. Moshe Arens, the defense minister who had come to Washington in a futile effort to win permission for Israeli retaliatory strikes against Iraq, thought Shoval "had been absolutely right" on the merits; he and other Israeli officials took offense at Baker's harsh reaction. "This Bush-Baker move against Israel's ambassador had, to the best of my knowledge, no precedent in modern diplomatic history," Arens said years later. "Never had an ambassador of a friendly country been publicly castigated in such manner in Washington, and this during a war in which we were supposed to be allies."

How much Baker was genuinely offended and how much he was throwing an elbow for strategic reasons can be fairly debated. Baker had a real temper, but for the most part he used it strategically. Sitting in a meeting where he did not feel the other side was being cooperative enough, he would dramatically slam his leather portfolio shut, declare that there was nothing else to talk about, and storm out of the room. More often than not, this resulted in an effort by the other side to calm him down and bring him back to the table, presumably offering more flexibility. "I think Baker scared the shit out of these people, I really do," said Aaron David Miller, his Middle East negotiator, "in part because I don't think they expected Americans to behave this way."

Even members of his own staff found themselves rattled by the rare but memorable moments when Baker exploded. "When he would blow up, it was scary even for people who knew him. He was scary," said Ross. "Two things would get him to blow up. One, if you went back on your word. Or two, if you accused him of going back on his. He would never go back on his, but one of those two things, he'd blow up and when he'd blow up, he'd erupt. He would smash his fist down on the table and you'd jump. It was real. I think it was oftentimes for effect, but it was for real."

Whether authentic or manufactured or some combination of the two, the spat with Shoval effectively laid down a marker, an opening salvo in a diplomatic campaign that Baker was already mapping out in his head even before the guns fell silent in Iraq. Although he had resolutely blocked Mikhail Gorbachev from publicly linking the conflict with Iraq to the Arab-Israeli dispute, Baker had also privately promised the Soviet leader that he would try to resolve the long-running conflict after the war ended.

With the decisive defeat of Saddam Hussein's armies, Baker saw an opening. The United States had generated enormous credibility in the Arab world by coming to Kuwait's rescue and Baker had done what no secretary of state had done before by assembling a coalition with the most powerful Arab states, including Egypt, Saudi Arabia, and Syria. Baker had spent months jetting from one sweltering Middle East capital to another, getting to know leaders like Hosni Mubarak, King Fahd, and Hafez al-Assad while collecting diplomatic chits for later.

Baker and his advisers had an idea of how to use those chits. On February 1, weeks before the end of combat in Kuwait, a memo hit Baker's desk listing opportunities for the postwar period. Among them was a sustained American push for a resolution between Israelis and Arabs. As the memo put it, "Can't underestimate difficulty but: May have more confident moderate Arabs. Renewed credibility of US security assurances for Israel. Opportunity for peace in the Middle East has often followed war." Baker had long been skeptical of getting "diddled," as he often put it to aides, in the Middle East peace bazaar, but he listened this time when Ross insisted this was the moment. "We've just seen an earthquake," Ross told him. "We have to move before the earth resettles, because it will, and it never takes long." At a meeting a month later with Bush and Brent Scowcroft, Baker emphasized the prospect, although Scowcroft was noticeably skeptical. "Take adv. of our unique position w/both Arabs & Israelis," Baker wrote in his notes during the meeting. "USE OUR LEVERAGE *NOW*!"

BAKER HAD SPENT his first two years as the nation's chief diplomat resolutely avoiding any major investment of time and energy in the search for
peace in the Middle East. Not that it was an unworthy goal, but Baker,
ever calculating, viewed it as a quagmire that had sucked in previous secretaries of state to little end. As seismic changes rippled through the Soviet
Union and Europe, there were other challenges that seemed more pressing and likelier to result in success.

The war between Israel and the Palestinians, sometimes hot, sometimes cold, had stretched on for decades and an agreement had eluded
many American statesmen. Harry Truman was the first world leader to
recognize the state of Israel in 1948, over the objections of his secretary of
state, George Marshall, and much of the State Department bureaucracy,
which was dominated by Arabists. When Israeli forces stormed into the
Sinai in 1956 as part of a secret alliance with Britain and France to secure
the Suez Canal, Dwight Eisenhower sided with Egypt and forced the
invaders to pull out of the peninsula. Lyndon Johnson failed to head off
the Six Day War in 1967 when Egypt, Syria, and Jordan mobilized against
Israel only to be destroyed in a pre-emptive attack by Israeli forces, who
went on to seize the Sinai, Gaza, Golan Heights, West Bank, and the eastern parts of Jerusalem. Henry Kissinger helped broker an end to the Yom
Kippur War in 1973 and Jimmy Carter negotiated peace between Israel
and Egypt at Camp David in 1978. Ronald Reagan was the most avowedly
pro-Israel president at least since Truman, but even he butted heads with
its government over his agreement to sell AWACS planes to Saudi Arabia.
That was the first time Baker encountered the treacherous politics of the
Middle East, as the White House chief of staff responsible for securing
congressional acceptance of the sale.

The situation he inherited in 1989 seemed no riper for progress than
it had in years past. The Israelis had given the Sinai back to Egypt in
exchange for a peace treaty as part of Carter's Camp David Accords, but
they still occupied Gaza, the West Bank, and the Golan Heights. They had
merged East Jerusalem and the Old City into West Jerusalem and pronounced the combined city the unified capital of Israel. They were building settlements in the West Bank for Jewish residents over the objections
of Palestinians who claimed the land for themselves, with an estimated
200,000 Jewish settlers living in the West Bank or East Jerusalem by the
time Baker decided to tackle the issue following the Gulf War. Life in the
occupied territories was a continuum of miseries, with few jobs, run-down
homes, and Israeli forces in charge. Militant groups such as Hamas, Hezbollah, and Yasser Arafat's Palestine Liberation Organization, or PLO,

and various offshoots had for years waged a pitiless terrorist campaign against Israeli targets, gunning down tourists, hijacking airliners, and even killing Olympic athletes. In 1987, an intifada, or uprising, erupted in the occupied territories as frustrated Palestinians took to the streets, throwing rocks and Molotov cocktails at Israeli soldiers and police officers.

In December 1988, just weeks before leaving office, Baker's predecessor George Shultz struck a deal with Arafat, who officially renounced terrorism and accepted the existence of Israel in exchange for the United States opening formal contacts with the PLO. Bush, then the president-elect, signed off on the agreement over the objections of Israel, but Baker had little interest in building on it. He was "not going to fly around the Middle East like George Shultz had done," Baker told Dennis Ross during the transition. Ross warned Baker that he "might want to ignore the Middle East, but it would not ignore him."

BUSH AND BAKER HAD a strained relationship with Israeli leaders from the start. Prime Minister Yitzhak Shamir came to visit the White House in April 1989, shortly after the new administration took office and whatever was said ended up driving an enduring wedge between the two sides.

To Bush and Baker, both Texans firmly convinced that the United States needed to remain on good terms with the Arab states that controlled so much of the world's energy supply, the settlements that Israel was building in the West Bank and Gaza were an impediment to peace, an attempt to unilaterally change the facts on the ground in a way that would make it more difficult to find agreement with the Palestinians and their Arab backers. The two largely subscribed to the approach laid out in United Nations Security Council Resolution 242, which had been passed in the aftermath of the Six Day War in 1967. It called on Israel to give back the territory it had seized and on its hostile Arab neighbors to recognize its sovereignty and right to live in peace within its boundaries. This land-for-peace formula was the bedrock of American thinking over the course of multiple administrations.

So when Shamir arrived at the White House in the early weeks of Bush's administration, the president pressed him on the West Bank settlements. Shamir told him he should not worry, that "settlements ought not to be such a problem." Bush interpreted that as a commitment to halt new construction in the occupied territory, but Shamir did not see it that way and just two weeks later still more settlements were announced. Shamir's defenders said he only meant that the United States should not concern itself with the settlements, not that he would stop them. "It's a misunderstanding," said Moshe Arens, who was then serving as foreign minister before becoming defense minister. "Shamir wasn't going to give him settlements." But Bush believed Shamir had lied to him and never forgave him. That Bush would rely on such a vague formulation without attempting to clarify what the prime minister actually meant remains surprising given the president's deep experience in international affairs, where ambiguity is often a tool for deflecting unwelcome pressure. The disconnect defined the Bush administration's relationship with Israel for the remainder of his presidency.

Baker gave his first major speech on the Israeli-Palestinian dispute in May 1989 before the American Israel Public Affairs Committee, the powerful advocacy group known as AIPAC that worked to make support for Israel an inviolable priority in Washington. In laying out his views, Baker intended to call on both Palestinians and Israelis to compromise. "The thing that he wanted was to put responsibility on everybody," said Dan Kurtzer, an aide who helped write the speech. Reading the draft, however, Dennis Ross feared that it might be seen as too tough on Israel, America's closest friend in the region. In the days before the speech, Ross tried to leaven the sharp language with expressions of solidarity with Israel and awareness of its history and vulnerability. But Baker took out "all the notes of warmth and acknowledgement of the United States' unique relationship with Israel," Ross said. When Ross appealed, "Baker replied that Bush would see that language as pandering and would instinctively oppose it."

Addressing the AIPAC crowd, Baker called for a "reasonable middle ground." He rejected the creation of a Palestinian state and called on the Palestinians to renounce violence and recognize Israel's existence. But what drew the most attention in Jerusalem was his tough remonstration of Israel's hard-line leadership. "For Israel, now is the time to lay aside, once and for all, the unrealistic vision of a Greater Israel," he said. "Forswear annexation. Stop settlement activity. Allow schools to reopen. Reach out to the Palestinians as neighbors who deserve political rights."

At first, the crowd responded politely. "The first twenty minutes after the speech, people were coming over to him and congratulating him," Kurtzer remembered. But then he noticed AIPAC officials wandering around the crowd of 1,200, stewing over the notion of an unrealistic Greater Israel. "What they were doing was building up the anger over the one phrase so that by the time we left that hotel where the speech was given, AIPAC was already in a bit of a frenzy." Baker knew it. "Nice job, fellas," he joked with advisers as they left.

During a flight later on Air Force One, Bush congratulated Baker for doing what he thought was the right thing. So did others. "Your Israeli-Arab speech was outstanding—candid, strong & fair," Richard Nixon wrote Baker. "You will get some heat but hold your ground."

The heat proved scalding, but Baker did hold his ground. Shamir took the speech as a personal attack. "Certainly, Baker's words were directed at me," he said later. Shamir had never heard anyone use the phrase Greater Israel and thought Baker had a poor grasp of the nuances and contradictions on the ground. "Most of all, for me personally, his phraseology confirmed that my feelings of disquiet after our initial meeting had some basis," Shamir said. Senators from both parties assailed Baker for the speech. After the warmth of the relationship with Reagan, Israeli leaders came to understand that Baker represented a less romantic, more traditional Republican view of their country. "I think he belongs to that school of Republicans who sees Israel as a small country, nothing special, small country, and it's a problem for the United States," said Moshe Arens.

Baker devoted only a modest amount of time in his first year in office to a halfhearted peace initiative by the Israelis and Egyptians, never convinced that it would lead anywhere and never willing to invest much political capital in it. The plan called for talks between Israel and a Palestinian delegation to establish the ground rules for elections in the West Bank and Gaza, which would legitimize a set of Palestinian leaders to negotiate a more lasting agreement.

The effort, such as it was, collapsed after Bush, at a news conference in March 1990, called for an end to settlement construction not just in the West Bank but in East Jerusalem too, the first time an American president had referred to housing in the city as settlements. Within days, Shamir's national unity government collapsed, ripped apart by deep divisions over the American peace effort.

BARELY A WEEK LATER, tension with Washington escalated again when a deputy foreign minister named Benjamin Netanyahu openly assailed the United States for being too gullible in its dealings with the Palestinians. "It is astonishing that a superpower like the United States, which was supposed to be the symbol of political fairness and international honesty, is building its policy on a foundation of distortion and lies," Netanyahu told the media.

Baker was furious. He summoned Dan Kurtzer and threw a copy of the news article at him.

"I'm going to kick out the ambassador," Baker fumed.

"Give me twenty-four hours to find out if it's a real quote," Kurtzer implored.

Baker pointed to his watch and tapped it. "Twenty-four hours," he said.

Netanyahu tried to minimize the blowup by insisting he meant only that the *policy* was based on lies, not that the Americans were lying. It was not a distinction that assuaged Baker. Rather than kick out the ambassador, Baker declared Netanyahu persona non grata, barring him from even entering the doors of the State Department. The ban drove some of Baker's aides crazy, as they feared it would make their jobs harder. Dennis Ross would go to Baker's seventh-floor office and say, "Come on, he's the deputy foreign minister of Israel, you gotta let him in," remembered William Burns, a rising-star young Arabist in the foreign service and Ross's deputy. "Baker would just smile and say nope." Eventually, Baker gave in a bit, allowing Netanyahu back into the building but only to see lower-level officials. He made it a policy never to personally meet with Netanyahu again while secretary.

Israel's defenders faulted Baker. When he appeared on Capitol Hill to testify before the House Foreign Affairs Committee on June 13, 1990, Representative Mel Levine, a California Democrat, chided the administration for trying to strong-arm Israel, singling out the president's statement on East Jerusalem. "When we move to direct public pressure on Israel, as has occurred several times in the course of the past year and a half, it serves to undermine the very solid progress you make through the private diplomatic efforts that you've been pursuing," Levine scolded.

Baker resented what he saw as an attack on Bush—and an effort to drive a public wedge between the president and his secretary of state. Ross, sitting behind him in the hearing room, sensed danger and slipped Baker a note offering a suggestion of how to respond carefully. Baker, peeved, tore the note into little pieces.

The problem, Baker told the committee, was not the president. It was the Israelis who were not serious about peace. He noted that he had asked them whether they would be willing to engage in dialogue with specific Palestinians and never got an answer.

"Now, with respect to whether or not we're willing to let bygones be bygones, you bet we are," Baker said. But he had just read news stories quoting officials from Shamir's freshly reconstituted government setting new conditions for any talks.

"Now, if that's going to be the approach and that's going to be the attitude, there won't be any dialogue," Baker said, his voice laced with anger.

"And there won't be any peace. And the United States can't make it happen. You can't, I can't, the president can't. And so it's going to take some really good faith, affirmative effort on the part of our good friends in Israel and if we don't get it and if we can't get it quickly, I have to tell you, Mr. Levine, that everybody over there should know that the telephone number is 1-202-456-1414. When you're serious about peace, call us."

The outburst was inspired in part by a conversation Baker had had with Thomas Friedman of *The New York Times*, who told the secretary that he could hardly make peace if the parties themselves did not want to. Still, it was not fully thought through—indeed, Baker could not even remember his own telephone number and gave the main switchboard number for the White House instead of the State Department. But he would not tolerate any attempt to separate him from Bush. "No one is going to create a hint of difference between him and the president," Ross observed.

Baker quickly found himself under fire from supporters of Israel who deemed his comments intemperate. But Baker won praise from others who thought that the United States had not done enough to push Israel to come to the table. His friend Robert Strauss, who had served as Jimmy Carter's Middle East envoy, called and left a message of support. "He said you have finally justified his (Strauss's) carrying you on his back for all these years and getting you elevated to this position of authority," an aide summarized the call for Baker. "He said it shows that even a yellow rat will fight if you corner him. In all seriousness, he was proud of you for having the guts to do what you did yesterday—it was the right thing to do."

The day after his testimony, Baker sent flowers to the White House operators to apologize for subjecting them to a flood of calls by giving out their phone number instead of his own. From 9 a.m. to 11:45 a.m. alone, the White House comment line received more than four hundred calls about Baker, two thirds of them positive, the rest negative. Among the words the White House staff wrote down: "Disgusting." "Distasteful." "Ill-informed." "Appalled." But also: "Proud that at last someone has the courage to say what Baker said."

EIGHT MONTHS LATER, Baker was ready to try again. During the Gulf War, Baker, up until then the preeminent public figure of the Bush administration, had to some extent taken a backseat to Dick Cheney and Colin Powell, who prosecuted the battle and became household names through their sober, careful daily briefings on television. But with the cease-fire, it was Baker's turn to take center stage again and he planned to make it his mission to reorder the Middle East at the bargaining table.

Baker was no expert on the region. But nobody came to the task with a more intuitive feel for negotiations or a better instinct for how to entice reluctant players to make compromises. "One reason he's been successful is that he actually listens to the other guy and looks for openings," said Condoleezza Rice, who had watched Baker up close during the German unification talks.

As he had demonstrated with the Soviets, Baker recognized that the person across the table had his or her own domestic politics to worry about and he made a point of looking for ways to satisfy those needs while still getting what he wanted. "Every one of his counterparts is also a political leader," said Dennis Ross. "What matters is he understands what are the pressures on them and what's going to matter to them sort of intuitively." Baker would give way on details while holding fast to essential priorities. He took the measure of the other person and determined in his own mind how far he could go. He knew the importance of saving face. "Everybody's got a red line, he would tell you," said Margaret Tutwiler. "And he would get as close as he could to that person's red line and he wouldn't push them beyond that because he knew they weren't going to be able to do it."

Somehow this tobacco-chewing, elk-hunting Texan who had never set foot in a synagogue growing up, much less a mosque, managed to make connections with Jews and Muslims as well as Christians of a far different type than he had encountered back in Houston. As unlikely a mediator as he might have seemed, Baker was almost chameleon-like in his capacity to adapt to his surroundings. "Jim has this ability to fit in and work with and get along with everybody," said Dick Cheney. "I've seen it with diplomats, with high society, and with the most powerful people in the world, wearing his black tie as a diplomat and a very smooth item. But I've also seen him in a duck camp in Louisiana and telling better jokes than the good old Cajuns who were there." Now Baker's targets were a disparate collection of kings, emirs, and prime ministers.

What the Soviet Union had pressed for in the run-up to the Gulf War was an international conference, which was the Arab preference as well. The Israelis, unsurprisingly not eager to be outnumbered by delegations from multiple Arab neighbors, favored direct negotiations with the Palestinians. Even then, they refused to talk with representatives of Yasser Arafat's PLO, unwilling to accept that his renunciation of terrorism was genuine. They would talk only with Palestinians from the occupied territories. Baker came up with a formula that gave both sides what they wanted and enough political cover to swallow what they did not. Under Baker's plan, the United States and the Soviet Union would jointly sponsor an international conference with the Israelis and Arab countries that would be followed by direct negotiations between Israel and the Palestinians and, separately, between Israel and Syria, perhaps its most virulent enemy at the time. The opening conference would be more ceremonial, a statement to the world that all sides were, at last, willing to come to the table in the interest of peace; the nitty-gritty bargaining would take place in the direct negotiations that would follow.

To make it all happen, Baker embarked on months of arduous shuttle diplomacy, racing from one Middle East capital to another in hopes of pulling together leaders who would just as soon slit each other's throats. He started with the Saudis, who clearly owed the United States plenty in the aftermath of the Gulf War. He arrived in Riyadh on March 8, 1991, barely a week after the shooting stopped and found a willingness to consider what he was proposing. Meeting with King Fahd and Prince Bandar bin Sultan, Baker outlined the two-track process.

Fahd expressed approval and said a day would come when Israel and the Arabs would live together in peace. Saudi Arabia, he added, would be inclined to open diplomatic and economic relations with Israel if a Palestinian homeland could be established. "We know there is a state called Israel," the king said. "No one is denying it and no one should deny it." For Baker, that was a remarkable step forward. Neither Saudi Arabia nor most of the Arab world had ever formally recognized Israel's existence.

But Baker soon found that for every couple steps forward, there would be at least one back. In the weeks to come, he grew so frustrated with the Saudis that he pounded on his desk in front of aides. "Those guys could fuck up a two-car funeral," he said. He had returned to the region and had dinner with Saud al-Faisal, the Saudi foreign minister, only to discover that the commitment that he thought he had from King Fahd to participate in the peace effort had vanished. The foreign minister explained that the Saudis would not attend the conference since they were not technically neighbors of Israel.

Baker was flabbergasted. "I guess that it was okay to be partners in war, but not in peace," he snapped.

He later confronted King Fahd directly, making the same point. "We were there for you," Baker said. "We need you to be there for us. How can we be partners in war but not in peace? If you can't do this, what do I say to your friend, George Bush?"

Baker and his team did not give up. Dennis Ross went to see Prince Bandar and suggested that the Saudis attend the international conference as members of a delegation from the Gulf Cooperation Council, a regional organization that they belonged to. What mattered to the Americans was that the Saudis be there, not in what form. This would allow the Saudis to claim they were not participating even though they were—a classic Baker sleight of hand of the sort that often provided a way out of international dilemmas that would frustrate less creative thinkers. Bandar embraced the solution and got it approved by the king. From then on, Bandar would be a key ally of Baker's in pressing other Arabs to join.

Baker had an easier time getting Egypt on board since it was the one Arab country that had a peace treaty and diplomatic relations with Israel thanks to Jimmy Carter's Camp David Accords. Hosni Mubarak would be a reliable ally throughout Baker's long efforts. With Saudi Arabia and Egypt signed up, Baker set out to leverage those commitments to persuade other Arab nations to follow suit. Syria would be the most important, and the most difficult. And then there was Israel.

ON MARCH 10, a Palestinian man stabbed four Jewish women to death at a bus stop in Jerusalem, saying that he was sending "a message to Baker," who was due to arrive the next day. Israelis later gathered at the bus stop to protest the killings, some of them blaming the secretary of state. "Baker go home!" they chanted. Cursing Baker, one of the men shouted, "You are responsible for the murder of Jews!"

Baker arrived the next day, shocked by the violence. It was his first trip to Israel since taking office and he was hoping to build on the momentum he thought he had from his visit to Riyadh, but the bus stop attack hardly encouraged the Israelis to break bread with the Arabs. Forced by his security agents to cancel a walking tour of the Old City, Baker made a point of laying wreaths at the graves of the victims. Yitzhak Shamir thought Baker seemed "visibly affected" by the attack, which "gave him an immediate sense of the horror of Arab terrorism and its impact on ordinary life."

In Shamir, Baker had a difficult and unenthusiastic partner. Born in a Russian-controlled town in Poland, he moved to the British mandate of Palestine before World War II, leaving behind a family that was later decimated by the Holocaust. A bookkeeper and construction worker, Shamir joined what became known as the Stern Gang, the more radical wing of the Jewish underground then fighting British rule by assassinating military and police officers. Hunted as a terrorist, Shamir learned to never talk about his work too loudly and stayed out of sight during the day. When he came out at night, he often disguised himself as a Hasidic rabbi. For all the hardship, he considered those "the best years of my life."

In the newly created Israel, Shamir eventually joined the Mossad, the intelligence service, and gravitated toward right-wing political parties that were emerging to take on the long-dominant left-wing Labor Party. He was elected to the Knesset, or parliament, in 1973 and served in several positions before taking his first turn as prime minister in 1983. Now seventy-five, he was quiet and not particularly charming, stubborn and uninterested in the sort of haggling that Baker was seeking. "I think Baker sized him up as a pretty ornery old man who was hard to deal with," Moshe Arens said.

When they first met in 1989, Shamir noted that Baker had been described as "an ever-flexible pragmatist" and he was sure he had been described to the American as an inflexible man of ideological principle. "Well, I think our informants were wrong in both cases," Shamir told Baker. "I am a man of principle but also a pragmatist when necessary. I know what political compromise means. And I am sure that you, Mr. Secretary, although a pragmatist, are a man of principle and that principle guides you in your approach to foreign policy."

Baker was determined to figure out if they really could find common ground. But just as he was negotiating with different Arab leaders with different vantage points, personalities, and priorities, he discovered that there was not a single Israeli voice either. While Shamir had cast off the national unity coalition, his narrow Likud-led right-wing government faced its own fissures. As hard-line as Shamir was, he was constantly buffeted by pressure from members of his own cabinet who took an even harder line, especially Ariel Sharon, a bluff former general and paratrooper who had fought in every war since Israel's independence and was now serving as housing minister.

Still, Shamir showed a little leg in that first visit, telling Baker in confidence during a private dinner at his house that he thought a confederal arrangement with Jordan, Israel, and the Palestinians could work. He also expressed openness when Baker suggested that the United States would guarantee Israel's security by posting American troops along the border with Syria if Israel would withdraw from the Golan Heights it had seized in 1967. But it was not to be that easy. Baker would have to return again and again.

During a follow-up visit to Jerusalem on April 26, Baker received a telephone call from home and stepped out of the prime minister's office to take it. His mother, Bonner Means Baker, had died at age ninety-six. For Baker it was a tough blow. Even though she had faded in recent years, she had taken real pride in him. "In my grandmother's later years," recalled Doug Baker, "I remember a time my dad was visiting in Houston and she's like, 'Jimmy, remind me, tell me what it is again that you do?' He said, 'Well, Mom, I'm secretary of state.' And she'd be like just beaming. I think she knew, but I think she just liked hearing it, just so proud. She'd say, 'Of the *whole* United States?' And he'd say, 'Yes, Mom, the whole United States.'" But then she would add something revealing. "She said, 'Well, you know, Jimmy, if your father was still around, he wouldn't have permitted it,'" Doug remembered. Even as the secretary of state for the whole United States, Baker was still in the shadow of his father. The family legacy loomed large. Baker could never quite escape the Warden's judgment.

Baker returned to the King David Hotel in Jerusalem, called Moshe Arens, and had his staff notify the Palestinians that he had to leave for Houston to bury his mother. Bush called Baker in his suite to express condolences. Shamir was moved by Bonner Baker's death and ordered a grove of ninety-six trees planted in Jerusalem in her memory, one for every year of her life. On her son's next visit, the prime minister gave him a certificate commemorating the moment. "He was genuinely touched," Shamir remembered, "but within minutes we were back to the arguments."

IF BAKER THOUGHT Shamir was vexing, he had yet to fully come to grips with Hafez al-Assad, the fighter pilot and ruthless autocrat who had ruled Syria for twenty-one years. Baker met Assad during the run-up to the Gulf War and convinced him to join the coalition against Iraq, with Syrian troops helping to liberate Kuwait despite years of hostility toward the United States. But cajoling Assad to sit down with Israel would prove to be far more daunting, the "toughest Arab domino to topple," as Baker put it.

Assad was born the ninth of eleven children in a mountain tribe family that belonged to the Alawite sect, a small branch of Shiite Muslims considered heretical by the Sunni majority in Syria. He grew up in a two-room stone house but managed to leave for an education and enlisted in the air force, where he learned to fly Soviet-made MiG jets. While in the military, he became radicalized by Syria's marginalization during a short-lived union with Egypt and joined a group of officers plotting to overthrow the government in Damascus. In the new regime, Assad became defense minister and then in 1970 staged a bloodless coup to take over the country on behalf of the Syrian Ba'ath Party. In 1973, Assad waged a fruitless war against Israel. In 1982, he put down an uprising in the Syrian town of Hama by killing ten thousand people and bulldozing a large swath of the city to the ground.

Over the course of 1991, Baker traveled repeatedly to Damascus for eleven meetings with Assad to bring him into the tentative peace process he was organizing. Each visit was an ordeal, the "ultimate endurance contest." Meetings lasted five or six hours, in one case nine hours and forty-six minutes, all in a room with barely working air-conditioning that challenged even the hardiest negotiators to keep alert. Baker and Assad were seated in two large easy chairs that made the secretary of state feel like a midget, positioned side by side so that Baker had to turn at an angle to see his interlocutor, leaving him with a sore neck every time. While Assad launched into long, repetitive lectures about the evils of the Sykes-Picot Agreement signed by Britain and France during World War I dividing up the Middle East as well as other crimes of Western imperialism, his guests gulped down sweetened lemonade and Turkish coffee to keep awake. But Assad never stopped for a bathroom break, almost as if it were a test of manhood. Finally, during one meeting, perhaps seven hours in, Baker pulled out a white handkerchief and waved it at Assad. "I give up," the secretary of state said. "I have to go to the bathroom." Baker and his staff dubbed this Bladder Diplomacy.

For his part, the diplomat from Texas sometimes threw Assad off with his foreign ways. "Well, you know, Mr. President," Baker told him at one point, "as we say in Texas, if a bullfrog had wings, it wouldn't scrape its ass on the ground."

Ed Djerejian, the ambassador to Syria, was so dumbfounded that he accidentally stuck his hand into a bowl of hummus. Gamal Helal, the State Department interpreter, turned to the secretary in abject confusion. "I can't translate that into English, much less Arabic," he said.

Assad was perplexed. "What does this mean? What does this mean?"

"Ed, I guess that's not translatable," Baker told Djerejian.

"I think not, Mr. Secretary," Djerejian replied.

So Baker tried another aphorism. "I'm reminded of what my father said when I was a young man," he said. "If the dog hadn't stopped running, he would have caught the rabbit." That one was lost in translation as well.

Baker advanced a version of the idea he had mentioned to Yitzhak Shamir—that if Syria would make peace, the United States would guarantee its border with Israel and perhaps the Golan Heights would be returned. Assad was impassive and Baker went home discouraged. The messages that followed were conflicting and confusing. A short while later, the Syrian government reported that Assad had agreed. But when Baker returned to Damascus, Assad said he had assented because of Baker's "guarantee" that Israel would pull out of the Golan Heights. Furious, Baker said he had made no such "guarantee"; he had talked about securing the border *if* Syria made peace with Israel. Baker concluded that Assad was feigning a misunderstanding to back out of the conference. On a later stop in Cairo, Hosni Mubarak urged Baker not to give up on the Syrian leader, but the secretary threatened to wash his hands of the whole project and leave "the dead cat" at Assad's door.

The "dead cat" became a favorite Baker metaphor as he raced around the Middle East. The point was who would be blamed if the peace effort collapsed. If there was to be no reconciliation, then each side wanted the other to be held responsible. No one wanted Baker leaving the feline corpse on his front step. "Underneath that Texas affability I think people could sense there was a really tough-minded guy there who would negotiate certainly, but there were certain boundaries and he simply would not go beyond that," said Robert Gates.

Baker's sessions with Assad were not only endless but circular. Whenever Baker thought he had gotten somewhere on an issue, Assad raised it again. Baker toggled between indulgent tolerance and strategic temper. "Baker was a master of the tactics of negotiating," said Richard Haass. "He knew when to hang tough and when to add a sweetener." After one more inconclusive session with Assad, Baker was summoned out of a meeting while in Lisbon on other business when Ed Djerejian called from Damascus and insisted the secretary be interrupted. Djerejian had in his hands a large white envelope with the presidential seal of Syria on it.

"This better be important, Ed," Baker said when he picked up the phone.

"Mr. Secretary, I just got the letter. It's on the cable traffic coming to you shortly. Assad has accepted the president's pitch."

"Are you sure?"

"I read it very carefully once, but it's a positive response, Mr. Secretary."

It had taken sixty-three hours of talks with Assad, but Baker had Syria on board. Now he needed to get Israel.

BAKER WAS in Moscow at the end of July, at a time of enormous danger in the Soviet Union, when hard-liners were gathering to take down Mikhail Gorbachev. But the secretary was also focused on pushing Israel to the bargaining table. He was talking by phone with Shamir constantly, three times in one day. He even canceled a visit to Moscow's Tomb of the Unknowns one morning to make another call to Shamir, this one resulting in a snap decision to travel to Israel the next day.

Shamir kept throwing out more conditions. On the phone he told Baker that he wanted the United States to press the United Nations to rescind its resolution equating Zionism with racism, a measure that had long infuriated the Israelis. Baker told him they were working to do just that, a promise he would deliver by the end of the year. But he added, it was time for Shamir to commit.

"I need for you to stand up with me and say yes, the same way Assad did," Baker said into the phone. He was playing to Shamir's pride, gambling that the Israeli did not want to look more intransigent than the Syrian. "If you do this, it will put the onus on the Palestinians. They are the only ones who have not responded."

Baker arrived in Israel the next day and headed into a ninety-minute meeting with Shamir. The real holdup was the nature of the Palestinian participation in the conference. In deference to Israeli objections to the Palestinians having their own delegation as if they were a nation, Baker had agreed to a joint Jordanian-Palestinian delegation, which in itself required making up with King Hussein, the Jordanian monarch who had sided with Saddam Hussein during the Gulf War. The Israelis insisted that none of the Palestinians on the joint delegation could be from the PLO; they would have to be residents of the West Bank or Gaza, not East Jerusalem. "We must be assured that we will not see PLO people," Shamir told Baker at one point. Baker could make that work. But when Shamir insisted that the Palestinian delegates would all have to actually renounce the PLO, the secretary of state drew the line. That would never fly, Baker said. Still, he promised that whoever was selected for the Palestinian seats would be acceptable to Shamir.

The prime minister's chief of staff interjected. That was not good enough.

Shamir waved him off. "Jim Baker's word—good enough," he said.

The Israelis were now in.

NEXT UP WERE the Palestinians. Meeting them in Jerusalem, Baker tried to leverage the yes he had just gotten from Shamir.

"Don't let the PLO block this process," he told Faisal Husseini, the Palestinian leader assigned to negotiate. "Yesterday afternoon, I had a yes from Israel."

Baker outlined a series of points that were meant to assure the Palestinians. "If this package I have prepared for you is not good enough, then we are out of steam," he said. Do not miss this opportunity, he urged them. "If you don't say yes, you will be the only one. I don't think we have ever been closer before to having a peace conference."

The Palestinians kept pressing for more—changes in American policy, PLO representatives on the delegation, even a visit by Baker to PLO headquarters in Tunis. All nonstarters, Baker said. They said they wanted someone from East Jerusalem in the delegation. Problematic, Baker said.

"I've stretched as far as I can," he said. "Look what I'm giving you. For God's sake, don't let this fall on the symbol of East Jerusalem."

With no final answer from the Palestinians, Baker returned home. He had been on the road for twenty-three days, his longest overseas trip as secretary of state. Ever solicitous of his traveling press corps, Baker presented wilted roses to David Hoffman of *The Washington Post*, the only reporter who lasted the entire journey. Aides marveled at Baker's stamina; Margaret Tutwiler called him "an endurance machine." Everywhere he traveled, he brought a cooler filled with Dr Pepper, Budweiser, and Diet Coke. After a particularly stressful meeting, he might indulge in a massage. While the travel and all the table-pounding had clearly taken a toll, he rarely looked haggard. At one point early in the process, his cousin Preston Moore expressed concern about Baker's health. "Take one hour per day and do it religiously—exercise, hit golf balls or backhands, jog, swim but *do it*!" he told Baker on his sixty-first birthday. "You can do anything you want to, but if you will do these things, you will be better in what you do *now*, and then you can do it better for a lot longer."

But the shuttle diplomacy was putting a strain on all of them. There were times that Margaret Tutwiler was not sure she could keep going. Aaron David Miller was away from home so long that when he returned from one trip, he found a note on his nine-year-old son's door: "I hate you. I hate Jim Baker. I hope he fires you."

FOR BAKER, arduous as the whole mission had been for him and his team, the pieces were beginning to fall into place. But just as he could see the picture coming into form, the puzzle was scrambled again.

With the changes in the Soviet Union, hundreds of thousands of Jewish immigrants were flooding into Israel and Shamir's government had been depending on the United States for financial assistance to provide housing for the new arrivals. The Israelis were requesting $10 billion in loan guarantees for 1991, but the timing could not be worse. Baker was concerned that at least some of the money would be used for settlement construction in the West Bank and Gaza. If the United States were to approve the $10 billion now, it could blow up the peace conference.

Baker convinced Bush to postpone the loan guarantees for 120 days and called Shamir to ask if they could wait until after the conference. Shamir seemed open to it at first, but within days, Israel's supporters in Washington opened a full-scale lobbying campaign pressing Congress to approve the money without delay. Bush and Baker pushed back, leaning on allies on Capitol Hill to put the issue off until the new year.

Bush did not help himself at a news conference on September 12 when he portrayed himself as a political David taking on a pro-Israeli Goliath. "We're up against a very strong and effective" lobby, the president told reporters. "I heard today there was something like a thousand lobbyists on the Hill working the other side of the question. We've got one lonely little guy down here doing it." Hardly. Not surprisingly, the president generated gales of anger with his comment, which seemed to perpetuate the old trope of an all-powerful Jewish lobby.

Besides, the whining was unnecessary. For all of Bush's complaints, in politics nothing comes close to a president with a 70 percent approval rating. The loan guarantees were put off. But the blowup over the housing assistance would leave a deep scar on the Bush-Israel relationship, evidence to many that the president was not on the side of America's closest partner in the Middle East.

For the moment, though, Baker wanted to take advantage of the delay to finally bring the last players to the table. Returning to the Middle East a few weeks later, he stopped in Damascus to iron out the latest objections raised by Assad. Once again, the Syrian leader was dancing around previous commitments, haggling over the wording of a letter of assurance, reopening issues Baker had thought were closed. At one point, the discussion devolved into whether negotiators would begin meeting within two weeks after the Madrid conference or simply begin organizing meetings within two weeks.

Baker was frustrated but determined to prevail. Back in his suite at the Sheraton that night after another long day of haggling, aides watched Baker, barefoot and in a white terry-cloth bathrobe, pace back and forth as the strategizing continued well after midnight. Then he started imitating the motions of a fly fisherman, reeling in a catch. "I'm gonna get him," Baker said to himself as much as anyone else. "I'm gonna get him."

Patience and power, knowing when to let the line out and when to yank it with all his might. And from time to time, an eruption of anger might work where finesse would not. Finally, when he met with Assad again the next day and again they went round and round, Baker had had enough. If most of the time the flashes of fury were calculated for effect, this time it was for real. Syria had lost on the battlefield to Israel. If Assad had any real hope of regaining the territory he had lost in 1967, Baker said, then he needed to take this process seriously and get on board. Assad did not seem to be listening.

"Go to hell," Baker finally snapped. "Go get your land yourself."

Gamal Helal, the interpreter, looked at him. "Mr. Secretary, do you want me to translate this?"

"I think they got it," Baker said.

They took a short break but when they returned to the discussion, Baker was still steamed. Assad brought up yet another petty point and the secretary of state came close to boiling over. The Syrian foreign minister sensed danger.

"Take care," he whispered in Arabic to Assad, "he is really angry."

"Why?" Assad asked. "We are negotiating!"

But Assad quickly recognized that Baker was on the edge and so, with that, abruptly declared that they were done. "I guess these are all the issues," Assad said.

Dennis Ross passed Baker a note. "Take the money and run," it read. Baker did.

BAKER FLEW NEXT to Jerusalem to meet again with the Palestinians. Baker told them that the Syrians had just committed to coming. It was time for the Palestinians to take yes for an answer.

"The ball is in your court," Baker told them. "Don't pass up this opportunity."

Faisal Husseini said there were still two provisions that "are essential to us"—the delegation must include a resident of East Jerusalem and Israel had to halt settlement construction. Husseini said he was being cast as a traitor to his people for not insisting on more.

"My people look at me like a Trojan horse," Husseini told Baker. "It is so difficult to be in this position for the first time in my life, in my career. Today, my daughter told me she couldn't go to school, couldn't face her classmates."

The room was silent. Baker aides thought the whole effort was over, all the work, all the travel, all the haggling and now it would fall apart. Baker, however, was not about to give up. Rather than confront the stalemate directly, he played for time. It was already 9 p.m. He stood up and said, "Let's eat."

After dinner, the two sides returned to the meeting room. Now Baker was ready to press for final acceptance.

"We come from different cultural backgrounds," he began. "I gave you everything I could on East Jerusalem and I'm not in the souk. The souk is closed. I've done all I can do for you. Israel doesn't know the extent of the guarantees I've given you. You are still hung up on symbols. I've stretched." Then he blew up. He shouted, pounded the sofa. "With you people, the souk never closes," he fumed. Storming out of the room, he called out, "I've had it. Have a nice life."

Stunned, the Palestinians asked Dennis Ross what they should do. "Do you think I'm going to go try to calm him down?" he replied. "No way." They had to drop their conditions and finish their delegation list. Finally, they agreed. Ross went to find Baker, who was pacing back and forth in another room and made no rush to return. "You could almost feel the steam coming out of his ears and he's muttering to himself," Ross said.

Nonetheless, it was done. Baker had brought everyone on board—the Israelis, the Saudis, the Syrians, the Egyptians, the Jordanians, the Soviets, the Europeans, and now the Palestinians. He huddled afterward with his team in his hotel room until past midnight. They had been debating sites for the conference for weeks, but now decided to go with Madrid, which would be neutral and closer to the region than, say, Washington. Rather than wait until morning, Baker called the Spanish foreign minister in the middle of the night to ask if he would host. He needed an answer in thirty minutes, Baker told him. The minister called back in twenty. Madrid would host.

It had taken eight trips to the region, endless cups of tea, a few portfolio-slamming eruptions, and countless diplomatic sleights of hand. All told, Baker would travel 251,134 miles and visit thirty-nine countries in 1991, the busiest year of his tenure. He had become such a constant presence that in the Middle East, Gamal Helal recalled, Baker was called "Mr. America."

The next day, as Baker was flying out of Israel, Ross told him that the Palestinians had asked if the announcement could say that they were the first to accept the invitation, not the last.

Baker laughed. "I guess we closed the souk," he said.

BAKER LANDED in Madrid on the morning of October 29, arriving with Bush on Air Force One the day before the formal opening of the conference. All of the competing parties were already there or on the way, a success cemented in part by sending each what were called letters of assurances intended to address their main concerns. Yet even at this late hour, Baker found himself juggling all sorts of petty disputes: Could this delegate attend? How many minutes was each delegation permitted to speak? What were the camera angles? Would there be small flags on the table in front of each delegation? The Israelis refused to sit at a table with the green, black, white, and red flag of the PLO, which the Palestinians would want in front of them. So flags were ruled out altogether. Making peace, as Baker discovered, was often about small points as well as large—before you could get to the momentous questions, you first had to decide on table decor.

The most persistent sticking point continued to be the presence of the Palestinians as part of the Jordanian delegation. The Israelis felt misled when they learned that the Palestinians would be allowed to speak for an entire forty-five minutes as if they were a delegation unto themselves, not simply split the time granted to Jordan. If the Palestinians got forty-five minutes, then the Israelis demanded sixty.

When Baker sat down with Yitzhak Shamir at 8 p.m. at the Palace Hotel, the prime minister also complained about the presence of Saeb Erekat, a Palestinian activist with ties to the PLO who showed up as deputy head of the delegation despite Baker's efforts to keep the organization out of the conference, or at least out of sight. Baker was not happy to see Erekat either and was especially irritated that the Palestinian was wearing a black-and-white checkered kaffiyeh, in the fashion of Yasser Arafat, a pointed jab on his part. Baker considered Erekat a "blowhard" and "irresponsible," complaining to the Egyptians, Soviets, and Europeans about his presence. Baker told the Palestinians that Erekat could not participate in the direct negotiations that would follow the conference.

But Baker told the Israelis that he was not about to change the format at the last minute. As it was, Jordan's King Hussein had already been forced to accept having the Palestinians as part of his delegation. Baker said he was not going to tell the king that he could only have half the speaking time as well. Shamir acknowledged that it was not such a make-or-break issue that the Israelis would walk out, but he pressed Baker to find a more satisfactory solution.

Then Baker sat down with Syria's foreign minister, Farouk al-Sharaa, who announced that he would not shake hands with the Israelis. You do not shake hands with someone occupying your land, he huffed. Margaret

Tutwiler passed Baker a note reminding him that he himself had shaken hands with Tariq Aziz just days before the United States went to war with Iraq. Baker made that point to Sharaa but it did not impress him. This is different, Sharaa insisted. They are occupying my land.

As aggravating as that was, the meeting nearly exploded when Sharaa defended the killing of an Israeli mother of seven children by saying that it was part of the fight against the occupation of their land. Baker erupted, calling that outrageous. You cannot tell me that you think killing a mother of seven on a bus was acceptable, he lectured Sharaa. The foreign minister squirmed in his seat but did not give in.

The conference formally opened the next day, October 30, with Bush and Mikhail Gorbachev delivering opening remarks. For the first time in history, Israel and its various Arab neighbors met in the same room and sat at the same table to talk about their fundamental differences rather than shoot at each other over them. They gathered in the eighteenth-century Hall of Columns in Spain's Royal Palace. With massive chandeliers hanging over the table, a bronze statue of Charles V overlooking the proceedings, and a frescoed ceiling featuring an allegory of the sun god Apollo, Shamir thought it was an "odd setting" for the warring Middle Easterners. But there, gathered together in the same room, were representatives from Israel, Syria, Jordan, Lebanon, Egypt, Saudi Arabia, and other Gulf states as well as the Palestinians.

Baker marked the history of the occasion in his comments to reporters afterward: ·

> Today, Israel and her Arab neighbors and the Palestinians all came together for the first time to begin the search for peace. That old taboo that Arabs and Israelis cannot meet and cannot talk is now something that we want to relegate to history. The road to peace will be very long and it will be very difficult. We have to crawl before we walk and we have to walk before we run, and today I think we all began to crawl.

The crawling was at times painful. The speeches over the next couple of days bristled with grievance and accusation, restating long-held positions without showing a lot of give. The Palestinians jabbed at their foes by effectively associating themselves with the PLO, daring the Israelis to walk out as they had threatened. Shamir remained in his seat but was equally truculent in his own address. Fatigued and aging, Shamir, now seventy-six, sometimes dozed during the other speeches.

Still, there was movement by inches. The Palestinians indicated that they could accept some form of limited self-rule in the West Bank and Gaza as an intermediate step to the full statehood they sought, coming closer to the Israeli position of partial autonomy for the Palestinians. And if the delegates maintained a show of distance or outright hostility during the public discussions, in private moments, during breaks, Israeli representatives chatted politely with their counterparts.

The exceptions were the Syrians, who kept to their corner, determined, it seemed, not only to avoid shaking hands but even to make eye contact. Perhaps unsurprisingly, Sharaa's speech was especially combative, accusing Shamir of "faking facts and history." As he kept talking, Sharaa went beyond his allotted time. Margaret Tutwiler passed a note alerting Baker when he was three minutes over, then again at four minutes over. Baker passed his own note to Sharaa at the podium telling him his time was up but he kept going. Boris Pankin, the new Soviet foreign minister, sent a note too, also to no avail. Agitated, the Israelis made a show of looking at their watches. When Sharaa finally finished, none of the Americans applauded. Baker considered it an ugly presentation and disappointing.

The multinational conference, of course, had been meant as the symbolic opening of a process that would then shift to direct negotiations between Israel and the Palestinians and separately with the Syrians. But even there, eleventh-hour snags threatened to unravel the whole plan. The main fight was over where these direct negotiations would be held.

The negotiators had already argued for weeks about whether they should be held in Washington, somewhere in Europe, in Cyprus, or in the region itself. Finally, it had been agreed that the opening round, at least, would be in Madrid. Now they were arguing about what *building* they would take place in. The United States had made arrangements for the three sets of talks to occur in three buildings, all starting at the same time, 10 a.m., but now the Syrians were threatening to pull out, seeing that somehow as a slight. Baker worked the phones feverishly to stage the talks in the same building but at different times. Baker told the quarreling parties that their intransigence would only benefit their foes. "Don't let them get public opinion advantage by not showing up," he lectured each of them. Eventually, the talks were back on. It was the start of what would be months of discussions.

Baker left Madrid with a sense of satisfaction, even though he knew much work lay ahead. The conference had brought together Israel with its myriad enemies for the first time and, if it did not guarantee peace, it suggested at least that peace was possible. Soon afterward, Baker received a handwritten letter on White House stationery from his old tennis partner.

Dear Jim,

    We just landed, and I'm listening to early returns from the Conference. The sun has set in Madrid, but before it sets here I want to get this letter off to you and the special team that put the conference together. You know how I feel about your perseverance and determination. You hung in against great odds and gave the "vision thing" a new dimension. . . .

See you soon—
George

For Baker, Madrid was the ultimate test of his ability to get people who hated each other to come to the table. Even Yitzhak Shamir, after all the scrapes, credited the conference to "Baker's remarkable, stubborn and gifted display of shuttle diplomacy." Mr. Caution had gambled and it had paid off. "One of the raps on me was that I was never willing to take on anything risky," Baker said shortly after leaving office. "I took on every damn risky thing there was during my tenure at State." He had tried to avoid getting bogged down in Middle East peace. "But when I could no longer avoid it, I jumped in with both feet and I really took it on even though there was scant chance of success and even though some in the administration didn't think I ought to do it."

    But he was not done yet. There were talks, but as of yet there was no peace. On the plane leaving Madrid, Baker ruminated with his team. In what was a surprise to some of his advisers, he seemed to recognize that he would eventually get drawn away to run Bush's campaign in 1992 for a second term.

    "I'm going to the White House to help the president get reelected," he said, "but then I'm coming back and we will do the peace treaties."

    Or so he hoped.

CHAPTER 25

A Call to Action

It was late and Baker was already in bed with his wife at his ranch in Wyoming in the summer of 1991, taking a break between shuttle missions to the Middle East, when the State Department operations center called. It was never good news when the ops center was on the line, especially at night. It meant something somewhere in the world was falling apart and, as often as not, it would be up to Baker to try to put it back together.

The news on this particular night, Sunday, August 18, was the most alarming of all. Mikhail Gorbachev had been removed from power in the Soviet Union, Baker was told. A group of senior Soviet officials calling themselves the State of Emergency Committee, including the vice president, prime minister, defense minister, KGB director, and even Gorbachev's chief of staff, had announced that it was in charge. They claimed that Gorbachev had fallen ill, but in fact they had put him under house arrest at his summer home in Crimea, cut off his telephones, and stripped him of the nuclear command codes.

"There goes another vacation," Susan Baker sighed, recalling the invasion of Kuwait the previous August.

Baker sought to reassure her. "Don't worry, honey," he said. "I'll be back here in no time."

As he began contemplating the alarming news from Moscow, Baker grabbed his hunter's notebook and began jotting down his initial thoughts on how to deal with the Soviet crisis. It should not have been a shock; there had been warnings in recent weeks. And yet it still came as a shock, all the more so because Baker immediately calculated that the options for the United States were limited. "No leverage. Certainly minimal," he wrote. "Will be hard to do business w/new guys for a while," he added. "Emphasize the lack of their political legitimacy." Baker, like the rest of the American government, could not tell in those early hours whether this was a new reality that he had to adjust to or in fact a coup attempt that was still reversible. "Yeltsin is key guy," Baker wrote. "Should stay in touch with him. Portray us trying to get info. Touch base w/reformer."

Boris Yeltsin was indeed the key guy. A farm boy turned construction boss from Sverdlovsk in the Ural Mountains, Yeltsin in recent years had become the champion of the reformers and perhaps the most popular figure in the new Russia. Brought to Moscow by Gorbachev, Yeltsin eventually turned on his patron, accusing the Soviet leader of moving too slowly on reforms and empowering the hard-liners. A large, lumbering figure with thick white hair and a thick white middle, Yeltsin was bombastic and fearless, his vodka-lubricated antics as thrilling to everyday Russians as they were offensive to the Soviet elite. Yeltsin publicly challenged Gorbachev, who slapped him down, only to find that it generated an even bigger following for Yeltsin. Ultimately, Yeltsin quit the Communist Party altogether and in June 1991 was elected president of the Russian Republic, which covered the vast bulk of the territory of the Soviet Union and included about half its population, making him the first popularly chosen leader in Russian history.

To Baker and most of Bush's advisers, Yeltsin was seen as an unreliable, mercurial, and at times even buffoonish figure. "What a flake!" Baker said after meeting him for the first time. "He sure makes Gorbachev look good by comparison." That was the equation that would then govern the administration's approach to Gorbachev and Yeltsin for years—Gorbachev was their man and Yeltsin would be kept politely at arm's length. When Yeltsin first visited the White House in 1989 as an out-of-favor politician, he was given an appointment with Brent Scowcroft. At first, Yeltsin refused to get out of the car parked next to the White House unless he got to see Bush. Eventually, he relented and entered the building, escorted in through the basement entrance to avoid offending Gorbachev, only to take offense himself. Petulant and loud, Yeltsin demanded again to see Bush and refused to go any further unless he was assured a meeting. Condoleezza Rice, his escort, told him that he would meet with Scowcroft and if that were not good enough, he could leave. Yeltsin backed down and Bush dropped by the national security adviser's office for a low-key greeting and a short chat. The spectacle left a deeply unfavorable impression with the Bush team.

Now, however, the future of the Soviet Union's transformation lay in the hands of this clownish champion of democracy, as Baker recognized on that uncertain August day. While the reunification of Germany and the Soviet-American collaboration against Iraq's invasion of Kuwait had seemed to signal a definitive end to the Cold War, it was certainly conceivable that it could resume under new management. The coup plotters, however, erred by not arresting Yeltsin at the same time they confronted Gorbachev. Yeltsin would make them pay for that mistake.

Baker talked by telephone with Bush, who was on vacation in Kennebunkport. Bush had met Vice President Gennady Yanayev, the putative face of the so-called emergency committee, during a visit to Moscow and Kiev just three weeks earlier and had found him "engaging and pleasant with a good sense of humor," a rather generous assessment of a chain-smoking apparatchik deemed by others to be mediocre and unimpressive. The real power behind the coup was Vladimir Kryuchkov, the KGB chief, a revanchist Soviet who opposed the sweeping changes Gorbachev had instituted.

For Bush and Baker, the initial instinct was to accommodate the new leadership rather than challenge it vigorously. They assumed the United States would have to work with whoever was in charge in Moscow—a case of expedience over principle. "Maybe the thing to do is go easy on him at first," Bush told Baker, referring to Yanayev. As with the Tiananmen Square massacre, Bush and Baker seemed to care more about maintaining stable relations than standing squarely with the people who shared America's Western liberal values. "We decided he should be condemnatory without irrevocably burning his bridges," said Scowcroft, who was in Kennebunkport with the president and recommended Bush describe the events as "extra-constitutional."

Meeting with reporters in Maine, Bush used the term three times but his tone was cautious and tempered. He lamented what he called the "disturbing development" and referred to Gorbachev as a "historic figure" while expressing hope that Yanayev would continue reforms. He acknowledged that he had not tried to reach Gorbachev. "We're not going to overexcite the American people or the world," he said. "And so we will conduct our diplomacy in a prudent fashion, not driven by excess, not driven by extreme."

Scowcroft quickly realized that the statement was not strong enough. Yeltsin was already in the streets mobilizing thousands of supporters against the coup plotters. The United States could not afford to be on the sidelines. This was not Tiananmen Square, at least not yet, and Bush could make a difference. The president cut short his vacation and flew back to Washington to address the situation. Baker and Bush decided to swear in Robert Strauss, Baker's old friend from Texas, who had already been tapped to be the next ambassador to the Soviet Union, and dispatch him to Moscow immediately. A plane was arranged to pick up Strauss in California, then stop in Wyoming for Baker and bring them both to Washington. Bush, in the meantime, made a second statement that day, taking a tougher position. The coup, he declared, was a "misguided and illegitimate effort" that "bypasses both Soviet law and the will of the Soviet peoples." At the embassy in Moscow, the diplomats on the ground were frustrated by the seeming equivocation. To some, it seemed as if Baker were waiting to see whether Yeltsin or Yanayev would win.

The CIA forecast that there was a 45 percent chance that the coup would fail, another 45 percent chance that it would devolve into a stalemate between hard-liners and democrats, and a 10 percent chance that the Soviet Union would return to its more oppressive, pre-Gorbachev days. What the agency could not tell Bush was what he should do to encourage the first alternative. "My problem is that, during Iraq a year ago, we knew what had to happen," Bush recorded in his diary that night. "What had to happen is Iraq had to get out of Kuwait. Here, I'm not sure what *has* to happen. What I'd like to see is a return of Gorbachev and a continuous movement for democracy. I'm not quite sure I see how to get there."

THE COUP CAPPED MONTHS of political tension in Moscow, where Gorbachev was trying to walk a perilous line between reformers and hardliners, satisfying neither. In January 1991, seven months before the coup plot, the confrontation in Lithuania had exploded at a time when Washington was focused on Kuwait and Iraq. Even as American warplanes were preparing to open Operation Desert Storm, Soviet troops assaulted independence activists in the Lithuanian capital of Vilnius in the middle of the night, storming through a human shield formed by protesters around a television tower, shooting some and crushing others under tank treads. Altogether, fourteen unarmed demonstrators were killed.

Gorbachev insisted that he had nothing to do with the attack, but the violence further isolated him from his friends overseas, especially in Washington, without actually stopping the nationalist movement in the Baltics. By March, both Latvia and Estonia had joined Lithuania in declaring independence. A month later, the Republic of Georgia, the home of Baker's old fishing buddy Eduard Shevardnadze, announced that it would break away from the Soviet Union and form its own country as well. The Soviet empire was falling apart, piece by piece, and Gorbachev seemed to be losing his grip on the cascading events. The Warsaw Pact formally disbanded. Yugoslavia was in the process of breaking apart more violently than the rest of Eastern Europe. And back in Moscow, an estimated 100,000 people were in the streets protesting Gorbachev, who was left trying desperately to stop the Soviet Union from collapsing by negotiating some form of new union with the key remaining republics.

The disarray accentuated a debate that had been raging in Washington for months. Had Baker and Bush invested too much in Gorbachev and Shevardnadze? Had they essentially gotten so close to their counterparts, so personally committed to their success, that they had lost sight of what was really going on and what really constituted America's interests? As the architect of the administration's foreign policy, Baker had long prized orderly change over radical transformation, fearing that the situation could easily spiral out of control and a weakened Soviet Union could lash out in Europe or beyond. Baker was less interested in accelerating the demise of the Soviet Union than managing it.

Among those who thought Baker and Bush had unwisely tethered themselves to Gorbachev and Shevardnadze was Richard Nixon, still eager to be seen as the Republican Party's foreign policy wise man from his self-imposed exile in New Jersey. Nixon had never liked Baker, an antipathy fueled by the sense that the secretary of state did not heed his advice. Nixon railed to his aide, Monica Crowley, that Baker did not "know anything about foreign policy—and what he does know is wrong." He had only gotten the job through friendship with Bush. "Baker was overrated as a strategist and now he's in totally over his head with foreign policy. He just looks like an amateur out there with Shevardnadze, holding his hand and sounding like he has no backbone." When Crowley arrived at Nixon's office one morning in December 1990, she found him pacing and fuming. "Monica," he said, "if Baker doesn't stop drooling over Shevardnadze, I am going to gag."

Shevardnadze's dictatorship-is-coming resignation soon afterward only reinforced the doubts. Dick Cheney, Dan Quayle, and other Cold Warriors in the American administration thought they should hedge their bets and build more of a relationship with Yeltsin, who, while more volatile, was emerging as a real force in Russian politics and its most determined anti-Communist. Gorbachev wanted to fix the Soviet Union; Yeltsin wanted to blow it up. "I thought we needed to spend time on him and treat him with a certain amount of respect," Cheney said later. "There was a conventional wisdom that this guy's limited, not a heavyweight in terms of where he was going." Bush and Baker, in this view, were making a mistake by disregarding Yeltsin in deference to Gorbachev. "They never really cottoned up to him because they had so much embedded friendship with Gorbachev and Shevardnadze," Quayle said.

The critics pushing Baker also included a member of the cabinet with no official role in national security. Jack Kemp, the former congressman now serving as secretary of housing and urban development, argued at a White House meeting that the United States should recognize Lithuania's independence. A handsome, square-jawed former Buffalo Bills quarterback who helped Ronald Reagan push through his tax cuts and then lost the 1988 nomination to Bush, Kemp was a supremely ambitious figure who got on Baker's nerves by weighing in on matters far afield of his area of responsibility. Although their wives were good friends, Baker privately referred to Kemp as High School Harry. "We'd have a cabinet meeting and he'd want to talk about the gold standard," Baker recalled.

Baker had little patience for anyone getting into his business, especially Kemp. The two were already at odds because Kemp had recently scheduled a meeting with Ariel Sharon, the Israeli housing minister who aggressively promoted settlements in the West Bank in defiance of American pressure. To Baker, this seemed like Kemp was running his own foreign policy; he insisted the Sharon meeting be canceled, but settled for forcing Kemp to move it to the Israeli embassy rather than receiving the Israeli minister at the Housing and Urban Affairs Department.

Now only two days later, Kemp was sticking his nose into Lithuania policy. Baker fumed and after the meeting marched into the Oval Office to complain about Kemp driving outside his lane again. Kemp, who happened to be scheduled to accompany Bush to a housing speech in St. Louis, overheard and told Baker he was wrong on Lithuania. Baker lost his cool.

"Fuck you, Kemp!" he shouted across the Oval Office.

The president and everyone else in the room stood frozen in shock. No one used four-letter words in the Oval Office. At least not in Bush's Oval Office.

As Baker stormed out, Kemp gave chase, reacting like "a quarterback who had just been victimized by unnecessary roughness," as Marlin Fitzwater put it. "He started running through the furniture, sidestepping the couch, dodging the end table and breaking into the clear near the door." Kemp caught up to Baker near Fitzwater's office, both men still dangerously hot. "I thought there was going to be a fistfight right there in the West Wing of the White House," Robert Gates said. Only when Scowcroft interceded did the two separate.

Kemp later apologized. "I deeply regret the 'altercation' & only ran you down to at least apologize for what I honestly believe was a misunderstanding," he wrote Baker. "You must know by now that I've had nothing but praise for you and the job you & the Pres. have done. I do understand your frustrations with events (and people) in Israel but I would never trespass on your vital responsibilities. Jim, I'm not only your friend, but I'm on the same team & while teammates can argue once in awhile (& even fight) you can be assured of my respect, friendship & loyalty."

Baker was gracious but terse in his reply, making no effort to accept responsibility for overreacting. "I have your very thoughtful handwritten note," Baker wrote back. "Thank you for it and for the apology which I fully accept. And for your 'respect, loyalty & friendship,' which I reciprocate. It's water over the dam."

THE SIGNS FROM MOSCOW were increasingly ominous in the weeks before the coup. Baker was meeting with his counterpart Alexander Bessmertnykh in Berlin in June when he received word from Jack Matlock, the American ambassador in Moscow, of a plot afoot aimed at toppling Gorbachev. Matlock had been tipped off by Gavriil Popov, the reformist mayor of Moscow, who showed up unannounced at Spaso House, the official American residence, and while carrying on a perfunctory conversation for the benefit of any bugs, scratched out on paper in Russian: "A COUP IS BEING ORGANIZED TO REMOVE GORBACHEV." He implored Matlock to get word to Yeltsin, who was visiting Washington, to return home immediately. Matlock scratched out his own response in Russian asking who was behind the putsch and Popov identified the KGB's Vladimir Kryuchkov, Defense Minister Dmitry Yazov, and a couple others.

Baker called the White House, where Matlock's alarming dispatch had also been received, and they discussed what to do. Baker wanted to warn Bessmertnykh and have Bush inform Yeltsin. They also decided that Matlock should tell Gorbachev directly. Baker put down the phone and called Bessmertnykh at his hotel not long after he had returned from their talks and implored him to come back. Bessmertnykh, thinking Baker just had another point to make about the issues they had been discussing, tried to put him off, but the secretary insisted it was urgent. The Soviet foreign minister jumped in an unmarked car and came to Baker, who repeated the message he had received and the urgency of reaching Gorbachev. But when Matlock arrived at the Kremlin to warn Gorbachev, the Soviet leader gave no indication of alarm and confidently made clear he thought he would be fine. Yeltsin likewise told Bush a coup could never happen. In the days to come, Baker could not be sure what to make of their calm assurance. Were they being naive and reckless for not taking the threat more seriously? No coup emerged in the subsequent weeks, but dark clouds appeared to be gathering.

While the developments in Moscow seemed increasingly grim, the outer edges of the old Soviet empire were pulling further away from their old masters. Baker took time out in June for a trip to celebrate the momentous changes in Eastern Europe with a stop in Albania, making him the first senior American official ever to travel there. More than perhaps any other Communist country in Europe, Albania had been a Stalinist outpost, virtually hermetically sealed to the outside world. But like the rest of the region, the coastal country of 3.2 million people was transforming itself and Baker wanted to go in person to give it a nudge.

The catch was that the rest of southeastern Europe surrounding Albania was on the verge of shattering into pieces. Yugoslavia, a multiethnic state artificially fused into a single country after World War I, was being ripped apart by the centrifugal forces of nationalism, tribalism, and religion. Slovenia and Croatia, two of the six republics that made up Yugoslavia, were moving rapidly toward independence despite threats by federal forces to crack down violently. James Dobbins, one of Baker's Europe advisers, told him that "he should not literally fly over Yugoslavia just as that country was about to descend into civil war" in order to get to Albania.

Baker reluctantly agreed to stop in Belgrade first. In a one-day visit on June 21, he met with the president of Yugoslavia as well as the leaders of each of the six republics, shuttling between rooms in an ugly Stalinesque government building over the course of ten hours in a condensed blitz of Balkan diplomacy. Baker bluntly condemned Slobodan Milosevic, the strongman leader of Serbia, whose brand of ethnic nationalism was fracturing the country. After their meeting, both Baker and Milosevic said that there should be no unilateral declarations of independence, but what Milosevic did not seem ready to listen to were Baker's warnings against using force to hold the splintering state together. The meeting was unhelpful in another way too: Milosevic came to the conclusion that whatever Baker's tough words, the Americans would "not use military force" and therefore he had a pretty free hand to shape events as he chose, as Milan Panic, a future prime minister, observed. He was right about that.

Influenced by Brent Scowcroft and Larry Eagleburger, who had both served in Yugoslavia earlier in their careers and had a jaundiced view of the place, Baker did not think the United States had a strong national interest in what happened there and not much capacity to shape events even if it did. "We don't have a dog in that fight," Baker was later quoted as saying privately by *Time* magazine, a phrase that would earn him endless denunciations for its cold cynicism.

Did he really say it? Several years later, Steven Weisman of *The New York Times* called Baker to double-check before mentioning it in a piece he was writing.

"You're the first journalist who ever asked me if I said that," Baker replied. "I've seen that quote all over. Let me tell you, I never said it."

"That's too bad," Weisman said, "because it's one of the most intelligent things you've ever said."

There was a pause. "Well," Baker said conspiratorially, "I'm not saying I didn't say it in *private*."

Indeed, he had said it in a private meeting with Bush, Scowcroft, and Eagleburger, as he would acknowledge years later. The one-day mission to Belgrade hardly persuaded him otherwise. While the other nations of Eastern Europe had turned away from authoritarian rule relatively peacefully, Yugoslavia seemed to be disintegrating into a miasma of violence. Baker's interest was mainly in preventing a bloodbath. The United States would not support unilateral changes in borders and would ostracize any republic that sought to impose its will on any other, he told the leaders. In the end, Baker realized, "I convinced no one." Talking with Milosevic in particular was like talking to "a wall with a crew cut."

Baker left Belgrade recognizing that he had not made a difference and he had little idea how to proceed. This was perhaps the first time he had been so thoroughly stymied in a diplomatic session. Milan Panic concluded that Baker's visit was "a major failure of U.S. diplomacy." Indeed, three days after Baker left Belgrade, Croatia and Slovenia declared their independence. War broke out the next day.

Baker's visit to Albania, on the other hand, proved a welcome tonic. Arriving ten days after the Communist government was replaced by a cabinet with half its members drawn from opposition parties, Baker found a small land breaking out of a forty-year dictatorship that left it one of the poorest places on the continent. About 300,000 people jammed the streets of Tirana, the capital, chanting, "U-S-A! U-S-A! U-S-A!" and "Baker! Baker! Baker!" Standing on a makeshift platform, with Susan Baker by his side, decked out in an outfit of red, white, and blue, Baker celebrated the change. "On behalf of President Bush and the American people," he said, "I come here today to say to you: Freedom works."

Back in Washington a few days later, glee gave way to gloom as Baker met with Bush at the White House along with NATO's secretary general to discuss the widening hostilities in Yugoslavia. The news from the region was grim but Bush shared Baker's view about the dog and the fight.

"We're not doing contingency planning," Bush said. "We're not thinking of intervening."

"Once the shooting starts, and I think it will, it'll be a mess," Baker warned. Various gangs will fight each other, he added, NATO will not get involved but the Conference of Security and Cooperation in Europe will be invoked.

"And do what?" Brent Scowcroft asked.

"Nothing," Baker said.

BAKER'S MAIN PRIORITY remained the Soviet Union, where the crisis, he felt certain, was coming. Amid the uncertainty, Baker thought it was important to lock in as much benefit for the West while still possible. Even before the coup, a CIA report on the latest events in the Soviet Union in January 1991 had made clear that prospects for continued peaceful reform and transition to a more democratic, market-based country were fading. "What you are telling us, fellas, is that the stock market is heading south," Baker told his staff after being briefed on the CIA assessment. "We need to sell." Share prices in Gorbachev were about to plummet.

One way to ensure some lasting benefit from Gorbachev's perestroika would be to seal the long-sought agreement on arms control. The START treaty that he had been negotiating for years now was meant to be the first time the world's two superpowers would actually shrink their long-range nuclear arsenals. The arms control treaties negotiated by Richard Nixon and Jimmy Carter in the 1970s merely aimed to limit the growth of nuclear weapons. The INF treaty signed by Ronald Reagan and Gorbachev was the first to eliminate an entire class of nuclear weapons, but even it did not deal with the massive fleets of intercontinental ballistic missiles, long-range bombers, and submarine-based nuclear forces that could destroy the world multiple times over.

For Baker, the START negotiations had been painstaking and protracted, with an accord at times so frustratingly out of reach despite the warm relations between Washington and Moscow. Baker was consumed with assembling the international coalition for the Gulf War and then bringing together the Arabs and Israelis in Madrid. But he was intent on securing a START pact before leaving office. In the weeks leading up to the coup, Baker pressed to resolve the last issues in the negotiations.

Meeting with Bessmertnykh again in London, this time on the sidelines of the annual Group of 7 meeting, Baker at last finalized the remaining elements of the treaty and then slipped into a separate meeting between Bush and Gorbachev to flash the president a thumbs-up sign. After nine years of negotiations that began under Baker's predecessor, the two superpowers had agreed to bring down their arsenals to no more than 1,600 deployed ICBMs, submarine-based missiles, and heavy bombers and 6,000 warheads, while instituting an inspection regime that would introduce a new level of transparency to their militaries. Overall, the treaty would cut the American and Soviet arsenals by roughly a third and, effectively, end an arms race that had consumed vast resources for four decades. For Baker, it was a landmark agreement, a legacy maker.

The deal cleared the way for Bush to travel to Moscow later that month to meet with Gorbachev for their first summit on Soviet soil. A grand treaty-signing ceremony was planned. Baker and Bush arrived on July 29, unsure what they would find. They were met at the airport by Gennady Yanayev, the first time Bush met the treacherous Soviet vice president who would become so important just three weeks later.

For the moment, the wild card seemed to be Yeltsin. Gorbachev was in the midst of negotiations with Yeltsin and the leaders of the other republics on a new treaty that would provide more autonomy to the Soviet outposts. But when Gorbachev invited Yeltsin to meet together with Bush, he brusquely refused, insisting on meeting with the American president separately. It did not go well. During their forty-minute discussion, Yeltsin asked Bush to open diplomatic relations with Russia, separate from the Soviet Union, which Bush curtly rejected, noting that America did not have such ties with the constituent republics of other countries. It would be like California opening an embassy in Moscow.

Undeterred, Yeltsin continued to act almost as if he were the head of state, not Gorbachev, or at the very least an equal to the Soviet president. Yeltsin asked if he could enter the State Dinner being thrown for the visiting American president alongside Bush and Gorbachev, a breach of protocol that the Soviet leader would not abide.

Yeltsin showed up at the dinner determined to assert himself anyway, approaching Barbara Bush and offering to escort her into the hall at the Grand Kremlin Palace as if he were the host. "Is that really all right?" she asked, sensing a breach of etiquette. Ultimately, she positioned herself so that Raisa Gorbachev would be between her and Yeltsin, but the maneuvering underscored how uncertain the power relationships in Moscow had become.

For Baker, the Russian scheming was just one of many intrigues to juggle. This was the same trip where he was on the phone constantly with Yitzhak Shamir and others in the Middle East trying to set up the peace conference, a negotiation that sent him to Israel immediately after Moscow. Bush went next to Kiev, the capital of the Soviet Ukrainian Republic, where nationalist sentiment was at a fever pitch. Unlike the Baltics or even Georgia, Ukraine was central to the fate of the Soviet Union. With some 50 million people, Ukraine was by far the second-largest republic and ethnically, historically, and culturally closer to Russia than almost any other part of the Soviet Union. If Ukraine were to break away, as its leaders were now suggesting, it would be a severe blow to Moscow.

The Soviets were unhappy that Bush was visiting Kiev, even just for a six-hour stop, seeing it as encouraging Ukrainian independence. They sent Gennady Yanayev to accompany him to reinforce that Moscow was still in charge. Sensitive to Gorbachev's concerns, Bush gave a speech that would come back to haunt him, essentially throwing cold water on Ukrainian nationalist aspirations. "Some people have urged the United States to choose between supporting President Gorbachev and supporting independence-minded leaders throughout the USSR," Bush told Ukrainian lawmakers in the Supreme Soviet Building, standing in front of a large statue of Lenin. "I consider this a false choice." But, he added, "Freedom is not the same as independence. Americans will not support those who seek independence in order to replace a far-off tyranny with a local despotism. They will not aid those who promote a suicidal nationalism based upon ethnic hatred. We will support those who want to build democracy."

The speech shocked and disappointed many in Ukraine as well as the large and politically important Ukrainian American community back in the United States. It sounded like a realpolitik Bush was trying to prop up a dying Soviet Union by trading away the self-determination of the Ukrainian people. In *The New York Times*, the columnist William Safire dubbed it the "Chicken Kiev" speech, a name that would stick.

At its heart, the Kiev speech reflected the fundamental divide within the administration about how hard to push as the Soviet Union seemed to be coming apart at the seams. "We were very nervous about Ukrainian independence," Baker acknowledged later. "We were working with Gorbachev effectively."

Cheney argued the opposite case in vain. He saw a longtime enemy on the ropes and felt the Americans should do everything they could to secure the victory. While Baker, Bush, and Scowcroft worried about Ukraine and the other republics breaking away from Moscow, Cheney thought the collapse of the Soviet Union would be to America's benefit. Even if Communist hard-liners managed to cut short Gorbachev's reforms and stage a comeback, he reasoned, America would be left with a smaller, fractured foe. "There's no question I was more of a hard-ass," Cheney said. "I looked at what was happening in the Soviet Union as a game apart, as a tremendous opportunity. And I didn't want to see it slip away and therefore I thought it was important for us to take steps to make certain that we took maximum advantage out of the breakup of the old Soviet Union."

THE RETURN OF THE COMMISSARS looked very real just seventeen days after Bush's Kiev speech when the coup began to the rumbling of tank treads in the streets of Moscow and the unnerving midday airing of *Swan Lake* on Soviet television. The question was whether the plotters would succeed. In Moscow, Boris Yeltsin rose to the occasion, inspiring a counterrevolution to face down the hard-liners intent on restoring the old Soviet Union. Racing to the Russian White House, then the home of parliament, Yeltsin clambered on top of a tank and rallied the nation to his side. Eventually, tens of thousands of people surrounded the White House, some of them armed. They erected barriers and waited, determined to stand against an anticipated assault.

Gennady Yanayev, the vice president serving as front man for the coup plotters, called a news conference to insist that Gorbachev was simply sick and that the emergency committee was committed to continuing his reforms. But no one believed him and, in one of the indelible images of the episode, his trembling hands captured on television convinced Russians and Westerners alike that the putschists did not have the will or ability to succeed. It was nervousness, not alcohol as many suspected, that made his hands shake like that, he later asserted. But either way, it gave the whole enterprise an amateurish quality.

On the morning of August 20, Bush reached Yeltsin by phone. Yeltsin filled the president in on what was happening. Tanks and troops were moving into Moscow but Yeltsin said 100,000 people had gathered to defend his headquarters at the Russian White House. He added that his people had tried to contact Gorbachev but were rebuffed.

"Mr. President," Yeltsin said, "it would be good if you yourself could demand to speak on the phone with Gorbachev and to rally world leaders to the fact that the situation here is critical."

Bush said he had tried to call already and failed but would try again.

"You have our full support for the return of Gorbachev and the legitimate government," he told Yeltsin.

Bush said he was thinking about calling Yanayev but was not sure that was a good idea.

"No, absolutely, you should not do that," Yeltsin replied. "An official call from you would legitimize them."

Bush agreed not to call. He signed off by praising Yeltsin's courage. "All the American people support you," he said. "What you're doing is absolutely right."

Most Russians thought so too—even the ones sent by the coup plotters to crush Yeltsin's defiance. When Sergei Yevdokimov, commander of the first battalion ordered to the White House, arrived and saw the crowds of Russians, he switched sides and ordered his tanks to turn their guns around to protect the demonstrators. Three men died in a skirmish with armored personnel carriers in front of the United States embassy not far away, but they would be the only fatalities of the whole confrontation.

The coup plotters lost their grip and their nerve. As the tide turned against them, they hurriedly dispatched a delegation to Crimea to meet with Gorbachev in what seemed to be a bid for forgiveness. Yeltsin sent his own delegation to Crimea in a surreal race to get to Gorbachev first. Baker received an update from an aide who handed him a note reporting that James Collins, the American deputy chief of mission, had tried to join the Yeltsin group but had missed the plane. "The Embassy's assessment is that the coup seems to be falling apart," the note reported.

Emboldened by Yeltsin's stout resistance, Bush and Baker had moved past their early ambivalence to more forcefully take sides. Baker flew to Europe for an emergency meeting of NATO foreign ministers to demand Gorbachev's restoration. Baker and the other NATO foreign ministers had just begun a discussion about the coup when someone slipped a message to Manfred Woerner, the secretary general, who was giving introductory remarks. "Excuse me, I've got to take a phone call," he said, and ducked out of the room. The ministers were flabbergasted—this sort of thing did not happen at ministerial meetings—but Woerner returned about ten minutes later with stunning news.

"I just got a call from Boris Yeltsin," he said. "The coup is over. Gorbachev has been released."

Baker went to find a phone and was on the line with one of Gorbachev's advisers when he saw CNN showing Bush back in Washington being asked by a reporter if he had spoken yet with the secretary of state.

"No," he said, "I have been trying to call him but have been unable to get through." Baker immediately hung up the phone and called the president back in Washington.

At 12:19 p.m. Washington time, the White House finally reached Gorbachev and patched him through to Bush at Kennebunkport.

"Oh my God, that's wonderful," Bush said as he picked up the phone. "Mikhail!"

"My dearest George," came the familiar voice, translated by a State Department interpreter. "I'm so happy to hear your voice again."

"My God, I'm glad to hear you. How are you doing?"

"Mr. President, the adventurers have not succeeded."

THAT NIGHT, as the coup collapsed and Gorbachev returned to the Kremlin, Baker was driven to the home of the American ambassador to NATO, set in several acres of parkland with a grazing herd of cows on the outskirts of Brussels. There he found a visitor, Andrei Kozyrev, a young Soviet diplomat who had been in charge of United Nations affairs but now was serving as foreign minister for Yeltsin's Russian republic. Kozyrev told Baker that Yeltsin could be erratic and difficult but wanted good relations with the West. He might not be the partner that Washington wanted, but he was the partner Washington had gotten. What a reflection of the changing order in Moscow, Baker thought, that he would be spending the very night that the coup fell apart meeting not with the Soviet foreign minister but the Russian one.

Yeltsin's on-the-tank defiance had made him a national hero but no one could say at first what that would mean and how he would handle the return of Gorbachev to the Kremlin. Gorbachev was free, but the crowds in the streets were chanting Yeltsin's name. Within days of Gorbachev's restoration, Ukraine and Belarus declared independence and the three Baltic states pressed the West for recognition. A seizure of power that had been intended to stop the collapse of the Soviet Union instead accelerated it. Rather than being replaced by the revanchists, Gorbachev increasingly found himself eclipsed by the democrats.

Under enormous political pressure, Bush formally recognized Lithuania, Latvia, and Estonia on September 2, but was reluctant to go further. A few days later, he met with Baker and the rest of the national security team to debate what else they should do. Cheney urged that they find ways to further encourage the Soviet breakup.

"We could get an authoritarian regime still," Cheney said. "I am concerned that a year or so from now, if it all goes sour, how we can answer
why we didn't do more."

One idea, advanced by Robert Gates and picked up by Cheney, was to
open consulates in each of the fifteen republics of the old Soviet Union,
establishing independent American representation and, in a sense, tacitly
offering a form of recognition.

"We ought to lead and shape the events," Cheney said.

Scowcroft pointed out that American aid programs were routed
through the central government.

"That's an example of old thinking," Cheney replied.

Baker was not yet ready to abandon their previous approach. He recommended caution. "We ought to wait on the consulates and do what we
can to strengthen the center," he said.

Cheney was frustrated. They should be engaging Ukraine and the others, he said. "The voluntary breakup of the Soviet Union is in our interest," he said. "If it's a voluntary association, it will happen. If democracy
fails, we're better off if they're small."

"The *peaceful* breakup of the Soviet Union is in our interest," Baker
countered. "We don't want another Yugoslavia."

The argument replayed itself again and again in the weeks that followed. In a meeting in October, Cheney once more pushed to reorient
their strategy toward the emerging republics.

"Support for the center puts us on the wrong side of reform," Cheney
said.

"The guys in the center *are* reformers," Baker countered.

At another meeting a month later, Cheney argued for recognizing
Ukraine's independence if its people approved it in an upcoming referendum. Baker argued for delay. "Mistake to say 'no' or quickly 'yes,'" he
wrote in notes of the meeting. "'Quick' or 'no' plays into hands of radicals." He added: "Run a risk by rushing to recog.—chaos & civil war—
whereas wait for a couple of weeks is *no risk*."

By this point, it was clear there would be a breakup of the Soviet Union.
The only question was what kind—peaceful, voluntary, or extremely ugly.
Gorbachev continued to act as the titular head of the union, showing up
in Madrid for the opening of the Middle East peace conference that Baker
organized. But at home, he was an increasingly marginalized figure as
Yeltsin drove the old Soviet state toward dissolution. On December 1,
Ukraine held its referendum and 90 percent voted for independence. By

this point, the vast bulk of the fifteen Soviet republics had announced that they were pulling out of the union.

A week later, on December 8, Yeltsin met secretly with two of his counterparts, Leonid Kravchuk of Ukraine and Stanislav Shushkevich of Belarus, in a hunting lodge in the Belavezha Forest near Brest and agreed to formally abandon the old Soviet Union altogether. In its place, they would maintain a loose affiliation through a newly created organization called the Commonwealth of Independent States open to all of the republics of the dying union. They did not bother to inform Gorbachev about what they were negotiating. In fact, after coming to agreement, Yeltsin called Bush to let him know before even calling Gorbachev. "The USSR, as a subject of international law and a geopolitical reality, is ceasing its existence," stated the preamble to the agreement, which was called the Belavezha Accords. Baker essentially adopted that language in a televised interview later that day. "The Soviet Union as we've known it no longer exists," he said on CBS's *Face the Nation*.

Baker remained no more certain what to do about it. He and Bush had elevated prudence and pragmatism as the cardinal American virtues but in reality the administration remained sharply divided over the Soviet collapse. Fear of chaos and civil war was real, but so too were the risks of sitting on the sidelines. Finally, in a memo, Baker prodded Bush to do more. "I think the Soviet situation is reaching a critical point," he wrote. "This weeks [*sic*] events will, in the end, mark the real collapse of the Soviet empire. But no one knows what will replace it. We face a great opportunity and equally great danger."

He went on:

Strategically, there is no other foreign issue more deserving of your attention or time. A Yugoslavia-type situation with 30,000 nuclear weapons presents an incredible danger to the American people—and they know it and will hold us accountable if we don't respond. Morally we stood with the democrats when they faced tanks in August; we must stand with them now to help them through the winter.

With Bush's permission, Baker decided to put a public marker down for American policy toward the breakup of the Soviet Union. He chose his alma mater, Princeton, in part because he was hoping that George Kennan, the legendary eighty-seven-year-old diplomat whose famed Long Telegram served as the foundation for the West's decades-long containment policy of curbing Soviet aggression, might attend. To Baker, it seemed like an apt bookend for the strategic architect of the beginning of the Cold War to essentially validate by his presence the strategy for the end of the Cold War.

Baker worked for days to find the right approach for what would be perhaps his most important speech as secretary of state. Baker, still very much a corporate lawyer by dint of training and inclination, was no great orator and he had left no other memorable addresses, so he wanted to get this right. He had long since adopted Reagan's technique of drawing lines through his texts to break up blocks of words to keep from one droning monologue, but he could never match the Gipper's natural skill.

At 4:30 in the morning on December 12, just hours before the speech, Baker suddenly bolted up in bed, worried about a single line in the text. The last draft had him pledging to work with Russia, Ukraine, and "the other republics." Baker feared that he might be leaning too far toward a complete breakup by forecasting collaboration with the republics and so in a mild panic he called Margaret Tutwiler to find out if the speech had already been released to reporters. It had not, so he added the infelicitous phrase "and any common entity" to allow for the possibility that a collective body might yet emerge from the ashes of the Soviet Union. The lawyer in Baker beat out the speechwriters every time.

A few hours later, Baker approached the lectern at Princeton, pleased that Kennan was indeed sitting in the front row. He opened by paying tribute to the master. "The simple fact of the matter is containment worked," Baker said. "The state that Lenin founded and Stalin built held within itself the seeds of its demise. And when pressure from the outside was maintained and windows to the West were created, the Soviet state broke up from the inside out."

Baker also offered praise for the Soviet leader that sounded a lot like an obituary. "These achievements were possible primarily because of one man, Mikhail Gorbachev. The transformations we are dealing with now would not have begun were it not for him. His place in history is secure." The paean was, essentially, a farewell to a partner. "It is a letting-go of Gorbachev," a Baker aide told a reporter. Baker went on:

If during the Cold War we faced each other as two scorpions in a bottle, now the Western nations and the former Soviet republics stand as awkward climbers on a steep mountain, held together by a common rope. A fall towards fascism or anarchy in the former Soviet Union will pull the West down too. Yet equally as important, a strong and steady pull by the

West now can help them to gain their footing so that they too can climb above to enduring democracy and freedom.

Baker's "call to action," however, was not matched by concrete ideas. He proposed a coordinating conference of Western nations to find ways of helping Russia and the other newly independent countries, but offered only small amounts of American aid, including $400 million to help secure and destroy old nuclear weapons and $100 million to help stimulate capitalist development. He said he hoped to send 250 Peace Corps volunteers to the former republics and C-5 cargo planes would bring leftover Gulf War military rations to feed the hungry in Moscow and Leningrad, now renamed St. Petersburg. The steps "seemed small compared with the huge problems in the Soviet Union," Thomas Friedman wrote in *The New York Times.* Doyle McManus of the *Los Angeles Times* called it "a Marshall Plan with other people's money."

The Marshall Plan that rebuilt Europe after World War II devoted $13 billion over four years, or the equivalent of $76 billion at the time of the Soviet collapse. Baker was convinced the American people would never support such an expenditure of money now on behalf of the faraway Russians, Ukrainians, and others, especially with a budget deficit of $269 billion, one of the largest such gaps in constant dollars since World War II. After the August coup, Americans remained deeply skeptical of Moscow; some 58 percent told pollsters that they opposed increasing financial aid to the Soviet Union while just 31 percent favored it. As the Cold War faded into history, Americans could identify plenty of needs to be addressed at home with what they expected to be a "peace dividend." Baker saw little chance of changing their minds.

SEVERAL INCHES OF SNOW covered Moscow when Baker's plane landed on December 15. The sky was dark and the air bleak. This was his tenth visit since becoming secretary of state but never had the atmosphere felt so fraught and so uncertain. He had come to find out whether the country still existed—and if so, who was in charge of it and its tens of thousands of nuclear weapons.

Gorbachev was angry with Baker. He felt that Baker's pronouncement on *Face the Nation* that the Soviet Union had ceased to exist effectively plunged a knife in his back. Summoning three American writers to the Kremlin a couple days before Baker's arrival, Gorbachev said the secretary of state had been "much too hasty in saying that the Soviet Union no longer exists." Gorbachev either did not know, or did not care, about Baker's qualifying phrase, "as we've known it." As Gorbachev said in the interview with Strobe Talbott and John Kohan of *Time* magazine and the historian Michael Beschloss, "Things are in flux here. While *we're* still trying to figure things out, the U.S. seems to know everything already! I don't think that's loyalty—particularly toward those of us who have favored partnership and full-fledged cooperation."

Talbott and Beschloss, who were working on a book about the end of the Cold War and had access to high-level players in both countries, came over to Baker's hotel shortly after he landed in Moscow that Sunday. They were delivering a message they had received the day before during lunch at the apartment of Pavel Palazchenko, Gorbachev's translator and confidant. Palazchenko said he had been told there were efforts to fabricate a criminal case against Gorbachev to discredit him. It was to be another August coup. Gorbachev was almost surely on the way out anyway, but he should not be prosecuted as if he were some banana republic dictator being shoved from power. Palazchenko wanted Baker to raise the issue with Yeltsin and seek assurances for Gorbachev's security.

Talbott and Beschloss passed along the warning and the request to Baker's team without revealing the source of the message. The secretary's aides wondered if Gorbachev himself was the author. In his memoir, Palazchenko denied that Gorbachev had asked him to reach out. "Nothing could be further from the truth," he said. Nonetheless, Baker took the message seriously and resolved to talk with Yeltsin about it.

Baker met that day with Andrei Kozyrev, the new Russian foreign minister, and then went to have dinner with Eduard Shevardnadze at the studio home of his friend, the Georgian artist Zurab Tsereteli. Shevardnadze had reassumed his post as Soviet foreign minister a month earlier, but the dinner was more of a reunion between two old friends reminiscing than a negotiation. Baker sat in a green plastic chair and Shevardnadze in a yellow one as they talked about everything that had happened. Shevardnadze looked thinner and he was clearly distressed by an illness that had sent his wife to San Francisco for tests. Baker tried to encourage him, telling Shevardnadze that he and Gorbachev would be remembered as enlightened leaders with unparalleled political courage.

"That will be the judgment of history," Baker said.

Shevardnadze lamented that they had not done more to preserve the union. They had underestimated the power of nationalism. And Gorbachev had refused to see the threat from the hard-liners that would ultimately manifest itself in the attempted coup.

"I warned him," Shevardnadze said. "We all did."

They then repaired to the dinner table for eight courses, including boar's head and tiny shot glasses of Georgian green vodka. There were many toasts.

Baker arrived for his meeting with Yeltsin the next day in St. Catherine Hall, the Kremlin chamber where he had met with Gorbachev so often over the previous three years. From the start, it was clear how much had changed.

"Welcome, you are on Russian soil," Yeltsin declared. Not Soviet soil. Meaning *he* was in charge now, not Gorbachev.

Baker pressed his questions: What would happen to the nuclear weapons now stationed in other republics? Who would hold the command codes? What about the newly signed START treaty and the conventional forces agreement? How should humanitarian aid be coordinated? And what about the Soviet Union's super-secret and very lethal biological weapons program?

Yeltsin assured him that Russia would remain a party to all international treaties and would assume exclusive control of the nuclear arsenal, which was deployed in four different republics. "Ukraine and others will not have their hands on the buttons," Yeltsin told Baker before quickly adding, "You should not tell them that right now, that they will not have their finger on the button." He was playing a dangerous game, but Baker was reassured to think that the nuclear commands would rest with just one government and not multiple new states.

Thinking ahead, Yeltsin pressed for Russia to be given the Soviet Union's seat on the United Nations Security Council and for the United States to extend diplomatic relations to Russia as a separate and independent country.

"It's a very important matter for you to recognize us," Yeltsin said. "It is indeed a serious matter for us and we would like the U.S. to be the first to recognize us. We don't want to see you wait too long."

Baker asked about Gorbachev.

"There will be no place for the president of the Soviet Union," Yeltsin answered bluntly. But he said Gorbachev would be treated with respect.

Listening to the conversation, Dennis Ross felt as though they were witnessing a peaceful coup right in front of their eyes—and, in fact, were being used to ratify its outcome.

After a quick tunafish lunch back at the United States embassy, Baker and his team returned to the Kremlin in the afternoon, entering the exact same hall, only this time finding Gorbachev waiting for them. It was midafternoon, but the sun outside had already disappeared and the room inside felt dark and gloomy. So did Gorbachev. He looked flushed, his eyes tired, but his manner was defiant. Gorbachev complained about the secret accord Yeltsin had struck with Ukraine and Belarus in the forest. "This is kind of a coup," he said, echoing Ross's unspoken thought. Gorbachev said such decisions should be made by the people. "Act like democrats, not highway robbers," he insisted. But it was clear he had no plan to reverse the outcome. "I emphasized that I saw my role as working to prevent further disintegration," he said later. It was too late for that.

As he was leaving, Baker knew he was seeing Gorbachev as president of the Soviet Union for the last time. He ran into Alexander Yakovlev, the longtime reformer and adviser to Gorbachev, and quietly asked if he was the one who had passed the private message through Strobe Talbott and Michael Beschloss. No, Yakovlev answered, but he agreed that he hated to see Gorbachev demeaned. Baker said he did too.

From there, Baker went to meet with Defense Minister Yevgeny Shaposhnikov, who took over after his coup-plotting predecessor was ousted. He assured Baker that the Soviet nuclear arsenal could only be launched with special telephones and equipment kept in briefcases. Right now, Shaposhnikov said, only three people had both: he, Gorbachev, and Yeltsin.

To mollify the leaders of the three other republics where nuclear weapons were stationed—Ukraine, Belarus, and Kazakhstan—Shaposhnikov said they might be given briefcases but not telephones, so they would *think* they controlled the weapons but would not really. Somehow this seemed less than comforting to Baker.

When Baker left the next morning, it was snowing again. Over the next couple days, he stopped in four other Soviet republics—Kyrgyzstan, Kazakhstan, Ukraine, and Belarus. As he boarded his plane to leave the territory of the dying Soviet Union, Baker and his team felt not triumph but melancholy.

Less than a week later, Gorbachev resigned and the red hammer-and-sickle flag flying over the Kremlin was taken down from its floodlit perch at 7:32 p.m. on December 25, 1991, Christmas in the West. The Soviet Union at last really was gone.

A MONTH LATER, Baker was back in Moscow, testing the new order. After a meeting with Yeltsin, he called Bush in Washington to report on "an extraordinary discussion" with the new Russian leader, who wanted "to dramatically demonstrate that we are allies, not enemies." Yeltsin signaled that he was ready to slash nuclear arsenals even more deeply than the START treaty. "We have a stake in moving quickly," Baker wrote in notes of his call with Bush. "One can't know how successful Yeltsin will be. But the more that can be done quickly, the better."

Others thought so too, but were unconvinced that Baker was actually demonstrating enough commitment or urgency. "The Bush and Baker idea of U.S. leadership is to collect the world together and let them all talk," Richard Nixon groused to Monica Crowley, his foreign policy assistant. "They're obsessed with the collective-action bullshit." Nixon later took his criticism public, arguing that Bush was not doing enough to help Russia and the other republics. "I don't have a blank check for all that," Bush answered. Indeed, by the time Baker cobbled together pledges from other Western countries three months would pass, and while he presented the accumulated promises as a $24 billion package to help steer the republics of the former Soviet Union through their wrenching transition, it was hardly transformative. The American share was just $4.35 billion, with less than half of that direct assistance.

Even that was hard to extract from a reluctant Congress. Baker was frustrated by the resistance. "Spent *trillions* of dollars to win Cold War," he wrote in talking points arguing for the Freedom Support Act, as the aid bill was dubbed. "Should be willing to spend few billion to *secure the peace*—or could have to spend far more again. (A *national security* issue!!) In *our* interests (the Am. people)." At a hearing barely a week later, though, members of his own party made clear they did not see it that way. "The American people are fed up with foreign aid," Senator Jesse Helms, the conservative Republican from North Carolina, griped at Baker, "and they want to know what the American people get out of it."

Baker wanted Congress to pass the aid by the time Yeltsin came to visit Washington in June. But the American presidential campaign was in full swing and Bush's poll numbers had plummeted along with the economy. Bush had little heft remaining to force lawmakers to follow his lead and Baker found his legendary lobbying skills unusually inadequate. Congress did not sign off on the package, modest as it was, until late October, more than ten months after Baker's speech at Princeton calling for expeditious action. Much of the rest of the $24 billion promised by the world's powers at Baker's behest never materialized either.

It was a moment of missed opportunity. Having presided over the largely peaceful conclusion of the Cold War, Baker failed to deliver a bold next step, letting political calculations about what was possible determine what he would even try to do. Yegor Gaidar and Andrei Kozyrev, two top advisers to Boris Yeltsin, remembered trying to engage Baker during his December 1991 visit to Moscow on the idea of a new Marshall Plan but felt rushed because the secretary of state was heading into other meetings. When Petr Aven, a prominent former Russian official under Yeltsin who had gone on to become a wealthy banker, asked Baker about this nearly a quarter century later, Baker flared. "They're justifying themselves" for their own failure to transform their country, he said dismissively of Gaidar and Kozyrev.

Baker insisted that he and Bush wanted to support Yeltsin. "But politically, yes, you're right, it was very difficult to justify economic assistance to Russia, with which we had fought for forty years," he told Aven. "A Marshall Plan at the time was absolutely out of the question. The American public would not support it—neither then, nor later."

CHAPTER 26

The Cruelest Turn

At night, before going home after a day of diplomacy, Baker would relax in his seventh-floor State Department office with a few of his more politically minded aides to chew over the latest developments on the domestic front. Bush was heading into 1992 with hopes of winning a second term, but the president's sky-high poll ratings had already faded into the distant past.

The sheen of victory in Kuwait had worn off and, with the Soviet Union now wiped off the map, many Americans were focusing on their own troubles. The economy was sagging. Bush was facing fire from the right, the left, and the middle. He was making political mistakes, giving ammunition to his enemies. Even worse, what Baker knew, and most others in the president's circle did not, was just how much a thyroid condition called Graves' disease was taking a toll on Bush, who was having trouble summoning his usual energy. In his office at night, Baker and his advisers would lament what they all saw as the screwups by the White House.

"Is there something that we can do?" Janet Mullins would ask Baker.

"This is not my thing," Baker would answer. "I can't get in the middle of this."

In fact, Baker could have intervened but he had no desire to descend back into the muck of political campaigning. He had run four presidential races by this point and had finally graduated, he thought, from fixer to statesman. Over the last three years, he had occupied the world stage at a time of profound change. He had presided over the end of the Cold War, helped reunify Germany, assembled a grand coalition to thwart the territorial schemes of a dictator, and organized a landmark Middle East peace conference. So while he watched the emerging campaign with the interest of a veteran—and the scorn of a been-there, done-that second-guesser—he desperately wanted to stay out of it.

Bush did not want to admit that he needed Baker any more than Baker wanted to dive back in. The president was a proud man and there was a part of him that resented the Georgetown cocktail chatter that Baker was the power behind his presidency. The doubles partners from the Houston Country Club had teamed up to run the world, but the subtle rivalry that had always shadowed the relationship kept both of them from making the decision that almost everyone else figured was inevitable. If Bush was to win a second term, the widespread consensus was that Baker had to help make it happen. The only people stopping that were Bush and Baker.

Any hopes that Baker harbored of avoiding the campaign probably evaporated when his partner in the 1988 campaign, Lee Atwater, was diagnosed with a brain tumor. If Atwater were able to oversee the 1992 campaign, then maybe Baker would not have to. But Atwater was dying and no longer able to run anything. In fact, his battle with cancer produced a remarkable late-in-life epiphany. Facing death, Atwater expressed regret for his take-no-prisoners approach to politics, even apologizing to Michael Dukakis. "In 1988, fighting Dukakis, I said that I 'would strip the bark off the little bastard' and 'make Willie Horton his running mate,'" Atwater told *Life* magazine in a confessional article. "I am sorry for both statements: the first for its naked cruelty, the second because it makes me sound racist, which I am not." He went on to agree that Bush captured the presidency on the back of a relentlessly negative campaign that was unworthy of the country. "In part because of our successful manipulation of his campaign themes, George Bush won handily," he said. The article was accompanied by photographs of Atwater, swollen from steroids and visibly ill, that shocked his friends.

By the spring of 1991, shortly after his fortieth birthday, Atwater was dead. He was buried in Columbia, South Carolina, wearing a jogging suit and holding a photo of his three daughters and a copy of *Red Hot & Blue*, a 1989 record album he cut with B.B. King and a roster of other all-star performers. Baker gave a eulogy at the memorial service. Atwater was "Machiavellian," Baker said, "in the very best sense of that term." He was "a pol's pol" who waged campaigns "by pushing it to the edge wholeheartedly and unabashedly, just the way he played guitar and just the way he lived." Baker added that he found it "hard to imagine a self-professed bad boy like Lee up there with the angels. But I am convinced that's exactly where Lee is and that the angels are simply going to have to adjust."

Still, Atwater's regrets were not Baker's. If the dying hatchet man had second thoughts about swinging the axe in 1988, his boss claimed to have none, at least none that he cared to share. Atwater was no rogue operator. Any bark-stripping he did with the permission, if not at the explicit direction, of Baker and Bush. And while Baker may have been too polished to use the sort of coarse language Atwater did, he saw nothing wrong with his approach to campaigns.

The question was whether he would do it all over again. Bush was slow to get started in putting his reelection operation together, determined to postpone the day he would go from being president to being a candidate again. Baker and other friends urged him to get going. They could see that Bush was making the climb more difficult for himself. As Susan Baker recalled it, "We were pulling our hair out." But when she urged Baker to step in, he resisted. "I would say to my husband, 'Honey, you've got to do something,' " she said. Baker, she added, would answer, "My brief is so big. Other people have to do that."

Reluctantly, Baker finally agreed to sit down with Bush for a private meeting in the living quarters of the White House just a few weeks after the Madrid conference and a few days before Thanksgiving 1991 to talk through the emerging campaign. They debated structure for the reelection organization. They talked about pushing out Treasury Secretary Nick Brady and making him general chairman of the campaign, to be replaced by a known, respected figure or business leader to send a signal to the markets. But Baker scribbled on his notepad: "(NOT RGD)," ruling out his longtime right-hand Dick Darman. And they talked about the White House chief of staff.

John Sununu had increasingly become the focus of widespread discontent among Bush's confidants, not just for mishandling the budget deal but for an imperious management style and a tin ear for politics. Curt and combative, Sununu styled himself as the "pit bull" of the White House and had alienated many of his colleagues and fellow Republicans around town. He drew fire for using government aircraft for personal trips and once taking a government car all the way to New York for a stamp auction. Worse, he angered Bush's inner circle and family when he blamed the president for ad-libbing remarks about credit card rates that sent the stock market into a downward spin, rather than taking the responsibility himself as a good chief of staff was supposed to do. Bush had not consulted Baker on the selection of Sununu in the first place but the secretary of state had been telling his friend for some time that it was time to cut the chief of staff loose. Bush had resisted. It went against his nature to throw people overboard. But Baker came back at him again, as did others.

Finally, the president commissioned George W. Bush to speak with six or seven family confidants on the pretense of gathering thoughts on the coming campaign but in reality to evaluate the chief of staff. The results were not positive. Reluctantly, the president realized that Baker was right and it was time for Sununu to go. In their meeting in the living quarters, Bush and Baker discussed how to handle it. Bush could move Sununu over to the campaign or the Republican National Committee, he could give him a cabinet spot like transportation secretary, or he could encourage the chief of staff to go home to New Hampshire and run for the Senate. More important was who would take over the White House. Bush and Baker talked about a few names, including longtime advisers like Craig Fuller, Fred Malek, and Will Ball. Baker, hoping to forestall being asked himself, proposed his friend Dick Cheney, who after all had done the job once before under Ford. But of course Baker's name came up as well. In the notes he took, Baker scribbled out conditions. "JABIII—for 1 year only—part-time," he wrote, and then added "DO BOTH," presumably meaning both running the White House and the campaign to improve coordination.

First, they would have to drop the hammer on Sununu. Never one for unpleasantness, the president tasked his son with delivering the message, which he did just before Thanksgiving. But Sununu did not take the hint and instead tried to fight back. It took three more emissaries from the Oval Office until Sununu finally got the message and resigned.

Baker sent Sununu a condolence note later that same day, a gesture that was either gracious or disingenuous or perhaps a little of both. "You have just done a very selfless thing by submitting your resignation to the president," Baker wrote Sununu. "It is not fair to you that it came to this but you have done the right thing by the president."

Baker had worked to get Sununu out but the victory came with the risk that he would be forced to come back as White House chief of staff himself. Baker had no interest so he pushed again for Cheney. When it came up at Camp David, Bush was willing to entertain it. Brent Scowcroft, who was also at the presidential retreat, called Cheney to ask if he would be open to a shift. "I've got major stuff I'm doing over here," Cheney replied, referring to his Pentagon post. "No, the answer's no."

Cheney understood what had happened—his friend Baker "threw me under the bus." In fact, he later heard that Baker had actually been in the room with Scowcroft when he called. "If Bush had called me and asked me, I would have had no choice," Cheney said. But he had no problem turning down Scowcroft—and Baker. With Cheney out and Baker resistant, Bush finally tapped Sam Skinner, a lawyer from Illinois serving as transportation secretary.

Bush was to some extent a victim of his own success—and Baker's. With the world situation looking brighter, Americans were wondering what the president was doing for them at home. Bush had assembled a significant record in domestic policy to take onto the campaign trail, having signed into law the Americans with Disabilities Act and new versions of the Civil Rights Act and Clean Air Act. But many Americans were more focused on the deteriorating economy. Bush was also in trouble on his right flank for breaking his famous "read my lips, no new taxes" campaign pledge.

Anger over the broken pledge generated a conservative challenge against Bush for the 1992 Republican nomination by Patrick Buchanan, a syndicated columnist and former Nixon and Reagan White House official whose self-branded pitchfork populism was aimed at upending the party establishment. A pugnacious brawler who loved mixing it up with fellow Republicans as much as Democrats, Buchanan decried "global bureaucrats," proposed building a "Buchanan Fence" along the border with Mexico, and made "America First" his campaign slogan.

Baker quietly pushed Bush to take on Buchanan's worldview. One day he sent the president a David Broder piece from *The Washington Post* in which the columnist suggested it would be "a wonderful fight for Bush" to have. Baker told Bush that he agreed. "I think it is important to your re-election that you run an *offensive* campaign based upon your strengths—one of which is leading America's leadership of the rest of the world!" Baker wrote in a cover note. "History shows us the dangers of *isolationism* and protectionism—both from a *security* & political standpoint and an *economic* one. (Remember the 30s?) The 'Put America First' argument is a phoney one. The way you Put America First is to maintain and not apologize for our engagement abroad."

Few gave Buchanan much chance of victory, but Bush was vulnerable following a recession that was pushing unemployment up to a high of 7.4 percent and left many Americans feeling that the president was more interested in what was happening overseas than at home. Bush struggled to pivot, admitting that he had failed to realize the economy was in a "freefall." But he was stilted and seemed out of touch. At one point, reading from notes prepared by his staff, he spoke out loud the stage directions he had been given. "Message: I care," he said. The message was not received. Baker was flying home from arms control talks in Moscow when he heard news that stunned the political world. Buchanan had mounted a strong showing against Bush in the New Hampshire primary, winning 38 percent of the vote against the incumbent president's 53 percent. "That was a wakeup call," Skinner said later.

With Buchanan at his heels, Bush disavowed the budget deal that included new taxes. "Listen," Bush told the *Atlanta Journal and Constitution* during the Georgia primary, "if I had it to do over, I wouldn't do what I did then for a lot of reasons, including political reasons."

Baker was aghast at Bush's reversal. "That admission is the worst political mistake I've ever seen," he said shortly afterward. Dick Darman felt abandoned by the president. To him, the deal was not a mistake, it was an act of leadership. Darman went to Bush to offer his resignation, which was rejected. But he remained bitter for years about the episode—including at his mentor, Baker, who he thought had opportunistically tried to present himself, after the fact, as a voice against the deal at the expense of Bush and Darman.

Baker was right about the politics, though. Renouncing the budget deal only made Bush look feckless and underscored how far he had fallen since the Gulf War victory. Back then, with the highest approval rating of any sitting president in the history of polling, he had seemed so formidable that first-tier Democrats with national profiles including Al Gore, Dick Gephardt, Mario Cuomo, and Senator Sam Nunn of Georgia all opted not to run against him. Instead, the Democratic field was filled with lesser-known lawmakers such as Senators Tom Harkin of Iowa and Bob Kerrey of Nebraska and former senator Paul Tsongas of Massachusetts; Governor Douglas Wilder of Virginia, the first African American ever elected to lead a state; retread candidates like former governor Jerry Brown of California and former senator Eugene McCarthy of Minnesota; and a backwater-Southern governor named Bill Clinton.

AT FORTY-FIVE, William Jefferson Clinton positioned himself as a generational agent of change, calling himself a New Democrat and promising that his formula of optimistic post–Cold War centrism and experience governing the conservative state of Arkansas would restore electability to a party that had lost five of the last six contests for the White House. A Yale Law School graduate and Rhodes Scholar, he nonetheless connected with everyday voters with his up-from-poverty life story and feel-your-pain empathy. He was not a stirring orator, but he had a youthful magnetism and roguish charm that captivated audiences.

A native of Hope, Arkansas, he would cleverly brand himself as the

Man from Hope, selling his upbeat vision to an electorate craving inspiration. With no experience on the world stage, he focused on the recession. At his Little Rock campaign headquarters, his strategist, James Carville, hung a sign on the wall reminding everyone of the candidate's priorities:

CHANGE VS. MORE OF THE SAME.

THE ECONOMY, STUPID

DON'T FORGET HEALTH CARE.

Before he could get the chance to take on Bush, Clinton had to overcome his biggest obstacle: himself. None of the other Democratic candidates could compete in terms of raw political talent, but he had outsized flaws too that could bring him down. When a lounge singer named Gennifer Flowers sold her story of a twelve-year extramarital affair with him to the *Star* supermarket tabloid and produced tapes of Clinton telling her to deny it, the candidate's future suddenly looked bleak. While womanizing by presidents and would-be presidents had been discreetly ignored in the past, the media environment had changed since Gary Hart's campaign imploded over his visit to the *Monkey Business* with Donna Rice; Clinton would get no pass for his sexual adventures. To save his campaign, Clinton went on *60 Minutes* on CBS, with his wife, Hillary Rodham Clinton, by his side, as he vaguely admitted "causing pain in my marriage."

But that was not the end of the scandals. He also had to deal with questions about dodging military service in Vietnam. A letter he had written in 1969 thanking the head of his university's Reserve Officer Training Corps for "saving me from the draft" gave the impression that he had pulled strings to avoid the war. He also had to fend off questions about drug use, admitting that he had tried marijuana while studying in England but insisting to no small amount of mockery that "I didn't inhale."

In effect, Clinton seemed to embody the baby boom generation—the libertine sexuality, the casual drug use, the feminist wife working as a lawyer, the lack of military service, the antiwar activism, the shaggy-haired pictures from school. For Bush and Baker and the older generation, there could hardly be a sharper contrast. Baker saw Clinton as sleazy. A straight arrow who never so much as loosened his tie in the White House, Baker was offended at the very notion of Clinton as president. But while his aides assumed that the Arkansas Democrat could never win the nomination, much less the general election, Baker warned against underestimating Clinton.

Indeed, through sheer grit and a relentless focus on the economic woes of voters, Clinton pushed through controversies that would have taken down a lesser candidate. Tom Harkin's victory in his home state of Iowa was written off, making the New Hampshire primary the first real contest of the year. While Paul Tsongas's eventual win there was likewise discounted because he came from next-door Massachusetts, Clinton's surprise second-place finish was treated as if he had actually won. At his election night party, he dubbed himself the "Comeback Kid." After trading victories in the next few contests with his rivals, Clinton finally secured the nomination by sweeping most of the Southern Super Tuesday states. Even though weakened by scandal, he presented a powerful threat to Bush—a Southern centrist Democrat during a recession amid public discontent with the direction of the country. He was "our worst political nightmare," in the words of Fred Steeper, the pollster for Bush's reelection campaign.

But Clinton would not be the only one to take on Bush. Ross Perot, an eccentric Texas billionaire with a penchant for publicity and a folksy critique of the president, jumped into the race as an independent candidate. Powered by his personal fortune and a growing popular disenchantment with the political status quo, he aimed to upend the two-party system that had enjoyed a monopoly on power in the United States for most of its history. Kicking off his candidacy on *Larry King Live* on CNN, Perot made clear that his would be an unconventional campaign, jumping from talk show to talk show while an army of supporters got his name on the ballot in all fifty states. He tapped into some of the same zeal for change as Clinton, promising to fix a broken system. "I'll be like a mechanic who's under the hood, working on the engine," Perot vowed.

By spring, with the help of Baker's old nemesis from the Reagan White House, Ed Rollins, Perot was actually leading polls in the three-way race, becoming the most potent independent presidential candidate since Theodore Roosevelt's Bull Moose comeback attempt in 1912. Baker considered Perot "weird" and even unstable, but he also saw him as a threat to steal away Republican votes that would otherwise go to Bush. What Baker did not know was that in private Perot was a big fan of his, even telling a friend that "if Jim Baker would just step up to the plate and the president would step down and say, 'Jim Baker's my favored successor,' I wouldn't even think about it." But of course, Bush was not stepping down.

AT A TIME when Baker was seen as the one figure who could save the White House for the Republicans, he also was costing Bush with a key constituency. One morning in March, he woke up to see a screaming headline on the cover of the *New York Post:* "BAKER'S 4-LETTER INSULT: Sec'y of State Rips Jews in Meeting at White House." Ed Koch, the former mayor of New York turned tabloid columnist, wrote that during a recent White House meeting Baker had responded to criticism of his tough approach to Israel by saying, "F—'em. They didn't vote for us." After "they," Koch or his editor inserted the words "the Jews" in brackets to explain what Baker presumably meant. As the quote spread, it would be repeated by others without the brackets, shortened to "Fuck the Jews," an even cruder version than Koch originally alleged.

The real story behind the inflammatory comment stemmed from Baker's long-running feud with Jack Kemp, who had told Koch about the episode. The White House and State Department quickly denied that Baker had said it, but William Safire, the *New York Times* columnist, followed with a piece saying that Baker had actually said something like it on two different occasions. Neither Koch nor Safire named a source, but the former mayor later acknowledged in a book that Kemp was the one who tipped him off.

Baker insisted the story was distorted at best. As he remembered it, the president's team was discussing a controversial policy in the Oval Office.

"Well, AIPAC won't like that," someone said, referring to the American Israel Public Affairs Committee.

"Screw them, they don't vote for us," Baker recalled replying.

In this telling, the target of his ire was an interest group, not Jews as a whole. "It was a political comment," Baker said, "not an anti-Semitic comment, not a slur."

Kemp had a different recollection. Asked about it years later, he remembered arriving at the White House one day and encountering Baker.

Kemp was in a light mood. "Hey Jimmy, I've got my Jim Baker green tie on," he joked.

Baker, however, did not seem amused. "Kemp, you're always trying to conduct not only housing policy but Treasury policy and Federal Reserve Board policy and State Department policy," he replied in Kemp's version.

Kemp, thinking Baker was just joking with him, said, "Well, somebody's got to do it, Jim."

Then they started arguing for real. Eventually, Kemp referred to his own Jewish roots. "Well, you're going to want me to campaign in the Jewish community for Bush's reelection," Kemp recalled saying.

"Well, they don't vote for us," he said Baker replied.

Kemp's G-rated version did not repeat the four-letter word. But either way, he said Baker's sentiment "got mischaracterized" by Koch and others as being anti-Israel. "I know he didn't mean it that way," Kemp said.

At the time, however, Baker was forced into serious damage control. "Nothing could be further from the truth than that story and nothing could be further from my beliefs or values," he wrote to Melvin Salberg and Abraham Foxman of the Anti-Defamation League. Representative Ben Gilman, a Republican from New York, told Baker that "irate constituents" were telling him that "as a result of your alleged statement they would not vote Republican in November." Gilman noted that 30 percent to 40 percent of Jews voted for Republicans. "I respectfully suggest that no potential source for votes should be summarily dismissed."

Bush came to Baker's defense. "I don't accept that Jim would say such a thing," he wrote Koch in a two-page letter. "He is working relentlessly to find a solution to a difficult problem—one that will benefit Israel and the cause of peace in the Middle East. He would not have had any White House meeting on the subject of loan guarantees except in my presence; and, Ed, I never ever heard such ugliness out of Jim Baker." Signing it "Warm Regards," Bush passed along greetings from Barbara in a handwritten note at the bottom: "P.S. In spite of this 'flap' your #1 fan remains BPB—she sends her best." A few days later, clearly hoping to ease the sting, Bush offered Baker and his family forty-eight hours at Camp David to get away.

After reading the Koch column, Foxman called Baker's good friend from Texas, Robert Strauss, now the ambassador to Moscow, and asked him what he made of the situation. While vouching for Baker, Strauss nonetheless told Foxman he had heard Baker tell jokes about Jews. It was just the way Baker was. Foxman decided to take the high road and let it go. "I don't believe he was an anti-Semite," he said years later. "That was part of the baggage that he carried."

Kemp later apologized to Baker and the two ostensibly made up, but the damage was done. Whatever Baker actually said, the line "fuck the Jews" would forever be cited by Israel's supporters as evidence of his supposed hostility to Israel. In June, Yitzhak Shamir's Likud Party was swept out of office in elections, a direct result, in his supporters' view, of Baker's refusal to provide the $10 billion for housing. "Shamir lost the election in part because he couldn't get the loan guarantee," said Moshe Arens. The money for resettling Soviet Jews was the one key political issue in Israel that year, Arens remembered, and the calculus of Israeli voters was simple: "if Shamir couldn't do it, better get somebody else who could do it."

That, in fact, was exactly the impression Baker wanted to leave with Israel. "Baker was determined not to do anything that might help Shamir," Dennis Ross remembered. Baker even rejected a compromise Ross had negotiated with Zalman Shoval, the Israeli ambassador, to provide just a single year's worth of loan guarantees, worth $2 billion, in exchange for greater assurances that the money would not be used for settlement construction.

Replacing Shamir was Yitzhak Rabin, leader of the Labor Party, who was far more open to the land-for-peace approach. Now Baker had a new partner waiting in the Middle East—if he could ever get the time to go back there.

AT THE STATE DEPARTMENT, the world had not stopped for America's political season. Baker was managing the new post-Soviet reality, trying to forge a working relationship with Boris Yeltsin and figure out how to maneuver the fifteen new nations that had emerged from the wreckage of the old union into a firm alliance with the West. With nuclear missiles stationed in four of those new states, he was working to persuade Ukraine, Belarus, and Kazakhstan to give up their arsenals and hand them over to Russia so that the United States was not suddenly dealing with four nuclear powers in place of one. He finalized a second Strategic Arms Reduction Treaty, or START 2, bringing down both American and Russian nuclear arsenals even further, a landmark pact that Bush and Yeltsin signed in June. He was also trying to move the Middle East peace process that he had midwifed to the next stage.

Then there was the collapsing Yugoslavia, which was descending deeper into civil war and ethnic cleansing. Baker's conclusion that the United States did not have a dog in that fight in the Balkans continued to drive administration policy despite growing atrocities. He rationalized that he had more than enough issues to confront, so the strategy was to leave the crisis to the Europeans to manage. It was their backyard, after all. "They wanted the lead, we gave them the lead," Baker reflected in retirement. "Should we have done that? Maybe not. Maybe we should have kept it. But I'll tell you, we had a hell of a lot of stuff on our plate." Among those pressing him at the time to take more of a leadership role was Margaret Tutwiler, who as with Tiananmen Square was deeply affected by the pictures of slaughter emerging from the Balkans. "Who's to say she might not have been right about Yugoslavia?" Baker allowed.

In the end, the wars would drag on for nearly a decade. Altogether, an estimated 140,000 people died and 4 million were displaced before the guns fell silent. The State Department desk officer in charge of Balkans policy resigned in protest in the summer of 1992, declaring that "the administration at high levels in the State Department and White House doesn't really want to get involved." Baker's response to a genocide in the making, he said, had been "ineffective" and "counterproductive." In the view of many, it was one of the darkest stains on Baker's record, a sign of his calculated or even cynical approach of only taking on problems he perceived as winners.

His detachment reflected the Bush team's drift away from statecraft back to electioneering. "The last year of the administration, it lost its footing a little bit," said Richard Haass, the aide to Brent Scowcroft. In part, he attributed that to the politics of the moment. As Bush faced increasing criticism on the campaign trail that he was more absorbed by foreign policy than events at home, neither he nor Baker would find it politically advantageous to be immersed in a major crisis in Europe. "The tennis equivalent would have been running away from your backhand," Haass said, "but the problem was foreign policy was the strength of the administration, so I thought it was a mistake to run away from it."

That was not how it seemed in the White House, where a low-grade sense of panic was settling in even after Bush, calling on all the ample advantages of incumbency, finally overcame Patrick Buchanan to secure the Republican nomination. The truth was the primary challenge had exposed him as vulnerable. His campaign was a mess. And so, increasingly, was Bush himself. Suffering from his thyroid condition, Bush could muster enough energy to get through the day, but not enough to think creatively, to use his imagination. Baker's team thought that Bush should announce a "Domestic Storm" to match the ambition of his foreign policy, but the president's campaign operation was too scattershot to come up with a compelling plan. Sam Skinner seemed ill suited for the role of chief of staff in the midst of a campaign. Bush had decreed that the reelection bid would be run outside the White House, leaving Skinner trying to manage the government separate from the political operation, with little coordination between the two. Skinner quickly found himself quarreling with Dick Darman, an accomplished bureaucratic knife fighter. By April, even Skinner had come to the conclusion that he should be replaced. His choice? The same as everyone else's. "I talked to the president about Baker coming back," Skinner said later. "I think everybody thought early on, why doesn't Jim come back and do it right away?"

Baker was hearing that from practically all quarters. "It's a bit unfair for your friends and admirers like myself to lean on you about the President's campaign," Gerry Bemiss, an old friend of his and Bush's, wrote to Baker in May. "But I suppose a lot of us think the President is in very bad shape and believe that your particular toughness and ability is necessary to salvaging the situation. From my viewpoint the Pres is in a miserable fix." Baker's cabinet colleague, Lynn Martin, the labor secretary and a veteran politician who had served in Congress, sent him a teasing, but also pleading, letter. "Your personality is improving," she wrote. "You're even getting better looking. But you'd become a '10' with a slight job shift, please." At the Pentagon, Colin Powell, overstepping his bounds as a uniformed general, asked Dick Cheney why that had not happened yet. "Dick, don't you see?" he asked. "It's not going well. It's all screwed up." Cheney mumbled that he knew but then changed the subject. Even Dan Quayle, no friend of Baker's, thought the old handler was needed. The vice president approached Bush about it in the spring around the same time as Skinner. "You need to ask Baker to come over and be chief of staff," the vice president told him. Bush's answer was maddeningly passive: "He'll do it when he thinks it's right."

Baker would never think it was right. Bush would not ask and Baker would not volunteer. The standoff rubbed some around Bush the wrong way. "I think they felt like Jim shouldn't have had to be begged," Powell said. But Baker was deeply reluctant. "He didn't want to leave the State Department to go back to the White House," said his son John Baker. "He really wanted to have people view him as a statesman, not a politician, and his view was if he went back to the White House he was always going to be viewed as a politician. That was a tough time for him. He knew he needed to help his friend but by the same token he really wanted to finish out his tour at the State Department."

So much so that he concocted schemes to get out of having to return to the White House. After Yitzhak Rabin's victory in Israel, Baker asked Dennis Ross if it would be possible to go on an extended trip to the Middle East to try to broker a major diplomatic breakthrough. If he were engaged in such a venture, Baker reasoned, then Bush could hardly ask him to leave the State Department. But Ross told him it would take Rabin a while to establish his government and by the time he did, it would be too late to avoid being summoned back to the White House. Baker embarked on a short trip to the Middle East anyway and Ross suggested what he called "one last Hail Mary"—Baker could invite regional leaders to a Washington summit in the first week of September, including Rabin, King Fahd, King Hussein, Hosni Mubarak, and Hafez al-Assad. During a stop in

Damascus, Baker pitched the idea to Assad, who said he would think about it. But weeks went by without a reply, effectively killing the idea.

The final act in this drama followed the pattern from four years earlier. With Democrats gathering for their convention in New York to nominate Bill Clinton, Baker invited Bush to go fishing in Wyoming, this time at Baker's own Silver Creek Ranch, where they would be blissfully out of touch. The two spent several days on the water with their sons Jamie Baker and Jeb Bush, a welcome relief from the tension of the previous few months. The air was clear and fresh, the weather warm, the politics far away. But one day, Bush asked Jamie and Jeb to excuse Baker and him. Baker sat down in a chair and Bush sank into the couch opposite him.

"You know," Bush said, "I think I really need some help."

It was the question Baker knew was coming but had dreaded for months.

And of course, he said yes. What else could he do?

AT THE DEMOCRATIC NATIONAL CONVENTION, Clinton tapped Al Gore as his running mate, assembling a next-generation ticket of two forty-something sons of the New South. The selection of Gore was awkward for Baker since their wives were such good friends and collaborators in the record album labeling project. The Clinton-Gore team breathed fresh energy into the campaign, so much so that Ross Perot, who had been leading in polls not long before, abruptly dropped out of the race, declaring that "the Democratic Party has revitalized itself."

When word of Perot's withdrawal reached Baker at the Wyoming ranch, he rushed down to the creek where Bush was fishing to share the news. He brought with him a satellite telephone and urged the president to call Perot immediately to try to win him over to their side. "Tell him you share his principles and values," Baker implored. "You hope he will support you."

Bush made the call, standing in a field by the stream in his fishing vest. Then they tried to patch him through to the White House press corps, which was staying a couple of hours away, to publicly appeal to Perot's supporters. But the line was scratchy, so they finally gave up and put the reporters on a bus to bring them to an air base near the ranch where Bush delivered the message on camera.

When they returned from the fishing trip, Baker was still not quite ready to reveal his own change of assignment. Even close friends, like

David Paton, were kept in the dark at first. Paton, in fact, had other ideas for his old roommate. "The president is obviously tired, distracted and perplexed," Paton wrote Baker as the Republican National Convention approached. "He has won a fine place in history and must quit the scene before he blows his record." Instead, Paton said, the party should nominate Baker. "Our country deserves you as its next president, goddamnit. Just four little months of rubber chicken and loudspeakers, you can do it easily."

Baker laughed it off as another missive from the "Daffy Doc," as he and the other Princeton roommates lovingly called Paton. But the truth was Paton had touched on an unresolved tension inside Baker. He cherished his relationship with Bush and revered him in a profound way. But he was frustrated with how Bush had let the situation get so out of control that he was on the verge of losing. Baker had quietly grown less impressed with Bush's political skills. There was a part of Baker that could not help thinking he could do it better himself. And he recognized that by leaving the State Department and returning to a staff job, he could jeopardize that possibility down the road. "In coming back, he knew very well that he would lose his potential to be a presidential candidate," said his cousin Addison Baker Duncan.

Baker, of course, would not displace his friend on the 1992 ticket. But Dan Quayle was another matter. With Bush trailing in the polls by 24 percentage points following the Democratic convention, a shake-up was the only way for Bush to present himself as an agent of change. It was not really fair to Quayle, Baker knew. He had been a loyal soldier. And for a long while, Baker had thought the possible benefit of a change on the ticket was not worth the risk. But with time running short and the odds worsening, Baker came to the conclusion that for the campaign to win, Quayle should go. So did others. Bob Teeter, the campaign chairman, commissioned a secret poll in July showing that Bush could gain a net of 4 to 6 percentage points if he pushed Quayle off the ticket, a significant bump if the race were tight. Teeter even tested possible replacements, including Colin Powell, who would be the first African American ever on a major party ticket, and Baker himself. Baker polled better than Quayle; Powell polled better than both of them. But Powell wanted no part of it and when he found out about the surreptitious research, he called Quayle to make clear he had nothing to do with it. But there was a full-on campaign to dump Quayle. Others pushing Bush to drop him included Gerald Ford and Richard Nixon. For his part, George W. Bush urged his father to replace Quayle with Dick Cheney. "I was just thinking of ways to help change the dynamic of a campaign that I thought was sinking," he said years later. "It had nothing to do with Quayle."

In his final weeks as secretary of state, Baker convened secret meetings at his Foxhall Road house to discuss how to dump Quayle. Baker knew the president would never explicitly push Quayle off the ticket—Bush felt he owed him better than that. But years later, Baker told the ghostwriter of his political memoir that the meetings were held "with George's knowledge and blessing" (although Baker refused to let that be published in his book). "Forty-one wanted him off, but didn't want to fire him," Baker confided to the ghostwriter. "He wanted him to take himself out." So the vice president would have to be convinced to do it on his own, to take one for the team. Baker and his allies thought that maybe they could get someone close to the president to approach Quayle and make clear it was time to go. Barbara Bush came to mind. "I told the president our first choice—the first lady," Baker informed the ghostwriter. Bush rejected the choice out of hand. "She's too close to me," he said. So were George W. and, for that matter, Baker himself, ruling out two other potential emissaries.

Baker never talked about the matter directly with Quayle but the vice president understood from newspaper speculation that he was in jeopardy. He had no intention of volunteering himself off the ticket. After days of twisting in the wind, Quayle finally forced the issue by going to see Bush to ask if the president wanted to replace him as his running mate. Bush could not bring himself to say yes. After the meeting, Quayle was asked by a reporter from *The Washington Post* if he would remain on the ticket. "Yes," Quayle answered, effectively putting an end to the coup attempt. With the die cast, Baker distanced himself from the effort. A White House official told the *Post* that "Baker had agreed that replacing Quayle, even if the move was orchestrated to make it look like Quayle's decision, would be a political mistake." In fact, the opposite was true.

ON AUGUST 13, Bush summoned his press secretary, Marlin Fitzwater, to the Oval Office and confirmed the worst-kept secret in town—Baker would be coming back to the White House as chief of staff and would run the reelection campaign from the West Wing. Fitzwater, like other top Bush aides, was relieved. "It was exciting to think that the old Baker efficiency was coming back to the White House," he wrote later.

Baker, of course, had already planned the rollout of the announcement in characteristically methodical fashion. Bush handed Fitzwater a written statement that Baker or his staff had obviously written. Just then, the phone in the Oval Office rang. Baker was on the line. Bush motioned for Fitzwater to get on the extension.

"Marlin, has the president laid this out for you?" Baker asked.

"Yes," he said.

"Take a look at the statement," Baker said. Then, teasingly, he added, "It has a lot of good things about me. You may want to tone it down."

Fitzwater laughed. "Sure," he said.

Bush jumped in. "See if it says anything good about me," he said.

"It gives him some credit," Baker said.

The jocular patter hinted at the relationship between the two men heading into this crucial period—at once lighthearted and affectionate yet edgy. Bush had to swallow his pride to ask Baker to come back and Baker had to swallow his ambition to say yes. He was giving up his platform as the world's most prominent diplomat to get back into the grubby business of electioneering. He would now become the only person ever to serve as White House chief of staff for two different presidents.

At the State Department, Baker gathered employees in the auditorium for a farewell speech that reviewed the accomplishments of the past three and a half years. All told, Baker had spent 283 days of his tenure out of the country, hunting for deals and heading off catastrophes as the Cold War melted away, logging more than 700,000 miles on his plane. Most of his time abroad was in Europe or the Middle East. In four years, he made just three stops in all of sub-Saharan Africa and five in Latin America, not counting Mexico. By comparison, he made twenty-nine stops in the Soviet Union and its successor states, as well as thirteen in Britain, eleven in Germany, and nine in France. Once he settled on a goal of Middle East peace, he concentrated his time there, including twelve visits each to Syria and Egypt, ten to Israel, and nine to Saudi Arabia. His twenty-three days straight on the road in the summer of 1991 trying to set up the Madrid conference was the second-longest single trip taken by any secretary of state in modern times, just behind Henry Kissinger's marathon shuttle diplomacy in the region during the Yom Kippur War of 1973.

Along the way, the world had changed—not because of him perhaps, but steered to some degree by him. The Soviet Union was no more. Eastern Europe was liberated. Germany was now one country again. Iraq was back in a box. Nicaragua's contra war was over. Panama's dictator was out of power. Israel was talking with its neighbors. Freedom was on the rise and nuclear arsenals were on the decline. A planet defined for four decades by a twilight struggle between two superpowers on hair-trigger alert was transforming itself. Not all the signs were encouraging. Yugoslavia was trapped in an orgy of ethnic hatred and bloodletting, Saddam Hussein was still in power, the Middle East had yet to find true reconciliation, and no clear strategy had been developed to help Russia evolve into a functioning capitalist democracy. But for Baker, there was more than enough to take pride in even as he unwillingly gave up the job that had absorbed him like no other.

The day he stepped down was perhaps the most painful he had experienced in public life—and the only one where he nearly lost his composure in public as he struggled to make it through his prepared remarks extolling the diplomats and their shared role navigating a "whirlwind of history." At the end, Baker received a standing ovation and waved his goodbye, ducking into an elevator, his eyes welling with tears. He had lunch with Dick Darman, Robert Zoellick, and Janet Mullins, then left the building at 2 p.m., went home to pack, and caught a 4:05 p.m. flight to Denver before switching to Jackson, Wyoming, for a rest at his ranch.

The applause in the State Department auditorium was genuine. The foreign service had been leery of Baker when he arrived and for years many resented his reliance on his close-knit team. But as he departed, many appreciated the fact that with Baker, the State Department had been at the center of the action in a way it often was not. "Jim," Bush wrote him in a note. "As I listened to that thunderous applause at State just now, I realized just how much you are giving up to come here. I am so very grateful. Get some rest. I'm glad we will be side by side in the battle ahead.— Your Friend, George."

The battle, of course, was not one Baker wanted to wage. He was tired of being a partisan warrior. Yet there was no one better at it, at least not in Bush's Republican Party. "That was the cruelest turn of the wheel," observed Aaron David Miller, the Middle East adviser. "It's almost as if he couldn't escape it in part because he was viewed to be so central, so irreplaceable, so necessary, that having become the most consequential secretary of state since Henry Kissinger in several years, with the world cooperating, he was forced back into the political game under very disadvantageous, unhappy circumstances." But this was the deal that Baker had made and, better than anyone, he knew that a deal always came with a price. As Miller reflected, "He couldn't escape his friendship with Bush, couldn't escape the political world, couldn't escape the four-year run of the electoral cycle."

BAKER'S RETURN to politics did not get off to a promising start. At the Republican National Convention in Houston just four days later, Patrick Buchanan was given a prime-time speaking slot, an effort at inclusion to bind the wounds of a rough nomination fight. But even as Buchanan dutifully pledged his support for Bush, he used the nationally televised platform to declare a "cultural war" in America, focusing on the sorts of divisive social issues that made Bush and Baker cringe.

Buchanan said the other side stood for "abortion on demand, a litmus test for the Supreme Court, homosexual rights, discrimination against religious schools, women in combat units" and other ideas he deemed radical. Bill Clinton's centrist message at the Democratic convention was fake, Buchanan added, "the greatest single exhibition of cross-dressing in American political history." As Baker watched in consternation, he knew this was hardly the message to win over America's swing voters.

Baker had washed his hands of the convention, which had been largely planned before he arrived on the scene. "You can bet your life Jimmy Baker won't be left holding the bag," Bush groused privately, a revealing comment hinting at years of resentment of his friend's remarkable ability to stay out of sight when things went wrong. But now Baker had to get serious. He could not disavow responsibility anymore and he had just ten weeks to turn the campaign around. Baker moved back into the corner office of the West Wing that he had occupied for four years accompanied once again by his plug-in unit. Four of his most trusted advisers at the State Department—Robert Zoellick, Dennis Ross, Margaret Tutwiler, and Janet Mullins—came with him to the White House. Larry Eagleburger was left behind to serve as acting secretary of state, a caretaker until Baker could return if they did manage to win a second term.

The Bush White House quickly discovered that Baker operated mainly through his own team, as he had throughout his meteoric Washington career. Dan Quayle, whose office was next door to the chief of staff's suite, noticed that Baker had the couch in his outer office removed "so that people couldn't hang around" while the door was closed when Baker's team met, creating "an us-versus-them atmosphere." Baker and his circle disparaged the old White House regime that in their view had botched things up so badly, privately referring to them as the Politburo. For their part, some of the West Wing staff resented the disdainful newcomers.

But Baker was genuinely shocked to discover how bad things were for the campaign, which heading into the final stretch had already burned through much of its money. The advertising effort was flagging. There was no clear theme as the fall sprint to Election Day opened. As he moved in, Baker insisted on more discipline and focus to the slipshod enterprise, convening meetings every day at 6 p.m. to coordinate White House and campaign activities and messaging. He pared attendance at key sessions from an unwieldy high of forty-three hangers-on to a tighter, more manageable ten participants. He insisted that Bush give him complete control of his schedule, right down to when the president would get a haircut. And his mere presence demanded better behavior. Dick Darman, a forceful, abrasive, table-pounding presence who had been at war with Sam Skinner before Baker's return, suddenly reverted to a deferential right-hand man. "When you got in a meeting with Baker, Darman was the polite little boy with his hands folded listening and was just another staffer," recalled Thomas Scully, a Darman aide.

To win, Baker knew that Bush had to persuade voters that he would do for America what he had done for the world, so Baker had his team develop an "Agenda for American Renewal," bringing together the president's trade and fiscal proposals into a single economic package. Bush would unveil the blueprint for this "Domestic Storm" at the Detroit Economic Club on September 10 and Baker would go on television to promote it.

But when the time came, Baker backed out of the public appearances and dispatched Nick Brady, the treasury secretary, instead. Baker reasoned that with all the glowing press he had been getting, taking on a high profile would feed the impression that he was really the one calling the shots, the "deputy president" theory again. Yet his decision to stay out of sight had the opposite effect—without Baker out front, the media did not take the economic plan as seriously as it would have had he invested his considerable credibility in it. Many in the White House saw Baker's absence as a desire not to be publicly associated with a losing effort or perhaps to preserve his image as a once and future secretary of state rather than a partisan hack. He did not do a single interview or television appearance in his first six weeks back at the White House.

His profile inside the building was often not much higher. Baker skipped some of the staff meetings in his office, leaving them to Zoellick to run. During the meetings he did attend, he sometimes seemed distracted, staring off into space. It was so clear that he did not want to be there. One White House official complained to Maureen Dowd of *The New York Times* that "Baker's been MIA." In a cheeky article that imagined the White House as a live-action version of the Clue board game, Dowd depicted Baker "hiding in the conference room with a candlestick."

Although Baker had run rings around Democrats in debate negotiations during previous campaigns, this time he handed off the task to Bob Teeter. Even when he approved letters, Baker insisted that aides take his name off them and put Teeter's on. At one point when Baker was referred to as the campaign manager, he sought a correction—he was the *White House chief of staff*. In the end, Teeter agreed to three debates, one of which would be a town-hall-style event—a format clearly more advantageous to Bill Clinton with his talk show style of politics and facility with words.

Quayle thought Baker's abrogation of responsibility for the debates was "pathetic," tossing away the one last chance Bush had to turn things around. In his view, Baker once again cared more about Baker than anyone else, even his great friend, the president. "Jim Baker told people what an impossible job he had," Quayle said later. "He set things up so that, if we managed to win, he would look like Houdini, whereas if we lost, as he seemed to expect, nobody would be able to blame him."

Quayle of course was already a decided adversary by this point. But even Baker's closest advisers like Tutwiler, Zoellick, and Darman could hardly help noticing Baker's disengagement. Several of them confronted him about it.

"What are you doing?" one of them demanded. You need to be *engaged*.

"I'm engaged," he insisted. "What do you think I'm doing?"

"No, you're not," the aide scolded.

The aide even called Susan Baker to see if she could intervene. "We're in trouble. We need help."

Help was not on the way.

IN MID-SEPTEMBER, Baker got a call out of the blue from Ross Perot asking to see him in secret. After checking with Bush, Baker invited the Texas businessman to his Foxhall Road house. When Perot arrived, he spun out a far-fetched story about how the Bush administration had been targeting him and tried to disrupt his daughter's wedding. He accused George W. Bush of investigating Perot's children. He theorized that Republicans had kept Gennifer Flowers in a warehouse to spring on Clinton when the time was ripe. That was the real reason he had dropped out, Perot claimed—Republican dirty tricks.

Baker rejected the accusations. "Ross, that's just bullshit," he said. "I don't know anything about that."

"Well, it's happening and I just felt you needed to know about it so you can take whatever action you think is necessary and you can tell the president."

To Baker, the whole thing was loony. Perot, the "juggy-eared prick," as Baker called him, had long been known for promoting wild conspiracy theories. Baker filled in Bush, who recorded the account of Perot's rant in his diary. "He waxed very emotional about the dirty tricks by the Republican Party—same old story," Bush dictated. But Baker realized Perot, by laying out his grievances against Bush and the Republicans, was setting the stage for the unthinkable—jumping back into the campaign. And that is what he did just weeks before Election Day.

So now there would be three onstage for the debates. Bush's presidency would ride on the outcome. Baker's team prepared for the showdowns with the sort of precision that had worked in the past. Recalling that the president had once been tripped up by seeming unfamiliar with a supermarket scanner, Baker's team pulled together a briefing book to keep him from looking out of touch again. Among other things, they drilled him on the prices of basic items he might be asked about, such as a dozen eggs (99 cents), a pound of hamburger ($1.59), a loaf of bread (59 cents), a quart of milk (92 cents), and a gallon of gasoline ($1.16).

They also tried to get him to speak in language that would resonate with everyday Americans, providing him a list of "effective" and "not effective" phrases.

Effective: "Open new markets." Ineffective: "Free trade."

Effective: "Put criminals behind bars." Ineffective: "Exclusionary rule."

Effective: "Stop outrageous lawsuits." Ineffective: "Legal reform."

Finally, under ineffective, it listed "capital gains tax cut." Under effective in that category, the briefing book bowed to political reality. It said, "[Nothing]."

On October 11, Bush and Baker flew to St. Louis for the first debate at Washington University, trailing badly and in need of a jolt. When Bush took the stage, however, the best he could offer was not a new plan but a new job for Baker. If he won, the president said, he would make Baker his economic czar in the second term. "What I'm going to do is say to Jim Baker when this campaign is over, 'All right, let's sit down now. You do in domestic affairs what you've done in foreign affairs. Be the kind of economic coordinator of all the domestic side of the house,'" Bush said. Watching with the rest of the campaign team, Baker was shocked. "Shit, we never talked about that," he recalled thinking. That was not what Baker wanted to do even if they could pull off an upset and win a second term. It was a stunning move, one intended to trade on Baker's stature but that in fact betrayed Bush's own weakness. After all, just a week earlier, Bush had told Larry King on CNN that Baker would be returning as secretary of state in a second term. As the political journalists Jack Germond and Jules Witcover later wrote, the surprise new assignment was "an incredible acknowledgment that his chief of staff had more credibility with the American people than he had himself." George Stephanopoulos, a young aide to Clinton, mocked the new arrangement, telling reporters that Bush was offering up "his handler-in-chief as a new de facto president," adding, "The big question is: Will James Baker offer George Bush a substantial policy role in his administration?"

The backlash stung. The campaign had scheduled Baker to give a speech on the second-term economic program, but over the next two weeks, it was postponed, revived, and canceled again as he uncharacteristically squirmed in the limelight. Already eager to avoid drawing too much attention to himself as the campaign headed toward seeming defeat, Baker argued that giving the speech would only draw more man-behind-the-throne coverage. When he was given a draft of the address, he demurred. "I like the speech," he said, "but the president should be giving it."

His vanishing act hardly went unnoticed. Among those angry at Baker for not stepping up was Barbara Bush, who took to calling him "the Invisible Man." When Baker stopped by the White House residence one night, she lit into him for not publicly standing up for her husband. "She was all over me about that," Baker recalled. Finally, the president meekly came to his defense. "Barb, get off his case," he told the first lady. But she was not the only family member furious with a savior who was not saving the president.

AS BAD AS the first debate had been, it would only get worse for Bush at the second debate, set in Richmond, Virginia, on October 15. Uncomfortable with the town-hall format, the first of its kind in presidential election history, Bush at one point was caught on camera stealing a glance at his wristwatch as if he were bored or eager to get the event over with. Clinton, on the other hand, was in his element, roaming the stage and responding directly to the "average citizens" recruited to pose questions.

When a woman asked, "How has the national debt personally affected each of your lives," Bush stumbled. The wording of the question confused him. He did not seem to understand at first that she was really asking how he himself had been affected by the recession, but instead started to discuss the debt itself, reflecting on its impact on interest rates.

"*You*, on a personal basis," the woman insisted. "How has it affected *you*?"

Bush seemed befuddled. "Help me with the question and I'll try to answer it."

She explained that friends of hers had been laid off.

Finally understanding, Bush sounded defensive, sensing that he was under attack for being an elitist far removed from the pain many Americans were enduring.

"Everybody cares if people aren't doing well," he said. "But I don't think it's fair to say, you haven't had cancer, therefore you don't know what it's like."

Clinton had no problem with the question, walking right up to the edge of the stage to talk with the woman. This was his moment and he knew what to do with it. Empathy was his brand.

"In my state, when people lose their jobs, there's a good chance I'll know them by their names," he said. "When a factory closes, I know the people who ran it. When the businesses go bankrupt, I know them."

Perot too hammered Bush for being oblivious to the experience of everyday Americans. He focused attention on the new North American Free Trade Agreement that Bush had negotiated in August, a pact that would essentially take the Canada–United States Free Trade Agreement that Baker had brokered during the Reagan administration and bring in Mexico. That "giant sucking sound," Perot said, would be the sound of American jobs heading south.

By the third debate in East Lansing, Michigan, on October 19, Clinton was openly mocking Bush's plan to turn the economy over to Baker.

"The person responsible for domestic economic policy in *my* administration will be Bill Clinton," the Democrat said.

"That's what worries me," Bush shot back.

It was a good riposte but Clinton's zinger still drew blood. No matter what Bush did, he could not convince a disenchanted public that he had a plan for a second term. When the three debates were over, only 15 percent believed Bush had won, while 39 percent said Clinton had prevailed and 31 percent picked Perot. Some in Bush's circle blamed it on Baker for outsourcing debate negotiations and effectively saddling his candidate with a format that did not play to his strengths. But in truth, Bush himself had lost and not only at the town hall.

Anxious to turn things around, Baker suddenly found an odd opportunity presented to him. Two days after the final debate, at the urging of Senator Arlen Specter, Baker got on the phone with Ken Langone, the cofounder of Home Depot and one of Perot's best friends. He proposed a far-fetched idea—Perot would drop out and support Bush for reelection if put in charge of the economic portfolio in the second term. Baker could go back to the State Department after all.

Baker was wary. Had Langone actually talked with Perot about this? "The man and I are very close," Langone assured him. He would not make the call unless he could deliver Perot. "The president's in trouble but he and Perot could be a dream team."

Baker informed Langone that it was illegal to trade a federal position for election support.

Langone suggested Bush could agree to "consult with Ross" on top economic appointments like the secretaries of treasury, commerce, and labor.

After they hung up, Langone reached out to Perot. The candidate told him that he had just gotten a call from someone at Goldman Sachs asking if he would drop out to support Bush. Langone concluded that Baker had leaked their conversation. "Ken, you can't trust these people," Perot said.

Langone called Baker at home that night and mentioned the Goldman Sachs call. Baker was confused, noting that he had never worked at Goldman Sachs. Either way, Langone said Perot had told him that if "those people" had any specific proposals, he would listen. But Baker concluded that Langone was "impetuous" and "sounded flaky," so he told him they would be better off not pursuing it. They were desperate, yes, but not enough to get in bed with Perot.

With time running short, Bush's only real recourse was to bring Clinton down. In a takeoff of James Carville's now famous maxim, someone wrote on a blackboard at campaign headquarters on Fifteenth Street, "Taxes and Trust, Stupid." Turning to some of the same sharp tactics that had worked against Michael Dukakis four years earlier, Baker's operation depicted Clinton as an unpatriotic, even un-American, liberal. While Bush ruled out attacks on Clinton's sex life, his team focused attention on the challenger's participation in a demonstration against the Vietnam War while in Britain for his Rhodes Scholarship. They insinuated nefarious motives behind a trip Clinton took in that era to Moscow and even pursued rumors that while in England he may have sought to revoke his American citizenship to avoid the draft.

At a campaign meeting at the White House early one morning in September, Bob Teeter raised the citizenship question. Journalists had filed requests for the Clinton passport file under the Freedom of Information Act. Baker asked Janet Mullins to check with the State Department on the status of the requests. Within a few hours, though, the alarm bell in his head that usually warned him of political danger finally went off and he reached out to Boyden Gray, the White House counsel. After checking with the Justice Department, Gray told Baker that releasing passport information could violate federal privacy law.

Baker quickly had Caron Jackson, his assistant, summon Mullins and Margaret Tutwiler back to his office. They found Baker standing in a tense and formal way and they quickly realized that it was an "on-the-record meeting," one meant to establish a record of deniability.

"I just need you to know it was inappropriate and you should not act on anything on Clinton's passports," Baker told the aides, in Mullins's recollection.

Tutwiler and Mullins left the office rolling their eyes. "We were like, 'Okay, I get what that was about,'" Mullins said later. "It was clearly a CYA." Baker was covering his ass.

Even so, in response to the Freedom of Information Act requests, State Department officials did eventually check the files and found nothing to verify the gossip.

Some of Bush's supporters were not willing to give it up. On October 6, four conservative Republican congressmen showed up in the Oval Office to urge the president to reach out to foreign governments for help. That was a line Baker was not willing to cross. "They wanted us to contact the Russians or the British to seek information on Bill Clinton's trip to Moscow," Baker later wrote in a memo to the file. "I said we absolutely could not do that."

Even without foreign assistance, the public attacks on Clinton may have been paying off anyway. Bush, who had governed as a picture of WASP rectitude, once again shed his gentlemanly reserve to slash at his Democratic challenger and his running mate. "My dog Millie knows more about foreign affairs than these two bozos," Bush said scornfully. The tough-guy nastiness may have been forced and unnatural, but he knew from 1988 that negative politics worked. By the end of October, Bush had trimmed his deficit to about 5 percentage points.

If Bush was indeed building toward a late comeback, however, it came to an abrupt halt the Friday before the election when Lawrence Walsh, the independent counsel, released a new indictment of Caspar Weinberger, Reagan's defense secretary, in the Iran-contra affair. The indictment referenced notes taken by Weinberger that undercut Bush's long-standing insistence that he had not known about the internal opposition to trading arms for hostages. "'86 Weinberger Notes Contradict Bush Account on Iran Arms Deal," a *New York Times* headline declared. "Bush Stance, Iran-

Contra Notes At Odds," reported *The Washington Post.* The prosecutor's October Surprise came at the worst possible moment for the president.

Appearing on *Larry King Live*, his campaign's favorite venue for softball interviews, Bush insisted there was nothing new in the court documents. George Stephanopoulos, the Clinton aide, telephoned into the show's call line to challenge the president's veracity. Walsh's office denied any political motivation in the indictment, but the timing just four days before the election convinced the Bush camp that the prosecutor was trying to sway the outcome.

Baker was furious. The Bush momentum was dead.

AT THE HOUSTONIAN HOTEL on Election Day, Tuesday, November 3, 1992, Baker joined Bush and his family as they awaited the public's verdict. After Bush got a haircut, it fell to Baker to deliver the bad news as the first wave of exit polls came in—Pennsylvania and Ohio looked bad, then more bad news from New Jersey and Michigan. "It looks like a blowout," Bush told his diary.

As the evening wore on, state after state that had gone Republican four years earlier switched to the Democrats, including California and the Pacific Northwest, New England, and even significant sections of the South. Bush held on to just eighteen states, fewer than half as many as in 1988. Clinton won 43 percent of the popular vote to 37 percent for Bush, the lowest for any incumbent president since William Howard Taft lost the three-way contest in 1912. The margin was even wider in the Electoral College, with Clinton capturing 370 votes to 168 for Bush. Perot took a whopping 19 percent of the popular vote, although he captured no states and therefore no electoral votes. Bush was crushed.

For Baker, it would always be an article of faith that Perot had cost them the election. "Had we not had Ross Perot, we would have won," Baker often said. Polling suggests otherwise. If Perot had not been in the race, 38 percent of his voters told interviewers as they left polling stations on Election Day that they would have voted for Bush and 38 percent said they would have voted for Clinton, with the rest generally saying they would not have voted at all. Of the eleven states that Bush lost by 5 percentage points or less, he would have had to flip ten of them to change the outcome in the Electoral College, a tall order to say the least.

There was no question, of course, that Perot had made Bush his main target in an effort that at times seemed more like a vendetta than a campaign. But Clinton was still beating Bush in the polls even during the several months that Perot had dropped out of the race and it was a one-on-one contest. Baker understood that their problems went beyond Perot—that Perot was a symptom, not a cause. Baker believed that the campaign had made a mistake not to go to Congress with a Domestic Storm economic program at the beginning of 1992. By the time they focused on it, it was too late. More broadly, after three straight terms, Baker concluded that the Republicans had simply worn out their welcome. Clinton represented a new generation pointing to the future. Bush was part of the same crowd that had been running Washington now for twelve years. "People were tired of us," Baker said.

When it was all over, Bush and Baker and their families looked for consolation. "Afterward, Barbara and I finished with all our tears, we said to each other, 'Well, our guys are going to live longer, that's the upside,'" said Susan Baker. But Jim Baker and his colleagues nursed grudges against those they blamed for helping to bring down Bush. At the top of their list was Lawrence Walsh, whose indictment of Weinberger seemed like a dastardly final blow and, indeed, was thrown out by a judge weeks after the election. Inside the White House, Baker went so far as to raise the question of whether Walsh himself had broken a law prohibiting government officials from trying to influence an election, an idea that ultimately led nowhere. Instead, Bush had his revenge by issuing last-minute pardons to Caspar Weinberger on previous charges as well as five other former Reagan-era government officials who had been prosecuted by Walsh, a decision that the independent counsel condemned as the completion of "the Iran-contra cover-up."

The election left another strain that was harder to resolve. The decades-long friendship between Baker and the Bush family was no longer the same. In the weeks after the election, recriminations followed Baker, as even some of Bush's closest family members piled on. Baker, they said, had lost his edge; he had never fully committed to the mission, he was too worried about his own reputation.

The most upset were Barbara Bush and George W. Bush. At various points over the years, Barbara had chafed at what she saw as Baker's opportunism, never forgetting that he had forced her husband to drop out of the 1980 presidential contest against Ronald Reagan and later took a job running Reagan's White House. This time around, as she and her son saw it, Baker had never invested in the campaign—he had resisted coming back to the White House until it was too late and even when he did come back, he acted as if it was someone else's mess that he was not going to be able to clean up.

"Everybody's emotions were raw," recalled Baker's son John. "Sometimes you say things, whether you meant them or not, you probably shouldn't have said them." It was "a fraught period," as Brent Scowcroft remembered it. "There was some sentiment," he said, "that Baker had had enough being in the shadow of the president and it was time for him to start going on his own."

Whatever his private feelings, George Bush himself never expressed the same bitterness toward Baker as his wife and son did. "Losing is hard, losing is tough," Baker observed. But "he never exhibited anything but love and appreciation to me." Dennis Ross suspected that Bush understood that he had put his friend in a no-win situation and therefore did not hold it against him. "I think Bush felt a certain degree of guilt because he knew that Baker didn't want to do this," Ross said. "He knew the only reason he would do it was because he was asking him to do it and so while the family felt that way, Bush didn't feel that way."

The hard feelings would fade over time and so would the memories of them. In the years before she died, Barbara Bush said she had no recollection of any recriminations against Baker, nor did she even recall calling him the Invisible Man. "I don't remember being upset with anybody," she said. "I was amused occasionally, but not upset—but not with Jimmy." Likewise, George W. Bush would also deny any ill will. His ire was directed at the campaign more generally, he said, not at Baker. "I was really frustrated because I could smell impending doom," the younger Bush said. In Dallas, where he was living at the time, the president's son saw people he considered natural supporters of his father putting Perot bumper stickers on their cars, which stuck with him. "I felt like the campaign was adrift, and so I was frustrated," Bush said. "But I wasn't angry at Baker. Nor did I blame Baker. How could you blame Baker?" What about resisting for so long the move from State? "Could he have come over earlier and made a difference?" Bush mused. "I don't know. It's hard to tell. Maybe it's one of these things where the whole thing was doomed from the beginning."

But at the time, in the moment, the tension was hard to miss. Baker watched the elder George Bush struggle with the sting of rejection and knew that he had failed to save his friend's presidency. After twenty-two years of working to advance Bush's political career, Baker saw his service as the family's consigliere coming to an end. He was sixty-two years old.

It was time to figure out what would come next. It was time to see if there was a future for Baker beyond Bush. He would always be close to the Bush family, but no longer would he be the one to rush to the rescue when times turned tough.

Or would he?

Part Five

CHAPTER 27

The Virus

Baker's last days in the White House were tortured. He and his team in the West Wing could hear the banging of the hammers outside their windows erecting what they morbidly called "the gallows"—the bandstand on Pennsylvania Avenue for Bill Clinton's inaugural parade. It was a dark time in a lame-duck presidency after an ignominious defeat. For Baker, the ten weeks between the election and the end of the administration were perhaps his toughest time in his public life.

The thrashing at the ballot box was bad enough. The strain with the Bush family was even worse. But on top of that, Baker now faced what he feared would be the unraveling of the reputation he had spent so many years polishing as an investigation was opened into the search of Clinton's passport files. The State Department inspector general, a quasi-independent watchdog within the building, had decided to refer the matter to the Justice Department for possible criminal prosecution. Suddenly, Baker and his team found themselves under investigation, suspected of dirty dealings.

Baker was distraught. Always exceedingly protective of his public image, he saw this as the humiliating end of twelve years in the top ranks of government, twelve years marked largely by one success after another, all coming down to what he considered a petty affair. Baker decided he could not take it. He sat down and drafted a letter of resignation. Being chief of staff was no longer worth it. He had not even wanted the job this time around. On the Friday before Thanksgiving 1992, he took the letter to Bush in his private study.

He was ending his career in shame, Baker told his friend, and he did not want to cause problems for the president. "Who needs this?" Baker asked.

Bush felt for Baker, but thought resigning was an overreaction. He refused to accept the letter. As long as he was president, Baker would be in the White House right alongside him.

But Baker could not let it go. "Jim Baker is still all uptight about the passport mess and there is nothing else that he can think of," Bush dictated to his diary a few weeks later. A few days after that, Bush returned again to Baker's state of mind: "Jim Baker has lost all interest in what's going on at the White House. There isn't much for him to do and he's worried about this passport deal still. He's got a lawyer and the lawyer tells him that they can't find anything that he could even be charged with and that it's most unlikely a special prosecutor will be appointed. He seems relieved but still totally preoccupied." Baker could hardly even concentrate on the farewell speeches they were trying to draft. "His heart isn't in any of that," Bush said. "It's just gone."

By happenstance, the law authorizing independent counsels was due to expire in mid-December, meaning that William Barr, the attorney general, had to decide by then whether to appoint a special prosecutor to look into the matter. As the deadline approached and Barr made no announcement, Baker and his aides thought that maybe they had escaped what they knew would be a costly and politically fraught ordeal. At dinner the night before the law was scheduled to lapse, Margaret Tutwiler and Janet Mullins were lifting glasses to toast their near-miss when suddenly word arrived—Barr had just requested the appointment of a prosecutor in the passport matter only hours before the deadline. He had acted on the recommendation of the head of the Justice Department's criminal division, Robert S. Mueller III. Tutwiler and Mullins were crushed. So was Baker. "Baker is a nervous wreck," Bush told his diary after Barr's announcement. The next day, Bush added, "It's ruining Jim Baker's life. Of all the clean honorable decent guys to have his Christmas ruined by this guy, it's too bad."

Baker's funk was noticed outside the White House. Under the headline "Missing and Presumed Injured," Mary McGrory, the *Washington Post* columnist, wrote that Baker had vanished along with his hopes for a Nobel Peace Prize or the White House. "His disappearance is the talk of the town's Christmas parties," she said. "No Republican wishes to be quoted—Baker is much feared and respected—but the general feeling is that he has suffered grave damage to his reputation and his quest for the presidency." She added that his relationship with Bush "is said to have cooled" and noted that Baker had hoped to be remembered as a statesman, not a political operative. "Now he may go down as a disdainful manager, a prime example of the Republican tendency to play dirty in politics."

Bush, who secretly consumed the columns of McGrory and other critical writers while publicly denying that he cared about their opinions, cringed as he read this one. "An ugly editorial by Mary McGrory," he told his diary, "and it will have Jim Baker climbing the wall." He added, "Jim is so sensitive about his own coverage that he will be really upset."

Joseph diGenova, a former United States attorney for the District of Columbia best known for investigating the capital's crack-smoking mayor, Marion Barry, was tapped as the independent counsel to investigate the passport flap. Baker knew diGenova, a Republican "prosecutor with a politician's flair for the spotlight," as the *Post* had recently called him, and thought he would be fair. But Baker recognized that once an investigation began, anyone in its sights faced danger, whether or not they had done anything wrong initially.

Baker still carried the scars from the long controversy over the 1980 campaign debate book and he knew from painful experience that even a seemingly minor matter could grow into a legal nightmare. He warned his team about what they could expect. "What Baker made perfectly clear and became obvious to all of us, the uninitiated, from the get-go is that this wasn't really about whether you did anything wrong in the first place," Mullins said. "This is a witch hunt."

Whether or not it was a witch hunt, the independent counsel statute was designed in a way that encouraged never-ending investigations in search of a crime. Under the law, an independent counsel essentially answered to no one and had no duties other than pursuing the assigned targets. Ordinary prosecutors with many issues on their plates had to make judgment calls about how much time and resources to devote to an investigation with thin prospects; an independent counsel had no such tradeoffs to worry about and, because any such investigation was by its very nature politically sensitive, there was great incentive to keep going rather than to let powerful figures off the hook.

Tutwiler, Mullins, and others suddenly had to find lawyers and were instructed not to talk with each other about the investigation. They knew they were not the real targets but could easily become collateral damage. "This wasn't about me," Mullins said. "It was about getting Baker." Baker felt mortified to have put them in that position. "We had just lost, his best friend was hurting, he had loyal staff members who were very, very vulnerable in a situation they didn't fully grasp," Mullins said. "And I think there was probably—guilt is probably not the right word but a sense of responsibility that he's the one who got this started."

Baker was ready when the investigators came knocking. As he sat down with diGenova's team, Baker pulled out a memo written contemporaneously documenting what he knew and when he knew it, effectively distancing himself from anything that might have crossed the line. The investigators were impressed. "At the end of the interview, we thought, 'This is not his first rodeo,'" Michael Zeldin, diGenova's deputy, said later. "He wrote that memo for self-protective purposes, knowing in some sense that we wouldn't necessarily be able to prove otherwise." The investigators left Baker's office "thinking this guy understands the way Washington works and what you have to do to protect yourself."

Even so, it would take three years for diGenova to investigate, three excruciating years for Baker and his circle. When the prosecutor finally did issue his report in November 1995, he cleared the Baker team, saying some of them had acted stupidly but not illegally. Indeed, diGenova went on to say that Barr should never have sought his appointment in the first place.

In his public remarks, diGenova expressed sympathy for those he had investigated. "Today, a Kafkaesque journey for a group of innocent Americans comes to an end," he said. "They did things that were stupid, dumb and partisan," he added, "but those things are not a crime."

Rarely if ever had a special prosecutor expressed regret at his own appointment. Exoneration proved a huge relief to Baker as well as Tutwiler and Mullins, but it did not take them long to grow outraged at what they had been put through. They thought Barr should never have subjected them to it. Word got back to Barr that Baker was angry at him, so when he visited Houston for other reasons, the former attorney general stopped in to see his cabinet colleague to make amends.

"I just want you to know that the reason I appointed the independent counsel a day before the statute expired was because you would have been in worse shape with the public integrity section of the Justice Department," Barr told Baker.

"I don't believe that for one minute," Baker shot back. "You should have had the balls to stand up," Baker added, but "you caved to the pressure."

Barr remembered that despite the dispute, Baker behaved like "a gentleman." But even years after the fact, Barr thought he did the only thing he could have under the circumstances. "I still think it was the right call," he said. Baker would never agree, or forgive.

AS HE PACKED UP his office in the West Wing under a cloud, Baker set about figuring out the rest of his life. After years devoted to public service,

Baker knew one thing—he was ready to cash in. For all of his family's one-time wealth, he had burned through much of his money during his years in government and figured it was time to refill the coffers. But he also knew that he did not want to become a lobbyist, one of those former somebodies who used to come see him asking for help during his years at the top. Baker cringed when he remembered Howard Baker, one of his successors as chief of staff, bringing clients to the Treasury Department. But beyond that, he was open to offers. James Baker was a capitalist and ready to make a buck, even if it meant trading on his connections in capitals other than Washington. Many firms were already beating down his door.

One decision was easy: He and Susan planned to stay in Washington for another two and a half years before returning to Houston so that Mary-Bonner could graduate from National Cathedral School. After that, Baker was pretty sure he would return to Houston, the only other place he had ever lived aside from Washington and school. But he was conflicted when his old Houston law firm, Andrews Kurth, approached him about coming back more than a dozen years after leaving. The managing partner wrote a powerful, heartfelt letter appealing to him to return to the place that had been his professional home as a young man. But Baker Botts, the family firm of his father, grandfather, and great-grandfather, also came calling. Barred from starting his career there because of the firm's nepotism rule, he now had the chance to end his career there. While his son Jamie—the fifth James Addison Baker and also now a practicing lawyer—was at the firm, the partners told Baker they would make a former-secretary-of-state exemption to the no-relatives policy.

Baker was not sure at first. "What would I be?" he asked Edward William Barnett, a law school classmate and the firm's managing partner. "Would people accept me? What do they want me to do?" Barnett assured him he would not be doing run-of-the-mill legal work, just high-stakes rainmaking. Baker was clear about his no-lobbying policy and he would agree to go on only two corporate boards chosen by the firm. On the other hand, Baker said, he did not mind lobbying foreign governments on behalf of American companies. "I would be happy to do that if I could," he said. But he warned, "I think you ought to explain to your partners that I am a depleting asset and whatever benefit I am to you, you got to get in the first two or three years. After that, people are going to forget me." Barnett said he understood. They came to an agreement. Finally, at age sixty-four, Baker would join the family business.

His Houston friend Robert Mosbacher, the fundraiser who had gone on to serve as George Bush's commerce secretary, let him know that the

Enron Corporation, the nation's largest natural gas company, based in their mutual hometown, wanted them both to join its board. Baker demurred. But Enron was persistent and Kenneth Lay, the firm's chairman and chief executive officer and a friend of Bush's, offered him a consulting contract instead to help the company develop projects around the world. At the time, Enron was seeking to build gas-fired plants or make deals in places where Baker might have particular sway, including Kuwait, Germany, and Russia. A month after leaving the White House, Baker signed on.

He also got a call from his old friend Robert Strauss, who told him a Democrat named David Rubenstein wanted to come see him. Baker agreed, so one day Rubenstein and two partners showed up at the White House. They knew the competition for Baker's service was hot when they found the next person waiting to see the outgoing chief of staff after them was David Rockefeller.

Rubenstein was a remarkable Washington success story. The son of a post office mail sorter and a homemaker, he had parlayed a fierce discipline and work ethic into a job as a domestic policy aide in Jimmy Carter's White House, where he was so committed that colleagues wondered whether he actually slept in his office. After leaving government, he transformed himself from a modestly paid public servant into a high-dollar private entrepreneur, trafficking in influence and access as cofounder of the Carlyle Group, a private equity firm based in Washington.

While he would become a billionaire, Rubenstein was a famous ascetic—he did not drink, smoke, or eat meat. But he collected people and one of the people he was intent on collecting was Baker. Rubenstein made his pitch, explaining that he would not make Baker lobby or do anything else that would make him uncomfortable. He noted that he already had Frank Carlucci, the former defense secretary under Ronald Reagan and Baker's Princeton classmate, helping to run the firm. Baker was polite but not all that interested. A relatively young investment firm with just $100 million under management? He could do better.

Unwilling to take no for an answer, Rubenstein approached Dick Darman to see if Baker's loyal consigliere could help persuade him. Darman told Rubenstein that he had made a mistake citing Carlucci as a draw; Baker and Carlucci did not get along particularly well, Darman explained. But the longtime Baker adviser agreed to talk with his old boss—and then asked whether there would be room for him to come too. Rubenstein quickly understood it was a package deal; if he wanted Baker, he would have to take Darman. He agreed. He would showcase Baker to attract wealthy clients who would be drawn to the former secretary's star power.

"It was a brilliant strategy that was about to make all of them very, very rich," wrote Dan Briody in a history of Carlyle.

For Baker, it was a good deal—plenty of cash with little real responsibility. "I didn't take up much of his time because I never asked him to ask for money," Rubenstein explained. "He never brought a deal in, he never worked on a deal, and I never asked him to ask for money. So what did he do? Well, I would basically have lunches and dinners and invite people to come to them who were prospective investors or people like that and if you were invited to a dinner in London where David Rubenstein is going to be the featured speaker, you probably wouldn't show up. If you're invited to hear Jim Baker, the great man, you would probably show up." He would take Baker once a year to the Middle East and once a year to Asia. In the Middle East, in particular, Baker was welcomed as royalty. "He was like a god there because he was the man who had saved the region to some extent," Rubenstein said.

Another opportunity soon came Baker's way as well, one that would prove irresistible given his family pedigree. George Rupp, the president of Rice University, reached out through intermediaries to see if Baker might be interested in establishing an institute at the Houston school. Preston Moore was asked to raise the idea with his cousin. At dinner at Baker's house a few days later, as Susan served fish around a wooden table, Moore mentioned the proposal. Baker's eyes lit up. This was, after all, the university founded and built from the ground up by Captain Baker with the William Marsh Rice estate he saved from turn-of-the-century fraudsters. "I knew what the answer was going to be," Moore recalled. Baker wanted to establish not just another think tank but an institute that would marry the world of ideas with the world of action, finding ways to translate theoretical policy positions into tangible deeds. What else would better reflect his view of policy and politics?

Baker asked Dennis Ross to come run it, but Ross did not want to move to Houston and opted instead to work for the incoming Clinton administration on the unfinished business of Middle East peace. John Rogers, Baker's longtime aide, agreed to help get it up and going and Baker then recruited Edward Djerejian, his former ambassador to Syria, to serve as the founding director. "Baker very cleverly approaches my wife and convinces her this is what we should be doing," Djerejian recalled.

Financed in part by some of the former secretary's wealthy friends, the Baker Institute for Public Policy at Rice University was inaugurated in the fall of 1993. At the formal groundbreaking ceremony a year later, Baker managed to draw four former presidents.

IN APRIL 1993, Baker boarded a Kuwait Airways flight specially arranged by the Kuwaiti government to fly Bush, several members of his family, and several of his former aides to the country they had liberated two years earlier. Bush was brought to Kuwait to be honored for all he had done for the tiny nation-state. He was awarded its highest medal by Jabir al-Ahmad al-Sabah, the emir restored to his throne by American troops. It was a valedictory moment for Bush and Baker, who were treated as conquering heroes. Only later would anyone learn that Saddam Hussein had reportedly sent a hit squad to kill the former president while they were in the region, a plot that never materialized but which prompted President Bill Clinton to launch a missile strike in retaliation.

All Baker knew at the time was that the trip had gone well. And for him, it was not over. After George and Barbara boarded the plane to head home, Baker stayed behind. Over the next two days, he met with the prime minister and other Kuwaiti officials as part of Enron's effort to win a contract to rebuild a 400-megawatt power plant at Shuaiba south of Kuwait City that had been destroyed by the Iraqis during the invasion, a project worth at least $600 million and possibly up to $1 billion. The competitor, a consortium led by Deutsche Babcock of Germany, had a bid that would cost Kuwait almost 50 percent less. But Enron had Baker, one of the heroes of the Gulf War. When he got together for breakfast with the Kuwaiti businessmen who were part of the Enron consortium, including a former foreign minister, they did not actually talk about the bid. That was not Baker's role. "We discussed the liberation, et cetera," the former foreign minister later said.

Still exceedingly sensitive about his reputation, Baker rejected the idea that he was making money off his time in public service, much less profiting off the war he had helped run. But of course he was, just as top officials from every administration in modern-day Washington had. No one was paying Baker millions of dollars because he had been a successful corporate lawyer in Texas. They were paying him millions of dollars because he had been secretary of the treasury and secretary of state—and might even be a presidential candidate soon. They did not want him to haggle over contracts or calculate bids. They wanted him to get people into the room, to tell stories, to backslap and reminisce and, eventually, to solve problems. He knew how things worked. He knew pretty much everyone who mattered. And Baker did not mind the perks that came with his new life. "There is nothing I enjoy more than having that jet at my disposal," he once told his cousin Addison Baker Duncan.

It should hardly have surprised him, then, that he would be accused of capitalizing on the Gulf War. In September 1993, the investigative reporter Seymour Hersh published a long piece in *The New Yorker* detailing Baker's work in Kuwait on behalf of Enron's bid for the power plant as well as the business dealings of Neil and Marvin Bush, two of the former president's sons. The Enron deal seemed to cross lines of propriety. "In seeking contracts to rebuild Kuwait so soon after American men and women risked their lives there—in using their sacrifice as a kind of calling card—haven't Baker, the two Bush sons, and the rest transgressed those bounds?" Hersh asked.

Baker later encountered Hersh on an airplane. "Seymour, you really tried to screw me on this," he remembered telling him. "I was trying to help an American company. There's nothing wrong with that."

Taken aback by Baker's anger, Hersh mumbled something about doing his job.

Hersh was not the only one to find it all just a little unseemly. Just a month after the *New Yorker* article, *The New Republic* weighed in with its own piece, this time focused on Baker's lucrative affiliation with Carlyle. David Rubenstein saw it first and sheepishly showed the article to Baker on a chartered jet heading to Europe in October. The cover included a cartoon drawing of Baker in front of a large bag of cash under the headline "The Access Capitalists: Influence-Peddling in the Nineties." As Baker flipped through the magazine, he found the cover story by a young writer named Michael Lewis lumping him together with other former senior government officials lured by Rubenstein to open doors for him around the world.

"The Carlyle Group, in short, has become a kind of salon des refusés for the influence-peddling class," Lewis wrote. "It offers a neat solution for people who don't have a whole lot to sell besides their access, but who don't want to appear to be selling their access." The article quoted Rubenstein saying, "Let's suppose you're the CEO of GM and you get a call from Baker. You think, 'Hey the former secretary of state wants to come out and have lunch with me. I'll get the photographer out . . . have my picture taken.'" Rubenstein seemed particularly pleased to have scored Baker, telling Lewis that while other top former officials had the ability to call any chief executive in the country, "Baker just puts us in a different league."

Baker fumed at the *New Republic* piece, blaming it on owner Martin

Peretz, a strong supporter of Israel who did not care for the Bush administration's approach to the Middle East. And he stiffened at the notion that he was exploiting his time in government. What was he supposed to do after stepping down? Be a hermit? "If the piece is suggesting that because you have held high political office, you are foreclosed from doing anything in business, I think that's bullshit," he said years later, as irritated about the criticism as he had been at the time.

The work sure was profitable, though. After years in public office, Baker was finally bringing home serious money. In the first nine months of 1994 alone, he earned $2.4 million from Baker Botts, Carlyle, Enron, paid speeches, and other income. Later that year, he collected $184,000 for a series of events over the course of a single week in Singapore, Taiwan, and Japan. By the end of that first full year out of office, his honoraria for speaking engagements came close to $900,000.

Baker's affiliation with Carlyle especially would make him a wealthy man, richer than his father or grandfather had ever been, and he would continue with the firm for more than a decade. But his arrangement with Enron would last only about two years. Baker was not earning the success fees he had thought he might and he later said that he felt queasy about the firm's bookkeeping. "I came home one day to Susan and I said, 'You know, honey, I don't understand this, the way they do the accounting at Enron,'" he recalled.

By 1995, he left the firm, once again saved by his instinct for trouble or self-preservation. Six years later, the firm went bankrupt with $74 billion in losses, the largest such filing in American history at the time, and multiple investigations were opened into Enron's finances. Kenneth Lay and Jeffrey Skilling, Lay's successor as chief executive officer, were convicted of conspiracy and fraud. Baker could only shake his head, glad he had cut his ties long before.

BUT BAKER MISSED his old life. Was he really done with politics? The past three Republican presidents had all leaned on him when election time came around. Now that Bush was done with campaigning, Baker thought of himself in some ways as the natural heir. At least, Baker no longer had to worry about crossing his friend Bush or being pressed back into service as a mere staffer. He had the name recognition, the experience—why should he not try himself? Only a few months into Clinton's presidency, Baker started exploring whether to run for president in 1996.

Baker had little doubt about his capacity to serve in the nation's highest office. He understood the presidency intimately as few others did. He had arguably acted as a shadow president during Ronald Reagan's first term and was often described as a virtual prime minister in Bush's administration. However exaggerated those descriptions were, Baker had learned better than anyone else of his generation how to acquire and wield power in Washington. He had been tempted by the idea of the presidency for years—keeping all those you-should-run letters from the 1980s in a file folder—but this, he knew, was the moment. Either he ran now or his chance would pass forever.

"When you see these people up close, you say, 'Wait a second, they're not that much better than I am; how did this guy get to be president?'" said Rubenstein, who talked about the prospect with Baker. "As they say, nobody's a hero to their valet, right? So you spend a lot of time in the White House and you know all the flaws of the person. So if you were chief of staff to Ronald Reagan and your best friend becomes president of the United States and you know what Reagan's flaws were and you know what Bush's flaws are and you certainly knew what Gerald Ford's flaws were, why would you say that you, who people say walk on water in all these great jobs, why would you say you shouldn't be president?"

In Washington, those who knew Baker considered him a potentially formidable president. Even before the 1992 election was over, *The New York Times* described him as one of about a half dozen potential candidates on "the A list" for Republicans in four years, along with his friend Dick Cheney and their mutual adversary, Dan Quayle. It was not hard, after all, to see Baker in the Oval Office in his own right, with his patrician mien, street savvy, commanding presence, and easy if controlled charm. What was hard to see was Baker as a candidate. His only run for public office, the Texas attorney general's race in 1978, had not exactly ended in glory and ever since then he had served on campaign staffs or in appointed jobs. He had little natural touch for campaigning. He was not an inspiring speaker. He did not especially like glad-handing strangers. And he was from a generation that would never have imagined sharing with the public whether they wore boxers or briefs as Clinton had.

If Baker was going to run, one thing he had to do was figure out how to purge the 1992 defeat from his record. At the annual Bohemian Grove encampment north of San Francisco in July 1993, he made an effort to laugh it off with a joke: Bush asks Baker what he would do after the election and Baker replies, "essentially do nothing." Bush then responds, "Hell, I thought that's what you did *during* the campaign."

It says much about what Baker had learned in his time in Washington that the joke, which had gone over well with the elite all-male audience where he told it, precipitated a lengthy, detailed debate inside his circle: Should he leak it? To *Newsweek*? What were the pros and cons? Andrew Carpendale, his State Department speechwriter, who had come to work for Baker in his new life, produced a full-page memo examining the merits, complete with three bullet points on why it would be beneficial to pass it to the magazine. Making the joke public would "show that you have a sense of humor about last fall, that you're not shirking responsibility, and that your relationship with George Bush remains steadfast and strong," Carpendale wrote. But Baker hesitated. The item never ran.

Baker began positioning himself in case he did run. As the 1994 midterm congressional elections approached, he campaigned for more than twenty Republican candidates around the country, including, of all people, Oliver North, who had nearly brought down Reagan and Bush during the Iran-contra affair. Convicted of lying to Congress, only to have the verdict overturned on a technicality, North was running for Senate in Virginia, a hero to the political right although still anathema to the party establishment. The state's silver-haired senior Republican senator, John Warner, refused to support North in the general election, sponsoring an independent candidate instead. Even Reagan issued a letter denouncing North. But Baker campaigned for him nevertheless, an act of pandering to conservatives so brazen that Maureen Dowd deemed it "the surest sign yet that he was seriously considering running for president in 1996."

North lost in November, but Republicans captured both houses of Congress anyway for the first time in forty years, providing a boost to the party heading toward 1996. They were a different breed of Republicans, though, and their leader was Newt Gingrich, the combative rebel who had pushed aside the long-reigning moderates and led the tax revolt against Bush that helped doom his presidency. In a revolutionary time inside his party, Baker was not much of a barricade stormer. When he gave a speech in Houston shortly after the midterm elections, teasing that he might run for president, he sounded out of touch with the new GOP zeitgeist as he talked about reaching across the aisle to Democrats. "In my view," he said, "the political center is where you win elections." Yet that was less and less the prevailing view.

As he explored the prospect, Baker examined the potential field. Bob Dole, the runner-up to Bush for the 1988 nomination, was the front-runner and early surveys showed him with 28 percent of the Republican vote. The only other potential candidate in double digits was Dan Quayle with 19 percent. Baker had just 4 percent, roughly the same as a passel of other possible contenders, including Dick Cheney. But Baker was not intimidated. Slowly, methodically, he took soundings for a possible campaign. He talked with political strategists such as Charlie Black to figure out what would be required. He thought through how much money he would need and how he could raise it. Some of his friends, like David Paton from Princeton, were enthusiastic and encouraged him to jump into the race. So did some of his close advisers, who believed he had all the right qualities of a president—seasoning, judgment, pragmatism, and the ability to see around corners.

But Baker found a lot of skepticism as well. David Rubenstein, Robert Zoellick, and Dennis Ross all thought that he would jeopardize his place in history as the secretary of state who helped end the Cold War. "You don't want your legacy to be a failed presidential candidate and in this case someone who didn't even get the nomination," Ross remembered telling him. "He said to me, 'Look, I can raise the money.' I said, 'That's not the issue.' I said, 'John Connally raised the money. You're never going to be the kind of person who's going to open up in a way and there's going to be a constant pressure to do that. It's just not you.'"

Baker invited Andy Card, Bush's former deputy chief of staff and transportation secretary, over to his office to talk about it. Card, like Ross, was skeptical: "What I told him was, 'You're standing on an amazing pedestal right now and it's flattering to be on that pedestal. But if you do run for president right now, your opponents would have the most fun trying to knock you off the pedestal and I'm not sure you could get back on that pedestal.'" He knew it was the right advice politically, but Card said years later, "I regretted saying that right after I walked out of his office." Baker, he thought, would have been a natural president.

One by one, Baker also talked with his eight children. Any campaign could potentially drag them into the unforgiving glare of publicity—their past drug use, divorces, and other difficulties. One of those he worried about most was Elizabeth Winston. He sat down with her at the Silver Creek Ranch and told her that her time at the Menninger Clinic would come up. Elizabeth said she was fine with that; she could help focus public attention on treatment. "I'll be your poster child for it," she told him.

For the frankest, most comprehensive assessment, Baker knew he could depend on Dick Darman and Margaret Tutwiler, who were the most trusted kind of Washington advisers, the ones who had the capacity to say things to him with bracing candor that others would not dare. In a pair of memos, they delivered on the candor, pointedly listing the tradeoffs as well as the possibilities of a presidential bid. Some of it was downright harsh. "First of all, you have passionate enemies far more than passionate supporters," Darman wrote in his. "Fairly or not, there are lots of reporters who believe that you skated through Washington for fourteen years as the 'velvet hammer' hoodwinking the press through your skillful manipulation of the media. They are out to settle scores." He noted that "the hardcore conservative wing of the party" despised Baker as did "the organized Jewish community." His reputation could be sullied by a failed run, just as it was for another former secretary of state who ran for president. "You do not want to be the Al Haig of the 1996" election, Darman wrote, a line that was sure to resonate with Baker. He would also have to be ready for attacks on Enron and the Carlyle Group, the passport case and his alleged "fuck the Jews" remark. "Frankly, you do not like criticism and you get on the defensive easily," Darman concluded. "I don't blame you, it makes you a human being, but the list of charges that every presidential candidate must deal with from the personal to the substantive grows with each election and you need to be ready for it."

In her own memo, Tutwiler echoed some of Darman's thoughts and told Baker he had to wrestle with questions like "what do I want to do for this country" and "Safire's old haunting question, 'What does he believe in?'" She noted that his baggage included a lack of elective experience, the "silver spoon" issue, and the perception that you "only care about yourself." Not to mention that he had no natural constituency. "Remember those in your economic bracket make up 1% of this country," she reminded him. At the same time, she told him she thought he would be a good president and a better campaigner than most expected. And so what if you try and fail, she wrote: "Those people who respect, admire, and like you for you and not for your previous titles will still be your friends win or lose—all the rest is shallow and artificial to begin with."

His advisers knew him well. Baker was not comfortable with the new politics of personal revelation, nor did he relish coming under attack. He had forged a formidable record as secretary of state and had a lot to lose from a failed campaign. There was a reason that Tutwiler had nicknamed him "Mr. Caution" all those years ago. And so, after months of deliberation, Baker opted against the race, putting an end to his never-off-the-ground campaign with an aside in the spring of 1995. "I'm over whatever short virus might have existed a year or so ago," he said publicly. Baker did in fact still have the bug. He would not entirely give up wanting to be president, but he knew that he did not have the wherewithal to do what it took to get the prize. "If he were *selected* to be president, he would have done it," David Paton said. "But he couldn't imagine going around and spending his time campaigning and saying the same thing again and again and having to weigh his opinion against what was politically savvy."

The simple truth was that Baker had accomplished too much to let it ride on a presidential campaign he was just as likely to lose. "What it came down to was, would he have rather been remembered as former secretary of state or as a failed presidential nominee?" his son Doug Baker said. "He was more comfortable with the former secretary of state."

In later years, his father would blame exhaustion after so long at the highest levels of government and national campaign politics. "I knew I could do that job," Baker said one day in retirement. "So why didn't I run for president? Because I was too damn worn out. We talked about it. We thought about it. My numbers were 83 percent name identification. We could have raised the money. But look, five campaigns—"

At that point, Susan Baker, who had been listening patiently, interjected a note of realism as only a spouse can. "But honey," she said, "the party was turning and it was getting much more conservative and they considered him very liberal." Tired, yes, but already a product of a different, fading time.

Baker shrugged. In the end, he said, "you've got to want to have it." And he did not want it enough to do what was required.

As it turned out, Dole did and asked Haley Barbour, chairman of the Republican National Committee, to reach out to Baker to see if he would be willing to be his running mate. Baker called Bush to ask his opinion. Bush first checked with his eldest son, George W. Bush, who had been elected governor of Texas in 1994 and was now entertaining his own national aspirations. "Yeah, I think you ought to do it," Bush told Baker, "and more importantly, George W. thinks you ought to."

The idea never went anywhere. The party was moving on. At age sixty-six, Baker found his style of Republicanism on the wane. "He could probably have gotten the *Democrat* nomination," Elizabeth Winston reflected. "He probably couldn't have gotten the Republican nomination because he wasn't far right enough."

AS HE DEBATED his future, Baker was also busy defining his past. While making money at Carlyle and dabbling in presidential politics, he was at work on a book about his time as secretary of state, intent on following Winston Churchill's maxim that "history will be kind to me for I intend to write it." It would not be a classic memoir and in fact on one letter from his publisher Baker made a point of circling the word and scribbled "stop calling it a memoir" in the margin. It would be, instead, his argument for history.

Baker made clear to the publisher that he did not want to write about his time as a campaign operative and political fixer; he wanted to frame his place in posterity as the diplomat who helped end the Cold War, so the book would only cover his nearly four years as secretary of state. "He wanted to be remembered for being a statesman," said Derek Chollet, an aide who worked on the book. "He didn't want to be remembered for being a political guy."

Baker set about the task with all the systematic organization and attention to detail that he brought to each of his government missions. He assembled a team, ordered up memos, collected documents, and researched books by other secretaries of state. To do the writing, he hired Tom DeFrank, the *Newsweek* correspondent who had first gotten to know Baker during the Ford campaign and was better wired in the Bush and Baker circles than perhaps any other journalist. Andrew Carpendale, the former State Department speechwriter, would oversee the project while Chollet, who had been in the State Department's policy planning office, would conduct research. Margaret Tutwiler would consult on drafts and from time to time Baker would send memos seeking input from Robert Zoellick, Dennis Ross, Robert Kimmitt, and others.

Baker approached the project as if it were an arms control treaty, negotiating each page, each word. No point was too small to deliberate. The title was the subject of furious debate. Memos flew back and forth proposing various alternatives. Many of the nine or ten that were considered included some variation of the word *whirlwind*. But Janet Mullins did not like the word. "Connotes victim of events," Baker jotted down as he took notes on her advice. "Everything I did was just accident. Was a witness not a catalyst." That struck too close to the right-place-right-time argument his critics made about his tenure—that he just happened to be there when the world changed, not that he had helped change it.

In the end, Baker opted for *The Politics of Diplomacy: Revolution, War & Peace, 1989–1992*. By marrying the words politics and diplomacy, he made no pretense to grand geopolitical vision, à la Henry Kissinger, but brought his own background in campaigns to the task of managing the turbulent forces of his era. He was, after all, a fixer, no matter how much he tried to break out of that straitjacket, but a fixer who shaped world events. And why not? Diplomacy was the practice of politics on a global scale.

The politics that erupted over the drafting of the book for Baker were instructive in their own way. Carpendale, a onetime graduate student on

Soviet and American politics under Dennis Ross at the University of California at Berkeley, was recruited to Bush's 1988 campaign despite being a lifelong Democrat and eventually rose to become Baker's chief speechwriter. "He was loud, he was boisterous, temperamentally about as opposite from Baker as you can imagine," recalled Peter Bass, his housemate at the time. He clashed in particular with DeFrank, a seasoned journalist who did not appreciate being lectured by the younger man. They ended up quarreling repeatedly over how long the writing was taking.

But Carpendale's biggest confrontation came with Baker himself over the former secretary's determination to scrub the book as if it were just another political document. Even after dropping the idea of a presidential campaign, Baker had little interest in an overly candid reflection of his life and times. "He was still then very much in the mind-set of a Washington figure where everything you say will be used against you eventually," Chollet said, "and so the caution was always there."

Baker was especially sensitive about the Persian Gulf War, making sure to expurgate any sense of doubt or uncertainty about the outcome. He took his dark black felt pen and crossed out a passage conceding that Robert Gates, Paul Wolfowitz, and other officials had urged the administration to ground all Iraqi helicopters after the cease-fire and shoot down those violating the order. He slashed a section recalling public statements that he, George Bush, and Dick Cheney made at the time encouraging Saddam Hussein's ouster. And finally he deleted this passage: "In retrospect, it may have been a tactical mistake to pull out of Iraq promptly and not exploit our military leverage. The Iraqi army was essentially prostrate at the time. If we had exerted a bit more pressure by slowing the pace of our withdrawal, it's at least possible Saddam may have been removed from power one way or the other."

The cleansing of the manuscript finally proved too much for Carpendale. He sat down at his computer to type out an angry dissent, the likes of which rarely reached Baker when he was secretary of state. "I want to register my vehement disagreement with several of the substantive changes you made in this chapter," Carpendale wrote, citing the Iraq deletions. "In short, you've cut almost all the sophistication and nuance out of the chapter." He went on. "It's obvious where these cuts came from: Margaret. And it's obvious why she would recommend them: they reveal a certain complexity to the post-war situation and imply that possibly we could have done things differently, even better. Undoubtedly, if she had her way, she'd do with this chapter what she recommended we do with the pre-August 2nd chapter: excise it from the book."

Carpendale saved the most stinging rebuke for his conclusion. "You alone will have to bear the burden when the lead review in *The New York Times Book Review* begins something like this: 'In a colorful and readable memoir, James A. Baker, III manages to do as an author what he did so well in over twelve years in power in Washington: glorify his own successes, avoid any hint of failure, and skirt the truth.'"

The clash finally played out one day in the office in a face-to-face blowup with Baker. "Andrew was saying something to him that was kind of disrespectful in some way and Baker just unloaded on him and I'm sitting there like, 'Oh shit,'" Chollet recalled. Baker pointed out the window of his grand Baker Botts office, gesturing toward the White House not far away. "I was goddamn White House chief of staff," Chollet remembered him erupting. "Don't you tell me what to do!"

Of course, Carpendale lost the battle. Baker was not about to cloud his legacy by publicly entertaining second thoughts about the end of the Iraq War. Carpendale was disappointed but not surprised. He respected Baker but understood his flaws as well.

His forecast of a brutal reception for a sanitized book proved eerily prescient. When the Baker book was published in September 1995, clocking in at a dutiful, carefully crafted 672 pages, the former secretary of state picked up *The New York Times* and found words that almost seemed as if they had come from Carpendale's memo.

"The man famous for spinning the message of the week is now spinning his own image for history," wrote Michiko Kakutani, the newspaper's famed book critic. "And yet, readers, like voters in the last presidential election, are unlikely to buy his message. In this case, it's clear the diplomat is still a politician."

CHAPTER 28

Scorched Earth

B aker was in a car heading into Houston from the airport when he got the call. It was the morning after the November 7, 2000, presidential election and he and Susan had just flown back from Austin, where they had spent the previous evening in a hotel suite at the Four Seasons with Dick Cheney, waiting like the rest of America for an election result that never came.

The Republican ticket had brought together George W. Bush and Cheney, two people close to Baker, yet for the first time in a quarter century, he had spent the campaign on the sidelines, neither operative nor prospective candidate, shunned as a relic of the past. Bush, the fifty-four-year-old governor of Texas, was running to become the first presidential son to follow his father to the White House since John Quincy Adams. He had picked Cheney as his running mate, but he was worried about the political optics and had not wanted to look too dependent on his father's old crowd, so the man who had run five Republican presidential campaigns had not been welcome.

But the day after the vote, Baker picked up the phone to hear Don Evans, a longtime friend of the younger Bush's and chairman of his presidential campaign, on the line. The election had been too close to call in several states, including in Florida, where fewer than two thousand votes separated the candidates. With its twenty-five electoral votes, Florida would determine the next president. While Bush had clearly lost the national popular vote, he was ahead at the moment in Florida, just barely, and the question was whether his narrow lead would withstand the challenges that were sure to come. As the vote headed to a recount, the Democrats had already sent a plane full of lawyers soaring through the predawn skies toward Florida and tapped Bill Clinton's former secretary of state,

Warren Christopher, to lead their efforts. The Republicans needed a secretary of state of their own. Evans had called Bush sometime after 4 a.m.
"What do you think about Baker?" he suggested. Bush said yes.

Baker did not hesitate when Evans called. He was in. Bush himself
then called. Yes, Baker told him, he would head right to Florida. Whatever
bitterness George W. had harbored toward Baker from the 1992 election
defeat was put aside in the interest of salvaging his own campaign. Within
hours, the campaign sent a borrowed jet to pick up Baker in Houston and
fly him to Tallahassee. For Baker, this was a chance to redeem himself in
the eyes of the elder Bush, to achieve what he had failed to do eight years
earlier. "When he went down to Florida," said David Rubenstein, "I think
this was his way to get back into the graces of The Man."

Baker had known George W. for four decades, going back to the days
when he was called "Junior," even though he was technically not one. As
a friend of the family, Baker had helped the young Bush along the way.
In 1962, he arranged for George W., then sixteen years old, to work as a
messenger for Baker Botts. Twenty years later, Baker steered a Princeton
friend to make the largest investment to that point in Bush's oil exploration
company, buying 10 percent of the firm for $1 million. And Baker had wel-
comed George W. into his father's campaigns, most notably in 1988 when
the son had an office at headquarters and served as chief loyalty enforcer.

Bush, though, no longer wanted to be called Junior. After too many
boozy years of mediocre business ventures and a failed campaign for Congress, George W. had quit drinking and gotten his act together. While his
father was in the White House, George W. put together a team of investors
to buy the Texas Rangers baseball team, making himself one of two managing partners and the team's public face in Dallas. He parlayed that into a
successful run for Texas governor in 1994 and four years later became the
first Republican to win a second consecutive term in the state, making him
the toast of a national party eager to reclaim the White House.

As the 2000 campaign approached, Baker understood that George W.
needed to establish himself on his own terms. "George W. Bush wanted to
prove it wasn't his dad's campaign," said Andy Card, who ran the convention for Bush that year and would become his first White House chief of
staff. "He was his own man. So there was some reluctance" to surround
himself with veterans of the first Bush administration, including and perhaps especially Baker.

For his part, Baker was sensitive about doing or saying anything that
would look presumptuous and either embarrass or aggravate the up-and-
coming candidate. Even an item in an obscure news outlet called *India*

Abroad, a weekly newspaper published in New York for the South Asian diaspora, caused a small kerfuffle in November 1998 when it quoted Baker saying he was going to run the young man's campaign. Baker, worried that it would upset Governor Bush, scratched out a handwritten note disavowing the article and faxed it to the prospective candidate's father.

"I think you know I would never say that because I've 'been there, done that'—for 3 Republican Presidents—and have no desire to ever do it again," Baker wrote former President Bush. While he regularly told everyone that George W. would be a fine president, Baker added, "he needs his campaign to be run by people in their 50s—not in their 70s." Baker asked Bush to pass along the note to his son.

The elder Bush wrote back to reassure Baker. "I read that nutty story out of India," he said. "Don't worry about it at all."

A media figure more widely read in the United States weighed in a few months later. Robert Novak, the conservative columnist, reported that George W. was assembling a coterie of advisers that pointedly excluded his father's closest confidants. "In international policy, the message is clearest about who is not on the new Bush team: James Baker and Gen. Brent Scowcroft, longtime collaborators of the elder Bush," Novak wrote.

Both Bushes quickly dashed off apologies to Baker and Scowcroft for what the father called that "horrible Novak column." In a note to Scowcroft that he sent to Baker as well, the former president said: "I am afraid this is just near the beginning of the attacks on my closest friends that will increase if George decides to run." He said he grew "furious" when he saw columns like Novak's. "I guess my message to you and to Jim Baker, too, is 'don't let the bastards get you down.'" In his own note to Baker, George W. wrote: "I feel badly about the slight in Novak's column. I value your friendship and advice."

Baker wrote back saying that he understood and would do anything the governor needed—or nothing at all, if that was more helpful. "It is important for you to have your own new and fresh team, but I think you know how much I love your family, and just don't want people to think I'm not 'on the team' (as the Novak article said) either because I don't want to be, or because you don't want me to be," Baker wrote. "All the Bakers are pulling and praying for your success."

WHILE THE CAMPAIGN did not want Baker out front, it did employ him for discreet missions behind the scenes. At one point, Karl Rove, the former aide to the elder Bush who had become the son's principal campaign strategist, sought Baker's advice about making contacts with former British prime minister Margaret Thatcher, an icon to many conservatives in America as well as Britain. She was friends with Steve Forbes, the publishing tycoon who was running against Bush for the nomination, and some in the governor's camp worried that she would become an overt supporter. Baker urged Charles Powell, a former foreign policy adviser to Thatcher, to convince her to stay neutral. Powell wrote to Baker saying he thought they had succeeded, but understood the sensitivity of anyone discovering their communication. "Probably best if you destroy this," Powell wrote.

Bush went on to bury Forbes and a clutch of other Republican candidates, including Dan Quayle, before outpacing Senator John McCain of Arizona through a series of fiercely contested primary battles to claim the nomination. Still, when Bush introduced a major foreign policy initiative in May 2000 as he pivoted to a general election campaign against Al Gore, it did not go unnoticed that arrayed behind him were some of the party's leading national security luminaries such as Henry Kissinger, Colin Powell, and George Shultz—with Baker nowhere to be seen.

On election night, Baker joined Cheney in the running mate's hotel to watch the results. Others from the old days were there too, including Nick Brady, Alan Simpson, and Donald Rumsfeld. As the votes rolled in, Cheney was keeping tallies of his own on a yellow legal pad. So was Baker, who a few days earlier had listed his predictions for the night, forecasting that Florida, Michigan, Wisconsin, and Tennessee would be the evening's decisive toss-ups. Some of Baker's predictions turned out to be on the money. While Michigan went for Gore and Tennessee went for Bush, Wisconsin was achingly tight, with Gore holding a lead of about 6,000 votes out of nearly 2.6 million cast, or 0.2 percent.

Then there was Florida, run by Jeb Bush, the candidate's brother, who had been elected governor in 1998. First, it was called for Gore, then the television networks took back the call. Later, they put it in Bush's column, led by Fox News, whose election decision desk was run by John Ellis, George W.'s cousin. When Cheney left the suite to drive across town and join Bush to claim victory, Baker stayed behind, suffering from a cold that made the prospect of standing in the rain for a middle-of-the-night victory rally unappealing. Then suddenly there was no victory rally. The vote count in Florida had narrowed. Gore retracted his concession. When Baker went to sleep, no one was sure who had won.

Less than twelve hours later, after a couple of phone calls, Baker found himself responsible for securing the victory. He was sidelined no more. Bush's lead in Florida stood at a meager 1,784 votes out of nearly 6 million cast, or roughly three hundredths of a percent. Baker quickly called Margaret Tutwiler, telling her to get to Florida and mobilize the rest of the old gang. It was 11:15 a.m. He grabbed a scrap of paper and scribbled out his initial thoughts: The recount should be conducted "Quickly, Openly, Calmly & In Acc w law," he wrote. "VP Gore campaign should share that goal," he added, then noted that he should ask to meet with Warren Christopher. "Now more of a LEGAL EXERCISE than POLIT. ONE," he wrote. "COUNTRY WON'T TOLERATE PETTY POLITICS." He knew better, of course. He was being asked to take charge in Florida not for his constitutional expertise but for his political acumen. This battle would be fought not just in the courts.

By around 2 p.m., when Joe Allbaugh, George W. Bush's campaign manager, arrived in Houston on a private plane borrowed from the media mogul Warren Tichenor to collect Baker for the flight to Florida, Baker was ready for a briefing. After forty-five minutes, he had heard what he needed to know. He knew where this would end up.

"We're heading to the Supreme Court," Baker said.

Really? Allbaugh asked.

"It's the only way this can end," Baker said.

ONE OF THE FIRST THINGS Baker did was call Warren Christopher. As it happened, Christopher's assistant, Kathy Osborne, had once been Ronald Reagan's secretary at the White House. She had been well liked around the West Wing, nicknamed the Cookie Lady because she used to feed snacks to those who stopped by her desk outside the Oval Office.

But if Baker thought he would have an inside track simply because he knew her back in the day, he was wrong. When she answered the phone, she told Baker that Christopher was not available.

"Where is he?" Baker asked.

"Oh, I don't know," she said nonchalantly. "I think he's traveling."

"To *Florida*?" Baker asked.

Osborne would not say, so Baker left a message.

After Christopher did not return the call promptly, Baker made a point of mentioning to reporters that he had reached out and not heard back, a small jab that did not go unnoticed at Democratic headquarters.

The two former secretaries of state had crossed paths over the years but could hardly be more different, the elk-hunting, cowboy-boot-wearing, dirty-joke-telling Texan and the gray, stoic, rigidly proper Californian. Where both had operated at the intersection of politics and policy, Christopher was at heart a technocrat. Baker was a political knife fighter.

At seventy-five, Christopher, or Chris as everyone called him, had been in and out of public life for decades. He had served in government inquiries after the Watts riots in 1965 and the Rodney King beating in 1991. He led the vice presidential selection teams that helped Bill Clinton pick Al Gore in 1992 and Gore pick Senator Joseph Lieberman of Connecticut in 2000. Most notably, as Jimmy Carter's deputy secretary of state, Christopher negotiated the release of the American hostages from Iran in the final minutes leading up to Reagan's inauguration in 1981. Twelve years later, he returned to Foggy Bottom for four distinguished but not especially memorable years as Clinton's secretary of state following Baker's whirlwind tenure.

Despite their missed telephone connection, a meeting between Baker and Christopher was set up for the next day, Thursday, November 9. They would sit down to take each other's measure in a small but well-appointed conference room at the Governors Inn, a boutique hotel in Tallahassee steps from the State Capitol.

Christopher had approached the meeting as if he were getting ready to negotiate with the Russians, thinking this would be a momentous event where the fate of the country would be worked out by two elder statesmen. Seasoned negotiator that he was, Christopher prepared a first offer to put on the table and, in case that was not accepted, a second offer as a backup and even a third offer.

Baker arrived for the encounter along with Allbaugh and Robert Zoellick, who had rushed down to Florida to once again serve at Baker's side. Christopher brought with him Bill Daley, chairman of Gore's campaign and a former commerce secretary under Clinton, and Ron Klain, who had served as Gore's chief of staff in the White House. Baker greeted Christopher politely. But he was not there to bargain. He had no first offer, much less a second or third. When Christopher suggested that Bush and Gore get together to agree upon a process to resolve the dispute, Baker shut him down.

"Well, Chris, we're not here to negotiate," he said. "Governor Bush won the election on Tuesday. The votes have been counted already. And we're going to stay here as long as needed to make sure they're certified. But we're not here to negotiate about ways to count the ballots. The ballots have been counted."

Christopher was flummoxed. He pressed again for a meeting between the candidates. Baker again rejected the idea.

"If you would like Vice President Gore to concede before that's finalized, that's fine," Baker said of the vote count. "But there's nothing to negotiate, nothing to talk about."

After they went back and forth in a similar vein three more times, the room fell silent.

"I guess there's nothing else to discuss," Christopher said.

"Well," Baker said, "if you have anything you need to discuss, you just call me."

The meeting had been scheduled to go to two hours. It lasted about twenty minutes. The Democrats were frustrated and impressed at the same time. Baker, as they saw it, was ruthlessly cynical. "He didn't spend one minute wondering if George Bush had gotten the most votes or not, or worry about the legitimacy of American democracy," remembered Klain. "He did not care one whit about any of those things. He was there to get his guy into the White House. Period." Truth be told, the Democrats wished Christopher had been of the same mind-set.

Baker wanted someone of heft to represent them in case the clash did end up in federal court, as he had predicted to Allbaugh—and not just a lawyer but someone with national stature and bipartisan respect. Jack Danforth came to mind. A former Republican senator from Missouri and ordained Episcopal priest, Danforth had a reputation for moral rectitude and political moderation that earned him admiration on both sides of the aisle. His nickname was "St. Jack," a sign of esteem though also a tweak at his righteous streak.

Danforth had been the runner-up to Cheney in George W. Bush's vice presidential selection process and now he was being tapped to defend the candidate who had passed him over. Danforth was tracked down in Cancún where he was on vacation. Don Evans called first and then Baker. But they were surprised when Danforth resisted. The former senator thought that going to federal court was a mistake and that Bush should avoid taking actions that would sully his image for any subsequent run for office.

"I just can't conceive that a federal court's going to take jurisdiction over a matter relating to state election law," Danforth said. "I just can't believe that." Bush was still young and had a future if he lost. If he was perceived as taking this recount fight too far, Danforth said, "it could affect his reputation."

Baker pressed Danforth to take the case anyway and the former senator relented. He began packing his bags and checking out of his hotel. But within a few minutes, Baker thought better of it and called back.

"It sounds like your heart's not in it," Baker said, "so we'll get somebody else."

The somebody else would be Theodore Olson, a former assistant attorney general and well-known Republican lawyer in Washington. The Baker team reached Olson on Thursday while he was on a plane to Los Angeles. As soon as he landed, he reboarded the same plane to head back east.

THE NEXT MORNING, Baker was having breakfast at the Governors Inn at the same time as the Democrats. Bill Daley, the son of the legendary Chicago mayor whose late votes in the razor-thin 1960 election had delivered the presidency to John Kennedy, came over to his table and joshed with Baker for a couple of minutes. At one point, Daley jokingly proposed a trade between states with close election night counts. "Come on, we'll give you Iowa and you give us Florida and we'll call it a day," Daley said.

Even two days after the election, neither Baker nor Daley nor anyone else had a full appreciation of the spectacle they were walking into in Florida. The first American presidential election to go into overtime since 1876 did not come with a script. Even for Baker, who had seen almost everything in his political career, this was new. Elections in the best of circumstances can be imprecise affairs. Ballots are thrown out because of voter errors and unclear instructions. Some voters are turned away on Election Day because of conflicting registration information. But the flaws rarely matter to the overall outcome because the margins of victory are typically wide enough to render them moot. In the case of Florida in November 2000, a microscope was trained on a process that did not stand up well to scrutiny. It was that rare situation where every vote mattered.

In Palm Beach County, for instance, a so-called butterfly ballot listed the names of candidates on opposing pages separated by a series of holes, leading to confusion and mistaken votes. On the left side, Bush was listed first and Gore second, but punching the second hole on the ballot would actually cast a vote for Patrick Buchanan, who was listed first on the right side. Improbably, 3,407 votes in heavily Democratic Palm Beach—more than three times as many as in any other Florida county—were cast for Buchanan, the old Bush family nemesis running as the nominee of the Reform Party, the last remnant of Ross Perot's two campaigns for the presidency. No one thought that many people had actually intended to vote for Buchanan, not even Buchanan himself. If he had gotten the same share he got elsewhere in the state, that would mean roughly 2,800 ballots were cast for Buchanan by mistake in Palm Beach, mainly by voters who otherwise supported Democratic candidates down the ticket, many of them elderly Jews excited about helping Al Gore's running mate, Joseph Lieberman, become the first Jewish vice president. Another 19,000 ballots in Palm Beach were thrown out because voters punched holes for two candidates. As problematic as the situation was, Gore had no real basis for complaint since the ballot had been approved by the county's Democratic supervisor of elections and there was no way to remedy it under Florida law once the vote was conducted.

In Duval County, a different kind of ballot created similar problems. Voters were told to choose one candidate on each page of the ballot, which covered races for Senate, House, and local offices, but there were so many minor candidates for president that they spread over two pages. Following instructions, some voters cast a vote on each page, meaning they inadvertently tried to vote for more than one candidate for president. More than 26,000 ballots were thrown out, largely because of double voting, and nearly 9,000 of them were in predominantly African American precincts where Gore was otherwise racking up huge margins. Other problems were reported elsewhere around the state. In Volusia County, a computer disk error initially gave nearly 10,000 votes to the Socialist Workers Party candidate by mistake. In one Palm Beach precinct, no votes were reported at all—the election worker feeding ballots into a counting machine had hit the "clear" button instead of the "set" button. In Broward and Miami-Dade counties and elsewhere, African American voters reported being turned away from the polls when their names were not on registration lists; some were denied ballots after being told that they were felons and thus disqualified, even though they had never been arrested before in their lives. Beyond the legitimate problems, people's imaginations ran wild— after Republican officials spotted an election worker in Volusia County leaving headquarters with two black bags that they suspected contained ballots, sheriff's deputies tracked down and stopped the worker's car twenty-five miles away, only to find personal clothing in the bags.

The broader issue was that in Florida at the turn of the century, about a third of voters across the state made their selections using paper ballots that they punched with a stylus, a system dating back more than a hundred years and open to misinterpretations. Most of the time, the stylus punched a clean hole in the ballot, but sometimes it did not. Tens of thousands of ballots then could be open to debate as to whether a vote had been properly cast or not. Not long after Baker ran into Daley at breakfast that Thursday, Warren Christopher's Democratic legal team requested a hand recount of paper ballots in four Florida counties—Palm Beach, Miami-Dade, Broward, and Volusia.

To Baker, this was a clear threat to Bush's victory. As he had told Christopher, his job was to preserve that win, not conduct an independent examination of what had really happened. In Baker's view, the Democrats were not really interested in a full inspection of the results either—they asked for a recount only in four predominantly Democratic counties where they were most likely to pick up votes to close the gap, which as of the automatic machine recount on Friday had already shrunk to a mere 327 votes. Democrats argued that they did not ask for a statewide recount because Florida law did not permit it; they would have had to file separate requests in each of the sixty-seven counties. Whatever their motives, the selective choices of where to recount would bolster Baker's conclusion that the effort was more about overturning the outcome than any genuine search for an accurate tally.

Under Florida law, overvotes—meaning ballots in which holes were punched for more than one candidate or, in some cases, where voters mistakenly wrote a name as well as punched a hole—were thrown out even if the intent was clear. Nothing more could be done about them. But undervotes—meaning ballots in which the stylus did not cleanly punch all the way through—could be counted depending on the circumstance. Thus Baker, no expert in election law, and the rest of the nation received a sometimes farcical tutorial in the oddities of Florida ballots. The word "chad," describing the tiny piece of the ballot punched out by the stylus, became a household term. A hanging chad had just one corner still attached to the ballot, while a swinging chad had two and a tri chad had three. When the chad remained fully attached to the ballot but had an indentation, indicating that someone at least tried to punch through, it was called a dimpled chad. If there was penetration but the chad was otherwise still fully attached, it was a pregnant chad.

Baker did not care about chads. He had one question and one only: how to stop the recounts. The Republicans had a built-in advantage in Florida given that the state was run by Jeb Bush. Indeed, Baker went straight to see Jeb as soon as he landed in Florida the day after the election. In addition, Katherine Harris, Florida's elected secretary of state, who oversaw elections, was a state co-chair of the George W. Bush campaign, and the state legislature, which had the power to appoint electors itself if it chose, was also controlled by Republicans. But the courts were a different story. Baker used to go hunting with his friend Lawton Chiles, the former Democratic governor of Florida, and remembered him boasting that he had appointed nearly every member of the Florida Supreme Court. The Florida judiciary was not going to be predisposed to rule in favor of a Republican effort to stop the recounts.

The other route would be federal court. Republicans had long railed against what they called activist federal judges intruding into state matters, yet now Baker was contemplating just that. As his team sat down to argue the merits of filing a federal lawsuit seeking to stop the selective recounts, some members were opposed, including Robert Zoellick and Joshua Bolten, the campaign's policy director, who cited the party's historical beliefs and expressed skepticism about their chances for success. "We run the risk that if we try to fight this battle at the Supreme Court, the liberals will vote against us because we're not liberals and the conservatives will vote against us because they're conservatives and will want to show constitutional deference to the state," Bolten remembered arguing. They speculated about whether Justice Antonin Scalia would decide that the court did not have jurisdiction and whether Justice Sandra Day O'Connor, a former state legislator, would resist federal intervention.

But Theodore Olson and others advocated trying anyway. Whatever the party's principles, they had to make a cold-blooded decision about the best way to achieve victory. Olson suggested taking a stand on equal protection and due process, making the case that each county would be judging ballots by different standards, with some accepting ballots with hanging chads, for instance, and others rejecting them. How could an election turn on such arbitrary differences between counties? How could the rules be changed after the election? Would that not disenfranchise some voters but not others?

Baker pressed Olson. "He asked tough questions," Olson said. "Should we, the Republicans, be running to court? Because the whole idea of, well, things should be decided in the political realm and we shouldn't run to federal judges for everything—so was it the wrong thing for Republicans to do? But we felt, and I felt, that we had to, because the thing was spinning out of control." Baker was not a constitutional scholar, but it sounded like a reasonable argument to him. And in keeping with a career of pragmatism over philosophy, he was perfectly comfortable dispensing with the federalism argument if it meant preserving Bush's victory. "At the end, he said something to the effect of, 'We've got a 30 percent chance of winning,'" recalled Benjamin Ginsberg, the campaign general counsel.

Baker took the matter to Bush and Cheney by telephone. Bush did not hesitate and signed off on the strategy. But the second-guessing continued even after the federal district court agreed to take the case, all the way to the morning of the hearing. "We were still debating this in the car on the way to court," Olson said. With Baker sitting next to him, on the phone with Austin as the campaign still argued about pulling the plug, Olson expressed exasperation. "We cannot have the whole world here watching and we decide we are going to do this thing and then decide we are not going to do this thing," he erupted.

As Olson got out of the car and made his way past all the television news trucks into the courthouse, the question was still unsettled. They arranged a system where the decision could be communicated to him in the courtroom. Finally, Ginsberg slipped in and gave him the word: "Yes, we are going forward." Olson stood up and made his argument.

LIKE OTHERS WHO had rushed to Florida in the crazy hours after the election, Baker did not imagine that he would be there for long. He had plans for a pheasant-hunting trip in Britain the following weekend with George H. W. Bush, Norman Schwarzkopf, and Prince Bandar bin Sultan, the Saudi ambassador. Cheney had originally been scheduled to go too, until he was tapped for the ticket. "My dad called and he goes, 'I have to go to Florida but just for a few days,'" Doug Baker said. "He goes, 'I'll be back, so still plan on going hunting this weekend.' And then about two days later, 'Well, we're going to push our hunting trip back.'"

Baker set himself up in the third-floor office of the George Bush Republican Center, the brick state party headquarters about three blocks from the State Capitol. Joe Allbaugh was in a corner office next to him, while Margaret Tutwiler was in a corner office across an open area and Robert Zoellick a little farther down. Among those who arrived to help were Frank Donatelli, who ran Baker's 1978 campaign for Texas attorney general and later worked in the Reagan White House, and John Bolton, a conservative Yale-trained lawyer with a trademark bushy mustache who had worked for Baker at the State Department.

Within a matter of days, Baker had not only reassembled much of his old team but essentially built a top-drawer law firm from scratch. By the end, he would enlist about fifteen lawyers, eight legal assistants, and seven secretaries from Baker Botts, not even counting Theodore Olson, the lawyers already on the ground like Benjamin Ginsberg, and the Florida lawyers who were recruited for their knowledge of state law. Joshua Bolten sent three aides who had been Supreme Court clerks. Doug Baker would come for a week to pitch in. Among those who worked on the effort were Republicans who would go on to serve as members of Congress, ambassadors, cabinet officers, and White House officials. Two of the attorneys on Baker's pickup team would later serve on the Supreme Court, John Roberts and Brett Kavanaugh.

As he had in two White Houses, three cabinet departments, and five presidential campaigns, Baker imposed a structure and order that resulted in crisp decisions. Where the Democrats had the same lawyers arguing in both state and federal courts, Baker assigned different attorneys to different courts so they could specialize. Every morning he had a meeting with top advisers and then convened a conference call with Bush back at his ranch in Crawford, Texas, or the governor's mansion in Austin, where he was awaiting the results of the recount, and Cheney, who had returned to Washington to begin assembling an administration in case they held on to their victory.

Baker was the field marshal mobilizing the troops, the chief strategist calling the shots. No one questioned his authority. "He can give you a look or a one-word response that puts you in your place," Andy Card remembered. When Karl Rove and Don Evans at the Austin campaign headquarters pushed back on one request during a phone call, "Baker's response," Rove recalled, "was swift and brusque: Hell, if we weren't going to agree, we could get our butts to Tallahassee and run the recount battle ourselves." Baker then hung up.

The flurry of activity kept everyone so busy that most days Baker and the team ate only delivered meals at the headquarters on paper plates using plastic utensils. On weekends, they broke up the tension by tossing around Nerf footballs—Baker had a tight spiral. Baker kept both Bush and his father up to date by telephone. At one point, the former president called for Baker seeking an update just before going into surgery at the Mayo Clinic for a hip replacement.

Tallahassee, a provincial state capital rarely at the center of the national universe, was not at all ready for the influx of high-profile Republicans and Democrats, and hordes of media who had descended to cover the never-ending 2000 election. On the second weekend in town, Baker and his colleagues were kicked out of their hotel rooms because of the annual Florida–Florida State football game; fans had booked the rooms months in advance. The Republicans eventually found a condominium where Baker would stay the rest of his time there.

Every day seemed to mix momentous legal clashes with circuslike political theater. Jesse Jackson came to lead a rally in West Palm Beach, complaining that black and Jewish voters were being disenfranchised. Baker sought his own street-level foot soldiers. Roger Stone, the self-described dirty trickster with a Richard Nixon tattoo who would later become famous as an adviser to Donald Trump convicted of lying to Congress, said he received a call from Margaret Tutwiler, who had been told by Baker to enlist his help. (Baker and Tutwiler later said they did not recall this but it was possible.)

Baker also deployed Republican heavyweights such as Bob Dole, Governor Christine Todd Whitman of New Jersey, and a slew of other politicians to argue their case to the broader public. He sent a young campaign aide named Ted Cruz to Philadelphia to bring Senator Arlen Specter down but Specter rejected the script and had his own points he wanted to make. "Baker says, 'No, no, that's not what we need you to say,'" Cruz recalled. Specter demurred, but then headed to the cameras and made his original points, saying "exactly what he wanted to say." One person Baker could not get to come to help validate the cause was his old friend Colin Powell, who had been tapped by George W. Bush as his prospective secretary of state and did not want to tarnish himself in partisan politics. Baker grumbled at that one; *he* was a former secretary of state and here he was doing his part.

The public perception, Baker understood, mattered as much as the legal skirmishing. It would do no good to win in a court of law but lose in the court of public opinion. The Democratic argument for recounts was compelling. "We're getting killed on 'count all the votes,'" Baker told his fledgling team on the day he arrived in Tallahassee. "Who the hell could be against that?" Baker likewise recognized that whatever happened, they had to preserve the count while Bush was still ahead. A Gore lead at any point would muddy Baker's message that Bush had won the election and the Democrats were trying to steal it. "We needed for Bush and Cheney to maintain their slim lead, because if the other side, Gore, ever got ahead, because of the way the press views Democrats versus Republicans, it wouldn't matter what we did after that because we would drown in negative publicity," said Irvin Terrell, a Baker Botts lawyer who joined the legal team in Florida. Eventually, Republicans printed up blue signs that looked at first like "Gore Lieberman" campaign placards but instead said, "Sore Loserman."

Warren Christopher was no match. Baker's Texas friend Robert Strauss used to call Christopher, invariably turned out in a fastidious pinstripe suit with a crisp pocket square, "the undertaker." Michael Powell of *The Washington Post* described him as "looking like one of those freeze-dried

Incan princes found atop an Andean volcano." At one point while Christopher was on television making a statement, someone watching at the Bush headquarters in Florida mused drolly about what would happen "if Warren Christopher were alive to see this."

None of which was especially fair or generous to Christopher; everyone on both sides considered him a thoroughly decent, honorable man. But he did not have Baker's political sense, or ability to project confidence and competence. "He looked strong, Chris looked weak," Bill Daley said years later. "Democrats started to trash Christopher as not mean enough, not tough enough, not nasty enough."

The difference resonated with the public. Some 51 percent of Americans in one poll said they agreed with the arguments that Baker had been making, compared with just 42 percent who sided with Christopher.

AS THE NATION WATCHED with a mix of fascination and horror, election officials in Florida went through the laborious process of recounting votes, holding disputed ballots up to see whether light would come through a punched card or not, while Republican and Democratic observers sat beside them arguing over practically each ballot.

By the time the recount battle was all over, forty-seven lawsuits had been filed by the various combatants. Baker's goal through these hand counts was to shut them down and, if that were not possible, at least to limit the number of new votes counted. His team argued for the most stringent standard possible to determine whether a ballot should be deemed valid, while Gore's lawyers maintained that every vote should be counted even if it required election officials to intuit the voter's intent.

When it came to absentee ballots sent from overseas, however, the two sides effectively switched positions. Knowing that most overseas ballots were mailed by members of the military who were likelier to support Bush, Baker and the Republicans argued that the authorities should bend over backward to count them, even if they came without a required postmark or signature or otherwise did not completely conform to state requirements. Gore, for his part, was left to argue for the strict letter of the law. By the time the absentee ballots were counted, Bush's lead crept back up to 930 votes, as Baker had imagined it would.

On the morning of November 20, the Florida Supreme Court took up the question of whether Katherine Harris should consider handrecounted ballots before she certified the results of the election. Baker and Christopher both arrived at the courthouse for the hearing but never shook hands and sat on opposite sides of the chamber. Just before the proceedings were to start, Benjamin Ginsberg handed Baker a typewritten note that he had been given by an intermediary showing that the justices had already decided informally among themselves in Gore's favor and had even written a draft opinion. Hand-counted ballots would be included and the deadline for certification would be extended until Sunday, November 26. The hearing was just a show.

Baker showed the note to Michael Carvin, a longtime Washington lawyer who was about to argue the case before the justices.

What should I do? Carvin asked.

"Just answer their questions and let's get out of here," Baker whispered.

Carvin did. "We all knew I was a sacrificial lamb before we saw the note," he said later, but his goal then "was to lose and lose big," to bait the Florida court into writing a decision so extreme that it would draw the United States Supreme Court into the fray.

The Florida court obliged; its decision came down late the next night. Baker was hardly surprised but he was still livid. When he appeared around midnight to address reporters, his anger showed. For the first time in the showdown, some of the journalists thought he looked his age. "Two weeks after the election, that court has changed the rules and has invented a new system for counting the election results," Baker told the reporters as cameras recorded the scene. "So one should not now be surprised if the Florida legislature seeks to affirm the original rules."

That was seen, rightly, as a threat—Baker was saying that if the Florida courts were going to try to take away the election, he had a trump card in the form of the state's Republican-controlled legislature. The specific remedy he seemed to be suggesting was that lawmakers could pass a bill effectively overruling the court's interpretation of the law.

But unspoken was an even more provocative scenario in which the legislature could vote to seat its own set of electors for the tally of the Electoral College, bypassing any further counting of the ballots and guaranteeing Florida's electoral votes for Bush. In truth, Baker did not want to pull the trigger on such a move; he knew it would hobble Bush's presidency by raising questions about its legitimacy from the start. "He wanted the threat but he didn't want the legislature to pick the electors," Frank Donatelli said years later. "But it did help to shape the overall environment."

When Baker strode back into the recount team's headquarters following his angry outburst, he received a standing ovation. But he drew condemnation from the other side. In *The New York Times*, the columnist Anthony Lewis wrote a piece headlined "Playing with Fire," going so far as to compare Baker to George Wallace and other Southern governors who defied court rulings ordering desegregation. "When a court speaks, presidents accept," Lewis wrote, listing several examples. "So it is dangerous business when a man who would be president tries to delegitimize a court. And it is despicable when a lawyer as senior and powerful as Jim Baker denounces a judicial decision against him and says it will be muscled in the legislature." In a subsequent book on the recount, the journalist Roger Simon wrote that the episode showed how far Baker was willing to take the fight. "Maybe Al Gore was afraid of scorching the earth, but not Jim Baker," Simon wrote. "He would not only scorch it, he would roast it in the fires of righteous indignation."

The day after the Florida Supreme Court ruling, hundreds of protesters massed on the plaza outside the office building where the Miami-Dade supervisor of elections was conducting the county's recount, egged on by Roger Stone and others. When the canvassing board decided to move the counting from the eighteenth floor, where observers were able to watch, to a smaller room on the nineteenth floor, anger exploded into shouts and threats. A couple dozen Republican protesters, many of them congressional aides or other operatives flown into the state, pounded on a desk, pumped fists in the air, and loudly demanded that the county's recount be halted. "Voter fraud!" they shouted. "Let us in!" The confrontation would later be dubbed the Brooks Brothers Riot. But it seemed to have an impact. Miami-Dade officials stopped their recount, attributing the decision to a determination that they would not meet the deadline even after it was extended by the Florida Supreme Court, although one official acknowledged the public pressure had been a factor.

AMID THE DRAMA, Baker learned that the Democrats had recruited David Boies, who rose to fame leading the federal government's landmark antitrust case against Microsoft and was considered perhaps the country's most celebrated trial lawyer. Baker decided he needed reinforcements. He had aides contact two partners from Baker Botts who had gone up against Boies before, Irvin Terrell and Daryl Bristow. Terrell, who had won two cases against Boies, was hesitant and put off the caller. The intermediary then called back "and delivered the following message with not a lot of finesse, and that was that Secretary Baker understood that in my business, trial lawyers prize courage and that if I was a trial lawyer, then I would come." Terrell got on a plane for Florida the next day. Bristow made the trip too. Soon after so did Phil Beck, another prominent attorney.

To the surprise of many, the United States Supreme Court agreed to hear the appeal. But then, on Sunday, November 26, before hearings could be held in Washington, Katherine Harris certified the results of the election concluding that Bush had won the state by 537 votes—and therefore the presidency. "I hereby declare Governor George W. Bush the winner of Florida's twenty-five electoral votes for the president for the United States," Harris proclaimed at 7:30 p.m. Her tally did not include new results from Palm Beach County, which missed the deadline by about two hours and would have given Gore another 192 votes, nor from Miami-Dade, which had halted its recount partway through after finding an additional 157 votes for Gore.

Nonetheless, Baker seized on the certification to declare victory and pronounce the contest over. Speaking with reporters, he noted that Bush had more votes on election night, more after the automatic machine recount, more in the returns initially submitted by the various counties, more after overseas absentee ballots were included, and more even after the Florida Supreme Court extended the deadline and Democratic counties employed what he called "a very loose standard" for counting ballots. "Ladies and gentlemen, at some point—at some point—there must be closure," he said. "At some point, the law must prevail and the lawyers must go home. We have reached that point."

Gore, however, was not about to surrender. He and his advisers were hardly going to accept the incomplete count certified by one of Bush's campaign co-chairs in a state government run by Bush's brother. And so they moved to challenge Harris's decision in Florida court. For the next week, lawyers were in and out of courthouses in both Florida and in Washington, following parallel tracks—Bush seeking to cement Katherine Harris's certification and Gore trying to throw it out and get the recounts going again. On December 4, Bush won in both venues. A Florida judge refused to overturn Harris's determination, a ruling that thrilled Baker's headquarters. It was almost an afterthought when the United States Supreme Court weighed in the same day by unanimously ordering the Florida Supreme Court to explain its earlier ruling extending the deadline for the hand recounts.

Gore went back to the Florida Supreme Court asking it to overturn the lower judge's ruling upholding the Harris certification. Despite Baker's antipathy toward the state high court, he and his advisers convinced themselves the Florida justices would have no choice but to uphold the ruling. Once they did that, it would be over and Bush would be president. But on December 8, the Florida Supreme Court ruled 4 to 3 to order manual recounts in all counties where the machine recount had flagged significant undervotes. Baker was beside himself. "Florida is a state where the zombies don't stay dead," he groused.

With Bush's permission, Baker ordered the legal team to go back to the United States Supreme Court; a day later, the high court voted 5 to 4 to halt the manual recounts until the justices could decide the case on the merits.

BAKER DID NOT GO to Washington for the oral arguments on December 11, leaving the case to Theodore Olson, at that point in his career already one of the country's most experienced Supreme Court litigators. Throughout the oral argument, the five most conservative justices seemed to signal sympathy toward the Bush case. At one point, when Olson might have been conceding a point, Justice Antonin Scalia interrupted and made sure to steer him back to his original position. At another, Justice Anthony Kennedy nudged Olson toward the argument that the justice himself considered most compelling. "I thought your point was that the process is being conducted in violation of the Equal Protection Clause and it is standardless," Kennedy told him. Taking the hint, Olson readily agreed.

The day after the arguments, Baker and the rest of the team in the Tallahassee headquarters settled in for hours of waiting, like an Election Day with nothing to do but sit tight until returns started coming in. Don Evans and Benjamin Ginsberg decided to walk up to Main Street to get their shoes shined on the theory that if they were out of touch something would inevitably happen. It did not. As evening approached, Baker and about a dozen others went out for dinner to a steakhouse popular with state lawmakers and lobbyists called the Silver Slipper, whose claim to fame was its bacon-wrapped prime rib—or, for the health conscious, its bacon-wrapped scallops. They got a private room and had the restaurant staff wheel in a television to watch in case the court delivered its ruling. After a meal spent swapping stories, no news had yet come in, so they returned to the Republican headquarters.

Back on the third floor, they closed the blinds to keep news cameras from getting candid shots. Then the phone rang. The court was about to deliver its decision. "That was one of those sort of heart-pounding moments and everybody got real tense and I remember things getting pretty quiet," Ginsberg said. Baker, wearing a green Michigan State sweat-suit, waited with the rest of the team until the fax machine began pump-ing out copies of the various opinions released by the justices. Joining by speakerphone was Theodore Olson, who had been having dinner at the McLean, Virginia, home of his friend, Kenneth Starr, the former indepen-dent counsel whose investigation of Bill Clinton in the Monica Lewinsky affair had led to impeachment.

The campaign aide Ted Cruz, who had previously served as a Supreme Court clerk, rushed into Baker's office with the opinions, which were com-plicated and unclear at first.

"What does it say?" Baker asked.

Cruz read for maybe five minutes, trying to make sense of it. Then he called out, "It says it's over, we won!"

The final decision was fractured and complicated. Seven justices accepted the equal protection argument that Baker and his team advanced, with Justices Stephen Breyer and David Souter joining the five more con-servative members of the court. But Breyer and Souter believed the solu-tion to the problem was to send the matter back to the Florida Supreme Court with instructions to set a single uniform standard for counting bal-lots. What no one outside the court knew at the time was that Anthony Kennedy, the swing vote, during a closed-door conference had seemed to agree with them, giving the liberals the majority. But Kennedy soon flipped back to join the other conservative justices, deciding that there was not enough time to rectify the matter before the legal deadline to certify the results. Therefore, on a 5 to 4 vote, the court ordered the count to simply stop. Harris's certification would stand.

Journalists on television struggled to make sense of the long opinions live on the air and it took a few minutes for the bottom line to sink in: The recount was over. Bush and Cheney had won. Baker had pulled it off.

The phone rang in Tallahassee. It was Bush calling from Texas.

"Good evening, Mr. President-elect," Baker said with a note of triumph. Around him, the room erupted in cheers.

Bush, who was already in bed in Texas when the ruling came down, had been watching the conflicting reports on television and wanted to be sure he understood what it all meant. Baker assured Bush that the fight was over. He was headed to the White House.

A couple minutes later, Don Evans's mobile phone rang. "It's Big Time," Evans said, using the wry nickname Baker had given to Cheney, who had been overheard using that phrase when Bush referred to a *New*

York Times reporter as a "major league asshole." Evans handed the phone to Baker.

"Hello, Mr. Vice President–elect," Baker said.

"Thank you, Jim," Cheney said. "And congratulations to you. You did a hell of a job." Teasing his old friend, Cheney added: "Only under your leadership could we have gone from a lead of 1,800 votes to a lead of 150 votes."

IN THE END, the official final margin was 537 votes out of nearly 6 million cast in Florida, a difference of just 0.009 percent. Bush and Cheney had lost the popular vote nationally but held on to the slimmest of leads in Florida to win the Electoral College with 271 votes, just one more than needed. The decision Baker had extracted from the Supreme Court accomplished what he needed it to do and he had won on the larger fairness point in a 7 to 2 vote. But since the five justices who made up the central majority in *Bush v. Gore* were the five most conservative on the court, the ruling was indelibly marked by the appearance of partisanship.

Indeed, the justices seemed as focused on the bottom line as they were on philosophical consistency. Conservatives who usually railed against federal court intervention in state matters embraced a novel equal protection argument that they had never before applied to the messy process of vote counting. Liberals who did not typically hold back when it came to second-guessing state decisions they deemed suspect suddenly argued for judicial restraint. As much as justices liked to present themselves as neutral arbiters, they were part of a political system too. Sandra Day O'Connor had been overheard at an election night party bemoaning Gore's apparent victory—"this is terrible," she had said before getting up and leaving the room—and all the justices seemed to be grasping for constitutional arguments to justify the outcome benefiting the candidate associated with their ideological leanings.

For years to come, disgruntled Democrats would accuse Baker of orchestrating the theft of an election. In reality, it was more complicated. Given the confusion of the butterfly ballot, problems with voter rolls, disenfranchisement of African American voters, machine errors, and other issues that resulted in tens of thousands of ballots being thrown out, it seems quite likely that more Floridians who showed up at the polls on November 7, 2000, intended to support Gore. But many of these problems were not resolvable by the counties or the courts in the days after the election. No one, for instance, could arbitrarily reassign votes for Patrick Buchanan in Palm Beach simply because it seemed implausible that they were actually meant for him.

As for the ballots that could be tabulated, two independent recounts later conducted by news organizations showed that Bush and Cheney would still have won even if the statewide hand recount of undervotes ordered by the Florida Supreme Court or the more limited recount in four Democratic counties sought by the Gore campaign had gone forward. Only if the overvotes statewide had been counted would Gore have had a chance—but neither he nor anyone else had requested such a recount given that it had no basis under Florida law. The Supreme Court's decision in Washington did not so much hand the election to Bush as it ended a flawed and problematic process—and did so without the virtue of certainty that would have given Bush's presidency more public legitimacy.

None of that, however, was a given during the climactic thirty-six days in Florida, which came down to a raw struggle for power by two parties willing to toss aside long-held convictions in the quest for victory. No one was better suited to lead such a contest than Baker, who even in the twilight of his career demonstrated his mastery of politics and flexible philosophical moorings. "It's easy to construct a scenario where if it had not been for Jim, we wouldn't have prevailed," Cheney said years after leaving office.

For Baker, it was a moment of vindication. He had rescued the Bush family after failing eight years earlier. There would be another Bush term in the White House after all, albeit for the son rather than the father. "I don't think it was a contrived second chance from the family or a contrived effort by Jim Baker to restore some relationship," Andy Card said. But whatever the intent, he added, that was the effect: redemption. "Once again," Card said, "Jim Baker rode the white horse to lead you to victory."

Was it statesmanlike? Maybe not. But Baker had proved once again that there was no better fixer in American politics.

CHAPTER 29

Grave and Deteriorating

On a blistering hot evening in Baghdad in summer 2006, Baker found himself dressed in a track suit, sitting in an air-conditioned trailer in a fortified compound. He was nursing a vodka, straight up, joined by a handful of other emissaries from Washington who had accompanied him halfway around the world to figure out just what the hell was going on in Iraq. One thing was clear about this latest American misadventure in the desert. "We've got a real mess on our hands," Baker said grimly.

America was in its fourth year of a war in Iraq that was profoundly different from the one that Baker and his generation had waged fifteen years earlier. Suicide bombers were ravaging the Iraqi capital. Guerrillas were ambushing American troops. Iraq was becoming a land of death squads, assassinations, beheadings, and mutilations. In the month before Baker arrived, sixty-six American troops had died, as had an estimated 2,865 civilians. The leadership in Washington was desperate for a way forward—or a way out.

That was where Baker and his companions came in. At the behest of Congress, Baker had agreed to lead the Iraq Study Group, a bipartisan, ten-member commission, along with Lee Hamilton, a distinguished former Democratic congressman from Indiana, to develop a plan to turn the situation around, one way or the other. In Baker's case, the assignment was all the more awkward given that the president he was being asked to aid was the son of his best friend and the man he had helped install in the White House during the Florida recount nearly six years earlier.

As central to his legacy as the first war in Iraq was, Baker had never been to Baghdad. He arrived on a military plane that performed a corkscrew landing, dropping out of the sky at a harrowing pace in tight spiraling circles to minimize the chances of enemy fire. At age seventy-six,

Baker sat up straight, stoic and outwardly unfazed, while some of the commission's young staffers less than half his age worried that they were about to lose their lunch. "It was like, shit! It was still pretty dangerous," recalled Leon Panetta, a former White House chief of staff under Bill Clinton and one of the Democratic members of the commission.

After landing at Baghdad's international airport, Baker and the others were given flak vests and helmets to wear for a nerve-wracking helicopter ride into the city since driving was far too dangerous. As they skimmed over neighborhoods scarred by war, a gunner perched himself at an open window scanning for danger while other helicopters fired off flares to draw away any heat-seeking missiles. Upon landing in the Green Zone, as the fortress section of Baghdad where the American military commanders and Iraqi leaders took refuge from the war was called, Baker and the others were ushered into armored Humvees accompanied by medics in case anything happened. The unsettling arrival made clear this would be unlike any diplomatic mission Baker had made before.

Once safely behind blast walls and barbed wire, Baker and the other commissioners began a nearly week-long investigation of a conflict that had become a festering wound for Washington. After a long day of interviews, they retreated each night to the trailer reserved for Baker to share their impressions over drinks. Baker was searching for a solution that had so far eluded everyone else. As Ben Rhodes, a young aide to Hamilton at the time, observed, "He looked like he was turning a problem in his head that he had never seen before."

While many veterans of the Baker plug-in unit had risen to top posts in the new Bush administration, including Robert Zoellick, Robert Kimmitt, Margaret Tutwiler, and even his son Doug Baker, the former secretary of state had spent the years since the Florida recount removed from the inner circle, watching with increasing alarm as the presidency he helped install headed off in worrisome directions. He had quickly learned there would be limits to his influence with the new team. When word got out during the transition that the incoming president was planning to ask Donald Rumsfeld to reprise his Gerald Ford administration role as secretary of defense, Baker tried to talk Bush out of it, reminding him how his father had believed Rumsfeld had maneuvered him out of the vice presidential sweepstakes in 1976 by shipping him off to the CIA. "All I'm going to say to you is, you know what he did to your daddy," Baker told him. But George W. Bush dismissed Baker's warning and appointed Rumsfeld anyway.

Like everyone else, Baker was shocked at the event that transformed the younger Bush's fledgling presidency. He was at the Baker Botts office in Washington on the clear, sunny morning of September 11, 2001, when he saw the television reports about a plane slamming into one of the World Trade Center towers in New York and then another one smashing into the other tower. From his hotel, he could spot a plume of smoke rising across the Potomac River where another plane struck the Pentagon. Baker had been scheduled to speak that morning at a conference sponsored by the Carlyle Group at the Ritz-Carlton hotel and he assumed it would be canceled but headed over just in case. He found John Major, the former British prime minister, another luminary on David Rubenstein's Carlyle payroll, and they talked about the attack and its implications. The conference ultimately was canceled and Baker spent much of the rest of the day giving interviews to television networks.

As it happened, one of the other people in town for the conference was Shafiq bin Laden, a half brother of Osama bin Laden who represented the family's sprawling, Saudi-based business empire, the Saudi Bin-laden Group. The bin Ladens were one of the most prominent families in the Middle East and Osama was one of more than fifty children of the patriarch Mohammed bin Awad bin Laden. Long estranged from Osama, the family had done business with Carlyle since the mid-1990s, when the American firm solicited $2 million for a fund that invested in buyouts of military and aerospace companies. Baker had visited the bin Laden headquarters in Saudi Arabia on behalf of Carlyle, as had the elder Bush, who had become a consultant to David Rubenstein's firm. With his extensive contacts in the Middle East and his gold-plated reputation in Saudi Arabia, Baker became the bin Laden family's favorite politician. In 1996, when the FBI was looking into the bin Laden family, Bakr bin Laden, another half brother of Osama's and head of the business, called Baker for advice. "Jim Baker is who we call when we need to do business with somebody," Bakr bin Laden told Charles Schwartz, a Houston lawyer who represented the family's interests in Texas.

But now the connection to anyone named bin Laden was instantly poison in the United States. Within a couple weeks of the attacks on New York and Washington, news stories suggested that the bin Laden investment in the defense-related Carlyle fund meant that Osama's relatives might profit from the massive spending on the new war on terror. Carlyle quickly disentangled itself and gave back the bin Laden investment. "The name turned out to be a real doody ball when he did what he did," Baker said later. But the divestment did not stop the conspiracy theories.

With the airports shut down after the attacks, Baker spent a few days marooned in Washington until eventually his longtime aide Caron Jackson and Ernie Caldwell, who had been driving Baker since his White House days, got a car, found some pillows, and stocked up on Oreo cookies. The group drove south until reaching an airport that had reopened. From Charlotte, they flew home to Houston. Over the weeks that followed, Baker watched from a distance as the younger Bush sent military forces into Afghanistan, swept the Taliban from power, and then turned his attention elsewhere in the Middle East.

The Baker family had its own personal tragedy soon after. In June 2002, Baker and his wife were visiting Mary-Bonner in London, where she had moved after graduating from Princeton to study at the Central School of Speech and Drama in hopes of a career in acting. The three of them were getting ready to go on to Greece for a vacation when a phone call came in the middle of the night. Baker's seven-year-old granddaughter, Graeme, Jamie's daughter, had died in a freak accident, drowning in a hot tub after she sat on the underwater floor drain and the powerful suction trapped her as her mother, Nancy, desperately tried to pull her to the surface.

Devastated, the Bakers caught a flight home. "I remember sitting with my dad and the two of us just bawling on the plane," Mary-Bonner said. In a note thanking President Bush for his condolences, Baker wrote: "She was as close to perfect as a child can be and of course our hearts are broken by her loss."

The heartbreak led to one more mission for the former secretary of state as he turned his energy to lobbying Congress to pass a new law requiring all public pools to install safety drain covers and shut-off valves to keep other children from meeting the same fate. It would take five years to overcome the resistance of the swimming pool industry before Congress passed the Virginia Graeme Baker Pool & Spa Safety Act.

BAKER HAD VIEWED the quickening march to war in Iraq with trepidation. He was never a believer in schemes to transform the Middle East and had thought the first President Bush made the right decision not to keep going to Baghdad. Now he saw the second President Bush seemingly eager to finish what his father had not. Baker was talking with the former president often enough to know that the elder Bush was anxious about what was happening too, worried about the possibility that ethnic tensions in Iraq might boil over. But Bush was in the awkward position of not wanting to second-guess his own son, even privately.

On August 15, 2002, Baker picked up *The Wall Street Journal* to find a column by his old friend Brent Scowcroft bluntly warning against war. "Don't Attack Saddam," the headline read. Scowcroft wrote that a war to topple Hussein "would be very expensive" and "could as well be bloody." Moreover, it could prompt Hussein to use his unconventional weapons and destabilize the whole region. George W. Bush was livid at the article, knowing it would be seen as a rebuke by his father's top adviser, and possibly an indirect message from his father himself. Bush railed at Condoleezza Rice, the Soviet expert from his father's administration who was now the national security adviser. She in turn railed at Scowcroft, her one-time mentor, for taking his views public without talking with her first. Scowcroft later dismissed the notion that his article was a proxy for 41, as the elder president was now nicknamed after his place in the presidential pantheon, to lecture 43, the newest president. Scowcroft maintained that he only sent a copy to the elder Bush on the same day he sent it to the newspaper and "he never commented on it one way or the other." But even if true, no one believed it. "The president was honked off, which is why Condi went crazy," said Colin Powell, who had his own qualms as secretary of state. "The real problem was they thought he was a stalking horse for 41."

Baker was also skeptical of the drive to war. But when he finally sat down at his Silver Creek Ranch to craft his argument, he avoided the head-on confrontation Scowcroft had employed, instead wrapping his warning in more diplomatic language. Rather than overtly opposing an invasion, he argued that if it were to be done, it should be done the right way—the way Baker and George H. W. Bush had done it. "Although the United States could certainly succeed, we should try our best not to have to go it alone and the president should reject the advice of those who counsel doing so," Baker wrote in *The New York Times* on August 25.

In the piece, headlined "The Right Way to Change a Regime," Baker urged the president to seek a United Nations Security Council resolution requiring Iraq to submit to anywhere-anytime inspections "and authorizing all necessary means to enforce it." *All necessary means*, of course, was the phrase Baker had used in the United Nations resolution authorizing the first war. "Some will argue, as was done in 1990, that going for United Nations authority and not getting it will weaken our case. I disagree," he added. Instead, having made the effort, he argued, America would "occupy the moral high ground" even if it did go to war.

Like Scowcroft, Baker later insisted he did not write the column at the behest of his friend in Kennebunkport. "I was really concerned that we were making a mistake, so I wrote the piece," Baker said. "I didn't talk to 41 about it. I didn't ask anybody about it. But I didn't write it in the way that Brent wrote some of his stuff." Scowcroft's message "was a little bit more 'how dumb can you be.'" Baker knew the Bushes well enough to know that would not go over well in the Oval Office. So rather than say *don't do it*, he laid out conditions for doing it that would be hard to meet. Some of his longtime confidants, like Margaret Tutwiler, urged him to take a harder line against the war, but that was not Baker's way. "Dad was smart enough to realize he could have been like Brent Scowcroft or Larry Eagleburger and burned the bridge," said Will Winston, his son. "No, you want to still have a dialogue."

Baker's dexterous approach spared him the excommunication inflicted on Scowcroft, who was removed as chairman of the president's intelligence board of outside advisers. Bush and Rice both said later that what made them so angry at Scowcroft was that he had not warned them about his article ahead of time, but neither they nor Andy Card, the White House chief of staff, nor Stephen Hadley, then the deputy national security adviser, could remember for sure if Baker did. "I'm confident that he gave me a heads-up and that'd be the difference," Bush said years after the fact. "The thing that upset us was that the Scowcroft piece came out of the blue." But it was more than that. "I don't remember a lot of people quoting the Baker article," Bush added. "I do remember quite a few quoting the Scowcroft article." In other words, part of what aggravated him was the impact Scowcroft's unvarnished language had on the debate. Baker had made his point without poking his finger in the president's eye. "It was subtle," Card said, "and it was a little more constructive."

Yet as he tried to avoid alienating the president, Baker was taking on his old friend Dick Cheney, the hawkish vice president who had been arguing against involving the United Nations, just as he had back in 1990. Already worried that Scowcroft's argument was gaining traction in Washington, Cheney decided to fight back publicly. Baker's piece only cemented his resolve. The day after it was published, Cheney appeared before the Veterans of Foreign Wars in Nashville and laid out the case against Hussein. Dispensing with the caveats of the intelligence professionals, Cheney stated flatly that Iraq not only had chemical and biological weapons but was trying to acquire nuclear weapons as well, going considerably beyond the consensus among the spy agencies.

"Against that background," he said, "a person would be right to question any suggestion that we should just get inspectors back into Iraq, and then our worries will be over. Saddam has perfected the game of cheat and retreat, and is very skilled in the art of denial and deception. A return of inspectors would provide no assurance whatsoever of his compliance with UN resolutions."

Baker and Cheney had been friends for a quarter century and now, even if they did not mention each other by name, they were conducting a public argument over matters of war and peace. Cheney was the one who got Baker into national politics by recruiting him to be Gerald Ford's delegate hunter. Baker later helped get Cheney into the cabinet by encouraging his selection as defense secretary. They shared a Western sensibility and a passion for hunting. While Baker had always been more moderate than Cheney and the two tussled from time to time in the first Bush administration, they had been partners in one crisis after another. But Baker saw a change. Cheney seemed increasingly hard-line, more rigid than before, and without the counterweight of more moderate figures like Baker and Scowcroft in this new administration, he seemed to hold more sway than ever. Baker figured Cheney had been transformed by the September 11 attacks; what else could it have been? But each of them said later that they never had it out directly. They knew what the other one felt without needing the confrontation. "I'm clearly more of a hard rock than he is," Cheney said with a shrug.

Bush took Baker's advice, but only so far. As Powell had recommended, the president went to the United Nations and won a fresh Security Council resolution demanding that Hussein give up any weapons of mass destruction. But when Bush went back for support for a military intervention, key European allies broke with him and refused to go along. Departing from Baker's script, Bush pushed ahead even without Security Council backing and in March 2003 gave the order that his father had not, sending American forces to Baghdad to topple Hussein once and for all.

IF THERE WERE any hard feelings toward Baker in the White House, they did not last long. Shortly after the invasion, Bush began turning to him for special assignments. One of the first was a personally difficult mission to head off a crisis in the former Soviet republic of Georgia, led by Baker's old friend, Eduard Shevardnadze. A champion of reform in Soviet days, Shevardnadze had now served as president of his home republic for a decade, presiding over a calcified, corrupt system that had become deeply unpopular. The Bush administration was worried that Shevardnadze, or his cronies, would subvert the country's fragile democracy to stay in power.

Baker showed up at Andrews Air Force Base outside Washington one day in July 2003 wearing a Naval Academy track suit, boarded a government plane, and headed off for Tbilisi, the Georgian capital. Along the way, he grilled the officials sent to accompany him as if he were secretary of state all over again.

"When I was secretary, the one thing I couldn't stand is I'd read the intelligence briefs and I'd pull a neck muscle reading 'on the one hand, on the other hand,'" he told Matt Bryza, the National Security Council expert on the region. "Give me your gut instinct. What's going to happen?"

Briefed by Bryza, Baker landed on July 4, America's Independence Day, and headed straight into meetings with Georgian opposition leaders. Then he joined Shevardnadze for dinner. It was an emotional reunion. Shevardnadze had been his partner in helping reunify Germany and bring the Cold War to an end. Baker considered Shevardnadze a close friend. But now it was his duty to deliver a tough message.

"They're looking at each other giving each other toasts," Bryza recalled later. "Shevardnadze's giving a toast and he's got tears in his eyes and he said, 'I really love you, Jim.' And Baker, I think he may have had a tear in his eye too, and he said, 'I love you too. But we've got to do these things.' He was emotional, but really sober."

Baker listed for Shevardnadze steps he should take to ensure a free and fair election. Shevardnadze agreed and Baker, relieved, headed home. But Shevardnadze was now an old man clinging to power. When elections were held four months later, they were widely dismissed as rigged and tens of thousands of Georgians took to the streets to protest. They were led by a flamboyant thirty-five-year-old former Shevardnadze minister named Mikheil Saakashvili. Holding a rose and backed by supporters, Saakashvili stormed into parliament. Shevardnadze gave up and resigned in what was called the Rose Revolution.

It was not lost on Baker that the man who had helped break the back of dictatorship in the Soviet Union had met a similar fate himself. But Baker chose to hang on to the memories of his partner from a different and more optimistic moment. Their meeting in 2003 was "the only negative experience I had with him," Baker said later, "the only time that he really ever stiffed me." When Shevardnadze died in 2014, President Barack Obama made Baker the head of the presidential delegation to the funeral. Baker stood at the service and wept openly for his friend.

Just after the Rose Revolution, Bush tapped Baker again, this time to seek debt relief for the newly emerging American-installed government in Iraq, which was saddled with some $130 billion in obligations from Saddam Hussein's era. Baker suited up and began jetting to Europe, Asia, and the Middle East, convincing the major powers to slash 80 percent of Iraq's debt and pressing its Arab neighbors to do the same. In some ways, it was a mirror image of his tin cup tour a dozen years earlier seeking financial contributions for the first Gulf War.

The larger mission, though, was to repair the damage from Bush's decision to invade Iraq over the objections of America's key allies. "You know, Jim, when you go around and do this debt relief stuff, I don't want you to just talk about debt relief," Condoleezza Rice recalled telling him. "I want you to try to smooth the waters in general."

Baker understood but set one condition. He knew that special envoys were a dime a dozen. He would do it only if he were to report directly to the president. He had to be able to look President Vladimir Putin of Russia or President Jacques Chirac of France in the eye and say he was delivering a message directly from the president. Bush and Rice agreed. To underline that message, they gave him the jet normally used as Air Force Two to embark on his mission—Baker *loved* that he had Cheney's plane—and assigned him a White House official, Gary Edson, as his traveling companion. Now Baker could say that the only other person in the room was an aide to the president; indeed, at each stop, he excluded the ambassador and made sure no cables were sent back to the State Department about his meetings, preserving his confidentiality, his maneuvering room, and his status of reporting only to Bush.

The administration did not make his task easy. Just three days after Baker's appointment in December 2003, Paul Wolfowitz, the deputy defense secretary, announced that firms from France, Germany, and Russia would be barred from competing for any of the $18.6 billion in reconstruction contracts in Iraq—a poke in the eye of the very allies Baker was to court. "This was literally a shit show," Edson recalled. Irritated, Baker nonetheless set out for Europe, stopping first in London, where the British were already on board, and then heading to Paris, where he met with the aggrieved Chirac. Baker's message: *We understand you're disgruntled but now we need to move on.* It was not an apology, no mistakes were admitted, but it was a recognition that the United States needed its friends and wanted to put the acrimony in the past.

Chirac agreed to a "substantial reduction" of Iraq's debt by the end of 2004. But rather than announce that right away, Baker put the commitment in his pocket and flew to Berlin, where he met with Chancellor Gerhard Schroeder. In the country that he had helped knit back together just a dozen years earlier, Baker was revered and so Schroeder agreed to the same language Chirac did. That allowed Baker to announce a three-way agreement all at once—the United States, France, and Germany were at last on the same page again. The announcement was made on December 16, just seven days after Wolfowitz's inflammatory move. "I don't think anybody else could have done this," said Edson.

From there, Baker flew to Moscow, where he got an earful from Putin, who made clear that, for all his public opposition to the war, what he really cared about were Russia's commercial interests in Iraq. Baker got it and within a week an Iraqi delegation made its way to Moscow to promise openings for Russian businesses. Putin was now on board with debt relief as well. Baker later flew to Asia, where there was more resistance. The Japanese agreed only to relieve "a majority" of Iraq's debt, which could be as little as 50 percent plus one dollar. Baker, all Texas charm, said that was wonderful, thank you very much and while we're at it, let's make it "*vast* majority." The Japanese agreed. The Chinese eventually did too, once they received commercial reassurances similar to those given to the Russians. Finally, Baker flew to the Middle East and got his old friends in Saudi Arabia, Kuwait, and elsewhere to jump on the train as well.

Baker's personal entanglements had become more complicated since his days in office. One day after he had been working on the debt relief project for ten months, he got a call from Lisa Myers, a reporter for NBC News who had covered Baker as a White House correspondent for *The Washington Star* during the Reagan era. She was working on a story suggesting that Baker was in the middle of a brazen conflict of interest. The liberal *Nation* magazine had obtained documents showing that the Carlyle Group was part of a consortium seeking to represent Kuwait in its efforts to recover $27 billion in war reparations from Iraq left over from the 1990–91 invasion and occupation. This was at the same time Baker was asking Kuwait to forgive its other Iraqi debt. In fact, the Carlyle consortium proposal was delivered to Kuwait's foreign minister on the *same day* Baker was in town to meet with him as Bush's special envoy.

Baker's mission for Bush did not technically cover Kuwait's war reparations, but his firm was marketing itself to the emirate as uniquely capable of resisting the spirit of forgiveness for Iraq that Baker himself was now promoting. It was beyond a conflict of interest; it seemed like the height of crass cynicism. Baker had spent a career cultivating a reputation for probity and now this deal made him look like just another double-dealer.

When Myers reached Baker, he told her he knew nothing about it. But he recalled adding, "I'll tell you one thing: I'm going to get it canceled before the day is over."

Baker called David Rubenstein. "Dave, you told me you would never embarrass me and you haven't until now," he said. But the proposal to Kuwait was "a direct conflict" with what he was doing for the president.

Rubenstein vowed to extricate the firm. "It will be canceled before the day is out," he promised Baker. And it was.

Rubenstein said years later that "I thought it was kind of a crazy deal" anyway and that "it was my mistake" because he should never have let it go forward.

Myers ran her piece on *NBC Nightly News* on October 13, 2004, and it did not make Baker or Carlyle look good, but she included Baker's denial that he knew anything about the deal. "This was like the most boldface influence peddling that I've seen in black and white over decades," Myers said years later. Yet she accepted Baker's denial. "One thing Jim Baker isn't is clumsy. That proposal is so over the top that it was really hard to believe that he or any of his immediate staff had ever signed off on it."

JUST BECAUSE he was jetting around the world on Dick Cheney's plane did not mean that Baker had finally gotten behind the whole Iraq adventure. He could hardly help being disturbed by the military setbacks as the scenes from the desert turned increasingly bloody.

While Saddam Hussein and his brutal Ba'athist regime had been shoved out of power, a collection of nefarious forces was building momentum against the foreign occupiers, including Iraqi troops left without work by the American-ordered de-Ba'athification program, Shiite extremists asserting themselves after decades of minority Sunni rule, and Al Qaeda terrorists flocking to Iraq from around the region eager for a showdown with the United States. Even worse, American inspectors had found no weapons of mass destruction, meaning the war had been waged by the Bush administration on false assumptions.

The ambivalence Baker felt at the time of his *New York Times* op-ed was hardening into a conviction that the war had been ill advised from the start. "I think he thought going into Iraq was a mistake," said his son John Baker. What the original Bush administration had worried about with Iraq in 1991—that if you break it, you own it, as Colin Powell had once told George W. Bush—had come to pass and there appeared no easy path to victory. The swift and satisfying removal of Hussein's government was evolving into a grinding guerrilla war. In hindsight, the decisions of his generation seemed vindicated. Since the end of the Gulf War, Baker had found himself constantly challenged by those asking why they did not keep going all the way to Baghdad. Lately, he noticed, no one was asking.

Not long after he visited Europe as part of his debt relief and relationship repair mission, Baker sat down with an old acquaintance and opened up about his frustrations with the Bush administration—and indulged in a little told-you-so valedictory. "The decision not to go to Baghdad in 1991 is looking pretty good right now, isn't it?" he told the acquaintance. The "big mistake" that the second President Bush had made in Iraq, Baker continued, was the decision to "go it alone" in the war. Baker noted that he talked all the time to people in the administration, including Powell, Rice, and others.

"You haven't mentioned the person who's actually running things," the acquaintance noted.

Oh, you mean my hunting partner? Baker said slyly. By which, of course, he meant Cheney.

Cheney, Baker said, had pushed similar views back during the first Bush administration. The difference was he did not prevail. Even before the first Gulf War, Baker recalled, Cheney did not want to go to the United Nations for support. "I won on that one," Baker recalled. Cheney did not want to force Israel to the table in Madrid after the war either. "I won on that too." The reason, he explained, was that the first President Bush protected Baker in a way that his son had not protected Powell. The problem for Powell now was that he had lost too many fights. "You can't be losing all those arguments and still be effective," Baker observed. "He should have said, 'I'm out of here,' a long time ago."

Cheney, on the other hand, should never have been allowed to have a sizable foreign policy staff of his own, Baker concluded. He was not supposed to be in the chain of authority, Baker noted. A seat at the table, yes, but not such a commanding one. If I were secretary of state, Baker added, I would not tolerate it. Could you imagine me permitting that sort of thing? Dan Quayle with a huge foreign policy staff?

Cheney and Donald Rumsfeld were the guys who handed George W. Bush this "doo-doo ball" in Iraq, Baker told his friend, and the president was well aware that Cheney and Rumsfeld were responsible for the mess. Let me tell you, Baker underlined, *he knows*.

Baker, of course, said none of this publicly. He remained a loyal soldier for the Bush family. He would stew and simmer in private, but he would not speak out. And Bush appreciated it. Baker's efforts to wipe away Iraq's debt reminded the president and his team how useful the former secretary of state could be. Bush made a point of stroking Baker, even inviting him and Susan to spend the night at the White House when they came to town for Ronald Reagan's funeral in June 2004—a gesture neither Reagan nor Bush's own father had ever extended to Baker.

A few days later, Bush went even further and tried to get Baker to join his team full-time. He had Cheney call to see if Baker would take over the CIA now that its director, George Tenet, was stepping down. Baker had little interest in running the spy agency, which hardly seemed like a step up after secretary of state. But he gave a political reason for declining the offer. "I don't think I should be considered for the CIA job, particularly at this time given the Florida recount events of 2000," he told Bush in a handwritten letter.

The president, however, was not done with Baker yet. A few months later, the former secretary of state was once again tasked with bringing finality to an election for Bush. The incumbent president had run a tough reelection campaign against Senator John Kerry of Massachusetts, one marked by ugly attacks on the Democrat's service in Vietnam. While Bush won Florida without a doubt this time, election night in November 2004 came and went without a concession or a claim of victory. This time, the race was close in Ohio, although nowhere near as tight as it had been in Florida four years earlier.

The morning after the election, as Kerry briefly contemplated seeking a recount, Andy Card called Baker from the White House, catching him on the way to the dentist. Recalling with dread the thirty-six days in Talla-hassee, Baker's first thought was: *Please, Andy, don't ask me to go to Cleveland.*

But Card was seeking a more modest intervention. Would Baker call Vernon Jordan, the longtime lawyer and power broker who had handled debate negotiations for the Democrats, and ask him to convince Kerry that it was time to fold his tent? Baker tracked Jordan down at the Amen Corner at the Augusta National Golf Club. Jordan agreed to call Kerry, but suspected the candidate was already getting ready to concede, which he did shortly thereafter.

With another term secured, Bush began contemplating changes to his team. Colin Powell had already said he would leave and Bush planned to replace him with Condoleezza Rice, who in turn would be succeeded as national security adviser by Stephen Hadley. The real question was whether he would take the opportunity to replace Donald Rumsfeld at the Pentagon as well. Brash and headstrong, Rumsfeld had been blamed by many for the deteriorating conditions in Iraq. Card suggested Bush tap Baker to take his place. But Rumsfeld had Cheney's unwavering support and Bush could not bring himself to fire his defense secretary, seeing it as an act of disloyalty.

Baker weighed in on the war from the outside from time to time, all the while careful to protect his relationship with the Bush family. In a speech in January 2005 at Rice University, Baker suggested it was time to begin getting out of Iraq. He was not advocating that America simply cut and run. "But we should be prepared to begin thinking about a phased withdrawal as Iraqi forces assume more of the burden and the security situation improves," he said. "Any appearance of a permanent occupation will both undermine domestic support here in the United States and play directly into the hands of those in the Mideast who, however wrongly, suspect us of imperial designs."

When the speech generated headlines, Baker quickly dashed off a letter to the president, disputing the interpretation of "some of our friends on the Left" that he was breaking with Bush's war policy. "I think you know I have always been very careful to avoid creating the perception that I am being critical of the administration in any way," he wrote. "And so I wanted you to know the truth."

Bush quickly reassured him with a handwritten note addressed to "Jimmy" that he was not upset. "Your 1/11/05 speech articulated our policy in Iraq. I could not have said it better. Thanks for the friendship."

If Bush were quietly perturbed, it did not stop him from circling back to the idea of bringing Baker into the government for a final tour at Washington's heights. As the war turned even bloodier, pressure mounted for Rumsfeld to go. Around Thanksgiving 2005, Bush again thought about replacing him with Baker. "He'd shown himself to be loyal and supportive of the president," said Hadley, "and nobody had any doubt that if Baker had been secretary of defense, he knew how the game works, he wouldn't be back-channeling advice from 41, he would be loyal and would serve 43 as president, no question about that."

One day, Baker got a call from said 41, telling him his son did in fact want him to take over as defense secretary. Baker thought about it for a couple days. If he took the job, he would be the only person in American history to serve as secretary of state, treasury, and defense. But Baker decided against it. Counting his time as acting commerce secretary, he had already run three cabinet departments. "I was seventy-five years old," he said later. "I said, 'Thank you, but I can't do it.' It would have been awfully hard to go back in government at that age." That was the reason he gave

Bush, anyway. What he did not say was that he knew his mission would be to salvage a war that he basically opposed. He did not relish the idea of fighting his friend Cheney day in and day out.

Few on the outside knew of the spurned entreaties. As the scale of the Iraq debacle became clear, Baker found himself regularly importuned to get involved. Sitting on an airplane in Washington waiting to take off one day, he was approached by Mark White, the Democrat who had beaten him for Texas attorney general in 1978 and later went on to become governor. The two had been friendly ever since their race. White gave him a little grief about his friend's son.

"Jim, you need to get off this plane and get down to that White House and straighten this thing," White said.

"They don't want me down there," Baker replied.

The truth was that they did.

THE ONES WHO did not want him anymore were his longtime patrons at the Carlyle Group. The past three years had been difficult for David Rubenstein and his partners as the private equity firm was associated first with Osama bin Laden's family and then with the increasingly unpopular Bush administration. The liberal provocateur Michael Moore highlighted Carlyle's since abandoned ties to Saudi Arabia in his 2004 antiwar movie *Fahrenheit 9/11*, essentially arguing that George W. Bush's administration had been soft on Saudi terrorism because of the financial interests of Baker and George H. W. Bush. The firm had come to be seen as something nefarious, "the CIA of the business world—omnipresent, powerful, a little sinister," as *The Washington Post* put it in 2003.

By the spring of 2005, Rubenstein decided it was time for a clean break. The elder Bush had already left the firm in 2003 and now Rubenstein approached Baker and asked him to step aside too. Rubenstein suggested that he could tie his retirement to his seventy-fifth birthday without drawing too much attention. It was an awkward conversation for Rubenstein, who still deeply admired Baker. The former secretary of state was not happy, but understood the situation. For Baker, it was the end of a lucrative arrangement that had put tens of millions of dollars in his pocket.

Turning his attention back to his legacy, Baker set about writing a second memoir, this one about his life in politics. If his first book was self-consciously sober and dutiful, this one would be a livelier account of his time in power. But Baker still wrote with the caution that had marked his long career. In particular, he went out of his way to avoid saying anything meaningful about the one issue that was dominating American society, the war in Iraq, much to the frustration of his publisher.

"You dip a very, very, very cautious toe into the water when addressing Iraq II" and in fact the draft of the book was "so cautious and nondescript that you might as well not be saying anything at all!" Neil Nyren, his editor, wrote him in an email. Nyren said he could understand loyalty "but when even Brent can no longer contain himself (among others), readers are simply going to expect something more from you." Without it, he added, he would be doing a "grave disservice" that "could have a serious effect on the book's reception as well."

Baker bristled. "I think what he really wants is for me to do something controversial. Iraq," he wrote his own team the next day. "Not going to do that."

His advisers tried to get him to change his mind. But Baker would not budge. He wrote Nyren saying that he had nothing new to say about foreign policy that was not in his original memoir. On Iraq, "we foresaw happening some of the problems that are occurring today, which is one reason we didn't go to Baghdad in '91" and why he wrote the 2002 op-ed. "The situation *is* evolving and just because Brent can no longer contain himself does not cut a lot of ice with me."

BUT BAKER COULD NOT escape the Iraq debate, try as he might. It was dividing America and increasingly consuming what remained of the Bush presidency. Once again, Baker would be called in to serve the Bush family. A Republican congressman from Virginia named Frank Wolf had returned from a trip to Iraq in September 2005 deeply disturbed by what he had seen and pushed Congress to form a commission to study the war. George W. Bush resisted. "The White House view was once you launch this torpedo, you never know what it's going to" hit, said Peter Feaver, the director of strategic planning at the National Security Council.

But with the war rapidly worsening, Wolf overcame White House opposition and pushed his Iraq Study Group through Congress. Bush grudgingly agreed to accept it as long as the panel was led by someone he trusted—someone like Baker. Before accepting the new post, Baker insisted on talking directly with the president to make sure this was what he wanted. Bush reassured him that he was on board even if others like Dick Cheney and Donald Rumsfeld were not. "We needed frankly a brand name that people would trust," said Condoleezza Rice, "and we needed someone that *we* could trust not just to make it a polemic and somebody to bring all those people together."

The assignment could hardly be more delicate. Baker was being asked to work with Lee Hamilton to find a consensus of Republicans and Democrats in a highly polarized atmosphere about how to turn around a losing war. And he had to do so without sacrificing his own credibility or alienating the family that he had been close to for decades. "It was extremely hard for him," said Ed Djerejian, the Baker Institute director who became a senior adviser to the commission. "This was tough for him because of the family connections. It was tough for him because of his relationship with 41, with Barbara, and then with the whole family and yet he took on this role. But he made every effort that W. blessed the Iraq Study Group formation and he was instrumental in getting W. to say okay."

Even so, Baker knew that it was a no-win assignment. Colin Powell could not believe he would agree to do it. He stopped by Baker's office one day and grilled him.

"You really going to take this on?" Powell asked.

"Yeah," Baker replied. "I hate it but I'm going to do it."

It did not help Baker that the media was heralding his selection as the father's team bailing out the bumbling son. (Not that Baker did not quietly enjoy the ego-stroking narrative; he collected and framed dozens of newspaper cartoons depicting him as the wise man schooling the baby Bush to add to his collection of cartoons from his long career.) "He obviously did not like the way things were going in Iraq, and yet was very loyal to the Bush family," said Hamilton. "Bush 43 would not have been president without Jim and the tie was really strong."

Baker had spent a lifetime navigating the crosscurrents of Bush family politics and figured he could manage this one as well. The main thing for Baker was to stay in touch with the president. That way, Baker thought, he could take Bush's temperature and shape the report so it would not be simply dismissed while making sure there would be no unpleasant surprises for the president. If the commission was not exactly an adjunct of the Bush White House, with Baker heading it, neither was it entirely independent.

Baker selected the other Republicans and Hamilton the Democrats. Baker picked Robert Gates, the old CIA Soviet hand who had been his colleague in the first Bush administration; Alan Simpson, the former senator from Wyoming who was close to the Bush family; Sandra Day O'Connor, the Supreme Court justice, who had recently retired; and Rudolph Giuliani, the former mayor of New York. Hamilton tapped Vernon Jordan; Leon Panetta; William Perry, Clinton's defense secretary; and Charles Robb, a former senator and governor from Virginia. When Giuliani failed to show up for meetings, Baker kicked him off the panel and replaced him with his old White House adversary Ed Meese, seeing him as a credible link to conservatives in Congress. It was a who's who list of Old Washington, like a Hollywood reunion of faded movie stars brought together for one more adventure. The average age on the commission was seventy-four. "The only thing we have in common is gray hair," Meese joked.

The commission was unveiled in March 2006 and the world did not exactly stop in its tracks. Its appointment merited just one paragraph in the next day's newspaper and it would take three months to even get modest financing. But Baker and Hamilton recruited four think tanks and a team of forty-four foreign policy and national security specialists to advise them. In the months to come, the advisers would prepare thirty-one papers for the panel and testimony would be taken from hundreds of Iraqi, Arab, European, and American officials, including Bush and Cheney. Baker made clear from the start that it would be a collaboration. At one point, Ben Rhodes, the young Hamilton aide, was told that he would take the lead in writing the eventual report. "I was a Democrat and they didn't care," said Rhodes. "In today's Washington," he reflected years later, after serving as a top adviser to President Barack Obama, "no Republican would let a Democrat write that."

Baker and the rest of the commission set about interviewing key players in the war. One of their most poignant interviews came with Powell.

Baker threw out the first question: Why did the United States go in with so few troops?

That prompted an impassioned, emotional monologue by Powell that went on for twenty minutes. Baker could see how angry the former secretary of state had become, bitter that he had been made front man for flawed intelligence justifying a flawed war. While Baker had emerged from his time as the nation's top diplomat with a storied place in history, Powell knew his long career would be tarnished by a now infamous appearance before the United Nations presenting what turned out to be false accusations against Iraq.

"Well, Colin," Baker said after it was over, trying to lighten the mood, "you're going to have a great book."

After Powell left, Baker turned to Panetta more mournfully. "He's the one guy who could have perhaps prevented this from happening," Baker said.

Whenever the commissioners ended up staying the night in Washington, Vernon Jordan invited them over to his house for dinner, a gathering of elders from across the partisan divide like the famous Sunday suppers at Joseph Alsop's house in Georgetown that Baker attended back in the day. "There was this palpable sense that 'it was better when we all ran things,'" said Ben Rhodes. Baker, first among equals in this group, would volunteer to say grace at Jordan's table. "He thought it was important to bless the food and this fellowship," Jordan said.

The fellowship's journey to Iraq from August 30 to September 4 provided a discouraging appraisal of the American war effort and the prospects for turning it around. Baker and six other commissioners who made the trip met with Shiite, Sunni, and Kurdish leaders as well as American military officers and the CIA station chief. The Iraqis seemed in denial while the Americans were straining to see through rose-colored lenses. The generals said they did not need more forces because this was a political problem that had to be solved by the Iraqis. But the Iraqis appeared unable to bridge their own divide, much less secure the population from attacks. Charles Robb, who had served as a Marine in Vietnam, ventured out of the Green Zone to look around for himself and came back with an even more dismal assessment.

When Baker and the others met with Nouri al-Maliki, the new prime minister, the Iraqi asked just one question.

"Are Americans—Republicans and Democrats—drawing close to withdrawing from Iraq?" he asked. It was a good question.

"You'll have your answer on November 7," Baker replied. Meaning the day of the 2006 midterm elections in America.

The answer on November 7 seemed clear. Tired of war and disenchanted with Bush, voters swept Republicans out of power in both houses of Congress. Democrats running on an antiwar message picked up thirty seats in the House and six in the Senate. For the first time since Bush took office, he faced a Congress controlled entirely by the opposition.

"Jim," Lee Hamilton said when he talked with Baker the day after the election, "I think we have a different ball game."

THE PRESIDENT THAT SAME DAY finally fired Rumsfeld, picking one of Baker's commissioners, Robert Gates, as the new defense secretary. Baker replaced Gates on the panel with Larry Eagleburger. Baker and the rest of his commission soon sat down to write a report that would fit the mood of the moment. Just as the country was increasingly looking for an exit, so was the commission. In a straw poll in September, only two of the panel's forty-four advisers favored a phased withdrawal; by November, just days before the election, half of them did.

Baker's view of the administration's handling of the war was as scathing as everyone else's. "Every interaction they had," said Ben Rhodes, who made a study of Baker as he deliberated with the commission, "betrayed a man who thought the Iraq war was a massive catastrophe, that people in charge should have listened to him and Scowcroft, that this was causing huge damage to American standing around the world, and had broken this delicate balance that he had personally built in the Middle East." It was time for an orderly way out and for Iraqis to take over.

But Baker carefully steered the drafting to avoid alienating Bush. "He didn't want to use language that would irk the president and cause him not to read it," recalled Robb. Some of the Democrats wanted to recommend withdrawing American combat forces by the first quarter of 2008. Baker argued against anything that seemed like a hard-and-fast deadline, knowing Bush would dismiss it out of hand. *Could* was okay, but not *should*. He wanted to condition any withdrawal on "the security situation on the ground." The Democrats went along. Baker also made sure to insert his personal priorities, urging Bush to reengage in the Israeli-Palestinian dispute and reach out diplomatically to Iran and Syria, both major players in Iraq and the broader region, an argument that irritated Condoleezza Rice. "That was really Baker's argument with Condi," observed Peter Feaver. "And that's the one that triggered her" anger.

Robb, a hawkish Democrat, was holding out. He could go along with a withdrawal but only if more American forces were sent first to secure Baghdad, what he and others would call a troop surge. Baker neither embraced nor rejected the idea at first, but it was clear his priority was a unanimous report that would lead America to the exit. "He wanted to make it a constructive vehicle so we could have an honorable disengagement," Robb said. "I thought if it's going to be an honorable disengagement, you've got to right the things that are wrong before you exit."

Throughout the process, Baker had kept in touch with the White House, letting Bush and his aides know where the commission was going even as they filled him in on their own secret internal policy review. Joshua Bolten, who had taken over as White House chief of staff, told Baker in confidence that rather than pull out, Bush might actually send more troops to Iraq. "Look, I think the president is actually going to double down," Bolten told him. Baker realized that if his report was not going to simply be put on a shelf, he had to accommodate that new reality.

Baker was open with Hamilton and the Democrats about his communications with Bush and his team and they viewed his contacts as an expedient way to make sure their recommendations would at least get a hearing in the Oval Office. "Jim knew his way around the White House, knew the players who were there," said Leon Panetta. "Jim wasn't two-timing us; he was basically trying to provide the intelligence on where the White House was going to make sure we would not do something that would be totally rejected." But when Ben Rhodes, young and passionately antiwar, spotted Baker in Hamilton's office on the telephone with Stephen Hadley at the White House going over possible lines for the report, he grew outraged, seeing it as a violation of the commission's independence. "I was upset," Rhodes later recalled. "I went to Lee Hamilton and complained. 'He's up there reading our text to Hadley.' And Hamilton doesn't give a shit because he knows how the world works." One of the ways the world works is that when you are a junior staffer who challenges Baker, there will be consequences. Baker heard about Rhodes's complaint and "he iced me for the rest of the time."

At the decisive meeting, Baker huddled with Hamilton, Ed Meese, and Bill Perry to hash out language that would keep Robb on board without alienating Perry and the other Democrats eager for a withdrawal. In the end, they included a single sentence in the report saying that the commission could "support a short-term redeployment or surge of American combat forces to stabilize Baghdad." Robb agreed.

In trademark Baker fashion, the report had something for everyone to hang on to—a declarative assertion that the war was being lost and that it was time to set a goal for getting out, yet an endorsement of a temporary troop reinforcement. What it lacked in consistency it made up for in consensus. At a time when the two political parties found it hard to agree on a post office renaming, Baker had put together a unanimous, bipartisan report on the most profound issue facing the country.

The day before the report was to be formally released, Baker visited the White House to have lunch with Bush and fill him in. Understanding where Bush was already heading, Baker urged him to read page fifty of the report, which included the sentence about the surge. "Baker hung a lot on that sentence," said Bolten. "Baker was selling that hard and really wanted the White House to embrace it. We didn't reject it. What he wanted and what he was selling, which I definitely didn't reject out of hand, was adopt the report and then do what you need to do and say you're doing this consistent with the report. This will all go down easier. I thought that was a reasonable argument."

But when the report was officially presented to Bush and Cheney in the Oval Office at 7 a.m. on December 6, all the attention focused on the suggested withdrawal in early 2008. "The situation in Iraq is grave and deteriorating," the report opened, offering an unmistakably stinging judgment of Bush's war. "We do not recommend a stay-the-course solution," Baker told reporters. "In our opinion, that is no longer viable." The next day's major newspapers barely noted the surge option, highlighting instead the proposed pullout.

Bush called the report "worthy of serious study" and insisted he too wanted American forces to come home. "I've always said we'd like our troops out as fast as possible," he told a news conference later in the day. But in fact, Bush had no interest in talking about withdrawal, much less Baker's pet priority of diplomacy with Iran or Syria. The report would be politely filed away. "It got characterized both in the press here and in the press overseas as a cover for a withdrawal, as basically a withdrawal strategy," said Stephen Hadley, "and once it got characterized that way, you could see why the president couldn't endorse it."

As Bolten had confided to Baker, Hadley and other White House officials were already developing a surge option. It was a huge gamble, investing even more in a war the American public had already given up on, but Bush announced it a month later during an address to Congress. It generated enormous opposition on the left and considerable skepticism on the right. But over the next year, the tide in Iraq seemed to turn with the influx of American troops along with a change in strategy by the new commander, General David Petraeus, and the enlistment of Sunni sheikhs to switch sides. Bombings, violence, and civilian casualties fell dramatically while American and Iraqi forces increasingly established control. And so, in keeping with John F. Kennedy's maxim that victory has a thousand fathers, the surge suddenly had many claiming paternity. Baker treated the single sentence on the surge as if it had been a major element of the report and advanced the notion that the Republicans on the study group had always pushed for a troop reinforcement, even bringing along Charles Robb in the end. In fact, the Baker-Hamilton report, as it was sometimes called, was seen as the embodiment of the conventional wisdom in Washington that it was time to get out of Iraq—a view shared nearly everywhere except in the West Wing.

In the view of Bush adviser Peter Feaver, the Iraq Study Group was never truly an effort to challenge the White House but rather to help the White House recalibrate the war in a way that would win more public support—or at least buy more time. Baker and the other commissioners were not rebels but institutionalists, and their recommendations were closer to what the White House wanted than was initially perceived. After the election, Bush's team made sure to tip off Baker about the direction the president was heading so the report would not be out of sync. "We could either attack the Baker-Hamilton report or we could smuggle our stuff into it," Feaver said. And through Baker, they smuggled it in.

FOR BAKER, the Iraq Study Group was an unsatisfying coda to a career spent at the center of the action, a master class in how he operated and yet evidence that the man who once ran Washington was no longer in charge. For three decades, he had his hand in nearly every major event in the nation's capital, from Gerald Ford's dramatic convention battle to the end of the Cold War. Time and again, he shaped events that shaped the world.

He was no visionary, no innovator. He articulated no grand plan for the country or the world. He did not start Reagan's revolution, nor the one that later swept Eastern Europe. Yet he figured out how to channel those forces, to harness them and focus them on constructive outcomes while averting potential disasters. He could bring together people who were more comfortable apart and find pragmatic ways to paper over any rifts. There was little idealism involved and a fair degree of opportunism. He was not above political hardball to advance his team's chances at the ballot box. He never lost sight of what was good for Jim Baker and he survived the ruthless arena of Washington. Asked in later years his biggest accomplishment, he regularly joked, "leaving Washington unindicted," a line he lifted from a *Doonesbury* cartoon. But somehow in the main, it worked. Things got done. Little wonder that the country would summon him out of retirement again to fix the Iraq War.

But the second Iraq War brought home what had shifted since his time in power. While Baker could be bold at times, he was driven by a desire to bring stability and order, not to shake things up. He never saw America's commitment to freedom as a mission statement to change a world that was not ready to change, as George W. Bush vowed to do in his second inaugural address. Going after Saddam Hussein for the sake of it was not a Baker goal. He knew the Middle East too well to want to send hundreds of thousands of American troops there for that. Yet he was too much part of the system—and too much part of the Bush ruling clan—to break with a president he had known since he was a boy. His op-ed before the invasion was classic Baker, written in a way so that he could later cite it no matter how things turned out. If the war went well, he could say that he did not oppose it, but only urged that it be conducted in the right way. If the war went badly, as it did, he could point to his piece as a prescient warning against unwise military adventurism. And he did it in a way that got him credit for speaking truth to power—without actually alienating the power.

The report he forged four years later at the depth of the misery in the Iraqi desert was also a deeply political document, unity its main goal over any particular prescription for change. His instinct was an orderly, face-saving retreat. Yet he was not willing to risk shouting into the wind to make a point. Baker, ever sensitive to the politics of the Oval Office, found himself urging more troops at the same time he was urging fewer troops in order to save his access to the president so that he could make a difference. But Washington tends not to look at the fine print. If all politicians were held to a strict interpretation of their own words, the capital would be an empty place.

Baker had tried to finesse the unfinesseable. You were either with Bush or against him on this one. Baker had tried to avoid taking sides, only to make himself and his work a cry in the wind. The Iraq Study Group received the ultimate presidential brush-off—"worthy of serious study," which was Washington-speak for *thanks for the report, we'll be sure to find some shelf space for it somewhere.*

The days were over when Baker's word shaped the outcome of global events. He was one more former, one more voice from the past, dismissed as out of date and out of touch with a ruling clique that he himself had helped install in the White House six years earlier. Iraq was not his fight. He would live with the memory of a better, more optimistic time for America and the world, when walls fell down, and wars were ending, not endless, and people wanted solutions and he was the one who provided them.

Three Funerals and an Election

In March 2016, Baker flew to California for a memorial service that would eventually bring him together with Donald Trump for the first time since the Reagan era. Baker was eighty-six years old by this point and much in demand on the funeral circuit, the "eulogist in chief," as he had taken to calling himself. This one was for Nancy Reagan, who helped bring him into her husband's White House and transformed his life. In his short speech, Baker paid tribute to the former first lady as President Reagan's "closest adviser," the vigilant "eyes and ears" of his White House, who was as "tough as a Marine drill sergeant" in service of her Ronnie. Baker was loyal to those who had been loyal to him and Nancy Reagan had been a patron he never forgot. Without her, he would have been just another corporate lawyer on the make in national politics. But with her support, and that of her husband, Baker had started as a staffer and ended up as a statesman.

At the VIP lunch afterward, though, the focus was on current-day politics and the strange nature of the moment. Trump was barreling toward the Republican nomination. He had demolished George Bush's son Jeb Bush, who had served two terms as governor of Florida and started the 2016 campaign as the front-runner only to be torn down by Trump, branded a low-energy tool of an outdated party establishment. Trump had derided Jeb's father and brother as well, the two presidents Baker had helped into office and with whom he was as closely identified as a family member. On his way out of the race, Jeb had warned—presciently, as it turned out—that Trump was a chaos candidate who would become a chaos president. But Baker was not ready to give up on the Republican Party just because it was embracing this crude outsider.

At the lunch, in a private room at the Ronald Reagan Presidential

Library and Museum where the service was held, Baker found himself with George Shultz, Newt Gingrich, and Brian Mulroney, the former Canadian prime minister who had served alongside Reagan in the 1980s. "I see some eerie parallels to the way Reagan came up and the way Trump is coming up," Baker told them. Not that Trump and Reagan were precisely the same, but they were both disruptors feared by the establishment, and entertainers before they were politicians. They both appealed to disaffected Rust Belt Democrats who saw in their make-America-great-again nationalism a reason to break with the recessionary politics of the recent past. "We thought he was a grade-B movie actor, *Bedtime for Bonzo*, he was going to get us in a nuclear war, and we were scared to death," Baker reflected. "And look at the people he brought into the Republican Party and then I see somewhat the same kind of phenomenon at work here."

As it happened, Mulroney was friendly with Trump, a neighbor in Palm Beach, Florida. When he got home, Mulroney called Trump and told him about what Baker had said. "I think that you should put in a call to Jim Baker and visit with him," Mulroney told him. "He'll give you nothing but the straight talk and good advice." Baker, he knew, was the antithesis of Trump's boorish personality but Mulroney hoped the candidate might take a little guidance from the most prominent Republican wise man.

Trump agreed and had his aide Hope Hicks call Baker's office to set up a telephone call. Baker and Trump ended up talking for twenty minutes.

"I really think you need to be thinking about pivoting to becoming more presidential," Baker told him.

"I hear that a lot," Trump said. "But when I'm under attack, I have to fight back." And as far as Trump was concerned, he was always under attack.

Not long after their phone conversation, Trump's campaign chairman, Paul Manafort, called Baker. Manafort, who had worked for Baker during the 1976 Republican convention before going on to a long, controversial, and ultimately criminal career as a big-spending lobbyist for an array of Russian-aligned interests, asked Baker to meet with Trump. Baker agreed, reasoning that he had met with other Republican candidates. One afternoon, he slipped into the offices of a Washington law firm that worked for Trump's campaign and the two sat down for about twenty-five minutes. Baker handed Trump a two-page list of suggestions for what to do now that he was becoming the nominee.

"You do not need to abandon your outsider/rebel persona. But you do need to bring on board other voters if you expect to win," Baker's memo said. Stop attacking people who might be allies, Baker urged. Don't feed the "shoot-from-the-lip big mouth" narrative he had developed. Reach out to women, minorities, and establishment Republicans. Steer clear of isolationism, embrace a more balanced immigration plan, stop talking about getting rid of NATO, do not advocate a new arms race. Baker recommended following his examples in negotiating the Social Security deal of 1983 and tax reform of 1986. "These suggestions," Baker concluded, "come to you from one who, at the age of 86, doesn't want anything except a Republican president in 2017 who is like the four I was privileged to have served."

The meeting was supposed to be off the record, but it naturally leaked almost immediately. That was why Baker gave Trump the two-page sheet, so that the campaign people could not spin the meeting as a quasi-endorsement. Baker had, in effect, laid out conditions for his support, conditions that Trump would never meet. Baker was recommending that Trump abandon the political formula that had taken him to the brink of the Republican nomination, that had enabled him to triumph over sixteen other GOP candidates. He would not pivot to the center, as the presidential candidates of Baker's day had invariably done. In fact, he would not try to appeal to the undecided middle of Americans, then or ever. He did not care about being presidential. He would never be like the four Republican presidents Baker had served.

Even Baker's flirtation with Trump caused heartache among his friends and family. He got a call one day from Tom Brokaw, the now-retired NBC anchor who had become a close friend to him. "Jim, you do not want to do this," Brokaw warned him. "You served your country nobly and your party admirably and you're at an age and stage, I'm telling you, as a friend, that this is not a good move."

Baker agreed not to endorse until he had thought it over. He was hardly convinced by Trump. "He's probably his own worst enemy," Baker reflected to us one day shortly before the Republican convention. "I don't think he's disciplined enough to do what he needs to do." But, Baker added, "I'm a Republican and I will tell you this—I've always believed at the end of the day there has to be a really overriding reason why you wouldn't support the nominee of your party."

Baker had a ready-made excuse to vote against Trump given the candidate's personal vilification of the Bushes. The Bush family loathed Trump. One day when we stopped by to visit, Barbara Bush scrunched her face in horror at the thought of Trump as president. "We're talking about ego that knows no bounds," she said. Months later, she wrote in Jeb's name on her ballot rather than vote for her party's nominee. The two former presidents likewise both voted against Trump—Bush 41 casting his ballot for Hillary Clinton, Bush 43 for "none of the above."

Yet Baker could not bring himself to. His compromise was not to publicly come out for Trump—no statement, no joint appearance. But in the privacy of the voting booth, Baker voted for Trump. "I'm a conservative," he explained almost with a shrug. Better to have a conservative in the Oval Office than a liberal, "even if he's crazy."

SHOULD THIS HAVE surprised anyone? It did many of Baker's friends and admirers. In recent years, Baker had come to personify an era in American politics when serious figures in both parties could put aside their differences in a crisis, bargain, and lead. He was seen as a representative of a time when Washington was still capable of coming together despite its ideological divisions, a Washington that now seemed gone. "The current sorry spectacle conjures nostalgia for James Baker," *Harper's* magazine lamented in Barack Obama's second term. "Time to talk to a wise man, someone from the days when government worked," Peggy Noonan wrote in *The Wall Street Journal* around the same time. In 2015, PBS produced a documentary entitled *James Baker: The Man Who Made Washington Work*, narrated by Brokaw. At a star-studded charity tribute to Baker at the Kennedy Center in Washington—notably sponsored by every living president and every living secretary of state, regardless of political party—Obama summed it up in a video shown to the audience. "You represent," he said, "what we need now more than ever."

But this was all before Trump. Trump is many things, one of which has been an extraordinary X-ray into the soul of others as they react to him and the challenges he poses to the American political system. In Baker's case, Trump had revealed the limits of the mythology that had grown up around the man. Democrats might embrace Baker's pragmatic approach to the world. But in the end, he was a Republican and that, he told us, was how he wanted to be remembered. His struggle reflected the larger one by the party he had helped build. Once anathema to its leaders, Trump effectively captured the party, forcing it to toe the line, with dissidents crushed or exiled. Much more than in Baker's time, Washington had become a place of tribes, with a permanent war of us against them.

But party loyalty was only part of the answer. For Baker, the decision to vote for Trump was as much about staying inside the tent. What he had learned in a lifetime of wielding power was that on the outside you had none. Becoming a Never Trumper would have meant giving up whatever modest influence he had left; whether he actually needed it anymore was not the point. Baker had succeeded by working within institutions, not by blowing them up. He worked fundamentally with the world as he found it. Baker never challenged the iron rule of his father and grandfather; he became a corporate lawyer and settled into a life of privilege and duty as a pillar of Houston. Had his first wife not died, perhaps he would have remained there.

Still, the ambivalence we found in all our conversations with Baker about Trump was real too. He was personally offended by the sheer incompetence of the man even more than by the outrageous tweets and statements. When we spoke with him shortly after the inauguration in 2017, Baker found the chaos of the opening days unforgivable. Mexico was never going to pay for Trump's border wall. Why would he keep saying that it would? His failure to hire an effective staff grated on Baker. He cringed at the insults to overseas allies and the rise of the same "America First" brand of isolationism and protectionism he had urged Bush to take on in 1992. For a man acutely conscious of the lines of propriety, the myriad ethical scandals surrounding Trump were head spinning, even as they ensnared old associates like Paul Manafort and Roger Stone. Nor was he encouraged when his old nemesis William Barr was tapped for a return engagement as attorney general.

Baker had recommended his friend Rex Tillerson, the chief executive of ExxonMobil, to become secretary of state. "I'm hopeful Trump will listen to him," Baker told us. Trump did not. Tillerson was eventually cast aside, as were so many others. Every few months, we sat down again and Baker would roll his eyes or make a face when asked about the latest Trump outrage. Baker the Handler, much as he hated being called that, seemed to imagine that in the right hands Trump could be managed, but no such handler emerged. Baker could hardly believe it when Trump said he "fell in love" with North Korea's dictator or tweeted in the middle of a special counsel investigation. Baker kept telling himself it was worth it to get conservative judges, tax cuts, and deregulation.

At one point over lunch in the summer of 2019, he confessed that he could potentially see himself voting for former Vice President Joe Biden if he won the Democratic nomination in 2020. By the fall, though, he had changed his mind again. "Don't say that I will vote for Biden," he told us. "I will vote for the Republican, I really will. I won't leave my party. You can say my party has left me because the head of it has. But I think it's important, the big picture." The big picture, he said, was Republicans controlling the executive branch.

Even Trump's pressure campaign on Ukraine to obtain help against his domestic rivals failed to change Baker's calculus. The man who refused to seek foreign help during the 1992 campaign disapproved of Trump's scheme to gain incriminating information on Biden and other Democrats. "Egregious. Inappropriate. Wrong," he said of the behavior that resulted in the president's impeachment, then added, "Not a crime." The Senate, he assumed correctly, would not convict. "But boy, it's hard to defend the antics," he allowed. "That's the only way to say it."

Within a couple months, he stopped even trying. As the country was suddenly ravaged in early 2020 by a devastating coronavirus pandemic that Trump had blithely predicted would simply vanish on its own, Baker went into isolation with Susan at Rockpile Ranch, where he celebrated his ninetieth birthday via a video call with his family. The economy collapsed and millions were put out of work in the worst such crisis since the Great Depression of Baker's youth. The police killing of an unarmed black man touched off street demonstrations and unrest unlike any in a half century. William Barr busied himself intervening in criminal cases to help Trump's friends. Trump fell way behind Biden in the polls. And Baker decided he had nothing more to say about any of it. At long last, he opted to keep out of politics as his grandfather had urged so many years ago.

THE IRONY, of course, was that Baker was an actual dealmaker, while Trump just played one on television. Unlike the forty-fifth president, Baker understood what it meant to get the other side to say yes. He did not view negotiation as a zero-sum exercise in which the only acceptable outcome was grinding someone else into dust. And even after leaving office, he never stopped looking for deals, for ways to make two seemingly irreconcilable positions reconcile. During the second Bush administration, he served as co-chairman of bipartisan commissions to reform the election system and to revamp war powers; his partner in the first was Jimmy Carter, the man he helped run two campaigns against, and his partner in the second was Warren Christopher, his adversary in Florida at the end of another campaign. In 2012, Baker found a way to keep the Episcopal Church of Texas from seceding from the national church over its support for same-sex marriage, letting individual parishes set their own policy for a transitional period. In 2016, he brokered an agreement ending a years-long stalemate over a monument to Dwight Eisenhower in Washington. And in 2017, he teamed up with other Republicans to propose a carbon tax plan to fight climate change.

His zeal for a deal was never as much about the details as about getting to the signature. To his critics, that was a form of cynical opportunism rooted in self-aggrandizement over principle. To his admirers, it was the foundation for progress in a polarized world. As time passed, some of his deals came under question. After Vladimir Putin rose to power in Russia, the former KGB officer pushed a revisionist history of the recent past in which the expansion of NATO into Eastern Europe had needlessly antagonized Moscow and driven it away from the West. Baker was a key figure in Putin's argument because he had told Mikhail Gorbachev during German reunification talks that NATO would not move "one inch to the east." Many papers have been written, think tank panels convened, and op-eds published arguing that Baker had made a commitment as part of what one research group, the National Security Archive, called "a cascade of assurances about Soviet security given by Western leaders to Gorbachev and other Soviet officials" that they did not live up to.

Never mind that it was Bill Clinton and George W. Bush who oversaw the absorption of Eastern Europe into the Atlantic Alliance years later, not Baker. Either way, it was a stretch to ascribe the worsening relations between Russia and the West to NATO's membership drive. It is true that Baker at one point during German unification talks had suggested that NATO would not extend its jurisdiction but he was talking about East German territory and soon backed off that. No such commitment was included in the final treaty that resulted in the German merger. The accord held that foreign troops could not be stationed in the territory of East Germany but German troops assigned to NATO could be deployed there as soon as Soviet forces withdrew. Gorbachev himself said later that "the topic of NATO expansion was not discussed at all and it wasn't brought up in those years," although he did think the approach of the alliance to Russia's front door was a "violation of the spirit" of reassurances.

A more difficult question emerges over the West's failure to do more to help Russia make a transition from its broken Communist system to a functional capitalist democracy. Baker talked about assisting the new state, but he never managed to extract adequate help from Congress or the allies. Even within the administration there was resistance because, in Brent Scowcroft's words, it seemed like "putting money down a rat hole." Baker had a point, of course, that the American people were in no mood to spend the peace dividend on their former enemy. Could Baker and George Bush have changed that sentiment through more assertive leadership? Left largely on its own, the newly democratic Russia in the 1990s ushered in a crony form of capitalism in which well-connected oligarchs made off with valuable state assets while many ordinary Russians lost their life's savings and the social safety net they had come to depend on. No wonder Russians soured on Western-style democracy and instead embraced Putin's authoritarian promises to make Russia great again.

Baker likewise lives with the legacy of his electoral endeavors. While he made a name for himself as a bipartisan compromise artist in odd-numbered years, he spent even-numbered years overseeing campaigns that pushed the boundaries. There is arguably a straight line from the racial fearmongering of Willie Horton and the questioning of Clinton's patriotism over his youthful Moscow trip to some of the uglier, nastier politics of today. Baker's give-no-quarter strategy in the 2000 Florida recount produced what many Americans viewed as a politicized outcome in the Supreme Court. His critics see that election as forever tainted.

Baker expresses regret for none of it. "Willie Horton, you could make the argument," he conceded. But when we spoke further about the 1988 campaign, Baker still wanted to argue his case, noting that Michael Dukakis did in fact run a furlough program and that the Horton ad was not aired by the Bush campaign itself. Would he have done anything differently? "Not a thing," he said. "We won a big victory. The name of the game is to win ethically and I think we did." He made the same argument about 1992, even when they did not win, and 2000, when they did. Indeed, he relished the tough-as-nails image generated by the Florida battle. When HBO aired the movie *Recount* in 2008 (with his actress daughter, Mary-Bonner Baker, appearing as a lawyer working for the Florida secretary of state, Katherine Harris), Tom Wilkinson played Baker as a ruthless, win-at-any-cost operative. Warren Christopher was depicted as a weak-kneed pushover. That was not especially helpful given that Baker at the time was co-chairing the war powers commission with Christopher. "I don't think I'm anywhere near as Machiavellian as they made me out to be," Baker said. But quietly he seemed to enjoy the portrayal.

AS THE END OF HIS ninth decade approached, he relished the opportunity to retreat to the Silver Creek Ranch in Wyoming, the remote spot two thousand miles from Washington that he and Susan had bought after the long, contentious 1988 campaign. On the rough dirt road leading up to the ranch was propped an old rusted door from a Model-T Ford with fading paint broadcasting its straightforward message to outsiders: "No Hunting or Fishing Allowed." The property itself was home to trout, magpies, elk, wolves, and bears, reserved for Baker and his family to hunt and fish. From the 1905 mountaintop homesteader's cabin where he and Susan stayed, Baker could peer out at the horizon in all directions without noticing any signs of human habitation.

Baker spent his summer days cruising across the open land in his Chevrolet Tahoe, past Tibble Rock, across from the jutting stone formation that his family dubbed the JAB Slab and through the meadow to check on his bear bait traps. Wearing a windbreaker with a Secret Service logo and the words "Jim Baker" stenciled on it, he took us on a tour one August day, speeding up and then braking seemingly at random to avoid hidden obstacles, completely familiar with every wrinkle in the land. "I know when to slow down and when to be careful," he told us, a self-assessment that could have applied to his long career in politics and diplomacy as well.

This was his refuge from politics. He did not use email and had never looked at Twitter. For years, he did not even have a television at the ranch, which had power for only a few hours a day from a small generator that he and Susan argued about what time to turn off each night. It had been many years since the government removed the special satellite equipment he had used to speak with the president during the dangerous twilight days of the Cold War.

The family, while still troubled by divorces and other challenges, had long since gotten past the worst of times and come together. At one Thanksgiving, John Baker, the son who had vowed to break up his father's second marriage but now had a job and a family of his own, said during the pre-dinner prayer, "I thank God that my parents didn't give up on me."

Baker spent time exploring. At age eighty-nine, he took an eleven-day driving trip by himself through the Rocky Mountains. He traveled with two of his sons to France to retrace his father's World War I experiences. He went fishing in the Russian Arctic and still drove out to the Eagle Lake Rod & Gun Club in Texas where, he liked to brag, he had been both the youngest member and now the oldest. He got together with the African American cousins he never knew he had until he went to Huntsville, Texas, one day, and met a distinguished-looking elderly black gentleman who told him that his name was James Baker too.

All the while, he worked to build the Baker Institute at Rice. For its twenty-fifth anniversary in 2018, he invited Barack Obama, who headlined a black-tie gala dinner in Houston. With Trump as the hate-tweeting context for their conversation, the Democratic former president and the Republican former secretary of state lamented the passing of a Washington where facts were facts and collective action had been hard, but still possible. "The responsible center in American politics has disappeared," Baker said. Obama nodded vigorously. While he was in town, Obama asked to visit George H. W. Bush, who was declining fast. Baker took Obama to see his old partner.

The Bakers and the Bushes, late in life, had returned to the close friendship of their pre-Washington days. The struggles of politics, of jockeying for power and credit, were long gone. They were, quite simply, family. Baker visited regularly or took the ailing former president out for oysters on the half shell. When Bush, suffering from a form of Parkinson's disease, was hospitalized at one point, Baker defied doctor's orders by smuggling in a small bottle of Gray Goose, his friend's favorite vodka. When Barbara Bush died in April 2018, Susan Baker gave one of the eulogies, recalling how the Bushes were the last ones outside the family to visit Baker's first wife, her close friend Mary Stuart, before her death. As Susan returned to her seat, Baker, tears in his eyes, mouthed the words to her, "You made me cry."

Three days after Obama's visit, on the last day of November 2018, Baker stopped by Bush's house to check on him. The ninety-four-year-old former president had stopped eating and was mostly sleeping. But he roused when Baker strode in.

"Where are we going, Bake?" he asked.

"We're going to heaven," Baker answered.

"That's where I want to go," Bush said.

Bush seemed to rally a bit, as he did again when Baker returned later in the day to see him. But as Baker and his wife were driving home that night after dinner with friends, he got a call urging him to come back. Baker rushed back to the house and found Bush fading fast. He held his friend's hand and rubbed his feet. At 10:10 p.m., with both Bakers and a few other friends and relatives at his bedside, the forty-first president died.

It was the end of an extraordinary friendship, one that had propelled both Bush and Baker to heights of power that neither might have attained without the other. "Having someone there that you totally trusted was a good thing for me," Bush told us before he died. In the end, the story of Bush and Baker is told by two bronze statues erected in recent years at opposite ends of a Houston park, facing each other for eternity.

In the days following Bush's death, the elaborate ritual and choreography of a state funeral kicked in—the lying in state at the Capitol, the televised service at Washington National Cathedral, the train ride across Texas. At the Washington service, Trump showed up, neglecting to shake hands with most of the other presidents. He was given no speaking role but instead listened to others extolling Bush in terms that seemed to emphasize the contrast between the forty-first and forty-fifth presidents.

The next day, at St. Martin's Episcopal Church in Houston, Baker offered his farewell, praising his friend's "decency," his "boundless kindness and consideration for others," his "courage" and "compassion." The contrast with the incumbent president was once again unmentioned and unmistakable.

As he came to his conclusion, Baker, the most disciplined and detached of men, choked up and struggled to finish. "We rejoice, Mr. President, that you are safely tucked in now and through the ages with God's loving arms around you," he said, his eyes welling with tears that few had ever seen, "because our glory, George, was to have you as our president and as such a friend."

ON A WARM TEXAS AUTUMN DAY, Baker took us to his own grave. He was not ready for it yet, but it was ready for him, whenever the time would come. It was in Glenwood Cemetery, the premier resting place for Houston's premier citizens. Located just a few miles from the home that Baker and his wife shared in their years after politics, its rolling ravines and curving pathways gave it the feel of a garden oasis in the middle of what had become a sprawling metropolis.

His father, the stern Warden of Baker's youth, was already there alongside his mother. Nearby was his grandfather, Captain Baker, the savior of the Rice fortune who had led a group of prominent Houstonians to rescue the very same Glenwood Cemetery from receivership shortly after the turn of the century. Baker's other grandparents were also there, as was Mary Stuart and her parents. Just two weeks after our visit, Baker's sister, Bonner, passed away and was buried in the family plot. Two months after that, his cousin, Preston Moore, once as close to him as the brother he did not have, died in a car accident and was laid to rest in the next lot over.

"This is where I'll be," Baker told us, pointing to a well-manicured spot in the ground, just a few feet from his parents. It was part of a small plot surrounded by a low brick wall, with a simple "BAKER" plaque affixed to it. He leaned down to tidy up the leaves.

He seemed content. James Addison Baker III had always known where he came from and he had always known where he would end up. It was everything in between that came as a surprise.

Acknowledgments and Notes

Most of all we want to thank James Baker. He embraced this project from the start, opening his world and the story of his remarkable ninety years to us. Over the course of seventy hours of interviews on twenty-five occasions starting in 2013, he welcomed us into his homes and offices in all the places that mattered to him—in Houston, Washington, and Wyoming. He gave us unfettered access to his archives at Princeton University, his files at Rice University and his most personal papers in his private collection. He provided all the time we requested for interviews and made it possible for us to speak with anyone in his life. He never shied away from any topic nor tried to put anything off limits. This is not an authorized biography—he did not read it before publication and had no veto over its contents (and no, there is no relationship with the authors). But what we discovered was a man confident in his life, assured that for any flaws or failings, his was a story that would hold up well in history, and we appreciated his faith that we would tell it honestly and straightforwardly.

We want to thank too all the people in his life who talked with us, sometimes repeatedly. Susan Baker could hardly have been more gracious with her time and her perspective, meeting us together with her husband and separately. She was candid, welcoming, and invaluable. Likewise, we are grateful to all eight Baker children, each of whom spoke with us, some more than once, and were remarkably honest and forthcoming about their shared experiences: Jamie, Mike, John, and Doug Baker; Elizabeth Winston Jones; Bo and Will Winston; and Mary-Bonner Baker Perrin. We were lucky too to meet and talk with Secretary Baker's cousin, Preston Moore, before he sadly passed away, and his childhood nanny, Bea Green, who was still in touch with the family as she approached her 107th birthday.

This book benefited from interviews with scores of others who interacted with Baker over the years, especially some of his closest advisers, including Margaret Tutwiler, Robert Zoellick, Robert Kimmitt, Dennis Ross, and Janet Mullins Grissom, all of whom were generous with their insights and memories. Presidents George H. W. Bush, George W. Bush, and Jimmy Carter, along with Vice Presidents Dick Cheney and Dan Quayle and Secretaries of State Henry Kissinger,

George Shultz, Condoleezza Rice, Colin Powell, and John Kerry all took the time to talk with us for the book. So did numerous other cabinet officers, White House aides, foreign officials, and even Baker's adversaries—all told, about 215 interviews with about 170 people.

Baker's current staff, including some who have been with him for decades going back to his days in Washington, were endlessly helpful. John Williams, a true professional, always had time for us and there was never a question he could not answer. We could not have hoped for more hospitality from Caron Jackson and Sandy Hatcher at Baker Botts, not to mention the terrific folks at the Baker Institute in Houston, led by Ed Djerejian and including Kim Murphy, Sonja Fulbright, and Ryan Kirksey.

We especially want to thank Daniel Linke, April Armstrong and everyone at the Seeley G. Mudd Manuscript Library at Princeton, which was like a home away from home for two dozen visits over the last seven years as we worked our way through Baker's archives and the remarkable oral history project the university conducted along with Rice University. Dan runs an outstanding institution and this book would never have come about but for him and the material that he made available. Likewise, the Miller Center at the University of Virginia has assembled the best presidential oral history collection in the nation. No book about the modern presidency would be complete without its incomparable work and we're grateful to Gerald Baliles, who has since passed away, along with Douglas Blackmon, William Antholis, Russell Riley, and the rest of the all-star team in Charlottesville.

Thanks too to a host of people who searched their organizations' files for us, including Tonia Wood at the Texas State Library and Archives Commission; Geir Gunderson at the Gerald R. Ford Presidential Library, and Donna Lehman, formerly of the library; Katie Henning at the University of Kentucky; Carol Leadenham at the Hoover Institution Archives; Kathy Ellingsworth at Akin Gump Strauss Hauer & Feld; Louis Jeffries at the Hill School; Sarah Gesell of the Kinkaid School; Joyce Lee of the *Houston Chronicle;* Seth Mandel of the *New York Post*; David Jackson of *USA Today*; Jake Tapper of CNN; Chuck Todd of NBC; and Robert Hendin of CBS. We relied as well on the National Security Archives at George Washington University; the Ronald Reagan Presidential Library; the George Bush Presidential Library; and the oral history project of the Association for Diplomatic Studies and Training.

A number of other researchers and historians gave us access to their files or provided material from their own work, to our enormous benefit, including Derek Chollet, Jonathan Darman, John Gans, Liviu Horovitz, Stuart Middleton, and James Wilson. Thanks especially to Jeffrey Engel, founding director of Southern Methodist University's Center for Presidential History, who knows more about Bush-era foreign policy than anyone and allowed us to profit off the prodigious work he did exploring those four years.

We had the support and guidance of a host of journalists and historians who covered Baker back in the day or have since written books about his time. We are particularly in the debt of Jon Meacham, Michael Beschloss, and Douglas Brinkley, three of the premier chroniclers of the American presidency, who took time out from their own research to advise us and keep us on track. Others who went out of their way to help included Jeffrey Birnbaum, Tom Brokaw, Lou Cannon, Maureen Dowd, Elizabeth Drew, Thomas Friedman, David Hoffman, Walter Isaacson, Andrea Mitchell, Alan Murray, Lisa Myers, Howell Raines, Hedrick Smith, Strobe Talbott, Evan Thomas, and Steven Weisman. Tom DeFrank, who covered Baker for *Newsweek* before becoming his writing partner, paved this ground long before us and his work showed us the way. Special thanks to Mark Updegrove, who in many ways steered us to this project in the first place and then supported it at every stage.

Once again, Cynthia Colonna was an inestimable help transcribing hundreds of hours of interviews. We had research assistance early on from Max Hill and Arthur Sanders Montandon. Kitty Bennett at *The New York Times* is an unparalleled resource for everyone who works with her. A fantastic team of fact-checkers came in at the end and saved us from more mistakes than we would like to admit, especially Chris Cameron, Hilary McClellen, Isabelle Taft, and Jordan Virtue, who looked over so many chapters, as well as Ruairi Arrieta-Kenna, Meg Bernhard, James Bikales, Molly McCafferty, Zach Montague, and Noah Weiland. Needless to say, any remaining errors are our own.

For a second time, Peter had the opportunity to spend a few months on fellowship at the Woodrow Wilson International Center for Scholars, one of the foremost places for research and study in Washington. We are grateful to Jane Harman, Rob Litwak, Aaron David Miller, Lindsay Collins, Laura Deal, and the whole team at the Wilson Center.

We have the incredible good fortune to work at two of the leading news organizations in the country. At *The New York Times*, A. G. Sulzberger and before him Arthur Sulzberger Jr. have not only steered the nation's greatest newspaper through some of the most tumultuous times in the news business, they have along with Mark Thompson built a strong foundation that will sustain it into the future. Dean Baquet and Joe Kahn have transformed the paper into an even more vital outpost of journalistic excellence than ever before, with the help of such talented senior editors as Matt Purdy, Alison Mitchell, Susan Chira, Phil Pan, and many others. Elisabeth Bumiller and Bill Hamilton run the Washington Bureau with tremendous energy, wisdom and determination and are the most supportive editors anyone could ask for. Michael Shear has been the best partner and friend since he and Peter covered local news together three decades ago. The team of Maggie Haberman, Katie Rogers, Annie Karni, and Michael Crowley, and previously Julie Hirschfeld Davis and Mark Landler, should be in the hall of fame.

At *The New Yorker*, David Remnick has proved time and again why he is the finest magazine editor of our time and has been unfailingly supportive throughout. Susan has been privileged to work with many wonderful colleagues there, including the great Dorothy Wickenden and *The New Yorker*'s tireless website editor, Michael Luo, and every week she is lucky to file her Letters from Trump's Washington to David Rohde, an advocate, partner and friend. Susan works beside some of the best writers in America in the magazine's Washington office, especially the indomitable Jane Mayer, Adam Entous, Evan Osnos, and Margaret Talbot.

Both of us have found second homes in the last couple of years in the unlikeliest of places for print reporters—at MSNBC for Peter and CNN for Susan. We're deeply grateful to the hosts, producers and bookers at both places, too many to name here, all professionals at the top of their game who have patiently tutored us in the challenges of live television. We are both grateful too to Jeff Bieber, Robert Costa, Sandy Petrykowski, and the crew at PBS's *Washington Week*, where we have appeared going back more than two decades.

This is the second book now that Kris Puopolo at Doubleday has edited from our household and she has been an unstinting supporter and wise counselor to us, always focused on the big picture, always making our work better. There is a reason she enjoys the sterling reputation she does in the book business. Bill Thomas, the editor in chief at Doubleday, sets the highest standards and we appreciate the faith he has shown in us. The rest of the team at Doubleday is a delight to work with, including the eternally patient Dan Meyer, Michael Goldsmith, Hannah Engler, Dan Zitt, and Michael Windsor. For more than twenty years now, Rafe Sagalyn has guided our literary ventures and no one ever had a more enthusiastic champion. Doug Mills, the most gifted news photographer of our generation, kindly took the author picture for the book jacket.

Our friends have sustained us through long days and nights devoted to this project, offering relief when we came up for air. We particularly cherish our neighborhood village of Martina Vandenberg and Alan, Marshall, and Max Cooperman. Our friends Heidi Crebo-Rediker and Doug and Charlotte Rediker have become like an extended family. So many others have supported us as well, including John Smith, our best man two decades ago and still the best of friends, and Jan Eckendorf; Heather McLeod Grant, who has been there since college and always will be no matter how far away she lives, and her wonderful family Elliott and Somerset Grant; Susan Ascher and Paul Kalb; Katy and Gary Bass; Sarabeth Berman; Leslie Crutchfield and Anthony, Caleigh, Quinn, and Finn Macintyre; Michael Grunwald and Cristina Dominguez; Julia Ioffe; Indira Lakshmanan and Dermot, Devan and Rohan Tatlow; Valerie Mann and Tim Webster; Toria Nuland and Bob Kagan; Nicole Rabner and Andie Kanarek; and Sabrina Tavernise and Rory MacFarquhar.

Our family has always been there for us, loving and supportive in every way possible and role models for life, especially Ted and Martha Baker; Linda and Keith Sinrod; Lynn and Steve Glasser; Karin Baker and Kait Nolan; Laura Glasser, Emily Allen and Will and Ben Allen-Glasser; Jeff, Diana, and Caroline Glasser; Jennifer Glasser and Matthieu, Alex, and Oliver Fulchiron; and Tiffany Hudson. Rosamaria Brizuela is family in every way that truly matters. Ellie patiently waited for walks and treats while we finished up the latest chapter.

Finally, but most importantly, there is Theo Baker. Born on the day we finished our last book together, he has now grown into a remarkable young man, with all the traits too often missing in today's Washington—not just smart and curious, but honest, decent, funny, thoughtful, loving, and eager. He inspires us and fills our lives with joy. It is to him this book is dedicated.

PROLOGUE: The Velvet Hammer

xiv "The point of holding power": James Baker, author interview.

xiv "The argument I've been making": Ibid.

xiv "The guy is nuts": Ibid.

xvii The man she profiled: Marjorie Williams, "Jim Baker Is Smooth, Shrewd, Tough and Cooly Ambitious. That's Why Washington Loves Him," *Washington Post*, January 29, 1989. This profile among others was later included in a classic collection published after her untimely death. See Marjorie Williams, *Reputation: Portraits in Power.*

xvii "a man in whom drive is more": Ibid.

xvii "In the two-party system": Haley Barbour, author interview.

xviii "He was the most important": Tom Donilon, author interview.

xix "Baker somehow understood": Hedrick Smith, author interview.

xxi "Did you get laid last night?": Ed Rogers, author interview.

xxi "A shrink would have a field day": Margaret Tutwiler, author interview.

xxi "somebody who likes making": Will Winston, author interview.

xxi "I didn't have any overarching": James Baker interview.

xxi "The Velvet Hammer": Louise Sweeney, "Reagan's Velvet Hammer," *Christian Science Monitor*, January 2, 1981.

xxi "a gentleman who hates to lose": Michael Kramer, "Playing for the Edge," *Time*, February 13, 1989.

xxii "This is not a man who sat back": David Gergen, author interview.

CHAPTER 1. In the Magnolia City

3 listed simply as "Lawher": Birth certificate, April 28, 1930, Rice University archive.

4 "you have quite a legacy": Preston Moore, author interview.

4 "He was the hero son": Stewart Addison Baker, James A. Baker III Oral History Project, Princeton and Rice.

5 "patriarchal migrations": John W. Thompson Jr., *Huntsville and Walker County, Texas*, p. 7, https://digital.sfasu.edu/digital/collection/Huntsville/id/22.

5 "to attain approbation of my suit": James A. Baker, handwritten letter to Anna McRobert Crawford, June 22, 1853, Rice archive.

5 Baker sat on the committee: J. H. Freeman, Texas State Historical Association, https://tshaonline.org/handbook/online/articles/fbacs.

5 "town of growing importance": Melinda Rankin, *Texas in 1850*, p. 138, https://texas history.unt.edu/ark:/67531/metapth6107/m1/135/zoom/?q=huntsville&resolution =2&lat=2617.5&lon=600.

7 "a place where *justice*": Baker personal files.

7 "oceans of mud, and submerged suburbs": Kenneth J. Lipartito and Joseph A. Pratt, *Baker and Botts in the Development of Modern Houston*, pp. 11–12.

8 "The law firm and the city": Ibid., p. vii.

8 "There is scarcely a great enterprise": Ibid., p. 47.

8 "a dashing handsome person": J. H. Freeman, *The People of Baker Botts*, p. 33.

9 "Residents of every section": "Celebrating Women Who Changed Houston for Good," a history produced by BakerRipley, a nonprofit that helps the less fortunate in Houston, March 8, 2017, https://www.bakerripley.org/blog/celebrating-women -who-changed-houston-for-good.

10 "America's most remarkable": Martin L. Friedland, *The Death of Old Man Rice*, p. ix.

10 "a penniless youth": Thomas M. Phillips, a partner at Baker Botts, in a paper he wrote on the life of Captain Baker, July 25, 1983, Princeton archive.

10 "under very suspicious circumstances": Ibid.

11 "wily, astute and crafty lawyer": Friedland, *The Death of Old Man Rice*, p. 208.

11 "gross miscarriage of justice": Ibid., p. 335.

11 A law professor who examined: Researching the case for his book nearly a century later, Friedland, a Toronto law professor, started out assuming that Patrick was guilty

of murder, but concluded that the chloroform story was likely "planted in Jones' mind by Captain Baker." Friedland, *The Death of Old Man Rice*, p. 377.

11 "Damn it, grow": Preston Moore, James A. Baker III Oral History Project, Princeton and Rice.

11 "the foster father of Rice Institute": Ed Kilman, "Work Hard, Study and Keep Out of Politics," *Houston Post*, October 3, 1937. Quoted by Phillips.

11 "barren wasteland": Susan Ripley Hilliard, "Rediscovering Historic Houston, http://rediscover.yourblvd.com/resources/rediscovering-historic-houston-boulevard-oaks-part-2/. Edgar Odell Lovett, the future president of Rice, sent the warning to his wife in a telegram, as relayed by the daughter of the Houstonian who took Dr. Lovett on a tour of the new institute's property.

11 "Baker and his friends literally": Lipartito and Pratt, *Baker and Botts in the Development of Modern Houston*, pp. 56–57.

12 The Oaks, a seven-acre property: In his will, the captain left The Oaks to Rice University as a residence for the school president but it was too far from campus to be practical and it was sold to the M. D. Anderson Foundation, which at the time was collaborating with the University of Texas to open a cancer hospital. What would become the world-renowned M. D. Anderson Cancer Center got its start on the Baker estate, converting the old house into offices and the stables into laboratories.

12 "could turn quickly": Lipartito and Pratt, *Baker and Botts in the Development of Modern Houston*, p. 49.

12 "He was a tough taskmaster": Moore interview.

12 "scare you to death": Addison Baker Duncan, James A. Baker III Oral History Project, Princeton and Rice.

12 "Work hard, study": Kilman, "Work Hard, Study and Keep Out of Politics." Quoted by Phillips.

13 "lose their Southern connection": Duncan oral history.

13 "the idolized treasure of a happy household": Kate Sayen Kirkland, *Captain James A. Baker of Houston, 1857–1941*, p. 121.

13 "the efficiency of its teaching": Kirkland, *Captain James A. Baker of Houston, 1857–1941*, p. 119.

13 "not particularly successful": James A. Baker III, *"Work Hard, Study . . . and Keep Out of Politics!,"* p. 8.

14 "bearing and deportment": James A. Baker, letter to James A. Baker Jr., August 27, 1917. Rice archive.

14 "bedraggled with mud": Alice Gray, letter to James A. Baker, November 5, 1918, Rice archive.

14 "There's nothing to do except": James A. Baker Jr., letter to sister, December 29, 1918, Rice archive.

15 "Houston: Where Seventeen Railroads": "Houston: Where Seventeen Railroads Meet the Sea," H. H. Tammen Company, Denver. University of Houston Digital Library, https://digital.lib.uh.edu/collection/p15195coll1/item/172.

15 "with rotary drill bits and derricks": "Oil and Texas: A Cultural History," Texas State Historical Association, https://texasalmanac.com/topics/business/oil-and-texas-cultural-history.

15 "Chicago of the South": Lipartito and Pratt, *Baker and Botts in the Development of Modern Houston*, p. 109.

15 "He was a central figure": Freeman, *The People of Baker Botts*, p. 43.

16 "He is a very, very competitive person": Moore interview.

16 "gave us real courage": Steven Fenberg, *Unprecedented Power*, p. 183.

16 "They were all about WPA": James Baker, author interview.

16 "Even if we win a military victory": "Neighbors of Note," *Houston Chronicle*, October 26, 1951.

17 "an austere demeanor": Baker, *"Work Hard, Study . . . and Keep Out of Politics!,"* p. 5.

17 "He was brought up in a": Moore interview.

17 "were a little bit afraid": Wallace Stedman Wilson, James A. Baker III Oral History Project, Princeton and Rice.

17 "He said, 'Let him stay' ": James Baker interview.
17 "The father was the person": David Paton, author interview.
18 "Darling, I had to be": Susan Baker, author interview.
18 "warm" and "spirited": Baker, *"Work Hard, Study . . . and Keep Out of Politics!,"* p. 4.
18 "It was demeaning": James Baker interview.
18 "sort of a Victorian": Ibid.
18 "That just killed me": Ibid.
18 "Few men have had so much": *Houston Chronicle,* August 3, 1941. Quoted by Phillips.
18 "was no commonplace life": Kirkland, *Captain James A. Baker of Houston, 1857–1941,* p. 345.
19 "It was segregated": Green interview.
19 "No one was talking politics": Ibid.
19 "The bus driver told us": Moore interview.
19 "Of course, World War II was": Edward W. (Mike) Kelly Jr., James A. Baker III Oral History Project, Princeton and Rice.
19 "I hope you will try": James A. Baker Jr., letter to James A. Baker III, June 21, 1941, Rice archive.
19 "I know you have been homesick": James A. Baker Jr., letter to James A. Baker III, July 14, 1941, Rice archive.
20 "I am very glad indeed": James A. Baker, letter to James A. Baker III, June 27, 1940, Rice archive.
20 "Please acknowledge receipt": James A. Baker, letter to James A. Baker III and three other grandchildren, June 27, 1940, Rice archive.
20 "His mother thought": Green interview.
20 "You have a son now": James Baker interview.
21 Allen Drury's classic political novel *Advise and Consent:* Governor Hunt went on to serve in the Senate, where he became a leading foe of Senator Joseph McCarthy's red-baiting campaign, until his son was arrested for soliciting sex from a male undercover police officer in Washington's Lafayette Square and Republican senators threatened to use the case against the senator if he did not resign. Hunt brought a .22 caliber Winchester rifle barely concealed by an overcoat to his Senate office and shot himself to death; the story of blackmail and suicide became the basis for Drury's novel, which won the Pulitzer Prize and was made into a movie starring Henry Fonda and Walter Pidgeon.
21 "Boy, that wasn't fair": James Baker interview.
21 "like a second father to me": Ibid.

CHAPTER 2. The Warden's Son

22 "It was the first time": Barney McHenry, author interview.
23 "There was no friction": Ibid.
23 " 'Smilin' Jim' ": *The Hill School News,* October 31, 1947, Princeton archive.
23 "Jim mused over the female situation": Ibid.
23 "Your subject and at times": Letters on file at the Rice archive.
23 "He is a fine boy": James A. Baker Jr., letter to Herbert B. Finnegan of the Hill School, Baker Institute, Rice University.
23 "I am sorry you thought": James Baker Jr., letter to James Baker III, February 25, 1948, Rice archive.
23 "Jimmy has always passed": James Baker Jr., letter to Radford Heermance, April 15, 1947, Rice archive.
24 "For someone who likes to hunt": James Baker, author interview.
24 "When I got to Princeton": Ibid.
24 "Obviously we were having": Ibid.
24 "If he was out to party": David Paton, author interview.
25 "first normal post-war class": *Nassau Herald,* 1952.
25 "a somewhat upsetting": Ibid.

25 Nearly one out of every five: Ibid. Of about 800 in the freshman class that arrived in 1948, 214 were Episcopalian, 201 were Presbyterian, and 66 were some other form of Protestant. Another 84 were Catholic and 54 were described as "Hebrew."

25 "Princeton was known as": Frank Carlucci, author interview.

26 His average for the first term: Princeton archive.

26 "There wasn't an awful lot": McHenry interview.

26 "I am greatly disappointed": James Baker Jr., letter to James Baker III, May 9, 1949, Rice archive.

26 "didn't pay much attention": James Baker interview.

26 "It took me about a couple hours": Ibid.

27 "Jimmy, you tell old John": Ibid.

27 "I have thought of you constantly": Bonner Baker, letter to James Baker III, July 9, 1949, Rice archive.

27 "We both feel that you": James Baker Jr., letter to James Baker III, July 8, 1949, Rice archive.

27 "Scott Fitzgerald was our hero": McHenry interview.

27 "They picked us up": James Baker interview.

28 "I've really been cruising": James Baker III, letter to James Baker Jr. and Bonner Baker, September 17, 1949, Rice archive.

28 "I've got the screaming A-Bomb hots": James Baker, letter to Mary Stuart McHenry, April 11, 1950, Rice archive.

28 "Mary Stuart, I've known": James Baker, letter to Mary Stuart McHenry, April 26, 1950, Rice archive.

28 "She was absolutely crazy": Patricia Honea Schutts, James A. Baker III Oral History Project, Princeton and Rice.

28 "It was just a wonderful love affair": Paton interview.

29 "We argued that": Don Oberdorfer, "Our Four Years on Campus," an excerpt from a book published by the *Daily Princetonian* called *The Orange and Black in Black and White: A Century of Princeton Through the Eyes of the Daily Princetonian*.

29 "ALL SOPHS GET BIDS!": *Daily Princetonian*, March 9, 1950.

29 "detached and breathlessly aristocratic": F. Scott Fitzgerald, *This Side of Paradise*, originally published in 1920. From Collector's Library reprint edition, published in 2013, p. 21.

29 "Ivy was the snobbish club": Richard Riordan, author interview.

30 "long uncombed gray hair": Undated Baker letter to parents. Judging from the folder it was in, it probably was written in the spring semester of 1952. Rice archive.

30 "Everybody had to scurry": McHenry interview.

30 "They told me it had been": Baker letter to Mary Stuart McHenry, December 26, 1950, Rice archive.

30 "Nobody questioned it": Riordan interview.

30 "In Princeton, the number one": Oberdorfer, "Our Four Years on Campus."

31 "The efforts of Jim Baker": *Nassau Herald.*

31 also finally buckled down: Princeton archive.

31 "probably the most popular teacher": Alexander Leitch, *A Princeton Companion*, Princeton University Press, 1978, http://etcweb.princeton.edu/CampusWWW /CompanioN/hall_walter.html.

31 "Things look darker": Baker letter to Mary Stuart McHenry, January 16, 1952, Rice archive.

32 "expert negotiator": James Baker, "Two Sides of the Conflict: Bevin vs. Bevan," April 21, 1952, Princeton archive.

32 "One of the questions": James Baker interview.

32 "sissified": Ibid.

33 "I get a little big": Ibid.

33 "Did an excellent job": Marine Leadership Performance Memorandum, October 14, 1952, Rice archive.

33 "I fought the Korean War": James Baker interview.

33 "time of tempest": Dwight D. Eisenhower, Inaugural Address, Online by Ger-

hard Peters and John T. Woolley, The American Presidency Project, https://www
.presidency.ucsb.edu/node/231580.

33 "I was sick the entire time": James Baker interview.
34 "But I can see where": James Baker III, letter to James Baker Jr. and Bonner Baker,
April 23, 1953, Rice archive.
34 "It was a disaster": James Baker interview.
34 "shattered, split wide open": "Ruinous Epilog to Homeric Drama," *Life*, August 31,
1953.
34 "I don't think the devastation": James Baker III, letter to James Baker Jr. and Bonner
Baker, August 30, 1953, Rice archive.
34 "It bolstered my sagging spirits": Ibid.
34 "that these sorry bastard Chinese": James Baker interview.
35 "I did it for my dad": Ibid.
36 "But he was smart enough": Ibid.
36 "Mr. Baker, Mr. James Addison": Robert S. Weatherall, James A. Baker III Oral History Project, Princeton and Rice.
36 near the top 10 percent: Ibid.
36 "You got good grades": Ibid.
36 "Everything I had ever known": Ibid.
36 "I was devastated": Ibid.

CHAPTER 3. God Came Today

37 "friend maker": Jonathan Bush, author interview.
38 Bush's was so weak: James Baker, author interview.
38 "powder puff serve": Doug Baker, author interview.
38 "Baker's the better tennis player": George H. W. Bush, author interview.
39 "They're both enormous": George W. Bush, author interview.
39 "I served him drinks": James Baker, Houston Oral History Project, Houston Public Library, http://digital.houstonlibrary.net/oral-history/james-addison-baker.php.
40 "why are you going": James Baker interview.
40 "anyone that doesn't come in": Robert S. Weatherall, James A. Baker III Oral History Project, Princeton and Rice.
40 "It's fair to say that": James Baker interview.
40 "You better start praying": Movie script, *Gunfight at the O.K. Corral*, 1957, https://www.springfield.co.uk/movie_script.php?movie=gunfight-at-the-o-k-corral.
40 "an almost impossible burden": James Baker, memo, September 25, 1957, Princeton archive.
41 "I became very disillusioned": James Baker interview.
41 "You have always been": James A. Baker Jr., letter to James A. Baker III, April 28, 1959, Princeton archive.
42 "Jimmy, I survived the Great Depression": Doug Baker interview.
42 "George had an eye for": Jonathan Bush interview.
42 "I have never hunted turkey": James A. Baker Jr., letter to James O. Winston Jr., January 3, 1962, Princeton archive.
43 "The country up there": James A. Baker Jr., letter to James Bertron, November 16, 1964, Princeton archive.
43 "both come from families": James A. Baker Jr., letter to the Houston Country Club on behalf of James O. Winston III and Susan Garrett Winston, January 14, 1966, Princeton archive.
43 "I could not at the last": Baker letter to J. T. Bagby, April 17, 1963, Princeton archive.
43 "Did I ever get my butt whipped?": John Baker, author interview.
43 "I remember him talking": George W. Bush interview.
44 "That was really the first": Jamie Baker, author interview.
44 "Well, here is the letter": Jamie Baker, letter to James A. Baker III, September 29, 1969, Princeton archive.

44 "I am glad that you finally": James A. Baker III, letter to Jamie Baker, October 6, 1969, Princeton archive.

44 "He told me that every": James A. Baker III, letter to Wallace Barry Wilson, September 16, 1969.

45 a convincing 56 percent: Bush pulled in 1,134,337 votes to Yarborough's 1,463,958. *Texas Almanac*, Texas State Historical Association, http://texasalmanac.com/topics /elections/senatorial-elections-and-primaries-1906-%E2%80%93-2018.

45 "My dear George": James A. Baker III, letter to George H. W. Bush, November 6, 1964, Princeton archive.

46 "one of the most vicious prosecutors": Mike Morris, "Ex-DA Frank Briscoe, Legal Heavyweight for Decades, Dies at 84," *Houston Chronicle*, January 5, 2011.

46 with 57 percent of the vote: The 1966 Election Results, *CQ Almanac*, https://library .cqpress.com/cqalmanac/document.php?id=cqal67-1311561.

46 "I was sort of in awe of him": James Baker interview.

46 "I'd get up in the middle": Jamie Baker interview.

46 "They were a great, great marriage": Jonathan Bush interview.

47 "It damn near killed her": James Baker interview.

47 the first successful adult: Thomas H. Maugh II, "Denton Cooley, Texas Surgeon Who Performed First Successful Heart Transplant in U.S., Dies at 86," *Los Angeles Times*, November 18, 2016.

47 "I could tell when he came out": James Baker interview.

47 "They just wanted our lives": Doug Baker interview.

47 "I thought the kids": James A. Baker III, letter to Mrs. A. C. McHenry, February 28, 1969, Princeton archive.

48 "didn't want to spend": Stewart Addison Baker, James A. Baker Oral History Project, Princeton and Rice.

48 "some pro, some con": Baker personal files.

48 "I'm really sure that G.": Barbara Bush, letter to Mary Stuart Baker, undated but postmarked May 7, 1969, Princeton archive.

48 "This is a big and difficult decision": James Baker, handwritten note to George Bush, Baker personal files.

48 "As I've mentioned before": James Baker, handwritten note to George Bush, August 22, 1969, Baker personal files.

50 "We do not have all of the": James Baker, letter to Jamie Baker, February 4, 1970, Princeton archive.

50 "Mary Stuart is in the hospital": James Baker, letter to David Paton, February 6, 1970, Princeton archive.

50 "Bush speech—Introduce him": James A. Baker III datebook, February 13, 1970, Princeton archive.

50 "She's not going to make it": Preston Moore, James A. Baker III Oral History Project, Princeton and Rice.

50 "things are not good": James Baker, letter to David Paton, February 17, 1970, Princeton archive.

50 "The treatment was so terrible": Barbara Bush, author interview.

51 "He prayed that she would not": Jamie Baker interview.

51 "God came today": Doug Baker interview.

51 "My dear sweet loving": Mary Stuart Baker, letter to James Baker, November 29, 1969, Baker personal files.

CHAPTER 4. A Long Dark Night

53 "He would go to the window": Beatrice Green, author interview.

53 "In line with our telephone conversation": James Baker, letter to Dossy Allday, February 26, 1970, Princeton archive.

53 "I am still swamped": James Baker, letter to Bonner Baker, March 5, 1970, Princeton archive.

53   "Bake, you need to take": James Baker, author interview.

55   "Jimmy, dear, it just doesn't": Mrs. John F. Bryan, letter to James Baker, July 17, 1970, Princeton archive.

55   "If I was ever going to become": James Baker interview.

55   "I hope you don't feel": James Baker, letter to Rosemary and Adams McHenry, April 9, 1970, Princeton archive.

56   "Bush and Bentsen seemed": Al Reinert, "The Unveiling of Lloyd Bentsen," *Texas Monthly*, December 1974.

56   53 percent of the vote: *Texas Almanac: 2018–2019*, Texas State Historical Association, https://texasalmanac.com/topics/elections/senatorial-elections-and-primaries-1906-2018.

56   60 percent, thanks in part: Harris County Clerk, certification of election results to Texas Secretary of State, December 4, 1970.

56   "I truly don't know what": James Baker, letter to Rosemary and Adams McHenry, November 10, 1970, Princeton archive.

56   "Right now I can't decide": George H. W. Bush, letter to James A. Baker III, November 11, 1970, Princeton archive.

56   "How sad I was to leave": Rosemary McHenry, undated letter to James A. Baker III, Princeton archive.

57   "Needless to say, I am": James Baker, letter to Jamie Baker, February 19, 1971. Princeton archive.

57   "I don't know why I did it dad": Mike Baker, undated handwritten note to James A. Baker III, Princeton archive.

57   "I don't think he really knew": Jamie Baker, author interview.

57   "like pulling teeth": James Baker interview.

57   "I had a little trouble": James Baker, letter to Rosemary and Adams McHenry, August 24, 1972, Princeton archive.

58   "He has stature, integrity": George H. W. Bush, letter to John Tower, February 22, 1973, Princeton archive.

58   "Things are about the same": James Baker, letter to Rosemary McHenry, June 19, 1972, Princeton archive.

58   "I know I have turned out": Bonner Moffitt, undated letter to James Baker, Princeton archive.

58   "You are right that his death": James Baker, letter to headmaster of the Hill School, March 8, 1974, Princeton archive.

59   "I'm pretty sure that every woman": Barbara Bush, author interview.

59   "one of those casserole ladies": James Baker interview.

59   "his voice was like": Susan G. Baker, *Passing It On*, p. 22.

59   "a drop-dead handsome dynamo": Ibid., p. 27.

59   "little church mouse": Susan Baker, unpublished interview with ghostwriter for Baker memoir, January 25, 2006, Princeton archive.

60   "Dad saw someone who": William Winston, author interview.

60   "Guess what we did?": Douglas Baker, author interview.

61   "sort of a communal type thing": James (Bo) Winston IV, author interview.

61   Johnny Baker asked Elizabeth Winston: Elizabeth Winston Jones, author interview. For clarity, she is referred to in the book by the name she used at the time, Elizabeth Winston.

61   "We had been a very happy": Ibid.

61   "When you have seven children": Susan Baker, author interview.

61   "I asked him, 'You're never'": John Baker, author interview.

61   "My grades suffered": Douglas Baker interview.

61   "Jimbo knew that he was not": Winston Jones interview.

61   "I think Dad was incredibly relieved": Bo Winston interview.

62   "Whatever it was": James Baker, letter to Dorothine Collins, September 10, 1974, Princeton archive.

63   "I said, 'Thank you very much'": James Baker interview.

63 "Age geography foreign affairs": James Baker, telegram to Gerald Ford, August 10, 1974, Princeton archive.

63 "Always bridesmaid": James A. Baker III, handwritten notes, August 16, 1974, Princeton archive.

63 "Dear Bake—Yesterday": George H. W. Bush, handwritten note to James A. Baker III, August 21, 1974, Princeton archive.

64 "Too bad about George": James A. Baker III, letter to Rosemary and Adams McHenry, August 21, 1974, Princeton archive.

64 "In spite of Princeton education": George H. W. Bush, cable to Donald H. Rumsfeld, February 1975, Gerald R. Ford Presidential Library and Museum.

64 "Geo Bush referred": Candidate Evaluation, James Baker, March 11, 1975, Ford Library.

64 "a high level job": George H. W. Bush, handwritten note to James A. Baker III, May 29, 1975, Princeton archive.

65 "We talked about the Under Secretary of Commerce": Donald Rumsfeld, Meeting with the President, June 7, 1975, Donald Rumsfeld papers, http://library.rumsfeld .com/doclib/sp/2376/1975-06-07.pdf#search="baker%20and%20houston".

65 "I am absolutely *elated*": George H. W. Bush, letter to James A. Baker III, June 27, 1975, Princeton archive.

65 "You were confirmed by Senate": Handwritten note, August 1, 1975, Princeton archive.

66 "We in this country": James Baker, commencement address, Northwest Academy graduation, May 28, 1976, Baker Institute. Baker delivered a similar address at Bo Winston's commencement from Eaglebrook School in Deerfield, Mass., three years later, on June 1, 1979, using some of the same passages, word for word. Princeton archive.

CHAPTER 5. Miracle Man

69 "Will Henry Kissinger be in": James Baker, author interview.

70 "he probably was some right-wing": Henry Kissinger, author interview.

70 "I understand you announced": James Baker interview; Dick Cheney, author interview.

71 "Oh, so you're Textile Baker": James Baker interview.

71 "I am calling for two things": Transcript of James Baker–Henry Kissinger call, April 5, 1976, 3:15 p.m., State Department.

72 "What's the deal with this Baker guy?": Pete Roussel, author interview.

72 more than $140,000 a year: Federal tax returns for 1974, Princeton archive. A little more than half of that came from his law firm, totaling twice as much as the $40,000 annual salary for his new Commerce job. The rest came from investments. Altogether, his net worth, after the mortgages on his Houston house and Rockpile Ranch, came to nearly $1.7 million (or more than $8.8 million in 2019 dollars). Most of his wealth, nearly $1 million, came from shares in the parent company of Texas Commerce Bank, the financial institution that had been the economic bulwark for his family for generations. He also owned $200,000 in WellTech, an energy firm, and he valued his shares in Graham Realty, the family holding company, at $150,000. In a letter he sent to the Senate committee considering his nomination, he noted that the ranch made little money from a stripper well but had potential. "A new well was just completed on May 16," Baker wrote, "and, if this new production holds up, the total production from the property will be substantially greater in the future." He agreed to put most of his investments in a blind trust, but when he tried to have Texas Commerce Bank administer it, senators objected so he was forced to hire another agent instead. James A. Baker III, letter to Senator Warren Magnuson, July 28, 1975, Princeton archive.

72 "This job is extremely": James A. Baker III, letter to David Paton, September 10, 1975, Princeton archive.

72	"man to watch": Kathy Lewis, "James A. Baker: A Man to Watch," *Houston Post*, September 21, 1975.

72	"He was so excited": Susan Baker, author interview.

72	"My feeling was that": James Baker interview.

73	"Maybe we hit it off because": James A. Baker III, *"Work Hard, Study . . . and Keep Out of Politics!,"* p. 38.

74	"They thought he was nothing": Stuart Spencer, Ronald Reagan Oral History Project, Miller Center, University of Virginia, November 15–16, 2001, https://millercenter.org/the-presidency/presidential-oral-histories/stuart-spencer-oral -history-campaign-advisor.

74	"If you want to win Texas": Baker, *"Work Hard, Study . . . and Keep Out of Politics!,"* p. 28.

74	"I'm talking to you now as": Ibid.

75	"We basically had to build": Cheney interview.

76	963 delegates to 879 for Reagan: James M. Naughton, "Ford Aides Still Confident Despite Setback in Missouri,": *New York Times*, June 15, 1976.

76	He brought eight delegates: Campaign memos, July 1976, Princeton archive.

76	"To bring them up here": James A. Baker III, memo to file, July 1, 1976, Gerald R. Ford Presidential Library and Museum.

76	"The worst thing that can happen": James A. Baker III, "Proposed Delegate Management Operation," Memorandum to Rogers C. B. Morton, Stu Spencer, and Roy Hughes, May 12, 1976, Ford Library.

76	"You'd have to go to pols": Tony Kornheiser, "Cutting Chaff and Shooting Straight with Jim Baker," *Washington Post*, January 18, 1981.

77	"Jim was in charge of every detail": Dick Cheney, *In My Time*, p. 96.

77	"there is a great degree": Jules Witcover, *Marathon*, pp. 467–70.

77	"A substantial portion of Baker's time": James Baker schedule, week of July 19, 1976, Princeton archive.

77	giving him a total of 1,135: R. W. Apple Jr., "Ford Aides Offer Delegate Totals Showing Victory," *New York Times*, August 14, 1976.

78	"In my judgment": Dick Mastrangelo, memo to James Baker, June 11, 1976, Princeton archive.

78	"'Miracle Man' Given Credit": *New York Times*, August 19, 1976, https://www .nytimes.com/1976/08/19/archives/miracle-man-given-credit-for-ford-drive-did -not-want-job-how-he-did.html.

78	"We had the incumbency": Stuart Spencer, author interview.

78	was just 9 percent: American Conservative Union, http://acuratings.conservative.org /acu-federal-legislative-ratings/?year1=1975&chamber=13&state1=0&sortable=1.

79	"looked the part": David Keene, then a Reagan aide, quoted in Craig Shirley, *Reagan's Revolution*, p. 284.

79	"I was really for Reagan": Clarke Reed, author interview.

79	a vote of 1,180 to 1,069: R. W. Apple Jr., "Ford Gains and Blocks Reagan on Disclosure of a No. 2 Choice; Baker or Ruckelshaus Favored," *New York Times*, August 18, 1976. (The Baker referred to in the headline was Howard Baker, the Republican senator from Tennessee.)

79	"I think we got it": John Baker, author interview.

79	"very ecstatic": Doug Baker, author interview.

79	"I could see a two-word plank": Witcover, *Marathon*, p. 500.

79	"Everybody thinks this was": James Baker interview. Much was made of the Mississippi delegation and Clarke Reed's role. In the end, the delegation split for Ford but was not decisive. Reed actually voted for Reagan in a "throw-away" ballot at the end of the vote to fulfill his commitment, but made a point of not actually trying to help the challenger win, to the satisfaction of Baker and the Ford team.

80	1,187 votes to 1,070 for Reagan: R. W. Apple Jr., "Ford Takes Nomination on First Ballot," *New York Times*, August 19, 1976.

80	"The guy that comes in second": Spencer, Miller Center oral history.

80	"Reagan was the dominating presence": William F. Buckley Jr., "The President

Comes Alive with the Conservative Spirit," *Los Angeles Times*, August 26, 1976, as quoted by Julian E. Zelizer, *Jimmy Carter*, p. 75.

80   "I'm not going to rearrange": *Washington Post*, May 16, 1976.

80   "I thought he'd be good": Spencer interview.

80   "Jim Baker had demonstrated": Gerald R. Ford, *A Time to Heal*, p. 410.

81   "That was one of the toughest things": James Baker interview.

81   "I remember being scared": Ibid.

81   33 percentage points: Gallup survey, July 16–19, 1976. Carter had the support of 62 percent to Ford's 29 percent, http://news.gallup.com/poll/23995/Gerald-Ford -Retrospective.aspx#1.

81   "The candidate who makes": Ford, *A Time to Heal*, p. 410.

81   "Blessed with good looks": *Newsweek*, September 6, 1976.

82   "He's honest, but clumsy": Malcolm D. MacDougall, *We Almost Made It*, p. 71.

82   "And these, remember, were the": Ibid.

82   "We actually quantified the fact": Mary Lukens, author interview.

82   "a little bit insulting": Ibid.

82   "You're a lousy fucking candidate": Stuart Spencer, unpublished interview with Stuart Middleton, University of Queensland, November 5, 2010.

83   "I'll tell you what coloreds want": "Rolling Stone's Biggest Scoops, Exposés and Controversies," June 24, 2010.

83   "Cheney and I slept in his office": Spencer, Middleton interview.

83   "as cold and arrogant": Ford, *A Time to Heal*, p. 414.

83   "avoided the word 'Republican' ": MacDougall, *We Almost Made It*, p. 197.

84   "With a Southerner leading the ticket": Undated, unsigned memo in Dick Cheney's files, Ford Library, https://www.fordlibrarymuseum.gov/library/document /0005/1561621.pdf.

84   reached nearly 20 percent: The concept of a "misery index" was devised in the 1970s by Arthur Okun, who served as a White House economist under Lyndon Johnson and later worked at the Brookings Institution. Ron Nessen, "The Brookings Institution's Arthur Okun—Father of the 'Misery Index,' " December 17, 2018, https:// www.brookings.edu/opinions/the-brookings-institutions-arthur-okun-father-of-the -misery-index/.

84   by 15 percentage points: Gallup survey, August 27–30, 1976. Carter had 51 percent to Ford's 36 percent, http://news.gallup.com/poll/23995/Gerald-Ford-Retrospective .aspx#1.

84   "almost like robots": Jimmy Carter, interview with Jim Lehrer. "Debating Our Destiny," PBS, April, 28, 1989, https://www.pbs.org/newshour/spc/debatingourdestiny /interviews/carter.html.

84   36 percent of Americans: Handwritten notes on memo on White House stationery, September 24, 1976, Princeton archive.

84   Ford had pared Carter's lead, "Carter Margin in Gallup Poll Is Cut to 50–42," *New York Times*, October 1, 1976.

84   "an agreement that the Russians": Transcript, Gerald Ford vs. Jimmy Carter presidential debate, October 6, 1976, American Presidency Project, University of California at Santa Barbara, http://www.presidency.ucsb.edu/ws/index.php?pid=6414.

85   "heart sank into my shoes": George Bush and Brent Scowcroft, *A World Transformed*, p. 20.

85   "Cheney and I were spastic": Spencer, Miller Center oral history.

85   "Dick and I say, 'Goddamn' ": Ibid.

85   "perspired heavily": Bush and Scowcroft, *A World Transformed*, p. 20.

85   "there was an air of exhilaration": Stuart E. Eizenstat, *President Carter*, p. 60.

85   "The data had totally flipped": Lukens interview.

85   "We came within two inches": Spencer, Miller Center oral history.

86   "We had anticipated it more": James A. Baker III, unpublished interview with Stuart Middleton, University of Queensland, November 8, 2010.

86   "How did we handle it?": Spencer, Middleton interview.

86   "To take the pardon issue on": Doug Bailey, unpublished interview with Stuart Middleton, University of Queensland, November 18, 2010.
86   7 percent of *Republicans*: Spencer, Middleton interview.
86   "We have come from a point": Transcript, *Issues and Answers*, ABC News, October 24, 1976.
86   "If he had traveled down to some": Gerald R. Ford, James A. Baker III Oral History Project, Princeton and Rice, May 23, 2006.
87   "Not one of the president's speeches": MacDougall, *We Almost Made It*, p. 198.
87   *"I'm feeling good about America"*: Unaired Ford campaign "Cherry Bomb" commercial, posted by PBS on YouTube, November 12, 2012, courtesy of Ford Library, https://www.youtube.com/watch?v=8mILEkcrHvQ.
87   "Neither the cherry bombs": Ibid.
87   "If you know or are 90 percent certain": Bailey oral history.
87   "nutty, absolutely screwy": Kaufman, *Ambition, Pragmatism and Party*, p. 298.
88   "If the former Georgia Governor": Witcover, *Marathon*, pp. 634–35.
88   "I resented one thing he did": Jimmy Carter, author interview.
88   "I quit smoking": James Baker interview.
89   48 percent of the popular vote: Election of 1992, American Presidency Project, University of California at Santa Barbara, https://www.presidency.ucsb.edu/statistics/elections/1976.
89   nine thousand voters in Ohio and Hawaii: Ibid. Carter won Ohio by 11,116 votes and Hawaii by 7,372 votes, for a combined margin of 18,488, meaning that if as few as 9,244 Carter voters had gone for Ford divided correctly between the two states, they would have flipped. Ohio's twenty-five electoral votes and Hawaii's four would have boosted Ford's total to 270 over 268 for Carter. This assumes that a rogue Ford elector from Washington State who cast a protest vote for Ronald Reagan would have stuck with Ford to reach the 270 needed.
89   "it would be very hard": Baker, *"Work Hard, Study . . . and Keep Out of Politics!,"* pp. 70–71.
89   "He was right, of course": Ibid.
89   "If he hadn't pardoned Nixon": James Baker interview. Over the years that followed, the country, and history, looked more generously on Ford's decision. By the time he died in 2006, even some of his fiercest critics came to believe he had been right. Roger Wilkins, then a *New York Times* editorial writer who repeatedly condemned Ford over the pardon, wrote a letter to the former president just a month before his death to say he had changed his mind. "Ford was right," Wilkins said shortly after the president passed away. Representative David Obey, a Democrat from Wisconsin, had thought at the time that the pardon was "the absolutely wrong thing to do," but later concluded that Ford "served as a healing agent for the country." Peter Baker, "38th President Leaves a Legacy of Healing," *Washington Post*, December 28, 2006.
89   "The best man did not win": James A. Baker III, letter to Gerald R. Ford, November 4, 1976, Ford Library.
89   "You were superb": Gerald R. Ford, letter to James A. Baker III, November 18, 1976, Ford Library.
89   "I was determined that the investigations": James Baker interview.
89   "When I found out there": Spencer interview.
90   "He did one superb job": Ford oral history.

CHAPTER 6. Out of the Back Room

91   "Grandma, what are those flags": Audio recording of Houston Chamber of Commerce debate, Texas State Library and Archives Commission.
91   "bitten by the bug": James Baker, author interview.
92   "He probably saw it": Doug Baker, author interview.
92   "reacquainted baby": James Baker interview.
92   "They're not printable": Marjorie Williams, "He Doesn't Waste a Lot of Time on

Guilt," *Washington Post*, January 29, 1989. Also in Marjorie Williams, *Reputation*, p. 65.

92 "One smart thing": Ibid.

93 "Jim Baker's election": Undated campaign memo with answers to potential questions, Princeton archive.

93 "He never said, 'and then' ": Charlie Black, author interview.

93 "Down here, Reagan routed us": Ibid.

94 "a little suspicious": Frank Donatelli, James A. Baker Oral History Project, Princeton and Rice.

94 "It's clear he did not have": Frank Donatelli, author interview.

94 "My first impression": Donatelli interview.

94 "Keep eye contact": James Baker, notes on draft of talk to the League of United Latin American Citizens, July 22, 1978, Princeton archive.

94 eventually threatened to burn: Tony Kornheiser, "Cutting Chaff and Shooting Straight with Jim Baker," *Washington Post*, January 18, 1981.

94 "candidate who brings his own baby": Laurence I. Barrett, *Gambling with History*, p. 382.

94 "I can remember their shooting": Doug Baker interview.

94 "If the Republicans had not fielded": Transcript of interview with Bob Bullock, *State Capital Dateline*, February 1978.

95 "We were competing": Pete Roussel, author interview.

95 "He's arrogant, shallow": Undated Baker campaign memo accompanying newspaper clips from February and March 1978, Princeton archive.

95 "Daniel May well be": April 1978 political guide, *Texas Monthly*, p. 119.

95 "I didn't know who the hell": Mark White, author interview.

96 "There's not much question": Earl Newlin, "White, Baker Address Press Club," *Port Arthur News*, February 23, 1978.

96 52 percent to 48 percent: White won 850,979 votes to 778,889 for Price. Dick J. Reavis, "A Death in the Family," *D Magazine*, August 1981. Two years later, at the age of thirty-nine, Daniel was shot to death at home by his second wife, Vickie, a former Dairy Queen waitress. She was charged with murder but acquitted after she testified that Daniel beat her during an argument about their pending divorce and she accidentally fired a gun at him. The story later became a made-for-television movie called *Bed of Lies*. "Wife Acquitted in Death of a Politician," Associated Press, October 31, 1981, https://www.nytimes.com/1981/10/31/us/around-the-nation-wife-acquitted-in-death-of-a-politician-in-texas.html.

96 "By all rights, he *should*": Jim Cicconi, "Opposition and Issues Report," May 8, 1978, Princeton archive.

96 8.6 percent of the more: Survey by Arthur J. Finkelstein & Associates, May/June 1978, Princeton archive.

96 "Jim Baker,": Finkelstein concluded: Ibid.

96 "I've been busting my ass": Frank Donatelli, author interview.

96 "One had the feeling": Jonathan Bush, author interview.

97 "I plunged out of the car": Ibid.

97 "Personally I oppose abortion": Campaign issues binder, Princeton archive.

97 "No," Baker's aides wrote: Letter drafted by James Baker aides to David Higdon, May 24, 1978, Princeton archive.

98 "This doesn't square": James Baker, handwritten note, May 24, 1978, Princeton archive.

98 "I feel that consenting adults": Campaign issues binder.

98 "I would be very concerned": Ibid.

98 Of the office's 14,922 pending cases: Jim Cicconi, memo to James Baker, January 27, 1978, Princeton archive.

98 Over the previous fifteen years: Texas Crime Rates 1960–2016, http://www.disaster center.com/crime/txcrime.htm.

98 One poll showed that: Texas Crime Poll, Texas Criminal Justice Center, Sam Houston State University, Fall 1977.

99   "I believe the fundamental problem": Patrick Martinets, "Candidate Assails System of Justice," *Fort Worth Star-Telegram*, March 22, 1978.

99   "specific instances where": James Baker, memo to Pete Roussel, Jim Cicconi, and Frank Donatelli, March 22, 1978, Princeton archive.

99   thirty-seven-page position paper: *Houston Chronicle*, September 6, 1978.

99   "My opponent, Mark White": Marjorie Williams, "Jim Baker Is Smooth, Shrewd, Tough and Cooly Ambitious. That's Why Washington Loves Him," *Washington Post*, January 29, 1989.

99   "If you write me off": Memo, Dary Stone to David Dean, Nola Haerle, Steve Some, Bill Clements campaign, August 7, 1978, Bill Clements papers, http://tx .clementspapers.org/clementstx/88222?solr_nav%5Bid%5D=f8d5884da0174265 e308&solr_nav%5Bpage%5D=0&solr_nav%5Boffset%5D=2.

100   "You should be aware": Ibid.

100   "Hey, no more debates": White interview.

100   "That was, sort of, the beginning": Michael Deaver, James A. Baker Oral History Project, Princeton and Rice.

100   "George Bush is my friend": Baker interview.

100   "You're never going to": John Baker, author interview.

101   "Most of the problems for Texas": Dee Steer, "White Criticizes Opponent Baker," *Tyler Morning Telegraph*, September 7, 1978.

101   "He's come down here from": "Mark White Blasts 'Unemployed Baker,'" Associated Press, printed in *Daily Telegram* of Temple, Texas, September 11, 1978.

101   "our chief vulnerability": Cicconi, "Opposition and Issues Report."

101   "He went through the roof": White interview.

101   "a killer issue": Cicconi interview.

102   "May I ask which party?": Cheryl Coggins, "Baker Attracts Demo Voters," *San Antonio Express-News*, October 15, 1978.

102   "almost as if Baker had just admitted": Ibid.

102   "He was the worst retail politician": Jim Barlow, author interview.

102   "We would be walking through": Ibid.

102   "The *Chronicle* was protecting": Ibid.

103   "I've always thought Baker": Ibid.

103   Baker took 999,431 votes: Texas State Library and Archives Commission.

103   "Jimmy is the only one": Fred McClure, author interview.

103   "Baker was a great politician": Dick Cheney, author interview.

103   "does not mean his exit": Jim Barlow, "Jim Baker's Defeat Tuesday Doesn't Mean He Will Be Leaving Politics," *Houston Chronicle*, November 11, 1978.

CHAPTER 7.   The Asterisk Club

104   "Bush cannot look too hungry": Undated memo, Baker files, Princeton archive.

105   the Asterisk Club: Richard Ben Cramer, *What It Takes*, p. 790.

106   "I had read Hamilton Jordan's book": James Baker, author interview.

106   "central casting's idea": James Baker, George H. W. Bush Oral History Project, Miller Center, January 29, 2000.

106   "lifelong Republican": Adam Clymer, "Bush, with a Promise of 'Candor,' Declares His G.O.P. Candidacy," *New York Times*, May 2, 1979.

106   "principled, stable leadership": Ibid.

107   "George, you've got to stop": James Baker, author interview.

108   "We didn't have a big gang": Pete Teeley, author interview.

108   "He doesn't pretend to be": David Keene, author interview.

108   "He didn't want to be": Ibid.

108   "George Bush is a wonderful guy": Ibid.

108   "Mount Vesuvius of press secretaries": Matt Schudel, "Vic Gold, GOP Consultant and Writer Who Reveled in Political Theater, Dies at 88," *Washington Post*, June 7, 2017.

108   "Vic was a sideshow": Teeley interview.
108   "shouting match": James Baker, handwritten note to Jonathan Bush, February 13, 1980, Princeton archive.
109   "I am sick and tired": Ibid.
109   "Forget about my comment": James Baker, memo to George Bush, February 14, 1980, Princeton archive.
109   "I have refereed my last argument": James Baker, memo to Jonathan Bush, Bob Mosbacher, and Fred Bush, February 14, 1980, Princeton archive.
109   "Let's put our differences": Jonathan Bush, handwritten note to James Baker, April 9, 1980, Princeton archive.
109   "The hatchet is buried": James Baker, handwritten note to Jonathan Bush, April 11, 1980, Princeton archive.
109   "Pres, that's not what we're": James Baker interview.
109   "There are no amateurs": Ibid.
109   Bush even called Fitzgerald: Susan Page, *The Matriarch*, pp. 103–4.
110   Both denied it: Jon Meacham, *Destiny and Power*, p. 310.
110   "He's a loser": Karl Rove, author interview. See also Rove's *Courage and Consequence*, p. 51, where Rove wrote that Fitzgerald also trashed both George H. W. Bush and George W. Bush. "We have a candidate who's a loser, who's got a son who's a loser and now we've got a campaign manager who's a loser," he quoted her saying.
110   "She thought she was": Keene interview.
110   "Have worst of all worlds": James Baker, undated notes on envelope, Princeton archive. In response to a message from the authors, Fitzgerald sent an email saying, "I greatly respect and admire Mr. Baker. He is an amazing gentleman." She did not respond to a follow-up email detailing specific incidents.
110   "She wants to run the campaign": James Baker, handwritten notes, May 6, 1979, Princeton archive.
111   "Honey, you have to talk": Susan Baker and James Baker, author interview.
112   "I'll make it sound like": Margot Hornblower, "Former 'Asterisk' Bush Basks in New Attention," *Washington Post*, January 23, 1980.
112   "The impossible dream": *Caucus Iowa*.
112   "I suppose I am out of the": Walter R. Mear, Associated Press, January 22, 1980.
112   "In Iowa, we defined": Baker interview.
112   "You're not out there": Jack W. Germond and Jules Witcover, *Blue Smoke & Mirrors*, p. 119.
113   "The clean fingernail Republican": Hornblower, "Former 'Asterisk' Bush Basks in New Attention."
113   "We propose this one-on-one encounter": Jon L. Breen, letter to Bush campaign, February 11, 1980, Princeton archive.
113   "Jim soon became an asterisk": Susan G. Baker, *Passing It On*, p. 53.
113   "I complained to him once": Tony Kornheiser, "Cutting Chaff and Shooting Straight with Jim Baker," *Washington Post*, January 18, 1981.
113   "I hope you each know": James Baker, typed letter to Jamie, Mike, John, and Doug Baker, February 19, 1980, Princeton archive.
114   "It doesn't work that way": Germond and Witcover, *Blue Smoke & Mirrors*, p. 127.
114   "It's important that we have": Baker interview.
114   "None of us tried to": Ibid.
114   "Turn Mr. Reagan's microphone off": Reagan's Nashua Moment, video posted on YouTube, https://www.youtube.com/watch?v=OO2_49TycdE.
115   "I'll get you someday": Craig Shirley, *Rendezvous with Destiny*, p. 154.
115   "You're never going to forget this": Baker interview.
115   "After the debate": Deborah Hart Strober and Gerald Strober, *Reagan*, p. 21.
115   Baker ran into David Broder: Baker interview.
115   "I don't think any of us appreciated": Ibid.
115   50 percent of the vote: Bill Peterson and Robert G. Kaiser, "The Eagle's Nose Dive,": *Washington Post*, March 22, 1980.
116   "What I'm saying is": George H. W. Bush, speech, Carnegie Mellon University,

April 10, 1980. Later, as vice president in 1982, Bush claimed he had never actually used the phrase "voodoo economics" and said no network had been able to find footage of him uttering it. Ken Bode at NBC News took up the challenge and unearthed a clip of the speech, https://www.youtube.com/watch?v=o8hnM6xNjeU.

116 list of banned words: Kornheiser, "Cutting Chaff and Shooting Straight with Jim Baker."

116 "It was a very good negative ad": Ibid.

116 "Pete, you've got to be": Teeley interview.

116 "Make sure Teeley doesn't": Ibid.

117 "Even with a Pennsylvania win": Rich Bond, memo to James Baker, April 16, 1980, Princeton archive.

117 Bush did go on to beat Reagan: David S. Broder, "Bush Wins Pa.; Democratic Race Tight," *Washington Post*, April 23, 1980.

117 "Bush's major objectives": Unsigned campaign memo, May 1, 1980, Princeton archive.

117 "I have never wanted to": Bill Frenzel, letter to James Baker, May 14, 1980, Princeton archive.

117 Reagan had secured 870 delegates: Unsigned campaign memo, May 19, 1980, Princeton archive.

117 Bush prevailed in Michigan: Bill Peterson, "Bush Scores Upset Victory in Michigan Primary," *Washington Post*, May 21, 1980.

117 They were running out of money: M. O. Hesse, memo to James Baker, May 12, 1980, Princeton archive.

118 "Jim turned off the phones": Keene interview.

118 "If you can't do California": Bill Peterson and David S. Broder, "Bush All but Abandons California Race, Plans Think Session," *Washington Post*, May 23, 1980.

118 "Baker says you don't have": Meacham, *Destiny and Power*, pp. 236–38.

118 "What in the hell": James Baker interview.

118 "George, I think it's time": Meacham, *Destiny and Power*, pp. 236–38.

118 "I WILL NEVER GIVE UP": Ibid.

119 "He is the most competitive guy": James Baker interview.

119 "Jimmy wasn't on the road": Kornheiser, "Cutting Chaff and Shooting Straight with Jim Baker."

119 "We still have a shot at it": George Bush, *Looking Forward*, pp. 3–4.

119 "That gives you one hell": James Baker interview.

119 "He had a hell of a tough job": Nick Brady, author interview. Pete Teeley remembered that "there was a bit of friction there" particularly between "Barbara and Baker." Teeley interview.

120 "My instinct was to keep fighting": Douglas E. Kneeland, "Bush Says He'll Quit Active Campaigning, Ending 2-Year Quest," *New York Times*, May 27, 1980.

120 "I may have been mad": Page, *The Matriarch*, p. 120.

120 He won seven contests: Bush won in Connecticut, the District of Columbia, Iowa, Maine, Massachusetts, Michigan, and Pennsylvania, along with the territory of Puerto Rico.

120 "I was so relieved": Susan Baker, James A. Baker III Oral History Project, Princeton and Rice.

120 "We had been married seven years": Susan Baker interview.

121 sounded like more of a "co-presidency": Haynes Johnson, David S. Broder, Lou Cannon, Bill Peterson, Martin Schram, and Felicity Barringer, "The Cement Just Wouldn't Set on GOP's Alliance," *Washington Post*, July 17, 1980.

121 "No, that's not right": Richard Allen, author interview. Also Richard V. Allen, "George Herbert Walker Bush: The Accidental Vice President," *New York Times Magazine*, July 30, 2000.

121 "Who else is there?": Ibid.

122 "Hold everything": Meacham, *Destiny and Power*, p. 252.

122 "It's not over yet": Louise Sweeney, "Reagan's Velvet Hammer," *Christian Science Monitor*, January 2, 1981. Bruce Gelb, a Bush campaign worker, later gave Baker a

framed medallion with a red, white, and blue ribbon emblazoned "Baker Says It's Not Over Yet."

122 "Is Ambassador Bush there?": Germond and Witcover, *Blue Smoke & Mirrors*, pp. 188–89.

123 "George's exodus was timely": Paul Laxalt, *Nevada's Paul Laxalt*, p. 312.

123 "What should I ask for?": Keene interview.

123 "the Reagan team was in charge": Margaret Tutwiler, the Association for Diplomatic Studies and Training Foreign Affairs Oral History Project.

123 "Jim Baker is the biggest phony": Strober and Strober, *Reagan*, p. 19.

124 combined rate reaching about 20 percent: In October 1980, inflation was 12.3 percent and unemployment was 7.5 percent. Bureau of Labor Statistics, https://data.bls.gov/pdq/SurveyOutputServlet.

125 "We can't run out the clock": Germond and Witcover, *Blue Smoke & Mirrors*, pp. 270–72.

125 "a stubborn man": Bill Peterson, "Anderson's Trying Days," *Washington Post*, October 2, 1980.

125 Baker gave Reagan a card: Bob Schieffer and Gary Paul Gates, *The Acting President*, p. 81.

125 "It sort of wiped Anderson out": James Baker interview.

125 Within fifteen minutes: Kathryn J. McGarr, *The Whole Damn Deal*, p. 264.

126 "We were outfoxed by Jim Baker": Stuart E. Eizenstat, *President Carter*, p. 878.

126 "His confidence in his candidate": Ibid., p. 873.

126 "He out-traded the people": Jimmy Carter, author interview.

126 "You are moderate": Debate Briefing Materials, Hoover Institution archive.

127 "Nancy looking daggers": David Gergen, *Eyewitness to Power*, p. 162.

127 "Reagan looked relaxed": Hamilton Jordan, *Crisis*, p. 355.

127 "There you go again": Presidential debate, October 28, 1980, https://www.youtube.com/watch?v=qN7gDRjTNf4.

127 "Are you better off": Ibid.

127 "Carter on the issues": Stuart Spencer, Ronald Reagan Oral History Project, Miller Center, University of Virginia, November 15–16, 2001.

127 "Are you serious?": Tutwiler, Association for Diplomatic Studies and Training oral history.

CHAPTER 8. Troika

129 "What are you getting me into?": Stuart Spencer, Ronald Reagan Oral History Project, Miller Center.

130 "Reagan's geographer": Lou Cannon, *Governor Reagan*, p. 328.

130 "Ed Meese couldn't organize": Stuart Spencer, author interview.

130 "a bumbling idiot": Bob Schieffer and Gary Paul Gates, *The Acting President*, p. 79.

130 "the guy who carried the suitcases": Ibid.

130 "Baker is a low-key": "Profiles of Key Members of the President-Elect's Transition Team," *Washington Post*, November 7, 1980.

130 "Yes," Deaver answered: Michael K. Deaver, *Behind the Scenes*, pp. 124–25.

131 "Dad looks at half a glass": Deborah Hart Strober and Gerald S. Strober, *Reagan*, p. 52.

131 "jump-off-the-cliff": Nancy Reagan, *My Turn*, p. 240.

131 "He was well mannered": Fred Ryan, author interview.

131 "Baker met her image": Ed Rollins, *Bare Knuckles and Back Rooms*, pp. 86–88.

131 "Oh no, no, no": Spencer interview.

131 "You'll guarantee he'll work": Ibid.

131 "If you become burdened": Michael Deaver, Ronald Reagan Oral History Project, Miller Center, September 12, 2002.

131 "I don't know whether I can": Ibid.

132 51 percent of the popular vote: The American Presidency Project, University of California, Santa Barbara, http://www.presidency.ucsb.edu/showelection.php?year=1980.

132   Reagan won 27 percent: "How Groups Voted in 1980," Roper Center for Public
        Opinion, https://ropercenter.cornell.edu/polls/us-elections/how-groups-voted/how
        -groups-voted-1980/.

132   picked up thirty-five seats: Office of the Historian, United States House of Rep-
        resentatives,   http://history.house.gov/Institution/Party-Divisions/Party-Divisions
        /Senate Historical Office, United States Senate. https://www.senate.gov/history
        /partydiv.htm.

132   "Let's Make America Great Again": "Political Ad: 'Let's Make America Great Again,'
        Reagan, 1980." Political Advertisement, New York, N.Y.; NBC Universal, Novem-
        ber 28, 1979. Accessed January 17, 2015 from NBC Learn: https://archives.nbclearn
        .com/portal/site/k-12/browse/?cuecard=4263.

132   "I woke up and I just cried": Susan Baker, author interview.

132   "The president's going to talk": Schieffer and Gates, *Acting President*, p. 81.

133   "I want you to be my chief of staff": James Baker, author interview.

133   "He really believes in saving face": Margaret Tutwiler, author interview.

133   had it typed up: Typewritten list of duties and responsibilities, signed by James Baker
        and Edwin Meese, November 19, 1980, Princeton archive.

133   "I don't want you in the room": Deaver, Miller Center oral history.

134   "Attend any meeting which": List of duties.

134   "I thought it over": Ed Meese, author interview.

134   "*OK—JAB III*": List of duties.

134   "It will become obvious": Douglas E. Kneeland, "A Tough but Tactful Tactician,"
        New York Times, November 15, 1980.

134   "In the White House, cabinet rank": Strober and Strober, *Reagan*, p. 62.

135   "Mike and Jim Baker hit it off": Margaret Tutwiler, Association for Diplomatic Stud-
        ies and Training Foreign Affairs Oral History Project.

135   "I went ballistic": Spencer, Miller Center oral history.

135   "Now that did piss off": Pete Teeley, author interview.

136   "Baker had a very different agenda": Richard Viguerie, author interview.

136   "bad mouthing JAB": Margaret Tutwiler, memo to Baker, undated on Office of the
        President-Elect stationery, taking dictation from Pete Teeley, Baker personal files.

136   "I was a sop": Lyn Nofziger, *Nofziger*, p. 271.

137   "Can't I just be": Elisabeth Bumiller, "Margaret Tutwiler, at Crisis Central," *Wash-
        ington Post*, October 9, 1984.

137   "Reagan pretty much gave": James Baker interview.

137   "Baker had all these lieutenants": David Gergen, author interview.

137   "one of the most powerful alliances": Schieffer and Gates, *The Acting President*,
        pp. 86–87.

137   "The worst thing Baker did": Viguerie interview.

137   conversation with a political scientist: James A. Baker III, interview with A. James
        Reichley, December 15, 1980, Gerald R. Ford Presidential Library and Museum.

138   "Let me tell you something": James Baker interview.

138   "Mr. President, I've given him": Susan Baker interview.

138   "What if Sherman Adams died": Michael Medved, *The Shadow Presidents*, p. 212.

138   roughly two-thirds bigger: The White House had roughly three hundred budgeted
        staff positions and others detailed from various departments at the beginning of
        Eisenhower's presidency and roughly five hundred when Reagan came into office.
        Samuel Kernell and Samuel L. Popkin, *Chief of Staff*, p. 201.

138   "This is a tough job": James Baker, letter to Mark White, December 6, 1980, Prince-
        ton archive.

139   "What happened to Jordan": Richard Cohen, "Unfair Battering Taken by Hamilton
        Jordan," *Washington Post*, December 7, 1980.

139   "Per JAB: clip & save": Copy of Cohen column, with handwritten note dated
        December 9, 1980, Princeton archive.

139   "Restore power and authority": James A. Baker III, *"Work Hard, Study . . . and Keep
        Out of Politics!,"* pp. 137–38.

139   "honest broker": Handwritten notes, Princeton archive.

139 "Rumsfeld's Rules": "Rumsfeld's Rules for 'The Assistant to the President,'" Princeton archive.
140 "He had one of the best antenna": Gergen interview.
140 "velvet hammer": Louise Sweeney, "Reagan's Velvet Hammer," *Christian Science Monitor,* January 2, 1981.

CHAPTER 9. Shit Detector

141 "In the present crisis": Ronald Reagan, Inaugural Address, January 20, 1981, American Presidency Project, University of California, Santa Barbara, http://www .presidency.ucsb.edu/ws/?pid=43130.
141 "a respectable seven": William Safire, "The Land Is Bright," *New York Times,* January 22, 1981.
141 "no brilliant Hollywood producer": James Reston, "Reagan's Dramatic Success," *New York Times,* January 21, 1981.
142 "About to inherit worst economic mess": Chris Whipple, *The Gatekeepers,* p. 109.
143 "We thought he was a nut": James Baker, author interview.
143 "We honestly thought he was": Ibid.
143 "Jim had tremendous respect": John Rogers, author interview.
143 "He was the most warmly ruthless man": Deborah Hart Strober and Gerald S. Strober, *Reagan,* p. 45.
143 "He wasn't buddy-buddy": Ed Meese interview.
143 "but he does not give back": Michael K. Deaver, *Behind the Scenes,* p. 104.
143 "Neither one of them let": Rogers interview.
143 "How many people do you know": Margaret Tutwiler, author interview.
144 "Sounds great": Bob Schieffer and Gary Paul Gates, *The Acting President,* p. 91.
144 "I ran the campaign that": James Baker interview.
144 "Jimmy didn't kiss his ass": Stuart Spencer, author interview.
144 "He could have a wicked tongue": Karen Morgan, author interview.
144 "that fucking Arab": James Baker interview.
144 "What is the difference": Transcript, *MacNeil/Lehrer Report,* January 26, 1981.
145 "didn't seem too worried": Larry Speakes, *Speaking Out,* p. 86.
145 "It was terrible": Rogers interview.
145 "very sure of his authority": Alexander M. Haig Jr., *Caveat,* pp. 74–75.
145 "reluctant to reveal": Ibid., p. 83.
145 "the second most important person": Martin Schram, "Inside Ed Meese Runs a Law-and-Order Streak," *Washington Post,* March 15, 1981.
145 "Every single day Ed Meese": Lou Cannon, *President Reagan,* p. 184.
146 "One by one, Baker gathered": Haig, *Caveat,* p. 83.
146 "to go talk to Haig": James Baker interview.
147 "He just had contempt for anyone": Richard Allen, author interview.
147 "That didn't go down real well": James Baker interview.
147 "Baker's a quicker study than Meese": Allen interview.
147 "dogged critique of the paper": Haig, *Caveat,* pp. 76–77.
147 "were disappearing in a haze": Ibid.
147 "the vicar of American foreign policy": George Gedda, "Haig Sworn in as 'Vicar' of Foreign Policy," Associated Press, January 22, 1981.
147 "a lack of enthusiasm": Bernard Gwertzman, "Haig Opposes Plan for New Bush Role but Reagan Moves," *New York Times,* March 25, 1981.
148 "would never have dared": Haig, *Caveat,* pp. 80–82.
148 "schoolboyish habit of scribbling": Ibid., p. 83.
148 "How did we get to WW III": James Baker personal files.
148 "A. Haig's Relative Degrees of Crises": Ibid.
148 "go to the source": Don Oberdorfer and John M. Goshko, "U.S. Gives Warning on Cuba-Salvador Arms Flow; Haig Warns U.S. Will 'Go to the Source' to Block Arms to Salvador," *Washington Post,* February 22, 1981.

148 "Give me the word": Cannon, *President Reagan*, p. 196.
148 "In essence, he said, 'Al, we agree' ": David Gergen, *Eyewitness to Power*, p. 172.
148 "He just thought he was crazy": Allen interview.
149 should have three priorities: Cannon, *President Reagan*, p. 107.
149 "Let me tell you something": Michael Deaver, James A. Baker Oral History Project, Princeton and Rice, January 30, 2007.
150 "Baker was constantly keeping": Hedrick Smith interview.
150 "Shit detector": Ibid.

CHAPTER 10. Big Leagues

151 "Do you know what's happened": Tom Matthews, "Reagan's Close Call," *Newsweek*, April 13, 1981.
151 "We don't know what": Del Quentin Wilber, *Rawhide Down*, p. 107.
152 "It doesn't look good": Michael K. Deaver, *A Different Drummer*, p. 137.
152 "P hit/fighting": Wilber, *Rawhide Down*, pp. 112–13.
152 "It looks quite serious": Herbert L. Abrams, *The President Has Been Shot*, p. 84.
153 "Now, he was ghostly pale": James A. Baker III, *"Work Hard, Study . . . and Keep Out of Politics!,"* pp. 142–44.
153 "Who's minding the store?": Michael K. Deaver, *Behind the Scenes*, p. 21.
153 "Doctors believe bleeding": Larry Speakes, *Speaking Out*, pp. 9–10.
153 "that the President is unable": United States Constitution, Twenty-fifth Amendment.
153 "I didn't want people thinking": James Baker, author interview
154 "I never talked to him": Ibid.
154 "This thing is out of control": Wilber, *Rawhide Down*, p. 186.
154 "Constitutionally, gentlemen": Video of Haig news conference, March 30, 1981, https://www.youtube.com/watch?v=zUKWofL-OqY. See also Steven R. Weisman, "Bush Flies Back from Texas Set to Take Charge in Crisis," *New York Times*, March 31, 1981.
155 mockery, including within the White House: Baker was forgiving of Haig's performance and defended him on television afterward. "Al Haig served the country well on March 30, 1981," Baker wrote in his memoir years after the fact. "At a very difficult time for our nation, he assured the people—on balance and despite the gaffe—that all was well." Baker, *"Work Hard,"* pp. 148–49. Not everyone was convinced. Reviewing that line in a draft of the memoir, Margaret Tutwiler jotted in the margin a note to Baker: "Why are you saying this? Do you really believe this?" She did not think so. And she had a point. While working on the memoir, Baker dismissed Haig. "He did such a shitty job," he told his ghostwriter, Tom DeFrank, in an unpublished interview, April 29, 1993, Princeton archive.
155 "The president is in good shape": Wilber, *Rawhide Down*, pp. 189–90.
155 "I think that's fine": Ibid.
155 "I got criticized roundly": James Baker interview.
155 "it turned out to be absolutely": Ibid.
156 "I want to tell you": Laurence I. Barrett, *Gambling with History*, p. 106.
156 "I am aren't alive aren't I": Peggy Noonan, *When Character Was King*, p. 188.
156 "I should have known": Matthews, "Reagan's Close Call."
156 "What makes you think": Howell Raines, "Reagan Making Good Recovery, Signs a Bill; White House Working, Bush Assures Senate," *New York Times*, April 1, 1981.
156 "I had hoped it was a KGB agent": Wilber, *Rawhide Down*, p. 215.
157 "The vice president is not": James Baker interview.
157 "I want you to stay here": Max Friedersdorf, Ronald Reagan Oral History Project, Miller Center, University of Virginia, October 22, 2002, https://millercenter.org/the-presidency/presidential-oral-histories/max-friedersdorf-oral-history-assistant-president.
157 "God bless you, Mr. President": Chris Matthews, *Tip and the Gipper*, p. 73.
157 "closer to death than": Tip O'Neill, *Man of the House*, p. 336.

158 "Speaker O'Neill will never be": Richard Williamson memo to David Gergen, December 29, 1980, Princeton archive.

158 "That was the minor leagues": O'Neill, *Man of the House*, p. 332.

159 "an exceptionally congenial": Ibid., p. 401.

159 "We need to get back": Agenda for April 6, 1981, Princeton archive.

159 rose from 55 percent: Gallup poll data collected by the American Presidency Project, University of California at Santa Barbara, http://www.presidency.ucsb.edu/data/popularity.php?pres=40.

159 "The honeymoon has ended": David S. Broder, "Reagan Shot: End of a Dream," *Washington Post*, April 1, 1981.

159 "Nobody was ever better": Speakes, *Speaking Out*, p. 112.

159 "It didn't matter how much": Ed Rogers, author interview.

160 "Deaver and Baker had the attitude": William Clark, Ronald Reagan Oral History Project, Miller Center, University of Virginia, August 17, 2003, https://millercenter.org/the-presidency/presidential-oral-histories/william-p-clark-oral-history-assistant-president.

160 "Poppin' Fresh, the doughboy": Speakes, *Speaking Out*, pp. 90–91.

160 Baker and Deaver "were furious": Bob Schieffer and Gary Paul Gates, *The Acting President*, pp. 112–13.

160 "It isn't really undercutting Meese": Hedrick Smith, author interview.

160 "Jim Baker looked like the efficient": David Stockman, *The Triumph of Politics*, p. 45.

161 "You'd walk into his office": Smith interview.

161 "Okay, what's our story today": Helene Von Damm, *At Reagan's Side*, p. 180.

161 "You could pretty well": Lou Cannon, author interview.

162 "Darman and I were sometimes": David Gergen, author interview.

162 "He would say, 'That's a good' ": Speakes, *Speaking Out*, p. 95.

162 "It was a tortured process": Larry Speakes, *Speaking Out*, p. 95.

162 "Candor and gentle persuasion": Deaver, *Behind the Scenes*, p. 128.

162 "Almost all the other great leakers": Marlin Fitzwater, author interview.

163 "I got the reputation": James Baker, unpublished interview with ghostwriter Tom DeFrank, May 12, 1993, Princeton archive.

163 "Baker is one of the great leakers": Deborah Hart Strober and Gerald S. Strober, *Reagan*, p. 108.

163 "The Baker team were masters": Ed Rollins, *Bare Knuckles and Back Rooms*, pp. 90–92.

163 "I would say that generally": Ed Meese, author interview.

163 "backstabbing by leak": Edwin Meese III, *With Reagan*, p. 109.

163 "It's inappropriate for you": Lesley Stahl, *Reporting Live*, pp. 166–67. According to the journalist Ann Devroy, the joke almost got out of control when a cameraman overheard Stahl taping her fake piece and tipped off Sam Donaldson of ABC News. ABC reporters fanned out on Capitol Hill trying to confirm it and Donaldson got through to Baker, who denied it but got suspicious as a result. See Devroy, "Prank News Report Has Press Buzzing, Reagan Laughing," *USA Today*.

164 "He always had the longer checklist": Deaver, *Behind the Scenes*, p. 174.

164 "His staff would tell him he": Ibid., pp. 134–35.

164 "He was absolutely tenacious": Ibid., p. 127.

164 "He doesn't ask you to come in": Margaret Tutwiler, author interview.

164 "It was the main policymaking": Kenneth Duberstein, author interview.

165 "a creature of the center": Richard Darman, *Who's In Control?*, p. 21.

165 "That gives my dad": Jonathan Darman, author interview.

165 "Reagan's in-box": Evan Thomas, "Remembering Dick Darman," *Newsweek*, January 24, 2008.

165 "He screams and throws paper": Marlin Fitzwater, *Call the Briefing!*, p. 98.

165 "He was the only guy": Stuart Spencer, Ronald Reagan Oral History Project, Miller Center, University of Virginia, November 15–16, 2001.

165 "a man whose talents": Rollins, *Bare Knuckles and Back Rooms*, pp. 90–92.

166 "Dick was somewhat insecure": Gergen interview.

166 "easily the most disliked man": Martin Anderson, *Revolution*, p. 240.
166 "Is The Big Tax Cut Dead?": Steven F. Hayward, "This Day in Gipper History," *National Review*, March 30, 2011.
166 "was a fly in New Deal amber": Stockman, *The Triumph of Politics*, p. 236.
166 "potentially gettable Democrats": Darman, *Who's In Control?*, p. 86.
167 "What's happening to me": Tony Kornheiser, "Tip O'Neill's Toughest Inning: The Sermon on the Mount," *Washington Post*, May 31, 1981.
167 "Leak story that White House": Unsigned memo, May 6, 1981, Princeton archive.
168 "could well ignite an inferno": Stockman, *The Triumph of Politics*, p. 188.
168 "They wanted the president": James Baker interview.
168 "If there's *any* doubt": Stockman, *The Triumph of Politics*, p. 189.
168 "I was furious": Ibid.
168 "Jim Baker carried around a bazooka": Ibid., p. 13.
169 "He knew you were never": Karen Morgan, author interview.
169 "Jim Baker made a few private runs": Stockman, *The Triumph of Politics*, pp. 245–46.
169 "We stroked and we stroked": Matthews, *Tip and the Gipper*, p. 126.
169 "Jim kept saying to me": Duberstein interview.
170 "They put only one legislative ball": O'Neill, *Man of the House*, p. 342.

CHAPTER 11. The Witches' Brew

174 "Not helpful": Richard Williamson, memorandum to James Baker, July 23, 1981, Princeton archive. Asked by the authors, Baker said he did not remember referring to them as "kooks" but acknowledged he could have.
174 "Reagan shares the view": Robert D. Novak, *Prince of Darkness*, pp. 370–71.
174 "With this, I burned bridges": Ibid.
174 "the air crackled": Sara Fritz, memorandum to colleagues, May 4, 1982, recording the party from the previous evening. Sara Fritz papers, Ronald Reagan Presidential Library and Museum.
174 "Dear Friend of Ronald Reagan": Clymer L. Wright Jr., letter to Republicans, May 14, 1982, Princeton archive.
175 "Yes, there is undermining": Ronald Reagan, letter to Clymer Wright, May 18, 1982, Princeton archive.
175 "Well—outa oily south Texas": Lyrics, "You Don't Mess Around with Jim," Princeton archive.
175 "The ceaseless sniping": Michael K. Deaver, *Behind the Scenes*, p. 128.
176 "I never knew until just": Peggy Noonan, author interview.
176 "The accusation used to drive me crazy": Stuart Spencer, author interview.
176 "On matters of policy": David Stockman, *The Triumph of Politics*, p. 83.
176 "Frankly, we weren't in a position": Richard Viguerie, author interview.
176 "we would have not": Noonan interview.
177 "tower over it like Ichabod Crane": Larry Speakes, *Speaking Out*, pp. 300–302.
177 "I want you to go into": Ibid., pp. 308–9.
177 "the highest negatives of any candidate": Elisabeth Bumiller, "Ed Rollins, Out on Front," *Washington Post*, December 19, 1983.
177 "You've gotta go to the woodshed": Ed Rollins, *Bare Knuckles and Back Rooms*, pp. 100–102.
177 "Now goddamnit, you walk out": Ibid.
178 "the left was inherently totalitarian": Stockman, *The Triumph of Politics*, pp. 1–2.
178 "a spare and stingy creature": Ibid., p. 8.
178 "Trojan horse to bring down": William Greider, "The Education of David Stockman," *Atlantic Monthly*, December 1981 (published in November).
178 "David Stockman stuck a knife": Michael K. Deaver, *Nancy*, p. 99.
178 "in that deliberate, dispassionate": Helene Von Damm, *At Reagan's Side*, p. 223.
178 "He didn't like to fire people": Ed Meese, author interview.
178 "I want you to listen up good": Lou Cannon, *President Reagan*, pp. 261–63.

178 "The menu is humble pie": Ibid.
179 "was politically disappointed": Robert Kimmitt, author interview.
180 "It is not the business": Ronald Reagan, News Conference, October 1, 1981, American Presidency Project, University of California at Santa Barbara, http://www.presidency.ucsb.edu/ws/index.php?pid=44327.
180 "We knew we had to win": Kimmitt interview.
181 "ill served by a staff": Charles Mohr, "Senate, 52–48, Supports Reagan on AWACS Jet Sale to Saudis; Heavy Lobbying Tips Key Votes," *New York Times*, October 21, 1981.
181 "not-quite-national-security adviser": David Rothkopf, *Running the World*, p. 224.
181 "regarded by his colleagues": Alexander M. Haig Jr., *Caveat*, p. 85.
181 "I could see he had": Richard Allen, author interview.
182 "decay of the Soviet experiment": Ronald Reagan, Address to Members of the British Parliament, June 8, 1982, American Presidency Project, University of California at Santa Barbara, http://www.presidency.ucsb.edu/ws/?pid=42614.
183 "a witches' brew of intrigue": James A. Baker III, *The Politics of Diplomacy*, p. 26.
183 "What an ego!": Speakes, *Speaking Out*, p. 96.
183 "I used to describe Al Haig": Deborah Hart Strober and Gerald S. Strober, *Reagan*, p. 86.
183 "I was convinced that": Michael Deaver, Ronald Reagan Oral History Project, Miller Center, University of Virginia.
183 He ordered the American ambassador: Patrick Tyler, *A World of Trouble*, p. 265.
183 "To me, the White House": Haig, *Caveat*, p. 85.
183 "That son of a bitch": Richard Reeves, *President Reagan*, p. 111.
183 "Happy birthday Jim": Michael K. Deaver, *Behind the Scenes*, p. 172.
184 "trying to irritate": Speakes, *Speaking Out*, p. 97.
184 "Clark told me that James Baker": Haig, *Caveat*, pp. 300–301.
184 "decided that Haig was not": James Baker, unpublished interview with ghostwriter Tom DeFrank, May 1993, Princeton archive.
184 "in a manner that seemed": Robert C. McFarlane, *Special Trust*, pp. 199–200.
184 "At least he's got a window": Laurence I. Barrett, *Gambling with History*, pp. 240–41.
184 "with a white-knuckled animus": McFarlane, *Special Trust*, pp. 199–200.
184 "I assumed that he": Alexander M. Haig Jr., *Inner Circles*, p. 547.
184 "I was in there when": James Baker, author interview.
185 "I don't think anyone": Margaret Tutwiler, author interview.
185 "We were all high-fiving": Deaver, Miller Center oral history.
185 "Whoa there": Peggy Noonan, *What I Saw at the Revolution*, p. 163.
185 "He gave only one reason": Ronald Reagan, *The Reagan Diaries*, ed. Douglas Brinkley, pp. 90–91.
185 "I was set up": Tyler, *A World of Trouble*, p. 281.
185 "Baker is solely in charge": Sara Fritz, memo summarizing interview with Fuller, June 17, 1982, Fritz papers.
186 fallen from 68 percent: Gallup poll data collected by the American Presidency Project, University of California at Santa Barbara, http://www.presidency.ucsb.edu/data/popularity.php?pres=40.
186 "All right, goddamn it": James Baker interview.
186 "extraordinarily cunning": Rollins, *Bare Knuckles and Back Rooms*, pp. 86–88.
186 "among the slickest": Lyn Nofziger, *Nofziger*, p. 280.
187 "The first was taking the job": Ibid., p. 273.
187 "I did make a mistake": James Baker interview.
187 "Why don't you ask Lyn": Nofziger, *Nofziger*, pp. 312–14.
187 "There's your pass": Ibid.
188 "He was right and we were wrong": James Baker interview.
188 "(1) I'm not running": Unsigned, undated memorandum showing poll numbers for trial heats in Texas Senate race, Princeton archive.
188 "Dad, why don't you run": Doug Baker, author interview.
189 "Had to expect that": Reagan, *The Reagan Diaries*, p. 110.

CHAPTER 12. The Ratfuck

190 "Without saying it": John Baker, author interview.

190 "They clearly knew": Ibid.

191 released on a $10,000 bond: "James Baker's Son Arrested," United Press International, December 10, 1982, https://www.nytimes.com/1982/12/10/us/james-baker-s-son-arrested.html.

191 "It was a BS thing": James Baker, author interview.

191 "Just say no": "Nancy Reagan's 'Just Say No' Campaign," Addiction.com, July 7, 2012, https://www.addiction.com/6662/nancy-reagans-just-say-no-campaign/.

191 Thirty-four percent of high school students: "Drugs and American High School Students, 1975–1983," National Institute on Drug Abuse, http://monitoringthefuture.org/pubs/monographs/mtf-vol1_1983.pdf.

192 "He had to balance": Doug Baker, author interview.

192 reached a plea bargain: United Press International dispatch, December 13, 1984, https://www.upi.com/Archives/1984/12/13/John-C-Baker-son-of-White-House-Chief-of/8615471762000/.

192 "When I saw my dad": John Baker interview.

192 "I think every one of our kids": James Baker interview.

192 "Bo was the *ringleader*": Susan Baker, author interview.

192 "people stabbing you in the back": Chris Whipple, *The Gatekeepers*, p. 113.

193 Baker was "*the* conduit": Alan Greenspan, author interview.

194 "This bill demonstrates": Francis X. Clines, "Pension Changes Signed into Law," *New York Times*, April 21, 1983.

195 "The commission he built was": Alan Greenspan, *The Age of Turbulence*, pp. 94–96.

195 "In our negotiations he was able": Robert M. Ball, *The Greenspan Commission*, p. 67.

195 "as if he had been run over": David Gergen, *Eyewitness to Power*, p. 152.

195 "Fellas, I've got a confession": Ibid.

195 "Reagan really needed a chief of staff": Whipple, *The Gatekeepers*, p. 111.

195 "rather like a grandfather": Paul Kengor and Patricia Clark Doerner, *The Judge*, pp. 151–53.

196 "Nancy felt terribly guilty": Deborah Hart Strober and Gerald S. Strober, *Reagan*, p. 52.

196 "I was just trying to keep": James Baker interview.

196 "Why don't you go talk": Whipple, *The Gatekeepers*, p. 139.

196 "He also cultivated the press": Nancy Reagan, *My Turn*, pp. 250–51. That did not keep her from appreciating Baker. After leaving the White House, the two kept in touch and when it came time to plan out her funeral, she asked Baker to deliver a eulogy.

197 "I think it is important that": Chase Untermeyer, *When Things Went Right*, p. 251.

197 "How long do I have to work": Ibid.

197 "out of control, screaming": Lyn Nofziger, *Nofziger*, pp. 286–87.

197 "Lynwood, what are we going to do": Ibid.

197 "I think we did what we should": Allen Pusey, "Aide Assesses Reagan at Midterm: Baker Admits Squabbles, Urges Donovan Resignation," *Dallas Morning News*, January 9, 1983.

198 "Ray Donovan shouldn't be": Ibid. Years later, after Donovan left office, he was brought to trial but acquitted of charges of corruption involving his construction company, after which he famously asked, "Which office do I go to to get my reputation back?"

198 "inadvertent and regrettable": James Gerstenzang, "Reagan Voices 'Full Confidence' in Donovan," Associated Press, January 11, 1983.

198 "Jimmy Baker at year end": Jon Meacham, *Destiny and Power*, p. 288.

198 "I think he should get out": Ibid.

198 "He was thrilled and went charging": Ibid.

199 "Let Reagan be Reagan!": Untermeyer, *When Things Went Right*, p. 262.

199 "This always struck me as odd": Ibid., p. 285.
199 "legislative wizardry": "Memo to Judge Clark," *Human Events*, April 23, 1983.
199 "Light reading": Meacham, *Destiny and Power*, p. 289.
199 "I want you to know": Ed Rollins, *Bare Knuckles and Back Rooms*, pp. 120–21.
200 "So *that's* where he went": Ibid.
200 "I got in this big argument": Stuart Spencer, author interview.
200 "We wanted to get Rollins offline": James Baker interview.
201 a 246-word item buried: David Hoffman, "Reagan Staff Had Carter Data Before '80 Debate, Book Says," *Washington Post*, January 9, 1983.
201 "a Reagan mole in the Carter": Laurence I. Barrett, *Gambling with History*, p. 382.
201 "Baker was really torn apart": David Keene, author interview.
201 "I came up through Watergate": James Baker interview.
201 "You build a reputation": Ibid.
201 "It is my recollection that": James Baker, draft letter to Don Albosta, "dictated over the telephone," June 22, 1983, Hoover Institution Library & Archives, Stanford University.
202 "I did not know then": James Baker, final letter to Albosta, June 22, 1983, Hoover archives.
202 "Say you saw it": Bob Woodward, *Veil*, p. 310.
202 "It put the fear of God in me": James Baker interview.
202 "He wasn't quite suave enough": Strober and Strober, *Reagan*, p. 67.
202 "It was a double mistake": Ibid.
203 "Baker was convinced": Ibid., pp. 165–66.
203 "God knows what he just approved": Robert C. McFarlane, *Special Trust*, p. 283.
203 "Stop these leaks": Speakes, *Speaking Out*, p. 114.
203 "We should turn this right back": Ibid.
203 "Anything Jim Baker says": James A. Baker III, *"Work Hard, Study . . . and Keep Out of Politics!,"* p. 119.
204 "I term Jim Baker an honest person": Steve Goldberg, "Debate Prober Backs Baker," Media General News Service, published in the *Richmond News Leader*, September 26, 1983.
204 "It wasn't worth a damn": James Baker interview.
204 But the *Post* examined it: Martin Schram, "Carter Book Seems to Have Aided Reagan in 1980 Debate," *Washington Post*, June 27, 1983.
204 "Reagan was quite well briefed": Jimmy Carter, author interview.
204 "rue the day": Francis X. Clines, "James Baker: Calling Reagan's Re-Election Moves," *New York Times Magazine*, May 20, 1984.
204 "It ate away at him": Jim Cicconi, author interview.
204 A poll showed that 70 percent: Harris Survey, Louis Harris & Associates, July 14–18, 1983.
204 "It ain't fun to see your name": John W. Mashek, notes from background interview with James Baker, July 8, 1983.
204 "He had months of hell": Susan Baker interview.
205 more believable than Casey's: Subcommittee on Human Resources, Committee on Post Office and Civil Service, House of Representatives, "Unauthorized Transfers of Nonpublic Information During the 1980 Presidential Election,": May 24, 1984, https://archive.org/stream/DebategateReport/Debategate%20Report%20volume%201_djvu.txt.
205 "professional services": Craig Shirley, *Rendezvous with Destiny*, p. 437.
205 "I was able to call Jim": Dick Cheney, author interview.
205 "little doubt": Shirley, *Rendezvous with Destiny*, p. 607.
205 "Jim, you succeeded in reviving": William Casey, draft letter to James Baker, March 25, 1985, Hoover archives.
205 "gets record straight": Casey notes, Hoover archives.
206 "the two most awful things": Susan Baker interview.
206 "Baker cared a great deal": Margaret Tutwiler, author interview.

CHAPTER 13. The Dark Side

207 "I'll be goddamned!": Francis X. Clines, "James Baker: Calling Reagan's Re-Election Moves," *New York Times Magazine*, May 20, 1984.

207 "Mr. President, Mike tells me": James Baker, author interview. Shultz later made a public threat to resign when the idea of a lie detector test came up again two years later. "The minute in this government I am told that I'm not trusted is the day that I leave," he told a news conference in December 1985. Norman Kempster, "Shultz Says He Will Resign if Ordered to Take Lie Test," *Los Angeles Times*, December 20, 1985.

208 "It's easy to start a war": James Baker interview.

209 "In short," he wrote: Robert McFarlane, secret memorandum, September 10, 1983, Princeton archive.

209 "Syrian takeover of this country": Second McFarlane memorandum, Princeton archive.

209 "I ask you to use all legitimate means": Ronald Reagan, memorandum to William French Smith, September 14, 1983, Princeton archive.

209 "We're seeking bipartisan support": Lou Cannon and George C. Wilson, "Reagan Authorizes Marines to Call In Beirut Air Strikes," *Washington Post*, September 13, 1983.

209 "Me": Copy of article, Princeton archive.

209 he did not tell the reporter: James Baker, handwritten notes on White House stationery titled "Lou" and dated September 15, 1983, Princeton archive.

210 "(1) only if *all* are": James Baker, handwritten notes on back of White House stationery, titled "Polygraph" and dated September 17, 1983, Princeton archive.

210 "We did not talk about matters": Lou Cannon, letter to James Baker, September 28, 1983, Princeton archive.

210 "There was no leak but a gush": David Gergen, memorandum, October 4, 1983, Princeton archive.

210 as close to Reagan as a "brother": Douglas Martin, "William P. Clark, Influential Adviser in Reagan White House, Is Dead at 81," *New York Times*, August 12, 2013.

210 "That's how we're going to": Michael Deaver, Ronald Reagan Oral History Project, Miller Center, University of Virginia, September 12, 2002.

211 "Mr. President, don't you think": James Baker interview.

211 "How do we roll Clark today": William Clark, Ronald Reagan Oral History Project, Miller Center, University of Virginia.

211 "It was the only time Baker lost": Paul Kengor and Patricia Clark Doerner, *The Judge*, pp. 247–48.

211 "Baker tried to convince her": Ibid.

211 "a user" who claimed: Nancy Reagan, *My Turn*, pp. 242–43.

211 "not the brightest bulb in the chandelier": Chris Whipple, *The Gatekeepers*, p. 113.

211 "rogue NSC adviser": James Baker interview.

211 "We never knew where Clark": Ibid.

211 "crime against humanity": "Transcript of President Reagan's Address on Downing of Korean Airliner," *New York Times*, September 6, 1983.

212 "If the best this president": "Insufficient Response," *Detroit News*, September 7, 1983. Copy with Gergen's notation in Princeton files.

212 "It just became almost intolerable": Deaver, Miller Center oral history.

213 "I have a black, I have a woman": Steven R. Weisman, "Watt Quits Post," *New York Times*, October 10, 1983.

213 "Baker knew just how much": Michael K. Deaver, *Behind the Scenes*, pp. 129–30.

213 "with brilliance" and a "deft touch": George P. Shultz, *Turmoil and Triumph*, pp. 320–21.

214 "roundtable" the decision: Deborah Hart Strober and Gerald S. Strober, *Reagan*, pp. 90–91.

214 "you can't have the biggest leaker": Edwin Meese 3rd, *With Reagan*, p. 114.

214   "I'm not sure that Mike Deaver": Ed Meese, author interview.
214   "That was a close call": Robert McFarlane, author interview.
214   "Fellas, I got a revolt": Clines, "James Baker."
214   "How could you do this?": Strober and Strober, *Reagan*, p. 92. Quoting Baker.
214   "This is the second time": Ibid., p. 90. Deaver recalls the story this way, but he appeared to be referring to Hedrick Smith's *The Power Game*, which actually quoted Deaver differently. In this account, Deaver yelled at Reagan, shouting, "You don't have enough confidence in me to make me chief of staff!" See Smith, *The Power Game*, p. 324.
215   "I would never say that": Ibid., *Reagan*, p. 90.
215   "I was getting mad": Deaver, Miller Center oral history.
215   "Mr. President, when I came here": Deaver, Miller Center oral history.
215   "God, what kind of jerk am I?": Ibid.
215   "Jim took it well but Mike was pretty upset": Ronald Reagan, *The Reagan Diaries*, ed. Douglas Brinkley, p. 187.
215   "If they hadn't had that debate": Robert Kimmitt, author interview.
216   "One thing I didn't understand": Peter Collier, *Political Woman*, p. 163.
216   "Iran-contra wouldn't have happened": Michael Deaver, James A. Baker Oral History Project, Princeton and Rice.
216   "My decision not to appoint": Ronald Reagan, *An American Life*, p. 448.
216   "How could this happen?": Robert C. McFarlane, *Special Trust*, p. 263.
217   "Bud, what is the light at": Lou Cannon, *President Reagan*, p. 453. Quoting McFarlane.
218   "This is not a consultation": Strober and Strober, *Reagan*, p. 273.
218   *You're on your own*: John A. Farrell, *Tip O'Neill and the Democratic Century*, p. 617.
218   "Preposterous, knock it down hard": Larry Speakes, *Speaking Out*, pp. 187–91.
218   "be careful what you say": Ibid.
218   "That was treatment about as unfair": Ibid.
218   "I may have made a mistake": James Baker interview.
219   "It wasn't *just* manufactured": Strober and Strober, *Reagan*, p. 289.
219   send over documents: James Baker files, Princeton archive.
219   "When I found out, I was ecstatic": Doug Baker, author interview.
220   "This is his life long dream": Ronald Reagan, *The Reagan Diaries*, pp. 213–14.
220   "I think the president would be better served": Lou Cannon, "Chief of Staff Baker Affirms Intention Not to Serve in a Second Reagan Term," *Washington Post*, January 14, 1984.
220   "So Jim Baker's going to get": Bob Woodward, *Veil*, pp. 429–31. The ally was Anthony Motley, an assistant secretary of state for Western Hemisphere affairs.
221   "I want to call your attention": James Baker, letter to Georgia Horner, August 28, 1984, Princeton archive.

CHAPTER 14. Morning in America

222   "amiable dunce": Arnold Sawislak, "Reagan Called 'Amiable Dunce' on New Washington Tape," United Press International, October 10, 1981, https://www.upi .com/Archives/1981/10/10/Reagan-called-amiable-dunce-on-new-Washington -tape/3026371534400/.
222   "It's true that hard work": Lou Cannon, "The Truth in Reagan's Humor," *Washington Post*, April 27, 1987.
224   "I'd rather get 80 percent": James Baker, author interview.
224   "That was Ronald Reagan": Jim Cicconi, author interview.
225   "Once more acquisition": Haynes Johnson, *Sleepwalking Through History*, p. 113.
226   expanding by 7.2 percent: Bureau of Economic Analysis, https://apps.bea.gov/iTable /iTable.cfm?reqid=19&step=3&isuri=1&1921=survey&1903=1#reqid=19&step=3 &isuri=1&1921=survey&1903=1.
226   Unemployment stood at 8 percent: Bureau of Labor Statistics historical tables, https://data.bls.gov/timeseries/LNS14000000.

226   according to a study: Robert Pear, "Study of Reagan Domestic Policy Finds Good
       and Bad News," *New York Times*, August 16, 1984.
226   "The debate in the last": David E. Rosenbaum, "In Four Years, Reagan Changed
       Basis of the Debate on Domestic Programs," *New York Times*, October 25, 1984.
226   Fifty percent of Americans: Gallup Poll, February 10–13, 1984. Fifty percent were
       satisfied, 46 percent were unsatisfied, and 4 percent had no opinion, https://news
       .gallup.com/poll/1669/general-mood-country.aspx.
227   "President Reagan has made": Richard Reeves, "The Ideological Election," *New York
       Times Magazine*, February 19, 1984.
227   "I can't make a fool of myself": David Stockman, *The Triumph of Politics*, pp. 374–75.
227   "was like a dog with a bone": Lou Cannon, *President Reagan*, p. 382.
228   "All this past weekend": Barry Goldwater, letter to William Casey, reproduced in *The
       New York Times*, April 11, 1984, https://www.nytimes.com/1984/04/11/world/text-of
       -goldwater-s-letter-to-the-head-of-cia.html.
228   "first acts of deception": Theodore Draper, *A Very Thin Line*, p. 22.
228   "I would like to get money": Minutes, National Security Planning Group Meet-
       ing, June 25, 1984, National Security Archive, https://nsarchive2.gwu.edu/NSAEBB
       /NSAEBB210/2-NSPG%20minutes%206-25-84%20(IC%2000463).pdf.
229   "we should take a very close look": Draper, *A Very Thin Line*, p. 76.
230   "If Reagan not run, what": James Baker, handwritten notes, undated, Princeton
       archive.
230   "99 percent" confident: Undated summary of a "deep background" dinner Baker
       had with a reporter for *U.S. News & World Report*. Sara Fritz files, Ronald Reagan
       Presidential Library and Museum, https://www.reaganlibrary.gov/sites/default/files
       /digitallibrary/personalpapers/fritz/box-004/40-414-004-005-2018.pdf.
230   to a dismal 35 percent: Gallup Poll, January 28–31, 1983. This was the lowest of Rea-
       gan's eight years in office. https://news.gallup.com/interactives/185273/presidential
       -job-approval-center.aspx.
230   Reagan's four most recent predecessors: Lyndon Johnson faced challenges for the
       Democratic nomination in 1968 from Eugene McCarthy and Robert F. Kennedy,
       ultimately convincing him to drop out of the race. Richard Nixon had to fend off two
       Republican congressmen who challenged him in 1972, Pete McCloskey of California
       from the left and John Ashbrook of Ohio from the right; neither was a serious threat,
       but Nixon growled about the "two gnats on my ass" and their campaigns delayed the
       time when the president could draw on the resources of the Republican National
       Committee, which had to stay ostensibly neutral. (See Jack W. Germond and Jules
       Witcover, *Wake Us When It's Over*, p. 327.) Gerald Ford, of course, had to first defeat
       Ronald Reagan in 1976 and Jimmy Carter had to get past Ted Kennedy in 1980.
230   "concrete steps we can take": Memorandum, unsigned and undated, in a folder from
       1983, Princeton archive.
230   "Ronald Reagan has always": Ed Rollins, memorandum, March 23, 1983, Princeton
       archive.
230   sixty-three-page memo: Germond and Witcover, *Wake Us When It's Over*, p. 89.
231   "Let me give you a bit": John Brady, *Bad Boy*, pp. 101–2.
231   "When her parents married": Elisabeth Bumiller, "Margaret Tutwiler, at Crisis Cen-
       tral," *Washington Post*, October 9, 1984.
232   "You're fifty-four years old": Ibid.
232   "tough and smarter": James Baker, "*Word Hard, Study . . . and Keep Out of Politics!*,"
       p. 284. This is a good example of how buttoned-down Baker was in his first memoir,
       The Politics of Diplomacy; in that book, he quoted Nixon saying Tutwiler was "tough,
       mean and devious," leaving out the more colorful term he later acknowledged. See
       Baker, *The Politics of Diplomacy*, p. 33.
232   "I've known Ronald Reagan": Ed Rollins, *Bare Knuckles and Back Rooms*, pp. 129–30.
232   "Baker might have been": Charles Black, author interview.
233   "Mondale—What If He's Worse": Clines, "James Baker."
233   "splash, dash and glitter": Germond and Witcover, *Wake Us When It's Over*, p. 179.

234   "hands that once picked cotton": Ibid., p. 74.

234   shot up to 55 percent: Gallup Poll, January 27–30, 1984, https://news.gallup.com /interactives/185273/presidential-job-approval-center.aspx.

234   from $74 billion: Historical Tables, Office of Management and Budget. See Table 1.1, Summary of Receipts, Outlays, and Surpluses or Deficits (-): 1789–2023, https:// www.whitehouse.gov/omb/historical-tables/.

235   "Let's tell the truth": Walter Mondale, "Address Accepting the Presidential Nomination at the Democratic National Convention in San Francisco," July 19, 1984, American Presidency Project, University of California at Santa Barbara, http://www .presidency.ucsb.edu/ws/index.php?pid=25972.

235   raising taxes by $50 billion: Impact of Budget Proposals on State and Local Issues, House Committee on the Budget, February 9, 1985, https://books.google.com /books?id=pBskMENSvIgC&pg=PA51&lpg=PA51&dq=deficit+reduction+act+of +1984+$50+billion+$11+billion&source=bl&ots=4D6MoGqoR7&sig=ACfU3Uo FpTovDjBYxaTBXoa2J_smowmsgw&hl=en&sa=X&ved=2ahUKEwjS_4_IoI_lAh VDmKoKHbxRAoQQ6AEwAnoECAcQAQ#v=onepage&q=deficit%20reduction %20act%20of%201984%20%2450%20billion%20%2411%20billion&f=false.

235   "In a very real sense": Germond and Witcover, *Wake Us When It's Over*, p. 466.

235   "(a.) don't say": James Baker, handwritten notes, undated, Princeton archive.

235   A memo prepared: Richard Reeves, *President Reagan*, pp. 226–27.

236   "My opponent has spent his": Germond and Witcover, *Wake Us When It's Over*, p. 418.

236   "The president is ordering you": Paul A. Volcker, *Keeping At It*, pp. 118–19.

237   speech from Pointe du Hoc: Ronald Reagan, "Remarks at a Ceremony Commemorating the 40th Anniversary of the Normandy Invasion, D-day," June 6, 1984, American Presidency Project, University of California at Santa Barbara, http://www .presidency.ucsb.edu/ws/index.php?pid=40018.

237   "First, the Olympics": Marcia Forbes, quoted in the Long Beach *Press-Telegram* and cited in Germond and Witcover, *Wake Us When It's Over*, p. 463.

237   "It's morning again in America": Ronald Reagan Videos, History Channel, https:// www.history.com/topics/us-presidents/ronald-reagan/videos/morning-in-america.

237   "It's all picket fences": Michael Beschloss, "The Ad That Helped Reagan Sell Good Times to an Uncertain Nation," *New York Times*, May 7, 2016.

238   "I ♥ U.S.": *Time* magazine, September 24, 1984, http://content.time.com/time /magazine/0,9263,7601840924,00.html.

238   55 percent to 37 percent: Cannon, *President Reagan*, pp. 538–39.

238   "Shut up!": Ibid.

238   "Reagan has been so cocooned": Ibid., p. 540.

238   "Doing everything we can": Video, Associated Press, August 1, 1984, https://www .youtube.com/watch?v=6JTtI3D6lqk.

239   "He didn't seem alert": Walter Mondale, *The Good Fight*, p. 300.

239   "I'm all confused now": Transcript, October 7, 1984, Commission on Presidential Debates, http://www.debates.org/index.php?page=october-7-1984-debate-transcript.

239   66 percent to 17 percent: Adam Clymer, "Poll Finds Debate Gave Mondale a Small Gain," *New York Times*, October 11, 1984.

239   "I stunk": Spencer interview.

239   "What have you done": Nancy Reagan, *My Turn*, p. 278.

239   "I had the briefing books": Stuart Spencer, James A. Baker III Oral History Project, Princeton and Rice.

239   "He was brutalized by": Lou Cannon, "Sen. Laxalt Hits Debate Briefing," *Washington Post*, October 12, 1984.

240   "What's up?" Darman asked: Richard Darman: *Who's In Control?*, pp. 132–35.

241   "cautioned him about Darman": Spencer oral history.

241   Nancy was "insane": Cannon, *President Reagan*, p. 546.

241   "took that very personally": Person close to Darman, author interview.

241   "There's a bear in the woods": The Living Room Candidate, Presidential Campaign

Commercials 1952–2016, Museum of the Moving Image, http://www.livingroom candidate.org/commercials/1984/bear.

242 financial questions about her husband: Zaccaro eventually did release his tax returns during the campaign. In January 1985, after the election, he pleaded guilty in New York to submitting fraudulent documents as part of a 1983 real estate deal. He was sentenced to 150 hours of community service. See Ralph Blumenthal, "Judge Sentences Zaccaro to Work in Public Service," *New York Times*, February 21, 1985. More than two years later, a jury acquitted him in an unrelated case in which he was charged with trying to extort a bribe from a cable television company. See George James, "Jury Acquits Zaccaro of Seeking to Extort Cable Television Bribe," *New York Times*, October 15, 1987.

242 "Let me help you with": Transcript, Vice Presidential Debate, Philadelphia, October 11, 1984, American Presidency Project, University of California at Santa Barbara, http://www.presidency.ucsb.edu/ws/index.php?pid=29425.

242 "We tried to kick a little ass": Dale Russakoff, "Bush Boasts of Kicking 'A Little Ass' at Debate," *Washington Post*, October 13, 1984.

242 Garry Wills compared Reagan's performance: Garry Wills, *Reagan's America*, pp. 228–30.

242 "Chuckle again": Ibid., p. 232.

243 "Is there any doubt in your mind": Transcript, October 21, 1984, Commission on Presidential Debates, http://www.debates.org/index.php?page=october-21-1984 -debate-transcript.

243 "Yes, age is an issue": Germond and Witcover, *Wake Us When It's Over*, p. 11.

243 "Well, I might just say": Ibid.

243 "You'll see that I was smiling": Walter Mondale, interview with Jim Lehrer, May 25, 1990, *Debating Our Destiny*, PBS, https://web.archive.org/web/20001212070100 /http://www.pbs.org/newshour/debatingourdestiny/dod/1984-broadcast.html.

243 He took a resounding 59 percent: Election of 1984, American Presidency Project, University of California at Santa Barbara, http://www.presidency.ucsb.edu/statistics /elections/1984.

244 "that's just been arranged": David S. Broder, "Reagan Wins Reelection in Landslide, Largest Electoral College Total Ever," *Washington Post*, November 7, 1984.

244 "We *have* to play down": Rollins, *Bare Knuckles and Back Rooms*, pp. 151–52.

244 "large lies told through": William Greider, "Reagan's Reelection: How the Media Became All the President's Men," *Rolling Stone*, December 20, 1984.

245 "As I remember it": James Baker, letter to Joseph Alsop, December 4, 1984, Princeton archive. Baker enclosed $200 worth of Susan B. Anthony dollar coins that he had won in another wager with a supporter of the Equal Rights Amendment plus a $50 check for the difference.

245 "I bet you didn't know your guests": James Baker, bcc copy of letter to Alsop, sent to Meg Greenfield, Princeton archive.

CHAPTER 15. Fencing Master

246 "Fuck yourself": Lou Cannon, *President Reagan*, p. 555.

246 "You're tired, aren't you?": James Baker, author interview. Also see Donald T. Regan, *For the Record*, pp. 243–45.

247 headed toward confirmation: Ed Meese was confirmed by the Senate on February 23, 1985, by a 63 to 31 vote, drawing the most negative votes of any attorney general nominee to that point since 1925. "Meese Confirmed After Delay of 13 Months," *CQ Almanac*, 1985.

247 "Both parties are tired": Memo, unsigned and undated, Princeton archive.

247 "Serious, substantive job": Handwritten notes, undated and unsigned. Green Post-it note on top says they were prepared by Dick Darman. Princeton archive.

248 "I've brought you a playmate": Bob Schieffer and Gary Paul Gates, *The Acting President*, p. 299.

248   "nodded affably": Regan, *For the Record*, pp. 254–57.

248   "I'd have flipped out": Stuart Spencer, Ronald Reagan Oral History Project, Miller Center, University of Virginia, November 15–16, 2001.

248   "If I was totally honest": James Baker confidant who asked not to be named, author interview.

249   "friendly session": Treasury Secretary Confirmation Hearing, C-SPAN, January 23, 1985, https://www.c-span.org/video/?125272-1/treasury-secretary-confirmation-hearing.

249   voting 95 to 0 to confirm: Presidential Cabinet Nominations, President Jimmy Carter through President George W. Bush, United States Senate, https://www.senate.gov/reference/resources/pdf/cabinettable.pdf.

249   "Isn't it something": Video of James Baker swearing-in, February 8, 1985, Ronald Reagan Presidential Library and Museum, https://www.youtube.com/watch?v=boKf-sfyOw4.

249   "He couldn't have been more": Margaret Tutwiler, author interview.

249   "I am instructing": Ronald Reagan, State of the Union address, February 6, 1985, American Presidency Project, University of California at Santa Barbara, http://www.presidency.ucsb.edu/ws/index.php?pid=38069.

250   about thirty thousand taxpayers: David E. Rosenbaum, "Treasury Study Cites Tax Disparity,": *New York Times*, August 2, 1985

250   just 6 percent in 1983: Jeffrey H. Birnbaum and Alan S. Murray, *Showdown at Gucci Gulch*, p. 11.

250   128 large, profitable companies: Robert S. McIntyre, "Corporate Income Taxes in the Reagan Years: A Study of Three Years of Legalized Tax Avoidance," Citizens for Tax Justice, October 1984, https://www.ctj.org/pdf/1984ReaganYears.pdf.

250   eight times as much money: In 1974, PACs gave $12.5 million to congressional candidates, compared to $104 million in 1984. Birnbaum and Murray, *Showdown at Gucci Gulch*, p. 18.

250   "I sort of like the tax code": David E. Rosenbaum, "A Tax Bill for the Textbooks," *New York Times*, October 23, 1986.

251   "It was a very apolitical": Ronald Pearlman, author interview.

251   "a tin ear for politics": James Baker interview.

251   "I've got to be the Sect.": James Baker, handwritten notes scribbled on White House cover sheet for joint statement, January 8, 1985, Princeton archive.

252   "Dad *hated* that": Jonathan Darman, author interview.

252   "Jimmy boy, you're massaging": Birnbaum and Murray, *Showdown at Gucci Gulch*, p. 77.

253   "There were times of stress": Pearlman interview.

253   "Ron, *you* describe this": Ibid.

254   "Death and taxes may be": Ronald Reagan, Address to the Nation on Tax Reform, May 28, 1985, American Presidency Project, University of California at Santa Barbara, https://www.presidency.ucsb.edu/documents/address-the-nation-tax-reform.

254   "If the president's plan": "Democratic Party's Response to the Tax Proposal," *New York Times*, May 29, 1985.

254   by 28 percent after inflation: Stanley L. Engerman and Robert E. Gallman, *The Cambridge Economic History of the United States*, Volume 3: *The Twentieth Century* (Cambridge, UK: Cambridge University Press, 2000), p. 500.

255   all-time record of $109 billion: United States Census, "U.S. Trade in Goods and Services—Balance of Payments (BOP) Basis," June 3, 2016, https://www.census.gov/foreign-trade/statistics/historical/gands.pdf.

255   One prominent economist: C. Fred Bergsten, director of what was then called the Institute for International Economics, quoted by Peter T. Kilborn, "Japan Invests Huge Sums Abroad, Much of It in U.S. Treasury Bonds," *New York Times*, March 11, 1985.

255   "The Japanning of America Today": Dave Schweisberg, "The Japanning of America Today," United Press International, in the *Durant (Okla.) Daily Democrat*, October 17, 1982.

255   appreciated another 20 percent: *American Economic Policy in the 1980s*, ed. by Martin Feldstein (Chicago: University of Chicago Press, 1994), p. 301.

255   "diffusing protectionist pressures": James Baker, memo to Ronald Reagan, September 20, 1985, Princeton archive.

256   10 percent to 12 percent: Jeffrey Frankel, *The Plaza Accord, 30 Years Later*, Harvard Kennedy School, September 20, 2015.

256   weaker dollar "is desirable": Peter T. Kilborn, "U.S. and 4 Allies Plan Move to Cut Value of Dollar," *New York Times*, September 23, 1985.

256   "What's new is that we're": Ibid.

256   "Shultz got livid at me": James Baker interview.

256   "I don't think we would": Martin Crutsinger, "U.S. Doesn't Plan to Intervene in Currency Markets in Major Way," Associated Press, September 24, 1985.

256   "EXTREMELY URGENT": James Baker, memo to Malcolm Baldrige, September 24, 1985, Princeton archive.

257   "doesn't speak for the administration": James Baker, interview with *U.S. News & World Report*, cited in "Baker Says U.S. Wants Gradual Drop in Dollar," United Press International, September 28, 1985.

257   slid by about 5 percent: Larry Thorson, "Dollar Slumps After Cooperation Agreement on Dollar," Associated Press, September 23, 1985.

257   depreciated by 40 percent: Frankel, *The Plaza Accord, 30 Years Later.*

257   "A lot of people are tired": Transcript, *Larry King Live*, CNN, September 2, 1987.

258   "I think I'd win": Katie Rogers, "How Donald Trump Used Hollywood to Create 'Donald Trump,' " *New York Times*, October 26, 2016.

258   "the Cadillac of committees": Richard E. Cohen, *Rostenkowski*, p. 137.

258   "Rostenkowski and Baker": Jim Jaffe, author interview.

259   "I have heard more about": Dick Gephardt, statement, undated, Princeton archive.

259   "Cheap shot": James Baker, handwritten note on Gephardt statement.

260   "Tax reform gets tougher": James Baker, letter to Will Winston, September 20, 1985, Princeton archive.

260   "He came in there": James Baker interview.

260   "We're going to oppose you": James A. Baker III, *The Politics of Diplomacy*, pp. 22–25.

260   "It was garbage": Dick Cheney, author interview.

260   "Tax reform is one of": James Baker, memo to Ronald Reagan, December 2, 1985, Princeton archive.

261   "suffer the worst defeat": Editorial, Baltimore *Sun*, December 6, 1985, Princeton archive.

261   "I think this editorial is right": James Baker, handwritten note to Nancy Reagan on a copy of the Baltimore *Sun* editorial, December 6, 1985, Princeton archive.

261   a vote of 223 to 202: David E. Rosenbaum, "Bill to End Budget Deficits Voted by House and Senate; Reagan Loses Key Tax Vote," *New York Times*, December 12, 1985.

261   "The rule is going down": Birnbaum and Murray, *Showdown at Gucci Gulch*, p. 165.

261   "that was a very dark day": James Baker interview.

261   "Mr. Speaker, when in your lifetime": Birnbaum and Murray, *Showdown at Gucci Gulch*, p. 168.

261   "He got up and talked about": Cheney interview.

261   *The president really needs you:* Birnbaum and Murray, *Showdown at Gucci Gulch*, p. 172.

262   258 to 168, with seventy Republicans: H.Res 343—A resolution providing for consideration of H.R. 3838, December 17, 1985, Congress.gov.https://www.congress.gov/bill/99th-congress/house-resolution/343.

262   "Obviously, a big part of that": Cheney interview.

262   "He had a great way of communicating": Bill Bradley, author interview.

263   "I was astonished to read": Jack Kemp, letter to James Baker, March 21, 1986, Princeton archive.

263   "If you are again 'astonished' ": James Baker, letter to Jack Kemp, March 24, 1986, Princeton archive.

263 "I've got to tell you": James Baker, draft letter to Bill Archer, undated, Princeton archive.

264 "He acted like he was": Jeffrey Birnbaum, author interview.

264 "Did I get them back or what?": James Baker interview.

265 "To hell with it": Bob Packwood, diary entry, April 18, 1986. Packwood read the diary entries to the author and later published excerpts on Bloomberg BNA in a series of three pieces: "Juggling Budget Numbers and Votes: How the Tax Reform Act of 1986 Made It Through the Finance Committee," January 19, 2017; "Juggling Budget Numbers and Votes: How the Tax Reform Act of 1986 Passed the Senate," January 23, 2017; and "Juggling Budget Numbers and Votes: How the Tax Reform Act of 1986 Made It Through Conference and Into Law," January 24, 2017.

265 "Bill and I in essence said": Packwood diary entry, April 29, 1986.

265 unanimous 20 to 0 vote: Rosenbaum, "A Tax Bill for the Textbooks."

265 "Jim, tell him to shut up": Packwood diary entry, May 6, 1986.

266 stunning 97 to 3 vote: The three dissenters, all Democrats, were Senators Carl Levin of Michigan, Paul Simon of Illinois, and John Melcher of Montana. H.R. 3838— Tax Reform Act of 1986, June 24, 1986, Congress.gov.https://www.congress.gov/bill /99th-congress/house-bill/3838/all-actions?overview=closed&q=%7B%22roll-call -vote%22%3A%22all%22%7D.

266 "After Danny and I agreed": Packwood diary entry, July 15–16.

266 *They said tax reform was dead*: "The Secretary Raps Tax Reform," *Washington Post*, September 17, 1986.

267 "This is this stick-up-his-ass": Jaffe interview.

268 "Jim is a relatively little part": Bob Packwood, author interview.

268 "We look forward to studying it": Birnbaum and Murray, *Showdown at Gucci Gulch*, p. 280.

268 "This is a triumph for": Ibid.

268 bipartisan 292 to 136 vote: H.R. 3838—Tax Reform Act of 1986, June 24, 1986, Congress.gov. September 25, 1986, https://www.congress.gov/bill/99th-congress /house-bill/3838/all-actions?overview=closed&q=%7B%22roll-call-vote%22%3A %22all%22%7D.

268 "All of us here today know": Ronald Reagan, "Remarks on Signing the Tax Reform Act of 1986," October 22, 1986, American Presidency Project, University of California at Santa Barbara, https://www.presidency.ucsb.edu/documents/remarks-signing -the-tax-reform-act-1986.

268 "For years to come": David E. Rosenbaum, "A Tax Bill for the Textbooks," *New York Times*, October 23, 1986.

CHAPTER 16. Black Monday

269 "Can you believe this arms": James Baker, handwritten note to Michael Deaver, November 14, 1986, Baker personal files.

270 there was a chance money: James Baker, Memorandum to the File, November 27, 1986, Baker personal files.

270 "We've got big problems": James Baker, Memorandum for the File, November 27, 1986, Baker personal files.

271 "we're dealing here with illegality": James Baker, Memorandum for the File, November 25, 1986, Baker personal files.

271 "that was the biggest favor": James A. Baker III, *"Work Hard, Study . . . and Keep Out of Politics!,"* p. 205.

272 "You don't hang up on": James Baker, author interview.

272 "If, by some miracle": Nancy Reagan, *My Turn*, p. 325.

273 "some overzealous investigation": Robert Kimmitt, Memorandum for the Record, December 19, 1986, Baker personal files. Kimmitt sat in on the interview, conducted on December 18 by FBI Special Agents James Beane and Dan Dreibelbis, and took notes that he then memorialized into this memo.

273 "It's the one lasting blot": James Baker interview.

273 "I didn't know the answer": Ibid.

273 "I think I let the president down": Robert McFarlane, author interview.

273 "I have wondered whether": Ibid.

274 "Who's This Man Calling?": *Time*, March 3, 1986. The article inside, titled "Peddling Influence," was written by Evan Thomas.

274 "Mike, you've made a big mistake": Associated Press, December 16, 1987, http://articles.latimes.com/1987-12-16/news/mn-19735_1_ronald-reagan.

274 convicted of three counts: Philip Shenon, "Deaver Is Sentenced to Suspended Term and $100,000 Fine," *New York Times*, September 24, 1988.

274 "I think he's had the fastest rise": Marjorie Williams, "The Perilous Rise of Michael Deaver," *Washington Post*, July 13, 1987.

274 "what's a virgin": Zach Schonfeld, "Parental Advisory Forever: An Oral History of the PMRC's War on Dirty Lyrics," *Newsweek*, September 19, 2015.

275 "We were just mad mamas": Ibid.

275 "modern-day witch hunt": Ibid.

276 "I couldn't understand how": Schonfeld, "Parental Advisory Forever."

276 "We don't question their right": Rock Lyrics Record Labeling, September 19, 1985, C-Span, https://www.c-span.org/video/?69484-1/rock-lyrics-record-labeling. See also Susan Baker, *Passing It On*, p. 80.

276 "an ill-conceived piece of nonsense": Schonfeld, "Parental Advisory Forever."

277 "I'm sure there are a lot": Maureen Dowd, "Limelight Falls Upon Susan Baker's Gospel Work," *New York Times*, April 9, 1985.

277 "Susan Baker visited and wrote me": Hillary Clinton, *Living History*, pp. 167–68.

277 "But there are none of us": Lois Romano, "Jim Baker and the Logistics of Power," *Washington Post*, April 30, 1985.

278 "We love you and we're proud": James Baker, letter to John Baker, May 28, 1986, Princeton archive.

279 "You can do what you want": William L. Silber, *Volcker*, p. 255.

279 "I'm resigning": Paul Volcker, author interview.

279 "Mr. Chairman, if you need": Wayne Angell, author interview.

279 "I don't know if he was in cahoots": Volcker interview.

280 "The only conversation Baker had": Angell interview.

280 "I don't remember getting": James Baker interview.

280 "Volcker is not cooperating": Ibid.

280 would you be interested?: Alan Greenspan, author interview.

281 "You know, Ron, this thing": Brian Mulroney, author interview.

282 "He was very much at ease": Derek Burney, *Getting It Done*, pp. 124–25.

282 "The congressional people": Mulroney interview.

283 "you can have your goddamn": Burney, *Getting It Done*, pp. 118–20.

283 North American Free Trade Agreement: As president, George Bush negotiated NAFTA with Canada and Mexico and signed it in December 1992 after losing reelection to Bill Clinton. Upon becoming president, Clinton secured revisions to the agreement that satisfied his labor and environmental concerns and then submitted it for approval in Congress. The House voted for it 234 to 200 and the Senate 61 to 38.

283 "Had it not been for Jim": Mulroney interview.

283 "as white as these walls": James Baker interview

283 "The market drops five": Ibid.

284 plunged by 508 points: Lawrence J. De Maria, "Stocks Plunge 508 Points, a Drop of 22.6%," *New York Times*, October 20, 1987.

284 "I never saw an elk": James Baker interview.

284 "I said, 'Put him on'": Alan Greenspan, author interview.

285 "I'm concerned about money supply": Ronald Reagan, *The Reagan Diaries*, ed. Douglas Brinkley, p. 538.

285 "should not expect us": Peter T. Kilborn, "U.S. Said to Allow Decline of Dollar Against the Mark," *New York Times*, October 18, 1987.

285 "There is nothing wrong": Ronald Reagan, Informal Exchange with Reporters,

Online by Gerhard Peters and John T. Woolley, American Presidency Project, University of California at Santa Barbara, https://www.presidency.ucsb.edu/documents /informal-exchange-with-reporters-27.

285 "a Herbert Hoover type of response": Greenspan interview.

285 "The way Jim set the thing up": Ibid.

286 "Stock market or no stock market": Ronald Reagan, *An American Life*, p. 695.

286 "If you're looking at the biggest": Robert Shiller, author interview.

286 "It conceivably could have made": James Baker interview.

287 "I didn't want to be the most": Ibid.

287 dozens of letters: A folder of these letters resides in the Princeton archive.

287 "People used to ask me": James Baker, unpublished interview with ghostwriter Tom DeFrank for his own memoir, May 1993, Princeton archive.

288 "a thin, tinny 'arf'": George Will, "George Bush: The Sound of a Lapdog," *Washington Post*, January 30, 1986.

288 "Fighting the 'Wimp Factor'": Margaret Garrard Warner, "Bush Battles the 'Wimp Factor,'" *Newsweek*, October 12, 1987. The cover line was "George Bush: Fighting the 'Wimp Factor.'"

289 "along the lines of": Tom DeFrank, author interview.

290 "Yeah, stop lying about my record": Bob Dole, interview with Tom Brokaw, NBC News, February 16, 1988, https://archives.nbclearn.com/portal/site/k-12/flatview ?cuecard=33616.

290 "I'm sort of running against": Bernard Weinraub, "Bush Nomination Seems Assured as Dole Leaves Republican Race," *New York Times*, March 30, 1988.

290 "We've got to get him over": Richard Ben Cramer, *What It Takes*, pp. 991–92.

290 "I don't want to do that": Pete Teeley, author interview.

290 "You *know* I really don't": Goldman et al., *Quest for the Presidency*, p. 312.

291 "The best thing I can do": Hugh Sidey, "The Presidency: What Friends Are For," *Time*, March 21, 1988.

291 "On reflection I think it would be": Richard Nixon, letter to George Bush, May 15, 1988, Princeton archive.

291 "I'm really going to need you": James Baker interview.

291 "He did it so softly": Kenneth Duberstein, author interview.

292 "He's taken his licks": President Reagan's Remarks Announcing the Resignation of James A. Baker III as Secretary of the Treasury and the Nomination of Nicholas F. Brady with James Baker and Nicholas Brady's Remarks in Press Room on August 5, 1988, https://www.youtube.com/watch?v=RPFwGRbfzLQ.

292 "I can promise you": James Baker interview.

293 "I'm sure you're not going": Alan Greenspan, *The Age of Turbulence*, pp. 111–13.

CHAPTER 17. The Handler

294 "born with a silver foot": Adam Clymer, "Democrats Use Humor and Scorn in Mounting Attack Against Bush," *New York Times*, July 20, 1988.

294 "a man who was born": Ken Herman, "Hightower: Bush Is a 'Toothache of a Man,'" Associated Press, July 20, 1988, https://www.apnews.com/fc25d54 b02502d315b62 bc9c5fo9doo9.

294 "in case George is too squeamish": Clymer, "Democrats Use Humor and Scorn in Mounting Attack Against Bush."

294 "Where was George?": Ibid.

295 "The good thing about": Tom Raum, "Bush Says Democrats 'Frantic Name-Callers,' Confirms Dole on Veep List," Associated Press, July 20, 1988, https://www.apnews .com/3b9c9f355d1066295656ab688163ddgo.

295 "This election is not about ideology": Michael Dukakis, Address Accepting the Presidential Nomination at the Democratic National Convention in Atlanta, July 21, 1988, American Presidency Project, the University of California at Santa Barbara, http://www.presidency.ucsb.edu/ws/index.php?pid=25961.

295   commanding 17-point: Dukakis led with 55 percent to 38 percent for Bush in a Gal-
      lup poll taken on July 21, 1988, the last day of the Democratic National Convention.
      "Dukakis Lead Widens, According to New Poll," *New York Times*, July 26, 1988.
296   "weak and intermittent": Gary MacDougal, memo to George Bush, July 8, 1988, cc'd
      to James Baker. Princeton archive.
296   "Lee was running on paranoia": Craig Fuller, author interview.
296   "nervous about getting layered": Ed Rogers, author interview.
296   "He was very upset": James Baker, author interview.
296   "They were very different personalities": Frank Donatelli, author interview.
297   "an insecure kid": *Boogie Man: The Lee Atwater Story*, a documentary produced by
      Stefan Forbes and Noland Walker, directed by Stefan Forbes. Interpositive Media
      Productions, 2008, https://www.youtube.com/watch?v=PmwhdDv8VrM.
297   "Southern pol": Rogers interview.
297   "Baker didn't know": Ibid.
297   "How do we know": George W. Bush, *Decision Points*, pp. 43–44.
297   "all blood on the floor": David Remnick, "Why Is Lee Atwater So Hungry?," *Esquire*,
      December 1986.
297   "You need to earn your spurs": Peter Goldman et al., *Quest for the Presidency, 1992*,
      p. 183.
297   "He was nervous about Baker": George W. Bush, author interview.
298   "We'd just come through": Janet Mullins Grissom, author interview. For clarity, she
      is referred to in the manuscript by the name she used at the time, Janet Mullins.
298   "I had my jacket off": Ibid.
298   "It was chaos": Robert Zoellick, author interview.
298   "a pretty loose ship": Donatelli interview.
298   leading in twenty-four states: John Dillin, *Christian Science Monitor*, September 19,
      1998, https://www.csmonitor.com/1988/0919/apolls.html.
299   "I wanted it totally kept": George H. W. Bush, author interview.
299   "If you're Bush, you don't like": Mullins Grissom interview.
299   "strange and unbelievable": George H. W. Bush diary, quoted in Jon Meacham, *Des-
      tiny and Power*, p. 326. Asked about it after Meacham's book was published, Trump
      asserted that Atwater asked him, not the other way around. *This Week*, ABC News,
      November 8, 2015, https://abcnews.go.com/Politics/week-transcript-donald-trump
      -ben-carson/story?id=35044135.
300   "surprisingly strong support": Gerald M. Boyd, "Bush Prunes Running-Mate List;
      Doles, Quayle and 3 Others Stay," *New York Times*, August 13, 1988.
300   "I don't know who leaked that": Dan Quayle, *Standing Firm*, pp. 23–24.
300   "There may be a problem": Craig Fuller, author interview.
301   "He thought it was unfair": George W. Bush interview.
301   "None of us were right": Fuller interview.
301   "By the time Bush said": Charlie Black, author interview.
301   "Dad you can tell me!": David Hoffman, "Bush Picks Quayle, 'Man of the Future,' As
      Running Mate," *Washington Post*, August 17, 1988.
301   "I thought, 'Oh crap, I lost'": Dan Quayle, author interview.
302   "Hang on for the veep": Ibid.
302   "this decision is revocable": Quayle, *Standing Firm*, pp. 4–6.
302   "it was the last laugh": Ibid.
303   "I have to get there": Quayle interview.
303   "Where's Quayle?": Hoffman, "Bush Picks Quayle."
303   "Hot" and "pumped up": Fuller interview.
303   "Let's go get 'em!": Hoffman, "Bush Picks Quayle."
304   "A Leader for the Future!": James Baker, handwritten notes, undated, Princeton
      archive.
304   "It was not a happy group": Dick Darman, *Who's In Control?*, pp. 188–90.
304   "there's a total meltdown": Quayle, *Standing Firm*, p. 24.
304   "This is totally ridiculous": Goldman et al., *Quest for the Presidency, 1992*, p. 326.

304 "Do you think you got": Campaign list of potential questions, undated and unsigned, Princeton archive.

305 "The intended effect": Quayle, *Standing Firm*, p. 37.

305 "There has been no serious discussion": Campaign talking points, August 18, 1988, Princeton archive. Although his skepticism was well documented and he later clashed in the Bush administration with Quayle, Baker later would insist he had not been flatly opposed to Quayle's selection as much as dubious about its advisability. "That's not true and I would argue to you that he was the right choice at that time," Baker told us in an interview. "Why do I say that? We won all but ten states." Baker said he was sympathetic to Bush's desire to bring in a new generation. "I can't say I was in favor of Quayle. I wasn't in favor of anybody."

305 "Through conversations with": Robert Kimmitt, memorandum to James Baker, August 25, 1988, Princeton archive.

306 "It was Dad who changed": George W. Bush interview.

306 "It was my decision": George H. W. Bush diary, August 21, 1988, as cited in Herbert Parmet, *George Bush*, p. 349.

306 "How dumb": James Baker interview.

306 "the vision thing": Robert Ajemian, "Where Is the Real George Bush?," *Time*, January 26, 1987.

306 "I want a kinder and gentler nation": George Bush, Address Accepting the Presidential Nomination at the Republican National Convention in New Orleans, August 18, 1988, American Presidency Project, University of California at Santa Barbara, http://www.presidency.ucsb.edu/ws/index.php?pid=25955.

307 "My opponent won't rule out": Ibid.

307 "We all knew it was a good line": Fuller interview.

307 "lips are organs": Peggy Noonan, *What I Saw at the Revolution*, p. 319.

307 "We got overruled": Fuller interview.

307 "the nature of the problem": Agenda for strategy session, James Baker office, August 25, 1988, Princeton archive.

308 "Our biggest prob.": James Baker, handwritten notes, August 25, 1988, Princeton archive.

308 "Anytime GB has been on attack": Ibid.

308 "Baker would oversee": John Brady, *Bad Boy*, pp. 179–80.

308 "driving up the opposition's negatives": Thomas Edsall, "Why Bush Accentuates the Negative," *Washington Post*, October 2, 1988.

309 "Lee, who was plenty happy": Black interview.

309 "What is it about the Pledge of Allegiance": Steven V. Roberts, "Bush Intensifies Debate on Pledge, Asking Why It So Upsets Dukakis," *New York Times*, August 25, 1988.

309 most states had similar programs: Robin Toner, "Prison Furloughs in Massachusetts Threaten Dukakis Record on Crime,": *New York Times*, July 5, 1988.

310 showing a series of inmates: Bush-Quayle 1988 Campaign, https://www.youtube.com/watch?v=PmwhdDv8VrM.

310 called "Weekend Passes": National Security Political Action Committee, https://www.youtube.com/watch?v=Io9KMSSEZoY.

310 Baker did not write his letter: Stephen Engelberg, Richard L. Berke, and Michael Wines, "Bush, His Disavowed Backers and a Very Potent Attack Ad," *New York Times*, November 3, 1988.

310 "Anybody who believes that": *Boogie Man: The Lee Atwater Story*.

310 "If I can make Willie Horton": Marie Cocco, Saul Friedman, Ellis Henican, Susan Page, Gaylord Shaw, Patrick J. Sloyan, Myron S. Waldman, and Catherine Woodard, "Smears and Fears: the '88 Campaign," *Newsday*, November 6, 1988.

310 "who for all I know": Sidney Blumenthal, "Willie Horton and the Making of an Election Issue," *Washington Post*, October 28, 1988.

310 "the only question is whether": Richard Stengel, "The Man Behind the Message," *Time*, August 22, 1988.

311 "the biggest mistake": Eric Benson, "Dukakis's Regret," *New York*, June 17, 2012. Just how decisive was the Willie Horton ad? John Sides, an associate professor of political science at George Washington University, argued in a piece on washingtonpost.com that the impact of the Horton ad was overstated: "It's Time to Stop the Endless Hype of the 'Willie Horton' Ad," January 6, 2016. He cited among other things a study by Tali Mendelberg that found that politicians use racial codes but that they lose their appeal once exposed. Mendelberg, "The Race Card: Campaign Strategy, Implicit Messages and the Norm of Equality, 2001, http://press.princeton.edu/titles/7090.html.

311 "the dark prince of political advertising": Stengel, "The Man Behind the Message."

311 "Baker and I would do": Doro Bush Koch, *My Father, My President*, p. 249.

311 "transcendent dorkiness": Bill Turque, a reporter with *Newsweek*, quoted in Thomas B. Rosenstiel and John Balzar, "'Mr. Malaprop': Poor Media Play May Be Bush's Bane," *Los Angeles Times*, June 29, 1988.

312 "sexy Reagan White House": Ibid.

312 "You cannot afford to lie back": "Strategy for September 25, 1988 Debate," Memorandum for Bush from "The Debate Team," September 20, 1988, Princeton archive.

312 "Prohibit nativity scenes": James Baker, handwritten notes on memorandum from Vic Gold to Baker for debate preparation, September 15, 1988, Princeton archive.

312 "brand a woman a criminal": Presidential Debate in Winston-Salem, North Carolina, September 25, 1988, American Presidency Project, University of California at Santa Barbara, http://www.presidency.ucsb.edu/ws/index.php?pid=29411.

312 "I'm going to do a heck of a lot better": Jack W. Germond and Jules Witcover, *Whose Broad Stripes and Bright Stars?*, p. 434.

312 "Energy Level: Slower to": James Baker, handwritten notes on Bush/Quayle stationery, September 30, 1988, Princeton archive.

313 "I served with Jack Kennedy": Video clip of vice presidential debate, October 5, 1988, https://www.youtube.com/watch?v=uWXRNySMW4s.

313 "knocked it right out": Richard Stengel, "Ninety Long Minutes in Omaha," *Time*, October 17, 1988.

313 "cheap shot": "'A Cheap Shot'—Reagan; 'A Plus for Us'—Dukakis: Bentsen's Quayle Jab Heats Race," *Los Angeles Times*, October 6, 1988.

313 "When you think about": E. J. Dionne, "Revival for Democrats," *New York Times*, October 7, 1988.

313 "snapping point": Cathleen Decker, "Declares He Reached a 'Certain Snapping Point': Quayle Says He'll Direct Own Campaign," *Los Angeles Times*, October 13, 1988.

313 "I am my own handler": Eileen Putman, "Quayle: 'I'm My Own Handler' Now," Associated Press, October 12, 1988.

313 "I've had all the advice": Quayle, *Standing Firm*, pp. 68–69.

313 "justified at being steamed": Germond and Witcover, *Whose Broad Stripes and Bright Stars?*, p. 444.

314 "threatens to dismiss": Lucy Howard, "Conventional-Wisdom Watch," *Newsweek*, October 24, 1988.

314 "Governor, if Kitty Dukakis": Presidential Debate at the University of California in Los Angeles, October 13, 1988, American Presidency Project, University of California at Santa Barbara, http://www.presidency.ucsb.edu/ws/index.php?pid=29412.

314 from 49 percent to 42 percent: Roger Simon, "Questions That Kill Candidates' Careers," *Politico*, April 20, 2007

314 "Well, this debate's gone": Goldman et al., *Quest for the Presidency, 1992*, p. 398.

315 "We're all sitting around the table": Sig Rogich, author interview. See also Brady, *Bad Boy*, p. 193. Craig Fuller said in an interview with the authors that Bush actually had a similar picture taken of him at a firing range "with one of those crazy hats." Fuller worried through the last days of the campaign that the picture would be found, making Bush look as foolish as Dukakis had, but it never was. Craig Fuller, author interview.

315 "Let's not forget, it's about winning": Rogich interview.

315 "I'm fed up with it": Josh King, "Dukakis and the Tank," *Politico*, November 17, 2013.
315 "How much lower": Transcript, *Face the Nation*, CBS News, October 30, 1988. A few days later, on November 3, Baker gave a speech at the National Press Club defending the campaign against the negativity critique as well, claiming the mudslinging of 1988 had really begun at the Democratic National Convention in Atlanta. But history has not accepted his version. James Baker, speech at National Press Club, November 3, 1988, transcript in Princeton archive.
316 "I just cannot let myself": John Balzar, "Already, Bush Camp Hears Whispers About Transition," *Los Angeles Times*, October 22, 1988.
316 "Nobody in this room believes me": George Bush press conference quoted in ibid.
316 "I am assuming that Jim said yes": Barbara Bush, *Barbara Bush*, pp. 240–41.
317 "Baker doesn't like it at all": Fuller interview.
317 "Battle of the Handlers": *Time*, October 3, 1988, http://content.time.com/time/covers /0,16641,19881003,00.html.
317 "That just cut me to the quick": James Baker interview.
317 "You need to think about this": Fuller interview.
317 "I'm a jealous wreck": James Baker interview.
318 "We walked into the Nebletts'": Barbara Bush, *Barbara Bush*, p. 246.
318 "We need to wait on Michigan": James A. Baker III, *"Work Hard, Study . . . and Keep Out of Politics!,"* p. 275.
318 forty states to take 426 electoral votes: Election of 1988, American Presidency Project, University of California at Santa Barbara, http://www.presidency.ucsb.edu/show election.php?year=1988.

CHAPTER 18. Jigsaw Puzzle

322 "the capital's leading wise man": Steven V. Roberts, "Out of Texas, the Capital's Leading Wise Man," *New York Times*, December 29, 1987.
322 "a close friend of the next president": Joe Holley, "Robert S. Strauss, Texas Lawyer and Political Insider, Dies at 95," *Washington Post*, March 19, 2014.
322 "I'm terribly partisan": Ibid.
322 "I want to get you and Jim Wright together": James Baker, unpublished interview with Peter Ross Range, ghostwriter for a never-completed memoir by Robert Strauss. Files at Akin Gump.
322 the new president was ready to talk: James A. Baker III, *The Politics of Diplomacy*, pp. 49–50.
323 "That was the holy grail": James Baker, author interview.
323 "very, very sensitive about": George H. W. Bush diary, July 16, 1989.
323 "the alternate president": Ibid., January 2, 1989.
324 "This is a very special occasion": George H. W. Bush, Remarks at the Swearing-in Ceremony for James A. Baker III as Secretary of State, January 27, 1989, American Presidency Project, University of California at Santa Barbara, http://www.presidency .ucsb.edu/ws/index.php?pid=16630.
324 "As you mentioned, Mr. President": Ibid.
325 "The totalitarian era is passing": George Bush, Inaugural Address, Online by Gerhard Peters and John T. Woolley, American Presidency Project, University of California at Santa Barbara, https://www.presidency.ucsb.edu/node/247448.
325 "moment rich with promise": Ibid.
325 "Now is *not the time*": Talking points for James Baker meeting with Yitzhak Shamir and Moshe Arens on April 5–6, 1989, Princeton archive.
326 "This is *not* a friendly takeover": Michael R. Beschloss and Strobe Talbott, *At the Highest Levels*, p. 26.
326 "I'm going to be": James Baker interview.
326 "Nothing comes between me": Ibid.
326 "mostly a bantering one": George Bush and Brent Scowcroft, *A World Transformed*, pp. 19–20.

326 "like an arm right into": Brent Scowcroft, author interview.
327 "Dick, damn it": Dick Cheney, author interview.
327 "We all knew each other": Ibid.
328 "He was so tightly wound": Lorne Craner, author interview.
328 "came to the State Department": David L. Mack, Association for Diplomatic Studies and Training Foreign Affairs Oral History Project, October 24, 1995, https://www.adst.org/OH%20TOCs/Mack,%20David%20L.toc.pdf.
328 "Jim Baker ran policy": Chas W. Freeman Jr., Association for Diplomatic Studies and Training Foreign Affairs Oral History Project, April 14, 1995, https://www.adst.org/OH%20TOCs/Freeman,%20Chas.toc.pdf.
329 "felt the action would be": Dennis Ross, *Doomed to Succeed*, p. 219.
329 "a disarming smile": Bush and Scowcroft, *A World Transformed*, pp. 3–4.
329 "empty cannons of rhetoric": Ibid., p. 5.
329 "Don't you think you all": Jeffrey A. Engel, *When the World Seemed New*, pp. 86–87.
330 the "Finlandization" of Eastern Europe: George H. W. Bush diary, January 9, 1989.
330 "Our purpose is to assure": George H. W. Bush, letter to Mikhail Gorbachev, January 13, 1989, Princeton archive.
330 "I lead a strange country": Henry Kissinger, Memorandum to Brent Scowcroft, January 17, 1989, Princeton archive.
330 "In my view Gorbachev is": Ibid.
331 "For Baker, the world was": Aaron David Miller, author interview.
331 "He has a less complicated approach": Henry Kissinger, author interview.
331 "He knew the time was right": Janet Mullins Grissom, author interview.
332 "Work w/Congress": James Baker, handwritten notes on a copy of talking points for cabinet meeting, January 23, 1989, Princeton archive.
332 "They couldn't just walk away": Bernard Aronson, author interview.
332 "It has now turned into": James Baker, talking points for call with George Mitchell, undated, Princeton
333 "We want to wind this thing down": Jim Wright, *Worth It All*, p. 223.
333 "This was to be the pattern": Ibid., pp. 224–25.
334 "Baker would tell a dirty joke": Mullins Grissom interview.
334 "He has a compelling presence": Maureen Dowd and Thomas L. Friedman, "The Fabulous Bush and Baker Boys," *New York Times Magazine*, May 6, 1990.
334 "I'm one of the few Republicans": James Baker interview.
334 "They were probably as close": Jimmy Carter, author interview.
335 "Baker knew we had a losing hand": Aronson interview.
335 "Today, for the first time": George H. W. Bush, Statement on the Bipartisan Accord on Central America, March 24, 1989, American Presidency Project, University of California at Santa Barbara, http://www.presidency.ucsb.edu/ws/index.php?pid=16840.
335 "We all have to admit": Bernard Weintraub, "Bush and Congress Sign Policy Accord on Aid to Contras," *New York Times*, March 25, 1989.
335 "Unease Is Voiced": Robert Pear, "Unease Is Voiced on Contra Accord," *New York Times*, March 26, 1989.
336 "Within minutes": Boyden Gray, author interview.
336 "Baker was absolutely livid": Aronson interview.
336 "up to the job": George H. W. Bush diary, February 10, 1989.
336 "This was the first": James Baker interview.
336 "He was mad": Gray interview.
336 "Basically, it's a restoration": Thomas L. Friedman, "Baker Says Accord on Contra Aid Enhances Powers of the President," *New York Times*, March 27, 1989.

CHAPTER 19. Fly-Fishing with Shevy

337 "I guess we bombed out there": Michael R. Beschloss and Strobe Talbott, *At the Highest Levels*, p. 39.

337 "Not really": Ibid.

338 "Everything is rotten": Carey Goldberg, "Reformer Turned Master Diplomat," *Los Angeles Times*, December 21, 1990.

338 "giving Jimmy a few suggestions": George H. W. Bush diary, March 4, 1989.

338 "sounds like an imperious demand": Pavel Palazchenko, *My Years with Gorbachev and Shevardnadze*, pp. 128–29.

338 he was "savaged": Richard Reeves, *President Kennedy*, p. 173.

339 "What were they waiting for?": Mikhail Gorbachev, *Memoirs*, p. 501.

339 "pragmatist," not a "zoological": Beschloss and Talbott, *At the Highest Levels*, 27–29.

339 "cold fellow": Ibid.

339 "Can't help but get impression": James Baker, "Key Impressions from the Trip," March 7, 1989, Princeton archive.

339 "decidedly listless debut": Beschloss and Talbott, *At the Highest Levels*, pp. 45–46.

339 "mush," as Baker put it: Jeffrey A. Engel, *When the World Seemed New*, p. 133.

339 "Don't just do something": Beschloss and Talbott, *At the Highest Levels*, p. 34.

340 "Cheney looked at Scowcroft": Robert M. Gates, *From the Shadows*, p. 462.

340 "If we don't regain leadership": Ibid.

340 "If I had to guess today": John M. Broder, "Cheney Predicts Gorbachev Will Fail, Be Ousted," *Los Angeles Times*, April 29, 1989.

340 "Cheney, you're off the reservation": Dick Cheney, author interview.

340 "I got it," he said: Ibid.

341 "Dump on Dick": Beschloss and Talbott, *At the Highest Levels*, pp. 54–55.

341 "his personal observations": Marlin Fitzwater, White House daily briefing, May 1, 1989, Federal News Service transcript.

341 "we wanted to see": Terence Hunt, "Bush Says He Hopes Gorbachev's Reforms Succeed," Associated Press, May 1, 1989.

341 "The president has said": James A. Baker III, speech to the Center for Strategic and International Studies, May 4, 1989, Federal News Service transcript.

341 "we damn near tanked": James Baker, author interview.

343 "You have to stay the course": James Baker, notes of meeting with Mikhail Gorbachev, May 11, 1989, Princeton archive.

343 "the Eeyore of Sovietology": David Ignatius, "Why Bob Gates Is the Eeyore of Sovietology," *Washington Post*, May 28, 1989.

343 "Baker is one of the foxiest": Don Oberdorfer, *The Turn*, pp. 344–45.

344 "invented reasons to come back": Ibid.

344 "We hope the Soviet changes": Engel, *When the World Seemed New*, pp. 137–39.

344 "Containment worked": George H. W. Bush, Remarks at Texas A&M University Commencement Ceremony, College Station, May 12, 1989, http://www.presidency.ucsb.edu/ws/index.php?pid=17022.

344 "drugstore cowboy": Bernard Weinraub, "U.S. Questions Moscow Pledge on Sandinistas," *New York Times*, May 17, 1989.

345 "a bit of a phony": "Quayle Calls Gorbachev's Proposals a Bit Phony," Cox News Service, May 20, 1989, https://www.deseretnews.com/article/47311/QUAYLE-CALLS-GORBACHEVS-PROPOSALS-A-BIT-PHONY.html.

345 "fought virtually every proposal": James A. Baker III, *The Politics of Diplomacy*, pp. 93–94.

345 "Don't keep telling me why": Ibid.

345 "The shorter the missile": James Graham Wilson, *The Triumph of Improvisation*, p. 133. Wilson traces the quote originally to Volker Rühe, a West German defense spokesman, during a 1987 trip by George Shultz to discuss the issue.

346 "Sometime very late tonight": Robert Zoellick, author interview.

346 "Let Europe be whole and free": George H. W. Bush, Remarks to the Citizens in Mainz, Federal Republic of Germany, May 31, 1989, American Presidency Project, University of California at Santa Barbara, http://www.presidency.ucsb.edu/ws/?pid=17085.

347 "Grab your sticks": Engel, *When the World Seemed New*, pp. 167–68.

348 "President Bush was the desk officer": James Baker interview.

348 "We deplore the decision": George H. W. Bush, President's News Conference, June 5, 1989, American Presidency Project, University of California at Santa Barbara, http://www.presidency.ucsb.edu/ws/index.php?pid=17103.

348 "While angry rhetoric might": George Bush and Brent Scowcroft, *A World Transformed*, p. 89.

348 "would like to not increase": Notes of meeting shared with the authors on condition that the note taker not be identified.

349 "I'm not briefing": Margaret Tutwiler, author interview.

349 "They may be able to clear": James Baker, Hearing of the House Foreign Affairs Committee, June 22, 1989, Federal News Service transcript.

349 "Jim Baker does not want": Bush and Scowcroft, *A World Transformed*, p. 104.

349 "Baker dropped China": David Rothkopf, *Running the World*, p. 290.

350 "I believe that the domestic situation": Transcript of meeting between James Baker and Qian Qichen, Waldorf-Astoria hotel, New York, September 28, 1989, Princeton archive.

350 "as friends, to resume": Toast by the Honorable Brent Scowcroft, Assistant to the President for National Security Affairs, Beijing, December 9, 1989, *New York Review of Books*, June 23, 2011.

351 "embarrassingly meager": Bush and Scowcroft, *A World Transformed*, pp. 112–14.

352 "My day in Paris": George H. W. Bush diary, July 31, 1989.

352 "almost passive stance": Thomas L. Friedman, "Senate Leader Asserts U.S. Fails to Encourage Change in East Bloc," *New York Times*, September 19, 1989.

352 "When the president": Don Oberdorfer, "Baker Answers Critics of U.S. Policy," *Washington Post*, September 20, 1989.

353 "I also believed we should": Bush and Scowcroft, *A World Transformed*, pp. 138–39.

353 "total autonomy": Oberdorfer, *The Turn*, pp. 371–72.

353 "crossed a threshold": Ibid. pp. 373–74.

354 "Can I tell you how difficult": Karen Groomes Morgan, author interview.

354 "We almost had major crisis": James Baker, handwritten note to Tom Brokaw, October 19, 1989, Princeton archive.

354 "That was a real bonding experience": Robert Gates, author interview.

354 "is likely to fall short": Robert Gates, draft of speech to 17th National Collegiate Security Conference, Georgetown International Relations Association, draft dated October 24, 1989, for conference on October 26, Princeton archive.

354 "I believe his text as revised": Brent Scowcroft, memo to James Baker, October 24, 1989, Princeton archive.

355 "No way," he scribbled: James Baker, handwritten note on Scowcroft memo, Princeton archive.

355 "in some places directly contradicts": James Baker, memo to George Bush, October 25, 1989.

355 "You're breaking a lot of china": James Baker interview.

355 the conflict found its way: Thomas L. Friedman, "Baker Blocks Expert's Speech About Gorbachev's Chances," *New York Times*, October 27, 1989.

355 "It is most unfortunate": Robert Gates, handwritten note to James Baker, October 28, 1989, Princeton archive.

355 "I felt I'd played by the rules": Gates interview.

356 "No, I don't want to be president": Morton Kondracke, "Quayle, Baker Square Off," *Washington Times*, October 31, 1989.

356 "Mr. P—We have successfully avoided": James Baker, handwritten note on copy of Kondracke column, Princeton archive.

356 "I keep hearing the critics": Bush and Scowcroft, *A World Transformed*, p. 148.

CHAPTER 20. The Curtain Falls

357 "The East German Government": J. Stapleton Roy, typed memo to James Baker, November 9, 1989, Princeton archive.

358 "Something we've wanted": James Baker, handwritten notes on a news dispatch dated November 9, 1989, Princeton archive.

358 images of jubilant crowds: The East German government had no intention of opening the wall dividing Berlin, but was merely issuing a new temporary travel regulation to take the pressure off as East Germans transited to the West via other countries. When government spokesman Günter Schabowski read the new regulation, he was asked when it would go into effect; he shrugged and said, *"Ab sofort":* Right away. Michael Meyer, "Günter Schabowski, the Man Who Opened the Wall," *New York Times*, November 6, 2015. See also the gripping account of the day by Mary Elise Sarotte in *The Collapse*.

358 "Of course, I welcome": George H. W. Bush, Remarks and Question-and-Answer Session with Reporters on the Relaxation of East German Border Controls, November 9, 1989, American Presidency Project, University of California at Santa Barbara, http://www.presidency.ucsb.edu/ws/index.php?pid=17783.

358 "This is a sort of great victory": Ibid.

359 "a historic moment": Tom Brokaw, *NBC Nightly News*, November 9, 1989, https://www.nbcnews.com/video/tom-brokaw-on-reporting-the-fall-of-the-berlin-wall-355151939923.

359 "God bless America": James Baker, handwritten notes, November 10, 1989, Princeton archive. See also Hans-Dietrich Genscher, *Rebuilding a House Divided*, p. 295.

359 last wall jumper: Sarotte, *The Collapse*, pp. 13–14.

360 *"Ich bin ein Berliner"*: John F. Kennedy, Remarks at the Rudolph Wilde Platz, Berlin, June 26, 1963, John F. Kennedy Presidential Library and Museum, https://www.jfklibrary.org/Research/Research-Aids/JFK-Speeches/Berlin-W-Germany-Rudolph-Wilde-Platz_19630626.aspx.

360 "tear down this wall": Ronald Reagan, Remarks on East-West Relations at the Brandenburg Gate in West Berlin, June 12, 1987, Ronald Reagan Presidential Library and Museum, https://www.reaganlibrary.gov/research/speeches/061287d. For a good account of the debate over including the line in Reagan's speech, see James Mann, *The Rebellion of Ronald Reagan*.

361 "given little thought": George Bush and Brent Scowcroft, *A World Transformed*, pp. 187–89.

361 "Virtually no West German": Philip Zelikow and Robert Blackwill, memo to Brent Scowcroft, March 20, 1989. Cited in Philip Zelikow and Condoleezza Rice, *Germany Unified and Europe Transformed*, p. 28.

361 "This is the real opportunity": Robert Zoellick, draft memorandum, May 15, 1989, Princeton archive.

362 "We were all caught": Dieter Kastrup, author interview.

362 "When Helmut Kohl gave": Horst Teltschik, author interview.

362 avoid being "stampeded": William J. Burns, *The Back Channel*, p. 55.

363 "the end of history": Francis Fukuyama, "The End of History?" *The National Interest*, Summer 1989.

363 "Germany will not unify": Francis Fukuyama, author interview.

363 "the triumph of the West": Fukuyama, "The End of History?"

363 "Mitterrand was not": Teltschik interview.

363 "We beat the Germans twice": Helmut Kohl, *Memoirs*, as quoted by Carsten Volkery, "'The Germans Are Back!,'" *Spiegel*, September 11, 2009.

364 "a possible PR ploy": Richard M. Nixon, letter to George H. W. Bush, November 16, 1989, Princeton archive.

365 "unprofessional at best": Bush and Scowcroft, *A World Transformed*, p. 160.

365 "This is the end of my non-agenda": Ibid., p. 163.

366 "I have been called cautious": Ibid., pp. 164–65.

366 "seasick summit": Michael R. Beschloss and Strobe Talbott, *At the Highest Levels*, p. 160.

366 "Mr. Baker, this is a drowning rat": Ibid., p. 161.

367 "We share the values": Zelikow and Rice, *Germany*, p. 18.

367　"What about calling them *democratic* values?": Beschloss and Talbott, *At the Highest Levels*, p. 162.

367　"Gorby went out of his way": James Baker, handwritten notes on cable by James Dobbins to United States Consulate in Leningrad, Princeton archive.

367　"inherited my tendency": Genscher, *Rebuilding a House Divided*, p. 15.

368　"What Baker learned very fast": Teltschik interview.

368　"If I'd been in Baker's position": Dan Quayle, *Standing Firm*, p. 145.

369　"We were in fact appalled": Kastrup interview.

369　Two previous secretaries of state: John Foster Dulles in 1954 and William Rogers in 1972 visited East Berlin but never left the city. In addition to being the first American secretary of state to visit East Germany outside Berlin, Baker was also the last. "Secretaries of State Visits Abroad," Department of State, https://1997-2001.state.gov /about_state/history/sectravels/dest7.html.

369　"would enhance the stature": James Dobbins, *Foreign Service*, pp. 108–9.

369　"Baker's mind was quick": Ibid.

369　"Baker seemed not to forgive me": Tom Heneghan, "Envoy Says Baker Froze Him Out Over German Unity," Reuters, February 24, 1994.

370　"It was terrible": James Baker, author interview.

370　"The process here is irreversible": Notes taken from the East Germany visit by an American official and shared with the authors on condition of anonymity.

370　"A lot of people wish": Ibid.

371　"If we had known": Bob Woodward, *The Commanders*, pp. 55–56.

371　"comic-opera coup": James A. Baker III, *The Politics of Diplomacy*, p. 186.

371　"I think we ought to go": Woodward, *The Commanders*, pp. 145–46.

371　"No news on #1": James Baker, handwritten notes, December 20, 1989, Princeton archive.

372　"You must understand that": James Baker, talking points, December 24, 1989, Princeton archive.

372　"It's not a political matter": James Baker, handwritten notes, December 24, 1989, Princeton archive.

372　"even a hypothetical possibility": Mark A. Uhlig, "Nicaraguan Opposition Routs Sandinistas," *New York Times*, February 27, 1990.

372　55 percent of the vote: "Observing Nicaragua's Elections, 1989–1990," The Carter Center, May 1990, https://www.cartercenter.org/documents/1153.pdf.

372　"the intelligence was given to me": George H. W. Bush diary, February 20, 1990.

372　"poisoning the well": Ibid.

373　"I hope that you'll make": Jimmy Carter, author interview.

373　"They were like sky high": Bernard Aronson, author interview.

373　"It was a much more important defeat": Ibid.

374　"Very close friend": George H. W. Bush, author interview.

374　"That empowered him": Aaron David Miller, author interview.

374　"Baker seemed to spend": Dobbins, *Foreign Service*, pp. 103–4.

375　"He'd tell it like it was": Bush interview.

375　"This is a place where you and I": George H. W. Bush diary, February 13, 1990.

375　"a visible lightness": Robert Kimmitt, author interview.

375　"Well, I'm not sure about Jim!": Notes of October 30, 1990, meeting shared with the authors on condition that the note taker not be identified.

375　"They're good friends": Dan Quayle, author interview.

375　"If you're so smart": James Baker interview.

376　"Like most siblings": Baker, *The Politics of Diplomacy*, p. 19.

376　"I hope that you can find": James Baker, letter to John Simpson, director of the Secret Service, January 3, 1990, Princeton archive.

376　"Brent and Jim did get": Bush and Scowcroft, *A World Transformed*, p. 36.

377　"He demanded more loyalty": Robert Gates, *From the Shadows*, pp. 456–57.

377　"Baker's frequent invoking": Quayle, *Standing Firm*, p. 101.

CHAPTER 21. Winners and Losers

378   "reunification appears inevitable": George H. W. Bush diary, February 7, 1990.
378   "We've got to lead": Ibid., February 24, 1990.
378   "We called it the cat table": Horst Teltschik, author interview.
378   "Hans-Dietrich, we understand you": Dieter Kastrup, author interview.
379   who exactly first conceived the idea: William J. Burns, *The Back Channel*, p. 55.
379   "You had to make it appear": Dennis Ross, author interview.
379   "Two Plus Four and not": Hans-Dietrich Genscher, *Rebuilding a House Divided*, p. 340.
380   "iron-clad guarantees": Memorandum of Conversation, James Baker and Eduard Shevardnadze, February 9, 1990. National Security Archive.
380   "Events are moving rapidly": Notes of meeting taken by an American official and provided to the authors on condition of anonymity.
380   "I saw our negotiator yesterday": Ibid.
380   "I say Four Plus Two, you say": Philip Zelikow and Condoleezza Rice, *Germany Unified and Europe Transformed*, pp. 182–83.
381   "A neutral Germany does not": Mikhail Gorbachev, *Memoirs*, pp. 528–29.
381   "The NSC got to him pretty quickly": Condoleezza Rice, author interview.
381   "membership, membership, membership": George H. W. Bush diary, February 10, 1990.
381   "Bye-bye, Commies!": Thomas L. Friedman, "Baker Asks Bulgaria for Fair Election," *New York Times*, February 11, 1990.
382   "wild and wooly": Andrew Carpendale, memorandum to ghostwriter Tom DeFrank, May 24, 1993, Princeton archive.
382   "Hit the roof twice": Notes by unnamed Baker aide written on announcement of conventional forces caps, Princeton archive.
383   "If I'm ever put": Ross interview.
383   "I had a long talk with Helmut Kohl": George H. W. Bush diary, February 13, 1990.
383   "He believed that Baker had": Zelikow and Rice, *Germany Unified and Europe Transformed*, p. 194.
383   "He said you had said": James Baker, handwritten note to Mikhail Gorbachev, March 28, 1990, Princeton archive.
384   "We must find a solution": Eduard Shevardnadze, *The Future Belongs to Freedom*, p. 139.
384   "Tell us what you need": Pavel Palazhchenko, *My Years with Gorbachev and Shevardnadze*, pp. 198–99.
384   for Gorbachev was now "critical": George H. W. Bush diary, March 7, 1990.
385   "another Munich": Andrew Rosenthal, "Bush Delays Action on Lithuania, Not Wanting to Harm Gorbachev," *New York Times*, April 25, 1990.
385   Senate voted overwhelmingly: The Senate voted 73 to 24 on May 1, 1990, to approve a nonbinding resolution urging Bush not to act on any trade agreements with the Soviet Union until it lifted its oil embargo and blockade on Lithuania. All but two Republicans voted against Bush on the measure. Joan Mower, "Senate Urges Halt to U.S.-Soviet Trade Agreement," Associated Press, May 2, 1990.
385   "After the Baker conversation": George H. W. Bush diary, April 18, 1990.
385   "Anchor Germany to West": James Baker, handwritten notes from meeting with Mikhail Gorbachev, May 18, 1990, Princeton archive.
386   "Taking Baker to the Cleaners": William Safire, "Taking Baker to the Cleaners," *New York Times*, May 21, 1990.
386   "The right wing is jumping on us": George H. W. Bush diary, May 22 and May 23, 1990.
386   "Jim would come to me": Colin Powell, author interview.
386   between 2,900 and 3,350 miles: Warsaw Pact Theater Forces—1985, Central Intelligence, September 1985, https://www.cia.gov/library/readingroom/docs/CIA-RDP 88T00565R000200250002-1.pdf. The CIA's own estimates were lower than those of the Defense Intelligence Agency, placing the range between 1,600 and 2,500 miles.

387   "It became a totem": Richard Burt, author interview.
387   "He looks at Baker": Ibid.
387   "Rick, you're probably pissed": Ibid.
388   would not a united Germany: George Bush and Brent Scowcroft, *A World Trans-formed*, pp. 282–83.
388   "It was as if everybody": Robert Blackwill, author interview.
389   "I'm gratified that you and I": Bush and Scowcroft, *A World Transformed*, pp. 282–83.
389   "practically assaulted": Zelikow and Rice, *Germany Unified and Europe Transformed*, pp. 276–79.
390   "They say Mitterrand has 1,000 lovers": James Baker, memo on conversation with Mikhail Gorbachev, Embassy in Paris, November 19, 1999, Princeton archive.
390   "Drinking decaffeinated coffee": American summary of Camp David meeting, June 2, 1990, Princeton archive.
390   "virtually open rebellion": Bush and Scowcroft, *A World Transformed*, pp. 282–83.
390   "We are in full agreement": Zelikow and Rice, *Germany Unified and Europe Trans-formed*, pp. 280–82.
391   "administration officials said they": Andrew Rosenthal, "Summit Talks End with Warmth but Fail to Resolve Key Issues," *New York Times*, June 5, 1990.
391   produced "no real progress": R.W. Apple Jr., "The Doubts That Linger: Question of Germany Remains Intractable," *New York Times*, June 4, 1990.
391   "deeply agitated": Genscher, *Rebuilding a House Divided*, p. 455.
391   "Well, *I* will disturb him": Kastrup interview.
392   "He was not in the best of moods": Ibid.
392   "a dour autumnal breakfast": Douglas Hurd, *Memoirs*, p. 389.
392   "taking into account": Agreed Minute to the Treaty on the Final Settlement with Respect to Germany, September 12, 1990, http://treaties.fco.gov.uk/docs/fullnames /pdf/1991/TS0088%20(1991)%20CM-1756%201990%201%20OCT,%20NEW %20YORK%3B%20TREATY%20ON%20GERMANY%20DECLARATION %20SUSPENDING%20OPERATION%20OF%20QUADRIPARTITE %20RIGHTS%20&%20RESPONSIBILITIES.pdf.
392   "The late night flurry": Hurd, *Memoirs*, p. 389.
392   "The new Germany is here": Thomas L. Friedman, "Four Allies Give Up Rights in Germany," *New York Times*, September 13, 1990.

CHAPTER 22. Desert Diplomacy

393   "He did not want to fail again": Pavel Palazchenko, *My Years with Gorbachev and Shevardnadze*, p. 205.
394   "Do you recall the subject": James A. Baker III, *The Politics of Diplomacy*, pp. 4–6.
394   "the State Department operations center": Palazchenko, *My Years with Gorbachev and Shevardnadze*, p. 206.
394   "I could not imagine": Eduard Shevardnadze, *The Future Belongs to Freedom*, pp. 99–100.
395   20 percent of the world's: World Proven Crude Oil Reserves by Country, 1980–2004, Organization of the Petroleum Exporting Countries (OPEC), https://www .opec.org/library/Annual%20Statistical%20Bulletin/interactive/2004/FileZ/XL/ T33.HTM.
395   "For several hours": Shevardnadze, *The Future Belongs to Freedom*, pp. 101–2.
396   "I gave him the assurance": James Baker, unpublished interview with ghostwriter Tom DeFrank, June 3, 1993, Princeton archive.
396   "It was one of the most difficult decisions": Shevardnadze, *The Future Belongs to Free-dom*, pp. 101–2.
396   "brutal and illegal invasion": Bill Keller, "Moscow Joins U.S. in Criticizing Iraq," *New York Times*, August 4, 1990.
396   "The Cold War breathed": Baker, *The Politics of Diplomacy*, p. 16.
396   "the first post–Cold War crisis": The State Department Policy Planning Office enti-

tled a memo "The First Post-Cold War Crisis" on August 4, 1991. William J. Burns, *The Back Channel*, p. 58.

397   "We didn't pay any attention": James Baker, unpublished interview with ghostwriter Tom DeFrank, June 1, 1993, Princeton archive.

397   While we take no position: R. Jeffrey Smith, "State Department Cable Traffic on Iraq-Kuwait Tensions, July 1990," *Washington Post*, October 21, 1991.

397   "we have no opinion on": Excerpts from Iraqi Document on Meeting with U.S. Envoy, *New York Times*, September 23, 1990. This was released by the Iraqi government, translated by ABC News, and published by the *Times*. The State Department never confirmed or denied its authenticity. Another version has circulated with somewhat different wording. https://www.nytimes.com/1990/09/23/world/confrontation-in-the-gulf-excerpts-from-iraqi-document-on-meeting-with-us-envoy.html. Glaspie later said the Iraqi account was doctored and omitted the first part of her sentence about Arab-Arab disputes in which she said she stressed "that we would not insist on settlements being made in a nonviolent manner, not by threats, not by intimidation and certainly not by aggression." See Thomas L. Friedman, "Envoy to Iraq, Faulted in Crisis, Says She Warned Hussein Sternly," *New York Times*, March 21, 1991.

398   "differences are best resolved": Rick Atkinson, *Crusade*, p. 52.

398   "She was lied to by him": George Bush and Brent Scowcroft, *A World Transformed*, pp. 310–11.

398   "What you want me to do": Jim Mann, "Baker Denies U.S. Misled Iraq About Stand on Invasion," *Los Angeles Times*, September 24, 1990.

398   "Washington's greatest self-positioner": Michael Kinsley, "James A. Baker, Please Resign," *Washington Post*, October 18, 1990.

398   "We were being accused": Baker interview with DeFrank, June 1.

398   "She didn't do anything wrong": James Baker, author interview.

399   "was invented by Tariq Aziz": Randa Takieddine, "The US Ambassador to Baghdad Tells the Story of Her Famous Meeting with Late Iraqi President," *Al Hayat*, March 15, 2008, http://www.informationclearinghouse.info/article19873.htm.

399   "She didn't tell us": Tariq Aziz, "The Gulf War: Oral History," *Frontline*, PBS, https://www.pbs.org/wgbh/pages/frontline/gulf/oral/aziz/1.html.

400   "Watch these guys": Dan Quayle, *Standing Firm*, p. 192.

400   "In the end, you will have": John Sununu, *The Quiet Man*, pp. 164–66.

400   "Too cute by half, Dick": James Baker interview.

400   "You've bought yourself": Richard Darman, *Who's in Control?*, pp. 264–65.

400   "prediction was closer": Ibid.

400   "He cut the deal because": Dan Quayle, author interview.

401   led the conservative opposition: The Senate approved the agreement 54 to 45, with nineteen Republicans siding with Bush and twenty-five opposing him. United States Senate, Roll Call on the Conference Report (H.R. 5835 Conference Report), October 27, 1990, https://www.senate.gov/legislative/LIS/roll_call_lists/roll_call_vote_cfm.cfm?congress=101&session=2&vote=00326. The House passed the deal 228 to 200, with just forty-seven Republicans voting yes and 126 voting no. United States House Clerk, Final Vote Results for Roll Call 528, October 26, 1990, http://clerk.house.gov/evs/1990/roll528.xml.

401   "He hated Newt after": Jonathan Darman, author interview.

401   "We just saw the train wreck": Janet Mullins Grissom, author interview.

402   "This will not stand": George Bush, Remarks and an Exchange with Reporters on the Iraqi Invasion of Kuwait, August 5, 1990, American Presidency Project, University of California at Santa Barbara, http://www.presidency.ucsb.edu/ws/index.php?pid=18741.

402   effectively declared war on Iraq: Colin L. Powell, *My American Journey*, pp. 466–67.

402   "What's the matter, Brent?": Quayle interview.

402   "arguably the most famous": Baker, *The Politics of Diplomacy*, p. 276.

402   "one smart son of a bitch": Colin Powell, author interview.

402   "I know you're aware of": Baker, *The Politics of Diplomacy*, p. 277.

402 "Jim Baker is worried that we": Jon Meacham, *Destiny and Power*, p. 441.

403 "a de facto member": George Crile, *My Enemy's Enemy*, p. 236.

403 "grave consequences": William Claiborne, "U.S. Ships Fire Warning Shots at Iraqi Tankers; Baghdad Escalates Threat Against Foreigners," *Washington Post*, August 19, 1990.

403 "Everybody said you've got": James Baker interview.

403 "We want one fact": James Baker, handwritten notes of call with Eduard Shevardnadze, August 22, 1990, Princeton archive.

403 "Jim Baker's many abilities": Margaret Thatcher, *The Downing Street Years*, pp. 782–83.

404 "Well, all right, George": Bush and Scowcroft, *A World Transformed*, pp. 351–52.

404 "the crunch point": James Baker, unpublished interview with ghostwriter Tom DeFrank, May 1993, Princeton archive.

404 "Jim, what do you really think": Quayle, *Standing Firm*, p. 208.

405 "It was at that point": Elizabeth Winston Jones, author interview.

405 "Jim really is an enigma": Powell interview.

405 "Look at Baker's relationship": Robert Zoellick, author interview.

405 "minister without portfolio": Elaine Sciolino, "Guardian of Baker's Door at State: A Quick Study Who Rose Rapidly," *New York Times*, February 23, 1990.

406 "A good age": Richard N. Haass, *War of Necessity, War of Choice*, pp. 80–82.

407 "Eduard, that would be": Baker, *The Politics of Diplomacy*, pp. 290–92.

407 "impassioned almost to the point": Ibid.

407 "You can't do that": Dennis Ross, *Doomed to Succeed*, pp. 237–38.

408 "to resolve all remaining conflicts": Baker, *The Politics of Diplomacy*, pp. 290–92.

408 "Why don't you just do it": Dennis Ross, author interview.

409 "Mr. President, isn't this": Baker, *The Politics of Diplomacy*, pp. 290–92.

409 "To bring it down to the": David Hoffman, "Baker Calls Iraqi Threat to 'Economic Lifeline,'" *Washington Post*, November 14, 1990.

409 "I knew what he was trying": Bush and Scowcroft, *A World Transformed*, p. 399.

409 "a brake on any immediate impulse": Thomas L. Friedman, "Baker Seen as a Balance to Bush on Crisis in Gulf," *New York Times*, November 3, 1990.

410 "the ablest of the president's men": Mary McGrory, "Baker's Tempering Touch," *Washington Post*, November 15, 1990.

410 $53.7 billion from other countries: William Diefenderfer and Robert Howard, "How to Fund a War,": *American Legion Magazine*, October 28, 2011.

411 "Why the hell do I have": Haass, *War of Necessity, War of Choice*, pp. 97–99. Also Richard Haass and Nicholas Burns, author interviews.

411 "He nearly threw me off": Haass interview.

412 "Gorbachev is close": Bush and Scowcroft, *A World Transformed*, p. 403.

412 "The first thing we must do": Michael Duffy and Dan Goodgame, *Marching in Place*, pp. 157–58.

412 "Mr. Secretary, you know you": Woodward, *The Commanders*, pp. 319–22.

412 "History now has given us": Paul Lewis, "U.N. Gives Iraq Until Jan. 15 to Retreat or Face Force; Hussein Says He Will Fight," *New York Times*, November 30, 1990.

413 "If Iraq does not reverse": Ibid.

413 "Yemen's perm. rep. just": James Baker, handwritten note to Robert Kimmitt, November 29, 1990, Princeton archive.

413 "Baker would have happily": David L. Mack, Association for Diplomatic Studies and Training Foreign Affairs Oral History Project, October 24, 1995, https://www.adst .org/OH%20TOCs/Mack,%20David%20L.toc.pdf.

413 warned against "hasty actions": Lewis, "U.N. Gives Iraq Until Jan. 15 to Retreat or Face Force."

413 "China can't go for military means": James Baker, handwritten note, November 29, 1990, Princeton archive.

413 approved the resolution 12 to 2: Lewis, "U.N. Gives Iraq Until Jan. 15 to Retreat or Face Force." The next day, Baker met with Qian Qichen in Washington, the first such official meeting in a year. Qian either forgot the deal Baker had offered or conveniently ignored it, because the Chinese protested when the minister was not

scheduled to see Bush too. Rather than cause a storm, Baker opted to take Qian to see the president even though the Chinese did not vote yes on the resolution.

413 "An historic moment": Robert Kimmitt, handwritten note to James Baker, November 29, 1990, Princeton archive.

414 "I want to talk to you": Baker, *The Politics of Diplomacy*, p. 346.

414 "He was more willing to": Brent Scowcroft, author interview.

415 "We wanted everybody in": Mullins Grissom interview.

415 "The threat of force is not": Notes of meeting shared with the authors on condition that note taker not be identified.

415 "I'm like, guys, we don't": Mullins Grissom interview.

415 "Bush did not like Mitchell": Ibid.

416 "That's part of why I knew": Ibid. Years later, Mitchell said he did not remember specifically sending messages to Baker through Mullins, but "that may well have occurred." From Mitchell's point of view, "it made sense to have continuing discussions to try to work things out." George Mitchell, author interview.

416 "dictatorship is coming": Bill Keller, "Shevardnadze Stuns Kremlin by Quitting Foreign Ministry and Warning of 'Dictatorship,'" *New York Times*, December 21, 1990. Keller translated the phrase as "dictatorship is approaching," though in the years since it has been more commonly rendered as "dictatorship is coming."

416 "Hard-liners are taking over": James Baker interview.

CHAPTER 23. Eyes of a Killer

417 "I was shitting in my pants": Stephen Hadley, author interview.

417 "I had to scrape an incensed Bandar": Richard N. Haass, *War of Necessity, War of Choice*, p. 103.

417 "I was extremely nervous": Brent Scowcroft, author interview.

417 "The whole world was looking": Gamal Helal, author interview.

418 "He never forgot that": Colin Powell, author interview.

418 "the eyes of a killer": Hadley interview.

418 "We wanted to make sure": Helal interview.

418 "I remember how urbane": James Baker, unpublished interview with ghostwriter Tom DeFrank, July 1, 1993, Princeton archive.

418 "He knew that the pictures": Karen Groomes Morgan, author interview.

419 "Our purpose ought not": Memorandum of Conversation, Intercontinental Hotel, Geneva, Switzerland, January 9, 1991.

419 "Unless you withdraw from Kuwait": "Text of Letter from Bush to Hussein," *New York Times*, January 13, 1991.

419 "That is why I can't accept": Memorandum of Conversation.

419 "sort of like the sword of Damocles": Hadley interview.

419 "The only question is by what path": Memorandum of Conversation.

420 "one of the toughest days": George Bush and Brent Scowcroft, *A World Transformed*, p. 444.

421 "You could tell by the look": Dick Cheney, author interview.

421 "Baker-Aziz meeting": Dan Quayle, *Standing Firm*, p. 223.

421 "in over six hours of talks": "Remarks by Baker at News Conference in Geneva on Standoff in the Gulf," *New York Times*, January 10, 1991.

421 "Everyone was, especially him": Groomes Morgan interview.

421 "When I talked to you": Thomas L. Friedman, "Baker Talks of Fast Strike if Kuwait Deadline Passes; Support in Congress Seen," *New York Times*, January 12, 1990.

421 "because I knew they were going": James Baker interview.

422 voted for the war resolution 250 to 183: Final Vote Results for Roll Call 9, H.J. Res. 77, House Clerk, January 12, 1991. Voting yes were 164 Republicans and 86 Democrats; voting no were 179 Democrats, three Republicans and one independent. http://clerk.house.gov/evs/1991/roll009.xml.

422 52 to 27, with ten Democrats: Roll Call Vote on the Joint Resolution, S.J. Res. 2,

United States Senate, January 12, 1991. Senator Chuck Grassley of Iowa was the only Republican to vote no. Senator Alan Cranston, a California Democrat, did not vote. https://www.senate.gov/legislative/LIS/roll_call_lists/roll_call_vote_cfm.cfm ?congress=102&session=1&vote=00002.

422 "I'm convinced I've done": James Baker interview.

422 "You could hear it in his voice": Zalman Shoval, author interview.

423 "so that I could try": Mikhail Gorbachev, *Memoirs*, p. 556.

423 "John, bring me a big martini": Ibid.

423 "The liberation of Kuwait has begun": Andrew Rosenthal, "U.S. and Allies Open Air War on Iraq; Bomb Baghdad and Kuwaiti Targets; 'No Choice' But Force, Bush Declares," *New York Times*, January 17, 1991.

423 "If they've been hit": Rick Atkinson, *Crusade*, pp. 82–85.

424 "We are going after western Iraq": Ibid.

424 "They were very, very funny": Robert Gates, author interview.

424 "You cannot do this, Prime Minister": James A. Baker III, *The Politics of Diplomacy*, p. 388.

424 "We may now have to act": Moshe Arens, *Broken Covenant*, pp. 205–6.

425 "I didn't sense any real sympathy": Moshe Arens, author interview.

425 "The Ministers continue to believe": James Baker and Alexander Bessmertnykh, joint statement, January 29, 1991, Princeton archive.

426 "Was Baker out of line?": Bush and Scowcroft, *A World Transformed*, pp. 460–61.

426 "His face turned ashen": Ibid.

426 "was furious": Ibid.

426 "got that steel jaw he gets": Marlin Fitzwater, author interview.

426 "Sorry about the way": James Baker, handwritten notes, January 30, 1991, Princeton archive.

426 "He should fire him for this": Monica Crowley, *Nixon in Winter*, p. 33.

426 "Baker bends over backward": Michael R. Beschloss and Strobe Talbott, *At the Highest Levels*, p. 335.

427 "What's it do for you": Michael Duffy and Dan Goodgame, *Marching in Place*, pp. 163–65.

427 "Margaret and I were both": Janet Mullins Grissom, author interview.

428 "We have done the job": Michael R. Gordon and Bernard E. Trainor, *The Generals' War*, pp. 414–16.

428 "We were all in agreement": Cheney interview.

428 "It hasn't been a clean end": George H. W. Bush diary, February 28, 1991. Cited by Bush and Scowcroft, *A World Transformed*, p. 487.

428 "the Iraqi military": George Bush, Remarks to Raytheon Missile Systems Plant Employees in Andover, Massachusetts, February 15, 1991, American Presidency Project, University of California at Santa Barbara, http://www.presidency.ucsb.edu /ws/?pid=19308.

428 "there's an incentive for some": Dick Cheney, interview with CNN, February 16, 1991.

428 "there would be no tears": James Baker, interview with CNN, February 17, 1991. 428 tried to immediately caveat that by adding, "That is a statement of fact, not a statement of a goal or a war aim." Nonetheless, it came across as something of a goal.

428 "Lebanonization of Iraq": James A. Baker III, "Why the U.S. Didn't March to Baghdad," *Los Angeles Times*, September 8, 1996.

428 "We are not prepared to go": Doyle McManus and John M. Broder, "Did Not Mislead Rebels, U.S. Says," *Los Angeles Times*, April 8, 1991.

429 "We are suffering": Thomas L. Friedman, "Baker Sees and Hears Kurds' Pain in a Brief Visit at Turkish Border," *New York Times*, April 9, 1991.

429 One hundred and forty-eight: Nese F. DeBruyne, "American War and Military Operations Casualties: Lists and Statistics," Congressional Research Service, April 26, 2017, https://fas.org/sgp/crs/natsec/RL32492.pdf.

429 about a quarter of them: Mark Thompson, "The Curse of 'Friendly Fire,'": *Time*, June 11, 2014.

429 shot up to 89 percent: Gallup Historical Presidential Job Approval Statistics: High Individual Measurements, https://news.gallup.com/poll/116677/presidential -approval-ratings-gallup-historical-statistics-trends.aspx.

429 enjoying an 84 percent: A *Newsweek* poll conducted by Gallup on March 1, 1991, found that 39 percent had a very favorable opinion of Baker and 45 percent a mostly favorable view for an overall 84 percent, compared with 8 percent who were unfavorable. Polls compiled by the Roper Center at the University of Connecticut, http:// www.ropercenter.uconn.edu/CFIDE/cf/action/ipoll/ipollBasket.cfm.

429 only 44 percent of Americans: ABC News/*Washington Post* poll, conducted March 1 to March 4. Roper Center.

429 "It doesn't get any better": James Baker interview.

CHAPTER 24. In the Souk

430 "has not received one cent": Clifford Krauss, "White House Rebukes Israeli Envoy," *The New York Times*, February 16, 1991.

430 "Baker took it personally": Dennis Ross, author interview.

430 "outrageous and outside": Statement by Press Secretary Fitzwater on Statements Made by Ambassador Zalman Shoval of Israel, George H. W. Bush Presidential Library and Museum, December 15, 1991, https://bush41library.tamu.edu/archives /public-papers/2712.

431 "Yesterday your Ambassador": James Baker, letter to Yitzhak Shamir, undated draft, Princeton archive.

431 "very laudatory towards Bush": Zalman Shoval, author interview.

431 "had been absolutely right": Moshe Arens, *Broken Covenant*, pp. 206–7.

431 "This Bush-Baker move against": Ibid.

431 "I think Baker scared": Aaron David Miller, author interview.

432 "When he would blow up": Ross interview.

432 "Can't underestimate difficulty": Memo titled "Post-Gulf War," February 1, 1991, Princeton archive.

432 "We've just seen an earthquake": William J. Burns, *The Back Channel*, p. 67.

432 "Take adv. of our unique position": James Baker, handwritten notes of discussion with George Bush and Brent Scowcroft, March 6, 1991, Princeton archive.

434 "not going to fly around": Dennis Ross, *Doomed to Succeed*, p. 218.

434 "settlements ought not": Ibid., pp. 220–21.

435 "It's a misunderstanding": Moshe Arens, author interview.

435 "The thing that he wanted": Dan Kurtzer, author interview.

435 "all the notes of warmth": Ross, *Doomed to Succeed*, p. 224.

435 "reasonable middle ground": Statement to AIPAC by Secretary of State Baker, 22 May 1989, Israel Ministry of Foreign Affairs, http://www.israel.org/MFA/Foreign Policy/MFADocuments/Yearbook8/Pages/59%20Statement%20to%20AIPAC %20by%20Secretary%20of%20State%20Baker-.aspx.

435 "For Israel, now is the time": Thomas L. Friedman, "Baker, in a Middle East Blueprint, Asks Israel to Reach Out to Arabs," *New York Times*, May 23, 1989.

435 "The first twenty minutes": Kurtzer interview.

435 "Nice job, fellas": William J. Burns, author interview.

436 "Your Israeli-Arab speech": Richard Nixon, letter to Baker, May 22, 1989, Princeton archive.

436 "Certainly, Baker's words": Yitzhak Shamir, *Summing Up*, pp. 200–3.

436 Senators from both parties: Kurtzer later concluded that the speech used unnecessarily inflammatory words and could have accomplished the same goal in a less provocative way. "You don't ask anybody to give up a dream," he said. Instead, Baker should have pressed Israel for specific, practical moves. "The idea was right but not the phraseology." Kurtzer interview.

436 "I think he belongs to that": Arens interview.

436 "It is astonishing that": "Israel Criticizes Report," *Washington Post*, March 22, 1990.

437 "I'm going to kick out": Kurtzer interview.

437 "Come on, he's the deputy": Burns interview.

437 "When we move to direct": Transcript, Hearing of the House Foreign Affairs Committee, Federal News Service, June 13, 1990.

438 "No one is going to create": Ross interview.

438 "He said you have finally": Note to James Baker, signed "csj," meaning probably Caron Jackson, June 13, 1990, Princeton archive.

438 "Disgusting." "Distasteful.": White House comment sheets, June 14, 1990, Princeton archive.

439 "One reason he's been successful": Condoleezza Rice, author interview.

439 "Every one of his counterparts": Ross interview.

439 "Everybody's got a red line": Margaret Tutwiler, author interview.

439 "Jim has this ability to": Dick Cheney, author interview.

440 "We know there is a state": Dennis Ross, *The Missing Peace*, pp. 68–69.

440 "Those guys could fuck up": Burns, *The Back Channel*, p. 73.

440 "I guess that it was okay": Ross, *The Missing Peace*, pp. 68–72.

440 "We were there for you": Ross, *Doomed to Succeed*, p. 246.

441 "a message to Baker": "Arab Stabs Four Women in Jerusalem, Three Dead," Associated Press, March 10, 1991. The fourth woman later died.

441 "visibly affected": Shamir, *Summing Up*, pp. 226–27.

442 "the best years of my life": Joel Brinkley, "Yitzhak Shamir, Former Israeli Prime Minister, Dies at 96," *New York Times*, June 30, 2012.

442 "I think Baker sized him up": Arens interview.

442 "an ever-flexible pragmatist": Shamir, *Summing Up*, pp. 200–201.

443 "In my grandmother's": Doug Baker, author interview.

443 "He was genuinely touched": Shamir, *Summing Up*, p. 230.

443 "toughest Arab domino": James A. Baker III, *The Politics of Diplomacy*, p. 447.

444 "ultimate endurance contest": Ibid., p. 454.

444 "I give up": Ibid.

444 "Well, you know, Mr. President": Ibid., p. 456.

445 "the dead cat": Ross, *The Missing Peace*, p. 76.

445 "Underneath that Texas affability": Robert Gates, author interview.

445 "Baker was a master of the": Richard Haass, *War of Necessity, War of Choice*, pp. 97–99.

445 "This better be important": Ed Djerejian, author interview.

446 "I need for you to stand up": Notes provided to authors on the condition that the note taker not be identified.

446 "We must be assured that": Zalman Shoval, *Jerusalem and Washington*, p. 185.

446 "Jim Baker's word—good": Ross, *Doomed to Succeed*, pp. 247–48.

446 "Don't let the PLO block": Notes provided to authors on the condition that the note taker not be identified.

447 "If this package I have prepared": Ibid.

447 "an endurance machine": Tutwiler interview.

447 "Take one hour per day": Preston Moore, letter to James Baker, April 25, 1991, Princeton archive.

447 "I hate you. I hate Jim Baker": Miller interview.

448 "We're up against": George Bush, The President's News Conference, September 12, 1991, American Presidency Project, University of California at Santa Barbara, http://www.presidency.ucsb.edu/ws/index.php?pid=19969.

448 "I'm gonna get him": Gamal Helal, author interview.

449 "Go to hell": Ibid.

449 "Take care": Ross, *Doomed to Succeed*, pp. 247–48.

449 "The ball is in your court": Notes provided to authors on the condition that the note taker not be identified.

449 "My people look at me": Ibid.

450 "We come from different": Ibid. See also Baker, *The Politics of Diplomacy*, p. 507.

450 "With you people, the souk never closes": Ibid. See also Ross, *Doomed to Succeed*, p. 249.

450 "Do you think I'm going to": Ross interview.
450 travel 251,134 miles: State Department count, Princeton archive.
450 "Mr. America": Helal interview.
450 "I guess we closed the souk": Ross, *Doomed to Succeed*, p. 249.
451 "blowhard": Ross, *The Missing Peace*, p. 275.
451 "irresponsible": Talking points for James Baker meeting with Feisal Husseini, October 30, 1991, Princeton archive.
452 "odd setting": Shamir, *Summing Up*, p. 237.
452 "Today, Israel and her Arab neighbors": Thomas L. Friedman, "Israel and Arabs, Face to Face, Begin Quest for Mideast Peace," *New York Times*, October 31, 1991.
453 "faking facts and history": R. W. Apple Jr., "Mideast Foes List Demands and Trade Angry Charges Across Conference Table," *New York Times*, November 1, 1991.
453 "Don't let them get public": Talking points for James Baker phone call to Yitzhak Shamir, November 3, 1991, Princeton archive.
454 "We just landed": George H. W. Bush, letter to James Baker, October 30, 1991, Princeton archive.
454 "Baker's remarkable, stubborn": Shamir, *Summing Up*, p. 228.
454 "One of the raps on me was": James Baker, unpublished interview with ghostwriter Thomas DeFrank, April 29, 1993, Princeton archive.
454 "I'm going to the White House": Kurtzer interview.

CHAPTER 25. A Call to Action

455 "There goes another vacation": Michael R. Beschloss and Strobe Talbott, *At the Highest Levels*, p. 423.
455 "No leverage": Serhii Plokhy, *The Last Empire*, pp. 75–77.
456 "What a flake!": Beschloss and Talbott, *At the Highest Levels*, p. 104.
457 "engaging and pleasant": George Bush and Brent Scowcroft, *A World Transformed*, pp. 510–11.
457 "Maybe the thing to do": Beschloss and Talbott, *At the Highest Levels*, p. 429.
457 "We decided he should": Bush and Scowcroft, *A World Transformed*, p. 520.
457 "disturbing development": George H. W. Bush, News Conference, Kennebunkport, Maine, August 19, 1991, Federal News Service transcript.
458 "misguided and illegitimate effort": Andrew Rosenthal, "Bush Condemns Soviet Coup and Calls for Its Reversal," *New York Times*, August 20, 1991.
458 "My problem is that, during": Bush and Scowcroft, *A World Transformed*, pp. 526–27.
459 "know anything about foreign policy": Monica Crowley, *Nixon in Winter*, pp. 20–21.
459 "if Baker doesn't stop drooling": Ibid., p. 25.
459 "I thought we needed to": Dick Cheney, author interview.
459 "They never really cottoned up": Dan Quayle, author interview.
460 "We'd have a cabinet meeting": James Baker, author interview.
460 "Fuck you, Kemp!": Robert Gates, *From the Shadows*, pp. 456–57. See also Morton Kondracke and Fred Barnes, *Jack Kemp*, 240–42.
460 "a quarterback who had just been": Marlin Fitzwater, *Call the Briefing!*, pp. 350–51.
460 "I thought there was going": Gates, *From the Shadows*, pp. 456–57.
460 "I deeply regret": Jack Kemp to James Baker, undated note, Princeton archive.
461 "I have your very thoughtful": James Baker to Jack Kemp, May 23, 1991, Princeton archive.
461 "A COUP IS BEING ORGANIZED": Jack F. Matlock Jr., *Autopsy of an Empire*, pp. 540–44.
462 "he should not literally": James Dobbins, *Foreign Service*, p. 117.
462 "not use military force": Milan Panic, *Prime Minister for Peace*, p. 42.
463 "We don't have a dog": J. F. O. McAllister, "Atrocity and Outrage," *Time*, August 17, 1992.
463 "You're the first journalist": Steven Weisman, author interview.
463 "I convinced no one": James A. Baker III, *The Politics of Diplomacy*, p. 480.

463 "a wall with a crew cut": Ibid., p. 481.

463 "a major failure of U.S. diplomacy": Panic, *Prime Minister for Peace*, p. 42.

463 "U-S-A! U-S-A! U-S-A!": "300,000 Albanians Pour into Streets to Welcome Baker," *New York Times*, June 23, 1991.

463 "On behalf of President Bush": Ibid.

464 "We're not doing contingency planning": The meeting took place on June 25, 1991. Bartholomew Sparrow, *The Strategist*, pp. 452–53.

464 "What you are telling us": Plokhy, *The Last Empire*, p. 78.

465 "Is that really all right?": Ibid., p. 26.

466 "Some people have urged": George H. W. Bush, Remarks to the Supreme Soviet of the Republic of Ukraine in Kiev, Soviet Union, August 1, 1991, American Presidency Project, University of California at Santa Barbara, https://www.presidency.ucsb.edu /documents/remarks-the-supreme-soviet-the-republic-the-republic-the-ukraine -kiev-soviet-union.

466 "Chicken Kiev" speech: William Safire, "Ukraine Marches Out," *New York Times*, November 1991.

466 "We were very nervous": James Baker interview.

467 "There's no question I was": Cheney interview.

467 "it would be good if you": Memorandum of Conversation, August 20, 1991, George H. W. Bush Presidential Library and Museum.

468 switched sides and ordered: Peter Baker, "Coup That Wasn't Stirs Russians' Mixed Emotions," *Washington Post*, August 17, 2001.

468 "The Embassy's assessment": Typewritten notes, undated and unsigned, Princeton archive.

468 "Excuse me, I've got to": James Dobbins, author interview.

469 "I have been trying to": Dobbins, *Foreign Service*, pp. 125–26.

469 "Oh my God, that's wonderful": Memorandum of Conversation, August 21, 1991, Bush Library.

470 "We could get an authoritarian": Bush and Scowcroft, *A World Transformed*, pp. 541–43.

470 "Support for the center": Plokhy, *The Last Empire*, p. 211.

470 "Mistake to say 'no'": Ibid., p. 264.

470 90 percent voted for independence: Francis X. Clines, "Ex-Communist Wins in Ukraine; Yeltsin Recognizes Independence," *New York Times*, December 3, 1991.

471 "The USSR, as a subject of": The Belavezha Accords, December 8, 1991, Russian Presidential Library, https://www.prlib.ru/en/history/619792.

471 "The Soviet Union as we've": David Hoffman, "'Soviet Union as We've Known It' Is Gone, Baker Says," *Washington Post*, December 9, 1991.

471 "I think the Soviet situation": James Baker, memorandum to George H. W. Bush, December 10, 1991, Princeton archive.

472 "The simple fact of the matter": James Baker, "America and the Collapse of the Soviet Empire: What Has to Be Done," address delivered at Princeton University, December 12, 1991, Federal News Service transcript.

472 "It is a letting-go": Doyle McManus, "Baker Appeals for Global Aid for Republics," *Los Angeles Times*, December 13, 1991.

472 "call to action": Baker, "America and the Collapse of the Soviet Empire."

473 "seemed small compared with": Thomas L. Friedman, "Baker Presents Steps to Aid Transition by Soviets," *New York Times*, December 13, 1991.

473 "a Marshall Plan": McManus, "Baker Appeals for Global Aid for Republics."

473 58 percent told pollsters: New York Times/CBS News poll, August 26–29, 1991, https://ropercenter.cornell.edu/public-perspective/ppscan/31/31025.pdf.

473 "much too hasty in saying": Beschloss and Talbott, *At the Highest Levels*, pp. 452–53.

474 "Nothing could be further": Pavel Palazchenko, *My Years with Gorbachev and Shevardnadze*, pp. 353–54.

474 "That will be the judgment": Notes shared with the authors on condition that the note taker not be identified.

475 "Welcome, you are on Russian": Ibid.

475 "Ukraine and others will": Ibid.

476 "This is kind of a coup": Ibid.

476 "an extraordinary discussion": James Baker, typewritten notes from telephone call with George H. W. Bush, January 29, 1992.

477 "The Bush and Baker idea": Crowley, *Nixon in Winter*, p. 75.

477 "I don't have a blank check": Thomas L. Friedman, "Bush Cites Limits on Aid to Russia," *New York Times*, March 12, 1992.

477 "Spent *trillions* of dollars": James Baker, handwritten notes on talking points, March 30, 1992, Princeton archive.

477 "The American people are fed up": Thomas L. Friedman, "Bush and Baker Press Aid to Russia but Meet Worries About Costs," *New York Times*, April 10, 1992.

478 "They're justifying themselves": Petr Aven and Alfred Kokh, *Gaidar's Revolution*, pp. 362–74.

CHAPTER 26. The Cruelest Turn

479 "Is there something": Janet Mullins Grissom, author interview.

480 "In 1988, fighting Dukakis": Donald M. Rothberg, "Ailing Republican Chairman Apologizes for Hardball Tactics," Associated Press, January 14, 1991.

480 Atwater was "Machiavellian": Neely Tucker, " 'Lee Atwater Story': Riveting Ruthlessness," *Washington Post*, September 26, 2008.

480 "by pushing it to the edge": Susan Baer, "Baker Praises Atwater at D.C. Memorial Service," Baltimore *Sun*, April 5, 1991.

481 "We were pulling our hair out": Susan Baker, author interview.

481 "I would say to my husband": Susan Baker, unpublished interview with ghostwriter for husband's second memoir, January 25, 2006, Princeton archive.

481 "(NOT RGD)": Handwritten notes, November 25, 1991, Princeton archive.

482 "JABIII—for 1 year only—part-time": Ibid.

482 "You have just done": James Baker, note to John Sununu, December 3, 1991, Princeton archive. Reflecting on his fall years later, Sununu did not blame Baker. In fact, he concluded that he should have emulated Baker and done more to reach out to reporters to build a better relationship. "Probably the biggest mistake I made was not taking his advice," Sununu said. "He really recommended I continue his practice of off-the-record briefings with the press, but the president didn't want me to do that." John Sununu, author interview.

482 "I've got major stuff": Dick Cheney, author interview.

482 "threw me under the bus": Ibid.

483 "global bureaucrats": Robin Toner, "Buchanan, Urging New Nationalism, Joins '92 Race," *New York Times*, December 11, 1992.

483 "America First": Maureen Dowd, "Buchanan's Alternative: Not Kinder or Gentler," *New York Times*, January 15, 1992.

483 "a wonderful fight for Bush": David S. Broder, "Shame of the GOP . . . ," *Washington Post*, December 7, 1991.

483 "I think it is important to your re-election": James Baker, handwritten note to George Bush, December 9, 1991, Princeton archive.

483 the economy was in a "freefall": Andrew Rosenthal, "Bush Camp Renews Strategy Debate," *New York Times*, January 25, 1992.

483 "Message: I care": Ibid.

484 winning 38 percent of the vote: New Hampshire Secretary of State's Office, https://sos.nh.gov/1992RepPresPrim.aspx.

484 "That was a wakeup call": Sam Skinner, author interview.

484 "if I had it to do over": Dick Williams, "Bush Sorry for Breaking Promise of No New Taxes; 'If I Had It to Do Over, I Wouldn't,' He Says," *Atlanta Journal and Constitution*, March 3, 1992.

484 "That admission is the worst": Bob Woodward, "Primary Heat Turned Deal into a 'Mistake,' " *Washington Post*, October 6, 1992.

485 "Change vs. more of the same": Michael Kelly, "Clinton and Bush Compete to Be Champion of Change," *New York Times*, October 31, 1992.

485 "causing pain in my marriage": Dan Balz, "Clinton Concedes Marital 'Wrongdoing,'" *Washington Post*, January 27, 1992.

485 "I didn't inhale": Gwen Ifill, "Clinton Admits Experiment with Marijuana in 1960's," *New York Times*, March 30, 1992.

486 "our worst political nightmare": Fred Steeper, Memorandum to Robert Teeter and Charlie Black, Re: Taking Risks, March 11, 1992, reproduced in the appendix of Peter Goldman et al., *Quest for the Presidency, 1992*, p. 648.

486 "I'll be like a mechanic": Susan Baer, "What Would Perot Do? Campaigner Has Record of Hands-On Style," Baltimore *Sun*, June 23, 1992.

486 "if Jim Baker would just step up": Goldman et al., *Quest for the Presidency, 1992*, p. 426.

487 "BAKER'S 4-LETTER INSULT": Ed Koch, "BAKER'S 4-LETTER INSULT," *New York Post*, March 6, 1992.

487 followed with a column saying: William Safire, "Blaming the Victim," *New York Times*, March 19, 1992.

487 acknowledged in a book: Edward I. Koch, *The Koch Papers*, p. 91.

487 "Well, AIPAC won't like that": James Baker, author interview.

487 "It was a political comment": Ibid.

487 "Hey Jimmy, I've got my": Jack Kemp, James A. Baker III Oral History Project, October 6, 2008, Princeton and Rice. Kemp's account raises some questions. He said that he had gone to the White House that day to accompany Bush on a trip to Los Angeles following riots sparked by the acquittal of police officers who beat African American motorist Rodney King. But the riots took place nearly two months after Koch's column was published. Since Kemp was speaking more than sixteen years later, it is possible he confused the timeline.

488 "Nothing could be further": James Baker, letter to Melvin Salberg and Abraham Foxman, March 5, 1992, Princeton archive.

488 "I respectfully suggest that": Benjamin Gilman, letter to James Baker, March 17, 1992, Princeton archive. According to exit polls, George Bush drew about 29 percent of American Jews in his 1988 contest with Michael Dukakis.

488 "I don't accept that Jim would": George Bush, letter to Ed Koch, March 6, 1991, Princeton archive.

488 "I don't believe he was": Abraham Foxman, author interview. A review of Baker's public life finds little if any convincing evidence beyond that disputed episode to suggest that Baker was overtly anti-Semitic. But it is true that he grew up in Texas in an era when he knew few if any Jews and he was not sensitized to the subject as Americans of later generations would be. And he remained deeply skeptical of some of Israel's policies, particularly under Yitzhak Shamir, which to some critics fed the impression of anti-Semitism.

488 "Shamir lost the election": Arens interview.

489 "Baker was determined not": Dennis Ross, *The Missing Peace*, pp. 82–84.

489 "They wanted the lead": James Baker, author interview.

490 an estimated 140,000: "Focus: The Former Yugoslavia," International Center for Transitional Justice, 2009, https://www.ictj.org/sites/default/files/ICTJ-FormerYugoslavia-Justice-Facts-2009-English.pdf.

490 "the administration at high levels": Don Oberdorfer, "U.S. Aide Resigns over Balkan Policy," *Washington Post*, August 26, 1992.

490 "The last year of the administration": Richard Haass, author interview.

490 "I talked to the president": Skinner interview.

490 "It's a bit unfair": FitzGerald "Gerry" Bemiss, letter to James Baker, May 31, 1992, Princeton archive.

491 "Your personality is improving": Lynn Martin, letter to James Baker, July 14, 1992, Princeton archive.

491 "Dick, don't you see?": Colin Powell, author interview.

491 "You need to ask Baker": Senior Bush administration official who asked not to be identified, author interview.

491 "I think they felt like Jim": Powell interview.

491 "He didn't want to leave": John Baker, author interview.

491 "one last Hail Mary": Ross, *The Missing Peace*, pp. 85–87.

492 "I think I really need some help": James Baker interview.

492 "the Democratic Party has revitalized itself": Steven A. Holmes, "Perot Says Democratic Surge Reduced Prospect of Victory, *New York Times*, July 17, 1992.

492 "Tell him you share his": James Baker, notes for ghostwriter, September 27, 2005, Princeton archive.

493 "The president is obviously": David Paton, letter to James Baker, July 22, 1992, Princeton archive.

493 "In coming back, he knew": Addison Baker Duncan, James A. Baker III Oral History Project, Princeton and Rice.

493 commissioned a secret poll: Fred Steeper, Memorandum Re: Vice President, July 20, 1992. Reproduced in the appendix of Goldman et al., *Quest for the Presidency, 1992*, pp. 703–4.

493 Baker polled better than Quayle: A public poll at that time showed that Baker polled better than Quayle. Gallup found that 40 percent of voters would be more likely to vote for Bush if Baker was his running mate instead of Quayle while 32 percent said they would be less willing and the rest said it would not make much difference or had no opinion. Gallup Poll, Gallup Organization, July 24–26, 1992.

493 called Quayle to make clear: Colin L. Powell, *My American Journey*, pp. 553–54.

494 "I was just thinking of ways": George W. Bush, author interview.

494 "with George's knowledge": Unpublished draft of memoir, September 20, 2005, Princeton archive.

494 "I told the president our": Ibid.

494 "Yes," Quayle answered: Ann Devroy and David S. Broder, "Private Talks Leave Quayle on Ticket; Departure Weighed in Discussions," *Washington Post*, July 25, 1992.

494 "Baker had agreed": Ibid.

494 "It was exciting to think that": Marlin Fitzwater, *Call the Briefing*, p. 354.

495 "Marlin, has the president": Ibid., p. 355.

495 more than 700,000 miles: Altogether, his staff calculated his total travel at 700,131 miles to 125 countries (many of them repeat visits). "Travel fact sheet—1989–1992," August 31, 1992, Princeton archive.

496 "whirlwind of history": Remarks of Secretary of State James Baker, The Loy Henderson Room, The State Department, Federal News Service, August 13, 1992.

496 "As I listened to that": George H. W. Bush, note to James Baker, August 13, 1992. In George Bush, *All the Best, George Bush*, p. 565.

496 "That was the cruelest": Aaron David Miller, author interview.

497 "abortion on demand": Pat Buchanan 1992 Republican Convention Address, C-SPAN, August 17, 1992, https://www.c-span.org/video/?31255-1/pat-buchanan-1992-republican-convention-address.

497 "You can bet your life": Goldman et al., *Quest for the Presidency, 1992*, p. 512.

497 "so that people couldn't": Dan Quayle, *Standing Firm*, p. 351.

498 "When you got in a meeting": Thomas Scully, George H. W. Bush Oral History Project, Miller Center, September 2–3, 1999.

498 "Baker's been MIA": Maureen Dowd with Thomas L. Friedman, "Baker Re-Emerges as Bush's Campaign Chief, Only to Be Hit with Criticism," *New York Times*, October 11, 1992.

498 "hiding in the conference room": Ibid.

499 "Jim Baker told people what": Quayle, *Standing Firm*, p. 351.

499 "What are you doing": Baker associate who asked not to be identified, author interview.

499 "Ross, that's just bullshit": James Baker interview.

500 "He waxed very emotional": Jon Meacham, *Destiny and Power*, p. 514.

500 "Open new markets": Bush Campaign Debate Briefing Book, Princeton archive.

500 "What I'm going to do is say": The First Clinton-Bush-Perot Presidential Debate, transcript, Commission on Presidential Debates, October 11, 1992, https://www.debates.org/voter-education/debate-transcripts/october-11-1992-first-half-debate-transcript/.

500 "Shit, we never talked about that": James Baker interview. The *Newsweek* reporters who compiled a book reconstructing the campaign after the election had a different version. They reported that Baker had known Bush would make the suggestion at the debate, although he was unhappy about it and groused to colleagues that he would only give the assignment a year before returning to the State Department. Along with Baker's appointment, Bush was supposed to announce that he would fire his current economic team of Nick Brady, Dick Darman, and Michael Boskin but forgot, leaving it to aides to put the news out after the debate. Goldman et al., *Quest for the Presidency, 1992*, p. 516. But in an interview with the authors, Baker insisted the idea "came as a total and absolute and complete surprise to me."

501 "an incredible acknowledgment": Jack W. Germond and Jules Witcover, *Mad as Hell*, pp. 475–76.

501 "his handler-in-chief": Greg McDonald, "Bush Has New Role in Mind for Baker; Economy May Be Next Duty," *Houston Chronicle*, October 13, 1992.

501 "I like the speech": Goldman et al., *Quest for the Presidency, 1992*, p. 516.

501 "the Invisible Man": Ibid.

501 "She was all over me": James Baker interview.

501 "Barb, get off his case": Ibid.

501 "How has the national debt": The Second Clinton-Bush-Perot Presidential Debate, transcript, Commission on Presidential Debates, October 15, 1992, https://www.debates.org/voter-education/debate-transcripts/october-15-1992-second-half-debate-transcript/.

502 "The person responsible for": The Third Clinton-Bush-Perot Presidential Debate, transcript, Commission on Presidential Debates, October 19, 1992, https://www.debates.org/voter-education/debate-transcripts/october-19-1992-debate-transcript/.

502 39 percent said Clinton: *New York Times*/CBS News Poll. Robin Toner, "Contest Tightens as Perot Resurges and Clinton Slips," *New York Times*, October 25, 1992.

503 "The man and I are very close": C. Boyden Gray, Memorandum to the File, October 22, 1992. Baker personal files. Baker had Gray, the White House counsel, listen in on the conversation, which took place on October 22, and make a record of it in writing.

503 "consult with Ross": Ken Langone, *I Love Capitalism!*, pp. 171–73.

503 "those people": James A. Baker III, Memorandum to File, October 21, 1992.

503 "impetuous" and "sounded flaky": Ibid. In his book, Langone concluded that Baker did not realize how close he was to Perot and had someone else reach out to the candidate. By doing so, Langone believed, Baker had scotched the possibility of a deal that would have saved Bush's presidency.

503 "Taxes and Trust, Stupid": Goldman et al., *Quest for the Presidency, 1992*, p. 591.

504 "I just need you to know": Mullins Grissom interview.

504 "They wanted us to contact the Russians": James Baker, Note for File, October 6, 1992. Baker personal files.

504 "My dog Millie knows more": Michael Wines, "Candidates Aim at Crucial States, and Each Other; Bush, Buoyed by Polls, Scrambles to Rebuild Winning Coalition," *New York Times*, October 30, 1992.

504 "'86 Weinberger Notes": Robert Pear, "'86 Weinberger Notes Contradict Bush Account on Iran Arms Deal," *New York Times*, October 31, 1992.

504 "Bush Stance, Iran-Contra": Walter Pincus and George Lardner Jr., "Bush Stance, Iran-Contra Notes at Odds," *Washington Post*, October 31, 1992.

505 "It looks like a blowout": Meacham, *Destiny and Power*, p. 521.

505 Clinton won 43 percent: Election of 1992, American Presidency Project, University

of California at Santa Barbara, http://presidency.proxied.lsit.ucsb.edu/showelection
.php?year=1992.

505 "Had we not had Ross Perot": James Baker interview.
505 38 percent of his voters: Steven A. Holmes, "An Eccentric but No Joke,": *New York Times*, November 5, 1992.
505 Of the eleven states: Bush lost Colorado, Georgia, Kentucky, Louisiana, Montana, Nevada, New Hampshire, New Jersey, Ohio, Tennessee, and Wisconsin by 5 or fewer percentage points. Together they had 107 electoral votes; if all of them flipped, Bush would have won with 275 to 263 for Clinton. From data posted by the American Presidency Project, University of California at Santa Barbara, http://presidency.proxied.lsit.ucsb.edu/showelection.php?year=1992.
506 "People were tired of us": James Baker interview.
506 "Afterward, Barbara and I finished": Susan Baker, author interview.
506 "the Iran-contra cover-up": The others pardoned were: Robert McFarlane, the former national security adviser; Elliott Abrams, former assistant secretary of state; and three former CIA officials, Clair E. George, Duane R. Clarridge, and Alan D. Fiers Jr. All five were charged, convicted, or pleaded guilty to various crimes related to misleading Congress. David Johnston, "Bush Pardons 6 in Iran Affair, Aborting a Weinberger Trial; Prosecutor Assails 'Cover-Up,'" *New York Times*, December 25, 1992.
507 "Everybody's emotions were raw": John Baker interview.
507 "a fraught period": Brent Scowcroft, author interview.
507 "Losing is hard, losing is tough": James Baker interview.
507 "I think Bush felt a certain degree": Dennis Ross, author interview.
507 "I don't remember being upset": Barbara Bush, author interview.
507 "I was really frustrated because": George W. Bush interview.

CHAPTER 27. The Virus

511 "Who needs this?": Bob Woodward, *Shadow*, p. 208.
512 "Jim Baker is still all uptight": Ibid., p. 210.
512 "Jim Baker has lost all interest": Ibid., pp. 211–13.
512 "Baker is a nervous wreck": Ibid.
512 "It's ruining Jim Baker's life": Ibid.
512 "His disappearance is the talk": Mary McGrory, "Missing and Presumed Injured," *Washington Post*, December 22, 1992.
513 "An ugly editorial by Mary McGrory": Woodward, *Shadow*, pp. 211–13.
513 "prosecutor with a politician's flair": Sharon LaFraniere, "DiGenova's Legacy," *Washington Post*, February 29, 1988.
513 "What Baker made perfectly clear": Janet Mullins Grissom, author interview.
513 "This wasn't about me": Ibid.
514 "At the end of the interview": Michael Zeldin, author interview.
514 "Today, a Kafkaesque journey": David Johnston, "File Search in 1992 Race Wasn't Illegal," *New York Times*, December 1, 1995.
514 "I just want you to know": James Baker, author interview.
514 "I still think it was the right call": William Barr, author interview. Janet Mullins Grissom was even less forgiving than Baker. When Barr came to see her to explain herself, she called him a coward. "You need to know that I will make it my mission in life that you will never, ever be confirmed for any office in any administration as long as I'm working in Washington, D.C.," she recalled telling him. As it happened, Barr managed to make a comeback in Washington anyway. In 2018, he was appointed to a second tour as attorney general by President Donald Trump and confirmed by the Senate in early 2019.
515 "What would I be?": Edward William Barnett, James A. Baker III Oral History Project, Princeton and Rice.
515 "I would be happy to do": Ibid.

515　"I think you ought to explain": Ibid.

517　"It was a brilliant strategy": Dan Briody, *The Iron Triangle*, p. 82.

517　"I didn't take up much": David Rubenstein, author interview.

517　"I knew what the answer was": Preston Moore, James A. Baker III Oral History Project, Princeton and Rice.

517　"Baker very cleverly approaches": Edward Djerejian, author interview.

518　"We discussed the liberation": Seymour M. Hersh, "The Spoils of the Gulf War," *The New Yorker*, September 6, 1993.

519　"There is nothing I enjoy more": Addison Baker Duncan, James A. Baker III Oral History Project, Princeton and Rice.

519　"In seeking contracts": Hersh, "The Spoils of the Gulf War."

519　"Seymour, you really tried": James Baker interview.

519　Taken aback by Baker's anger: Seymour Hersh, email to authors.

519　"The Carlyle Group, in short": Michael Lewis, "The Access Capitalists," *The New Republic*, October 18, 1993.

520　"If the piece is suggesting": James Baker interview.

520　he earned $2.4 million: General Summary, 1994 Payments Received. This year-to-date summary included $1,010,921 from Baker Botts through August, $374,994 from Enron through September, and $173,076 from Carlyle. A separate summary of honoraria prepared by the Washington Speakers Bureau showed that Baker earned $893,000 in fees in 1994, Princeton archive.

520　"I came home one day to Susan": James Baker interview.

521　"When you see these people": Rubenstein interview.

521　"the A list" for Republicans: Andrew Rosenthal, "While in Houston to Help Bush, Many Have Eyes on 1996," *New York Times*, August 17, 1992.

521　"essentially do nothing": Andrew Carpendale, memo to James Baker, July 28, 1993, Princeton archive.

522　"show that you have a sense": Ibid.

522　"the surest sign yet": Maureen Dowd, "Baker, Lieutenant to Reagan, Salutes North," *New York Times*, October 5, 1994.

522　"In my view": Rad Sallee, "Baker Acts Like Contender but Ducks Question; Candidacy 'Not Ruled Out,' He Says in Speech," *Houston Chronicle*, November 22, 1994.

522　with 28 percent of the Republican vote: CBS News Poll, January 2–3, 1995.

523　"You don't want your legacy": Dennis Ross, author interview.

523　"What I told him was": Andy Card, author interview.

523　"I'll be your poster child": Elizabeth Winston Jones, author interview.

524　"First of all, you have passionate enemies": Unsigned and undated memo to James Baker. Margaret Tutwiler identified its author as Dick Darman, Princeton archive.

524　"what do I want to do": Unsigned memo to James Baker, June 10, 1994. Margaret Tutwiler confirmed that she was its author, Princeton archive.

524　"I'm over whatever short virus": "Former Secretary of State No Longer Interested in Presidential Run," Associated Press, May 10, 1995.

524　"If he were *selected* to be": David Paton, author interview.

525　"What it came down to was": Doug Baker, author interview.

525　"I knew I could do that job": James Baker and Susan Baker, author interview.

525　"But honey," she said: Ibid.

525　"Yeah, I think you ought to": James Baker interview.

525　"He could probably have gotten": Winston Jones interview.

526　"stop calling it a memoir": James Baker, handwritten note on letter from Neil Nyren, Putnam publisher, January 17, 1995, Princeton archive.

526　"He wanted to be remembered": Derek Chollet, author interview.

526　"Connotes victim of events": James Baker, handwritten notes on memorandum from Andrew Carpendale, January 17, 1995, Princeton archive.

527　"He was loud, he was boisterous": Peter Bass, author interview.

527　"He was still then very much": Chollet interview.

527　"In retrospect, it may have been": Draft manuscript pages, Princeton archive.

527 "I want to register": Andrew Carpendale, memorandum to James Baker, January 23, 1995, Princeton archive.
528 "You alone will have to bear": Ibid.
528 "Andrew was saying something": Chollet interview.
528 Of course, Carpendale lost: As it was, Carpendale was wrestling with his own demons, a bipolar disorder that he had hidden from friends who only in hindsight would recognize the signs. After Baker's book was done, Carpendale headed back to California but never got over being absent from the center of the action. After the attacks of September 11, 2001, he tried to enter government again, only to have his calls go unreturned. In May 2002, at age forty-one, he committed suicide in Palo Alto. See Tia O'Brien, "'Brilliant' Foreign Policy Analyst Remembered as Sharp Wit, Playful," *San Jose Mercury News*, May 26, 2002.
528 "The man famous for spinning": Michiko Kakutani, "A Political Insider with Bush Tells of the Outside," *New York Times*, October 5, 1995.

CHAPTER 28. Scorched Earth

530 "What do you think about Baker?": George W. Bush, author interview.
530 "When he went down": David Rubenstein, author interview.
530 he arranged for George W.: Bill Minutaglio, *First Son*, pp. 64–65.
530 Baker steered a Princeton friend: Ibid., pp. 202–3.
530 "George W. Bush wanted": Andy Card, author interview.
531 "I think you know I would": James Baker, handwritten note to George H. W. Bush, November 11, 1998, Princeton archive.
531 "I read that nutty story": George H. W. Bush, handwritten note to James Baker, November 13, 1998, Princeton archive.
531 "In international policy": Robert Novak's syndicated column ran in various newspapers across the country, including in the *New York Post* on February 22, 2001, under the headline "George W.'s Righty Brain Trust."
531 "horrible Novak column": George H. W. Bush, letter to Brent Scowcroft, cc'd to James Baker, February 25, 1999, Princeton archive.
531 "I feel badly about the slight": George W. Bush, handwritten note to James Baker, February 25, 1999, Princeton archive.
531 "It is important for you": James Baker, handwritten note to George W. Bush, March 2, 1999, Princeton archive.
532 "Probably best if you destroy this": Charles Powell, letter to James Baker, September 2, 1999, Princeton archive.
532 listed his predictions: James Baker, handwritten notes, November 2, 2000, Princeton archive.
532 Michigan went for Gore: 2000 Official Presidential General Election Results, Updated December 2001, Federal Election Commission, https://transition.fec.gov/pubrec/2000presgeresults.htm.
532 a lead of about 6,000 votes: Abby Goodnough, "Recounting Becomes Issue, Not Just in Florida," *New York Times*, November 10, 2000.
533 a meager 1,784 votes: David Barstow and Don Van Natta Jr., "How Bush Took Florida: Mining the Overseas Absentee Vote," *New York Times*, July 15, 2001.
533 "Quickly, Openly, Calmly": James Baker, handwritten notes, November 8, 2000, Princeton archive.
533 "We're heading to the Supreme Court": Gloria Borger, *Bush v. Gore: The Endless Election*, CNN documentary.
533 "Where is he?": James Baker, author interview.
534 "Well, Chris, we're not here": Ron Klain, author interview.
535 "He didn't spend one minute": Ibid.
535 "I just can't conceive that": Jack Danforth, author interview. Ultimately, Theodore Olson would prove Danforth wrong. The federal courts took the case. "The next time I saw Jim Baker," Danforth said later, "he said, 'I told you so.'"

536 "Come on, we'll give you": Bill Daley, author interview.

536 go into overtime since 1876: In 1876, Democrat Samuel Tilden beat Republican Rutherford B. Hayes in the national popular vote, but disputes in Florida, Louisiana, and South Carolina left the winner of the Electoral College undecided for weeks after Election Day. Congress set up a special electoral commission composed of lawmakers and Supreme Court justices, which ultimately voted 8 to 7 to award the disputed Electoral College votes to Hayes, putting him in the White House.

536 Improbably, 3,407 votes: Jonathan N. Wand, Kenneth W. Shotts, Jasjeet S. Sekhon, Walter R. Mebane Jr., Michael C. Herron, and Henry E. Brady, "The Butterfly Did It: The Aberrant Vote for Buchanan in Palm Beach County, Florida," *American Political Science Review*, April 25, 2001, http://sekhon.berkeley.edu/elections/election2000/butterfly.april.pdf.

537 roughly 2,800 ballots: Ibid.

537 Another 19,000 ballots in: Don Van Natta Jr., "Democrats Tell of Problems at the Polls Across Florida," *New York Times*, November 10, 2000.

537 More than 26,000 ballots: Raymond Bonner with Josh Barbanel, "Democrats Rue Ballot Foul-Up in a 2nd County,": *New York Times*, November 17, 2000.

537 nearly 10,000 votes: Van Natta, "Democrats Tell of Problems at the Polls Across Florida."

537 hit the "clear" button: Ibid.

537 sheriff's deputies tracked down: Ibid.

538 shrunk to a mere 327 votes: David Firestone and Michael Cooper, "Bush Sues to Halt Hand Recount in Florida," *New York Times*, November 12, 2000.

539 appointed nearly every member: In fact, Chiles had appointed five of the seven members of the Florida Supreme Court and had jointly appointed the sixth along with Jeb Bush. The seventh was appointed by another Democratic governor, Bob Graham.

539 "We run the risk that if": Joshua Bolten, author interview.

539 "He asked tough questions": Theodore Olson, author interview.

539 "At the end, he said something": Benjamin Ginsberg, author interview.

540 "We were still debating this": Olson interview.

540 "Yes, we are going forward": Ibid.

540 "My dad called and he goes": Douglas Baker, author interview.

541 "He can give you a look": Card interview.

541 "Baker's response": Karl Rove, *Courage and Consequence*, p. 201.

542 said he received a call: Jeffrey Toobin, "The Dirty Trickster," *The New Yorker*, May 23, 2008.

542 "Baker says, 'No, no' ": Ted Cruz, author interview.

542 "We're getting killed": Jeffrey Toobin, *Too Close to Call*, pp. 45–47.

542 "We needed for Bush and Cheney": G. Irvin Terrell, James A. Baker III Oral History Project, Princeton and Rice, February 6, 2014.

542 "the undertaker": Rubenstein interview.

542 "looking like one of those": Michael Powell, "The Wise Old Men, Leading Us Through Gray Areas," *Washington Post*, November 15, 2000.

543 "if Warren Christopher were": Republican in the room at the time who asked not to be named, author interview.

543 "He looked strong": Daley interview.

543 Some 51 percent of Americans: American Viewpoint poll, November 22, 2000.

543 forty-seven lawsuits: Steve Newborn, "Why So Many Recount Lawsuits? Go Back to 2000," WLRN Miami, November 15, 2018, https://www.wlrn.org/post/why-so-many-recount-lawsuits-go-back-2000.

544 "Just answer their questions": Michael Carvin, author interview. See also Toobin, *Too Close to Call*, pp. 133–34.

544 "We all knew I was a sacrificial lamb": Carvin interview.

544 "Two weeks after the election": Baker Reaction to FL Supreme Court, November 21, 2000, American Presidency Project, University of California at Santa Barbara, https://www.presidency.ucsb.edu/documents/presidential-documents-archive-guidebook/documents-related-the-2000-election-dispute/1121.

544 "He wanted the threat": Frank Donatelli, author interview.
545 "When a court speaks": Anthony Lewis, "Playing with Fire," *New York Times*, November 25, 2000.
545 "Maybe Al Gore was afraid": Roger Simon, *Divided We Stand*, p. 276.
545 "Voter fraud!": Dana Canedy and Dexter Filkins, "A Wild Day in Miami, with an End to Recounting, and Democrats' Going to Court," *New York Times*, November 23, 2000.
545 "and delivered the following message": Terrell oral history.
546 "I hereby declare Governor George W. Bush": Harris Declares Bush Florida Winner, November 26, 2000, American Presidency Project, University of California at Santa Barbara, https://www.presidency.ucsb.edu/documents/presidential-documents-archive-guidebook/documents-related-the-2000-election-dispute-29.
546 "a very loose standard": Baker on Florida Results, November 26, 2000, American Presidency Project, University of California at Santa Barbara, https://www.presidency.ucsb.edu/documents/presidential-documents-archive-guidebook/documents-related-the-2000-election-dispute-23.
547 "Florida is a state where": Robert Zelnick, *Winning Florida*, p. 138.
547 "I thought your point was": Transcript of Oral Argument, *Bush v. Gore*, December 11, 2000, https://www.supremecourt.gov/oral_arguments/argument_transcripts/2000/00-949.pdf.
547 "That was one of those": Ginsberg interview.
548 "What does it say?": Cruz interview.
548 seemed to agree with them: David Margolick, "The Path to Florida," *Vanity Fair*, March 19, 2014.
548 "Good evening, Mr. President–elect": James A. Baker III, *"Work Hard, Study . . . and Keep Out of Politics!,"* p. 362.
548 "It's Big Time": Ibid.
549 "Hello, Mr. Vice President-elect": Ibid. See also Dick Cheney, *In My Time*, pp. 296–97.
549 the five justices who made up: Chief Justice William Rehnquist and Justices Sandra Day O'Connor, Antonin Scalia, Anthony Kennedy, and Clarence Thomas voted in the majority while Justices John Paul Stevens, David Souter, Ruth Bader Ginsburg, and Stephen Breyer were in dissent.
549 "this is terrible": She later explained that she was not upset about the outcome but because the networks were calling the election before the polls closed in California. Her husband, John O'Connor, however, told others at the party that she had been distressed by Al Gore's apparent victory because she would not be able to retire if a Democrat were in the White House to pick her replacement. Evan Thomas, *First*, p. 323.
550 two independent recounts: The first study, by *USA Today*, the *Miami Herald*, and Knight Ridder, found that Bush would have actually increased his vote margin under the counting standards advocated by the Gore campaign. If every hanging chad and dimpled ballot had been counted, Bush would have won by 1,665 votes, instead of 537, the study found. The only scenario that would have possibly given Gore a chance was if only ballots with a clean punch were counted, the opposite of what Gore sought. In such a case, the study found Gore with three more votes than Bush out of 6 million cast—so razor-thin close that it would be impossible to conclude that Gore would necessarily have won, because different counters might have assessed the ballots differently enough to change the margin by four votes. http://www.usatoday.com/news/washington/2001-04-03-floridamain.htm. The other study, by a consortium of eight news organizations, including *The New York Times*, *The Washington Post*, and CNN, found that neither the limited statewide recount ordered by the Florida Supreme Court nor the recount sought by Gore in the four Democratic counties would have changed the ultimate outcome. The only scenario for a Gore victory in this study was if Florida had conducted a broader recount in every county, something neither sought by Gore nor ordered by the Florida Supreme Court. Judge Terry Lewis, who was overseeing the recount, said later that he was thinking about ordering a reex-

amination of ballots rejected by machines. The machines had purportedly recorded more than one vote for president, which theoretically might have resulted in a Gore victory, but neither side had asked that such ballots be counted. In other words, if the U.S. Supreme Court had not issued its controversial ruling in *Bush v. Gore* and the process had gone forward as ordered by the Florida high court, Bush still would have won, http://www.factcheck.org/2008/01/the-florida-recount-of-2000/ or http://www .nytimes.com/images/2001/11/12/politics/recount/preset.html.

550 "It's easy to construct a scenario": Dick Cheney, author interview.
550 "I don't think it was a contrived": Card interview.

CHAPTER 29. Grave and Deteriorating

551 "We've got a real mess": Ben Rhodes, author interview.
551 sixty-six American troops: http://icasualties.org.
551 estimated 2,865 civilians: Iraq Body Count, https://www.iraqbodycount.org/data base/.
552 "It was like, shit!": Leon Panetta, author interview.
552 "He looked like he was turning": Rhodes interview.
552 While many veterans: Robert Zoellick served as trade representative and deputy secretary of state, Robert Kimmitt as deputy treasury secretary, Margaret Tutwiler as ambassador to Morocco and undersecretary of state, and Doug Baker as a deputy assistant commerce secretary and White House aide.
552 "All I'm going to say to you is": Robert Draper, *Dead Certain*, p. 282.
553 "Jim Baker is who we call": Charles Schwartz, author interview. Schwartz described Baker as the bin Laden family's "favorite politician": Steve Coll, *The Bin Ladens*, pp. 425–26.
553 "The name turned out to be": James Baker, author interview.
554 "I remember sitting with my dad": Mary-Bonner Baker, author interview.
554 "She was as close to perfect": James Baker, letter to George W. Bush, June 20, 2002, Princeton archive.
555 "would be very expensive": Brent Scowcroft, "Don't Attack Saddam," *Wall Street Journal*, August 15, 2002, http://www.wsj.com/articles/SB1029371773228069195.
555 "he never commented on it": Brent Scowcroft, author interview.
555 "The president was honked off": Colin Powell, author interview.
555 "Although the United States could": James A. Baker III, "The Right Way to Change a Regime," *New York Times*, August 25, 2002.
555 "I was really concerned": James Baker interview.
556 "Dad was smart enough": Will Winston, author interview.
556 "I'm confident that he gave me": George W. Bush, author interview. Authors also spoke with Condoleezza Rice, Andy Card, and Stephen Hadley and none remembered specifically whether Baker got in touch first.
556 "It was subtle": Andy Card, author interview.
556 "Against that background": Remarks by the Vice President to the Veterans of Foreign Wars, 103rd National Convention, August 26, 2002, https://georgewbush -whitehouse.archives.gov/news/releases/2002/08/20020826.html.
557 "I'm clearly more of a hard rock": Dick Cheney, author interview.
558 "When I was secretary": Matt Bryza, author interview.
558 "They're looking at each other": Ibid.
558 "the only negative experience": James Baker interview.
558 some $130 billion in obligations: Martin A. Weiss, "Iraq's Debt Relief: Procedure and Potential Implications for International Debt Relief," Congressional Research Service, March 29, 2011, https://fas.org/sgp/crs/mideast/RL33376.pdf.
559 "You know, Jim": Condoleezza Rice, author interview.
559 "This was literally a shit show": Gary Edson, author interview.
560 "I don't think anybody else": Ibid.

560 The liberal *Nation* magazine: Naomi Klein, "James Baker's Double Life," *The Nation*, October 12, 2004, https://www.thenation.com/article/james-bakers-double-life/.

560 "I'll tell you one thing": James Baker interview.

561 "Dave, you told me you would": Ibid.

561 "I thought it was kind of a crazy deal": David Rubenstein, author interview.

561 Myers ran her piece: Lisa Myers, "Influence Peddling Charged over Iraq's Debt," NBC News, October 13, 2004, http://www.nbcnews.com/id/6242360/ns/nbc_nightly_news_with_brian_williams-nbc_news_investigates/t/influence-peddling-charged-over-iraqs-debt/#.VxmVdGMydg3.

561 "This was like the most boldface": Lisa Myers, author interview.

561 "I think he thought going into": John Baker, author interview.

562 "The decision not to go": Baker acquaintance, notes provided to author.

563 "I don't think I should be considered": James Baker, letter to George W. Bush, June 16, 2004, Princeton archive.

563 *Please, Andy, don't ask me*: James A. Baker III, *"Work Hard, Study . . . and Keep Out of Politics!,"* p. 390.

564 "But we should be prepared to": James Baker, letter to George W. Bush, January 18, 2005, Princeton archive.

564 "some of our friends on the Left": Ibid.

564 "Your 1/11/05 speech": George W. Bush, handwritten note to James Baker, January 19, 2005, Princeton archive.

564 "He'd shown himself to be": Stephen Hadley, author interview.

564 "I was seventy-five years old": James Baker interview.

565 "Jim, you need to get off": Mark White, author interview.

565 "the CIA of the business world": Greg Schneider, "Connections and Then Some," *Washington Post*, March 16, 2003.

566 "You dip a very, very, very": Neil Nyren, email to James Baker, November 8, 2005, Princeton archive.

566 "I think what he really wants": James Baker, note to staff, November 9, 2005, Princeton archive.

566 "we foresaw happening some": James Baker, email to Neil Nyren, November 28, 2005, Princeton archive. Nyren then retreated. "I understand what you're saying and I've said my piece," he replied. But as with his first memoir, Baker's advisers warned him that he was opening the door to legitimate criticism if he ignored other items. Hancock noted that Baker did not disclose that the conference he was to attend on the day of the September 11 attacks was sponsored by the Carlyle Group and included investors with the last name of bin Laden. "If I were a critical reviewer and I wanted to argue that you were not telling 'the whole truth,' I would use this as an example," Hancock wrote. He won half the battle. In the final version, Carlyle's role in sponsoring the conference was included, but the name bin Laden was nowhere to be found. Daryl Hancock, note on draft of chapter 13, dated March 12, 2006, Princeton archive.

566 "The White House view was": Peter Feaver, author interview.

566 "We needed frankly a brand name": Rice interview.

567 "It was extremely hard for him": Ed Djerejian, author interview.

567 "You really going to take this on?": Powell interview.

567 "He obviously did not like": Lee Hamilton, author interview.

568 "The only thing we have in common": Peter Baker, Robin Wright, and Dafna Linzer, "From Hundreds of Sources, Panel Forged Consensus," *Washington Post*, December 7, 2006.

568 "I was a Democrat": Rhodes interview.

568 "Well, Colin," Baker said: Bob Woodward, *The War Within*, p. 52.

568 "He's the one guy who could": Ibid.

569 "There was this palpable sense": Rhodes interview.

569 "He thought it was important": Vernon Jordan, author interview.

569 "Are Americans—Republicans": Woodward, *The War Within*, pp. 110–11.

569 voters swept Republicans out: John M. Broder, "Democrats Gain Senate and New Influence," *New York Times*, November 10, 2006.

569 "I think we have a different ball game": James Baker interview. In a separate interview, Hamilton did not recall the line but did not dispute it.

570 two of the panel's forty-four advisers: Baker, Wright, and Linzer, "From Hundreds of Sources, Panel Forged Consensus."

570 "Every interaction they had": Rhodes interview.

570 "He didn't want to use language": Charles Robb, author interview.

570 "That was really Baker's argument": Feaver interview.

570 "He wanted to make it": Robb interview.

570 "Look, I think the president": Joshua Bolten, author interview.

571 "Jim knew his way around": Panetta interview.

571 "I was upset": Rhodes interview.

571 "support a short-term redeployment": Iraq Study Group report, p. 50, https://www.thepresidency.org/sites/default/files/pdf/iraq_study_group_report.pdf.

571 "Baker hung a lot on that sentence": Bolten interview.

572 "The situation in Iraq is grave": Iraq Study Group report, p. 6.

572 "We do not recommend": David E. Sanger, "Panel Calls for New Approach to Iraq," *New York Times*, December 6, 2006.

572 "worthy of serious study": Peter Baker and Robin Wright, "Bush Appears Cool to Key Points of Report on Iraq," *Washington Post*, December 8, 2006.

572 "It got characterized both": Hadley interview.

573 "We could either attack": Ibid.

573 "leaving Washington unindicted": In the *Doonesbury* cartoon that ran on March 29, 1987, Garry Trudeau's characters host a radio show offering a "salute to Jim Baker" which starts, "Born in a log cabin in 1930, James A. Baker III has never been indicted . . ."

EPILOGUE: Three Funerals and an Election

575 "eulogist in chief": James Baker, author interview.

575 "closest adviser": Nancy Reagan Funeral Service, C-Span, March 12, 2016. https://www.c-span.org/video/?c4584653/user-clip-nancy-reagan-funeral-service.

576 "I see some eerie parallels": James Baker interview.

576 "We thought he was a grade-B": Ibid.

576 "I think you should put in a call": Brian Mulroney, author interview.

576 "I really think you need": James Baker interview.

576 "You do not need to abandon": James Baker, memo to Donald Trump, Baker personal files.

577 "Jim, you do not want to do this": Tom Brokaw, author interview.

577 "He's probably his own worst enemy": James Baker interview.

577 "none of the above": Mark K. Updegrove, *The Last Republicans*, p. 398.

578 "I'm a conservative": James Baker interview.

578 "The current sorry spectacle": Andrew Cockburn, "Kerry, Iran and the Wisdom of James Baker," *Harper's*, November 15, 2013.

578 "Time to talk to a wise man": Peggy Noonan, "To Lead Is to Negotiate," *Wall Street Journal*, October 4, 2013.

578 "You represent": Barack Obama, video tribute, Kennedy Center, November 12, 2013.

579 "I'm hopeful Trump will listen": James Baker interview.

579 "Don't say that I will vote": Ibid.

580 "Egregious. Inappropriate. Wrong": James Baker interview.

580 "one inch to the east": Philip Zelikow and Condoleezza Rice, *Germany Unified and Europe Transformed*, pp. 182–83.

581 "a cascade of assurances": National Security Archive, "NATO Expansion: What Gorbachev Heard," December 12, 2017, https://nsarchive.gwu.edu/briefing-book

/russia-programs/2017-12-12/nato-expansion-what-gorbachev-heard-western
-leaders-early.

581 "the topic of NATO expansion": Maxim Korshunov, "Mikhail Gorbachev: I Am
Against All Walls," *Russia Beyond the Headlines*, October 16, 2014.

581 "putting money down a rat hole": Bartholomew Sparrow, *The Strategist*, p. 445.

582 "Willie Horton, you could": James Baker interview.

582 "I don't think I'm anywhere": Ibid.

583 "I know when to slow down": Ibid.

583 "I thank God": Susan Baker, *Passing It On*, p. 36.

583 "The responsible center in American politics": Peter Baker, "From Obama and
Baker, a Lament for a Lost Consensus," *New York Times*, November 28, 2013.

584 "You made me cry": Witness who asked not to be named, author interview.

584 "Where are we going, Bake?": James Baker interview.

584 "Having someone there": George H. W. Bush, author interview.

584 his friend's "decency": James Baker, eulogy for George H. W. Bush, St. Martin's Episcopal Church, Houston, December 6, 2018.

585 "This is where I'll be": James Baker interview.

Bibliography

Abrams, Herbert L. *The President Has Been Shot: Confusion, Disability, and the 25th Amendment in the Aftermath of the Attempted Assassination of Ronald Reagan.* New York: W. W. Norton, 1992.

Anderson, Martin. *Revolution.* New York: Harcourt, 1988.

Arens, Moshe. *Broken Covenant: American Foreign Policy and the Crisis Between the U.S. and Israel.* New York: Simon & Schuster, 1995.

Atkinson, Rick. *Crusade: The Untold Story of the Persian Gulf War.* New York: Houghton Mifflin, 1993.

Aven, Petr, and Alfred Kokh. *Gaidar's Revolution: The Inside Account of the Economic Transformation of Russia.* London: I. B. Tauris, 2015.

Baker, James A. III. *The Politics of Diplomacy: Revolution, War & Peace, 1989–1992.* New York: Putnam, 1995. With Thomas M. DeFrank.

———. *"Work Hard, Study . . . and Keep Out of Politics!": Adventures and Lessons from an Unexpected Public Life.* New York: Putnam, 2006. With Steve Fiffer.

Baker, Susan G. *Passing It On: An Autobiography with Spirit.* Houston: Bright Sky Press, 2010.

Ball, Robert M. *The Greenspan Commission: What Really Happened.* New York: Century Foundation Press, 2010.

Barrett, Laurence I. *Gambling with History: Reagan in the White House.* New York: Doubleday, 1983.

Beschloss, Michael R., and Strobe Talbott. *At the Highest Levels: The Inside Story of the End of the Cold War.* New York: Little, Brown, 1993.

Birnbaum, Jeffrey H., and Alan S. Murray. *Showdown at Gucci Gulch: Lawmakers, Lobbyists, and the Unlikely Triumph of Tax Reform.* New York: Random House, 1987.

Boies, David. *Courting Justice: From NY Yankees v. Major League Baseball to Bush v. Gore, 1997–2000.* New York: Miramax Books, 2004.

Bolton, John. *Surrender Is Not an Option: Defending America at the United Nations.* New York: Threshold Editions, 2007.

Bradley, Bill. *Time Present, Time Past: A Memoir.* New York: Alfred A. Knopf, 1996.

Brady, John. *Bad Boy: The Life and Politics of Lee Atwater.* New York: Addison-Wesley, 1996.

Brands, H. W. *Reagan.* New York: Doubleday, 2015.

Brinkley, Douglas. *The Unfinished Presidency: Jimmy Carter's Quest for Global Peace.* New York: Viking, 1998.

Briody, Dan. *The Iron Triangle: Inside the Secret World of the Carlyle Group.* Hoboken, N.J.: John Wiley & Sons, 2003.

Burney, Derek H. *Getting It Done: A Memoir.* Montreal: McGill-Queen's University Press, 2005.

Burns, William J. *The Back Channel.* New York: Random House, 2019.

Bush, Barbara. *Barbara Bush: A Memoir.* New York: Charles Scribner's Sons, 1994.

———. *Reflections: Life After the White House.* New York: Scribner, 2003.

Bush, George [H. W.]. *All the Best, George Bush: My Life in Letters and Other Writings.* New York: Scribner, 1999.

———. *Looking Forward.* New York: Doubleday, 1987. With Victor Gold.

Bush, George [H. W.], and Brent Scowcroft. *A World Transformed.* New York: Alfred A. Knopf, 1998.

Bush, George W. *Decision Points.* New York: Crown, 2010.

———. *41: A Portrait of My Father.* New York: Crown, 2014.

Cannon, James. *Gerald R. Ford: An Honorable Life.* Ann Arbor: University of Michigan Press, 2013.

Cannon, Lou. *Governor Reagan: His Rise to Power.* New York: PublicAffairs, 2003.

———. *President Reagan: The Role of a Lifetime.* New York: Simon & Schuster, 1991.

———. *Reagan.* New York: G. P. Putnam's Sons, 1985.

Cheney, Dick. *In My Time: A Personal and Political Memoir.* New York: Threshold Editions, 2011.

Clinton, Hillary Rodham. *Living History.* New York: Simon & Schuster, 2003.

Cohen, Richard E. *Rostenkowski: The Pursuit of Power and the End of the Old Politics.* Chicago: Ivan R. Dee, 1999.

Coll, Steve. *The Bin Ladens: An Arabian Family in the American Century.* New York: Penguin, 2008.

Collier, Peter. *Political Woman: The Big Little Life of Jeane Kirkpatrick.* New York: Encounter Books, 2012.

Cramer, Richard Ben. *What It Takes: The Way to the White House.* New York: Random House, 1992.

Crile, George. *My Enemy's Enemy: The Story of the Largest Covert Operation in History.* London: Atlantic Books, 2003.

Crowley, Monica. *Nixon in Winter: The Final Revelations.* London: I. B. Tauris, 1998.

Daalder, Ivo, and I. M. Destler. *In the Shadow of the Oval Office.* New York: Simon & Schuster, 2009.

Darman, Richard. *Who's in Control? Polar Politics and the Sensible Center.* New York: Simon & Schuster, 1996.

Deaver, Michael K. *Behind the Scenes: In Which the Author Talks About Ronald and Nancy Reagan . . . and Himself.* New York: William Morrow, 1988. With Mickey Herskowitz.

———. *A Different Drummer: My Thirty Years with Ronald Reagan.* New York: Harper, 2001.

———. *Nancy: A Portrait of My Years with Nancy Reagan.* New York: William Morrow, 2004.

DeYoung, Karen. *Soldier: The Life of Colin Powell.* New York: Alfred A. Knopf, 2006.

Djerejian, Edward P. *Danger and Opportunity: An American Ambassador's Journey Through the Middle East.* New York: Threshold Editions, 2008.

Dobbins, James. *Foreign Service: Five Decades on the Frontlines of American Diplomacy.* Washington: Brookings Institution Press and RAND Corporation, 2017.

Donaldson, Sam. *Hold On, Mr. President!* New York: Random House, 1987.

Draper, Robert. *Dead Certain: The Presidency of George W. Bush.* New York: Free Press, 2007.

Draper, Theodore. *A Very Thin Line: The Iran-Contra Affairs.* New York: Hill & Wang, 1991.

Drew, Elizabeth. *Portrait of an Election: The 1980 Presidential Campaign.* New York: Simon & Schuster, 1981.

Duffy, Michael, and Dan Goodgame. *Marching in Place: The Status Quo Presidency of George Bush.* New York: Simon & Schuster, 1992.

Eizenstat, Stuart E. *President Carter: The White House Years.* New York: Thomas Dunne, 2018.

Engel, Jeffrey A. *When the World Seemed New: George H. W. Bush and the End of the Cold War.* Boston: Houghton Mifflin, 2017.

Farrell, John A. *Tip O'Neill and the Democratic Century: A Biography.* New York: Little, Brown, 2001.

Fenberg, Steven. *Unprecedented Power: Jesse Jones, Capitalism, and the Common Good.* College Station: Texas A&M University Press, 2011.

Fitzwater, Marlin. *Call the Briefing!: Bush and Reagan, Sam and Helen: A Decade with Presidents and the Press.* New York: Times Books, 1995.

Ford, Gerald R. *A Time to Heal: The Autobiography of Gerald R. Ford*. New York: Harper & Row, 1979.

Freeman, J. H. *The People of Baker Botts*. Houston: Baker Botts, 1992.

Friedland, Martin L. *The Death of Old Man Rice: A True Story of Criminal Justice in America*. Toronto: University of Toronto Press, 1994.

Gates, Robert M. *From the Shadows: The Ultimate Insider's Story of Five Presidents and How They Won the Cold War*. New York: Simon & Schuster, 1996.

Genscher, Hans-Dietrich. *Rebuilding a House Divided: A Memoir of the Architect of Germany's Reunification*. New York: Broadway, 1998.

Gergen, David. *Eyewitness to Power: The Essence of Leadership, Nixon to Clinton*. New York: Simon & Schuster, 2001.

Germond, Jack W., and Jules Witcover. *Blue Smoke & Mirrors: How Reagan Won and Why Carter Lost the Election of 1980*. New York: Viking, 1981.

———. *Mad as Hell: Revolt at the Ballot Box, 1992*. New York: Warner Books, 1993.

———. *Wake Us When It's Over: Presidential Politics of 1984*. New York: Macmillan, 1985.

———. *Whose Broad Stripes and Bright Stars: The Trivial Pursuit of the Presidency, 1988*. New York: Warner Books, 1989.

Goldman, Peter, Thomas M. DeFrank, Mark Miller, Andrew Murr, and Tom Mathews. *Quest for the Presidency, 1992*. College Station: Texas A&M University Press, 1994.

Gorbachev, Mikhail. *Memoirs*. New York: Doubleday, 1996.

Gordon, Michael R., and Bernard E. Trainor. *The Generals' War: The Inside Story of the Conflict in the Gulf*. New York: Little, Brown, 1995.

Greenspan, Alan. *The Age of Turbulence: Adventures in a New World*. New York: Penguin, 2007.

Gutman, Roy. *Banana Diplomacy: The Making of American Policy in Nicaragua, 1981–1987*. New York: Simon & Schuster, 1988.

Haass, Richard N. *War of Necessity, War of Choice: A Memoir of Two Iraq Wars*. New York: Simon & Schuster, 2009.

Haig, Alexander M. Jr. *Caveat: Realism, Reagan and Foreign Policy*. New York: Scribner, 1984.

———. *Inner Circles: How America Changed the World: A Memoir*. New York: Warner Books, 1992. With Charles McCarry.

Hartmann, Robert. *Palace Politics: An Inside Account of the Ford Years*. New York: McGraw-Hill, 1980.

Hayes, Stephen F. *Cheney: The Untold Story of America's Most Powerful and Controversial Vice President*. New York: HarperCollins, 2007.

Hoffman, David. *The Dead Hand: The Untold Story of the Cold War Arms Race and Its Dangerous Legacy*. New York: Doubleday, 2009.

Hurd, Douglas. *Memoirs*. London: Little, Brown, 2003.

Iraq Study Group. *The Iraq Study Group Report: The Way Forward—A New Approach*. New York: Vintage, 2006.

Isaacson, Walter. *Kissinger: A Biography*. New York: Simon & Schuster, 1992.

Johnson, Haynes. *Sleepwalking Through History: America in the Reagan Years*. New York: W. W. Norton, 1991.

Jordan, Hamilton. *Crisis: The Last Year of the Carter Presidency*. New York: G. P. Putnam's Sons, 1982.

Kaufman, Scott. *Ambition, Pragmatism and Party: A Political Biography of Gerald R. Ford*. Lawrence: University Press of Kansas, 2017.

Kengor, Paul, and Patricia Clark Doerner. *The Judge: William P. Clark, Ronald Reagan's Top Hand*. San Francisco: Ignatius Press, 2007.

Kernell, Samuel, and Samuel I. Popkin. *Chief of Staff: Twenty-five Years of Managing the President*. Berkeley: University of California Press, 1986.

Kirkland, Kate Sayen. *Captain James A. Baker of Houston, 1857–1941*. College Station: Texas A&M University Press, 2012.

Knott, Stephen, and Jeffrey Chidester. *At Reagan's Side: Insiders' Recollections from Sacramento to the White House*. Lanham, Md.: Rowman & Littlefield, 2009.

Koch, Doro Bush. *My Father, My President: A Personal Account of the Life of George H. W. Bush*. New York: Warner Books, 2006.

Koch, Edward I. *The Koch Papers: My Fight Against Anti-Semitism.* New York: St. Martin's Press, 2008. With Rafael Medoff.

Kondracke, Morton, and Fred Barnes. *Jack Kemp: The Bleeding-Heart Conservative Who Changed America.* New York: Sentinel, 2015.

Kozyrev, Andrei. *The Firebird: The Elusive Fate of Russian Democracy.* Pittsburgh: University of Pittsburgh Press, 2019.

Langone, Ken. *I Love Capitalism!: An American Story.* New York: Portfolio, 2018.

Laxalt, Paul. *Nevada's Paul Laxalt: A Memoir.* Reno: Jack Bacon & Company, 2000.

Lipartito, Kenneth J., and Joseph A. Pratt. *Baker & Botts in the Development of Modern Houston.* Austin: University of Texas Press, 2011.

MacDougall, Malcolm D. *We Almost Made It.* New York: Crown, 1977.

Major, John. *John Major: The Autobiography.* New York: Harper, 1999.

Mann, James. *The Rebellion of Ronald Reagan: A History of the End of the Cold War.* New York: Viking, 2009.

Matlock, Jack F. Jr. *Autopsy on an Empire: The American Ambassador's Account of the Collapse of the Soviet Union.* New York: Random House, 1995.

———. *Reagan and Gorbachev.* New York: Random House, 2004.

Matthews, Chris. *Tip and the Gipper: When Politics Worked.* New York: Simon & Schuster, 2013.

McFarlane, Robert C. *Special Trust.* New York: Cadell & Davies, 1994. With Zofia Smardz.

McGarr, Kathryn J. *The Whole Damn Deal: Robert Strauss and the Art of Politics.* New York: PublicAffairs, 2011.

Meacham, Jon. *Destiny and Power: The American Odyssey of George Herbert Walker Bush.* New York: Random House, 2015.

Medved, Michael. *The Shadow Presidents: The Secret History of the Chief Executives and Their Top Aides.* New York: Times Books, 1979.

Meese, Edwin 3rd. *With Reagan: The Inside Story.* New York: Regnery Gateway, 1992.

Menges, Constantine C. *Inside the National Security Council: The True Story of the Making and Unmaking of Reagan's Foreign Policy.* New York: Simon & Schuster, 1988.

Miller, Aaron David. *The Much Too Promised Land: America's Elusive Search for Arab-Israeli Peace.* New York: Bantam, 2008.

Minutaglio, Bill. *First Son: George W. Bush and the Bush Family Dynasty.* New York: Times Books, 1999.

Mondale, Walter. *The Good Fight: A Life in Liberal Politics.* New York: Scribner, 2010.

Morris, Edmund. *Dutch: A Memoir of Ronald Reagan.* New York: Random House, 1999.

Nelson, Michael, and Barbara A. Perry, editors. *41: Inside the Presidency of George H. W. Bush.* Ithaca, N.Y.: Cornell University Press, 2014.

Nessen, Ronald. *It Sure Looks Different from the Inside.* New York: Simon & Schuster, 1978.

———. *Making the News, Taking the News: From NBC to the Ford White House.* Middletown, Conn.: Wesleyan University Press, 2011.

Nofziger, Lyn. *Nofziger.* New York: Regnery, 1992.

Noonan, Peggy. *What I Saw at the Revolution: A Political Life in the Reagan Era.* New York: Random House, 1990.

———. *When Character Was King: A Story of Ronald Reagan.* New York: Viking, 2001.

Novak, Robert D. *Prince of Darkness: Fifty Years of Reporting in Washington.* New York: Crown, 2007.

Oberdorfer, Don. *The Turn: From the Cold War to the New Era.* New York: Poseidon Press, 1991.

O'Neill, Tip. *Man of the House: The Life and Political Memoirs of Speaker Tip O'Neill.* New York: Random House, 1987. With William Novak.

Ottaway, David B. *The King's Messenger: Prince Bandar bin Sultan and America's Tangled Relationship with Saudi Arabia.* New York: Walker, 2008.

Page, Susan. *The Matriarch: Barbara Bush and the Making of an American Dynasty.* New York: Twelve, 2019.

Palazchenko, Pavel. *My Years with Gorbachev and Shevardnadze: The Memoir of a Soviet Interpreter.* State College: Penn State University Press, 2009.

Panic, Milan. *Prime Minister for Peace: My Struggle for Serbian Democracy.* Lanham, Md.: Rowman & Littlefield, 2015.

Parmet, Herbert S. *George Bush: The Life of a Lone Star Yankee.* New York: Scribner, 1997.

Plokhy, Serhii. *The Last Empire: The Final Days of the Soviet Union.* New York: Basic Books, 2014.

Popadiuk, Roman. *The Leadership of George Bush: An Insider's View of the Forty-first President.* College Station: Texas A&M University Press, 2009.

Powell, Colin L. *My American Journey: An Autobiography.* New York: Random House, 1995. With Joseph E. Persico.

Power, Samantha. *A Problem from Hell: America and the Age of Genocide.* New York: Basic Books, 2002.

Quayle, Dan. *Standing Firm.* New York: HarperCollins, 1994.

Reagan, Nancy. *My Turn: The Memoirs of Nancy Reagan.* New York: Random House, 1989. With William Novak.

Reagan, Ronald. *An American Life: The Autobiography.* New York: Simon & Schuster, 1990.

———. *The Reagan Diaries.* New York: Harper, 2007. Edited by Douglas Brinkley.

Reeves, Richard. *President Kennedy: Profile of Power.* New York: Simon & Schuster, 1993.

———. *President Reagan: The Triumph of Imagination.* New York: Simon & Schuster, 2005.

Regan, Donald T. *For the Record: From Wall Street to Washington.* New York: Harcourt, 1988.

Rhodes, Ben. *The World as It Is: A Memoir of the Obama White House.* New York: Random House, 2018.

Rice, Condoleezza. *No Higher Honor: A Memoir of My Years in Washington.* New York: Crown, 2011.

Rollins, Ed. *Bare Knuckles and Back Rooms.* New York: Broadway, 1996.

Ross, Dennis. *Doomed to Succeed: The U.S.-Israel Relationship from Truman to Obama.* New York: Farrar, Straus & Giroux, 2015.

———. *The Missing Peace: The Inside Story of the Fight for Middle East Peace.* New York: Farrar, Straus & Giroux, 2004.

Rothkopf, David. *Running the World: The Inside Story of the National Security Council and the Architects of American Power.* New York: PublicAffairs, 2005.

Rove, Karl. *Courage and Consequence: My Life as a Conservative in the Fight.* New York: Threshold Editions, 2010.

Rumsfeld, Donald. *Known and Unknown: A Memoir.* New York: Sentinel, 2011.

Sarotte, Mary Elise. *The Collapse: The Accidental Opening of the Berlin Wall.* New York: Basic Books, 2014.

Schieffer, Bob, and Gary Paul Gates. *The Acting President: Ronald Reagan and the Supporting Players Who Helped Him Create the Illusion That Held America Spellbound.* New York: Dutton/Plume, 1989.

Schwarzkopf, H. Norman. *It Doesn't Take a Hero: The Autobiography.* New York: Bantam, 1992.

Schweizer, Peter, and Rochelle Schweizer. *The Bushes: Portrait of a Dynasty.* New York: Doubleday, 2004.

Shamir, Yitzhak. *Summing Up: An Autobiography.* London: Weidenfeld & Nicolson, 1994.

Sherman, Gabriel. *The Loudest Voice in the Room.* New York: Random House, 2014.

Shevardnadze, Eduard. *The Future Belongs to Freedom.* New York: Free Press, 1991. With Catherine A. Fitzpatrick.

Shirley, Craig. *Reagan's Revolution: The Untold Story of the Campaign That Started It All.* Nashville: Thomas Nelson, 2005.

———. *Rendezvous with Destiny: Ronald Reagan and the Campaign That Changed America.* Wilmington, Del.: Intercollegiate Studies Institute, 2009.

Shoval, Zalman. *Jerusalem and Washington: A Life in Politics and Diplomacy.* New York: Rowman & Littlefield, 2019.

Shultz, George P. *Turmoil and Triumph: My Years as Secretary of State.* New York: Scribner, 1993.

Silber, William L. *Volcker: The Triumph of Persistence.* New York: Bloomsbury, 2012.

Simon, Roger. *Divided We Stand: How Al Gore Beat George Bush and Lost the Presidency.* New York: Crown, 2001.

Simpson, William. *The Prince: The Secret Story of the World's Most Intriguing Royal, Prince Bandar bin Sultan.* New York: Regan, 2006.

Smith, Hedrick. *The Power Game: How Washington Works.* New York: Random House, 1988.

Sparrow, Bartholomew. *The Strategist: Brent Scowcroft and the Call of National Security.* New York: PublicAffairs, 2015.

Speakes, Larry. *Speaking Out: Inside the Reagan White House.* New York: Scribner, 1988.

Stahl, Lesley. *Reporting Live.* New York: Simon & Schuster, 1999.

Stockman, David A. *The Triumph of Politics: Why the Reagan Revolution Failed.* New York: Harper & Row, 1986.

Strober, Deborah Hart, and Gerald S. Strober. *Reagan: The Man and His Presidency. The Oral History of an Era.* New York: Houghton Mifflin, 1998.

Sununu, John H. *The Quiet Man: The Indispensable Presidency of George H. W. Bush.* New York: Broadside Books, 2015.

Taylor, Paul. *See How They Run: Electing the President in an Age of Mediaocracy.* New York: Alfred A. Knopf, 1990.

Thatcher, Margaret. *The Downing Street Years.* New York: HarperCollins, 1993.

Thomas, Evan. *First: Sandra Day O'Connor.* New York: Random House, 2019.

Thompson, John W. Jr. *Huntsville and Walker County, Texas: A Bicentennial History.* Huntsville, Tex.: Sam Houston State University Press, 1976.

Toobin, Jeffrey. *Too Close to Call: The Thirty-six Day Battle to Decide the 2000 Election.* New York: Random House, 2001.

Tyler, Patrick. *A World of Trouble: The White House and the Middle East—from the Cold War to the War on Terror.* New York: Farrar, Straus & Giroux, 2009.

Untermeyer, Chase. *When Things Went Right: The Dawn of the Reagan-Bush Administration.* College Station: Texas A&M University Press, 2013.

Volcker, Paul A. *Keeping At It: The Quest for Sound Money and Good Government.* New York: PublicAffairs, 2018.

Von Damm, Helene. *At Reagan's Side: Twenty Years in the Political Mainstream.* New York: Doubleday, 1988.

Von Drehle, David, and Staff of The Washington Post. *Deadlock: The Inside Story of America's Closest Election.* New York: PublicAffairs, 2001.

Walsh, Lawrence E. *Firewall: The Iran-Contra Conspiracy and Cover-up.* New York: W. W. Norton, 1997.

Weinberger, Caspar. *Fighting for Peace: Seven Critical Years in the Pentagon.* New York: Grand Central, 1990.

Weisberg, Jacob. *Ronald Reagan.* New York: Times Books, 2016.

Whipple, Chris. *The Gatekeepers: How the White House Chiefs of Staff Define Every Presidency.* New York: Crown, 2017.

White, Andrea. *The Very Long Life of Alice's Playhouse: A Survivor's Story.* Houston: Sam Houston Park Publishing, 2012.

Wilber, Del Quentin. *Rawhide Down: The Near Assassination of Ronald Reagan.* New York: Henry Holt, 2011.

Williams, Marjorie. *Reputation: Portraits in Power.* New York: PublicAffairs, 2008.

Wills, Garry. *Reagan's America: Innocents at Home.* New York: Doubleday, 1986.

Wilson, James Graham. *The Triumph of Improvisation: Gorbachev's Adaptability, Reagan's Engagement, and the End of the Cold War.* Ithaca, N.Y.: Cornell University Press, 2014.

Witcover, Jules. *Marathon: The Pursuit of the Presidency, 1972–1976.* New York: Viking Penguin, 1977.

Woodward, Bob. *The Choice.* New York: Simon & Schuster, 1996.

———. *The Commanders.* New York: Simon & Schuster, 1991.

———. *Maestro: Greenspan's Fed and the American Boom.* New York: Simon & Schuster, 2000.

———. *Plan of Attack.* New York: Simon & Schuster, 2004.

———. *Shadow: Five Presidents and the Legacy of Watergate.* New York: Simon & Schuster, 1999.

———. *State of Denial: Bush at War, Part III.* New York: Simon & Schuster, 2006.

———. *Veil: The Secret Wars of the CIA, 1981–1987.* New York: Simon & Schuster, 1987.

————. *The War Within: A Secret White House History, 2006–2008*. New York: Simon & Schuster, 2008.

Woodward, Bob, and David S. Broder. *The Man Who Would Be President: Dan Quayle*. New York: Simon & Schuster, 1992.

Wright, Jim. *Worth It All*. McLean, Va.: Brassey's, 1993.

Yergin, Daniel. *The Quest: Energy, Security, and the Remaking of the Modern World*. New York: Penguin, 2011.

Zelikow, Philip, and Condoleezza Rice. *Germany Unified and Europe Transformed: A Study in Statecraft*. Cambridge: Harvard University Press, 1995.

Zelizer, Julian E. *Jimmy Carter*. New York: Times Books, 2010.

Zelnick, Bob. *Winning Florida: How the Bush Team Fought the Battle*. Palo Alto, Calif.: Hoover Institution, 2001.

Index

ABOUT THE AUTHORS

PETER BAKER and SUSAN GLASSER are longtime Washington journalists who have written for years about the intersection of politics and the world. Baker is the chief White House correspondent for *The New York Times* and an MSNBC political analyst. He has covered the last four presidents for the *Times* and *The Washington Post* and is the author or coauthor of six books, including *Days of Fire: Bush and Cheney in the White House*, a *New York Times* top-ten book of the year, and *The Breach: Inside the Impeachment and Trial of William Jefferson Clinton*, a *New York Times* bestseller.

Glasser is a staff writer for *The New Yorker* and author of the weekly "Letter from Trump's Washington" as well as a global affairs analyst for CNN. She previously was the editor of *Politico* and founder of *Politico Magazine*. Before that, she was editor in chief of *Foreign Policy* magazine following a long stint at the *Post*, where she was assistant managing editor for national news and editor of the paper's Outlook section. Together, Baker and Glasser were Moscow bureau chiefs for the *Post* and authors of *Kremlin Rising: Vladimir Putin's Russia and the End of Revolution*.

A NOTE ON THE TYPE

This book was set in Janson, a typeface long thought to have been made by the Dutchman Anton Janson, who was a practicing type-founder in Leipzig during the years 1668–1687. However, it has been conclusively demonstrated that these types are actually the work of Nicholas Kis (1650–1702), a Hungarian, who most probably learned his trade from the master Dutch typefounder Dirk Voskens. The type is an excellent example of the influential and sturdy Dutch types that prevailed in England up to the time William Caslon (1692–1766) developed his own incomparable designs from them.

Composed by North Market Street Graphics,
Lancaster, Pennsylvania

Printed and bound by LSC Communications,
Harrisonburg, Virginia

Designed by Cassandra J. Pappas